# FIX YOUR

## V8'S AND 6'S
### 1978 TO 1968

By
Bill Toboldt

Member, Society of Automotive Engineers
Associate Member, Automotive Engine Rebuilders Association

SOUTH HOLLAND, ILLINOIS
THE GOODHEART-WILLCOX COMPANY, INC.
Publishers

Copyright 1978

By

**THE GOODHEART-WILLCOX CO., INC.**

Printed in the United States of America

All Rights Reserved

Library of Congress Catalog
Card Number: 61-9347
ISBN 0-87006-254-9
12345-78

# INTRODUCTION

FIX YOUR FORD is a handbook of time and money-saving service information for car owners who want to do their own repairing. It also provides helpful tips for experienced mechanics interested in doing a better job in less time.

This book tells you how to make emergency repairs if your car "conks out." It shows you how to locate trouble and how to make many adjustments and repairs without the use of expensive equipment.

FIX YOUR FORD gives simplified tune-up procedures; explains shortcut methods of removing and installing parts; reveals how to get better than normal speed, power and economy. It includes detailed specification charts and separate chapters on Pinto and Fiesta service.

When engine service procedures are given, the Ford engine under discussion usually is identified by displacement - 250, 302, 351, etc. - rather than by names such as Mustang, Torino or LTD. These names identify model lines and refer to the complete chassis which, in most cases, is available with a choice of engines. For this reason, you must determine the displacement of the engine to be repaired so you can select the repair procedure which is applicable.

FIX YOUR FORD is based on material obtained from many sources, particularly from topflight Ford mechanics throughout the country, from the Ford Motor Co. and Ford Customer Service Div., and from many tool and equipment manufacturers.

*Bill Toboldt*

# Fix Your Ford

Above. 1974-1978 Mustang II and 1975-1978 Pinto feature this 2800 cc V-6 engine. Below. 2300 cc in-line Four is first Ford-built engine assembled with metric fasteners. Engine has five main bearings, hydraulic valve lifters, overhead camshaft and cogged belt drive. (Courtesy Ford Customer Service Div.)

# CONTENTS

| | |
|---|---|
| TUNE-UP TIPS | 7 |
| IGNITION TUNE-UP | 13 |
| CARBURETOR AND FUEL SYSTEM SERVICE | 47 |
| REDUCING ENGINE EMISSIONS | 79 |
| SHORTCUTS ON ENGINE DISASSEMBLY | 93 |
| SIMPLIFIED ENGINE REPAIRS | 113 |
| ADJUSTING VALVE TAPPETS | 157 |
| COOLING SYSTEM KINKS | 167 |
| EXHAUST SYSTEM SERVICE | 179 |
| QUICK TESTS ON BATTERIES | 185 |
| SIMPLIFIED ALTERNATOR SERVICE | 191 |
| KINKS ON STARTER TESTING | 201 |
| LIGHTING SYSTEM SERVICE | 207 |
| ACCESSORY AND INSTRUMENT SERVICE | 221 |
| OVERHAULING FORD CLUTCH | 233 |
| MANUAL SHIFT TRANSMISSION | 239 |
| AUTOMATIC TRANSMISSION SERVICE | 251 |
| PROPELLER SHAFT AND UNIVERSAL JOINTS | 267 |

REAR AXLE SERVICE KINKS . . . . . . . . . . .271

QUICK SERVICE ON SHOCK ABSORBERS
   AND SPRINGS. . . . . . . . . . . . . . . . . . . . .285

SHORTCUTS ON WHEEL ALIGNMENT . . . . .295

QUICK SERVICE ON BRAKES . . . . . . . . . . .311

LUBRICATION AND TIRES. . . . . . . . . . . . .343

EMERGENCY TROUBLE SHOOTING
   AND REPAIRS . . . . . . . . . . . . . . . . . . . .349

TIPS ON BODY SERVICE . . . . . . . . . . . . . .355

SERVICING THE PINTO . . . . . . . . . . . . . .361

QUICK SERVICE ON FIESTA . . . . . . . . . . .378

SPECIFICATIONS. . . . . . . . . . . . . . . . . . .391

INDEX . . . . . . . . . . . . . . . . . . . . . . . . . .396

# TUNE-UP TIPS

To get maximum engine performance and fuel mileage, special care must be taken when doing a tune-up job. Tuning Ford engines is not difficult. However, on cars equipped with exhaust emission controls, carefully follow factory specifications provided on a decal in the engine compartment. Carburetor and ignition units are readily accessible. Spark plugs, particularly on the Four and Six, can be removed and replaced without difficulty.

## WHEN TO DO TUNE-UP JOBS

A tune-up job is needed in order to get maximum performance and best fuel mileage. No great skill is required to do a tune-up job on these engines and only simple hand tools are required. A tune-up is needed when fuel mileage and performance drop below acceptable standards. On late models, perform a tune-up before misfiring occurs or unburned fuel will reach the catalytic converter and cause it to overheat.

Fuel consumption is so dependent on type of driving, it is impossible to state what fuel mileage can be expected from a car. Fig. A-1 shows how fuel economy will vary with speed of driving.

As shown in the illustration, maximum economy can be expected at about 30 mph. This will vary somewhat with different cars, the equipment, the load, and the terrain over which the car is driven.

Engineers have found that at higher speeds a car equipped with an automatic transmission will get about one mile per gallon more than a car with a conventional three speed transmission. However, cars equipped with overdrive or a four speed transmission get better fuel economy.

Power steering also affects fuel economy. At low speeds a loss of about one mile per gallon of fuel can be expected and this drops until at eighty mph the loss will be approximately one-quarter mile per gallon.

Air conditioning also takes its toll. At 20 mph about two and one-half miles per gallon of fuel are required, over that required to operate the vehicle. This drops to about one mile per gallon at speeds of 70 mph.

It is also important to note that maximum economy is not reached until the engine has reached full operating temperature or after about seven or eight miles of operation. At the start of the drive, only 25 percent of fuel economy is obtained. After three miles of driving, the fuel economy is only about 50 percent of its maximum.

# Fix Your Ford

All such points must be considered when deciding on the need of a tune-up job and when making comparisons between different cars.

It will be found that cars used mostly in city type, stop-and-go driving will require a tune-up job more frequently than cars used mostly on trips of ten miles or more. A Ford Motor Company engine engineer pointed out at a meeting of the Society of Automotive Engineers that after only 10,000 miles of operation a modern engine will lose 11.7 percent of its torque because of accumulations in the combustion chamber. Also, the loss in power resulting from combustion chamber deposits is accompanied with a three-to-four percent loss of economy.

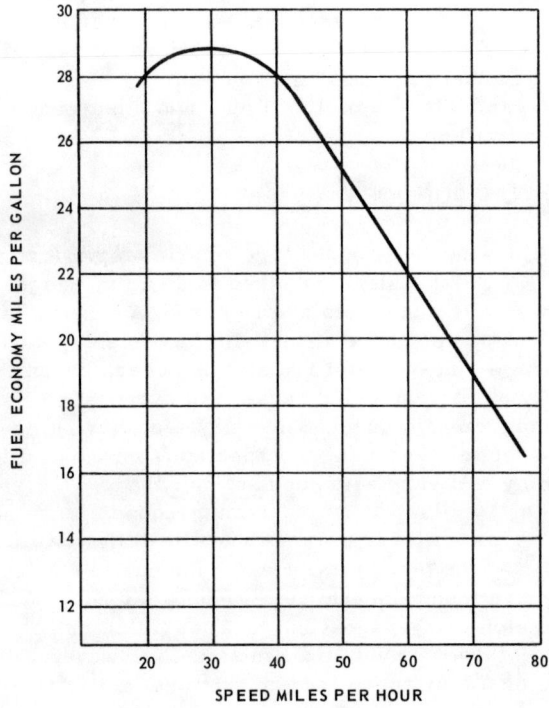

*Fig. A-1. Typical curve showing how fuel economy varies with car speed.*

Short trip driving and idling of the engine also result in sticking valves. These, in turn, result in a loss of compression.

A tune-up job is advisable every 10,000 miles or sooner. However, with breakerless ignition, a greater interval is possible. But, leaving the tune-up job go too long will result in hard starting, poor fuel economy and possible roadside failure.

# Tune-Up Tips

## FIRST STEP IN TUNE-UP

The first step in an engine tune-up job is to make sure the valves are not sticking. Sticking valves usually are indicated by noisy action, particularly in the case of mechanical valve lifters.

The best way to be sure that all engine valves are free is to use one of the special oils that are available and designed to free sticking valves. DO NOT, however, use this tune-up oil in cars that are equipped with a catalytic converter. The exhaust flow during this treatment will have a damaging effect on the catalyst.

Instructions vary, but a good method of treatment is to run engine at fast idle to normal operating temperature. Remove air cleaner and pour tune-up oil slowly and steadily into carburetor. Move throttle rod to speed up engine. Smoke will come from tail pipe, so perform this operation outdoors. Also, do it when car will not be needed for several hours, so oil will have time to dissolve the lacquer.

A simpler method of treatment for sticking valves is to pour tune-up oil into fuel tank. It will remove accumulations of lacquer from valve stems and carburetor during normal engine operation.

When restarted, the engine will idle more smoothly and have stepped-up performance. Now you can make the compression test and assume that there will be no compression loss due to sticking valves.

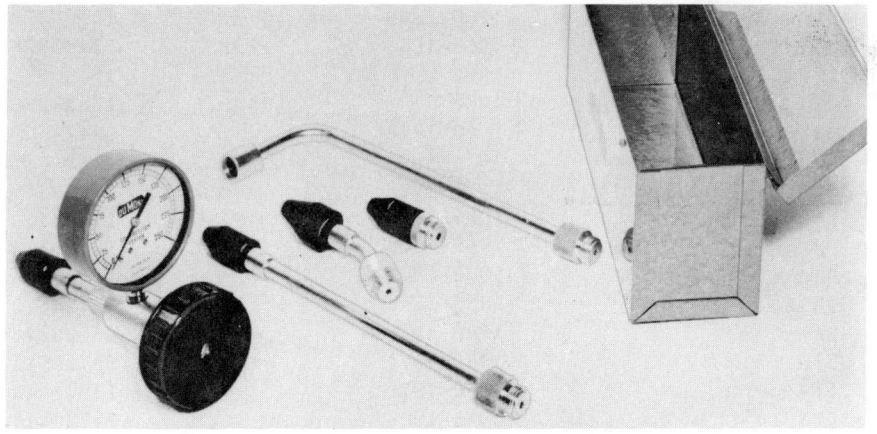

Fig. A-2. Gauge used for checking compression.

## HOW TO MAKE A COMPRESSION TEST

When making a compression test, first bring the engine to operating temperature, and then shut off the ignition. Remove the air cleaner, and block the throttle and the choke in wide-open position. Remove all the

**Fix Your Ford**

## COMPRESSION PRESSURES AT CRANKING SPEED AND FIRING ORDER

| Displacement | Year | Compression Pressure | Firing Order |
|---|---|---|---|
| 144 cu. in. | 1965-1960 | 170 lb. | 153624 |
| 170 cu. in. | 1967-1960 | 170 lb. | 153624 |
| 170 cu. in. | 1968 | 175 lb. | 153624 |
| 200 cu. in. | 1967-1965 | 170 lb. | 153624 |
| 200 cu. in. | 1968 | 175 lb. | 153624 |
| 221 cu. in. | 1963-1962 | 150 lb. | 15426378 |
| 223 cu. in. | 1964-1956 | 150 lb. | 153624 |
| 240 cu. in. | 1968-1965 | 175 lb. | 153624 |
| 250 cu. in. | 1971-1976 | * | 153624 |
| 260 cu. in. | 1965-1963 | 150 lb. | 15426378 |
| 289 cu. in. | 1968-1965 | 150 lb. | 15426378 |
| 292 cu. in. | 1963-1956 | 160 lb. | 15486372 |
| 302 cu. in. | 1968 | 170 lb. | 15426378 |
| 352 cu. in. | 1966-1958 | 180 lb. | 15426378 |
| 390 cu. in. | 1968-1961 | 180 lb. | 15426378 |
| 390 (4V) cu. in. | 1968-1964 | 190 lb. | 15426378 |
| 410 cu. in. | 1966 | 195 lb. | 15426378 |
| 427 cu. in. | 1966-1964 | 180 lb. | 15426378 |
| 428 cu. in. | 1968-1966 | 195 lb. | 15427378 |
| 429 cu. in. | 1968 | 190 lb. | 15426378 |
| 462 cu. in. | 1968 | 180 lb. | 15426378 |
| 122 cu. in. (2000 cc) | 1973-1974 | * | 1342 |
| 140 cu. in. (2300 cc) | 1974-1978 | * | 1342 |
| <u>170.8 cu. in. (2800 cc) V-6</u> | 1974-1978 | * | 142536 |
| Six cyl., in-line | 1969-1978 | * | 153624 |
| 302 cu. in. | 1969-1978 | * | 15426378 |
| 390 cu. in. | 1969-1974 | * | 15426378 |
| 428 cu. in. | 1969-1974 | * | 15426378 |
| 429 cu. in. | 1969-1974 | * | 15426378 |
| 351C cu. in. | 1969-1974 | * | 13726548 |
| 351W cu. in. | 1969-1978 | * | 13726548 |
| 351M cu. in. | 1975-1978 | * | 13726548 |
| 400 cu. in. | 1971-1978 | * | 13726548 |
| 460 cu. in. | 1969-1978 | * | 15426378 |

*In 1969-1978, instead of providing the actual compression pressures of the individual engines, Ford stated that when checking compression, "Take the highest compression reading and compare it to the lowest reading. The lowest should be within 75 percent of the highest." For example: If the highest reading is 200 psi, then the lowest reading permissible would be 150 psi.

# Tune-Up Tips

spark plugs, and then with the compression gauge, Fig. A-2, firmly inserted in one spark plug hole, crank the engine to at least four compression strokes to obtain the highest possible compression reading.

Check and record the compression of each cylinder and compare it with the specified value for that particular engine.

If one or more cylinders read low or uneven, inject about a tablespoonful of engine oil on top of the pistons of the low reading cylinders. Crank the engine several times and recheck the compression.

If the compression is higher than it was originally, it indicates that the piston rings or cylinders are worn and should be serviced.

If the compression does not improve after putting the oil in the cylinders, it indicates that the valves are sticking or are seating poorly.

If two adjacent cylinders have low compression, and injecting oil in the cylinders does not increase compression, the probable cause is a defective head gasket between the cylinders.

A compression check is of value because an engine with low or uneven compression cannot be tuned successfully to give maximum performance and economy.

If a weak cylinder cannot be located with a compression test, a cylinder balance test can be made which will help pinpoint the trouble.

## MAKING A CYLINDER BALANCE TEST

It is often difficult to locate a weak cylinder, especially in an eight cylinder engine. The reason is that while a compression test will show cylinders that are low in compression, it will not show any of the other causes that might result in uneven firing. For instance, a compression test will not locate a leaking intake manifold, a valve that does not open properly due to a worn camshaft or a defective spark plug.

A cylinder balance test will show the output of one cylinder as it is checked against another cylinder. This is done by means of grounding several spark plugs at a time, so that the engine will operate on only one or more cylinders at a time.

Do not perform a cylinder balance test on late model engines in cars equipped with a catalytic converter. Misfiring created by the test would cause unburned fuel to be exhausted from the cylinder which, in turn, would result in overheating of the catalytic converter.

As a further caution on catalytic converter equipped cars, never remove a cable from a spark plug for more than 30 seconds. Again, the converter would overheat if raw fuel reached the catalyst. Be sure to check the chapter on REDUCING EXHAUST EMISSIONS for additional cautions.

The equipment used when making a cylinder balance test is shown in Fig. A-3. To determine which cylinder should be grounded first, the usual procedure is to divide the firing order in half and arrange one-half over the other. For example: on a six cylinder engine with a firing order of 1-5-3-6-2-4, place the numbers 1-5-3 over the numbers 6-2-4. The

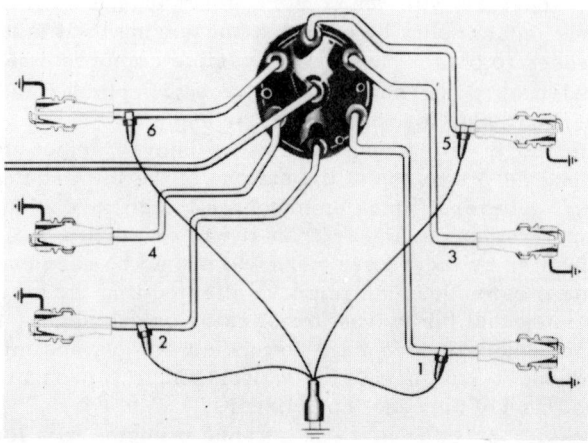

*Fig. A-4. Method of making a cylinder balance test to locate weak cylinders.*

cylinders to be tested together appear one over the other. That is, you would first test cylinders 1 and 6, next test cylinders 2 and 5, then test cylinders 3 and 4. If the power output of one pair of cylinders does not equal the others, the engine will run at lower rpm and with reduced vacuum. To detect this, connect a tachometer to primary ignition and ground; connect a vacuum gage to the intake manifold. The same two-cylinders-at-a-time testing procedure can be followed for V-8 engines.

Start testing a six cylinder engine for unbalance by connecting the special cylinder balance testing wiring harness to ground out cylinders 2-3-4-5. Operate the engine on cylinders 1 and 6, taking note of rpm and vacuum readings. Then shut off the engine and reconnect the special wiring harness to ground out cylinders 1-3-4-6. Operate the engine on cylinders 2 and 5, again taking rpm and vacuum readings. Shut off the engine.

Finally, reconnect the wiring harness to ground out cylinders 1-2-5-6 as in Fig. A-4. Run the engine on cylinders 3 and 4, again taking rpm and vacuum readings. Shut down and compare the three sets of readings. A variation of more than 40 rpm between pairs of cylinders being tested indicates that at least one of those cylinders is weak.

The reading on the vacuum gage should be essentially the same for each pair of cylinders being tested. If one pair of cylinders shows a vacuum reading materially lower than the others, that pair is weak and should be further checked to see which cylinder is at fault. This can be done by first increasing the speed of the engine and then shorting first one cylinder and then the other. The cylinder which gives the lowest vacuum reading is then at fault. A tachometer can be used instead of the vacuum gage.

The difficulty may be caused by low compression, faulty ignition to that cylinder, or possibly an air leak at the intake manifold.

# IGNITION TUNE-UP

The ignition system supplies the spark that ignites the air-fuel mixture in the combustion chamber. Two basic Ford systems are used, Fig. B-1: conventional or breaker point type; breakerless or solid state type (used on some models in 1973-74 and adopted on all models in 1975-76). A higher voltage Dura-Spark system was introduced in 1977.

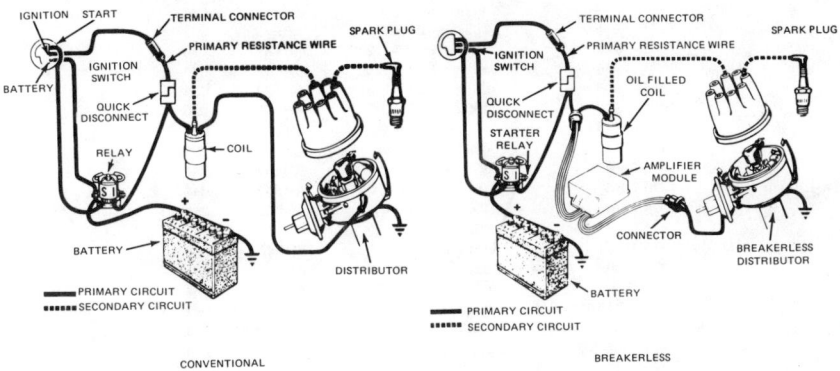

*Fig. B-1. Conventional ignition system is shown at left, breakerless type at right.*

The ignition system is easy to service and only simple tools are required. Service procedures for the conventional system follow; "breakerless" service begins on page 31. CAUTION: On late model cars equipped with catalytic converters, any misfiring should be corrected immediately or unburned fuel reaching the converter will cause it to overheat.

Ford uses a spark ignition system. There are many types of expensive equipment available for testing the spark. A satisfactory method requiring no equipment is to disconnect the high tension cable at one of the spark plugs. With the engine operating, hold the end of the spark plug wire about 1/4 in. away from some metal part of the engine. A strong, steady spark should jump from the end of the wire to the engine. If not, or if it is weak, thin or intermittent, the ignition system requires servicing. Do not make this test if there is any gasoline leakage present.

## SPARK PLUG TYPES
### (Original Equipment)

| Year—Model | Displacement | Spark Plug | Gap (In.) |
|---|---|---|---|
| 1962–1970 | 170 cu. in. Six | BF82 | .034 |
| 1962–1966 | 352 cu. in. V8 | BF42 | .034 |
| 1962–1970 | 390 cu. in. V8 | BF42 | .034 |
| 1964–1968 | 427 cu. in. V8 | BF32 | .034 |
| 1966–1970 | 240 cu. in. Six | BTF42 | .034 |
| 1969–1970 | 250 cu. in. Six | BF82 | .034 |
| 1964–1968 | 289 cu. in. V8 2V | BF42 | .034 |
| 1964–1968 | 289 cu. in. V8 4V | BF42 | .034 |
| 1968–1970 | 429 cu. in. V8 | BF42 | .034 |
| 1966 | 410 cu. in. V8 | BF42 | .034 |
| 1966–1969 | 428 cu. in. V8 | BF42 | .034 |
| 1968–1970 | 302 cu. in. V8 4V | AF32 | .034 |
| 1969–1970 | 302 cu. in. V8 2V | BF42 | .034 |
| 1969–1970 | 351 cu. in. V8 C-4V | AF32 | .034 |
| 1970 | 351 cu. in. V8 W-2V | BF42 | .034 |
| 1970 | 428 cu. in. V8 4V | BF32 | .034 |
| 1970 | 428 cu. in. Cobra | AF32 | .034 |
| 1971–1972 | 170 cu. in. Six | BRF82 | .034 |
| 1971–1976 | 200 cu. in. Six* | BRF82 | .034 |
| 1971–1972 | 240 cu. in. Six | BRF42 | .034 |
| 1971–1976 | 250 cu. in. Six* | BRF82 | .034 |
| 1971–1974 | 302 cu. in. V8 2V* | BRF42 | .034 |
| 1971 | 302 cu. in. V8 4V | ARF42 | .034 |
| 1969–1972 | 351 cu. in. V8 C-2V* | ARF42 | .034 |
| 1971–1974 | 351 cu. in. V8 W-2V* | BRF42 | .034 |
| 1971–1973 | 351 cu. in. V8 C-4V*+ | ARF42 | .034 |
| 1971–1974 | 400 cu. in. V8 2V | ARF42 | .034 |
| 1971–1973 | 429 cu. in. V8 4V | BRF42 | .034 |
| 1971 | 429 cu. in. Cobra | ARF42 | .034 |
| 1974 Ford | 351 cu. in. V8 C-2V | ARF42 | .044 |
| 1974 Ford | 351 cu. in. V8 C-4V | ARF42 | .034 |
| 1974 Ford | 460 cu. in. V8 4V | ARF52 | .054 |
| 1974 Ford (Cal) | 460 cu. in. V8 4V | ARF52 | .044 |
| 1974 Torino | 351 cu. in. V8 2V | BRF42 | .034 |
| 1974 Torino | 351 cu. in. V8 C-2V | ARF42 | .034 |
| 1974 Torino | 400 cu. in. V8 2V | ARF42 | .044 |
| 1974–1976 Mustang II | 2300 cc Four 2V | AGRF52 | .034 |
| 1974–1976 Mustang II | 2800 cc V6 | AGRF42 | .034 |
| 1974 Maverick | 302 cu. in. V8 2V | BRF42 | .034 |
| 1975–1976 | 2300 cc | AGRF52 | .034 |
| 1975–1976 | 2800 cc | AGR42 | .034 |
| 1975–1976 | V6-170 | AGR42 | .034 |
| 1975–1976 | 200 cu. in. | BRF82 | .044 |
| 1975–1976 | 250 cu. in. | BRF82 | .044 |
| 1975–1976 | 302 cu. in. | ARF42 | .044 |
| 1975 | 351M cu. in. | ARF42 | .044 |
| 1975 | 351W cu. in. | BRF42 | .044 |
| 1976 | 351M cu. in. | ARF52 | .044 |
| 1976 | 351W cu. in. | ARF42 | .044 |
| 1975–1976 | 400 cu. in. | ARF42 | .044 |
| 1975–1976 | 460 cu. in. | ARF42 | .054 |
| 1977–1978 | 2300 cc | AWRF42 | .034 |
| 1977–1978 | 2800 cc | AWRF42 | .034 |
| 1977–1978 | 200 cu. in. | BRF82 | .050 |
| 1977–1978 | 250 cu. in. | BRF82 | .050 |
| 1977–1978 | 302 cu. in. | ARF52 | .050 |
| 1977–1978 | 351 cu. in. | ARF52 | .050 |
| 1977–1978 | 400 cu. in. | ARF52 | .050 |
| 1977–1978 | 460 cu. in. | ARF52 | .050 |
| 1977–1978 | Cal V8 | ARF526 | .060 |

\* With air conditioning
+ Manual transmission

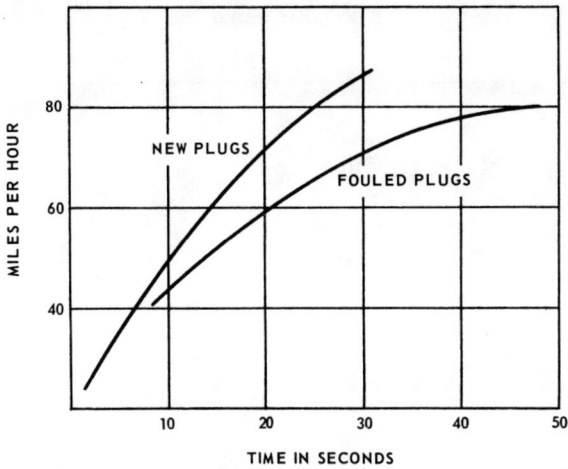

*Fig. B-2. Note how acceleration improves with new spark plugs.*

## WHAT TO DO ABOUT SPARK PLUGS

Spark plugs should give at least 10,000 miles of satisfactory service, provided they are the correct heat range for the engine and fuel of the proper octane rating is used. Continued use of old plugs results in hard starting, poor acceleration and reduced power at high speeds, Fig. B-2. To help diagnose ignition problems, compare the appearance of the old plugs with conditions shown in Fig. B-3.

A normal spark plug in good condition can be identified by a light tan or gray deposit on the firing tip. Severely eroded or worn electrodes will result from extended operation. If the center electrode is rounded and the side electrode is grooved, install new plugs.

Dry, fluffy carbon desposits indicate that the plug is either too cold or the air-fuel mixture is excessively rich. Wet, black deposits result from oil entering the combustion chamber. If the plug gap is bridged over with deposits, it is a sign of either oil or carbon fouling.

When highly leaded gasoline is used, it may result in a fused, glazed coating on the insulator tip. Overheated spark plugs can be identified by a white or light gray insulator with a bluish burnt appearance of the electrodes. Preignition will cause the electrodes to melt and possibly blister the insulator.

## CLEANING AND CHECKING SPARK PLUGS

The only satisfactory way to clean spark plugs is by means of abrasive particle blasting equipment. If such equipment is not available, scrape the soot from the insulator and from the interior of the shell (metal body) of the spark plug. Then, carefully examine the insulator for cracks or any other defects.

Also, check the condition of the firing points or electrodes.

# Fix Your Ford

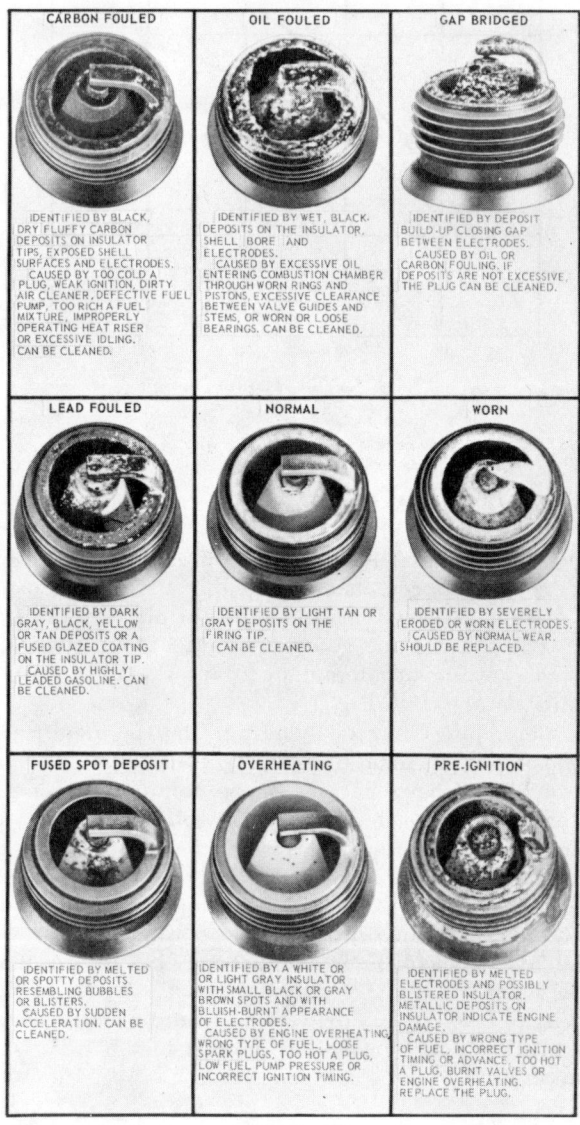

Fig. B-3. Different types of spark plug failure.

When the electrodes are worn, Fig. B-4, an excessive amount of voltage is required to jump the gap. Misfiring and loss of fuel economy will result. Usually, it is advisable to install new plugs. In an emergency, dress both electrodes with a small file to obtain flat, parallel surfaces, Fig. B-5.

## Ignition Tune-Up

Fig. B-4. Note worn condition of electrodes.

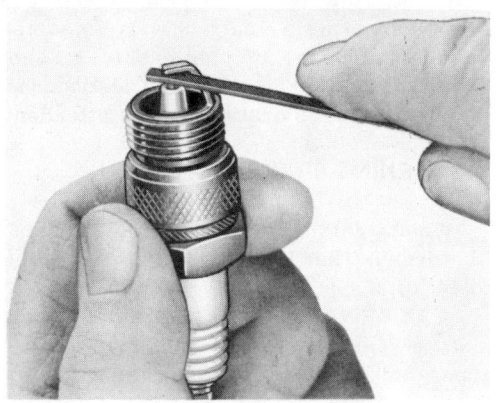

Fig. B-5. Truing electrodes by filing firing points will improve ignition.

## ADJUSTING AND INSTALLING SPARK PLUGS

When adjusting a spark plug gap, bend the side electrode only. Attempting to bend the center electrode invariably results in breaking the insulator. Never open the gap enough to try to make a wide gap plug from a conventional (.035 in.) gap plug, Fig. B-6. Wide gap plugs are used on later engines to keep exhaust emission levels low.

Combination gauges and adjusters are available for accurately setting the spark plug gap. A round wire gauge, Fig. B-7, is preferred over the blade type feeler gauge.

When installing spark plugs, first be sure that the area surrounding the spark plug hole in the cylinder head is clean and free from dirt. Also

Fig. B-6. Widening gap of old type plug will lead to early failure.

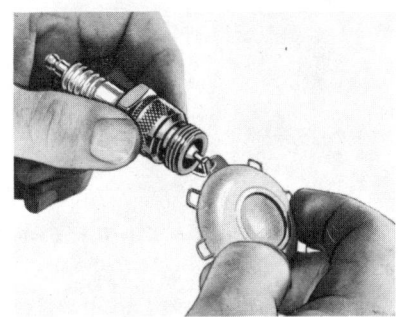

Fig. B-7. Using a combination spark plug gap gauge to check and adjust the gap.

make sure that the spark plug threads and the surface contacting the head are clean. This is particularly important on Ford cars of recent manufacture, as no spark plug gasket is used. Any dirt will not only result in compression leakage, but will also tend to make the plug operate at higher than normal temperatures, with attendant misfiring and short life.

## TIGHTENING SPARK PLUGS

When tightening the spark plugs, the Ford factory specifies 15 to 20 ft. lb. torque. That is 15 to 20 lb. exerted at the end of a 1 ft. wrench, or 30 to 40 lb. at the end of a 6 in. wrench.

A 13/16 in. long socket wrench should be used when removing and replacing spark plugs. Special long sockets with sponge rubber lining in the upper end, designed to grip the insulator of the plug, and also to reduce the possibility of cracking the insulator, are available.

## REMOVING THE DISTRIBUTOR CAP

In order to replace an ignition condenser, a rotor, or install new ignition breaker points, it is first necessary to remove the distributor cap.

To remove the distributor cap, snap back the hold-down clips and the cap can then be lifted off the distributor body, Fig. B-8.

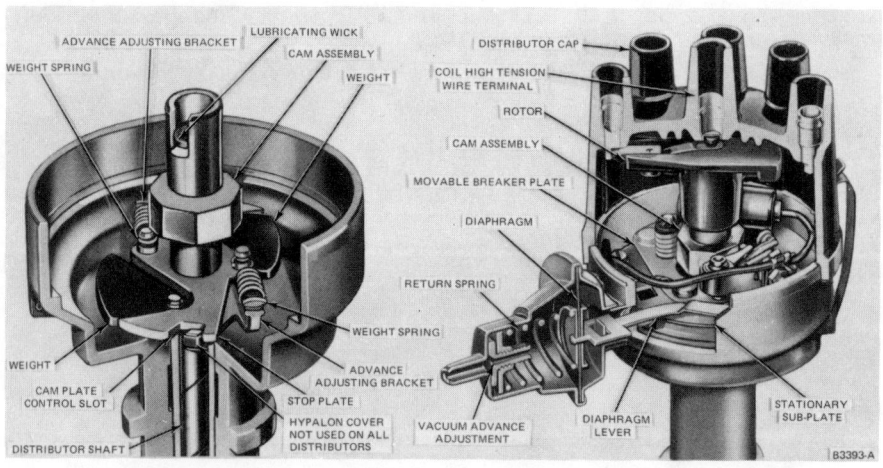

*Fig. B-8. Details of single-diaphragm dual advance distributor.*

Carefully clean the distributor cap and then examine it thoroughly to be sure that it is not cracked at any point. Particular attention should be paid to any evidence of charring between the firing points on the interior

## Ignition Tune-Up

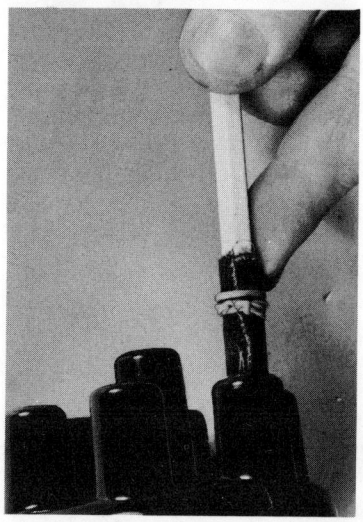

*Fig. B-9. Cleaning the towers of a distributor cap with fine emery cloth wrapped around a pencil.*

of the cap. Such a condition results from arcing of the spark. Also make sure the interior of the towers are clean and are not corroded. If there is any evidence of such corrosion, it should be removed. The easiest way of doing this is to roll some fine grain abrasive paper around a pencil, and use it as a hone to remove the corrosion, Fig. B-9. If the cap is cracked, or if there is any arcing between points in the interior of the cap, or if the interior of the towers cannot be cleaned, a new cap should be installed.

*Fig. B-10. Note pitted condition of these breaker points. Such points should be replaced.*

# Fix Your Ford

After the cap has been removed, the rotor, Fig. B-8, can be pulled vertically from the top of the distributor shaft. If the spring contact on top of the rotor is defective, a new rotor should be obtained. Also if the firing end of the rotor is badly eroded, the rotor should be discarded.

## CHECKING BREAKER POINTS

Normally, ignition breaker points should give good service for about 15,000 miles, but it pays to make more frequent checks. The solid state and Dura-Spark systems do not employ breaker points.

Breaker points in good condition have an even gray appearance without pitting or metal transfer from one point to the other. Also, the points should have been contacting over their entire area.

As shown in Figs. B-10 and B-11, any discoloration other than the frosted slate gray should be considered as a burned condition. Burned points can result from excessive voltage or a defective condenser. Excessive metal transfer or pitting can result from incorrect alignment, incorrect voltage regulator setting, radio condenser installed to the distributor side of the coil, the ignition condenser may be of an incorrect capacity, or extended operation of the engine at high speeds.

| CONDITION | CAUSED BY |
|---|---|
|  BURNED | Any discoloration other than a frosted slate grey shall be considered as burned points. |
| 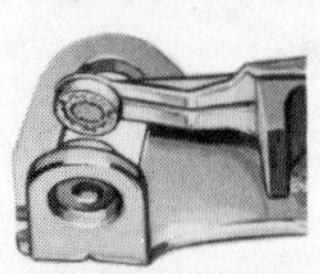 EXCESSIVE METAL TRANSFER OR PITTING | Incorrect alignment. Incorrect voltage regulator setting. Radio condenser installed to the distributor side of the coil. Ignition condenser of improper capacity. Extended operation of the engine at speeds other than normal. |

Fig. B-11. Worn ignition breaker points, together with cause of failure.

Special care must be taken to be sure that the breaker points are correctly aligned. Not only must the contact area be centered, but the rubbing block must contact the distributor cam fully.

The vented type breaker points used on Ford cars must be accurately aligned and strike squarely in order to realize the full advantage of the design and assure normal breaker point life. Any misalignment will cause short life, overheating and pitting.

While points are manufactured to close limits for alignment, they must

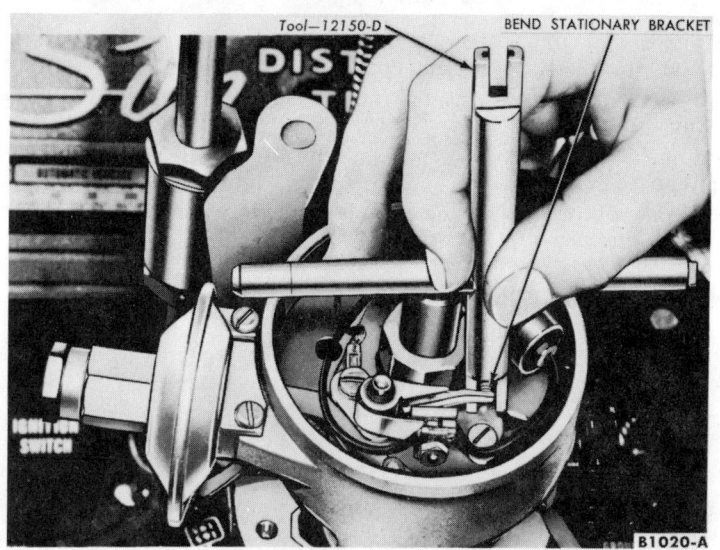

*Fig. B-12. To align breaker points, adjust stationary point only.*

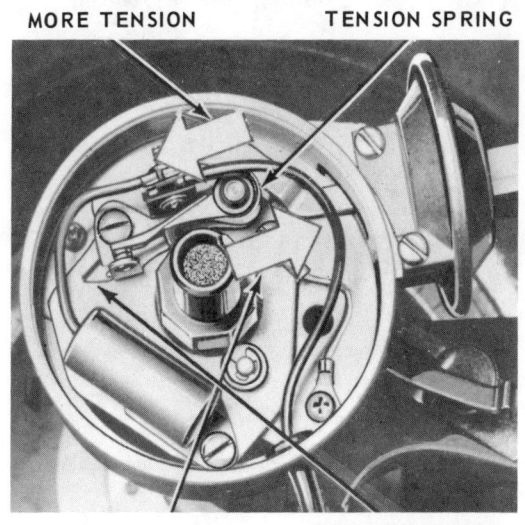

*Fig. B-13. Method of adjusting breaker spring tension.*

always be checked. Turn cam until points close. Check alignment.

With distributor in place, crank engine in short spurts until it stops with points closed. A dental mirror helps in this application. Align breaker points.

## Fix Your Ford

To adjust breaker point gap, rotate distributor until rubbing block is on high point of cam. Loosen locking screw that secures point assembly to breaker plate. Adjust gap width by turning adjusting screw or by inserting a screwdriver in adjusting slot, Figs. B-17 and B-18. Use a feeler gauge to measure the gap or, if available, use a dwell meter. In general, dwell angle is: V-8 engine, 28 deg.; six cylinder engine, 37 deg.; four cylinder engine, 39 deg.

## SETTING BREAKER POINT SPRING TENSION

In addition to accurately aligning the breaker points, it is also important that the breaker point spring tension be correct. If the tension is too great, rapid wear of the breaker arm rubbing block will result, causing the breaker gap to close up and retard the spark timing. If the spring tension is too weak, the breaker arm will flutter at high speed resulting in an engine miss.

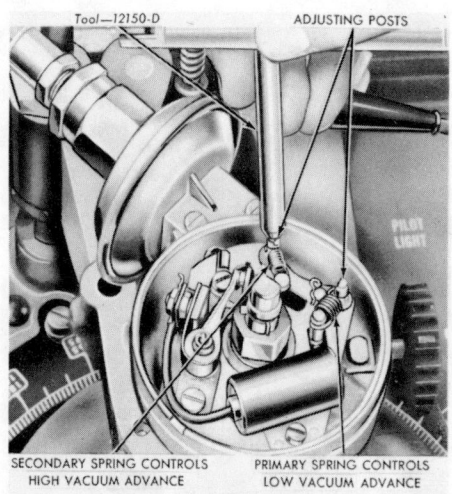

Fig. B-14. Advance on Loadomatic distributor is controlled by tension of two springs. Late model cars with automatic transmissions use only one spring.

To check the spring tension on either the pivot-type or the pivotless breaker points, place the hooked end of the spring tension gauge over the movable breaker point. Pull the gauge at a right angle to the movable arm until the breaker points just start to open. If the tension is not within specifications, adjust the spring tension on the pivot-type points, or replace the breaker point assembly on the pivotless points.

To adjust the spring tension, disconnect the primary (distributor

## Ignition Tune-Up

transistor lead wire), the condenser, if so equipped, and the jumper strap on the centrifugal advance distributor at the breaker point assembly primary terminal.

Loosen the nut holding the spring in position. Move the spring toward the breaker arm pivot to decrease tension and in the opposite direction to increase tension, Fig. B-13. After tightening the lock nut, check the spring tension. Repeat the adjustment until the specified spring tension is obtained. The correct tension should range between 17 and 20 ounces for all distributors, except the distributor with dual breaker points. In that case it should range between 27 and 32 ounces.

## QUICK SERVICE ON THE LOADOMATIC DISTRIBUTOR

The Loadomatic distributor, Fig. B-14, is used primarily on the six cylinder engines and smaller V-8s prior to 1975. The varying requirements of speed and load are satisfied by the action of the breaker plate which is controlled by a vacuum actuated diaphragm working against the tension of one or two coil springs mounted on the breaker plate.

On 1961 and later Loadomatic distributors used on cars with automatic transmissions, only one coiled spring is used, Fig. B-15. On manual transmission equipped cars, and all cars prior to 1961, two coiled springs are used, Fig. B-14.

On distributors on six cylinder engines, the diaphragm moves the breaker plate counterclockwise to advance the spark, and the springs move the breaker plate clockwise to retard the spark. The amount of spark advance is therefore controlled by the strength of the vacuum.

For eight cylinder engines equipped with quick Loadomatic distributors, the spark is advanced by the diaphragm moving the breaker plate clockwise and retarded by the spring moving the plate counterclockwise.

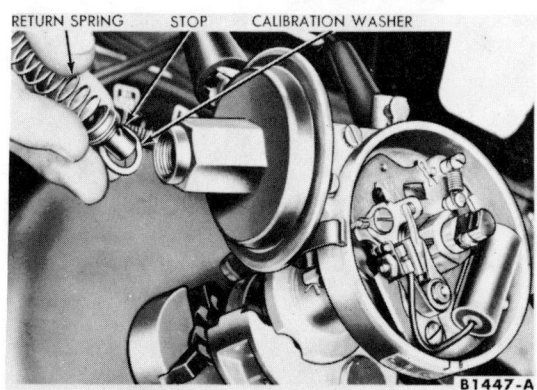

*Fig. B-15. Loadomatic distributor as used on cars equipped with automatic transmission. Degree of vacuum advance is controlled by shims or washers as indicated.*

# Fix Your Ford

Six cylinder distributors rotate clockwise and eight cylinder distributors counterclockwise.

For all eight cylinder distributors, a vacuum actuated spark control valve is attached to the carburetor throttle body to control manifold vacuum to the distributor and regulate spark advance.

The springs on the breaker plate are precision adjusted at the factory and should not require any further attention.

To replace the breaker points on the Loadomatic distributor, first remove the distributor cap and rotor. Then disconnect the condenser and primary lead wires from the breaker point assembly. Remove the screws retaining the breaker point assembly and condenser, which will permit lifting the breaker point assembly out of the distributor.

Installation of new breaker points is accomplished by placing the breaker point assembly and the condenser in position on the breaker plate and installing the screws. Be sure that the ground wire is under the breaker point assembly screw nearest the breaker point contacts. Align and adjust the breaker points as previously described. Then connect the primary and condenser wires to the breaker point assembly. Installation of the rotor and distributor cap completes the job.

Setting the vacuum advance on the Loadomatic distributor should be done on a distributor test bench. On the conventional Loadomatic with two coil springs on the breaker plate, such as is used on cars with manual shift transmissions, the primary spring should be adjusted first, Fig. B-14, and the secondary spring last. If a distributor test bench is not available, an approximate setting can be made and checked by driving the car. The procedure is to start with little tension on the two springs. After each test acceleration, the spring tension is increased a slight amount, until the engine starts to "ping."

On models starting in 1960, an additional adjustment is provided by means of washers behind the stop in the diaphragm housing, Fig. B-15. The addition of a washer will retard the spark.

On 1961 and later Loadomatic distributors used on cars with automatic transmissions, there is only one coil spring on the breaker plate. The other adjustment is by means of washers and shims used to adjust the tension of the diaphragm spring, Fig. B-15. This controls the spark advance at high engine speed.

After making sure the breaker points are correctly aligned, as previously described, the gap between the points must be accurately adjusted. The procedure is as follows: A dwell meter or a feeler gauge can be used to measure the gap. Rotate the distributor until the rubbing block of the point assembly rests on the peak of a cam. If the distributor is still in the engine, the distributor can be rotated by cranking the engine. So the engine will not start, ground the lead from the ignition coil on any convenient part of the engine. Then crank the engine in spurts, until it stops with the rubbing block on the high point of the cam. Loosen the screw holding the breaker point assembly to the breaker plate. Then adjust the point opening by inserting a screwdriver in the notch at the point end of the breaker

## Ignition Tune-Up

assembly. With the screwdriver pry the assembly back and forth until the desired gap as measured by the feeler gauge is obtained. Tighten the screw holding the breaker point assembly to the breaker plate, taking care not to alter the breaker point gap.

If a dwell meter is available, adjust the gap until the desired dwell is obtained.

### QUICK SERVICE ON THE DUAL ADVANCE DISTRIBUTOR

The dual advance distributor, Fig. B-8, provides both centrifugal and vacuum advance. The centrifugal advance is provided to control spark advance according to engine speed, and the vacuum advance to regulate the advance according to engine load.

The unusual feature of this distributor is that provision is made for adjusting the centrifugal advance as well as the vacuum advance.

The centrifugal advance is adjusted through a slot in the breaker plate Fig. B-16, and the vacuum is adjusted by varying the number of shims placed behind the vacuum advance spring, Fig. B-15.

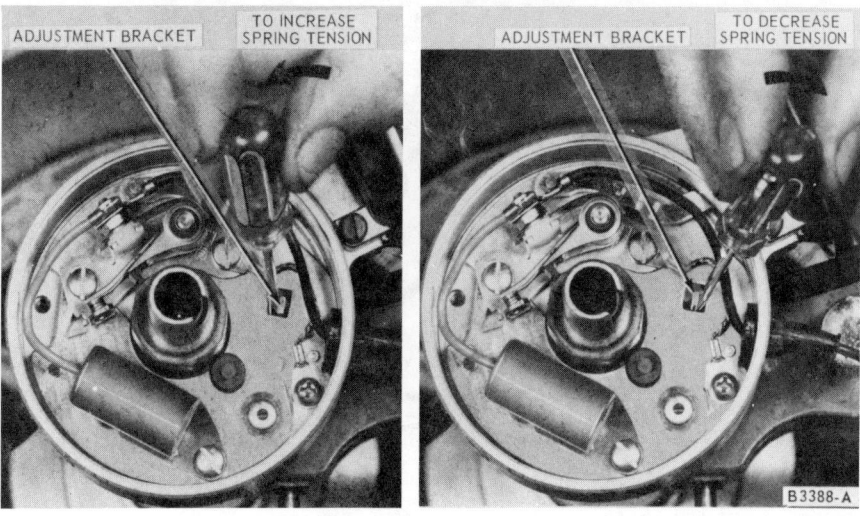

*Fig. B-16. Showing procedure for changing centrifugal advance on distributors for six and V-8 engines.*

To remove and install the ignition breaker points on the dual advance distributor, first remove the distributor cap, rotor and dust cover (if installed). Disconnect the distributor-transistor wire from the breaker point assembly. Remove the retaining screws from the breaker point assembly and lift the breaker point assembly out of the distributor.

Installation of a breaker point is accomplished by placing the breaker point assembly in position, and installing the retaining screws. Be sure to place the ground wire under the breaker point assembly screw farthest from the breaker point contacts. Align and adjust the breaker point assembly.

Adjustment of the ignition breaker point gap is accomplished by first loosening the screw securing the point assembly to the breaker plate, and then using a tool to engage the adjusting slot at the breaker point end of the assembly. The width of the gap is measured by means of a feeler gauge as shown in Fig. B-17.

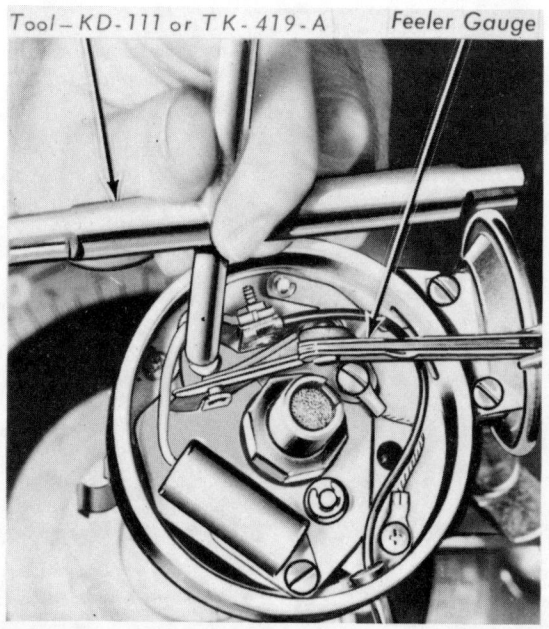

*Fig. B-17. Adjusting breaker point gap. A feeler gauge is used to measure the gap.*

## QUICK SERVICE ON THE CENTRIFUGAL ADVANCE DISTRIBUTOR

The centrifugal advance distributor, Fig. B-18, has two breaker point assemblies and is used primarily on high performance engines.

To remove the breaker point assemblies on the centrifugal advance distributor used on the conventional ignition system, first remove the distributor cap and the rotor. Disconnect the primary lead, Fig. B-18, the jumper strap and the condenser lead from the breaker point assemblies. Remove the retaining screws from the breaker point assemblies and the condenser. Lift the breaker point assemblies and the condenser out of

## Ignition Tune-Up

the distributor.

Installation of the new breaker point assemblies is accomplished by reversing the procedure. After aligning the breaker points, the gap is adjusted as follows:

After accurately aligning the breaker point assemblies, rotate the distributor cam until one of the rubbing blocks rests on the peak of a cam lobe.

If the car is equipped with a transistor ignition system, and the starter is going to be tapped to place a breaker point assembly on the peak of the cam, proceed as follows:

Connect a jumper between the S-terminal of the solenoid and the battery with the ignition switch off and the coil lead (ground wire) disconnected from the solenoid.

Insert the correct blade of a clean feeler gauge between the breaker points. Insert the blade of a screwdriver at the gap adjustment slot indicated in Fig. B-18 and by turning the screwdriver, adjust the gap to the specified amount of .020 in. Then adjust the other set of points in the same manner, taking care to carefully lock the adjustment by turning down the screw which fastens the breaker point assembly to the plate.

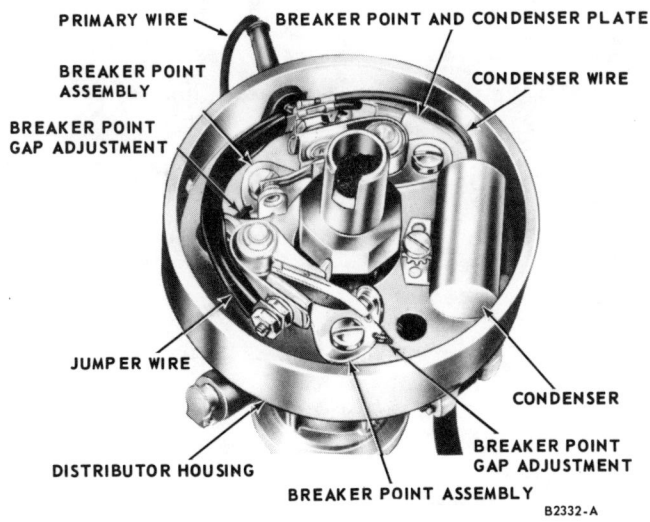

Fig. B-18. Details of centrifugal distributor with dual breaker points.

Apply a light film of distributor cam lubricant to the cam when new points are installed. Never use engine oil for that purpose.

The centrifugal advance adjustment is reached through a hole in the breaker plate, as shown in Fig. B-16.

The distributor should be placed in a distributor test bench when adjusting the centrifugal advance, and the adjustment is made by bending one spring adjustment bracket to change its tension, as shown in Fig. B-16. Bend the adjustment bracket away from the distributor shaft to decrease advance (increase spring tension), and toward the shaft to increase advance (decrease spring tension). After each adjustment check the advance point, as indicated by the meters on the test bench.

The vacuum advance is adjusted by means of spacing washers between the vacuum chamber spring and nut, Fig. B-15. The addition of a washer will decrease advance, and the removal of a washer will increase advance.

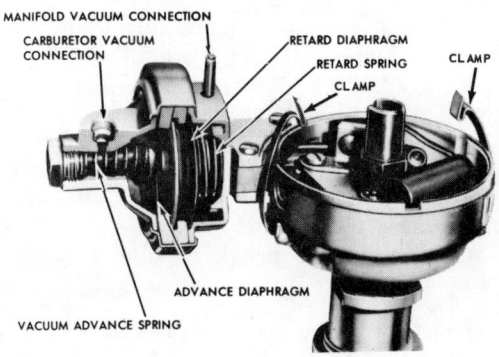

*Fig. B-19. Details of a dual diaphragm distributor.*

## QUICK SERVICE ON DUAL DIAPHRAGM DISTRIBUTOR

The 1968-1974 exhaust emission control systems require a specially retarded spark for more complete combustion at idle and low speed, combined with the usual spark advance at normal speeds. On some models, this is obtained by means of a dual diaphragm distributor, Figs. B-19 and B-20. With the exception of the diaphragm assembly, the rest of the distributor is similar to the Autolite unit used previously.

The outer diaphragm, Figs. B-19 and B-21, controls the spark advance in the same manner as the single diaphragm did in an older model. The other, or retard diaphragm, operates to retard the spark at low engine speed and during deceleration.

To remove the breaker points and condenser from the dual diaphragm distributor, remove the distributor cap and rotor. Disconnect the primary and condenser wires from the breaker point assembly. Remove the breaker point assembly and condenser retaining screws which will permit the breaker point assembly and condenser to be lifted from the distributor. Installation of the breaker points is accomplished by reversing the procedure. However, be sure to place the ground wire under the breaker point assembly screw farthest from the breaker point contacts on an

## Ignition Tune-Up

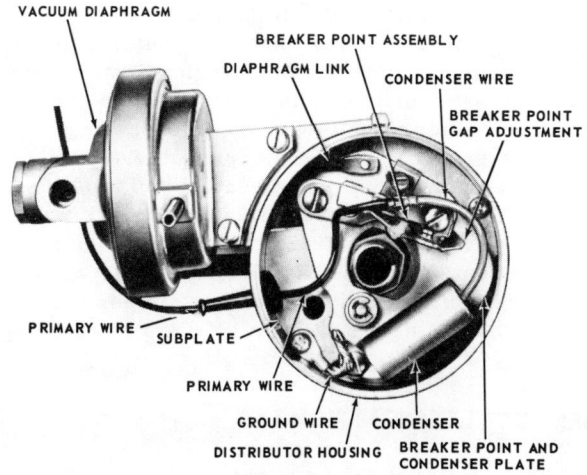

*Fig. B-20. When replacing points on a dual diaphragm distributor, place ground wire under breaker plate assembly screw farthest from points on V-8 engines or under condenser retaining screw on six cylinder engines.*

eight cylinder engine distributor, or under the condenser retaining screw on a six cylinder engine distributor. After carefully aligning the breaker points, the gap should be adjusted.

To adjust the breaker points, rotate the distributor until the rubbing block rests on the peak of the cam. Insert the correct blade of a clean

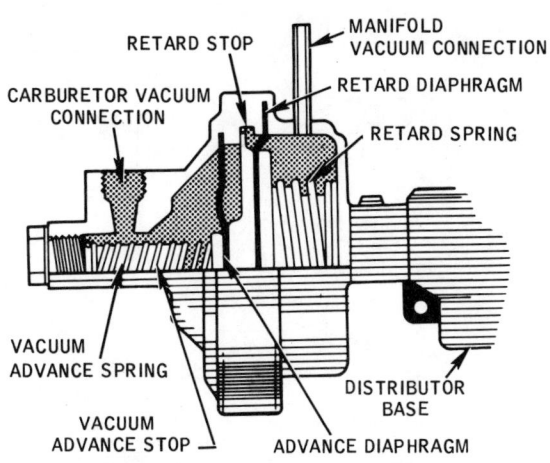

*Fig. B-21. Sectional view of dual diaphragm vacuum advance assembly.*

feeler gauge between the breaker points and adjust the gap by inserting a screwdriver at the point indicated in Fig. B-20.

On dual diaphragm vacuum advance distributors, the centrifugal advance unit is the same as on single diaphragm vacuum advance distributors. However, the outer primary diaphragm utilizes carburetor vacuum to advance ignition timing, while the inner or secondary diaphragm is actuated by intake manifold vacuum to provide additional timing retard during periods of closed throttle deceleration and idle, thereby assisting in the reduction of exhaust system hydrocarbons.

The distributor vacuum control valve used on some IMCO Ignition Systems is incorporated in the distributor vacuum advance supply line to provide advance ignition timing under certain engine operating conditions. It is installed in the coolant outlet elbow to sense engine coolant temperatures.

## 1973-1978 BREAKERLESS IGNITION

The breakerless (solid state) ignition system is found on some 1973-74 models and on all 1975-76 models. Earlier vehicles have the conventional breaker point type ignition system. The breakerless system retains most of the features of the conventional system, but employs a unique armature and magnetic pickup coil, Fig. B-22, and a solid state amplifier module. Starting in 1977, the higher voltage Dura-Spark system became standard equipment on all models.

The armature turns with the distributor shaft, causing fluctuations in the magnetic field generated by the pickup coil assembly. These fluctuations cause the amplifier to turn the ignition current off and on, causing

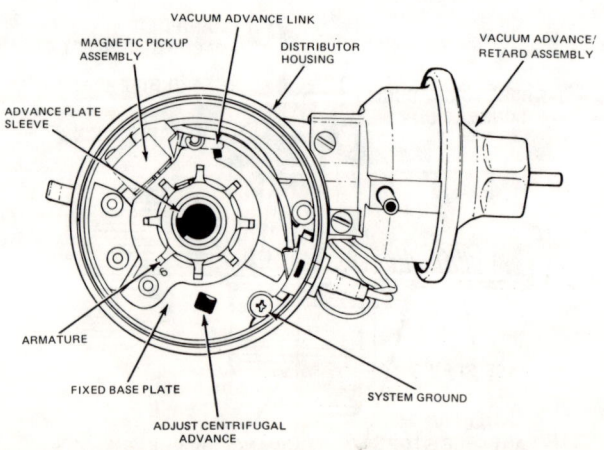

*Fig. B-22. Breakerless ignition distributor installed on some 1973 and 1974 models. "Breakerless" ignition has been used on all models since 1975.*

## Ignition Tune-Up

the high tension spark to jump the gap at the plugs. The distributor is provided with a conventional cap and rotor; also with vacuum and centrifugal spark advance units. See Fig. B-16 for adjustments.

The rotor of the distributor on six cylinder engines rotates in a clockwise direction. To advance timing, move the distributor counterclockwise. The rotor of the distributor on V-8 engines rotates in a counterclockwise direction, so the spark is advanced by moving the distributor clockwise.

The distributor can be removed in the usual manner: Remove air cleaner and disconnect wiring and vacuum lines. Scribe a mark on distributor body and cylinder block indicating position of rotor in distributor and distributor in engine block. Marks will serve as a guide when reinstalling distributor. Remove hold-down bolt and clamp, then lift distributor out of block.

To install the distributor: First be sure No. 1 piston is at TDC after compression stroke. Then align correct initial timing mark on timing pointer on crankshaft damper. Position distributor in block with one armature segment and rotor at number one firing position, Fig. B-23.

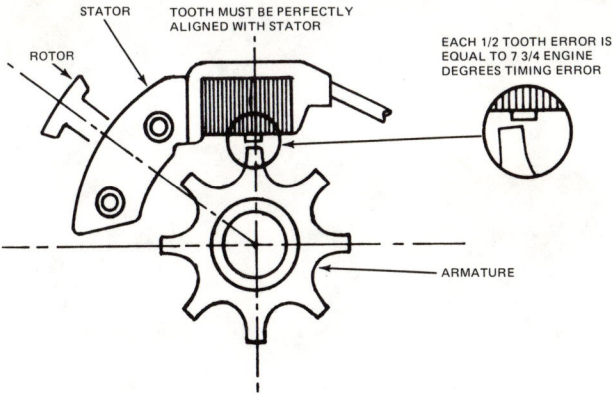

*Fig. B-23. Note alignment of tooth with stator.*

Make sure oil pump intermediate shaft properly engages distributor shaft; it may be necessary to crank engine with starter after distributor is partly engaged. Turn distributor to advance timing until an armature tooth is aligned correctly, Fig. B-23.

### V-SIX DISTRIBUTOR

The 1975 V-Six breakerless ignition system was described in previous paragraphs. To adjust the centrifugal advance unit on the 1974 V-Six, work through the side of the distributor, Fig. B-24. Bend one spring of adjustment bracket away from distributor shaft to decrease advance; toward shaft to increase advance.

## Fix Your Ford

The vacuum advance diaphragm assembly is factory preset and cannot be adjusted. If tests indicate that the diaphragm is inoperative or out of calibration, install a new unit.

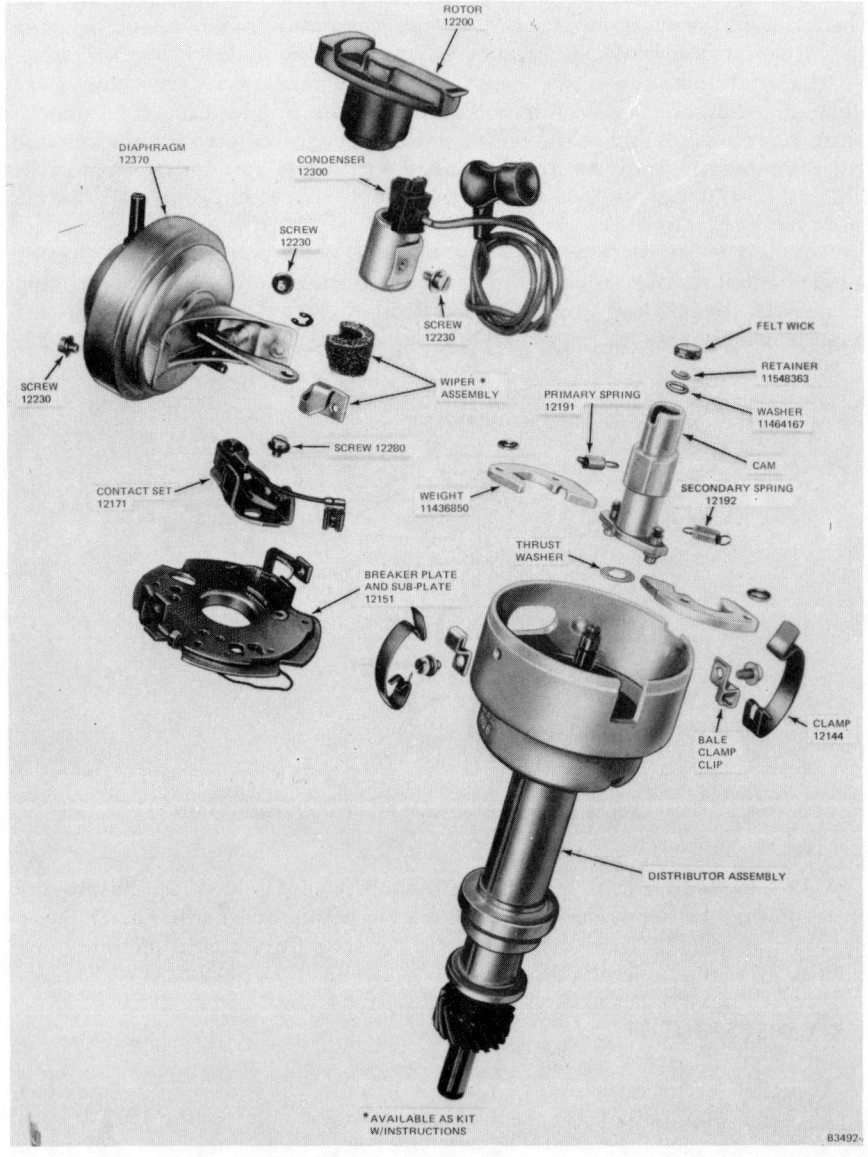

Fig. B-24. Details of V-Six distributor.

## Ignition Tune-Up

### 2300 cc 4-CYLINDER DISTRIBUTOR - 1974

Correct point gap on the 2300 cc distributor is .027 in. Dwell is 35 to 41 deg. at idle speed. Firing order is 1-3-4-2. See decal in engine compartment for initial ignition timing. Replacement parts for distributor shaft, drive gear or cam are not available. Breakerless ignition used on 1975 2300 cc engine was described in previous paragraphs.

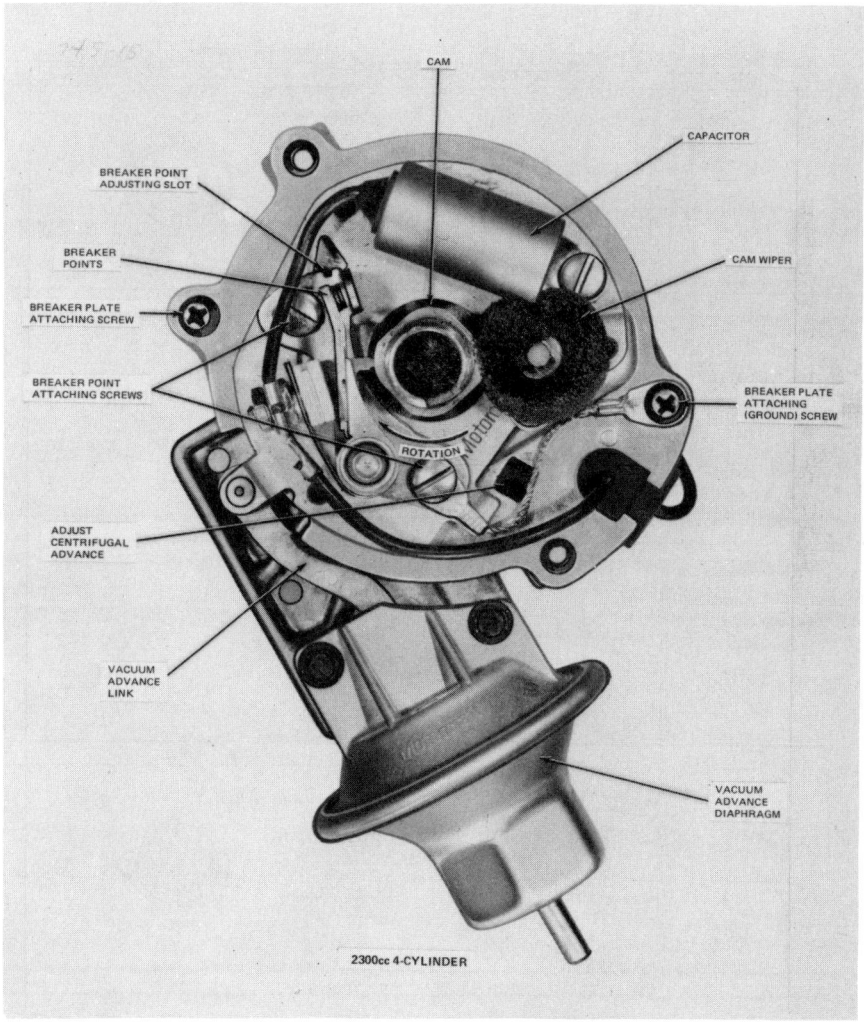

*Fig. B-25. Construction of distributor for 2300 cc engine is typical of other distributors installed on older Ford engines.*

# Fix Your Ford

## FORD ENGINE IGNITION TIMING

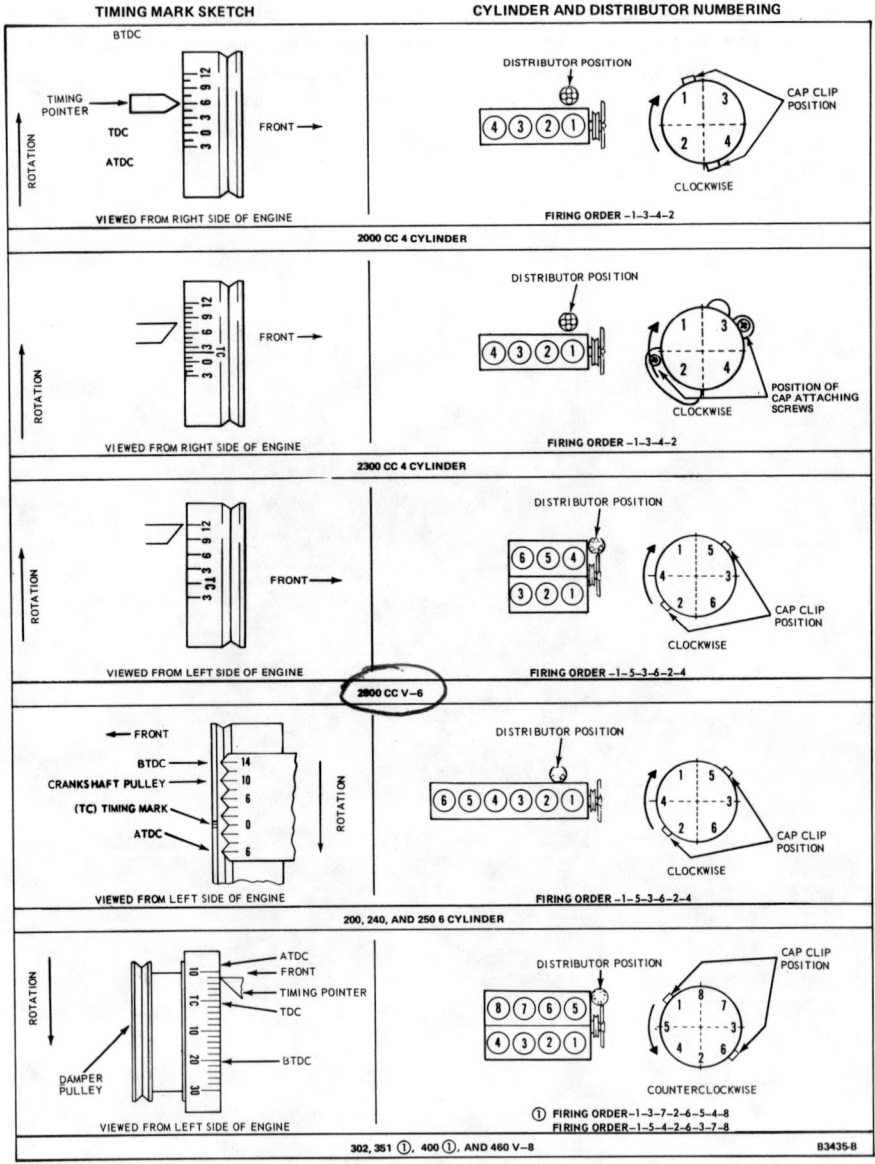

Fig. B-26. Ignition timing and firing order of recent Ford engines.
(Courtesy Ford Customer Service Div.)

## Ignition Tune-Up

## DURA-SPARK IGNITION SYSTEM

Dura-Spark ignition, introduced in 1977, is similar to 1975-1976 breakerless system. However, Dura-Spark has higher voltages and comes in two versions: 1-For California vehicles. 2-For other 49 states.

|                              | Start (10V) at 200 rpm | Run (14V) at 800 rpm |
|------------------------------|------------------------|----------------------|
| 1976 Breakerless System      | 32,000V                | 26,000V              |
| 1977 49 State Dura-Spark     | 42,000V                | 36,000V              |
| 1977 California Dura-Spark   | 47,000V                | 42,000V              |

The higher voltages provided by the Dura-Spark system permit a much wider spark plug gap, which is needed to ignite the leaner fuel mixtures and help handle the increased exhaust gas recirculation in California engines. New components include: a solid state module; ignition coil; distributor cap and adapter; ignition wiring.

The new module analyzes system requirements and supplies the required spark plug voltages. It includes an integrated circuit with a built-in regulator that reduces the temperature of the coil and module.

The coil windings are designed to provide the needed voltages. The distributor features the basic spoked armature design. The new cap and adapter are larger, higher and more durable. The spark plug towers offer positive locking of the terminal and a better boot seal.

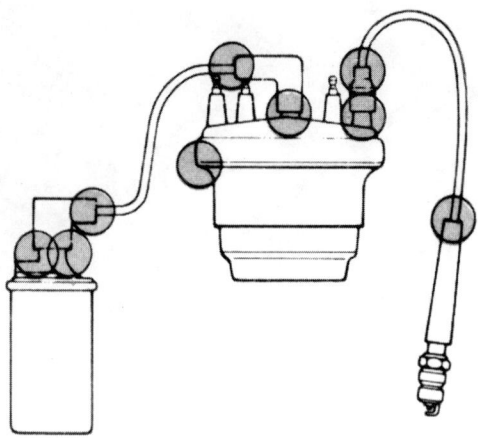

Fig. B-26a. Dura-Spark ignition system. Maintain at least 3/4 in. clearance at indicated points to prevent arcing.

The rotor gap is .096 in., which reduces radio frequency interference. The ignition cables have been increased in size from 7 mm to 8 mm in diameter. When servicing the Dura-Spark system, be sure to maintain at least 3/4 in. clearance at the key points shown in Fig. B-26a.

# Fix Your Ford

## TIMING BREAKER POINT TYPE DISTRIBUTORS

First clean and chalk the timing mark located on the vibration damper or fan pulley, Fig. B-26. Disconnect the vacuum line (single diaphragm distributor) or vacuum lines (dual diaphragm distributor) and plug the disconnected vacuum line or lines.

Connect a timing light, Fig. B-27, to the No. 1 spark plug wire. If available, connect a tachometer to the engine. Start the engine and reduce the idle speed to 600 rpm to be sure the centrifugal advance is not operating. Aim the timing light at the timing mark, Fig. B-27. The chalk mark

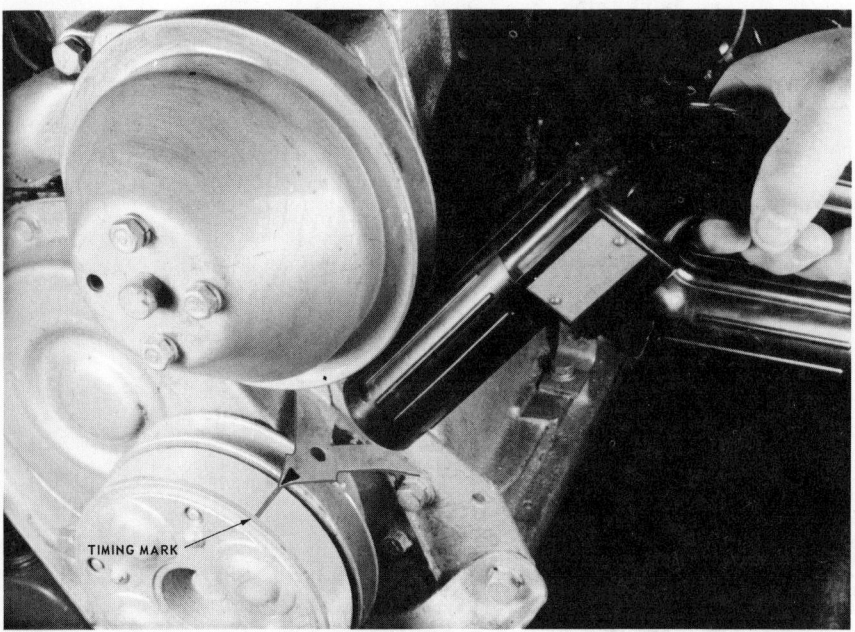

*Fig. B-27. Using timing light to time ignition.*

should line up with the pointer. If not, rotate the distributor until it does, Fig. B-26. Ignition timing is correct if the breaker points "break" just as the piston reaches the end of its compression stroke and the specified degree mark aligns with the pointer, Fig. B-26.

Check the centrifugal advance for proper operation by starting the engine and raising the speed to approximately 2000 rpm. If the ignition timing advances as indicated by the timing light directed on the timing marks, the centrifugal advance is operating correctly. Note engine speed when the advance begins and the amount of total advance which will be shown by the number of degrees the timing beam moves. Stop the engine.

## Ignition Tune-Up

Unplug the vacuum line and connect it to the distributor vacuum advance unit, (outer diaphragm on dual diaphragm distributors). Start the engine and accelerate it to approximately 2000 rpm. Note the engine speed when the advance begins and the total amount of advance. Advance of the ignition timing should begin sooner and advance further than when checking centrifugal advance alone. Stop the engine.

Check the vacuum retard operation on dual diaphragm distributors as follows: Connect the intake manifold vacuum to the inner (retard) diaphragm side of the vacuum advance. Reset the carburetor to normal idle speed. The initial timing should retard to approximately top dead center. On some engines it will go as low as 6 deg. after top dead center.

If the vacuum advance or vacuum retard (dual diaphragm distributors) is not functioning correctly, remove the distributor and test it on a distributor test stand. Replace the dual diaphragm unit if the retard portion is out of calibration or if either diaphragm is leaking.

On recent model engines, look for tune-up and timing instructions on a decal in the engine compartment.

## HOW TO REMOVE THE DISTRIBUTOR

To remove distributor: Disconnect primary wire leading from distributor to ignition coil. Remove distributor cap. Disconnect vacuum line at distributor. Scribe a mark on distributor housing indicating position of rotor. Scribe a mark on distributor body and another on engine block, indicating relative position of distributor in block. Use these marks when replacing distributor.

Remove retaining bolt and lock washer (screws and lock washers on Loadomatic distributor). Lift distributor out of block. Do not rotate crankshaft while distributor is removed, or it will be necessary to re-time engine.

## HOW TO INSTALL THE DISTRIBUTOR

To install distributor: Position distributor in block with rotor aligned with mark previously scribed on distributor body. Install distributor retaining screw. If crankshaft has been rotated while distributor was out of engine, rotate crankshaft until number one piston is on top dead center, after compression stroke.

Position distributor in block with rotor at number one firing position. Make sure oil pump intermediate driveshaft is properly seated in oil pump. Install, but do not tighten, distributor retaining bolt. Rotate distributor clockwise until breaker points are just starting to open. Tighten retaining bolt. Connect distributor primary wire and install distributor cap.

Start engine and adjust ignition timing to specifications. Reconnect distributor vacuum line and check advance with timing light when engine is accelerated.

## Fix Your Ford

## TIMING WITHOUT A TIMING LIGHT

If a timing light is not available, another method can be used which requires no special equipment. The procedure is to crank the engine until No. 1 piston is coming up on its compression stroke. Remove the spark plugs and the compression can be felt by holding a thumb over the spark plug hole when the piston is coming up on the compression stroke. Both intake and exhaust valves will be closed at that time. Continue cranking until the desired timing mark aligns with the index. Connect No. 1 cable to the spark plug and place the spark plug on some metal part of the engine. Then loosen the distributor hold-down clamp and rotate the distributor body. At the same time observe the spark plug. When a spark jumps the plug gap the timing will then be set at the correct position. Tighten the distributor in position.

## EMISSION CONTROLS

Because of exhaust emission control requirements, various devices have been installed which are designed to supplement the vacuum controls which have been installed on the distributors in the past. These devices regulate the distributor timing by changing the vacuum forces applied to the distributor diaphragms. Also, number and type of supplemental devices vary with different car models and also with year of installation.

Such devices include the distributor vacuum deceleration valve, distributor vacuum control valve, transmission spark control system, electronic spark control system, distributor modulator, thermal sensing valve, electric assisted choke, spark delay valves, PCV valve, crankcase valve, ported vacuum switch and Thermactor air injection system. For maximum engine performance, these devices must be kept in proper working order, along with maintaining the correct carburetor air-fuel mixture and engine speed adjustments. Emission control material begins on page 79; carburetor service, page 47, tune-up specifications, page 391. For specifications on recent models, see decal in engine compartment.

## ELECTRONIC SPARK CONTROL SYSTEM (1972-1973)

The electronic spark control system helps to control exhaust emissions by delaying vacuum to the ignition distributor advance unit as required. It consists of a speed sensor, ambient air temperature switch, distributor modulator valve (solenoid) and an electronic amplifier.

The vacuum is retarded by use of the vacuum control valve inserted in the vacuum line between the carburetor vacuum advance port and the distributor primary vacuum advance connection. The valve is normally open and when energized electrically, it closes to cut off the vacuum supply from the carburetor to the primary vacuum advance unit on the distributor and prevents vacuum advance.

An ambient temperature switch in either the right or left A-piller is

## Ignition Tune-Up

necessary to sense outside air temperature. At temperatures below 49 deg. the switch contacts open and allow normal vacuum at all speeds. At temperatures above 65 deg. the switch contacts close and cut off the vacuum to the vacuum diaphragm unit on the distributor, and retard ignition. As the vehicle accelerates, a voltage that is proportional to the speed of the vehicle is generated by the speed sensor and transmitted to the electronic amplifier. When the vehicle reaches a predetermined speed which varies with different vehicles, the control amplifier causes the distributor modulator valve to deenergize, restoring distributor advance from the carburetor venturi port to the distributor primary diaphragm. At speeds below 18 mph the electronic amplifier causes the modulator valve to close, so at that speed and below, no vacuum is applied to the primary side of the distributor and spark is retarded.

### DISTRIBUTOR VACUUM CONTROL VALVE

The distributor vacuum control valve, Fig. B-28, also known as the coolant temperature sensing valve, is included in the distributor vacuum advance supply line of certain engines to provide advance ignition timing under prolonged idling conditions and is installed in the coolant outlet.

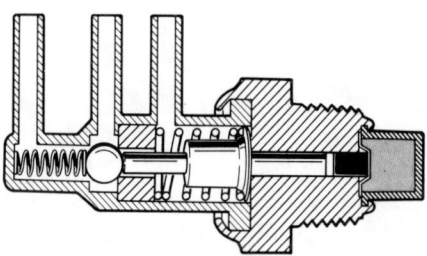

*Fig. B-28. Distributor vacuum control valve.*

When checking the operation of this control, first make certain all vacuum hoses are properly installed and routed. Attach a tachometer to the engine and bring engine to operating temperature. Be sure choke plate is fully open. Engine must not be overheated. Note engine idle rpm with transmission in neutral and carburetor throttle in curb idle position. Disconnect the vacuum hose from the intake manifold at the temperature sensing valve and plug the hose. Note engine idle rpm with the hose disconnected. If no change in idle rpm, the valve is acceptable up to this point. If there is a drop in idle speed of 100 rpm or more, the valve should be replaced. Install vacuum line on manifold fitting; then verify that all season coolant is up to specifications and correct radiator cap is installed.

Cover radiator sufficiently to induce high temperature condition. Continue to run engine until the high temperature light comes on. If engine idle has by this time increased 100 rpm or more the temperature sensing valve is satisfactory. If not, install a new valve.

## TRANSMISSION REGULATED SPARK CONTROL SYSTEM

The transmission regulated spark control system (TRS System) consists of a distributor modulator valve, ambient temperature switch, transmission switch and in some applications a spark delay switch is used.

To check the operation on cars with automatic transmissions, connect a vacuum gauge between the distributor and the modulator valve. Then with the temperature switch temperature known to be above 65 deg. F., start the engine with transmission in NEUTRAL. No vacuum should be indicated. With the foot brake applied shift into reverse. At low rpm, the gauge may or may not register a vacuum reading. If no vacuum reading is obtained, perform a vacuum test as follows: Disconnect one wire from the distributor modulator valve. Shift into NEUTRAL and increase engine speed from 1000 to 1500 rpm. Vacuum should be indicated. Reconnect the wire. Malfunction of the electrical circuit affects the vacuum, but vacuum portion has no effect on the electrical. Therefore if the distributor modulator valve does not function as outlined above, neither will the vacuum. In this event, there is either an absence of electrical feed or a poor ground is indicated and each component should be checked.

Check the system on a car with a manual transmission is basically similar.

## DECELERATION VALVES

Excessively high engine idle speeds can be caused by a hanging or maladjusted deceleration valve. Binding throttle linkage is another possible cause.

Make the following tests: Attach tachometer to ignition system and operate engine until it reaches operating temperature (approximately 20 min.) Disconnect rubber hose between deceleration valve, Fig. B-29, and carburetor at decelerator valve end. Cap the nipple on the valve and verify that ignition timing, engine idle speed and carburetor mixtures are set to specifications.

Increase engine speed to 3000 rpm, hold for approximately 5 seconds, then release the throttle. If engine does not return to normal idle speed, check for throttle linkage hang-ups. Correct if necessary.

Remove cap from deceleration valve nipple. "Tee" a vacuum gauge into hose between deceleration valve and carburetor. On 2300 cc engines, verify that a 3/16 in. vacuum hose is connected between small nipple on valve and manifold vacuum source. Increase engine speed to 3000 rpm and hold for approximately 5 seconds. Release throttle and measure time require for vacuum to drop to zero. It should take from 2 to 5 seconds.

Replace the deceleration valve on 2300 cc engines if valve is not within

## Ignition Tune-Up

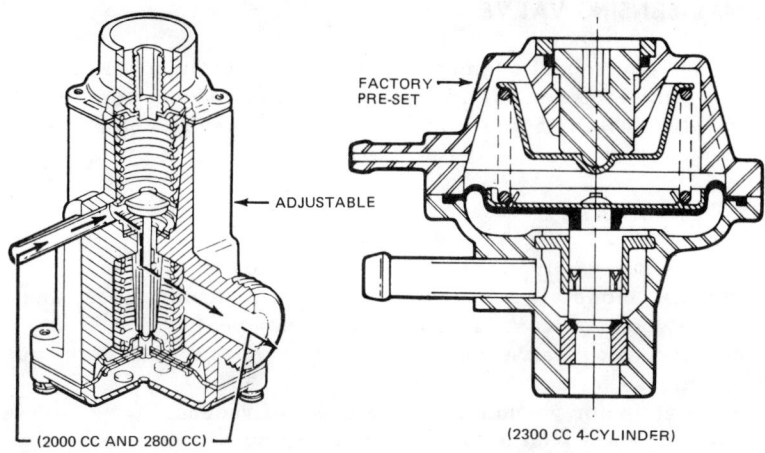

*Fig. B-29. Two types of deceleration valves: adjustable valve introduced in 1973; nonadjustable type on 1974 2300 cc engines.*

specifications. On 2000 cc and 2800 cc engines, adjust as required to meet specifications of 2 to 5 seconds. Turning the adjusting screw inward reduces time the valve is open; outward increases open time. If the deceleration valve cannot be adjusted to specifications, install a new valve.

## DISTRIBUTOR SHAFT ROTATION

The distributor shaft on all four and six cylinder engines, regardless of size, rotates in a clockwise direction. All V-8 engines, regardless of size, rotate in the counterclockwise direction.

## DISTRIBUTOR MODULATOR 1970-1971

The distributor modulator is a device for reducing engine emissions by close control of the distributor spark advance during certain conditions of acceleration and deceleration. It consists of a speed sensor; a thermal switch; an electronic control amplifier and a three-way solenoid valve controlling vacuum applied to the distributor. The control amplifier and the three-way valve are combined in a unit and are mounted inside the passenger compartment on the dash panel. The speed sensor is connected to the speedometer cable. The thermal switch is mounted near the front door hinge pillar on the outside of the cowl panel. The device operates to prevent spark advance below a specified speed when accelerating and also prevents advance below a specified value on deceleration. Operating speeds vary according to engine. See also Chaper on "Reducing Engine Emissions."

## THERMAL SENSING VALVE

On some late model engines, the distributor vacuum will be obtained from either the intake manifold or the carburetor vacuum port. A thermal sensing valve installed in a heater water system will control the source of the vacuum pick-up.

## SPARK DELAY VALVE

The spark delay valve is found in many places on 1974 engines. Basically, the SDV slows air flow in one direction in vacuum lines, thus providing closer control on vacuum-operated equipment.

The spark delay valve can be checked for operation with the aid of a vacuum gauge as follows:
1. Set distributor vacuum gauge to 10 in. of vacuum.
2. Connect black side of delay valve to vacuum source.
3. Connect a 24 in. hose from gauge to colored side of delay valve.
4. Apply vacuum and observe time for gauge to reach 8 in. of vacuum with a 10 in. vacuum source.

When checking the delay valve, care must be exercised to prevent oil or dirt from getting into the valve.

## CHECKS AND CARE OF IGNITION CABLE

When ignition cables are disconnected from spark plugs, or from the distributor, special care must be taken not to pull on the wires, but only on the moulded cap. This applies particularly to radio resistor wire which has been used on all Ford cars since 1958. These wires can be identified by the word radio stamped on the covering of each cable. The conductors of these cables are made of fabric which is impregnated with graphite or other material to make it a conductor of high tension current. Pulling on the cable may separate it from the connector at the end, or the weather seal may be damaged. Arcing within the cable will occur. Misfiring and hard starting will result. Special pliers are available to assist in pulling caps and cables from the spark plugs. Never pull directly on the cable.

Starting in 1974, cable resistance should not exceed 5000 ohms per inch of length. Never substitute conventional cables for resistance cables, and never puncture the cable insulation with a probe when testing.

If there is any doubt as to the condition of the radio type ignition cable, and there is no ohmmeter available for checking resistance, it is always a safe plan to install new wire. Or, you can have the wire tested in a shop which has the necessary equipment. It is very important that the insulation on the cable from the distributor to the spark plugs, and from the coil to the distributor, be examined carefully, because if this insulation has deteriorated, current will leak and misfiring will result.

The engineers at the Champion Spark Plug Co., suggest a way of check-

## Ignition Tune-Up

ing the cables which does not require elaborate equipment or excessive time. The procedure requires a jumper wire with a clip on each end and a screwdriver. Fasten one clip to a good engine ground. Then clip the other end to the screwdriver shank, which will serve as a probe. Start the engine and remove one cable from a spark plug. With the engine running, probe around the coil high tension lead and its boot, Fig. B-30. If any spark jumps from the coil boot or lead, it is a sign that the cable and boot need replacement. With the engine still running, probe around the disconnected plug cable and boot looking for sparks. If any sparks occur, replacement is needed. Reconnect the cable and check the remaining cables in the same manner.

*Fig. B-30. Method of checking ignition cable insulation for leaks.*

When high tension cables are removed or disconnected, special care must be taken to replace them in their original positions. That applies not only to the actual connections from the distributor to the spark plugs, but also to their positions in their grommets and clips. Should they be placed in the wrong grommet or clip, cross-firing from one cable to another will occur, causing misfiring. Fig. B-31 shows the cable arrangement on engines with the firing order of 1-5-4-2-6-3-7-8.

Two types of secondary ignition cables are used on most 1975 engines: Hypalon and silicone. The silicone type is identified by the letter "S" stamped in white on the insulation. Make sure that these heat resistant cables are installed in their original position.

## IGNITION RESISTORS

A resistance wire, shown in Fig. B-1, is incorporated in the primary ignition circuit. This primary resistance is cut in the circuit

*Fig. B-31. Location of ignition cables on V-8 engines with firing order 1-5-4-2-6-3-7-8. (Typical.)*

while the engine is being cranked, but as soon as the engine starts all the current from the ignition coil passes through the resistor. In that way, the full twelve volts is supplied to the coil for easy starting.

Should this resistance, either block type or wire type, become defective, engine misfiring and eventual complete failure of engine will result, so be sure to check this resistance when an elusive misfiring occurs.

## CHECKING PRIMARY IGNITION CIRCUIT

Except for defective resistors in the line from the ignition switch to the coil, trouble in the primary ignition circuit is usually confined to loose or dirty connections. Pay particular attention to battery and battery ground connections, making sure they are tight and show no evidence of corrosion.

Make sure the terminal marked "D" on the coil is connected to the distributor and the one marked "B" is connected to the ignition switch. If this is not done, the polarity of the ignition coil will be reversed and misfiring, particularly at high speeds, will occur.

If a voltmeter is available, the voltage drop throughout the primary ignition circuit can be measured. This should not exceed 0.3 volts for any wire. Make sure the wires are correctly located, otherwise there will be cross-firing. The correct location for high tension wiring on V-8 engines with a firing order of 1-5-4-2-6-3-7-8 is shown in Fig. B-31.

## TRANSISTOR IGNITION

The transistor ignition system used on some recent model Ford cars is shown in Fig. B-32. In this system, the primary circuit of the ignition coil draws a peak current of 12 amp. or approximately 5.5 amp. average current to provide the high voltage required at high engine speed.

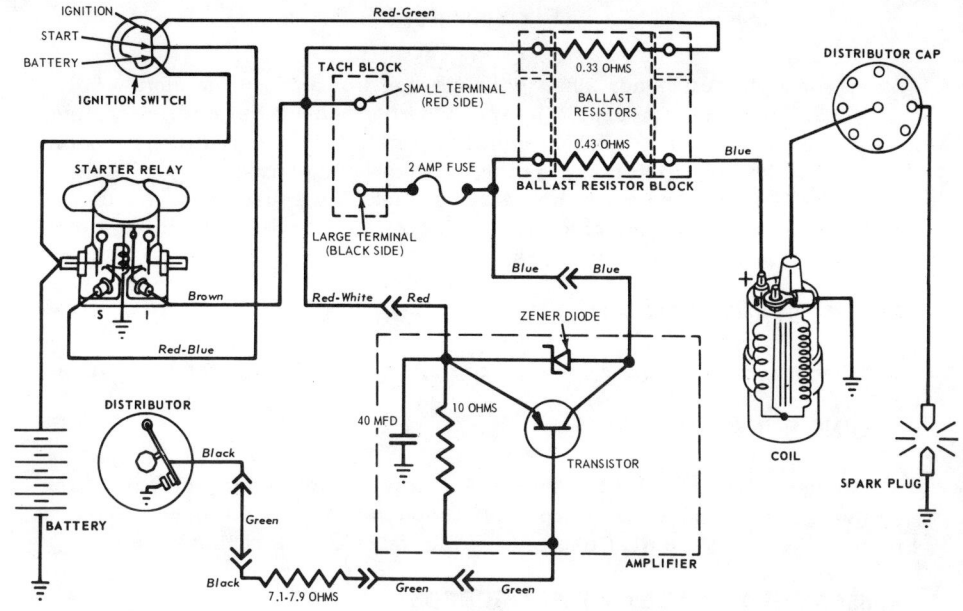

*Fig. B-32. Typical transistor ignition system.*

This system uses the normal ignition distributor and the transistor in the system acts as a switch or relay. As shown in the diagram, the transistor is connected between the battery and the coil and is used to make and break the coil primary circuit.

The transistor is controlled by the conventional distributor breaker points and a resistor limits the transistor control current to 0.5 amp. Because of the low current passing through distributor breaker point, pitting and erosion of the points is practically eliminated assuring long life.

The amplifier assembly is provided with fins to promote cooling and is mounted under the instrument panel to further protect it from engine heat. The ceramic ballast resistor block and a tachometer connector block are mounted in the engine compartment.

To prevent the transistor from being damaged by the application of external devices and accessories other than normal testing equipment, a two ampere fuse is placed between the large terminal of the tachometer block and the coil primary circuit. The tachometer block is provided so that a tachometer or other test equipment can be connected in the circuit.

## IGNITION TROUBLE SHOOTING
Also see carburetor section for causes of poor performance.

### ENGINE CRANKS NORMALLY BUT WILL NOT START

To determine if the trouble is in the primary or secondary circuit, pull the coil wire from the top of the distributor and hold it 3/16 in. away from the cylinder head. Then with the ignition on and the engine being cranked, check for a spark. If the spark is good, check the ignition timing.

If the spark is good and the ignition timing is not at fault, the trouble may be in the distributor cap, rotor, or spark plug wires.

If there is no spark or the spark is weak, the cause of the trouble is probably in the primary circuit. Check coil, coil to distributor high tension lead, ignition breaker points, condenser.

## ENGINE STARTS BUT FAILS TO KEEP RUNNING

Check ignition breaker points, spark plugs, leaks in high tension wiring.

## ENGINE RUNS BUT MISSES

Misses steady at all speeds: If the miss is isolated to one particular cylinder, check spark at spark plug. If a good spark does not occur, trouble is in secondary circuit. Check spark plug wire and distributor cap.

## MISSES ERRATICALLY AT ALL SPEEDS

Check breaker points, condenser, secondary wiring, side play in distributor shaft, coil, spark plugs. Check for high tension leakage across wires, coil, rotor and distributor cap. Make sure wires are correctly routed to plugs to avoid cross fire.

## MISSES AT IDLE SPEED ONLY

Check: Coil, condenser, breaker points, rotor, ignition wiring, distributor shaft for side play, spark plugs, distributor cam for wear.

## POOR ACCELERATION

Check: Ignition timing, spark plugs, breaker points, distributor advance, spark control valve.

## LACK OF POWER AND LOW TOP SPEED

Check: Ignition timing, coil, condenser, rotor, distributor advance, distributor shaft for excessive side play, distributor cam, spark plugs.

## EXCESSIVE FUEL CONSUMPTION

Check: Ignition timing, spark plugs, distributor advance.

## ENGINE OVERHEATING

Check: Ignition timing, cooling system.

# CARBURETOR AND FUEL SYSTEM SERVICE

The Ford carburetor and fuel systems, as a rule, give very little trouble and require a minimum of attention. The basic systems include:

    Fuel Tank        Carburetor       Intake Manifold
    Fuel Lines      Fuel Filter       Fuel Gage
    Fuel Pump      Air Cleaner

In addition, since 1968 additional equipment has been added and which is designed to reduce exhaust and crankcase emissions.

## TUNE-UP TIPS 1970-1977

In order to meet the Federal requirements of exhaust emissions, carburetor adjustments and ignition timing must be held within very close limits. To insure that specifications are not exceeded, idle mixture screws are "limited" for adjustment through a very narrow range. Specifications

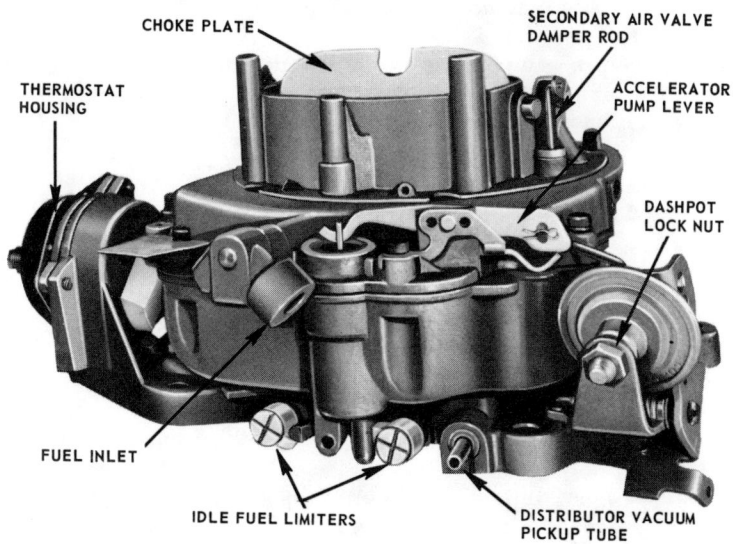

Fig. C-1. Details of Autolite model 4300 carburetor.

governing idle speed, ignition timing and other adjustable conditions are printed on a decal in the engine compartment. Follow these instructions.

In the case of a complete carburetor overhaul, it is necessary to remove the limiters placed on the idle mixture adjustment screws, Fig. C-1. New limiters are provided in the better grade of carburetor repair parts kits, along with complete instructions governing overhaul and adjustment of the unit. After the work is completed, new limiters must be placed on the idle mixture adjustment screws.

Ford service bulletins advise:
1. Adjust all idle speeds with headlights OFF, automatic transmission in DRIVE or manual transmission in NEUTRAL. If air conditioner equipped, place A/C controls in OFF position.
2. Adjust HIGH IDLE SPEED with throttle solenoid operating by using solenoid adjustment.
3. Adjust LOW IDLE SPEED, using carburetor idle speed screw with lead wire disconnected from throttle solenoid.

The distributor DIAPHRAGM HOSE OR HOSES must be disconnected and plugged when setting timing.

## ADJUSTING THE CARBURETOR 1968-1978

Starting with the 1968 models, Ford engines were designed to operate within the limits of the Federal Government regulations in regard to exhaust gas emissions. As a result, all carburetors were equipped with idle fuel mixture adjusting limiters and a more detailed adjusting procedure is required. The simpler procedure to be followed when adjusting older carburetors will be given later. The procedure for cars with exhaust emission control systems is as follows:

All carburetors are equipped with idle fuel mixture adjusting limiters. The limiters control the maximum idle richness and help prevent unauthorized persons from making overly rich idle adjustments. There are two types of idle limiters: external and internal.

The external type plastic idle limiter cap, Fig. C-1, on the idle mixture adjusting screw, or screws, is used in all Autolite and Motorcraft carburetors. Any adjustment made on carburetors having this type of limiter must be within the range of the idle adjusting limiter. Under no circumstances are the idle adjusting limiters or limiter stops on the carburetor to be mutilated or deformed to render the limiter inoperative. On Autolite models 2100 2-V and 4100 4-V carburetors, the power valve cover must be installed with the limiter stops on the cover in position to provide a positive stop for tabs on the idle adjusting limiters.

The internal needle type limiter used on the Carter model YF 1-V carburetor is shown in Fig. C-2 and is located in the idle channel which is not visible. The limiter is installed and sealed during manufacture.

A satisfactory idle should be obtainable within the range of the idle adjusting limiters, if all other engine systems are operating within specifications.

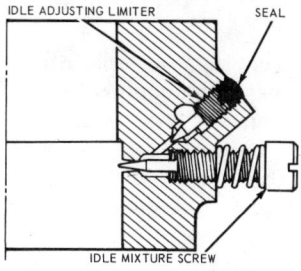

*Fig. C-2. Carter model YF 1-V sealed idle adjusting limiter, as installed on carburetors used with special exhaust emission control systems.*

## ADJUSTING CARBURETORS HAVING LIMITERS

Following are the normal procedures necessary to properly adjust the engine idle speed and fuel mixture on cars equipped with carburetors having idle fuel mixture adjusting limiters. The specific operation should be followed in the sequence given whenever idle speed or fuel adjustments are made.

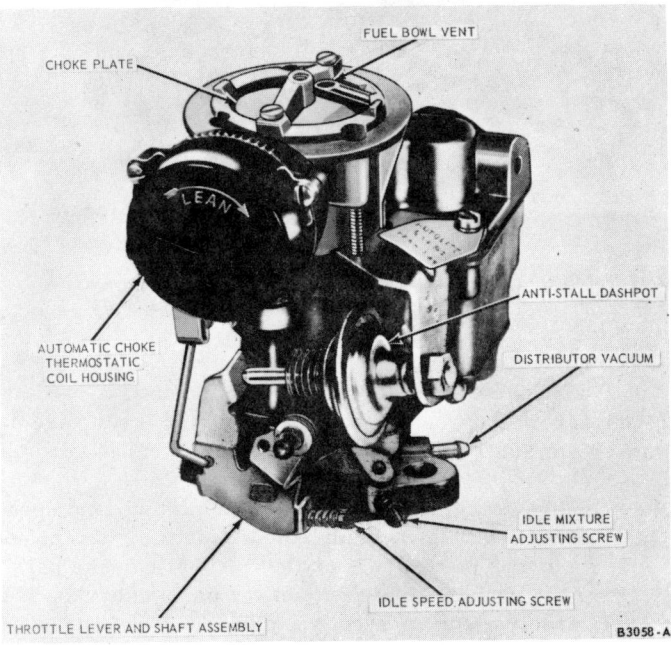

*Fig. C-3. The idle mixture limiter on the 1968-1972 Carter YF1-V carburetor is of the internal needle type. The 1971-1973 model Carter YF1-V carburetor is also equipped with a solenoid throttle positioner.*

## Fix Your Ford

With the engine not running, set the idle fuel mixture screws, Figs. C-1, C-2, and C-3, to the full counterclockwise position of the limiter caps. On vehicles not equipped with exhaust emission control systems, establish an initial idle mixture setting by turning each screw inward until lightly seated, then turn outward 1 1/2 turns.

On all cars, back off the idle speed adjusting screw, Fig. C-3 until the throttle plates seat in the throttle bore. Be sure the dashpot or solenoid throttle positioner (if so equipped) is not interfering with the throttle lever. It may be necessary to loosen the dashpot or solenoid to allow the throttle plate to seat in the throttle bore.

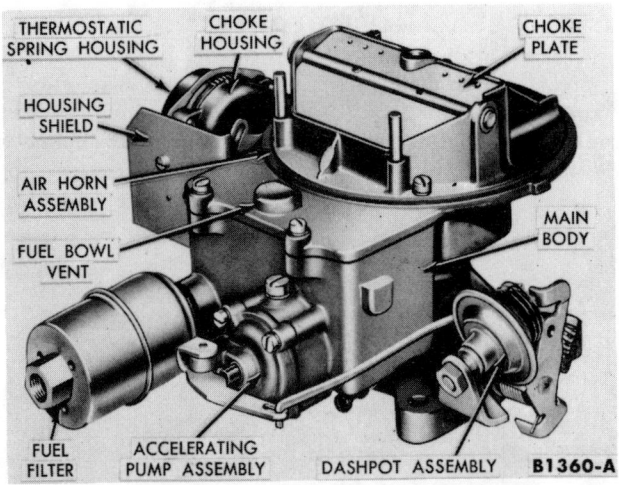

*Fig. C-4. Note fuel filter, dashpot, automatic choke and accelerating pump assembly on the Ford dual carburetor. The Autolite carburetor is similar.*

Turn the idle speed adjusting screw inward until it just makes contact with the screw stop on the throttle shaft and lever assembly. Then turn the screw inward 1 1/2 turns to establish a preliminary adjustment of the idle speed.

Set the parking brake while making idle mixture and speed adjustments. On a vehicle with a vacuum release parking brake, remove the vacuum line from the power unit of the vacuum release parking brake assembly. Plug the vacuum line, then set the parking brake. The vacuum unit must be deactivated to keep the parking brake engaged when the engine is running with the transmission in drive.

Start the engine and run until the underhood temperature is stabilized which requires a minimum of 20 minutes at 1500 rpm. Check the initial ignition timing and distributor advance. On vehicles with a manual shift

## Carburetor, Fuel System Service

transmission, the idle setting must be made when the transmission is in neutral. On vehicles with automatic transmissions, the idle setting is made with the selector lever in Drive position, except when using an exhaust gas analyzer.

Be sure the choke plate is in the full open position. Turn on the headlights (high beam). Adjust engine idle speed to specifications. Tachometer reading is taken with the air cleaner installed. If not possible to adjust idle speed with air cleaner in position, remove it and make the adjustment. Then replace air cleaner and recheck speed.

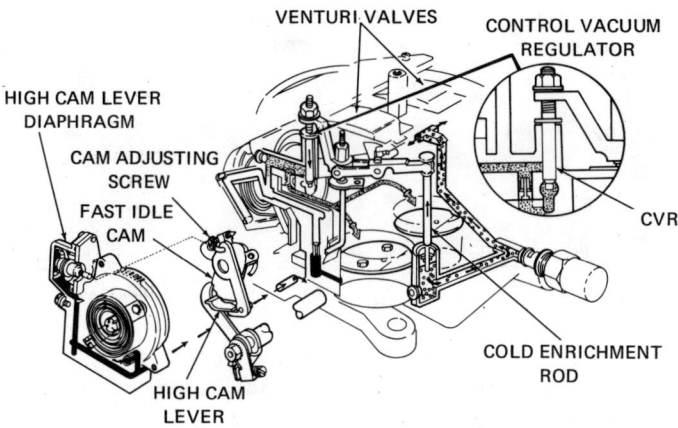

*Fig. C-5. Cold enrichment system used on Motorcraft variable venturi carburetor installed on 1978 Mustang II, Granada and Pinto cars.*

On carburetors equipped with a solenoid throttle positioner, Fig. C-7, turn the solenoid assembly in or out to obtain the specified curb idle rpm. Then tighten lock nut. Disconnect the solenoid lead wire at the bullet connector, then adjust the carburetor throttle stop screw to obtain 500 rpm. Connect the solenoid lead wire and open the throttle slightly by hand. The solenoid plunger will follow the throttle lever and remain in the fully extended position as long as the ignition is on and the solenoid is energized.

Turn the idle mixture adjusting screws inward to obtain the smoothest idle possible within the range of the idle limiters. Turn the idle mixture adjusting screws inward an equal amount. Check for idle smoothness only with air cleaner installed.

On 2 and 4 venturi carburetors, turn the idle mixture adjusting screws inward an equal amount.

After final adjustment of idle rpm and mixture, stop engine and adjust carburetor fuel bowl vent valve, Fig. C-4. All carburetors have this fuel bowl vent valve, except Autolite model 4100 4-V and Carter model YF.

If satisfactory idle condition is not obtained after performing the preceding normal idle fuel adjustments, check the entire system for vacuum leaks, the ignition timing, breaker point gap, spark plugs, and ignition system wiring continuity.

## MOTORCRAFT MODEL 2700 VV CARBURETOR

The Motorcraft 2700 VV carburetor used on 1978 Pinto, Mustang II and Granada engines is the variable venturi type (see page 69 for details). The VV carburetor is able to vary the area of its venturi according to engine load and speed. In that way, it differs from other types of carburetors which have a fixed area venturi.

The variable venturi carburetor uses a dual element venturi valve that moves in and out of the air flowing into the two throats of the carburetor.

The venturi valve is controlled by engine vacuum and throttle position, and it is connected to two main metering rods which control airflow.

## ADJUSTING 2V/4V CARBURETORS

To adjust the idle fuel mixture on two and four barrel carburetors, first turn both adjustments all the way in until they seat lightly. Then back out approximately one and one-half turns. Bring the engine up to operating temperature and then turn one adjustment in until the engine falters, then back out until the engine runs smoothly. Follow same procedure with other idle mixture adjustment. Repeat procedure on both needles. Final setting may vary one-half turn difference between two adjustments.

After the idle mixture has been adjusted, the idle speed should be adjusted. This should preferably be done with a tachometer, but if one is not available the idle speed screw should be adjusted until the engine runs smoothly without racing. If the car has an automatic transmission, the idle speed should be such that the car does not creep with the transmission shift in drive position.

## LATE MODEL IDLING SPEED ADJUSTMENTS

Idling speed on late model Ford engines varies with application. Factors include whether or not the car is equipped with a manual or automatic transmission; whether it has a solenoid throttle positioner; whether the solenoid is connected or disconnected during the idling test. Check the decal in the engine compartment for specific settings.

## SPARK CONTROL VALVE

A spark control valve is used on engines equipped with the Loadomatic distributor. It controls the throttle bore, throttle plate and venturi

## Carburetor, Fuel System Service

## EARLIER MODEL IDLING SPEED ADJUSTMENTS

| Year and Displacement | | Idle Speed with Manual Trans. | Idle Speed with Auto. Trans. |
|---|---|---|---|
| 1971 | 351 C 2-V | 700-500* | 625-500* |
| 1971 | 351 C 4-V | 825-400* | 625-500* |
| 1971 | 390 2-V | ...... | 600-475* |
| 1971 | 400 2-V | ...... | 625-500* |
| 1971 | 429 | ...... | 600 |
| 1971 | 429 Cobra | 700 | 650 |
| 1970-1971 | 170, 200, 250 | 750e | 550e |
| 1970-1971 | 240 | 800e | 550e |
| 1970-1971 | 302 | 800-500ge | 600-500ge |
| 1970-1971 | 351 W, 351 C | 700-500e | 600-500e |
| 1970 | 428 | 725 | 675 |
| 1970-1971 | 429 | 850-500e | 600e |
| 1968-1969 | 170, 200 Six | 700a | 550i |
| 1968-1969 | 240, Six | 600a | 500i |
| 1968-1969 | 302 V-8 | 625a | 550fi |
| 1968-1969 | 390 V-8 | 625a | 550i |
| 1968-1969 | 428 V-8 | 625a | 550i |
| 1969 | 250 1-V | 700 | 550 |
| 1969 | 351 2-V | 650 | 550 |
| 1969 | 351 4-V | 675 | 550 |
| 1965-1967 | 170, 200 | 575-600 | 500-525(D) |
| 1966-1967 | 170, 200(a) | 625-650 | 550-575 |
| 1965-1967 | 240 | 500-525 | 500-525(D) |
| 1966-1967 | 240(a) | 625-650 | 525-550 |
| 1964 | 223 | 525-550 | 525-550(D) |
| 1964-1967 | 289, 352, 390 | 575-600 | 475-500(D) |
| 1966-1967 | 289, 390, 410, 428(a) | 610-635 | ...... |
| 1966-1967 | 410, 428 | 575-600 | 475-500 |
| 1964-1966 | 427 | 700-800 | ...... |
| 1964-1965 | 390 Intercep. | ...... | 550-575(D) |
| 1964-1965 | 289 Hi Perf. | 700-800 | ...... |
| 1962-1964 | 144, 170 | 500-525 | 475-500(D) |
| 1963 | 406 | 675-700 | 475-500(D) |
| 1963 | 223, 260, 352, 390 | 500-525 | 475-500(D) |

a — Applies to cars with Thermactor.
D — Automatic transmission shift lever in drive.
e — With headlights on and air conditioner off.
f — Headlights on; auto. trans. in drive and air conditioner full on.
g — With solenoid throttle positioner.
i — IMCO emission control.
* — Higher rpm, solenoid energized — Lower rpm, solenoid deenergized.

vacuums reaching the vacuum diaphragm of the ignition distributor. In that way the degree of spark advance or retard is adjusted to engine requirements. All passages within the carburetor and connecting tubing must be kept unobstructed. In addition, they must be kept tight so that no leakage of vacuum occurs. Should these passages become clogged or the spark valve become defective, the spark will not be advanced sufficiently.

A spark control valve is included in the kit of carburetor repair parts and should be installed whenever the carburetor is overhauled. A defective spark valve will usually be indicated by severe pinging under acceleration.

## CARTER MODEL YFA 1-V CARBURETOR

The Carter model YFA 1-V carburetor used on the 1978 Ford in-line 250 cu. in. (4.1 L) six cylinder engine is made up of three major assemblies: air horn, main body and throttle body. See Fig. C-7. Most adjustments on this carburetor are factory set. The required manual adjustments of the automatic choke, engine idle speed and carburetor air-fuel mixture must be performed in that order. Specifications may vary by model application. See the decal in the engine compartment.

To adjust fast idle speed, first adjust curb idle speed and mixture to specifications. With engine at operating temperature, disconnect EGR vacuum and run a jumper vacuum line to distributor. Remove air cleaner and attach a tachometer. Manually rotate fast idle cam until fast idle screw rests on kickdown step of cam. Then, adjust fast idle speed to specifications.

Adjust automatic choke by loosening retaining screws that attach choke housing. Then, turn spring housing to alter choke setting.

To adjust dechoke, first remove air cleaner. Hold throttle plate fully open and close choke plate as far possible without forcing it. Use a drill of correct diameter to check clearance between lower edge of choke plate and air horn. Adjust dechoke by bending arm on choke trip lever of throttle lever.

## AUTOLITE MODEL 1101-V CARBURETOR

On 1969 models with a solenoid throttle modulator, when adjusting the idle speed and mixture, turn the solenoid assembly, Fig. C-8, in or out of the bracket to obtain the specified curb idle rpm, then tighten the lock nut. Disconnect the solenoid lead wire at the bullet connector, then adjust the carburetor stop screw to obtain the specified rpm. Connect the solenoid lead wire and open the throttle slightly by hand. The solenoid plunger should follow the throttle lever to increase the engine rpm to specifications.

When adjusting the cold engine idle speed, Fig. C-5, on 1969 and earlier models the engine should be operating at normal temperature. With the air cleaner removed, manually rotate the fast idle cam until the

## Carburetor, Fuel System Service

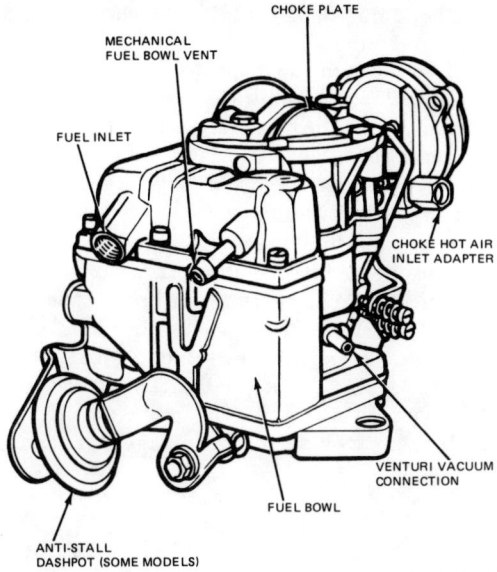

*Fig. C-7. Carter model YFA 1-V carburetor. Note anti-stall dashpot used on some models.*

fast idle adjusting screw rests on the center step of the cam. Then start the engine and turn the fast idle adjusting screw inward or outward as required to obtain the specified idle speed.

To adjust the anti-stall dashpot, hold the throttle in the closed position and depress the plunger with a screwdriver blade. Measure the clearance between the throttle lever and the plunger tip which should check with the

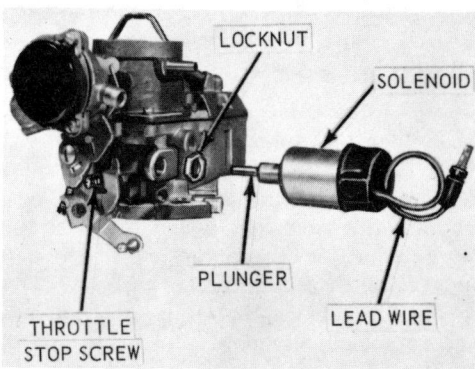

*Fig. C-8. Autolite model 1101-V with solenoid throttle modulator.*

clearance given in the accompanying table. Turn the anti-stall dashpot in a direction to provide the desired clearance and then tighten the lock nut.

The fast idle speed adjustment on the Autolite 1101-V is made with the engine at operating temperature, and the air cleaner removed. Manually rotate the fast idle cam until the fast idle adjusting screw rests on the center step on the cam. Start the engine and turn the fast idle adjusting screw inward or outward as required, to obtain the specified idle rpm given in the Engine Idling Speed Table.

The anti-stall dashpot adjustment is made with the air cleaner removed from the vehicle. With the engine idle speed and mixture properly adjusted, and the engine at normal operating temperature, loosen the anti-stall dashpot lock nut, Fig. C-9. Hold the throttle in the closed position and depress the plunger with a screwdriver blade. Measure the clearance between the throttle lever and the plunger tip. This should check with the specified clearance given in the table on page 60. Turn the anti-stall dashpot in the direction to provide the specified clearance, then tighten lock nut.

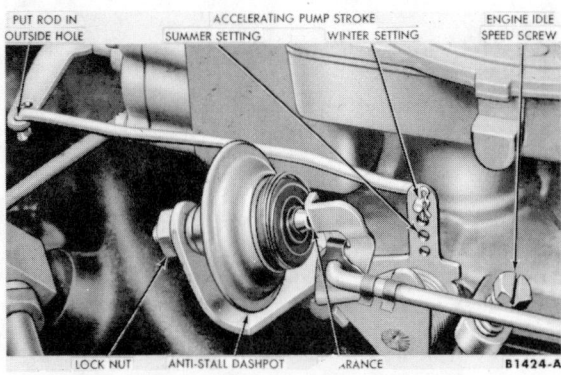

*Fig. C-9. Location of anti-stall dashpot, idle speed and accelerating pump adjustments on Ford dual and 4-V carburetors.*

Accelerating Pump Adjustment: Insert the roll pin in the lower hole position in the accelerating pump lever. Hold the throttle plate in the closed position. Position a gauge or drill of the specified thickness between the roll pin and the cover. Bend the accelerating pump actuating rod to obtain the specified gauge or drill clearance between the pump and the roll pin in the pump lever. The accelerating pump should not be changed from the specified setting.

After adjusting the accelerating pump the vent valve can be adjusted. With the air cleaner removed, set throttle linkage to the idle position. The groove in the vent valve rod should now be evened with the open end of the vent. Bend the arm on the vent valve rod actuating lever where it contacts the accelerating lever, to align the groove with the edge of the bore.

## Carburetor, Fuel System Service

To adjust the float level remove the carburetor air horn and gasket and measure the distance from the gasket surface of the upper body to the top of the float. If the float adjustment is not within specified dimensions, bend the float arm tab as necessary. Do not apply pressure on the float inlet needle.

## AUTOLITE 2100 2-V CARBURETOR

The fast idle adjustment is made in the same manner as is described for the Autolite model 1101 Carburetor.

The anti-stall dashpot is adjusted in the same manner as described for the Autolite model 1101 Carburetor.

The vent valve, Fig. C-10, must be closed during normal and wide-open throttle operation, and open to the specified clearance at closed throttle or idle operation. Bend the vent rod at the rod attaching bracket to obtain the specified clearance.

The dry float adjustment is a preliminary adjustment only. The final adjustment must be made after the carburetor is on the engine. With the air horn removed, the float raised and the fuel inlet needle seated, check the distance between the top surface of the main body and the top surface of the float with the gauge which accompanies the replacement part kit. Take the measurement near the center of the float at a point 1/8 in. from the free end of the float. The gauge which is included in the replacement part kit should be placed in the corner of the enlarged end section of the fuel bowl. The gauge should touch the float near the end but not on the end radius.

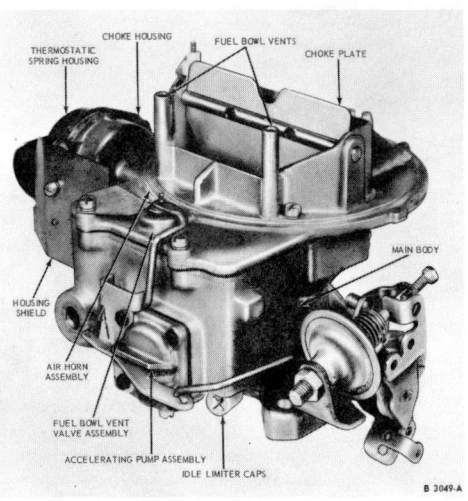

*Fig. C-10. Note idle limiter caps on the idle mixture adjustments on this 1968–1971 Autolite 2100 2-V carburetor.*

# Fix Your Ford

## AUTOLITE 4100 CARBURETOR

The engine fast idle speed adjustment and the anti-stall dashpot adjustment are the same as described for the Autolite 1101 carburetor. To adjust the accelerating pump, the operating rod should be in the specified hole in the over-travel lever and the inboard hole nearest to

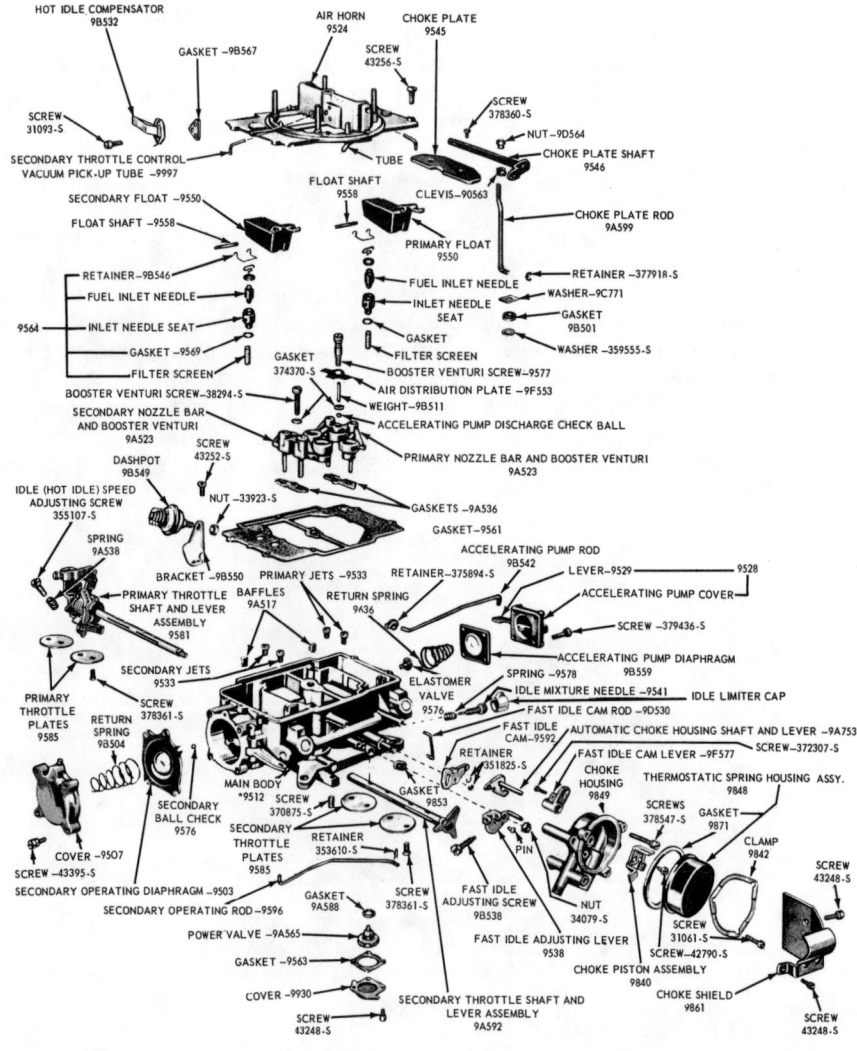

*Fig. C-11. Autolite model 4100 4-V carburetor.*

## Carburetor, Fuel System Service

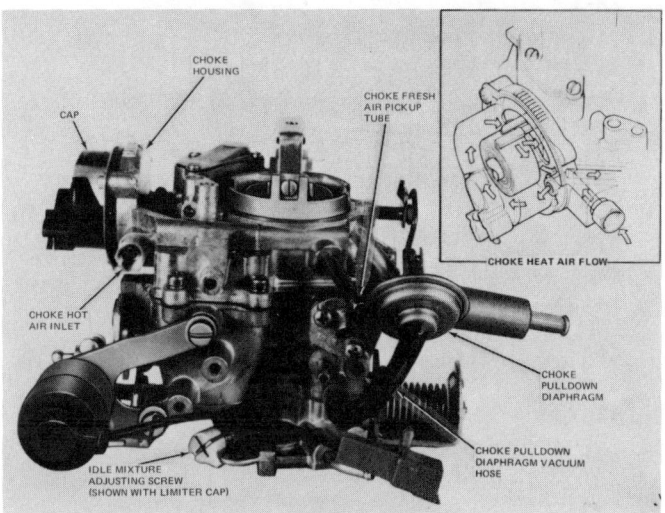

*Fig. C-12. Holley model 1946 1-V carburetor as installed on 1978 Fairmont with 200 cu. in. six cylinder engine. Note idle mixture adjusting screw and choke heat airflow.*

the pump plunger in the accelerator pump link. To release the rod from the retainer clip, Fig. C-11, press the tab end of the clip toward the rod, then at the same time press the rod away from the clip until it is disengaged. Position the clip over the specified hole in the over-travel lever. Press the end of the clip together and insert the operating rod through the clip of the over-travel lever. Release the clip to engage the rod.

The fuel bowl vent valve is not adjustable on the Autolite model 4100 carburetor. To adjust the wet fuel level, remove the carburetor air cleaner and the air horn retaining screws. Temporarily replace the air horn and gasket in position on the carburetor main body and start the engine. Let the engine idle for several minutes, then rotate the air horn and remove the air horn gasket to provide accessibility to the float assemblies. While the engine is idling, use a standard depth gauge to measure the vertical distance from the top machined surface of the carburetor main body to the level of the fuel in the fuel bowl. The measurement must be made at least one-quarter inch away from the antivertical surface. To assure an accurate reading, refer to the specifications for the correct fuel level setting. If any adjustment is required, stop the engine and bend the float tab contacting the fuel in that valve upward in relation to the original position to raise the float level.

The dry float level is checked with the air horn removed and the float raised and the fuel inlet needle seated. Use the gauge which accompanies the kit of replacement parts to check the distance between the top surface of the main body and the top surface of the float.

## ANTI-STALL DASHPOT ADJUSTMENT

| Year | Model | Clearance | Year | Model | Clearance | |
|------|-------|-----------|------|-------|-----------|---|
| 1970-1971 | 170 | 7/64 in. | 1969 | 302 V-8 X | .125 in. | |
| 1970-1971 | 200 | 7/64 in. | 1969 | 390 V-8 | .125 in. | |
| 1970-1971 | 240 | 7/64 in. | 1969 | 429 V-8 | .125 in. | |
| 1970 | 250 | 7/32 in. | 1968-1969 | 170 Six | .100b | 100c |
| 1971 | 250X | 0.10 in. | 1968-1969 | 200 Six | 2a b | 2a c |
| 1970-1971 | 302 2V | 1/8 in. | 1968 | 240 Six | .080b | .100c |
| 1970 | 351 2V | 1/8 in. | 1968 | 289 V8 | .125b | .125c |
| 1970 | 351 4V | 0.80 in. | 1968 | 302 V8 2V | .125b | .125c |
| 1970-1971 | 351 W | 1/8 in. | 1968 | 302 V8 4V | .093b | .062c |
| 1970 | 390 | 1/8 in. | 1968 | 390 V8 2V | .125b | .125c |
| 1970 | 428 CobraM | 0.14 in. | 1968 | 390 V8 4V | ... | .100c |
| 1970 | 428 CobraX | 0.20 in. | 1968 | 427 V8 4V | ... | .100c |
| 1971 | 400 | Solenoid | 1964-1967 | Ford 1V | Foot note* | |
| 1970-1971 | 429 2V | 1/8 in. | 1965-1967 | Ford 4V | .060-.090 | |
| 1970-1971 | 429 4V | 1/16 in. | 1965-1967 | Ford 2V | .060-.090 | |
| 1970 | 429 Cobra | Solenoid | 1964-1960 | V-8's | .060-.090 | |
| 1971 | 429 CobraM | 7/64 in. | 1963-1960 | 223 Six | .060-.090 | |
| 1969 | 200 Six X | 2a | 1963 | 260 V8 | .060-.090 | |
| 1969 | 200 Six M | 3a | 1963-1960 | Falcon | .120-.150 | |
| 1969 | 240 Six | .080 in. | 1959 | All | .035-.050 | |
| 1969 | 250 Six X | .080 in. | 1958 | Holley | .045-.064 | |
| 1969 | 250 Six M | .080 in. | 1958 | Ford | .060-.090 | |
| 1969 | 302 V-8 M | .125 in. | 1958 | Carter | 7/16 in. | |

\* - 3 1/2 turns in after initial contact of adjusting screw with diaphragm.
a - Turns after contact.   b - IMCO.   c - Thermactor.
M - Manual Transmission.   X - Automatic Transmission.

## HOLLEY MODEL 1946 1-V CARBURETOR

The Holley 1946 1-V carburetor, Fig. C-12, is installed on the 1978 Fairmont when equipped with the 200 cu. in. (3.3 L) in-line six cylinder engine with automatic transmission. It uses seven basic systems to provide correct air-fuel ratios for varying operating conditions. The idle mixture adjusting screw is located in the throttle body near the mounting stud. This adjusting screw is equipped with a limiter cap, which must not be removed unless the official procedure for initial adjustment of the air-fuel mixture is followed.

The bimetal spring of the automatic choke is inside the choke housing (part of air horn). The spring exerts closing pressure on the choke valve at temperatures below 75 deg. F. (24 C). As the engine heats up, the spring uncoils and opens the choke valve.

## CARTER MODEL RBS 1-V

The Carter model RBS 1-V carburetor, Fig. C-13, is installed on the 1970 250 cu. in. Ford engine. The basic instructions for adjusting this carburetor are given on page 47. However, the adjustment of the accelerating pump and float level differ from usual practice.

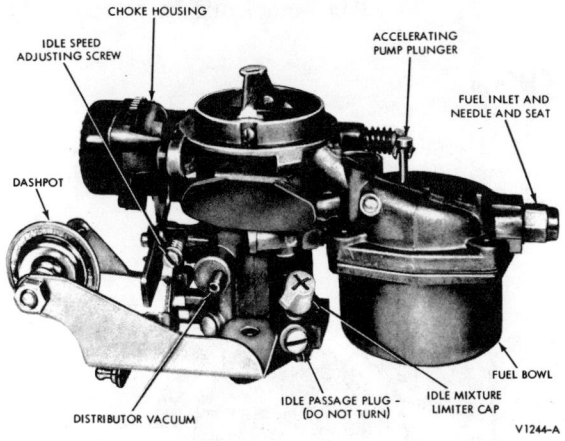

*Fig. C-13. Details of Carter model RBS carburetor. Some models have solenoid throttle positioner instead of dashpot.*

To adjust the accelerating pump, back off the idle speed adjustment screw and open the choke plate to allow the throttle plate to rest in the bore. Measure the height from the flat surface of the main body casting to the top surface of the pump stem. Open the throttle wide. Then measure the height again. The pump stroke is the difference in the two readings. To adjust the stroke to the specified value of 0.40 in., open or close the pump connecting link at the offset portion.

To adjust the float level, remove the float bowl and gasket. With main body inverted and only weight of the float assembly pressing against the inlet needle and seat, measure the vertical distance from the main casting to the raised lips in the outer ends of the float. While holding the tab, adjust float to 9/16 in.

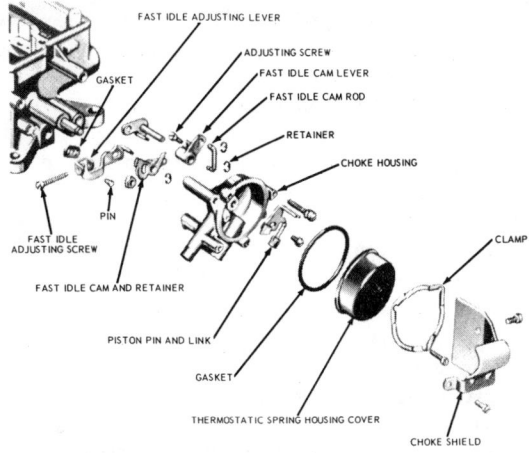

*Fig. C-14. Choke housing assembly as used on Autolite 2100 and 4100 carburetors.*

# Fix Your Ford

## AUTOMATIC CHOKE

The automatic chokes used on Autolite 2100 and 4100 carburetors are similar. Both depend on both carburetor vacuum and exhaust heat for their operation, Figs. C-14 and C14a.

*Fig. C-14a. Sectional view of Autolite automatic choke. Typical of model 2100 and 4100 carburetors.*

The automatic choke is equipped with a bimetal thermostatic spring and a vacuum piston, Fig. C-14a. The bimetal thermostatic spring mechanism winds up when cold and unwinds when warm. When the engine is cold, the thermostatic spring holds the choke piston upward and closes the choke plate.

When the engine is started, manifold vacuum acting directly on the piston in the choke housing moves the choke plate (against spring tension) to partly open position to prevent stalling. As the engine continues to operate, manifold vacuum draws heated air from the exhaust manifold heat chamber and heats the thermostatic spring, causing it to unwind. The tension of the spring gradually decreases as the temperature rises, allowing the choke plate to open.

When the engine reaches normal operating temperature, the choke is in the full-open position and the choke piston is at its lowest point in the cylinder. Slots in the piston chamber wall allow sufficient air to bleed past the piston and into the intake manifold, causing a continual flow of warm air to pass through the thermostatic spring housing. In that way,

## Carburetor, Fuel System Service

the spring remains heated and the choke plate remains fully open until the engine is stopped and allowed to cool.

When trouble occurs in the operation of this type choke, it is therefore important to check both the vacuum and the heat. In the case of the vacuum, this is supplied to passages in the carburetor. In the case of the heat, this is carried to the carburetor by a tube connected to a heat stove in the exhaust manifold.

Difficulties in the operation of this type of choke usually result from clogged vacuum or heat lines. In addition, accumulations of carbon within the choke housing will make it inoperative.

To adjust this type of thermostat, loosen the clamp screws that retain the thermostatic spring housing to the choke housing. The spring housing can be turned to alter the adjustment. Turning the housing in a counterclockwise direction will require a higher thermostatic spring temperature (cool weather operation), to fully open the choke plate. Turning the spring housing in the opposite direction, (clockwise) will cause the choke plate to be fully opened at a lower thermostatic spring temperature (hot weather operation). This is the lean direction as indicated by the arrow on the choke thermostatic spring housing.

The automatic choke used on a Holley carburetor, Fig. C-15, uses both vacuum and heat. The vacuum, in addition to drawing warm air from the heat chamber, acts on a small piston which is linked to the choke plates in the carburetor. When servicing this thermostat, be sure all carbon and dirt are removed from the assembly, and that the piston works freely in the cylinder. Also be sure that all vacuum and heat passages are clear and unobstructed. To adjust the Holley automatic choke, loosen the three screws that retain the thermostatic spring housing to the choke housing, Fig. C-17. The spring housing can then be turned to alter the adjustment. Turning the housing in the counterclockwise direction results in a higher thermostatic spring temperature being required to open the choke plate. Turning the spring housing in the opposite direction, or clockwise, causes the choke plate to open at a lower thermostatic spring temperature.

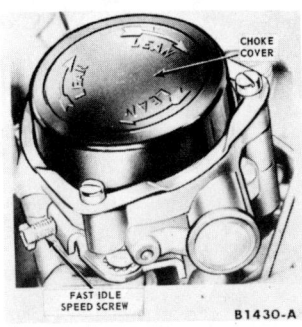

*Fig. C-15. Fast idle and choke adjustments on Holley four barrel carburetor.*

## ELECTRIC CHOKE

The 2100-D 2-V and 4300 4-V carburetors are provided with an electric choke system. The system consists of a choke cap, thermostatic spring, a bi-metallic temperature sensing disc (switch) and positive coefficient ceramic heater, Fig. C-16.

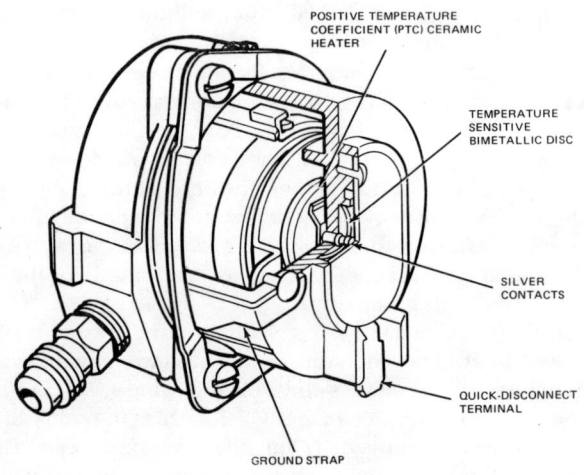

Fig. C-16. Details of electric assist choke.

The electric choke is powered from the center tap of the alternator as current is constantly supplied to the temperature-sensing switch. The system is grounded through a ground switch connected to the carburetor body.

At temperatures below approximately 60 deg. F., the switch is open and no current is supplied to the ceramic heater. Normal thermostatic spring choking action occurs.

At temperatures above approximately 60 deg. the temperature-sensing switch closes, and current is supplied to the ceramic heater. As the heater warms, it causes the thermostatic spring to pull the choke plates open in 1 1/2 minutes. In that way, an overrich mixture is prevented and exhaust emissions are reduced.

## HOLLEY DUAL CARBURETOR ADJUSTMENT

The idle speed and idle mixture adjustments on the Holley Dual Carburetor, Fig. C-17, are made in the same manner as described in the paragraph headed "Carburetor Adjustments 1967 and Earlier." When

## Carburetor, Fuel System Service

preparing to adjust the float level, invert the fuel bowl and check the setting with the cardboard gauge that is provided in the overhaul repair kit of parts. Set the float so that there is .735 to .766 in. clearance between the bottom of the float and the fuel bowl, with the fuel bowl held in the inverted position.

The fast idle speed adjustment on the Holley dual carburetor is made

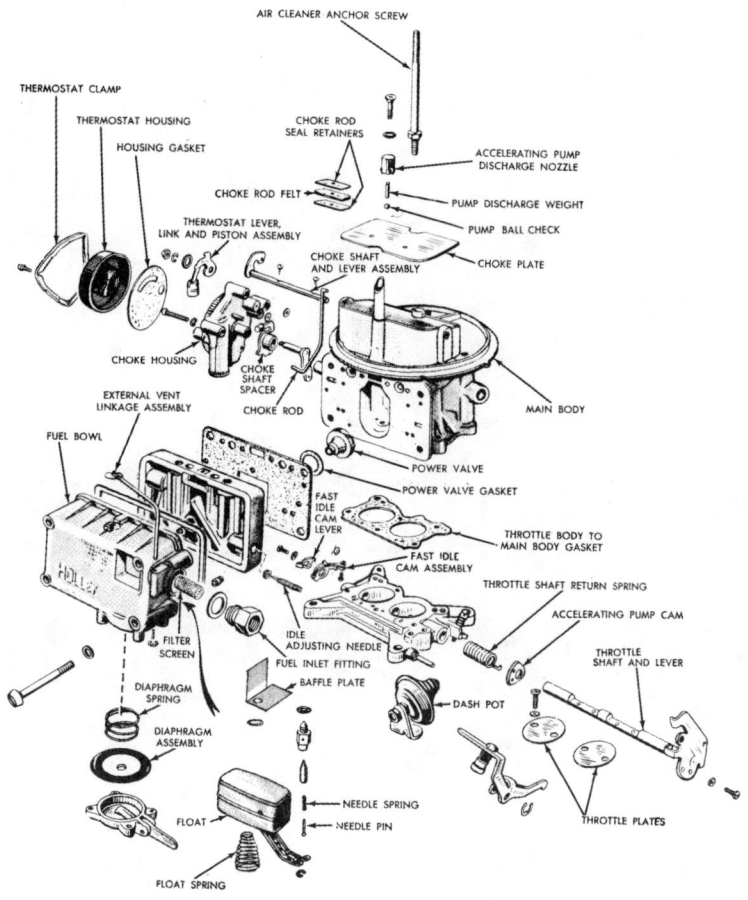

*Fig. C-17. Exploded view of Holley dual carburetor.*

with the engine turned off. Manually rotate the fast idle cam until the fast idle speed stop screw rests on the lowest step in the fast idle cam. Turn out the stop screw until clearance exists, then screw it in until it just touches the lowest step in the cam. Then carefully back off this adjustment one-quarter to one-half turn.

## Fix Your Ford

The accelerating pump adjustment is made by placing the pump link in the proper hole in the pump cam. The top hole in the cam is for hot weather operation. It also is the most economical adjustment, providing minimum pump discharge. The bottom hole is for extreme cold weather operation. It provides maximum pump discharge.

The anti-stall dashpot adjustment is made with the air cleaner removed from the engine. With the engine idle speed and air-fuel mixture properly adjusted, and the engine at normal operating temperature, loosen the dashpot lock nut, Fig. C-9. Hold the throttle closed and depress the dashpot plunger with a screwdriver blade. Measure the clearance between the throttle lever and the plunger tip. It should be .045 to .064 in. If not, turn the dashpot in its bracket in the correct direction to obtain the specified clearance. Tighten the lock nut and test the retarding action of the dashpot diaphragm.

The fuel bowl external vent adjustment is made with the throttle plate closed. Then, the clearance between the vent button and the top of

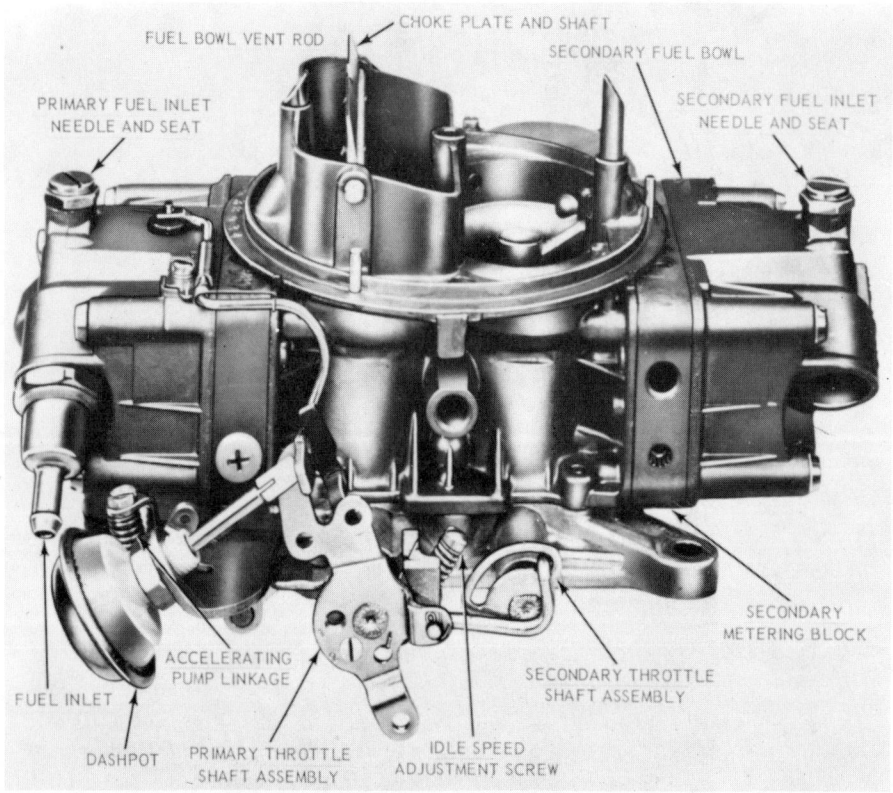

*Fig. C-18. Details of Holley four barrel carburetor.*

## Carburetor, Fuel System Service

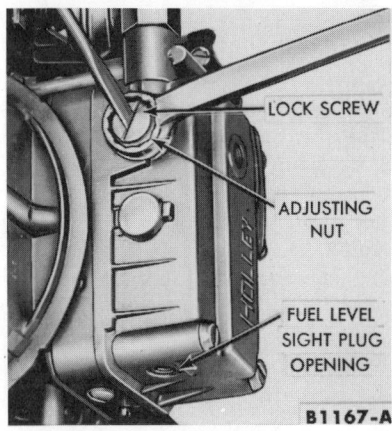

*Fig. C-19. Method of adjusting fuel level on Holley carburetors.*

the fuel bowl should be 1/16 in. To adjust the clearance, bend the horizontal arm on the accelerator pump operating lever.

## FOUR BARREL CARBURETORS

The idle speed and idle mixture adjustments are made in the same manner as described in the paragraph headed "Carburetor Adjustments 1967 and Earlier." The accelerator pump is adjusted in the same manner

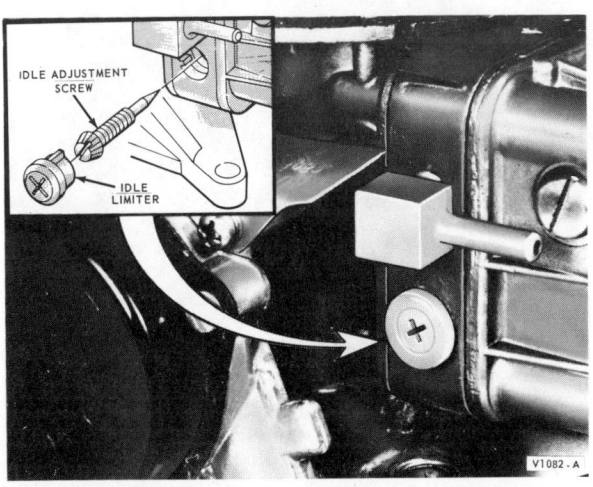

*Fig. C-20. Holley model 4100-C 4-V Cobra Jet carburetor idle limiter.*

as described for the Holley dual carburetor.

To adjust the fuel level on the Holley four barrel carburetor, Fig. C-18, position the car on a level floor. Make sure that fuel pump pressure is correct (4 to 6 psi). Bring the engine to operating temperature. Place a suitable container below the fuel level sight plug, Fig. C-19, to collect any spilled fuel. Check each fuel bowl separately. With the engine stopped, remove fuel level sight plug and gasket and check fuel level which should be at lower edge of the sight plug opening. If the fuel level is too high, drain the bowl and recheck. Fuel level is adjusted by turning the adjusting nut, Fig. C-19. Turning the adjusting nut 1/6 turn will change fuel level 3/64 in. After each adjustment, operate engine and recheck level. Details of the idler limiter screw as installed on the Holley 4150-C 4-V Cobra Jet carburetor are shown in Fig. C-20.

The Rochester 4 MV carburetor is used exclusively on the 429 cu. in. Cobra Jet engine. This is a 4-venturi two-stage carburetor. The primary fuel inlet has 1 3/8 in. bores and the secondary side has 2 1/4 in. bores. The air valve is used in the secondary side for metering control and operates tapered metering rods. All metering systems receive fuel from a centrally located float chamber. See Fig. C-21.

Idle speed, idle mixture, fast idle speed and anti-stall dashpot adjustments are covered at the start of this chapter.

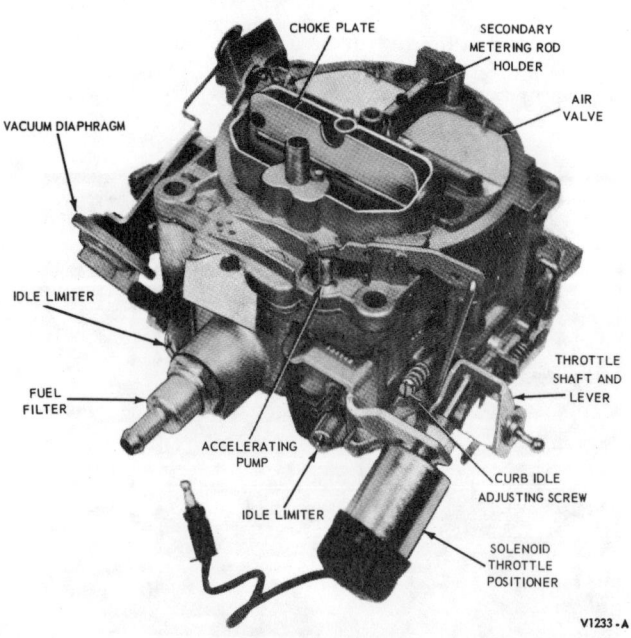

*Fig. C-21. Showing the adjustments on Rochester Quadrajet 4MV carburetor.*

# Carburetor, Fuel System Service

## VARIABLE VENTURI CARBURETOR

The 1977 2.8 litre (170.8 CID) V-6 engine and the 302 CID engine in California cars are equipped with a Motorcraft model 2700 variable venturi carburetor. See Fig. C-21a. This carburetor varies the airflow through the venturi in accordance with the requirements of engine speed and load.

The variable venturi feature is designed to increase the speed of the air passing through the carburetor. This increase in speed of airflow is accompanied by a decrease in pressure, which draws fuel out of the float bowl and into the air entering the carburetor.

The Motorcraft 2700 carburetor utilizes a venturi valve to change the area of the venturi. Tapered metering rods are attached to the venturi valve. The rods move back and forth in the jets as the air valve moves. When the venturi valve is closed, the largest portion of the rod is in the jet. Therefore, effective metering of the fuel is controlled by the rod position in the jet.

The venturi valve controls the venturi area and the main jet area. With this setup, an extremely efficient air-fuel ratio is maintained throughout the range of engine speed and load.

Special gauges and a dial indicator are required when making a complete adjustment of the carburetor. Curb idle adjustment is made in accordance with the instructions given on the decal in the engine compartment.

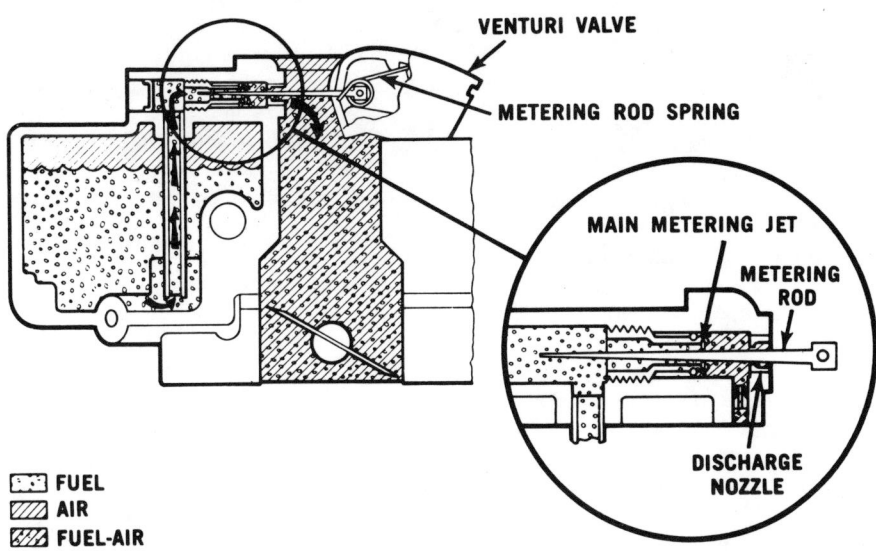

Fig. C-21a. Details of variable venturi carburetor as installed on California engines. Note tapered metering rod.

## HIGH ALTITUDE OPTION

Certain counties in the Western United States have been designated as high altitude areas by the U.S. Environmental Protection Agency. According to the EPA, all cars and trucks under 6000 lb. GVW sold for use in those counties must be certified to meet normal EPA exhaust emission standards while operating in high altitudes.

To meet this EPA requirement, Ford Motor Co. has developed a High Altitude option for all its cars and light trucks. This option consists of a special high altitude compensating carburetor, which is designed to supply the same relative air/fuel mixture at high and low altitudes.

As the car ascends in altitude, the atmospheric pressure drops and becomes less dense. This change in air density causes the air/fuel mixture to become richer at the same throttle opening with an attendant increase in exhaust emissions.

In operation, the change in atmospheric pressure is sensed by an aneroid valve. When the valve detects lower atmospheric pressure, it opens and allows air to be pulled through a bypass circuit. The bypass circuit, in turn, discharges below the venturi but above the throttle plates, thereby leaning the mixture.

## HOT AND COLD AIR INTAKE

The amount of air-fuel mixture that can be drawn into the cylinders will vary greatly with the temperature of the air. To provide a uniform combustible mixture for the engine, it is, therefore, highly desirable that the temperature of the air entering the carburetor be controlled within narrow limits. This is accomplished by the hot and cold air intake system which forms part of the carburetor air cleaner and is used on most of the 1968-1977 Ford lines except some of the high performance engines. It is an essential part of the exhaust gas emission control system.

This is a thermostat-vacuum controlled unit which is attached to the air cleaner and controls the temperature of the air entering the air cleaner for improved combustion.

The assembly takes air from the engine compartment, or heated air from a shroud around the exhaust manifold. This tempered air is then passed through the air cleaner and into the carburetor.

A thermostat, Fig. C-22, in the air duct is exposed to the air and the action of the thermostat controls the position of the valve plate so that the hot and cold air are blended to maintain a temperature of approximately 100 deg. F. The valve plate should be in the "heat on" position, Fig. C-22, when the temperature is 100 deg. F. or less and in the "heat off" position, Fig. C-23, when the temperature exceeds 135 deg. F.

Make sure that a vacuum of 15 in. reaches the vacuum motor. To check the vacuum motor, remove it from the assembly and connect it to a vacuum source of 15 in. The motor should then move the motor rod one-half in. If not, replace the motor.

## Carburetor, Fuel System Service

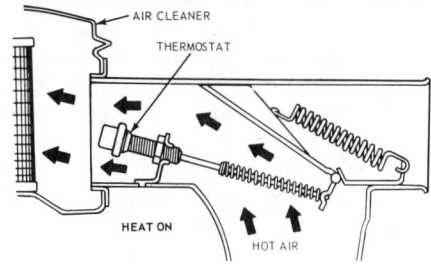

Fig. C-22. Duct and valve assembly in "Heat On" position – Warm-up.

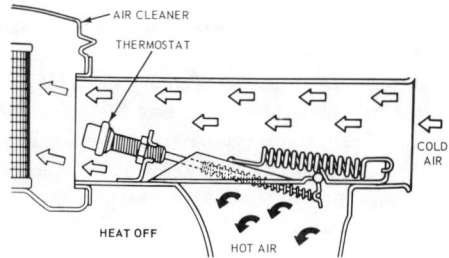

Fig. C-23. Duct and valve assembly in "Heat Off" position – Warm engine.

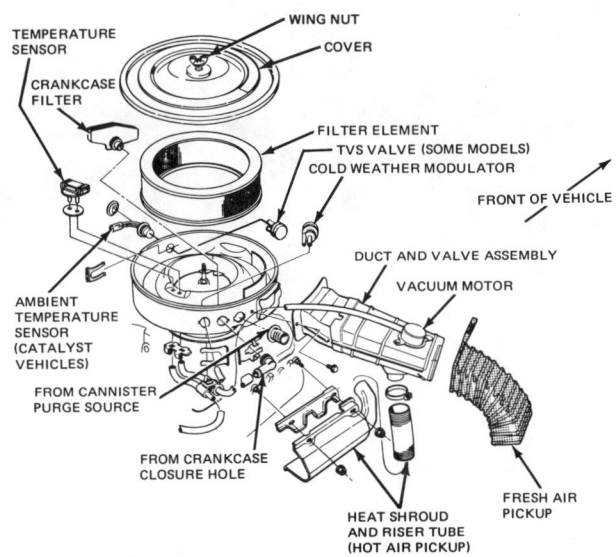

Fig. C-24. Details of air cleaner assembly used on late model cars.

## Fix Your Ford

When the engine is cold and ambient temperature in the engine compartment is less than 100 deg. F., the valve plate should be in the "heat on" position. See Fig. C-22. If not, check for possible interference of plate and duct, which would cause the plate to bind in its given travel. Check operation of the duct assembly by immersing it in water of specified temperature and noting position of valve plate.

Recent models with emission control equipment have special air cleaners with thermostatic control, Fig. C-24. Cars equipped with catalytic converters have an ambient temperature sensor, TVS valve and cold weather modulator.

## CLEANING THE AIR CLEANER

Cleaning the air cleaner is an important part of servicing the carburetor and should be a part of every tune-up job. Several different types of air cleaners have been used on Ford cars. Currently, the cars are equipped with a dry type air filter that has a replaceable cellulose fiber filtering element, Fig. C-25. This type air filter element should be cleaned every 4000 miles, and replaced every 12,000 miles. To remove the air filter, remove the wing nut which is in the center of the top of the unit. The air cleaner can then be lifted from the carburetor. After lifting the cover from the air cleaner, the filtering element can be lifted out for cleaning. On recent models, it is also necessary to disconnect the vacuum hose and the vacuum control motor, and also disconnect the crank case ventilating system hose from the air cleaner before the unit can be removed from the carburetor.

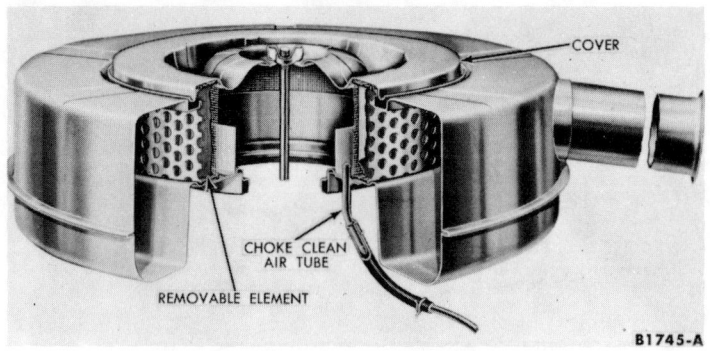

*Fig. C-25. Sectional view of typical air cleaner. Removing wing nut at center, permits removal of cleaning element.*

Cellulose fiber filter elements must not be cleaned with a solvent or cleaning solution. Also oil must not be added to the surface of the filter element or air cleaner body. One method of cleaning the element is to

## Carburetor, Fuel System Service

hold the element in a vertical position and tap it lightly against a smooth horizontal surface to shake the dust and dirt out. Do not deform the element or damage the gasket surfaces by tapping too hard. Rotate the filter after each tap until the entire outer surface has been cleaned. Another method of cleaning is to direct a stream of compressed air to the element in the direction opposite that of the intake air flow. Extreme care mut be exercised to prevent rupture of the element material.

Hold the filter in front of a bright light and carefully inspect it for any splits or cracks. If the filter is split or cracked, replace it.

Previously, an oil bath type unit was employed as an air cleaner. This unit is attached to the carburetor in the same manner as just described. To clean the unit, empty the oil and clean out the accumulated dirt from the bottom of the pan. Then refill to the indicated level with heavy engine oil. The wire mesh element should be washed in kerosene and then dipped in light engine oil.

It is important to keep the air filter clean. If it becomes clogged with dirt, the free flow of air is obstructed, resulting in an excessively rich mixture, loss of power, and greatly reduced fuel economy.

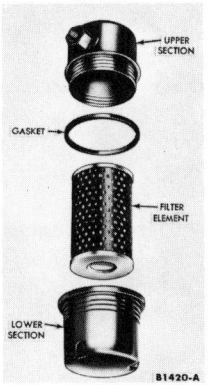

*Fig. C-26. Can type fuel filter.*

## CLEANING THE FUEL FILTER

Recent model Ford engines are equipped with in-line fuel filters. Fig. C-4. These are of one piece construction and cannot be cleaned. Replace the filter at 25,000 mile intervals, or when it becomes clogged or restricted.

A can type filter has also been used and is shown in Fig. C-26. This type filter is mounted in different positions. In some installations it is in the line or at the base of the fuel pump, Fig. C-27.

# Fix Your Ford

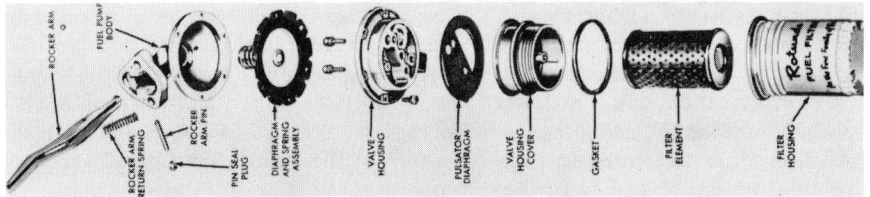

Fig. C-27. Note fuel filter mounted in the base of this fuel pump. (Carter)

## TIPS ON CARBURETOR SERVICE

Most difficulties encountered in the operation of carburetors result from dirt and other foreign material that gets past the fuel filters and forms in the carburetor. It is therefore important to make sure that fuel filters are cleaned at least once each year.

One of the major difficulties arises from moisture that accumulates in the system. This results from condensation. The difficulty, however, is easily overcome by using some of the special preparations that are designed to absorb moisture. The moisture will then pass through the fine mesh of the filters, and the tiny jets of the carburetor. Such chemicals have various names, and their descriptions imply that freezing of the fuel line will be prevented. Obviously, if this moisture is allowed to accumulate in the fuel system, it will freeze in cold weather, with the result that the car will not operate. In addition, the fuel pump, filter and carburetor may be damaged. Moisture that collects in the die cast fuel pumps and in carburetors will cause corrosion, which will be a cheesy like substance, which effectively clogs the system.

When overhauling the carburetor becomes necessary, this will be indicated usually by poorer fuel economy, rough running engine and

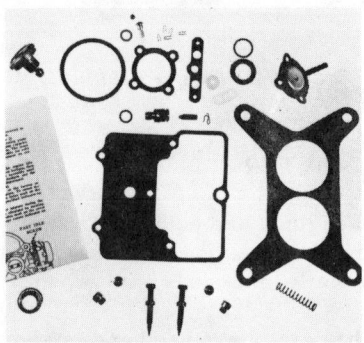

Fig. C-28. Typical of parts included in carburetor repair kit. Note instruction sheet.

# Carburetor, Fuel System Service

particularly a rough idle. When overhauling a carburetor, the owner has the option of installing a rebuilt unit, or purchasing a kit of repair parts and installing it. One of the kits is shown in Fig. C-28, and as shown in the illustration, the necessary instructions are included.

Before installing any new parts in a carburetor, it is important the main body, float bowl and air horn be carefully cleaned and all the internal passages cleared by blowing out with compressed air. A gummy substance frequently forms in the carburetor. It is important that all of this is removed. This is most easily done by using a special solvent designed for cleaning carburetor parts. However, do not immerse any rubber parts such as diaphragms in the solvent.

Also before installing new parts in the carburetor, the mating surfaces of the main body and the air horn should be checked to be sure they are true and not warped. This is done with a straightedge as shown in Fig. C-29. In addition, the two parts should be held together and checked. If one can be "rocked" on the other a new unit should be obtained.

Unless these two surfaces are true and flat, air leaks will occur and the carburetor will not operate correctly.

When disassembling the carburetor, carefully note the position of the various parts and at the same time study the illustration included in the parts kit, and the illustrations in this text, so that there will be no confusion when reassembling the unit. Pay particular attention to the location of the ball checks.

## QUICK SERVICE ON MANIFOLD HEAT CONTROL VALVE

A valve is placed in the exhaust system to direct hot air around the intake manifold and to aid in the vaporization of the fuel. The exhaust

*Fig. C-29. Checking the surface of a carburetor with a straightedge to make sure it is not warped.*

gases are directed into passages around the intake manifold by means of a thermostatically controlled valve. In the case of V-8 engines, this is located at the outlet of the right exhaust manifold. On the six cylinder engines the heat control valve, Fig. C-30, is in the exhaust manifold directly below the carburetor. When the valve is closed, or in the "heat on" position, warm air from the exhaust is directed through the passages provided around the intake manifold. After the engine reaches operating temperature, the valve is opened so the exhaust gases pass directly to the muffler. It is important that this valve be kept free and in good operating condition. The shaft has an external extension or counterweight, which can be easily swung back and forth when the valve is in operating condition. If it is rusted and will not move freely, some penetrating oil should be poured on the shaft, and the ends of the shaft tapped back and forth until the shaft can be rotated freely.

If this shaft is not free to operate, heat will usually be supplied all the time with the result that power and performance will not be normal.

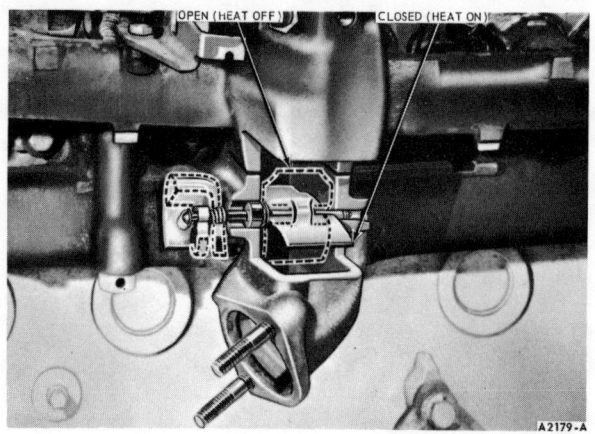

Fig. C-30. Manifold heat control valve as used on a 240 cu. in. Six.

## QUICK SERVICE ON FUEL PUMPS

Failure of the fuel pump, Figs. C-27, C-31, C-33, and C-34, is one of the major causes of roadside failures. Its operation should be checked each year and particularly before starting on a long trip. Fortunately, a fuel pump is easily checked. However, before checking the fuel pump it is advisable to check the fuel filters to make sure they are free and not obstructing the flow of fuel.

If a pressure gauge is not available to check the operation of the fuel pump, the pump can be checked by measuring the quantity of fuel it

## Carburetor, Fuel System Service

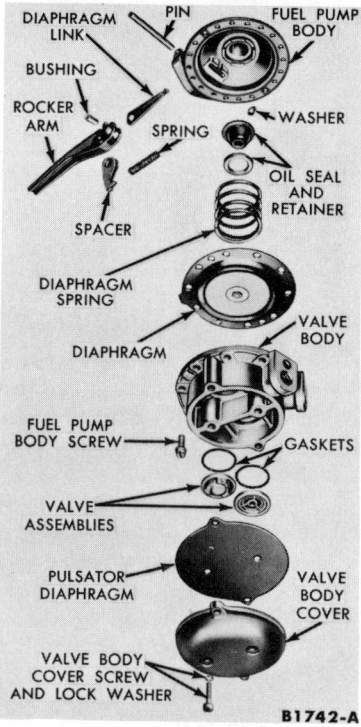

Fig. C-31. Details of AC fuel pump as used on many V-8 engines.

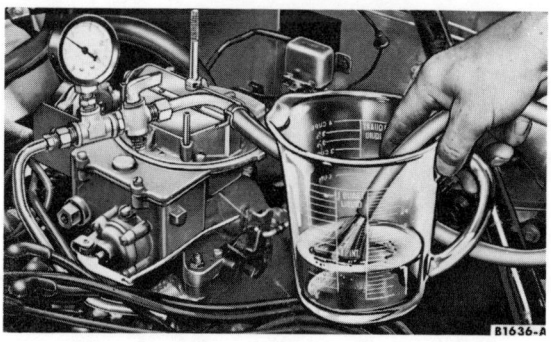

Fig. C-32. One method of checking the operation of a fuel pump.

pumps. Disconnect the fuel line at the carburetor and place the end of the fuel line in a suitable container, Fig. C-32. Then start the engine. Note the time required to pump one pint of fuel. Fuel pumps on smaller engines

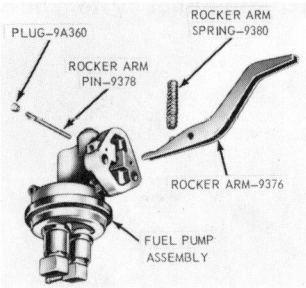

*Fig. C-33. Carter permanently sealed fuel pump installed on V-8 engines.*

should pump one pint of fuel every thirty seconds, and on larger engines one pint in twenty seconds. There will be ample fuel in the carburetor float bowl to operate the engine for sufficient time to make such a check.

If a pressure gauge is available to check the fuel pump, disconnect the fuel line at the carburetor and connect the pressure gauge (zero to 15 lb.) to the line. Start the engine. A pressure of 3-1/2 to 5-1/2 lb. should be obtained on engines of 240 cu. in. displacement or less. The fuel pumps on larger engines should have 4 to 6 lb. pressure.

On recent models the Carter permanently sealed type fuel pump, Figs. C-33 and C-34, is installed. On this type fuel pump only the rocker arm spring, pin and the rocker arm are replaceable.

However, regardless of type, most mechanics prefer to install a new or rebuilt pump rather than take the time to repair the original pump.

## EVAPORATIVE EMISSION SYSTEM

Recent model vehicles are equipped with fuel evaporative emission systems which are designed to prevent the escape of fuel vapors into the atmosphere. Fuel vapors trapped in the sealed fuel tank are vented through the orifice vapor separator assembly in the top of the tank. The vapors leave the separator assembly through a single vapor line and continue to the carbon canister in the engine compartment for storage until such time as they are purged to the engine by means of a tube connected to the air cleaner.

*Fig. C-34. Carter permanently sealed fuel pump installed on smaller Ford engines.*

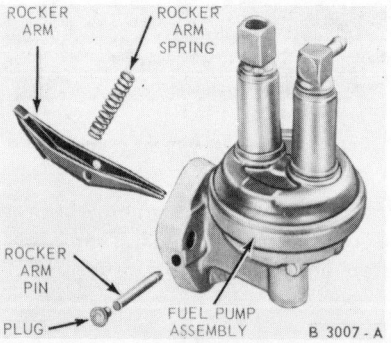

# REDUCING EXHAUST EMISSIONS

In addition to the material presented in this Chapter, the reader should also study the Chapter on Ignition and the Chapter on Carburetion.

In order to meet Federal regulations covering crankcase and exhaust emission of noxious gases, all cars are now equipped with special devices or are so designed to reduce the emission of such gases from the crankcase and from the exhaust system.

Crankcase ventilating systems have been in use for many years. The purpose of this original system was to remove the blow-by gases and water vapor from the crankcase and in that way reduce the tendency toward oil dilution. In that system, air entered through the oil filler in the rocker arm cover, passed through the valve chamber into the crankcase and then to the atmosphere through the road vent tube.

More recently, the Closed Crankcase Ventilating system was adopted. In this system, Fig. D-1, the crankcase ventilating air source is the carburetor air cleaner. The air passes through a hose connecting the air cleaner to the oil filler cap, Fig. D-1. The cap is sealed at the filler opening to prevent the entrance of unfiltered air. The air then passes

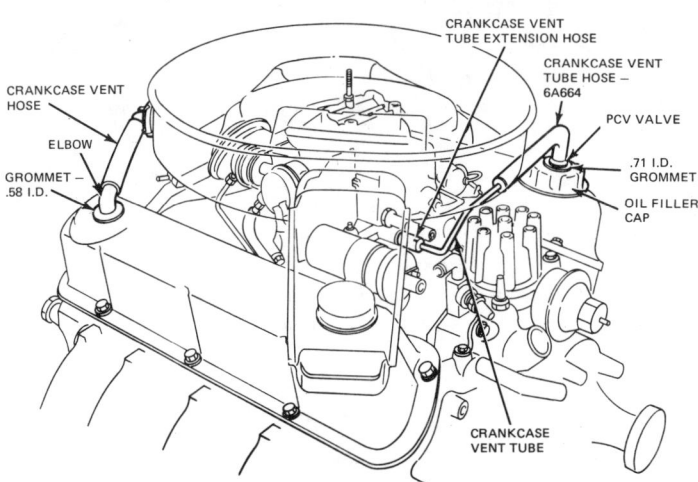

*Fig. D-1. Late type positive crankcase ventilating system, showing location of PCV valve.*

# Fix Your Ford

down past the valve push rods and into the crankcase and valve timing case cover. Then to the rear of the crankcase and up to the valve rocker cover. The air then flows through the oil separator (except on the 428 police) to the spring loaded regulator valve, Fig. D-2, which regulates the amount of air flow to meet changing operating conditions. The air is then directed to the intake manifold or carburetor spacer through the crankcase vent hose, tube and fittings.

At idle speed, intake manifold vacuum is high. This high vacuum overcomes the tension of the spring pressure and moves the valve to the low speed position, Fig. D-2. With the valve in this position, the ventilating air passes between the valve and the outlet port, providing a minimum of ventilation.

As engine speed increases and manifold vacuum decreases, the spring forces the valve to the full open position, Fig. D-2, which increases the flow of ventilating air.

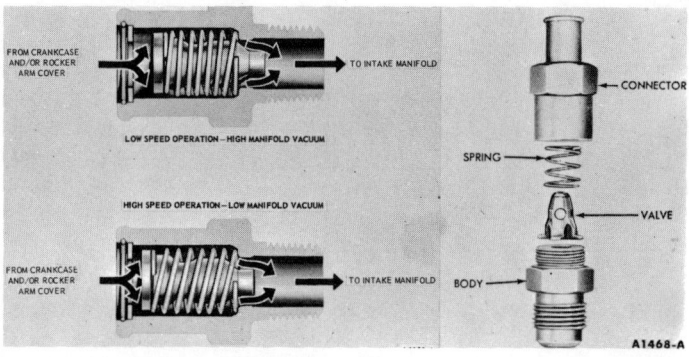

*Fig. D-2. Details of crankcase ventilating valves. Late type is shown at the left and early type at the right.*

When servicing these systems, it is important that all connecting tubing be clear, unobstructed and without leaks.

A defective closed crankcase ventilating system, or when the valve is stuck in the open position, will cause the engine to idle unevenly. If the valve is stuck in the closed position, fumes will issue from the oil filler pipe.

If there is any doubt as to the condition of the valve, install a new one and compare engine performance. Do not attempt to recondition defective regulator valves.

A malfunctioning closed crankcase ventilating system may be indicated by loping or rough engine idle. Do not attempt to compensate for this idle condition by disconnecting the crankcase ventilating system and making carburetor adjustment. The removal of the crankcase ventilating system

## Reducing Exhaust Emissions

from the engine will adversely affect fuel economy and engine ventilation with resultant shortening of engine life.

To determine whether the loping or rough idle condition is caused by a malfunctioning crankcase ventilating system, perform either of the following tests.

Install a known good regulator valve in the crankcase ventilating system. Start the engine and compare the engine idle condition to the prior idle condition. If the idle condition is found to be satisfactory, replace the regulator valve and clean the hoses, fittings, etc.

If the loping or rough idle condition remains when the good regulator valve is installed, the crankcase ventilating regulating valve is not at fault. Check the crankcase ventilating system for restriction at the intake manifold or carburetor spacer. If the system is not restricted, check engine compression, ignition and carburetion.

Some 1971 models have an electronically controlled distributor modulator which consists of an electronic speed sensor in the speedometer cable assembly; a combination electronic module and solenoid vacuum switch which controls carburetor spark port vacuum to the distributor; and an ambient temperature switch connected to the ground. When the car is in motion, the speed sensor in the speedometer cable supplies a frequency signal to the electronic module. This activates the module and the solenoid vacuum switch to close the distributor vacuum advance at speeds below 18 mph on deceleration and below 23 mph, or 28 mph (depending on the engine model) on acceleration.

## THERMACTOR EXHAUST EMISSION CONTROL SYSTEM

Control of exhaust emitted gases by the Thermactor System, Fig. D-3, is achieved by burning the hydrocarbon and carbon monoxide concentration in the exhaust ports of the cylinder head. To accomplish this burning of the contaminants, air under pressure is injected into the exhaust ports near each exhaust valve. The oxygen of the air, plus the heat of the exhaust gases in each exhaust outlet port, induces combustion during the exhaust stroke of the piston. The burned gases then flow out the exhaust manifold into the exhaust system.

The Thermactor system, Fig. D-3, consists of: An air supply pump, and air bypass valve, check valve, air manifolds for the cylinder heads, air supply tube for the exhaust port of each engine cylinder, the connecting air supply hoses and vacuum sensing hose.

A sectional view of the air bypass valve is shown in Fig. D-4. The Thermactor installation, as installed on the 390 cu. in. V-8 engine is shown in Fig. D-3, which is typical of the Thermactor installations on other Ford engines.

Air under pressure from the pump, flows through the bypass valve, Fig. D-3, to the air manifolds that distribute the air to the air supply tube in each exhaust port, Fig. D-3. A check valve in the inlet air side of each air manifold prevents a back flow of exhaust gases into the air pump when

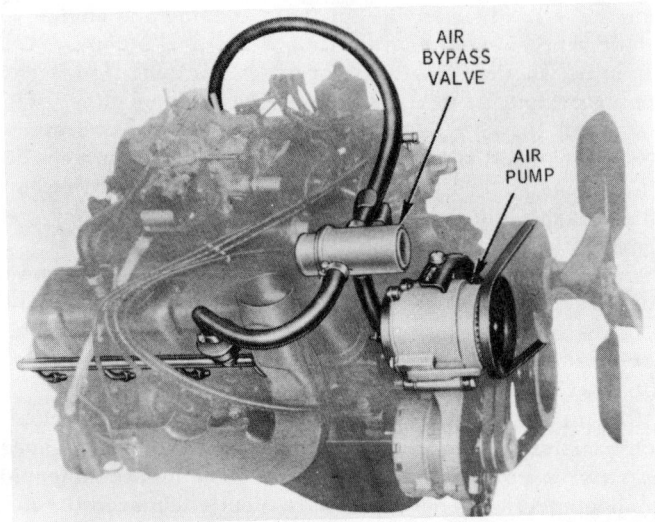

*Fig. D-3. Thermactor crankcase emission control system as installed on V-8 engine.*

the exhaust back pressure exceeds the air pump delivery pressure. Earlier models had a backfire suppressor valve which was incorporated in the bypass valve.

All the air from the air supply pump passes through the air bypass valve. Normally, the air is directed to the check valves and into the air

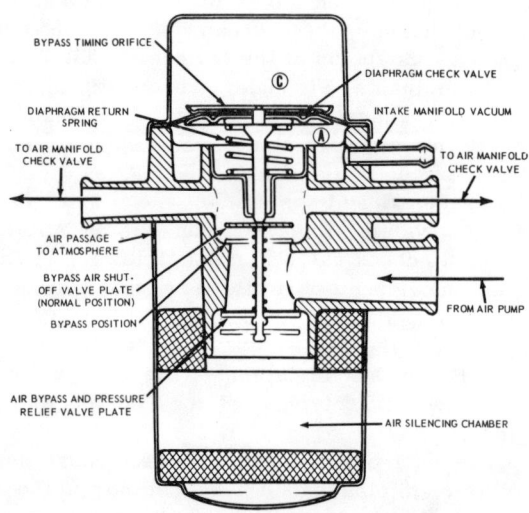

*Fig. D-4. Sectional view of air bypass valve.*

## Reducing Exhaust Emissions

manifold. During engine deceleration periods, air delivery to the air manifold is momentarily interrupted and the air is diverted to the atmosphere.

When servicing the Thermactor system, the first step is to make sure that the drive belt is properly adjusted. A loose drive belt causes improper air pump operation and a belt that is too tight places a severe strain on the air pump bearings. If adjustment is necessary, loosen the air pump mounting and the adjusting arm bolts. Move the air pump forward or away from the engine until the correct tension is obtained. With a suitable bar, pry against the pump rear cover to hold the belt tension when tightening the mounting bolt. Do not pry against the pump housing.

To check the valve, operate the engine until it reaches normal operating temperature. Inspect all hoses and hose connections for obvious leaks and correct as necessary, before checking the check valve operation. Disconnect the air supply hoses at the check valve. Visually inspect the position of the valve plate inside the valve body. It should be lightly positioned against the valve seat.

Insert a probe into the hose connection on the check valve and depress the valve. It should freely return to the original position against the valve seat when released. If equipped with two check valve assemblies, check both valves for free operation.

Leave the hose, or hoses, disconnected and start the engine. Slowly increase the engine speed to 1500 rpm and watch for exhaust gas leakage at the check valve or valves. There should not be any exhaust leakage. The valve may flutter or vibrate at idle speed, but this is normal due to the exhaust pulsations in the manifold. Defective check valves should be replaced as they cannot be repaired.

To determine if the air bypass valve is operating correctly, remove the air bypass valve to air manifold check valve hose at the bypass valve hose connection. Then with the transmission in neutral and the parking brake on, start the engine and operate at normal engine idle speed. Verify that air is flowing from the air bypass valve hose connection. Air pressure should be noted, as this is the normal delivery flow to the air manifold or manifolds. Momentarily (approximately 5 seconds) pinch off the vacuum hose to the bypass valve to duplicate the air bypass cycle. Release the pinched vacuum hose. Air flow through the air bypass valve should diminish or stop for a short period of time. The length of time required to resume normal flow cannot be specified, since the time interval is dependent on engine vacuum and length of time the vacuum line is pinched off.

To check the bypass valve for diaphragm leakage, first remove the vacuum supply hose to the air bypass valve at the bypass valve connection. Insert a tee connection in the vacuum supply hose. Connect a vacuum gauge to one of the remaining connections of the tee, insert a short length of hose on the remaining connection. Insert a suitable plug in the open end of the short length of hose. Start the engine and note the vacuum gauge reading. Remove the plug from the short length of hose and connect to the air bypass valve vacuum connection. Observe vacuum gauge reading. If the indicated vacuum reading does not correspond with the previous reading after approximately sixty seconds, replace the air bypass valve.

If air supply hoses are baked or burned, the trouble would be due to defective check valve on air supply manifold. If there is excessive backfire in the exhaust system on 1967 models equipped with Thermactor, the cause will be a collapsed, plugged or disconnected suppressor valve vacuum line. A defective fire suppressor valve will also cause trouble.

## IMCO EXHAUST EMISSION CONTROL

The IMCO exhaust emission control system uses a specially calibrated carburetor and distributor in conjunction with retarded ignition timing. This reduces the exhaust contaminations by burning them within the cylinder combustion chamber before reaching the exhaust manifold.

Servicing this system, therefore, involves careful ignition and carburetor adjustment which is described in appropriate chapters.

## DISTRIBUTOR MODULATOR 1970-1971

The distributor modulator system should be checked when loss of engine performance and excessive fuel consumption are noted. Road tests would be similar to those of retarded spark. To check the system, connect a vacuum gage to the large hose connection of electronic module which is mounted on the dash inside the passenger car compartment. Raise the rear wheels. Start the engine and with the transmission in neutral, the vacuum gage should read zero. With the transmission in gear, slowly accelerate to 40 mph. The vacuum should cut in between 21 and 31 mph at which point the vacuum should drop to zero. Allow the engine to coast down from 25 to 15 mph and the vacuum should drop to zero and remain there. With the transmission in neutral, chill the thermal switch (mounted near the front door hinge pillar on the outside of the cowl panel) with the engine operating at 1500 rpm. There should be a vacuum reading. If these checks are satisfactory, the system is in good condition. If not proceed as follows: Voltage at red wire leading to control module with ignition switch on should show full battery voltage. Disconnect multiple plug and insert an ohmmeter from the grey wire to the ground. Place one hand on the thermal switch to warm it and switch should open at temperature above 68 deg. F. Apply ice to thermal switch and switch should close at temperatures below 58 deg. F.

To check control module, leave plug disconnected. Place a jumper between two red wires where wires are joined at plug. Operate engine at 1500 rpm. Connect vacuum gage at carburetor spark port vacuum connection. Record reading. Reconnect vacuum line to carburetor. Connect vacuum gage to large hose connection of solenoid valve. Gage should indicate zero. Ground system end of grey wire at thermal switch multiple

## Reducing Exhaust Emissions

plug where switch is unhooked from circuit. Reading should be zero.

To check speed sensor, remove jumper from grey wire. Leave switch disconnected. Raise vehicle and operate engine in gear to 32 mph. Some vacuum should be indicated. Check speed sensor for continuity. Resistance of sensor is 40 to 60 ohms.

## EXHAUST GAS RECIRCULATION

The exhaust gas recirculating (EGR) system and the coolant spark control (CSC) are installed on most 1973-1978 engines. These systems regulate both spark advance and EGR operation according to coolant temperature by switching vacuum signals. EGR routes part of the exhaust gas back to the carburetor air intake system. This lowers combustion temperatures, slows the combustion process and reduces nitrous oxide ($NO_x$) emissions.

Major EGR/CSC system components, Fig. D-5, include a 95 deg. F. EGR-PVS valve, spark delay valve (SDV) and vacuum check valve. When the engine is operating at about 2500 rpm and the temperature is below 82 deg. F., the EGR-PVS valve admits carburetor EGR ported vacuum directly to the distributor advance diaphragm through a one-way check valve. At the same time, the EGR-PVS valve shuts off the EGR valve and transmission diaphragm.

When the engine coolant temperature is 95 deg. F. and above, the EGR-PVS valve directs carburetor EGR vacuum to the EGR valve and transmission. At temperatures between 82 and 95 deg. F., the EGR-PVS valve may be open, closed or in mid-position.

In 1977 engines, the EGR and transducer valves are combined, Fig. D-5a. Cleaning the valve is not recommended. If dirt impairs the operation of the valve, install a new unit.

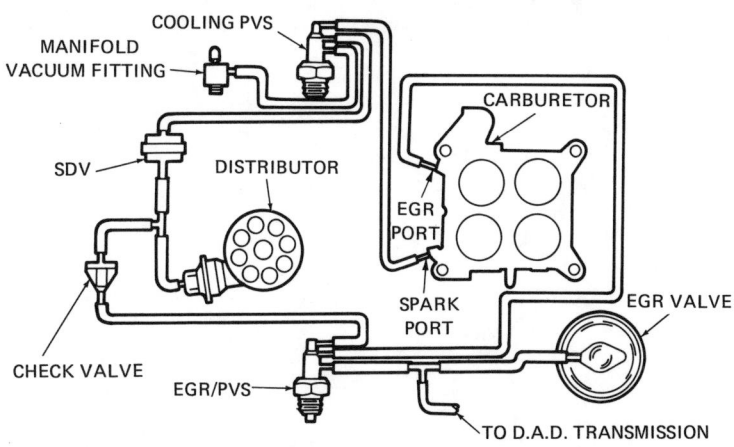

*Fig. D-5. Exhaust gas recirculating (EGR) system used on 1978 engines.*

# Fix Your Ford

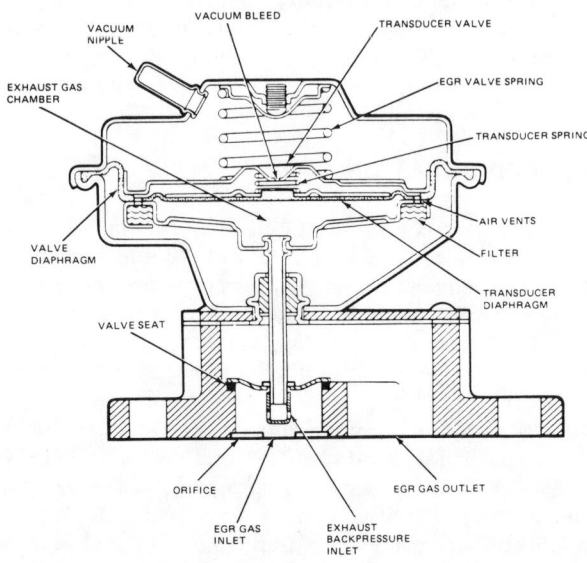

*Fig. D-5a. Sectional view of EGR and transducer valve assembly used in 1977 models. No service adjustments are required.*

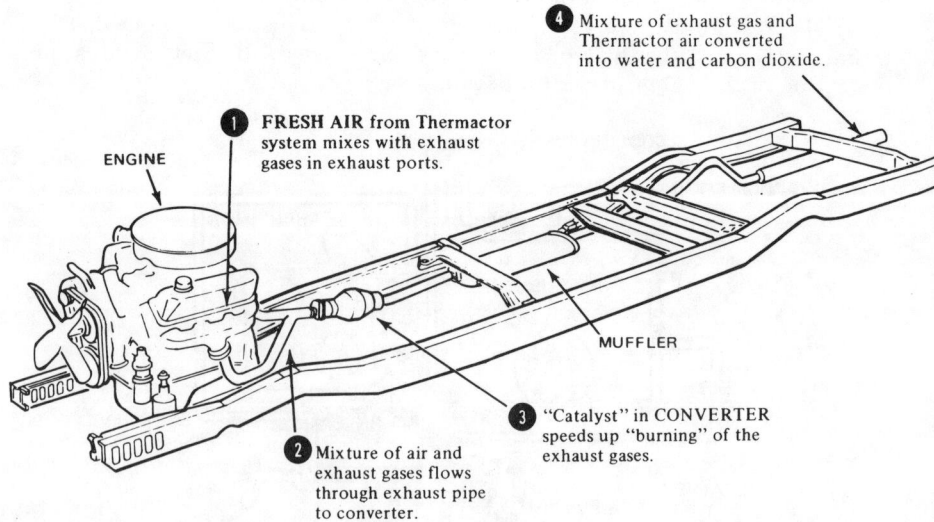

*Fig. D-6. Location of catalytic converter and how it operates. Some cars have two converters, one in each exhaust line.*

# Reducing Exhaust Emissions

## 1974-1978 CTAV SYSTEM

The Cold Temperature Actuated vacuum system (CTAV) is used to more accurately match spark advance to engine requirements under cold outside temperature conditions. The system can select from two vacuum sources for spark advance, depending on the temperature of air in the air cleaner. If the ambient air temperature is below 49 deg. F., the system will select exhaust gas recirculating vacuum for distributor modulation. If the temperature is above 65 deg. F., the system will select spark port vacuum. In between these two temperatures, the system will select either port, depending on which cycle it is in.

The CTAV system consists of an ambient temperature switch, Fig. D-7, a three-way vacuum switch, an inline vacuum bleed and a latching relay.

Vacuum both for the spark port and the EGR port is supplied to the three-way solenoid valve. The ambient temperature switch provides the signal that determines which source will be selected. The latching relay provides for one cycle each time the ignition switch is turned on.

The temperature switch activates the solenoid. It is calibrated to open at 49 deg. F., and below, and to close at 65 deg. F. and above. Thus, at air temperatures within the air cleaner below 49 deg. F., the system is inoperative and the distributor diaphragm receives spark port vacuum while the EGR valve receives carburetor EGR port vacuum, Fig. D-7.

When the temperature switch closes above 65 deg. F., current from the battery energizes the three-way solenoid vacuum valve and carburetor EGR port vacuum is delivered to the distributor advance diaphragm, as well as the EGR valve. The latching relay (normally off) is also energized by the closing of the temperature switch. However, once ON, it receives its energy through the ignition switch and stays ON until the ignition switch is turned OFF, whether the temperature switch is open or closed.

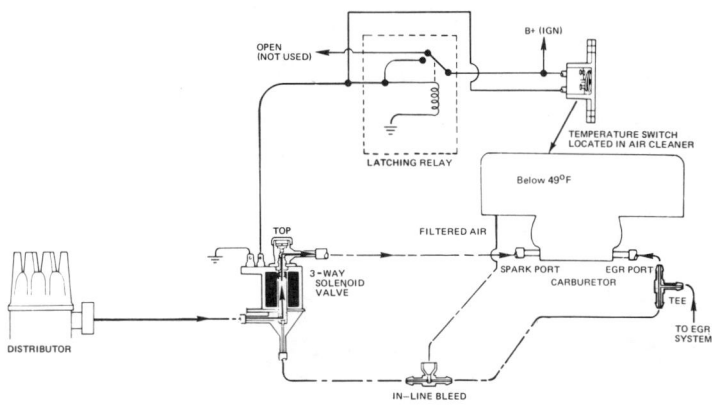

*Fig. D-7. Circuit showing details of Cold Temperature Actuated vacuum system.*

# Fix Your Ford

## 1974-1978 EMISSION CONTROL SYSTEM

Beginning with 1974 models, each passenger car is equipped with a special decal in the engine compartment, providing engine tune-up specifications and emission control data. These vital statistics specifically apply to that particular vehicle, and the printed instructions should be followed.

The complete emission control system installed on most 1975-1977 Ford cars includes catalytic converter, vacuum-operated exhaust heat control valve, ported vacuum switch, electric PVS, cold weather modulator, temperature switch, solenoid vacuum valve, Thermactor air injection system, exhaust gas recirculating system, fuel decel valve system, decel throttle modulating system and cold start spark advance system. Devices used in earlier models have been described.

The catalytic converter, Fig. D-7, is a device designed to convert noxious hydrocarbons and carbon monoxide in the exhaust gases to harmless water and carbon dioxide.

Lead-free gasoline must be used in catalytic converter equipped engines. Avoid running out of fuel, and keep the engine tuned and in good operating condition. Any misfiring will cause overheating of the converter. Refer to the decal on the glove compartment door or in the engine compartment for proper maintenance schedules.

Do not operate the engine for more than 30 sec. with one or more spark plugs shorted out, or with a plug cable removed.

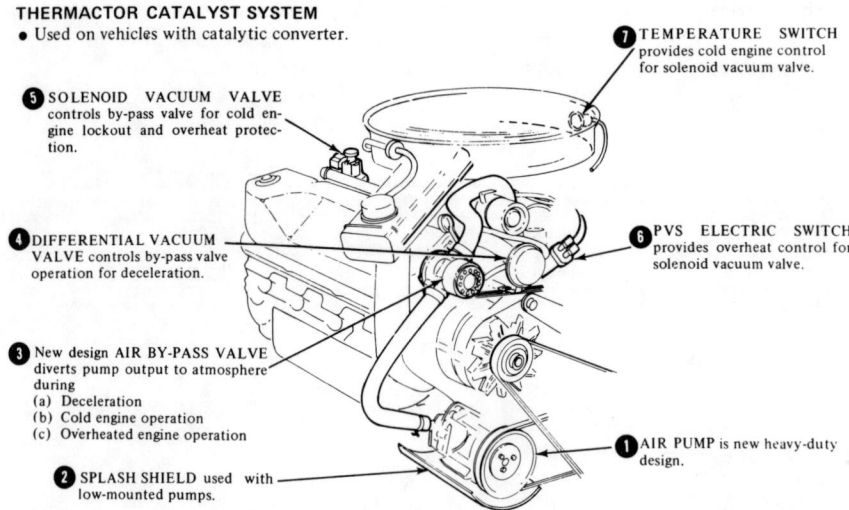

*Fig. D-8. Callouts explain function of components of Thermactor catalyst system used on engines equipped with a catalytic converter.*

## Reducing Exhaust Emissions

No converter maintenance is necessary, but the Thermactor system and allied emission controls do require service.

## THERMACTOR SYSTEM SERVICE

The Thermactor system used on cars without a catalytic converter is basically the same setup used on previous models, Figs. D-3 and D-4. The Thermactor catalyst system used on vehicles with the catalytic converter is shown in Fig. D-8.

Noisy operation in either system may result from a worn air pump or worn drive belt. Be sure drive belt tension is correct. If adjustment is necessary, pry against the end plate of the air pump, not against the pump body. An air pump in good condition should provide a pressure of 2 1/2 psi at 1000 rpm. Make tests with the engine at normal operating temperature. Also make sure all hoses are in good condition, with no leakage.

To check operation of air bypass valve: Run engine to normal operating temperature. With transmission in neutral and engine running at 1500 rpm, remove hose from upper end of bypass valve, Fig. D-9. Check for air flow from valve outlet. If there is no flow, check vacuum supply and vacuum circuit. Then, remove and plug vacuum hose. Check for air flow from vent (front of valve). If there is no flow, replace air bypass valve.

To make air bypass valve pressure test: Remove hose from air by-

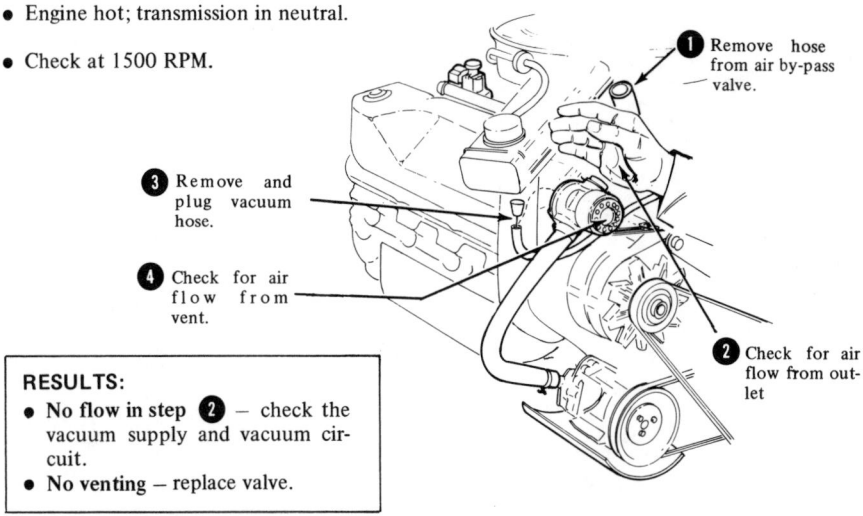

**AIR BY-PASS VALVE FUNCTIONAL TEST (CATALYTIC)**

- Engine hot; transmission in neutral.
- Check at 1500 RPM.

❶ Remove hose from air by-pass valve.

❸ Remove and plug vacuum hose.

❹ Check for air flow from vent.

❷ Check for air flow from outlet.

**RESULTS:**
- No flow in step ❷ — check the vacuum supply and vacuum circuit.
- No venting — replace valve.

*Fig. D-9. Steps are given for making functional test of air bypass valve.*

## Fix Your Ford

pass valve outlet. Attach pressure gauge to outlet. With engine running at 1000 rpm at normal operating temperature, gauge should show 2 1/4 psi. If less, and previous tests have shown pump to be satisfactory, replace valve.

To check vacuum differential valve, Fig. D-8: Remove hose from air bypass valve outlet. Start engine. Air should flow from valve. Cycle vacuum differential valve by accelerating engine to 2500 rpm, then release throttle to idle. Air flow should change from outlet to vent momentarily. If not, check for strong vacuum at vacuum differential valve. If vacuum is present, replace valve. If not, check vacuum supply.

To test vacuum reservoir: Disconnect hoses. Connect a vacuum gauge to one opening and apply vacuum to other opening. A vacuum of 12 in. Hg. should be maintained for at least one minute.

There are two types of solenoid vacuum valves, Fig. D-8, used in the 1975-1976 system. Type one is normally closed, while type two is normally open. Tests on either type are made with the engine at idle and air temperature above 65 deg. F.

To test closed solenoid vacuum valve: Momentarily disconnect hose from air bypass leading to vacuum differential valve. If valve dumps (releases) air, hose connections to solenoid valve are satisfactory. If not, check vacuum supply and hose connections. Disconnect wires from solenoid vacuum valve. Bypass valve should dump air.

To test open solenoid vacuum valve: First disconnect wiring to solenoid vacuum valve. Then reconnect "hot" wire and ground other terminal with a jumper wire. Bypass valve should dump air. If not, replace solenoid vacuum valve.

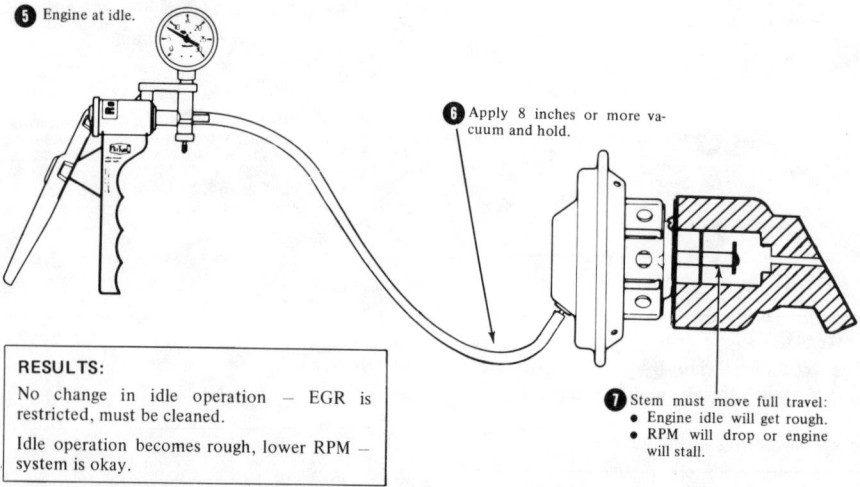

*Fig. D-10. Method is shown for checking 1975 exhaust gas recirculation valve.*

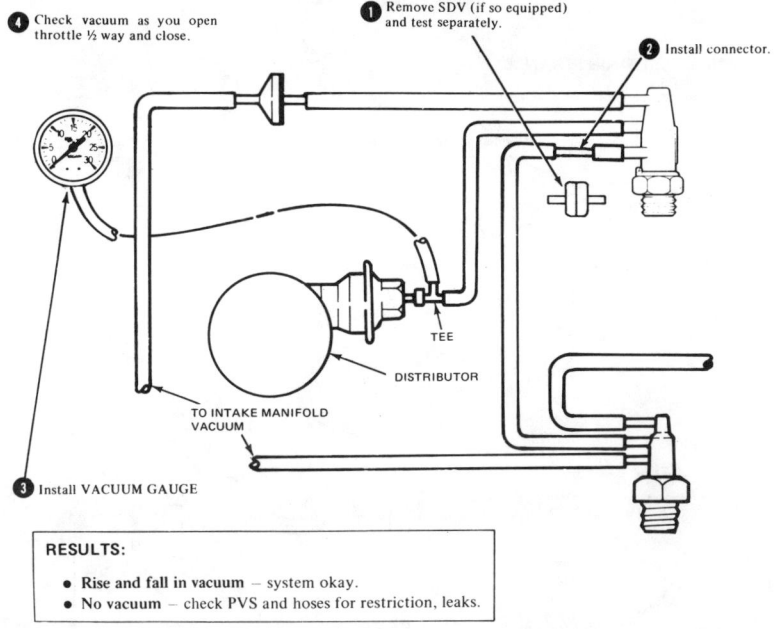

*Fig. D-11. Follow sequence of steps for testing cold start spark advance system as installed on 2300 cc (California) and 460 CID engines.*

## 1975-1978 EXHAUST GAS RECIRCULATING SYSTEM

To test EGR system: First disconnect EGR valve, Fig. D-10, from system. With engine off, apply a vacuum of 8 in. to valve. Close off vacuum supply; valve must hold vacuum for at least 30 seconds. If not, replace EGR valve.

Another test is made with the engine idling. Again apply 8 in. of vacuum to EGR valve. Hold vacuum and note stem of EGR valve. It should move smoothly for full travel, and engine idle should get rough and drop in rpm. If there is no change in engine rpm, EGR valve is restricted. Clean or replace EGR valve.

Ford emphasizes that the use of unleaded fuel will avoid the formation of deposits in the EGR valve. To clean the valve, use a small gauge wire or small drill to clean the orifice. Take special care not to enlarge the orifice. With the EGR valve removed, use compressed air to clean the exterior, taking care to first mask the diaphragm. Apply 15 in. of vacuum to the hose connection to retract the valve, then use compressed air to clear the valve seat.

## COLD START SPARK ADVANCE

To test CSSA system: Remove SDV (spark delay valve), if so equipped, and insert a vacuum gauge, Fig. D-11. Then, with engine at normal

# Fix Your Ford

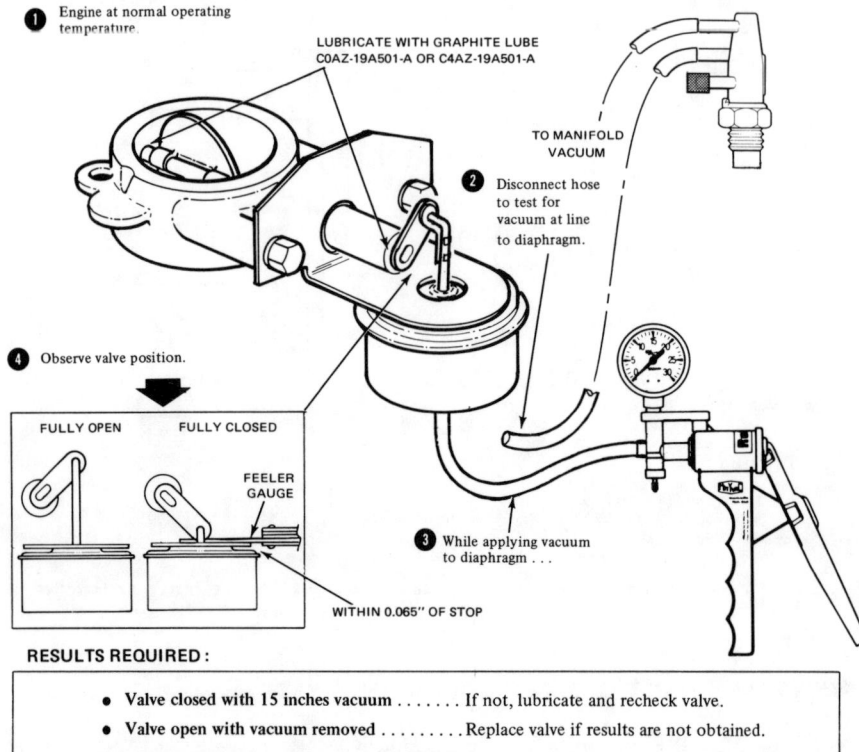

Fig. D-12. Test vacuum-operated exhaust heat control valve in sequence shown. Compare test results with results required.

operating temperature with transmission in neutral, note vacuum as throttle is opened half way, then closed. If system is satisfactory, vacuum will rise and fall. If not, check PVS (ported vacuum switch) and hoses for restrictions and leaks.

## VACUUM-OPERATED HEAT CONTROL VALVE

The vacuum-operated exhaust heat control valve, Fig. D-12, is designed to provide better evaporation and distribution of the air-fuel mixture. To test this valve, run engine to normal operating temperature. Disconnect hose at diaphragm. Apply 15 in. Hg. to valve. Valve should close. If not, lubricate shaft as shown in Fig. D-12. Recheck operation of valve. If valve is closed when vacuum is removed, install a new valve. On 302 and 351W CID engines, valve should start to close at 1-3 in. Hg. On all other applications, it should start to close at 3-6 in. Hg.

# Shortcuts on
# ENGINE DISASSEMBLY

This chapter will deal with shortcut methods of removing different engine parts and their reinstallation. Details of servicing procedures for repairing these individual parts, together with further information on disassembly after these parts have been removed, are given in the Chapter on Simplified Engine Repairs.

## CYLINDER HEAD REMOVAL

Briefly, to remove the cylinder head, it is necessary to first drain the cooling system, disconnect the radiator hose connection, carburetor linkage, battery ground cable and any electrical wiring that is attached to the cylinder head. Also, remove the intake and exhaust manifolds and remove the valve rocker cover. On engines with rocker arm shafts, the shaft and rockers should be removed. On the heads on engines with rocker arm studs, loosen the adjustment and swing the arm to one side. If car is equipped with air conditioner, it is usually necessary to remove the compressor. Similarly, on cars with Thermactor exhaust emission control, it is necessary to remove the compressor and disconnect the hose and manifold.

After the cylinder head nuts or studs have been removed, the head can then be lifted from the cylinder block. In case the head sticks to the block, do not pry between the head and block, as that would mar the gasket surface of the head or cylinder block. If necessary, place a block of wood so that it will act as a fulcrum, and with a lever, pry against some protruding area of the cylinder head which will not be damaged.

After removing carbon and reconditioning the valves, make sure that the gasket surface of head and block are smooth and not marred. If necessary, remove any roughness with a fine file or abrasive stone.

When removing the cylinder head, make a careful check to be sure there are no cracks. Pay particular attention to the areas around the valve seats. If any cracks are found, it is generally advisable to obtain a new cylinder head. In some cases, small cracks can be sealed by means of special cooling system sealing compounds or by mechanical means.

Detailed instructions for removing the cylinder heads of various engines follow.

# Fix Your Ford

## HOW TO REMOVE THE CYLINDER HEAD

240 CU. IN. 1965-1971: Drain cooling system and remove air cleaner together with heat stove for hot and cold air intake, Fig. E-1. Disconnect radiator upper hose and heater hose from coolant outlet housing. Disconnect wire from temperature sending unit. Disconnect battery ground cable. Remove carburetor fuel inlet lines and distributor vacuum lines. Disconnect other vacuum lines for accessibility and identify each one for correct replacement. Remove accelerator cable retracting spring and disconnect accelerator cable from carburetor. Disconnect accelerator cable bracket from cylinder head. On vehicles with automatic transmission, disconnect kickdown rod at bell crank. Pull crankcase ventilating valve from rocker cover and remove vent hose and valve.

*Fig. E-1. Typical 240 cu. in. six cylinder engine. Insert shows Thermactor air injection into exhaust manifold which was a feature of some recent models.*

## Engine Disassembly

On Thermactor engines, disconnect air pump outlet hose at manifold and remove manifold. Disconnect air bypass valve and vacuum lines at intake manifold. Disconnect power brake vacuum line at intake manifold.

Remove the rocker arm cover. Loosen rocker arm stud nuts so the rocker arms can be rotated to one side. Remove the valve push rods in sequence and identify each one so they can be replaced in their original positions. Disconnect spark plugs. Disconnect muffler inlet pipe from exhaust manifold. Discard inlet pipe gasket.

Remove cylinder head bolts. Tapped holes are provided in head so lifting eyes can be installed. Remove cylinder head. When replacing the cylinder head, tighten the bolts to 70 to 75 ft. lb. torque and in the sequence shown in Fig. E-2.

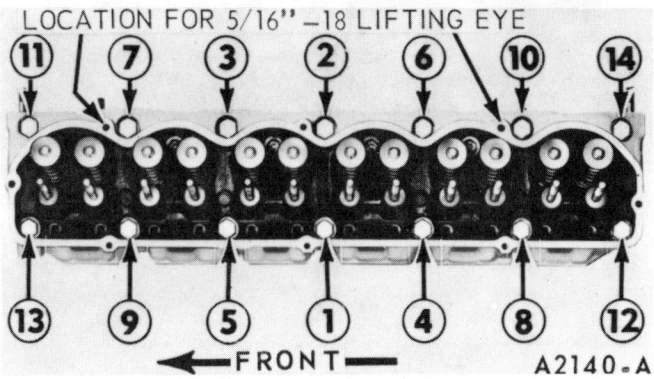

*Fig. E-2. Cylinder head bolt tightening sequence for 240 and 250 cu. in. engines.*

When reconditioning the cylinder head, make a careful check to be sure there are no cracks. Pay particular attention to areas around the valve seats. If any cracks are found, it is generally advisable to obtain a new cylinder head. In some cases small cracks can be sealed by means of special cooling system sealing compounds.

144, 170, 200 and 250 CU. IN. SIX: Drain the cooling system. Remove the air cleaner, Fig. E-3. Disconnect the upper radiator hose at the engine. Disconnect battery ground cable. Disconnect the muffler inlet pipe at the exhaust manifold. Pull the muffler inlet pipe down. Remove the gasket.

Disconnect the accelerator retracting spring. Disconnect the accelerator rod at the carburetor.

On IMCO exhaust emission equipped engines, disconnect the transmission kickdown rod. Disconnect the accelerator linkage at the bell crank assembly.

Disconnect the fuel inlet line at the fuel filter hose and the distributor

# Fix Your Ford

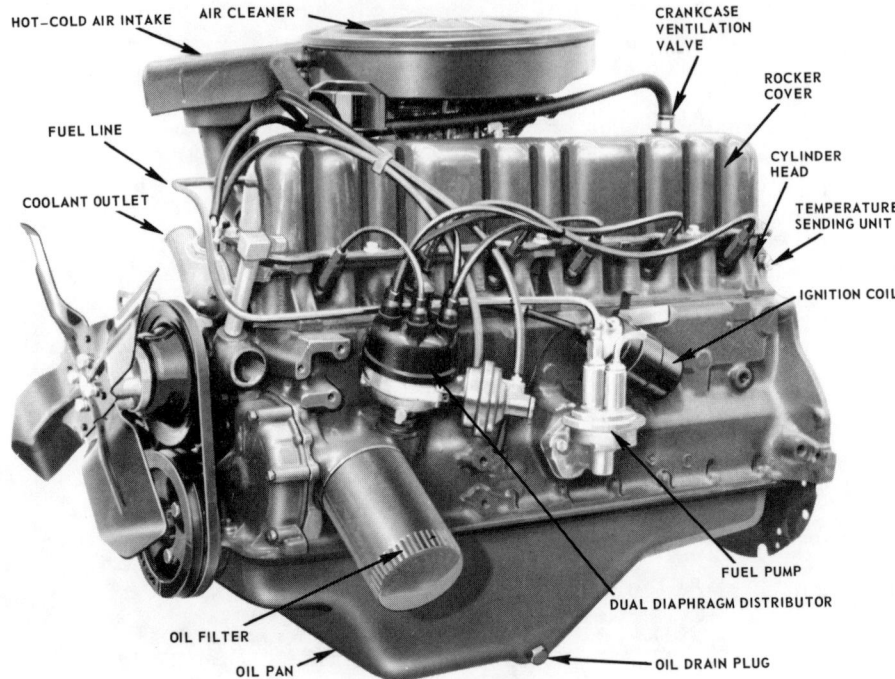

*Fig. E-3. 170 cu. in. engine with IMCO exhaust emission.*

vacuum lines. Disconnect vacuum lines, as necessary, for accessibility and identify them for proper connection.

Disconnect the distributor vacuum line at the distributor. Disconnect the carburetor fuel inlet line at the fuel pump. Remove the lines as an assembly.

Disconnect the spark plug wires at the spark plugs, and the temperature sending unit wire at the sending unit.

Remove the crankcase ventilating system. On Thermactor engines disconnect the air hose at the check valve. Remove the intermediate exhaust air supply tube assembly. Remove the valve rocker arm cover. Remove the round rocker arm shaft assembly. Remove the valve push rods in sequence, taking care to identify each one so that they can be replaced in their original position.

Remove the remaining cylinder head bolts and remove the cylinder head. Do not pry against the cylinder head and block, as the gasket surfaces may become damaged.

When installing the cylinder head on the 170 cu. in. Six engine, apply cylinder gasket sealer to both sides of the new gasket. Spread the sealer evenly over the entire surface. Tighten cylinder head bolts to correct torque in recommended sequence.

## Engine Disassembly

*Fig. E-4. On the 144, 170, 200 and 250 cu. in. engines, tighten cylinder head bolts in the order indicated.*

The hydraulic valve lifters on these engines can be lifted from the cylinder block by means of a strong magnet, Fig. E-15.

Early models of these engines were provided with adjustable rocker arms so that valve lash could be easily adjusted. On recent models, valve lash is adjusted by selecting push rods of the correct length. Check clearance between the rocker arm and the valve stem tip with a feeler gauge. If clearance is less than specified amount, install an undersize push rod. If clearance is greater, install an oversize push rod.

When replacing a cylinder head, make sure that all gasket surfaces are clean and that the head is not warped, as described in the chapter on Basic Engine Repairs. Tighten cylinder head bolts to a torque of 70-75 ft. lb., in the sequence shown in Fig. E-4.

2800 cc V-6: Remove air cleaner. Disconnect battery and carburetor linkage. Drain coolant. Remove distributor cap and cables. Remove distributor vacuum line, distributor, coolant outlet hose, rocker arm covers, fuel line and filter, carburetor, intake manifold and EGR tube. Remove rocker arm shaft by loosening two bolts at a time in sequence. Remove push rods and keep in sequence, front to rear. Remove exhaust manifold. Remove cylinder head bolts and lift off heads.

260, 289, 302, 351 and 400 CU. IN. V-8 ENGINES: The following steps apply particularly to the 1968-1974 302 cu. in. engine, Fig. E-5, and with the exception of the Thermactor and other accessory equipment, is typical of other engines. The procedure for removing the cylinder head is as follows: Drain cooling system. Disconnect automatic choke. Remove air cleaner and air duct assembly. Disconnect accelerator rod at carburetor. Remove retracting spring. Disconnect any vacuum lines for accessories. Disconnect wires at coil. Disconnect spark plugs and remove high tension wires and distributor cap. Remove carburetor inlet line and automatic choke heat tube. Disconnect vacuum hoses from distributor and remove distributor. Disconnect upper radiator hose and temperature sending unit. Remove heater hose from choke housing and disconnect hose from intake manifold. Remove water pump bypass hose. Disconnect crankcase vent hose, Fig. E-5. On Thermactor engines, remove air manifold hoses at air bypass valve. If equipped with air conditioner, remove compressor to intake manifold brackets. Remove intake manifold assembly, being careful not to damage gasket surfaces. Remove EGR cooler, if equipped.

## Fix Your Ford

Disconnect battery ground at cylinder head. Isolate, then remove, air conditioner compressor. Disconnect power steering pump bracket and remove drive belt. Move pump out of the way, positioning it so that oil will not drain. On Thermactor engines, disconnect air hoses from check valves and remove valves. Remove air bypass valve, air pump and bracket. Remove alternator bracket bolt and spacer, ignition coil and air cleaner inlet duct. Disconnect exhaust manifolds. Remove alternator.

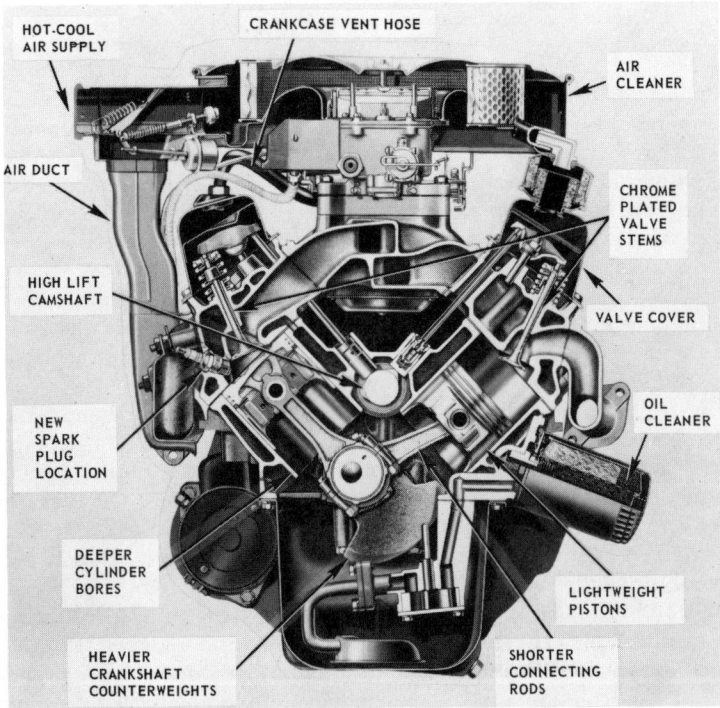

*Fig. E-5. Sectional view of 302 cu. in. engine. Typical of 289 and 260 cu. in. engines.*

Remove rocker arm covers. Loosen rocker arm stud nuts so that rocker arms can be swung to one side. Remove push rods in sequence and identify them so they can be replaced in their original positions. Remove the cylinder head retaining bolts and lift the heads off the cylinder blocks. Do not pry off the cylinder head as it may mar the gasket surfaces. On 302-2V engines, remove exhaust valve stem caps.

When installing cylinder head, torque all bolts in three steps and in sequence, shown in Fig. E-6. Tighten 260 and 289 to 65-70 ft. lb., 302 to 65-72 ft. lb., 351C to 95-105 ft. lb., 351W to 105-112 ft. lb., 400 to 95-105 ft. lb. After torquing, bolts should not be disturbed.

## Engine Disassembly

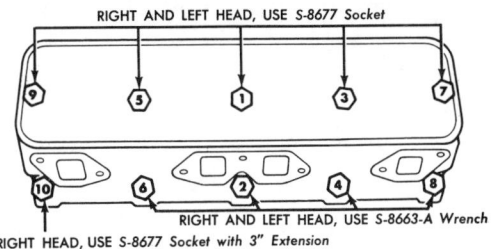

Fig. E-6. Tightening sequence of cylinder head bolts on 260, 272, 289, 302, 312, 351, 352, 390, 406, 410, 427, 428 and 429 cu. in. V-8 engines.

352, 390, 406, 410, 427, 428, 429, 460 CID V-8 CYLINDER HEADS: Drain cooling system and remove air cleaner, Fig. E-7. Disconnect carburetor linkage. Disconnect battery ground cable. On 1968-1970 models remove engine hood and hot air duct. On vehicles with automatic transmission, remove kickdown rod retracting spring. Disconnect the kickdown rod at the carburetor. Disconnect the transmission vacuum line.

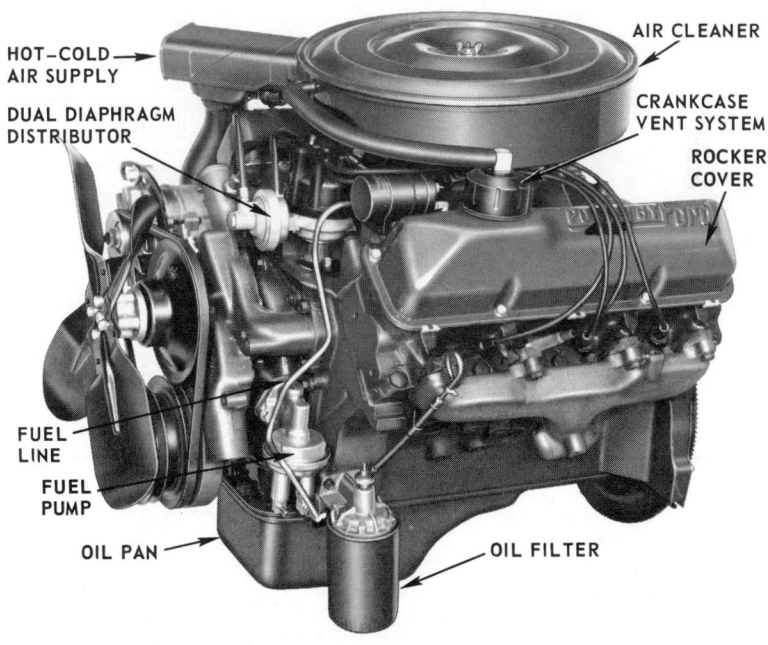

Fig. E-7. Typical 390 cu. in. engine.

## Fix Your Ford

Disconnect the coil high tension lead and the primary wire at the distributor. Disconnect the oil pressure sending unit wire at the sending unit (and oil temperature sending unit wire on the 390, 427, 428 and 429 V-8 engines if so equipped).

Disconnect the spark plug wires at the spark plugs and remove the wires from the ignition harness brackets on the valve rocker arm covers. Remove the distributor cap and spark plug wire assembly. Disconnect the distributor vacuum hoses at the distributor. Remove ignition coil.

Remove the carburetor fuel inlet line at the fuel filter, the automatic choke air heat tube and the heat chamber air inlet tube. Disconnect the brake booster vacuum line at the intake manifold and at the flexible hose. Remove the vacuum line. Remove the distributor hold down bolt and clamp and remove the distributor. Disconnect the radiator upper hose at the thermostat housing. Disconnect the heater hose from the inlet manifold. Disconnect the water temperature sending unit wire at the sending unit. Disconnect the heater hose at the water pump and remove it from the automatic choke housing bracket.

Loosen the clamp on the water pump bypass hose and slide it toward the water pump. Remove the crankcase ventilation regulator valve from the right valve rocker arm cover or oil separator. On Thermactor engines, disconnect the air lines and hoses as necessary for accessibility. Remove the valve rocker arm covers. Position the wire loom attached to the left valve rocker arm cover out of the way. Remove the valve rocker arm shaft assemblies and the push rods in sequence and place them in a rack so that they can be installed in the same location. Remove the intake manifold retaining bolts and lift off the intake manifold.

Remove the intake manifold, crankcase ventilation system components, carburetor, and thermostat housing as an assembly.

On the 390 and 428 cu. in. V-8 engines, disconnect the exhaust manifolds at the muffler inlet pipes. Remove the exhaust control valve. Leave the manifolds attached to the cylinder heads.

On the 427 V-8, remove the exhaust manifold to cylinder head retaining bolts. Leave the manifolds attached to the muffler inlet pipes and secure them to the car frame with wire.

Remove ignition coil and identification tag. Remove power steering pump mounting bracket bolts and position pump and bracket out of way. Leave fluid lines attached to pump. If equipped with air conditioning, isolate compressor at service valves and remove valves and hoses from compressor. Remove nuts attaching compressor support bracket to water pump. Remove bolts attaching compressor to upper mounting bracket and position compressor out of way. Remove compressor upper mounting bracket from cylinder head. Remove cylinder head bolts and lift off head.

When replacing the cylinder head, apply gasket sealer to both sides of the gasket for the 427 engine. On engines with specially treated composition gasket, do not apply sealer. Guided by the word "front" on the gasket, install the gasket over the cylinder head dowels.

Torque all the bolts in sequence, as indicated in Fig. E-6, first to 70

## Engine Disassembly

ft. lb., then to 80 ft. lb. and finally to 90 ft. lb., with the exception of the 427 which should have a final torque of 100 ft. lb.

## OIL PAN REMOVAL KINKS

200, 250 CU. IN. IN-LINE SIX 1970-1978 except Granada and Fairmont: Drain crankcase. Remove oil dipstick and flywheel housing cover. On Mustang, disconnect stabilizer bar and pull it downward out of way. Remove one bolt and loosen other on cross member No. 2, then lower it out of way. Remove oil pan.

200, 250 CU. IN. SIX 1975-1978 Granada: Disconnect oil cooler lines at radiator. Remove radiator top support. Remove dipstick. Drain crankcase. Detach sway bar from chassis. Remove starter. Remove nuts attaching engine mounts to support brackets. Loosen rear insulator to cross member bolts. Raise engine and place 1 1/4 in. block on chassis bracket. Place jack under transmission and raise slightly. Remove pan attaching bolts. Lower pan to cross member. Place transmission cooler lines out of way and lower pan.

200, 250 CU. IN. SIX 1978 Fairmont: Disconnect oil cooler lines at radiator. Remove radiator top support. Remove oil level dipstick. Raise vehicle on hoist and drain crankcase. Remove bolts attaching sway bar to chassis. Remove K-brace. Lower front steering rack and pinion. Remove starter. Remove nuts attaching engine mounts to support brackets. Remove two rear insulator-to-cross member attaching bolts. Raise engine and place 1 1/4 in. spacer between support insulator and chassis bracket. Place jack under transmission and raise slightly. Remove oil pan attaching bolts and lower pan to cross member. Position oil cooler lines out of way and remove oil pan.

302, 351 CU. IN. V-8 1978 Fairmont: Disconnect battery positive cable. Remove fan shroud and position it over fan. Raise vehicle. Drain crankcase. Remove two bolts attaching steering gear to main cross member and let steering gear rest on frame. Remove bolts attaching engine mounts. Raise engine and place two 2 in. x 4 in. wood blocks between engine mounts and frame. Remove K-braces. Remove oil pan attaching bolts and lower pan to frame. Remove oil pump bolts and lower pump into pan. Remove pan.

2800 cc V-SIX: Remove oil level dipstick. Drain cooling system. Remove radiator shroud. Remove upper and lower radiator hoses. Raise vehicle and disconnect automatic transmission cooler hoses. Remove steering gear hoses. Disconnect sway bar. Drain oil from crankcase. Remove splash shield protecting starter. Remove starter. Remove engine front support nuts. Raise engine and place wood blocks between supports and chassis. Remove oil pan bolts and oil pan.

144, 170, 200 and 250 CU. IN. SIX, 1964-1972: Drain the crankcase, Fig. E-3. Remove the oil level dipstick and flywheel housing inspection cover. Remove oil pan retaining screw and remove oil pan. On 1967-71 Mustang, remove stabilizer bar. Also remove one bolt and loosen another on No. 2

cross member and lower it out of the way. Then remove oil pan and gasket. Remove oil pump inlet tube and screen assembly.

1972 Mustang: To remove oil pan, drain cooling system. Remove radiator. Drain engine crankcase. Remove bolts and nuts retaining sway bar to the chassis and allow sway bar to hang. Remove both engine support through bolts and nuts and raise front of engine. Place 2 in. blocks between engine supports and chassis brackets. Remove starter. Remove oil pan retaining bolts, lower pan. Remove oil pump pickup tube and screen assembly. Position the oil cooler lines up and out of the way. Push oil pan forward over the front cross member and into the radiator area to allow the oil pan to clear the cross member and be removed from the bottom.

240 CU. IN. 1966-1973: Drain crankcase and remove radiator, after disconnecting hose connections and automatic transmission cooler lines. On vehicles with air conditioning, remove condenser attaching bolts and position condenser to one side for accessibility. Do not disconnect refrigerant lines. Raise vehicle on hoist. Disconnect and remove starter. Remove engine front support insulator to intermediate support bracket nuts on both supports. Remove the engine rear support insulator to cross member bolt and insulator to transmission extension housing bolts. Raise the transmission, remove the support insulator and lower transmission to the cross member. Raise the engine with a transmission jack and place 3 in. thick wood blocks between both front support insulators and intermediate support brackets. Remove stabilizer bar. Remove oil pan attaching bolts, allowing pan to rest on cross member. Remove oil pump attaching bolts and place it in bottom of pan. Rotate crankshaft as required to remove oil pan.

260, 302 AND 289 CU. IN. V-8, 1963-69: Drain crankcase, Fig. E-5, and remove dipstick. Lower stabilizer bar. On Mustang, also lower idler arm. Remove oil pan bolts and lower pan. Crank engine to obtain necessary clearance. On older models, remove oil inlet tube retaining bolt and loosen other bolts and swing inlet tube out of the way permitting pan removal.

352, 390, 410, 427, 428, 1964-1971: Raise the car and drain the oil. On engines with air conditioning remove shroud from the radiator. Remove stabilizer bar and connecting links and pull ends down. Remove engine front support insulator to frame nuts. Raise engine and insert 1 in. block of wood between the insulators and the frame cross member. Remove oil pan retaining screws and lower pan to frame cross member. Crank engine to obtain necessary clearance between crankshaft and rear oil pan and remove the oil pan.

On 1967 390 CU. IN. engine, it is necessary to remove the sway bar.

302, 302 Boss, 351W 1970-1975 Ford: Remove dipstick. Remove bolts attaching fan shroud and position shroud over radiator. Raise vehicle. Drain crankcase. Remove bolts and nuts retaining engine supports to chassis. Raise engine and place wood blocks between engine supports and

## Engine Disassembly

chassis brackets. Disconnect stabilizer from lower control rods and pull ends down. Remove pan attaching bolts and position pan on cross member. Position stabilizer bar for clearance and remove oil pan.

302, 302 Boss, 351W 1970-1971 Fairlane, Falcon, 1972 Mustang, Torino: Remove dipstick. Remove bolts attaching fan shroud to radiator. Place fan shroud over radiator. Raise vehicle. Drain crankcase. Remove stabilizer bar. Remove engine front support through bolts. Raise engine and place wood blocks between engine supports and chassis brackets. On automatic transmission cars, disconnect oil cooler lines at radiator. Remove oil pan bolts and lower pan to cross member. Remove oil pump pickup tube and screen from oil pump. Rotate crankshaft as needed and remove oil pan.

302, 302 Boss, 351C 1970-1975 Mustang: Remove dipstick. Raise vehicle. Drain crankcase. Remove bolts retaining stabilizer to frame. Remove two bolts retaining number 2 cross member to chassis. Remove oil pan attaching bolts. Turn crankshaft as needed. Remove oil pan.

302 and 351 1975-1978 Mustang: Disconnect battery. Remove fan shroud. Raise vehicle. Drain oil. Remove cross member. Remove attaching screws from steering shaft and bolts attaching steering gear to frame. Remove bolts from sway bar. Remove starter. Remove oil pan bolts and oil pan.

429, 460 1969-1977 Ford, LTD: Disconnect battery. Remove radiator shroud. Raise vehicle. Drain oil. Remove sway bar bolts and move bar forward on struts. Remove bolts from engine supports. Raise front of engine. Insert 1 1/4 in. wood blocks between insulators and bracket. Remove oil filter. Remove oil pan bolts and oil pan. Rotate crankshaft as needed.

351C and 400 1970-1971 Mustang: Remove dipstick. Raise vehicle. Drain crankcase. Disconnect and remove starter. Remove bolts retaining sway bar to chassis. Remove the two bolts retaining No. 2 cross member to chassis. Remove oil pan attaching bolts. Turn crankshaft as needed and remove oil pan.

351C, 351M, 400 1970-1978 Fairlane, Torino, Ford, Granada: Remove dipstick. Remove fan shroud and position shroud over fan. Raise vehicle. Drain crankcase. Disconnect and remove starter. Remove sway bar attaching bolts from lower control arms and lower sway bar. Remove engine front support through bolts. Raise engine and place wood blocks between engine supports and chassis brackets. Remove oil pan attaching brackets. On automatic transmission cars position oil cooler lines out of the way. Remove oil pan.

## HOW TO REMOVE CONNECTING RODS

Before removing the connecting rods and piston assemblies, Figs. E-1, E-5 and E-8, it is first necessary to remove the cylinder head and oil pan. The procedure for removal of those units has just been explained. After removing the head and oil pan, the next step is to remove the ridge from the top of the cylinder bore, Fig. E-9. This ridge, which has been

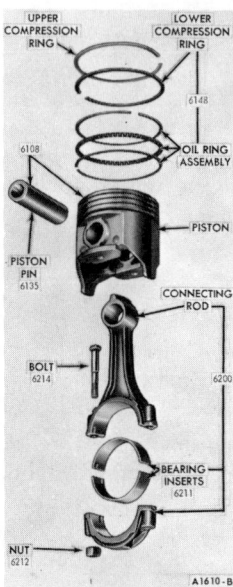

*Fig. E-8. Typical connecting rod and piston assembly.*

worn by the piston rings, is located about 3/8 in. below the top of the cylinder. The ridge must be removed, otherwise the ring striking the ridge will break the piston ring lands as the pistons are pushed up through the cylinder bore. This would make it necessary to install new pistons.

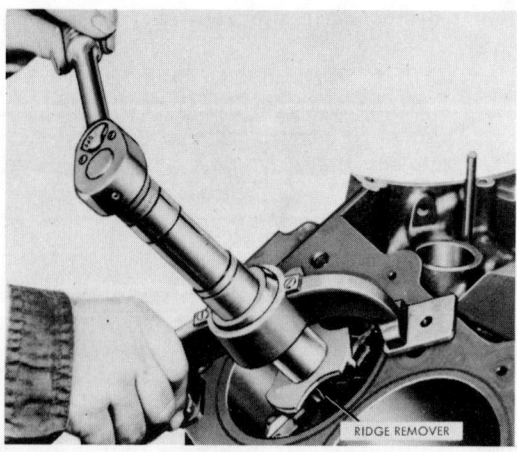

*Fig. E-9. Ridge worn at top of piston travel in cylinder must be removed with a special cutter before attempting to remove pistons.*

## Engine Disassembly

There are many types and makes of cylinder ridge removing tools on the market. One type is illustrated in Fig. E-9.

When removing the ridge at the top of the cylinder bore, first crank the engine until the piston in that particular cylinder is at the bottom of the travel, or stroke. Place a cloth on top of the piston head to collect the cuttings. Remove the cylinder ridge with a ridge cutter, following the instructions furnished by the tool manufacturer. Never cut into the ring travel areas in excess of 1/32 in. when removing the ridge.

After removing the ridge from the top of the cylinder bore, examine the lower ends of the connecting rods and make sure they are marked clearly. Every manufacturer marks the lower end of the connecting rod and cap with a number corresponding to the cylinder in which the rod is installed. If the marks are not clear, it is advisable to mark each rod and cap with a prick punch, or a file, using one mark for each cylinder. In other words, mark No. 1 cylinder with one prick punch mark, and No. 2 with two marks, etc. This is necessary so that the connecting rods and pistons can be reinstalled in their original cylinders. However, care must be taken not to make the marks too deep, as heavy blows from the hammer and prick punch would tend to distort the bearing bore at the big end of the connecting rod.

After making sure that the connecting rods are properly marked, remove the connecting rod cap bolts and shove the piston and rod assembly up through the cylinder bore and out of the top. After each piston and connecting rod assembly has been removed to the top of the cylinder bore, replace the cap on the corresponding rod so that it will not become mixed with the other piston and rod assemblies. Also make sure the bearing shells do not become mixed but remain in their respective connecting rod bores.

The connecting rod assemblies on all Ford engines are removed to the top of the cylinder block.

When installing pistons and connecting rod assemblies, be sure the indentation on the top surface of the piston, Fig. E-10, is installed toward the front of the engine. On six cylinder engines, the piston and connecting

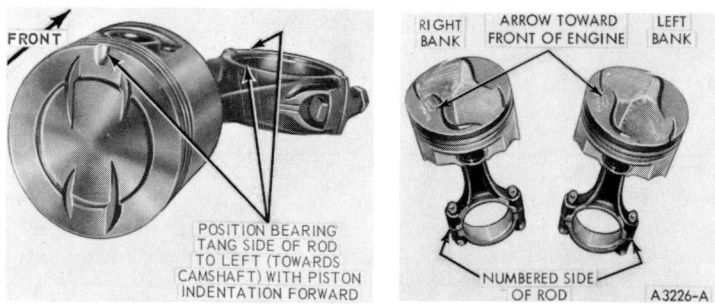

Fig. E-10. Left. Notch on some pistons must be toward front of engine. Right. On others, an arrow used must point toward front.

rod should be assembled with the bearing tang notches in the connecting rod (at the parting line of the cap) and the indentation notch in the piston position as shown in Fig. E-10. On V-8 engines, the pistons and connecting rods should be assembled so that the notch in the piston is toward the front of the engine and the number side of the connecting rod will be placed on the outside of the engine "V." Always be sure to install the pistons in the same cylinders from which they are removed, or to which they were fitted.

Make sure the ring gaps are properly spaced around the circumference of the piston and install the assembly as described in the section dealing with piston rings.

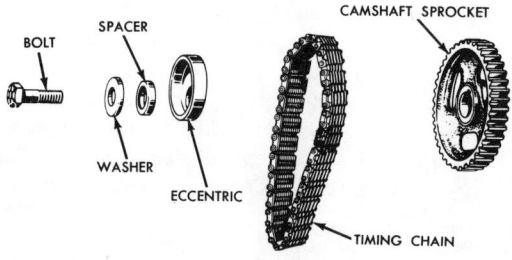

Fig. E-11. Typical timing chain and sprocket.

## REMOVING TIMING CHAIN AND COVER

In order to replace the timing chain, Figs. E-11 and E-13, or to stop a leak at the front end of the crankcase, it is necessary to remove the timing case cover. On the 351C and 400 CID engines however, the front oil seal can be replaced after removing the vibration damper.

The following instructions apply in general to all Ford vehicles. Drain the cooling system and crankcase. Disconnect the radiator lower hose from the water pump, and the heater hose from the water pump. Slide the water pump bypass hose clamp toward the water pump. Loosen the alternator to cylinder head mounting bolt. Remove the alternator bracket bolt at the water pump and cylinder front cover. Remove the bracket. On Thermactor engines, remove the air pump and brackets. On a vehicle with power steering and/or air conditioning, loosen the drive belt tension and remove the belts. Remove the fan, spacer, pulley and drive belt.

Using a puller, Fig. E-12, remove the crankshaft pulley from the crankshaft vibration damper. Remove the damper retaining screw and washer. Using a puller, remove the crankshaft vibration damper.

Disconnect the fuel pump outlet line from the fuel pump and remove the fuel pump retaining bolts and lay the pump to one side with the flexible fuel line still attached.

Remove oil level dipstick. Remove oil pan to cylinder front cover retaining bolts. Remove cylinder front cover and water pump as an assembly.

## Engine Disassembly

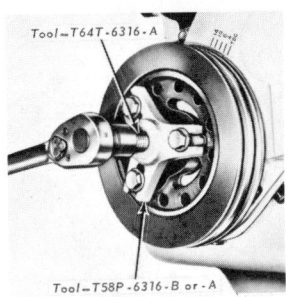

*Fig. E-12. Type of special puller used when removing fan drive pulley from crankshaft.*

## REPLACING THE TIMING CHAIN

If the timing chain is to be replaced, first remove the timing chain front cover as just described and then crank the engine until the timing marks on the sprockets or gears are positioned as shown in Figs. E-13 and E-14.

Remove the crankshaft sprocket cap screw, washers and fuel pump eccentric. Slide both sprockets and timing chain forward and remove them as an assembly. The timing chain is installed by reversing the process, taking care that the timing marks on the sprocket are in correct alignment or position.

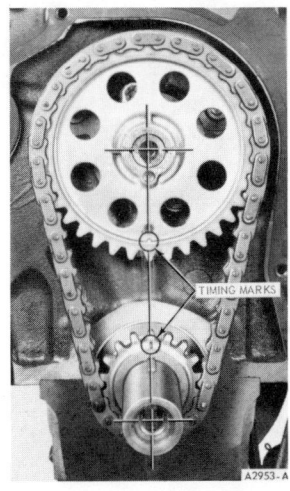

*Fig. E-13. Correct timing mark location on 289, 302, 312, 332, 351, 352, 390, 400, 410, 427, 428, and 429 cu. in. engines.*

## CAMSHAFT REMOVAL

It is seldom necessary to remove the camshaft from any Ford engine unless one or more of the cams have become worn to such an extent it does not raise the valves as much as specified. In order to check the valve lift, a dial indicator is required. On engines with hydraulic valve lifters, it is necessary to first install a solid tappet-type push rod in the push rod core of the camshaft to be checked. The dial indicator should be installed in such a manner as to have the actuating point of the indicator in the push rod socket and in the same plane as the push rod movement. Then

*Fig. E-14. Showing marks on timing gears used to drive camshaft on the 2800 cc V-Six engine.*

turn the crankshaft slowly in the direction of normal rotation until the tappet or lifter is on the base circle of the camshaft lobe. At this point, the push rod will be in its lowest position. Zero the dial indicator and then continue to crank the engine slowly until the push rod is in the fully raised position. Compare the total lift recorded on the indicator with the specifications, or with the lift of other valves of the same engine. On individual engines, intake valve lift should not vary more than 0.005 in., and exhaust valves should not vary more than 0.005 in.

To remove a camshaft, first remove the timing case cover and the

## Engine Disassembly

timing chain and sprocket as previously described. On V-8 type engines remove the intake manifold and oil pan and also the grille, and grille center support from the front of the vehicle. Remove the valve rocker arm covers and release the spring tension on the valve rocker arms by loosening the adjusting screws. On engines with valve rocker arm shafts, loosen the valve rocker arm shaft support bolts in sequence, two turns at a time. Then remove the valve rocker arm assemblies and oil tubes. Remove the push rods in sequence.

Turn the camshaft until the tappets can be lifted with the fingers or with a magnet, Fig. E-15. Then with the tappets raised clear of the camshaft lobes, secure them in the raised position with spring-type clothes pins. The camshaft can then be drawn forward and out of the cylinder block after removing the camshaft thrust plate and spacer. When pulling the camshaft forward, be careful to avoid damaging the camshaft bearings by striking them with the camshaft lobes.

The preceding procedure, while applying particularly to the 302 V-8 engine, applies also in general to the other engines as well. When replacing the camshaft, be careful not to force the camshaft back against the plug which seals the bearing at the rear end. Too much force will tend to loosen this sealing plug, with the result that an oil leak will occur. So proceed carefully because seal replacement is a time consuming task.

Fig. E-15. Using a magnet to remove a valve lifter.

## REMOVING THE ENGINE

When the engine is badly worn, as indicated by excessive oil consumption, severe knocking, or when the water jacket is cracked, many car owners prefer to install a rebuilt engine rather than attempt to overhaul the original unit. Rebuilt engines are available at larger automotive parts jobbers, and also from Ford dealers.

When removing the engine from a chassis, Fig. E-16, a chain hoist is needed. This hoist must be supported by a strong beam over the engine. It must be remembered that the engine will weigh approximately 500 lbs.

## Fix Your Ford

and therefore the beam must be of sufficient strength to support such a weight.

The following instructions, while applying particularly to the 390 and 428 cu. in. V-8 engines, will also apply in general to the other Ford engines.

Drain the cooling system and the crankcase. Remove the hood. Remove the air cleaner and disconnect the battery positive cable.

Disconnect the radiator upper hose at the engine and the radiator lower hose at the water pump. On a vehicle with automatic transmission, disconnect the transmission oil cooler lines from the radiator.

Remove the cooling fan and spacer (or fan drive clutch) and power steering pump drive belt, if so equipped. Remove the radiator and the oil level dipstick.

Disconnect the oil pressure sending unit wire at the sending unit and the flexible fuel line at the fuel tank line.

Disconnect the accelerator cable at the carburetor and remove the accelerator retracting spring. Remove the accelerator cable bracket from the intake manifold. Position the accelerator cable and body ground strap out of the way.

On a vehicle with automatic transmission, disconnect the kickdown rod at the carburetor. Remove the kickdown rod retracting spring. Disconnect the transmission vacuum line at the engine.

On a vehicle with power steering, remove the power steering pump from the mounting bracket. Remove the power steering hose bracket bolt. Wire the power steering pump in a position that will prevent the oil from draining out. Remove the power steering pump bracket, coil bracket and compressor bracket, and compressor assembly if equipped with air conditioning. Remove the ignition coil. Position the compressor (with lines attached) out of the way. On a vehicle with power brakes, disconnect the brake vacuum hose at the pipe and position the hose out of the way.

Disconnect the heater hose at the water pump and intake manifold and remove the heater hose from the automatic choke bracket. Disconnect the coolant temperature sending unit at the sending unit. Remove the wire loom from the clips on the left valve rocker arm cover and position it out of the way.

On a vehicle with air conditioning, remove the compressor from the mounting bracket and position it out of the way, leaving the refrigerant lines attached.

Remove the battery ground cable and alternator ground cable bolt at the engine. Remove the alternator grounding bolt and spacer, and position the alternator out of the way.

Disconnect the fuel inlet line at the pump. Raise the front of the vehicle and remove the starter.

Disconnect the muffler inlet pipe from the exhaust manifold.

Remove the engine support insulator to intermediate support bracket nuts, and loosen the right side support insulator to engine bolts.

On an engine with an automatic transmission, remove the flywheel

## Engine Disassembly

housing cover. Remove the oil cooler lines retaining clip from the engine block. Disconnect the convertor from the flywheel. Secure the converter assembly in the housing. Remove the remaining flywheel housing to engine bolts and remove the transmission fluid filler tube bracket.

On a vehicle with a manual shift transmission, remove the flywheel housing inspection cover and the clutch pedal retracting spring. Disconnect the clutch release bracket at the equalizer rod and remove the bracket from the engine. Remove the remaining flywheel housing to engine bolts.

Lower the vehicle, then support the transmission. Install the engine left lifting bracket on the front of the left cylinder head, and install the engine right lifting bracket at the rear of the right cylinder head. Then attach an engine lifting sling, Figs. E-16 and E-17.

Remove the flywheel or converter housing to engine upper bolts. Raise the engine slightly and carefully pull it from the transmission. Lift the engine out of the engine compartment.

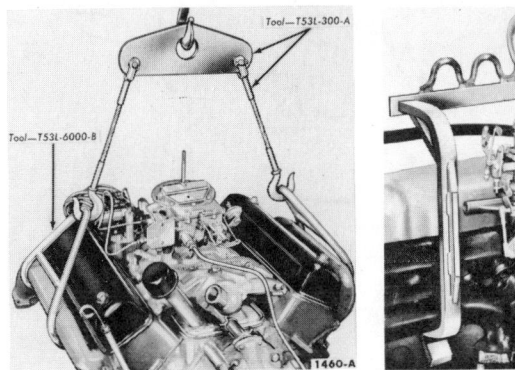

*Fig. E-16. Left. Lifting a V-8 engine from the chassis. Fig. E-17. Right. Method used to lift six cylinder engine.*

## TROUBLE SHOOTING

For engine trouble shooting see the end of the Chapter on Simplified Engine Repairs.

# Fix Your Ford

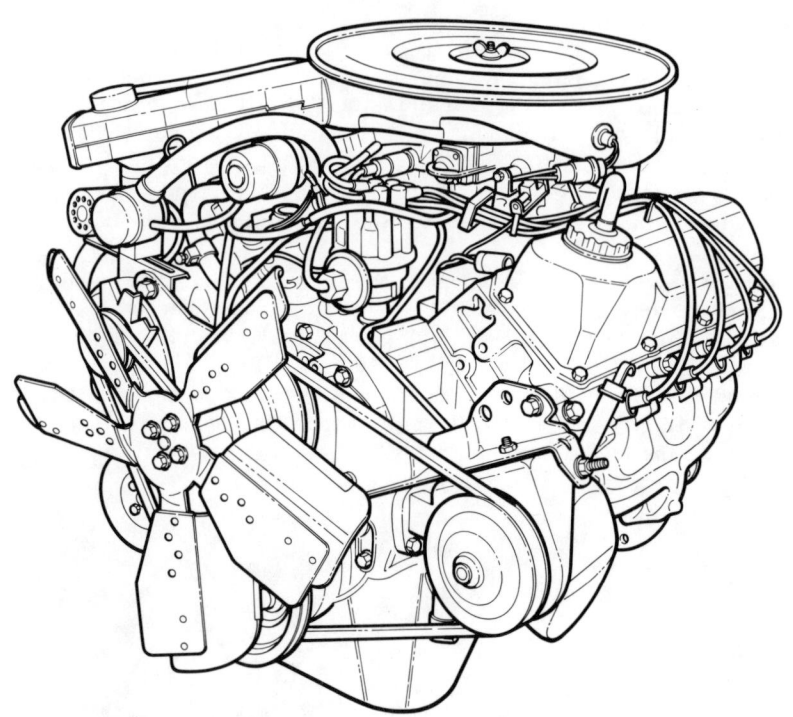

Engine shown is typical of 1976–1978 351W and 400 CID V-8s.

The 1978 Fairmont Wagon has 140 cu. in. (2.3 L) engine as standard equipment with 200 cu. in. (3.3 L) Six or 302 cu. in. (5.0 L) V-8 optional.

# Simplified
# ENGINE REPAIRS

General repair work on Ford engines is not difficult. The detailed and simplified instructions given here are applicable to all Ford engines.

Many car owners and smaller repair shops do not rebuild the complete engine nor recondition the cylinder heads. Rather, they remove the unit and have the work done by a local automotive machine shop.

In order to recondition or replace an engine part, it is, of course, necessary to first disassemble the engine, either partly or completely. The procedure for such disassembly is discussed elsewhere in this book, while this chapter will be devoted exclusively to the servicing and repairing of the different parts after they have been removed from the engine.

## WHEN VALVES SHOULD BE RECONDITIONED

Due to incorrect valve tappet clearance, gummy valve stems, the use of low octane fuel, unequal tightening of the cylinder head bolts, incorrectly adjusted carburetors, etc., valve life will be materially shortened. As a

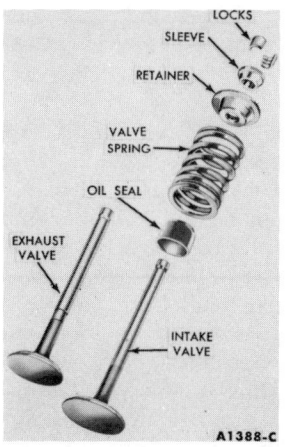

Fig. F-1. *Typical valve assembly.*

## Fix Your Ford

result, the face and seat of the valve, Fig. F-1, become burned and pitted, as shown in Fig. F-2. As a further result, the compression of the combustible gases will not reach its maximum value. In extreme cases, it will be necessary to replace the valve and also the valve seat. In cases not so extreme, the valve and valve seat can be reconditioned to give many more thousands of miles of useful service.

It is necessary to recondition the valves of the Ford engine when compression tests indicate that the valves are leaking. Leaking valves will also be indicated by loss of power and reduced fuel economy.

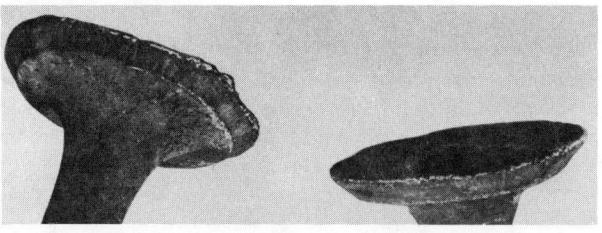

*Fig. F-2. Example of burned valves.*

## HOW TO REMOVE THE VALVES

Before removing the valves, it is first necessary to remove the cylinder head. On engines with the rocker arm and shaft construction, Fig. F-3, such as the 170, 200, 223, 352, 370, 390, 427, 428 cu. in. engines it is necessary to remove the rocker arm and shaft assembly, Fig. F-4. On other engines such as 221, 240, 260, 289, 302, 351, 429 C.I.D. engines with spherical socket type rocker arms, Fig. F-5, the rocker arm stud nut must be removed from each of the rocker arms which will permit the removal of the rocker arm.

In case of the engine with conventional rocker arm and shaft construction, Fig. F-4, remove the rocker arm support bolts, permitting the removal of the shaft and rocker arm as an assembly.

Note: If it should ever be desired to remove the rocker arm shaft while the head is still installed on the engine, loosen the bolts two turns at a time in sequence until all are loose. This procedure must be followed to avoid damage to the valve mechanism.

After the rocker arm and shafts are removed, the valves can be removed from the cylinder heads. To remove the valves from the cylinder head, a C-type valve spring compressor is used, Fig. F-6. While it is possible to compress the springs by pressing down on the valve spring retainers with two screwdrivers, this is a difficult and tedious method.

With the valve spring compressed, the valve locks and keeper are removed as shown in Fig. F-7.

## Engine Repairs

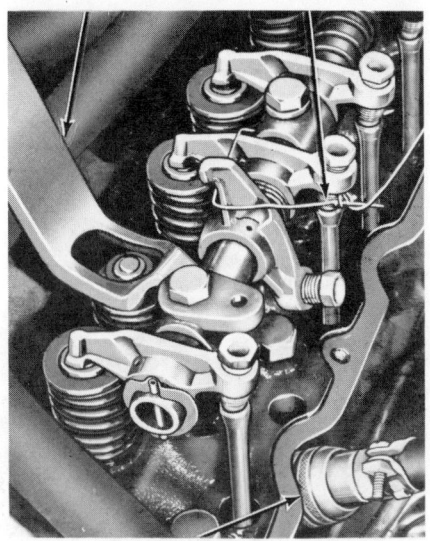

*Fig. F-3. Typical rocker arm and shaft construction.*

Any valve which has a bent stem, or requires refacing so that the edge of the face is less than 1/32 in. thick, should be replaced, Fig. F-8. In addition, no more than .010 in. should be removed from the end of the valve stem, in case it is rough.

After removing the valve from the cylinder head it must be thoroughly cleaned. All carbon and gummy varnish-like material must be removed from the valve and the stem, so that it can be inspected to determine if it is fit for further use.

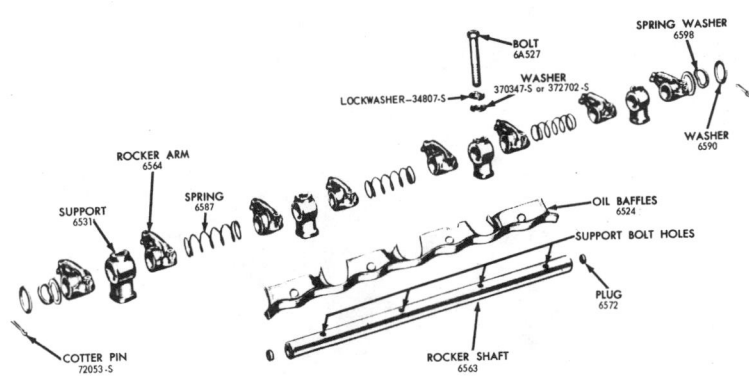

*Fig. F-4. Exploded view of typical rocker arm and shaft assembly.*

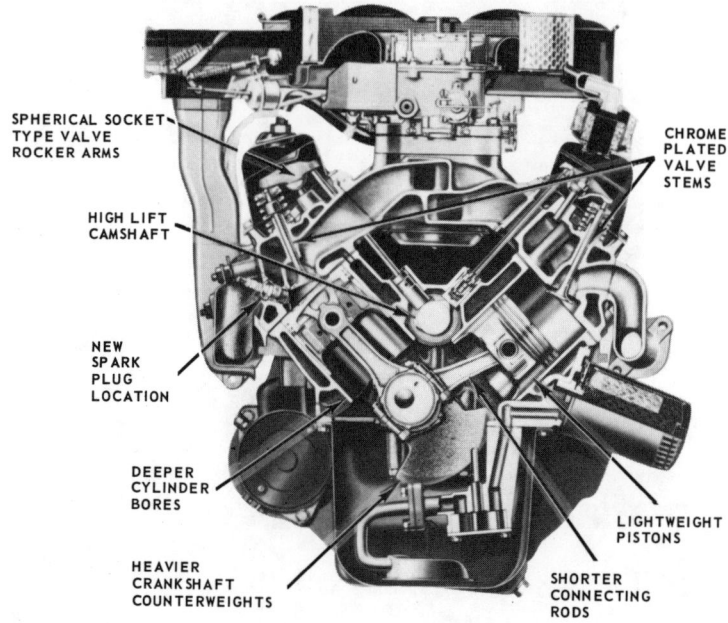

*Fig. F-5. Note spherical socket type of valve rocker arms.*

The easiest way to clean valves is to use one of the special cleaning compounds that is available. Or, if preferred, the valves can be held against a power driven rotary wire brush. If that is not available, the

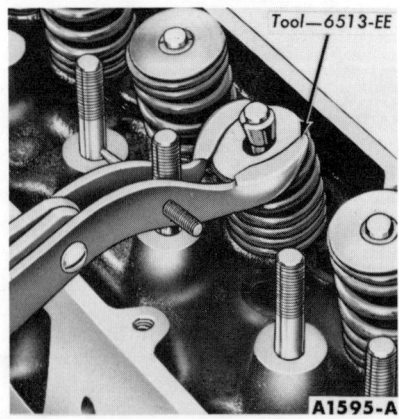

*Fig. F-6. "C" type valve spring compressor being used to compress valve spring.*

## Engine Repairs

valve can be scraped with the blade of a penknife and then finally cleaned with some extremely fine emery paper. Care must be exercised so that no metal is actually removed from the valve stem.

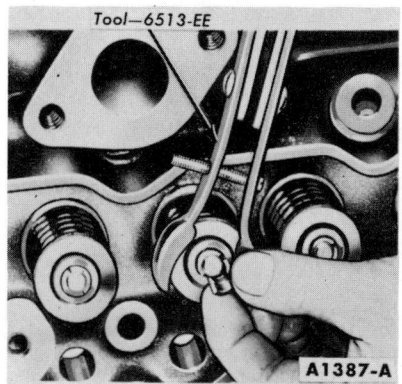

*Fig. F-7. Removing valve locks after having compressed valve spring.*

After cleaning the valves, the valve stems should be checked to see if they are bent or worn. Valve stems are sometimes bent if considerable force is required to remove them from the cylinder head. To check for a bent valve stem, place the valve stem on the face of a surface plate or other true surface with the valve head over the edge. Then by rolling the valve along the surface of the plate, a bent stem which will not roll freely, will be quickly found.

Micrometers are used to measure valve stem wear. Measure the diameter of the valve stem of a new valve, or the unworn portion of a used valve. This is then compared with the measured diameter of the worn portion of the used valve. The wear on the valve stem should not exceed .002 in.

Greater wear will result in poor seating of the valve, plus the fact that air and oil will be drawn past the valve stems resulting in a weak fuel mixture and stepped up oil consumption.

If the valve stem is not bent, nor worn more than .002 in., the valve may be refaced as shown in Fig. F-9. This is done on a valve refacing machine. Most automotive machine shops will perform this operation at small cost.

After the valve is refaced, the valve head should be examined to make sure it is not too thin. If the edge of the valve head is less than 1/32 in., Fig. F-8, the valve should be discarded, as a valve in that condition will quickly warp and burn.

In addition to refacing the valve, the valve seat must also be reconditioned. Special valve seat reconditioning equipment is available for such

# Fix Your Ford

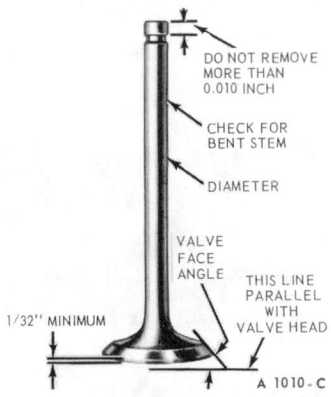

Fig. F-8. Critical valve dimensions.

work. By using 30 deg., 45 deg., and 60 deg. seat cutters, the proper seat width can be obtained, and at the same time the seat can be raised or lowered as desired, Fig. F-10.

## RECONDITIONING VALVES WITHOUT SPECIAL EQUIPMENT

It is possible to recondition valves and valve seats without the use of special equipment, but the final job is not as satisfactory as is the case when special equipment is used. However, this procedure is often resorted to when an auto machine shop is not immediately available, or when

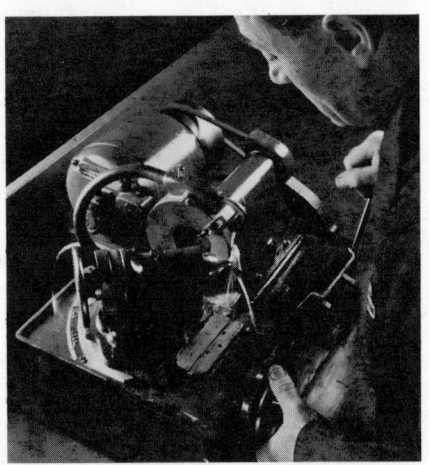

Fig. F-9. Refacing valve on valve refacer.

## Engine Repairs

repair costs must be kept to a minimum.

The procedure is to use fine carborundum powder, or special valve grinding compound and grind or lap the valves to the seat. A very light coating of the valve grinding compound is placed on the face of the valve, and the valve is then placed in position in the cylinder head. Using a valve lapping tool on the valve head, the valve is rotated back and forth on its seat. The valve grinding compound grinds away the metal of both the seat and the valve until they are smooth, and without any pits or other defects.

To keep the valve grinding compound evenly distributed, the valve should be raised occasionally from its seat and then given half a turn before the lapping process is resumed. Only light pressure should be placed on the valve during the grinding process.

The lapping is continued until all of the pit marks are ground away from both the valve and its seat. If the valves are badly pitted, it will be found that a groove will be ground in the face of the valve during the lapping process. Such a condition is not desirable, as the valve will then quickly pit again, as the groove affords a place for carbon and other combustion products to lodge. That is why refacing of valve and seat is the preferred method.

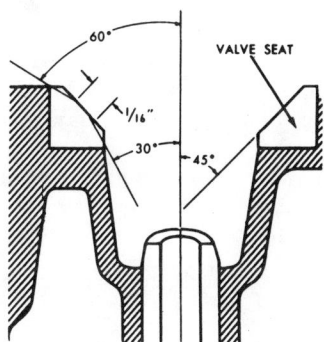

*Fig. F-10. Cutters of 30 deg. and 60 deg. are used to raise or lower the valve seat which should be 1/16 in. wide.*

When the lapping process is completed, great care must be exercised to remove all traces of the grinding compound. Should any of the compound remain on the intake valve seat, it will be drawn into the engine, and cause rapid wear of all parts. On the exhaust valve it will cause the stem to be worn, and in turn the valve will seat poorly. This results in compression loss, followed by burning of the valve seat and face.

The width of the intake valve seat should range from .060 in. to .080 in., while the limits for the exhaust valve should range from .070 in. to .090 in. This is important because if the seats are too narrow, the valves will operate at too high a temperature and will soon become burned. If the valve seat is too wide, there is a tendency for carbon to lodge on the seat, and the valve will soon become pitted and not hold compression.

While the angle of the intake and exhaust valve seats of virtually all Ford built engines is 45 deg., there are some engines with intake seats of 30 deg. Care must therefore be taken when reconditioning the valves to first check the angle of the valve seats and faces so they can be reconditioned to the correct angle. So that valves may seat quickly, the face of the valve is usually finished to an angle of one degree less than the seat. For example: a 45 deg. valve seat would have a valve with a 44 deg. face.

The finished valve seat should contact the approximate center of the valve face. This can be checked by placing a slight amount of Prussian blue on the valve seat, then set the valve in position and rotate the valve with light pressure. The blue will be transferred to the face of the valve and show clearly whether it is centered or not.

Another point to check on engine valves is the condition of the valve stem. If the end of the valve stem is rough, it will make it difficult to accurately adjust the valve tappet clearance. When necessary, the end of the valve stem can be ground on the same machine that refaces the valve face. However, not more than .010 in. should be removed from the end of the valve stem.

As pointed out previously, it is possible to recondition valves by hand grinding, but a much better job can be done by using specialized equipment. Consequently, many car owners and operators of small garages, not having their own equipment, take advantage of the facilities of an automotive machine shop. This is particularly true in the case of the overhead valve type engine.

In such cases, all that is necessary is to remove the cylinder heads from the engine and take them to the machine shop where the heads are completely disassembled, cleaned and reconditioned.

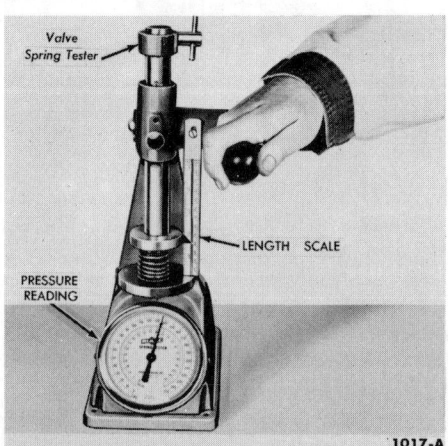

*Fig. F-11. One method of checking pressure of a valve spring.*

## Engine Repairs

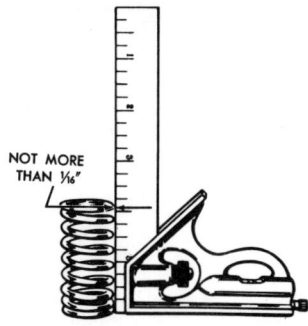

*Fig. F-12. Checking valve spring for length and flatness of end.*

## QUICK CHECKS ON SPRINGS

It is also important to check the condition of the valve springs, for if any of them are weak, full power will not be developed, particularly at higher engine speeds. Special testers are available for testing the compression strength of valve springs, Fig. F-11. However, a fairly accurate check can be made by comparing the length of a used spring with that of a new spring, as shown in Fig. F-12. The end of the valve spring must also be flat, and neither flatness nor length should vary more than 1/16 in.

After valves and seats have been reconditioned, the valve springs will not exert as much pressure as they did originally because the assembled height of the spring will be greater. In other words, it will not be compressed as much as it was originally.

It is necessary, therefore, to measure the length of the valve spring after it is reassembled in the engine. If it exceeds a certain specified amount, it is necessary to install spacers between the cylinder heads and

*Fig. F-13. Correct valve spring height must be maintained if maximum power is to be obtained.*

the valve spring, in order to restore compression. Fig. F-13 shows a method of measuring the assembled height of the valve spring. The specified valve spring height of various engines is shown below.

### VALVE SPRING ASSEMBLED HEIGHT

| Engine Displacement | Valve Spring Assembled Height |
|---|---|
| 2000 cc Four | 1 25/64 - 1 27/64 in. |
| 2300 cc Four | 1 35/64 - 1 37/64 in. |
| 2800 cc V-6 | 1 35/64 - 1 39/64 in. |
| 144, 170, 200 cu. in. | 1 9/16 - 1 39/64 in. |
| 200 cu. in. 1971-1978 | 1 9/16 - 1 19/32 in. |
| 240 cu. in. 1967-1969 | 1 35/64 - 1 39/64 in. |
| 250 cu. in. | 1 9/16 - 1 39/64 in. |
| 260, 289, 292 cu. in. | 1 3/4 - 1 25/32 in. |
| 302 cu. in. 2V | 1 5/8 - 1 11/16 in. |
| 302 cu. in. 1970 Boss-1971 HO | 1 13/16 - 1 27/32 in. |
| 302 cu. in 1972-1973 | 1 21/32 - 1 23/32 in. |
| 302 cu. in. 2V Intake 1975-1978 | 1 43/64 - 1 45/64 in. |
| 302 cu. in. 2V Exhaust 1975-1978 | 1 19/32 - 1 34/64 in. |
| 332 cu. in. | 1 13/16 - 1 27/32 in. |
| 351 cu. in. | 1 25/32 - 1 13/16 in. |
| 351C cu. in. 1970-1974 | 1 13/16 - 1 27/32 in. |
| 351M cu. in. 1975-1978 | 1 3/4 - 1 13/16 in. |
| 351W cu. in. 1970-1978 | 1 3/4 - 1 13/16 in. |
| 352 cu. in. | 1 13/16 - 1 27/32 in. |
| 390 cu. in. ml | 1 5/16 - 1 21/64 in. |
| 390 cu. in. 1970-1971 | 1 13/16 - 1 27/32 in. |
| 400 cu. in. 1971-1978 | 1 13/16 - 1 27/32 in. |
| 410 cu. in. | 1 13/16 - 1 27/32 in. |
| 427 cu. in. | 1 51/64 - 1 53/64 in. |
| 428 cu. in. | 1 13/16 - 1 27/32 in. |
| 429 cu. in. 1970-1973 | 1 51/64 - 1 53/64 in. |
| 460 cu. in. 1975-1978 | 1 51/64 - 1 53/64 in. |

ml - mechanical lifters.

## WHAT TO DO ABOUT VALVE GUIDES

Ford engines of the overhead valve type are not provided with removable valve guides. Instead, holes in the cylinder head are accurately reamed directly in the cylinder head. This has the advantage of cooler operating valves. However when the valve guide holes in the cylinder head become worn more than .0045 in., it is necessary to recondition the holes by reaming, installing new valves with oversize valve stems. As this is a precision operation, it is generally necessary to have such work done by an automotive machine shop.

Another method of reconditioning the valve guides is by knurling. This requires special equipment which produces a raised pattern on the valve guide. This permits the use of valves with standard size stems and improved lubrication is claimed for the process.

## Engine Repairs

Fig. F-14 shows a guide being reamed. Valves with oversize stems are available in .003 in., .015 in., and .030 in. oversize. The stem to guide clearance should be .0010 to .0024 in.

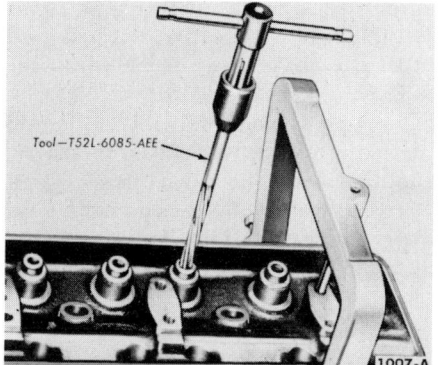

*Fig. F-14. Reaming valve stem guide before installing new valves with oversize stems.*

## CLEANING CYLINDER HEAD

Before assembling the valves to the cylinder head, the head should be thoroughly cleaned. Carbon and combustion deposits should be removed from the combustion chambers. This can be done by scraping with a putty knife, or by means of an electric drill equipped with a wire brush. Be sure all carbon accumulations are removed, as any particles remaining may result in preignition. All grease should be removed from the outside of the cylinder head, and the water jacket flushed thoroughly to remove all traces of rust accumulation.

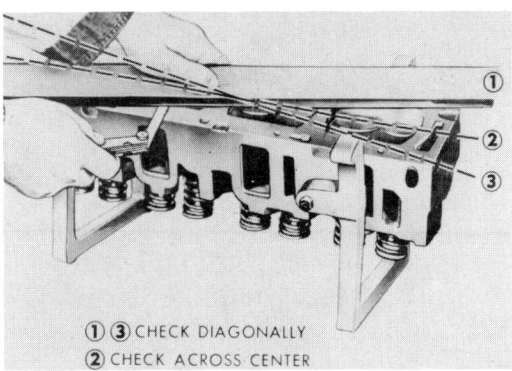

*Fig. F-15. Gasket surface of cylinder heads must be checked for flatness both diagonally and across the center.*

# Fix Your Ford

It is also important to check the surface of the cylinder head that mates with the cylinder block. This can be done with a straightedge and a feeler or thickness gauge as shown in Fig. F-15. The straightedge should be held diagonally and then across the center while checking the clearance between the straightedge and the cylinder head at various points. Warpage should not exceed .003 in. in any six inches, or .006 in. overall. In addition, the cylinder head should be carefully examined for any cracks, particularly around the valve seats, and around the water jacket. A strong magnifying glass is helpful in locating such leaks, and automotive machine shops have special equipment designed to locate the finest cracks. While the cylinder head is off, it is also an excellent time to check and make sure the core plugs are tight and have not rusted. If there is any indication of rust around any of the core plugs, they should be replaced, as explained in Chapter on Cooling Systems.

## HOW TO INSTALL PISTON RINGS

After the connecting rods, Fig. F-16, are removed from the engine, they should be thoroughly cleaned in a solvent designed for cleaning engine parts. If such special solvent is not available, kerosene can be used, but that is not as effective as commercial cleaning solvents.

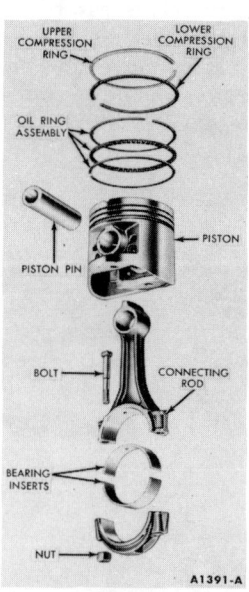

*Fig. F-16. Typical piston, connecting rod, bearing inserts, piston pin and ring assembly. Some types use snap rings at ends of piston pins.*

## Engine Repairs

After the connecting rod and piston assemblies have been cleaned, the rings can be removed as they will not be used again. The usual practice is to grasp the end of a ring with a pair of pliers and pull out. In the case of cast iron rings, this will break the rings so that both parts are easily removed from the groove. Steel rings are removed in the same manner but instead of breaking, the ring can be easily worked out of the groove. Once one end is free, the rest will easily spiral out of the groove. Always be sure to remove the steel expander ring from the bottom of each groove where such rings have been used. Then with the rings removed from each piston, the grooves should be cleaned. The preferred method of cleaning is to use one of the special ring groove cleaning tools, such as is illustrated in Fig. F-17. Such tools quickly cut the carbon from the groove without danger of scratching or otherwise damaging the sides of the ring grooves.

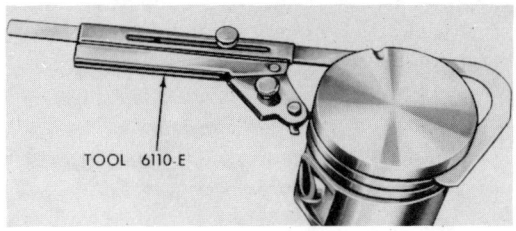

*Fig. F-17. Using special tool to clean piston ring grooves. If tool is not available, use a broken cast iron ring.*

If such a tool is not available, a substitute method is to use a broken segment of a cast iron piston ring. This is used as a scraper. However, this method is long and tedious and there is always the possibility of marring the surface of the sides of the ring grooves. This would result in loss of compression, and also tends to increase oil consumption.

It should be pointed out that if new piston pins are to be fitted, that most shops will not bother to clean the piston and rod assemblies. Instead, they send them to an automotive machine shop to clean the assemblies and install the new pins and rings. Or, if desired, the ring installation can be left to the mechanic doing the actual overhaul job. In general, whenever new rings are found to be necessary, it is advisable to install new piston pins at the same time. The reason being that the pins generally wear out at about the same time as the rings.

Before installing new rings on the pistons, or fitting new piston rings, the pistons should be carefully checked to make sure they are in good condition and are still serviceable. In addition, the clearance between piston and cylinder wall should be checked.

When examining the pistons, make sure the ring grooves are in good condition, that the sides of the grooves are smooth, and without any grooves worn by the rings. The sides of the grooves must also be at right angles with the center line of the piston. A good method of checking grooves is to roll a new piston ring around the groove. It should roll freely, without binding and without any side play. If the clearance between the side of the ring and the piston groove exceeds .005 in., Fig. F-18, the piston should be discarded. However, if desired, the pistons can be placed in a lathe, and the grooves trued. A spacing ring is then inserted to compensate for the amount of metal removed from the side of the groove. When checking the piston, also make sure there are no burned areas around the ring lands. In addition make sure that there are no cracks anywhere. If the piston is of the steel strut type, make sure the strut has not loosened.

Spongy, eroded areas near the edge of the top of the piston are usually caused by detonation, or preignition. A shiny surface on the thrust surface of the piston, offset from the center line between the piston pin holes, can be caused by a bent connecting rod. Replace pistons that show signs of excessive wear, wavy ring lands, fractures and/or damage from detonation or preignition.

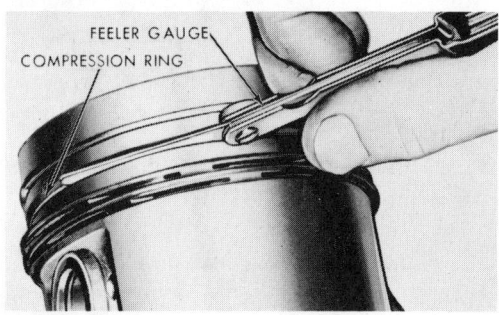

Fig. F-18. Using thickness gauge to check side clearance of piston ring.

## FITTING PISTON RINGS

Replacement type piston rings are designed to compensate for a certain amount of wear in the cylinders. The claims made by some manufacturers are quite extreme, but in general replacement type rings should not be installed in cylinders that have more than .010 in. taper or .005 in. out-of-round. For details on measuring cylinder clearance see piston clearance tables on page 126.

When selecting a piston ring set for an engine, it is necessary to select the proper size. To do this, position the ring in the cylinder bore in which it is going to be used. Push the ring down into the bore area where normal ring wear is encountered. Use the head of a piston to position the ring in the bore so the ring is square with the cylinder wall.

## Engine Repairs

Measure the gap between ends of ring with a feeler gauge, as shown in Fig. F-19. The size of this gap is dependent on make of the piston ring, and also on the diameter of the cylinder bore. In general, gap should be .003 in. for each inch of diameter. In other words, the correct ring gap for a 3 in. bore cylinder should be 3 times .003 in. or .009 in.

Current specifications for the piston ring gap on Ford engines follows:

| Engine | Compression Ring | Oil Ring |
|---|---|---|
| 2000 cc | .0150 - .0229 in. | .0160 - .055 in. |
| 2300 cc | .0100 - .020 in. | .0150 - .055 in. |
| 2800 cc | .0150 - .0229 in. | .0150 - .055 in. |
| 144 cu. in. | .010 - .031 in. | .015 - .055 in. |
| 170 cu. in. | .010 - .020 in. | .015 - .055 in. |
| 200 cu. in. | .008 - .016 in. | .015 - .055 in. |
| 221 cu. in. | .010 - .020 in. | .015 - .055 in. |
| 223 cu. in. | .010 - .031 in. | .015 - .066 in. |
| 239 cu. in. | .010 - .027 in. | .015 - .066 in. |
| 240 cu. in. | .010 - .020 in. | .015 - .055 in. |
| 250 cu. in. | .008 - .016 in. | .015 - .055 in. |
| 260 cu. in. | .010 - .032 in. | .015 - .067 in. |
| 272 cu. in. | .010 - .027 in. | .015 - .066 in. |
| 289 cu. in. | .010 - .020 in. | .015 - .069 in. |
| 292 cu. in. | .010 - .027 in. | .015 - .062 in. |
| 302 cu. in. | .010 - .020 in. | .015 - .069 in. |
| 312 cu. in. | .010 - .027 in. | .015 - .062 in. |
| 332 cu. in. | .013 - .030 in. | .015 - .062 in. |
| 351 cu. in. | .010 - .020 in. | .015 - .055 in. |
| 352 cu. in. | .010 - .020 in. | .015 - .066 in. |
| 390 cu. in. | .010 - .031 in. | .015 - .066 in. |
| 400 cu. in. | .010 - .020 in. | .015 - .055 in. |
| 410 cu. in. | .010 - .031 in. | .015 - .066 in. |
| 427 cu. in. | .010 - .031 in. | .015 - .060 in. |
| 428 cu. in. | .010 - .020 in. | .010 - .035 in. |
| 429 cu. in. | .010 - .020 in. | .010 - .035 in. |
| 460 cu. in. | .010 - .020 in. | .015 - .055 in. |

Those specifications apply to rings supplied by Ford. If rings of other manufacture are used, their specifications should be followed.

The side clearance of the piston rings in the grooves should not be less than .002 in. for the smaller engines, or more than .004 in. for the larger engines. The side clearance for oil rings should be a snug fit for all engines.

Piston rings are easily installed on the pistons. Some mechanics use special ring spreader tools which, of course, make the installation quite simple and without any danger of breaking the ring. Other mechanics will not use the special tools but will spread the rings by hand. On the cast iron type rings, the procedure is to place a thumb on each end of the ring and spread the end of the rings apart. This will enlarge the diameter sufficiently so that it can be slid down over the piston to its proper groove.

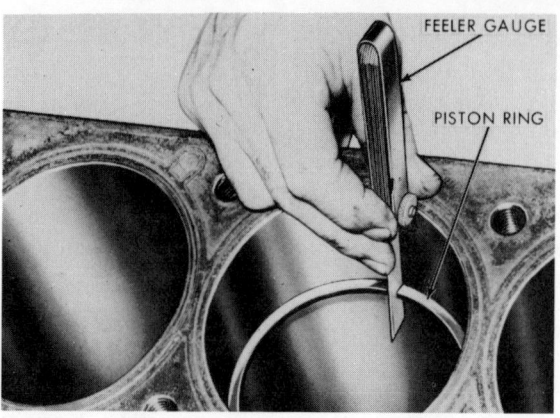

*Fig. F-19. Measuring end gap clearance of piston ring. Note location of ring in cylinder where normal wear occurs.*

Be careful to follow the manufacturer's instructions so each ring is placed in the correct groove. With some make of rings it is necessary that one side of the ring be toward the top of the piston. If rings are not placed in proper groove with right side up, excessive oil consumption will result. Ring gaps should be staggered, not in alignment.

Instructions for installing the piston with its connecting rod in the cylinder bores are given in the paragraph entitled "Installing Connecting Rod Assemblies."

## CHECKING PISTON CLEARANCE

There are several ways to check piston clearance. An easy way is to use a half-inch wide strip of feeler gauge approximately the same length as the cylinder. Place this strip on one side of the cylinder wall (not front or rear, but on one side), then insert the piston from the top of the cylinder and slide it down by pressing on the connecting rod. The piston should not

*Fig. F-20. Measuring piston skirt clearance with thickness gauge and spring scale.*

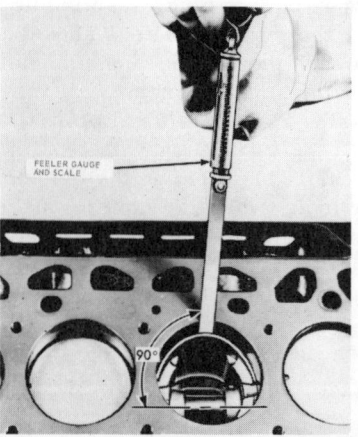

## PISTON CLEARANCE TABLES

Gauge .0035 thick
and .500 in. wide

| Pull | Clearance | Engine Displacement | Piston Clearance |
|---|---|---|---|
| ... | .... | 2000 cc | .001 - .002 in. |
| ... | .... | 2300 cc | .0013 - .0021 in. |
| ... | .... | <u>2800 cc</u> | .001 - .002 in. |
| 12 lb. | .0014 in. | 144 cu. in. | .0018 - .0036 in. |
| 10 lb. | .0018 in. | 170 cu. in. | .0018 - .0036 in. |
| 8 lb. | .0023 in. | 200 cu. in. | .0018 - .0036 in. |
| ... | .... | 200 cu. in. (74) | .0013 - .0021 in. |
| 7 lb. | .0025 in. | 223 cu. in. | .0008 - .0060 in. |
| ... | .... | 240 cu. in. | .0014 - .0022 in. |
| ... | .... | 250 cu. in. | .0014 - .0020 in. |
| 6 lb. | .0027 in. | 260 cu. in. | .0021 - .0039 in. |
| 5 lb. | .0030 in. | 289 cu. in. | .0020 - .0038 in. |
| ... | .... | 302 cu. in. | .0018 - .0026 in. |
| 3 lb. | .0033 in. | 332 cu. in. | .0015 - .0021 in. |
| ... | .... | 351 cu. in. | .0018 - .0026 in. |
| ... | .... | 351 W | .0018 - .0026 in. |
| ... | .... | 351 C and M | .0014 - .0022 in. |
| 2 lb. | .0036 in. | 352 cu. in. | .0015 - .0023 in. |
| 1 lb. | .0038 in. | 390 cu. in. | .0015 - .0023 in. |
| ... | .... | 400 cu. in. | .0014 - .0022 in. |
| ... | .... | 410 cu. in. | .0015 - .0023 in. |
| ... | .... | 427 cu. in. | .0042 - .0066 in. |
| ... | .... | 428 cu. in. | .0015 - .0023 in. |
| ... | .... | 429 cu. in. | .0014 - .0022 in. |
| ... | .... | 460 cu. in. | .0034 - .0042 in. |

have the rings installed but should be inserted upside down from the top of the cylinder. Measure the pull required to pull the thickness gauge from between the cylinder wall and the piston, Fig. F-20. The pull required to remove the gauge varies with the clearance.

To measure the amount of wear, use a dial gauge and measure across the piston as shown in Fig. F-21. To measure the amount of taper in the cylinder, first place the dial gauge close to the top of the cylinder so that it measures the diameter across the engine as shown as C and D in Fig. F-22. Then slide the dial gauge down to the bottom of the cylinder bore and note the difference between that reading and the reading made at the top of the bore.

To measure the amount of out-of-round of the cylinder, the dial gauge is first set to note the diameter across the cylinder, and is then rotated to measure the diameter parallel to the engine axis. The difference between those two readings is the amount of out-of-round.

Another method of determining piston clearance is to use a micrometer, Fig. F-21, and measure the diameter of the piston across the thrust

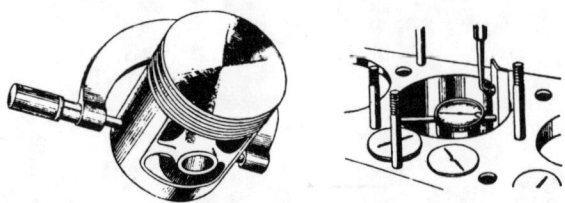

*Fig. F-21. Left. Measuring piston diameter with micrometer. Right. Measuring cylinder taper with dial gauge.*

faces, that is, at right angles to the piston pin. Also, an internal micrometer or dial gauge may be used to measure the diameter of the cylinder bore. This diameter should be measured at a point approximately 2 in. from the top of the cylinder, and across the cylinders, Fig. F-22. The difference between the diameter of the piston and the diameter of the cylinder is the piston clearance.

## EXPANDING PISTONS

Usually when an engine requires new piston rings, it is also necessary to expand the pistons so the clearance between the piston and the cylinder wall is not excessive. In the past various methods have been devised to expand the pistons. However, most of these methods have been virtually discarded in favor of one of the peening methods. This is done by using special equipment which will be found in many automotive machine shops.

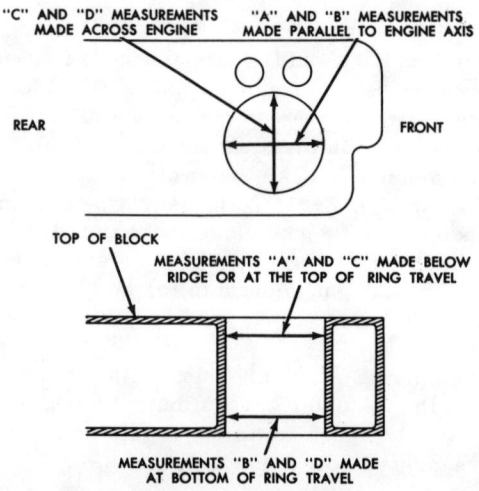

*Fig. F-22. Method of making measurements to determine amount of cylinder wear.*

## Engine Repairs

### CHECKING PISTON PINS

It is often difficult to determine whether a piston pin requires replacement. In general, a piston pin knock will sound very much like a loose valve tappet. In many cases it is worse when the engine is cold than after it has reached operating temperature.

When a car has traveled a distance sufficient to require replacement of piston rings and bearings, it would be poor economy not to replace the piston pins also. Furthermore, when new piston rings have been installed, and particularly when pistons have been expanded, piston pins with only a slight amount of excess clearance will knock. This knock will in some cases disappear after the piston and rings have been run in.

When examining the condition of piston pins, any appreciable looseness or wear is sufficient cause for rejection. An inexperienced mechanic will sometimes confuse side play of the pins in the piston boss with pin wear.

### BE SURE TO CHECK ROD ALIGNMENT

Along with the job of fitting the piston pin, is the job of checking the connecting rod for alignment. Obviously if the rod is bent or twisted, the piston will not move in a straight line at right angles to the center line of the crankshaft. Equipment for aligning connecting rods forms part of every well equipped shop.

If the equipment is not available, an approximation of the trueness of a connecting rod can be obtained by viewing the movement of the upper end of the connecting rod as the engine is cranked. To do this, the oil pan is removed and the rod and piston assemblies are in position on the crankshaft. While the engine is cranked by the starter, the mechanic underneath the engine views the movement of the upper end of the connecting rod. This should remain centrally located on the piston pin, with equal clearance on each side of the piston pin bosses, and the end of the connecting rod. If the upper end of the connecting rod moves back and forth between the piston bosses, or if it remains pressed firmly against one of the bosses, it indicates that the rod is bent.

### TIPS ON REPLACING ENGINE BEARINGS

After the connecting rod has been removed from the engine, it is important to check the rod bearings to determine whether they can be used again. It is often difficult to determine the condition of a bearing and many bearings are discarded when actually they still retain many miles of useful life. First of all, the color of the bearing surface is no gauge of the condition of the bearing.

In many cases the bearing surface will be stained a dark gray or black. Such bearings are still serviceable. However, if any of the bearing metal has dropped from the backing, the bearing should be discarded. Also if the

## Fix Your Ford

*Fig. F-23. Illustrating a badly scored crankshaft journal.*

bearing surface is deeply grooved, scratched or pitted, Fig. F-23, replacement is indicated. If the back of the bearing which contacts the connecting rod or cap shows areas that are black, it indicates that there was dirt between the shell and the rod, and the bearing should be replaced. If there are groove marks on the back of the bearing shell, the shell has been slipping in the rod, and such bearing should also be replaced. Several types of conditions of bearings which have failed are illustrated in Fig. F-24.

One of the best methods of determining the condition of a bearing is to make an oil leak test. This test is described later in this chapter.

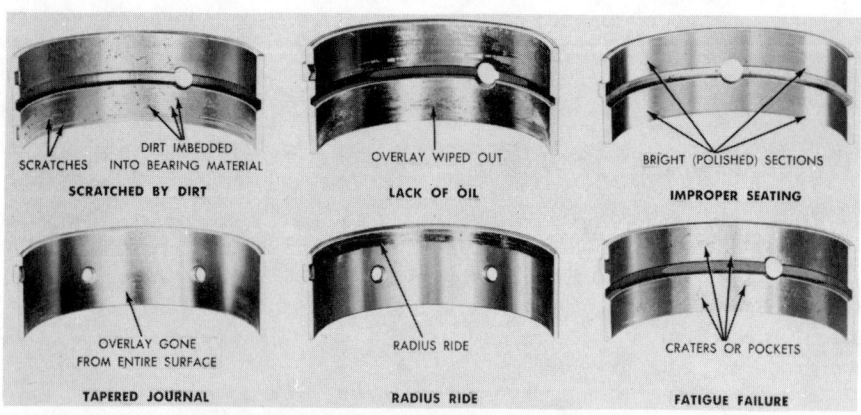

*Fig. F-24. Showing different types of wear on engine bearings.*

## Engine Repairs

### CHECKING THE CRANKSHAFT

Before replacing any connecting rod bearing, the connecting rod bearing journals should be carefully measured for wear and roughness. Ordinary 3 in. outside micrometers are used for measuring the connecting rod bearing journals. The throws or journals should be measured at several points along their length to check for any taper, and also measured at two points at right angles to each other to see if there is any out-of-round.

Generally accepted limits for taper and out-of-round are .001 in. and .0015 in. respectively. If the wear exceeds these values the crankshaft should be reground. If there is any roughness, as shown in Fig. F-23, the journal should, of course be reground. When journals are tapered, out-of-round or scored, it will be impossible to fit a bearing correctly, with the result that the bearing will knock, lose an excessive amount of oil, and will soon fail completely.

Equipment is available for turning the connecting rod bearing journals without removing the crankshaft from the engine.

### RODS MUST FIT THE BEARINGS

When overhauling an old engine, it is often found that a previous mechanic has filed down the bearing caps in an effort to make a worn out bearing last a little longer. The result of this is that the end of the connecting rod is no longer round, and it will be impossible to install a new bearing shell properly. When such a condition is found, new connecting rods should be obtained, or in some cases it will be possible to remachine the old connecting rod so that the big end of the connecting rod is round and can again receive a bearing shell.

It is important that the bearing shell be a snug fit in the connecting rod. To insure such a fit in the conventional connecting rod, such as has been used in Ford engines since 1949, bearing manufacturers make the bearing half slightly higher than an exact half. As a result the bearing half will extend slightly beyond the edge of the bearing cap. This is known as bearing crush and is illustrated in Fig. F-25.

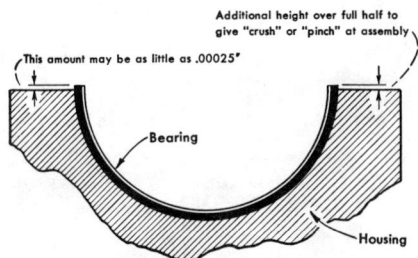

*Fig. F-25. Bearing shells should protrude approximately .00025 in. above bearing cap or housing.*

*Typical 351C engine.*

*Details of accessory drives on 2800 cc V-Six engine.*

# Engine Repairs

## HOW TO FIT THE ROD BEARINGS

Conventional type bearings are keyed to the rod and clearance is often checked by the feel or drag as the rod is swung back and forth on the connecting rod journal.

Some mechanics use Plastigage for checking the fit of these bearings. Plastigage consists essentially of slender rods of plastic. A short length of the Plastigage is placed between the bearing journal and bearing, Fig. F-26, and the connecting rod caps are tightened to approximately 45 ft. lb. tension. The connecting rod is then removed and the width of the crushed Plastigage is compared with a gauge provided by the manufacturer. The gauge reading gives the clearance of the bearings directly in thousandths of an inch.

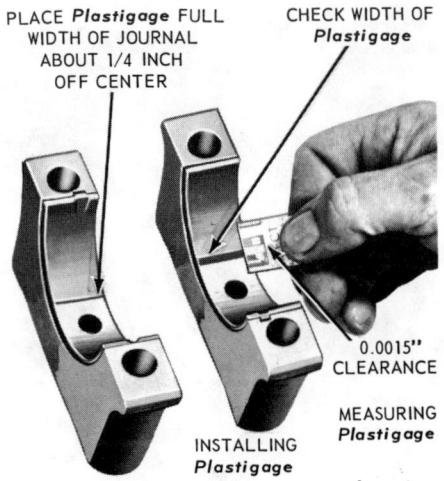

Fig. F-26. Using Plastigage to measure bearing clearance.

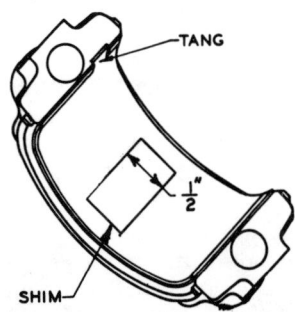

Fig. F-27. Piece of .002 in. shim stock may be used to adjust bearing clearance.

# Fix Your Ford

Another method of fitting the connecting rod bearings is to place a piece of .002 in. metal feeler stock that is 1/2 in. wide and 1 in. long between the bearing and the crank pin, as shown in Fig. F-27.

Bolt the rod on the crank pin, but with the piston end down, instead of in the conventional manner. Then with the rod bolts tight, the piston end of the rod is swung back and forth presenting some resistance. If no resistance is felt, the clearance is excessive and obviously, if the rod cannot be swung back and forth on the crank pin, the clearance is too little. The correct clearance is obtained when the piston is swung to an approximate horizontal position and then will gradually sink to a vertical position.

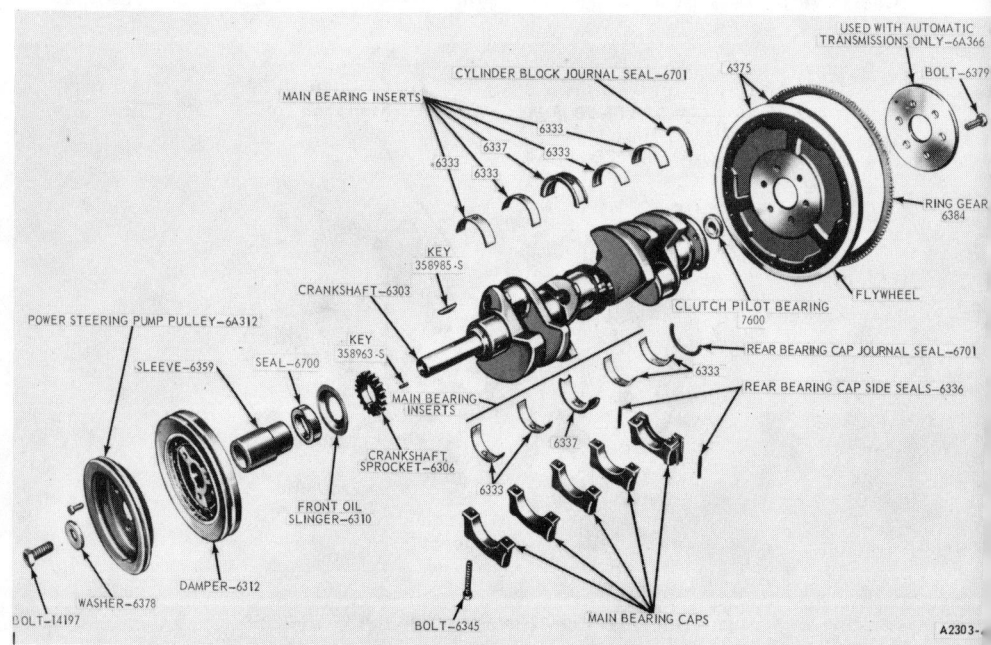

*Fig. F-28. Typical crankshaft of 390 and 428 cu. in. V-8 engines. Note type of bearing seals.*

## USE TORQUE WRENCH ON ROD NUTS

After all the rod bearings have been carefully adjusted, it is essential that the connecting rod bolt nuts be correctly tightened to the specified torque. The specifications are for clean, undamaged and lightly oiled threads. Dry, dirty or damaged threads produce increased friction which prevents accurate measurement of tightness with the torque wrench.

## Engine Repairs

## ENGINE TORQUE TABLES

Other torque specifications are given on page 393

| Engine Displacement Cu. In. | Connecting Rod Bolt Torque ft. lb. | Main Bearing Bolt Torque ft. lb. |
|---|---|---|
| 140, 170, 200 | 19-24 | 60-70 |
| 240 | 40-45 | 60-70 |
| 250 | 21-26 | 60-70 |
| 289 | 19-24 | 60-70 |
| 302 1970-1977 | 19-24 | 60-70 |
| 312 | 45-50 | 95-105 |
| 332 | 45-50 | 95-105 |
| 351 | 40-45 | 95-105 |
| 351C 1970 | 40-45 | 60-70 |
| 351C 1971-1974 | 40-45 | 95-105* |
| 351M 1975-1977 | 40-45 | 95-105 |
| 351W 1971-1977 | 40-45 | 95-105 |
| 390 | 40-45 | 95-105 |
| 390 police | 53-58 | 95-105 |
| 400 1971-1977 | 40-45 | 95-105* |
| 410 | 40-45 | 95-105 |
| 427 | 53-58 | 95-105 |
| 428 | 40-45 | 95-105 |
| 429 Boss 1970 | 85-90 | 70-80 |
| 460 1973-1977 | 40-45 | 95-105 |
| 2000 cc | 29-34 | 60-75 |
| 2300 cc | 30-36 | 80-90 |
| 2800 cc | 21-25 | 65-75 |

*3/8-16    35-45

## CHECKING AND REPLACING MAIN BEARINGS

The main bearings used on all Ford engines are of the "slip-in" type. The crankshaft and main bearing as used in the 302 cu. in. Ford V-8 engine are shown in Fig. F-28, while the crankshaft used in the six cylinder 240 cu. in. engine is shown in Fig. F-33. Note that on the 427 cu. in. engine there are side bolts in the main bearing caps as well as vertical bolts for increased strength, Fig. F-29.

The usual procedure when replacing the main bearings, is to replace one bearing at a time, leaving the other bearings to support the shaft. After removing the bearing cap, the upper half of the bearing shell must be removed from the cylinder block. There are several ways in which this can be accomplished. A putty knife or some similar tool with a bent blade can be used to rotate the bearing shell around the shaft until it can be

## Fix Your Ford

removed. Another method is to bend a cotter pin, as shown in Fig. F-30. Insert the eye end in the oil hole in the bearing journal. Rotate the crankshaft and the bent end of the cotter pin will force out the bearing shell.

After both halves of the bearing shell have been removed, the crankshaft journal should be checked for wear. Special micrometers are required to check these journals, one type being shown in Fig. F-31. Conventional micrometers cannot be used as they will not reach up and measure the full diameter.

If the journal has more than .001 in. taper, or is more than .0015 in. out-of-round, the crankshaft should be reground. To do this it will have to be removed from the engine. However, if only the connecting rod crank pins require reconditioning, this can be done with the crankshaft in the engine. Special equipment is required to do this job. When the proper size main bearing shells are obtained, the upper one is slid into place on the upper half of the bearing journal. Then the lower half is placed in the cap and the cap installed.

After installing one main bearing, replace the others, one at a time.

It is essential that main bearing bolts be tightened to the specified torque listed in the engine torque table. The specifications are for clean, undamaged and lightly oiled threads, otherwise increased friction will prevent accurate measurement of tightness with the torque wrench.

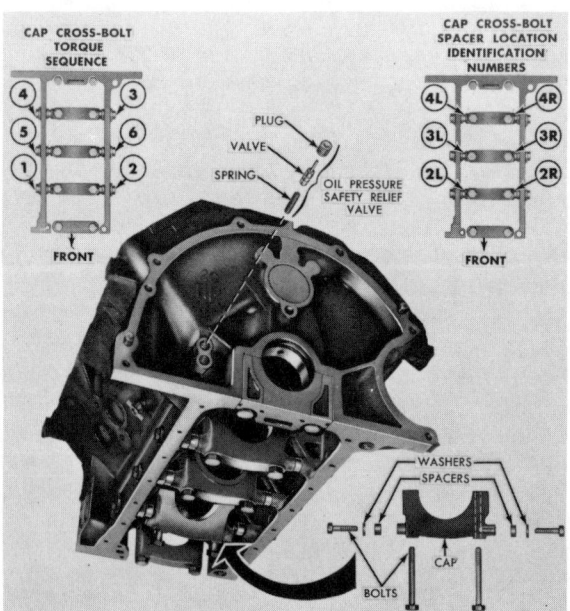

*Fig. F-29. Crankcase of 427 cu. in. engine. Note side bolts on main bearing caps.*

## Engine Repairs

When replacing the bearings of a 427 cu. in. V-8, the main bearing cap cross bolts, washers and spacers, Fig. F-29, should be removed before removing the cap retaining bolts.

Ford main and connecting rod bearings are a selective fit. Do not file or lap bearing caps or use shims to obtain the proper clearance.

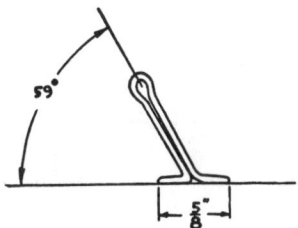

*Fig. F-30. Method of bending cotter pin to remove main bearing shells.*

Selective fit bearings are available for service in standard and .001 in. and .002 in. undersize. Standard bearings are divided into two sizes and are identified by a daub of red or blue paint. Red marked bearings increase clearance and blue marked bearings decrease the clearance. Undersize bearings which are not a selective fit are available for use on journals that have not been refinished.

*Fig. F-31. Special gauge for measuring diameter of main bearing journals without removing crankshaft from engine.*

# Fix Your Ford

## WHEN SHOULD MAIN BEARINGS BE REPLACED

Main bearings should be replaced when they are worn to such an extent that the engine will knock or leak oil in excessive amounts. Such knocks will become most evident when the engine is under a heavy load such as when pulling a steep grade. Another method is to make a check and see how much oil they are leaking.

## HOW TO MAKE AN OIL LEAK TEST

One of the best methods of checking the engine bearings for proper fit, and also to determine when they need replacing, is to make an oil pressure or oil leak test, as shown in Fig. F-32. This test will also show whether the entire engine lubricating system is clear and unobstructed.

The equipment for making such a test is illustrated and is designed to supply oil under pressure to the engine lubricating system.

*Fig. F-32. Making an oil leak test on an engine to determine main bearing clearance.*

Basically the equipment consists of a small tank of about 5 gal. capacity. This is partly filled with oil of SAE 30 grade. Compressed air is then applied to the tank until the pressure reaches approximately 25 lb. or the normal oil operating pressure. By means of suitable tubing, the tank is connected to the engine oil system. The engine is then cranked slowly and at the same time the engine bearings and the entire oiling system are carefully observed.

Under these conditions, copper alloy bearings in good condition will leak at a rate of approximately 50 drops per min. Bearings leaking oil at

## Engine Repairs

a faster rate, particularly those leaking in a steady stream have too much clearance. Bearings showing a slower leakage than 30 drops per min. may have insufficient clearance, or the oil line to bearing may be clogged. Babbitt type bearings should leak at a rate of 20 to 150 drops per min.

In addition to the main and rod bearings, it is important to observe other bearings which may receive pressure lubrication, such as camshaft bearings and wrist pin bearings. It is also important to check the plug at the rear of the camshaft rear bearing. This plug will occasionally get loose and excessive oil leakage will occur. As this will drop down past the rear main bearing, it is often mistaken for a leaking rear main bearing.

Instead of a pressure tank for making this test, some mechanics will use an oil pump. The intake of the pump is immersed in a pan of oil, and the outlet is connected to the engine oiling system. An electric drill is then used to drive the pump.

Regardless of the type of equipment used in making this test, it is important that the oil used is not heavier than SAE 30. In addition, it is important that the oil is not cold. It should be at least 75 deg. F.

## REPLACING REAR MAIN OIL SEALS

To prevent the leakage of oil from the rear main bearing and out past the oil pan, the rear main bearing is provided with an oil seal. There are three general types of oil seals used in the various Ford engines; the ring type used on the 240 cu. in. Six, the braided rope type used on such engines as the 260, 289, 292, 302 and 312 cu. in. V-8 engines and the split-lip type used on the 390, 410, 427 and 428 cu. in. V-8 engines.

RING TYPE OIL SEAL: To replace the ring type oil seal, Fig. F-33, as used on the 240 cu. in six cylinder engine, it is normally necessary to remove the engine from the chassis, and remove the crankshaft from the cylinder block. However, if the crankshaft rear oil seal is the only operation being performed, the following procedure can be used. Remove the starter.

On automatic transmission cars remove fluid level dipstick and tube. Disconnect transmission shift linkage and drive shaft. Support transmission on a jack. Disconnect transmission at the engine and at support insulator. Move transmission to one side. Do not drain. On manual shift transmission, remove the pressure plate and cover assembly. Remove flywheel and engine rear cover plate.

Use an awl to punch two holes in crankshaft rear seal on opposite sides and just above the bearing cap split line. Use two large screwdrivers and pry against the two screws at the same time to remove seal. Do not mar crankshaft surface.

Clean oil seal recess before installing new seal. Coat seal contact surface of the oil seal with Lubriplate. Then carefully start seal in the recess and tap it in position with a tool of the same diameter as the seal.

# Fix Your Ford

When installed, the seal should be flush to 0.005 in. below surface of cylinder block.

BRAIDED TYPE OIL SEAL: The braided type seal is shown in Fig. F-28. Normally this is removed after the crankshaft is removed from the engine. However, in an emergency it can be replaced by using the following procedure. Remove the engine oil pan and then the rear main bearing cap. To remove the upper seal from the cylinder block use a pair of long-nose pliers to grasp one end of the seal. As pull is exerted on the seal, rotate the crankshaft in the direction that pull is being exerted which will help draw the seal from the engine block.

To install the upper half of the seal in the engine block, fasten a piece of strong string or thin wire to one end of the seal. Coat the seal with Lubriplate. Thread the end of the string or wire over the crankshaft and in the groove provided for the seal. Then pull on the string and at the same time rotate the crankshaft which will help to draw the seal into position. Cut off the ends of the seal flush with the engine block.

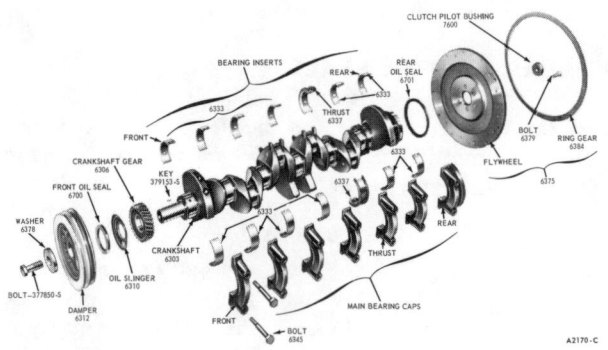

*Fig. F-33. Crankshaft and main bearing assembly of 240 cu. in. engine. Note ring type rear bearing seal.*

In regard to the replacement of the lower half of the seal, in some installations this is a special retainer and in others the seal is held in a groove which forms part of the rear main bearing cap. In either case pull the old seal from its groove and proceed as follows. Carefully clean the old groove and press the new seal into position. Then drive the seal into position, using a piece of round stock of the correct diameter, or a special tool as shown in Fig. F-34.

SPLIT-LIP TYPE REAR OIL SEAL: This type seal is used on 351, 390, 410, 427, 428, 429 and 460 cu. in. engines, Fig. F-35. As shown in the illustration, side seals are also employed in the rear main bearing cap. To replace these seals without removing the engine from the chassis, first remove the oil pan and oil pump as required. Loosen all main bearing cap bolts, thereby lowering the crankshaft slightly but not to exceed 1/32 in.

Remove the rear main bearing cap and remove the oil seal from the

## Engine Repairs

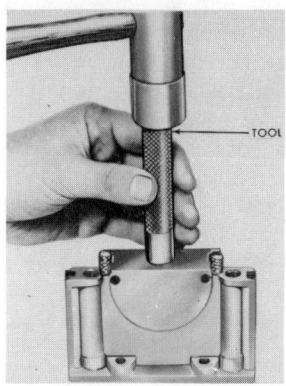

*Fig. F-34. Method of seating wick-type rear bearing seal in cap.*

cap and the block. On the block side if a seal removing tool is not available, install a small sheet metal screw in one end of the seal and pull on the screw to withdraw the seal. Be careful not to scratch or otherwise damage the crankshaft seal surfaces.

Clean all the surfaces of cap and block with a brush and solvent. Dip the new split-lip type seals in engine oil. Carefully install the upper seal in the cylinder block into its groove with the undercut side of the seal toward the front of the engine, Fig. F-35, by rotating it on the seal journal of the crankshaft until approximately 0.375 in. protrudes below the parting surface. Be sure no rubber has been shaved from the outside

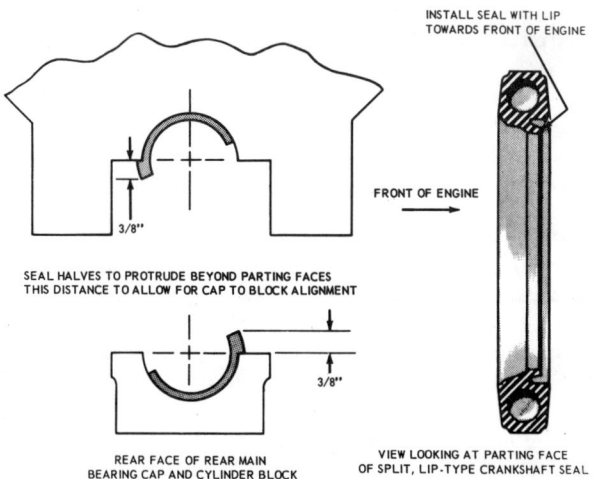

*Fig. F-35. Details of split-lip type bearing seal.*

diameter of the seal by the bottom edge of the groove.

Tighten the remaining bearing bolts and torque to specifications.

Install the lower seal in the bearing cap with undercut side of seal toward the front of the engine, Fig. F-35.

Apply a thin coating of oil resistant sealer to the rear main bearing cap mating surface. Do not apply sealer to the area forward of the side seal groove. Torque the cap bolts to specifications.

Dip the rear bearing side seals in light engine oil and immediately install them in the grooves. Do not use sealer on the side seals. It may be necessary to tap the seals the last 1/2 in. of travel. Do not cut the projecting ends of the seal.

Check the retainer side seals for leaks by squirting a few drops of oil into the parting lines between the retainer and the cylinder block from the outside. Blow compressed air against the seals from the inside of the block. If air bubbles appear in the oil, it indicates possible oil leakage. This test should not be performed on newly installed seals until sufficient time has been allowed for the seal to expand in the seal grooves.

## CYLINDER RECONDITIONING

In most cases cylinders will require reconditioning only after 100,000 miles of operation, when the cylinder is more than .003 in. out-of-round, or when the taper exceeds .006 in.

It should be pointed out that when the car is used mostly in city driving, which consists of short trips of less than five miles, that engine wear increases much more rapidly than it does on long trips of many miles duration.

The most satisfactory method of determining the wear in a cylinder is to use a dial gauge. This was explained in a previous paragraph.

Cylinders can be reconditioned either by means of a boring bar, or by means of a cylinder hone. Boring bars are usually used when considerable metal has to be removed. Final finish is usually secured by means of a hone.

However, even when cylinder wear is not excessive the glaze should be removed from the cylinders before installing new piston rings. If the glaze is not removed from the cylinders, the engine will continue to use considerable oil.

Removing the glaze is accomplished by means of a deglazing hone. The hone is driven by an electric drill and all that is necessary is to move the rotating hone up and down the cylinder several times until the glaze is removed.

Before deglazing the cylinders, cloths should be placed over each of the crankshaft throws so that abrasive particles from the hone will be caught on the cloths.

If a deglazing hone is not available, it is advisable to use some relatively fine sandpaper or emery paper, and rub the surface of the cylinder to remove the glaze. The abrasive paper should be moved spirally around the cylinder bore when doing the deglazing by hand.

## Engine Repairs

### INSTALLING CONNECTING ROD ASSEMBLIES

After the proper size rod bearings have been selected, pins fitted, pistons expanded and rings installed on the pistons, and main bearings replaced, the connecting rod and piston assemblies are ready to be installed in their original cylinders. To do this it is necessary to use a ring compressor, as shown in Fig. F-36. This is essentially a sleeve which compresses the piston rings in their grooves, so that the pistons can be replaced in the cylinders. Before compressing the rings, however, the piston and rings should be given a liberal coating of engine oil. Similarly, the cylinders should be covered with oil. With the rings compressed, insert the connecting rod and piston assembly in the top of the cylinder. The assembly will be prevented from dropping through the cylinder by the pressure of the expanded piston against the cylinder walls and by the ring compressor. The assembly is driven the rest of the distance into the cylinder by tapping the top of the piston with the handle of a heavy hammer, Fig. F-36. Be sure that the indentation mark on the top of the piston is toward the front of the engine, Fig. E-15. When installing the rod and piston assemblies, one mechanic should be underneath the engine to guide the lower end of the connecting rod, so it does not strike and mar the connecting rod throw on the crankshaft.

If it is difficult to force the piston fully into the cylinder, the trouble is probably caused by the piston rings not having been compressed into their grooves, with the result that the rings are extending over the edge of the cylinder. In such cases, remove the ring compressor, make sure that none of the rings have been damaged, again compress the rings carefully, and install the piston assembly in the cylinder.

Not only must the indentation on the top of the piston be toward the front of the engine, but the oil squirt hole on the lower end of the connecting rod must be toward the right side of the engine.

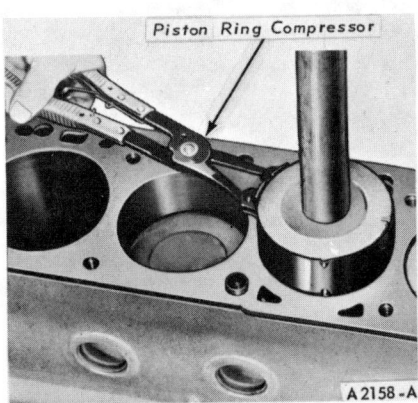

*Fig. F-36. Using piston ring compressor while installing piston and connecting rod assembly.*

## REPLACING CONNECTING ROD CAPS

When installing and tightening connecting rod caps, it is important to place the caps on the rods from which they were originally removed. Be sure to apply a liberal coating of oil to the crankshaft throw before attaching the connecting rod and cap. The socket used to tighten the nuts must be of the thin-wall type as there is very little clearance. The usual socket does not slide over the nut fully. Many mechanics will tighten these nuts as much as possible. This is poor practice as it distorts the bearings and connecting rod caps with the result that they are no longer round. Under such conditions, oil leaks from the bearings and their life will be materially shortened and oil consumption increased.

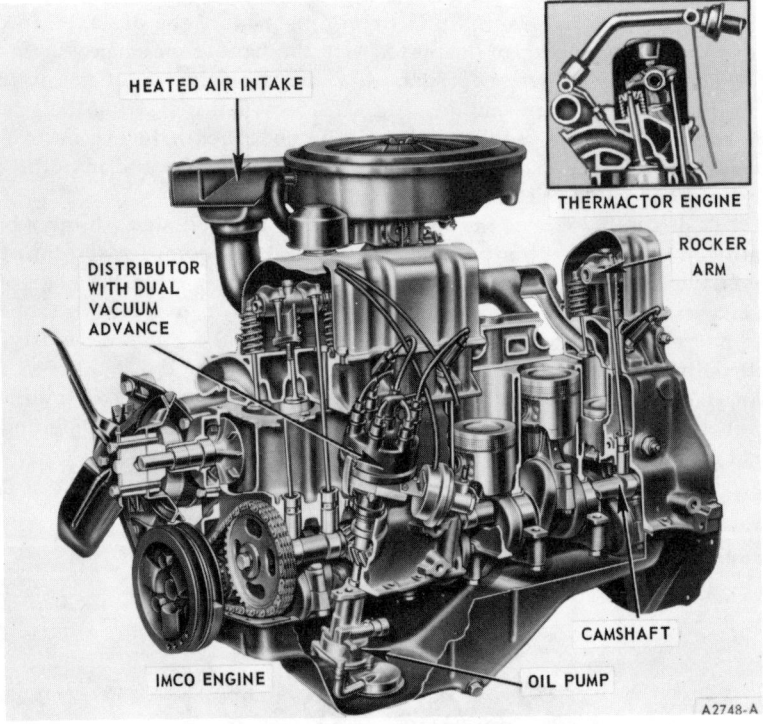

*Fig. F-37. Sectional view of 200 cu. in. six cylinder engine. Typical of six cylinder construction.*

A torque wrench should always be used to tighten connecting rod nuts. The correct tension for tightening connecting rod bolt nuts is given in the table on page 135. Be sure to follow the instructions given under the heading "Use Torque Wrench on Rod Nuts," page 134.

# Engine Repairs

## WHEN TO REPLACE TIMING CHAINS

The life of a timing chain, Figs. F-37 and E-16, is normally in excess of 100,000 miles. However, to determine when a timing chain should be replaced, first remove the timing chain cover to expose the chain, and then rotate the crankshaft in a clockwise direction to take up the slack in the chain on the left side.

Establish a reference point on the cylinder block and measure from that point to the timing chain, Fig. F-38. Then rotate the crankshaft in the opposite direction to take up the slack on the right side of the chain. Force the left side of the chain out with the fingers and measure the distance between the reference point and the chain. The chain deflection is the difference between the two measurements. If it exceeds 0.5 in., the timing chain should be replaced.

*Fig. F-38. When timing chain deflection exceeds 1/2 in. it should be replaced.*

The timing chain should not be permitted to become slack as it is likely to jump on the timing sprockets, and in that way alter the ignition and valve timing so that the engine will either stop completely or run at very reduced power.

## SERVICING OIL PUMP

Two types of oil pumps have been used on Ford cars; the rotor type, Fig. F-39, and the gear type.

It is important that the oil pump develops sufficient pressure to force oil through the entire engine lubricating system, otherwise, bearings will be burned.

In the case of the rotor type pump, the end clearance of the rotor assembly should be .0011-.0041 as illustrated in Fig. F-39. On this same type pump, the clearance between the outer race to the housing should be .006-.012 in.

On gear type pumps, the clearance between the face of the gears and the pump cover should be .001-.003 in. This clearance is measured in the same manner as illustrated in Fig. F-39.

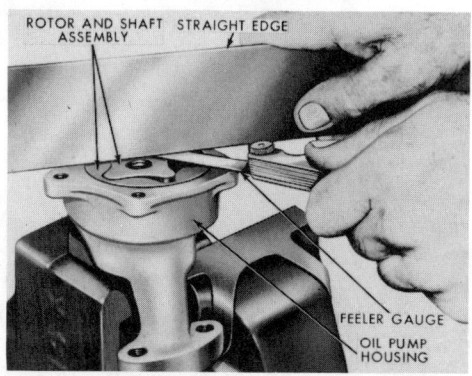

*Fig. F-39. End play of oil pump rotor shaft should be .0011 to .0041 in. on all engines.*

## SERVICING HYDRAULIC VALVE LIFTERS

Hydraulic valve lifters seldom require attention, particularly if the engine oil is changed frequently. Several different hydraulic valve lifters are used in Ford engines. While they differ in detail, they are similar in principle. A typical hydraulic valve lifter is shown in Fig. F-40 and the operation is shown in Fig. F-41. The complete units are interchangeable. An easy way to locate a noisy lifter is to use a piece of garden hose, placing one end to your ear and the other at each rocker arm in turn. Defective lifters will give a clicking noise, each time the valve is opened and closed. Another method is to place a finger on the edge of the valve spring retainer, on each valve in turn. Lifters not operating correctly will give a distinct shock each time the valve seats.

The easiest method of removing the hydraulic valve lifter is by means of a magnet, as shown in Figs. E-23 and F-42. To do this, remove the valve rocker arm covers and the valve rocker arm shaft assemblies, which will then permit reaching the hydraulic valve lifters with the magnet, as shown in Figs. F-42 and E-23.

Each hydraulic valve lifter is a matched assembly. If the parts of one lifter are intermixed with those of another, improper valve operation will result. Disassemble and assemble each lifter separately to be sure that parts are not mixed. Keep the lifter assemblies in proper sequence so

## Engine Repairs

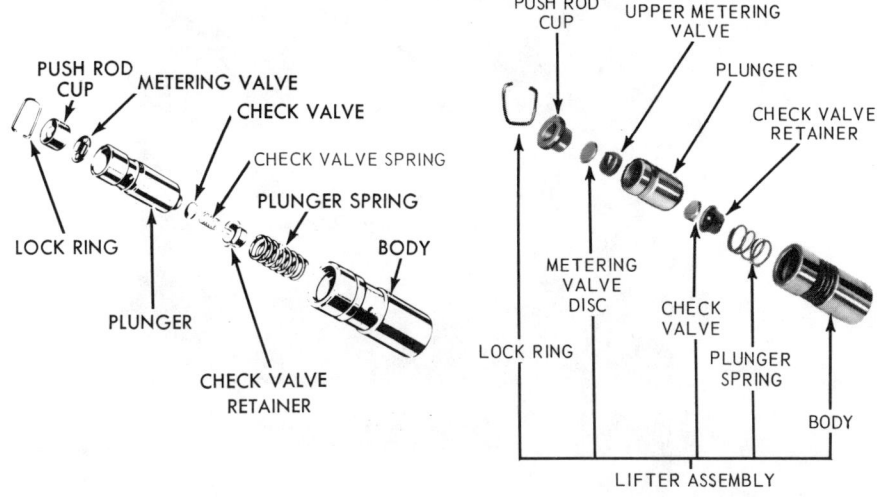

*Fig. F-40. Two types of hydraulic valve lifters used on Ford engines.*

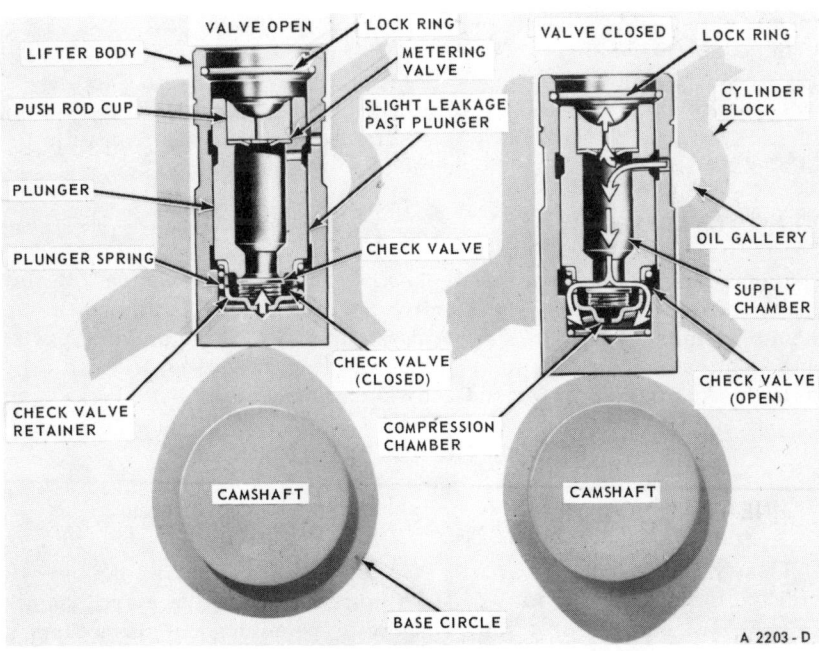

*Fig. F-41. Showing the operation of the hydraulic valve lifter, with the valve in the open and closed positions. Removal of the lock ring permits disassembly.*

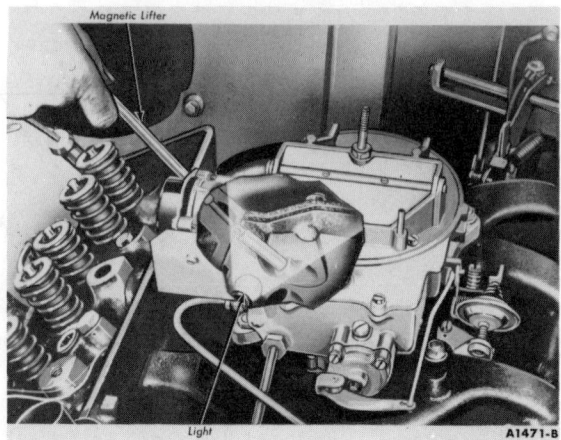

*Fig. F-42. A magnetic lifter may be used to lift hydraulic valve lifters from the cylinder block.*

that they can be installed in their original bores. To disassemble, grasp the lock ring at the upper end of the lifter with a pair of long-nose pliers to release it from the groove. It may be necessary to depress the plunger slightly in order to release the lock ring. After removing the lock ring, the other parts should be easily removed from the lifter body.

In general, when hydraulic valve lifters have seen enough mileage that they are no longer operating correctly, it pays to install complete new units rather than to attempt to salvage the old ones. However, in many cases, by thoroughly cleaning the individual parts of the hydraulic lifter with solvent, they can be reassembled and placed back in service.

## DO NOT MIX PARTS

Regardless of what part of the engine that is being repaired, it always pays to carefully observe the relative position of each part, and the parts should be marked so they can be reassembled in their original position. This applies particularly to such parts as engine valves, hydraulic lifter parts, rocker arms, piston and rod assemblies, etc.

## ENGINE TROUBLE SHOOTING

## ENGINE WILL NOT CRANK

This type of trouble is usually in the starting system and the reader is referred to that chapter for additional suggestions. If the starting system is not at fault, check for a seized engine by removing the spark plugs and then attempting to crank the engine. If the engine now cranks, it indicates that water is leaking into the cylinders. Remove cylinder heads and check for defective head gasket or cracks in the water jacket.

## Engine Repairs

### ENGINE CRANKS, BUT WILL NOT START

Check the fuel supply. If there is sufficient fuel in the tank, the cause of the trouble is probably in the ignition system. To determine which system is at fault, check the intensity of the spark by disconnecting wire from spark plug and holding wire 1/4 in. away from exhaust manifold. If spark jumps, ignition is OK, and trouble is probably in the fuel system. If spark is weak or no spark, then the ignition system should be checked as described in the Chapter on Ignition Tune-Up.

Check choke system for binding. If engine is hot, choke plate should be in open position. If the plate is not open, the engine will load up due to excessively rich mixture.

To check the fuel supply at the carburetor, remove the air cleaner and work the throttle by hand. Each time the throttle is actuated, fuel should spurt from the accelerating pump discharge nozzles which can be seen by looking down into the air intake of the carburetor. If fuel is discharged, the engine is probably flooded and engine should be cranked with the throttle wide open, or wait 15 minutes to give the excess fuel in the engine a chance to evaporate. For additional checks see the ignition and fuel sections.

### ENGINE STARTS, BUT FAILS TO KEEP RUNNING

Idle fuel mixture incorrectly adjusted. Idle speed set too low. Choke not operating properly. Float setting incorrect. Dirt or water in fuel lines. Clogged muffler. Carburetor icing. Clogged air cleaner. Leakage in high tension wiring.

### ENGINE RUNS, BUT MISFIRES

Determine if the miss is steady or erratic and at what speed it occurs.

IF THE MISS IS CONSTANT AND AT ALL SPEEDS: Isolate the miss by operating the engine with one cylinder not firing. This is done by disconnecting the wire from one spark plug at a time until all the cylinders have been checked. Ground the removed spark plug wire. If the engine speed changes when a particular cylinder is cut out, that cylinder is delivering power. If no change in engine operation is noticed, then the miss is occuring in the cylinder that is cut out.

If the miss is isolated in a particular cylinder, check the spark at that particular cylinder. If a good spark does not occur, check the spark plug wire and the distributor cap. If a good spark occurs, check the spark plug. If the spark plug is in good condition, a valve in that particular cylinder is sticking, or some other mechanical part of the engine is at fault.

Perform a compression test on the engine to locate the cause.

IF MISS IS ERRATIC AT ALL SPEEDS, CHECK THE FOLLOWING: Exhaust system restricted. Defective breaker points, condenser, second-

## Fix Your Ford

ary wiring, coil or spark plugs. High tension leakage across coil, rotor or distributor cap. Also check float setting and make sure fuel line and filter are clear. Check for leakage of water from water manifold into engine.

IF MISS IS AT IDLING ONLY: Check carburetor adjustment. Check for excessive play in distributor shaft and for worn distributor cam.

IF MISS IS AT HIGH SPEED ONLY: Check power valve in carburetor. Check fuel pump pressure which may be low. Fuel filter may be restricted.

## ROUGH ENGINE IDLE

FUEL SYSTEM: Idle speed too low. Idle mixture incorrect. Float level incorrect. Air leaks between carburetor, spacer and manifold. Air leaks in accessory equipment that is vacuum operated. Fuel leakage at carburetor fuel bowl. Power valve leaking fuel. Idle fuel system air bleeds or fuel passages restricted. Fuel bleeding from accelerating pump discharge nozzles. Improper secondary throttle plate stop adjustment, (four barrel carburetor). Incorrect idle speed setting of the secondary carburetors on cars with more than one carburetor. Leaking fuel pump, lines or fittings.

IGNITION SYSTEM: Defective breaker points. Defective spark plugs. Incorrect ignition timing.

EXHAUST SYSTEM: Exhaust gas control valve inoperative or sticking.

ENGINE: Loose engine mounting bolts or worn insulator. Cylinder head bolts not properly torqued. Valve lash too close on engines with mechanical lifters. Crankcase ventilation regulator valve defective.

## POOR ACCELERATION

IGNITION SYSTEM: Incorrect ignition timing. Defective spark plugs. Defective breaker points. Defective automatic advance.

FUEL SYSTEM: Inoperative accelerating pump. Fuel setting incorrect. Throttle linkage not properly adjusted. Leaking power valve. Distributor vacuum passages in carburetor blocked on Loadomatic carburetor. Restricted fuel filter.

COMPRESSION: Compression may be low as the result of leaking or sticking valves, leaking head gasket, worn cylinders and pistons and rings.

EXHAUST SYSTEM: Manifold heat control valve stuck.

BRAKES: Dragging.

CLUTCH: Slipping.

TRANSMISSION: Improper band adjustment on automatic transmissions. Also check converter one-way clutch.

## DOES NOT DEVELOP FULL POWER

FUEL SYSTEM: Restricted air cleaner or fuel filter. Clogged or undersize main jets. Low float setting. Clogged or undersize secondary jets on four barrel carburetors. Power valve defective. Secondary throttle

## Engine Repairs

plates on four barrel carburetor not opening. Fuel pump pressure incorrect. Distributor vacuum passage in carburetor incorrect.

IGNITION SYSTEM: Incorrect ignition timing. Defective coil, condenser or rotor. Incorrect distributor advance. Distributor cam worn. Excessive play in the distributor shaft. Defective spark plugs. Defective ignition breaker points.

EXHAUST SYSTEM: Clogged exhaust system. Exhaust gas control valve inoperative.

COOLING SYSTEM: Thermostat defective. Check system for a condition that prevents engine from reaching normal operating temperature.

ENGINE: Perform an engine compression test. Also check for worn cams on camshaft.

## EXCESSIVE FUEL CONSUMPTION

Check tires for proper inflation. Front wheel alignment. Brake adjustment. Check for exhaust system restriction. Check exhaust gas control valve operation. Check ignition system and timing. Crankcase ventilator regulator valve and tubes. Fuel pump pressure. Engine idle speed. Idle mixture. Automatic choke. Accelerating pump. Anti-stall dashpot. Air cleaner for restrictions. Float setting. Jets for wear. Power valve operation. Air bleeds for obstructions. Spark control valve for proper seating.

IGNITION SYSTEM: Check spark plugs. Distributor advance.

ENGINE: Check compression and valve lash.

COOLING SYSTEM: Check thermostat.

TRANSMISSION: Check band adjustment.

## ENGINE OVERHEATS

Check engine sending unit and gauge. Valve lash. Oil and oil level.

COOLING SYSTEM: Insufficient coolant. Cooling system leaks. Drive belt tension. Radiator fins obstructed. Check thermostat. Clogged radiator and water jacket. Radiator of insufficient capacity on car with air conditioning.

IGNITION SYSTEM: Timing.

## NOISY VALVES

Noisy valves often result from problems in the engine lubricating system. Also, on engines having either hydraulic or solid lifters, check for wear or misalignment in the valve train.

## NOISY HYDRAULIC LIFTERS

LUBRICATION SYSTEM: Check for high or low level of oil in crankcase, which could result in air bubbles in oil. Thin or diluted oil. Low oil pressure. Dirt or other foreign material in valve lifters. Sticking lifters due to "varnish" coating plunger and cylinder of lifters (caused by overheating of oil).

## NOISY SOLID LIFTERS

VALVE TRAIN: Check for incorrect valve lash. Worn lifters. Broken or weak valve springs. Bent push rods. Worn rocker arms and/or shafts. Excessive runout of valves and seats. Worn camshaft lobes.

## ENGINE KNOCKS

LOOSE CONNECTING RODS: A connecting rod bearing that is slightly loose will usually knock loudest around an engine speed of 45 mph and of greatest intensity just as the engine goes from a pull to a coast. A rod bearing in very bad condition will be heard at all speeds.
LOOSE MAIN BEARINGS: A main bearing knock is more of a bump than a knock and can be located by shorting out the plugs. It is loudest when the engine is under heavy load at low speed.
PISTON SLAP: Piston slap is usually worse when the engine is cold and will decrease in intensity as the engine becomes warm.
LOOSE PISTON PINS: Using a stethoscope is sometimes helpful as a piston pin may sound loudest when the instrument prod is placed on the cylinder block. The rod knock is usually loudest when the prod is on the crankcase. Shorting out the spark plug on one cylinder will change the intensity of the knock but will not always eliminate it completely.

## HIGH OIL CONSUMPTION

Among the more important causes of high oil consumption are the following: Worn cylinder walls. Worn piston rings. Worn pistons. Incorrectly installed piston rings. Worn connecting rod and main bearings. Worn crankshaft journals. Worn intake and exhaust valve stems. Defective valve stem seals. Defective vacuum booster in fuel pump. Excessive oil pressure. Clogged oil return from valve chamber. Clogged crankcase ventilating system. Oil leakage.

## REPLACING VALVE SPRINGS AND SEALS

Broken valve springs or defective seals on the valve stems may be replaced without removing the cylinder head by the following procedure:
Remove the rocker arm cover and on engines with rocker arm shafts force the rocker arm to one side and wire it to an adjacent rocker arm, Fig. F-43. On engines with spherical socket type rocker arms, remove the stud nut and rocker arm, fulcrum seat and both push rods from cylinder being serviced. Place transmission in drive position.
Install an air line adapter in spark plug hole and connect air line, Fig. F-43. With a lever type tool, Fig. F-43, compress the valve spring

## Engine Repairs

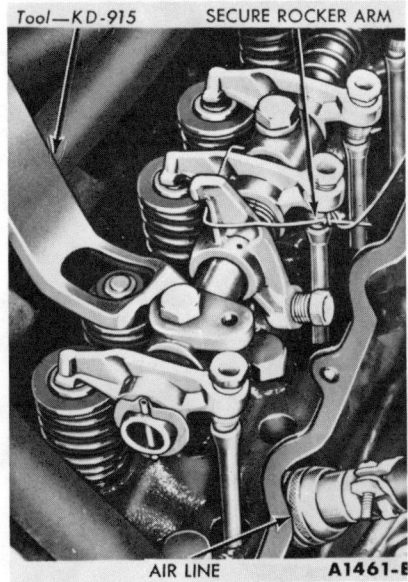

*Fig. F-43. Method of replacing valve stem seals and/or spring without removing cylinder head. Air pressure of approximately 100 psi is applied to cylinder as indicated.*

and remove the retainer locks, spring retainer and spring. Remove and discard valve stem seal.

Check condition of valve stem and if in good condition, install a new valve stem seal and spring. Then replace other parts. If valve stem is scored, a new valve should be installed, making it necessary to remove the cylinder head.

While replacing valve stem seal and/or spring be sure that ample air pressure is maintained in cylinder, otherwise, valve will drop into cylinder.

### ENGINE KEEPS RUNNING

If engine keeps running after the ignition is turned off, it may be due to overheating. Or, if engine temperature is normal, there may be excessive carbon accumulations in the combustion chamber. However, this condition is not unusual in late model engines with exhaust emission equipment. A change to higher octane fuel will help in many cases. If trouble continues after checking emission controls and general tune-up, leave the transmission in drive before turning off the ignition.

*1970–1971 390 cu. in. engine which develops 270 hp @ 4400 rpm.*

# ADJUSTING
# VALVE TAPPETS

Accurate adjustment of the clearance between the end of the rocker arm and the push rod, Fig. G-1, is very important if maximum performance and economy are to be obtained. This clearance, known as valve lash, or tappet clearance, is measured with a feeler gauge of the proper thickness. An error of only one or two thousandths of an inch will result

Fig. G-1. Typical rocker arm and shaft construction with adjustable rocker arms, illustrating method of making valve lash adjustment.

in considerable loss of power, and if the clearance is more than specified, the valves will be noisy. If the clearance is less than specified, the valves will be burned, and soon will have to be replaced.

Most engines today are equipped with hydraulic valve lifters. However, some current engines (1600 cc, 2000 cc, 2300 cc and 2800 cc) and many of the older models have mechanical valve lifters. In addition, many of the older models used mechanical lifters for some years, then they were converted to hydraulic lifters.

Valve lash adjustments are necessary after the valves have been reconditioned, or after about 10,000 miles of service. In some cases, adjustments can be made with the engine operating; in others, with the engine cold and not operating. (See Engine Tune-up Specifications near back of book.) When adjusting valves on an engine that is not operating, make sure the valves are fully closed. Instructions for adjusting valve lash are as follows:

## Fix Your Ford

To adjust the valve lash on six cylinder engines with mechanical type lifters, first locate the timing mark on the vibration damper, Figs. G-2 and B-31, at the front of the engine. Then make two chalk marks on the damper, spaced 120 deg. from the timing mark. This will divide the face of the damper into three segments, each 120 deg., Fig. G-2.

Proceed according to the six steps shown in Fig. G-2.

**STEP 1**—SET NO. 1 PISTON ON T.D.C. AT END OF COMPRESSION STROKE ADJUST NO. 1 INTAKE AND EXHAUST

**STEP 4**— ADJUST NO. 6 INTAKE AND EXHAUST

**STEP 2**— ADJUST NO. 5 INTAKE AND EXHAUST

**STEP 3**— ADJUST NO. 3 INTAKE AND EXHAUST

**STEP 5**— ADJUST NO. 2 INTAKE AND EXHAUST

**STEP 6**— ADJUST NO. 4 INTAKE AND EXHAUST

*Fig. G-2. Marking the front pulley as an aid when adjusting valve lash on six cylinder engines.*

Valve lash is adjusted by means of a setscrew and lock nut located at the push rod end of the rocker arm, Fig. G-1. The procedure is to first crank the engine until the piston is at top center with both valves closed. Then insert the blade of the feeler gauge between the end of the valve stem and the rocker arm, Fig. G-1, and turn the setscrew until the gauge is a snug fit between the valve stem and the rocker arm. The adjustment is then locked with the lock nut.

## Tappet Adjustment

The detailed procedure for adjusting the valve lash on a six cylinder engine is as follows: Rotate the crankshaft until No. 1 piston is near top center at the end of the compression stroke, then adjust the intake and exhaust valve lash for No. 1 cylinder. This operation is done with the engine not operating, as it is much easier that way. Repeat this procedure for the remaining set of valves, turning the crankshaft one-third turn at a time as indicated by the chalk mark on the vibration damper. Adjust the valves in the firing order sequence 1-5-3-6-2-4.

To check on the adjustment, operate the engine for approximately thirty minutes, and then with the engine idling check the valve lash. This will not be too easy, because of the movement of the rocker arms, and if a change in adjustment is necessary, it is easier if one individual turns the adjusting screw while the other operates the feeler gauge to note the adjustment.

To adjust the valves on the V-8 engines with mechanical lifters, the procedure is similar except the order in which the valves are adjusted. In the case of the V-8, first locate the timing marks on the vibration damper, and make three chalk marks, each spaced 90 deg. from the timing mark, so that the damper is divided into four equal parts.

On the 272, 292 and 312 cu. in. engines which have mechanical valve lifters, and a firing order of 1-5-4-8-6-3-7-2, crank the engine until No. 1 piston is near top center on the end of the compression stroke and adjust

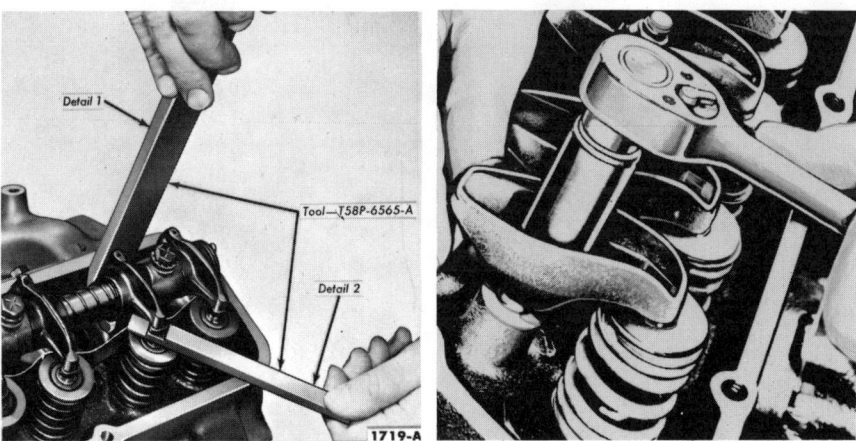

*Fig. G-3. Left. Method of collapsing hydraulic valve lifters operated by forged rocker arms, when checking valve lash. Fig. G-4. Right. Adjusting clearance of hydraulic lifter by means of stud nut.*

the following valves: No. 1 exhaust, No. 4 exhaust, No. 5 exhaust, No. 1 intake, No. 2 intake, No. 7 intake. Rotate the crankshaft 180 deg. or one-half turn which puts No. 4 piston on T.D.C. then adjust the following valves: No. 6 exhaust, No. 8 exhaust, No. 4 intake, No. 5 intake. Rotate the crankshaft 270 deg. or three-quarter turn from 180 deg. which puts

No. 3 piston on top center, then adjust the following valves: No. 2 exhaust, No. 3 exhaust, No. 7 exhaust, No. 3 intake, No. 6 intake, No. 8 intake. Valve lash should be adjusted to specified value.

On 332, 352, 390, 406, 427 and 428 cu. in. V-8 engines when equipped with mechanical lifters, and which have a firing order of 1-5-4-2-6-3-7-8 and a valve arrangement of E-I-E-I-I-E-I-E, crank the engine until No. 1 piston is on T.D.C. on its compression stroke and adjust the following valves: No. 1 exhaust, No. 4 exhaust, No. 5 exhaust, No. 1 intake, No. 7 intake, No. 8 intake. Rotate the crankshaft 180 deg. or one-half turn which puts No. 4 piston on T.D.C. and adjust the following valves: No. 2 exhaust, No. 6 exhaust, No. 4 intake, and No. 5 intake. Rotate the crankshaft another three-quarter turn, placing No. 3 piston on T.D.C. and adjust the following valves: No. 3 exhaust, No. 7 exhaust, No. 8 exhaust, No. 2 intake, No. 3 intake, No. 6 intake.

## HYDRAULIC VALVE CLEARANCE SIX CYLINDER ENGINES

The specified clearance between the end of the rocker arm and the valve stem on Ford six cylinder engines with hydraulic lifters is:

| Displacement | Year | Clearance |
|---|---|---|
| 170 cu. in. Six | 1965-1967 | .066-.216 in. |
| 170 cu. in. Six | 1968-1969 | .066-.166 in. |
| 170 cu. in. Six | 1970-1971 | .066-.117 in. |
| 170 cu. in. Six | 1972 | .100-.150 in. |
| 200 cu. in. Six | 1965-1969 | .066-.216 in. |
| 200 cu. in. Six | 1970-1971 | .095-.145 in. |
| 200 cu. in. Six | 1972-1976 | .079-.129 in. |
| 200 cu. in. Six | 1977-1978 | .110-.160 in. |
| 240 cu. in. Six | 1965-1971 | .082-.152 in. (1t) |
| 240 cu. in. Six | 1972 | .100-.150 in. |
| 250 cu. in. Six | 1969-1971 | .095-.195 in. |
| 250 cu. in. Six | 1972-1976 | .095-.045 in. |
| 250 cu. in. Six | 1977-1978 | .096-.184 in. |

(1t) = One turn down after contact.

To check clearance, crank engine until No. 1 piston is on TDC on compression stroke. Check clearance between rocker arm and end of valve stem on No. 1 intake, No. 1 exhaust, No. 2 intake, No. 3 exhaust, No. 4 intake and No. 5 exhaust. Crank engine one revoltuion until No. 6 piston is on TDC. Then, check clearance on No. 2 exhaust, No. 3 intake, No. 4 exhaust, No. 5 intake, No. 6 intake, No. 6 exhaust.

On engines with forged type rocker arms, Fig. G-3, apply pressure to slowly bleed down valve lifter until plunger bottoms. Hold lifter and check clearance between rocker arm and valve stem tip. If clearance is less than specified, install undersize push rod. If clearance is greater than specified, install oversize push rod.

On engines such as the 240 cu. in. Six, or 289 cu. in. V-8, Fig. G-4, which have the rocker arms mounted on an adjustable stud, instead of

## Tappet Adjustment

installing new push rods, adjust the ball stud nut by loosening the adjustment until there is clearance between the rocker arm and the push rod. This will be indicated by being able to rotate the push rod. Then tighten ball stud nut until all clearance is removed, Fig. G-4. Then tighten adjustment the number of turns indicated in the specification table at the end of this book.

### HYDRAULIC VALVE CLEARANCE V-8 ENGINES

The hydraulic valve lifter adjusting procedure on Ford V-type engines varies. On some engines, it is necessary to install push rods of the desired length to obtain the specified clearance. On other engines, a threaded adjustment is provided. Another variation is "positive stop" rocker arm studs.

To check existing clearance, the piston of the cylinder being checked must be at top center on the compression stroke. Then, bleed down the lifter by applying pressure with a tool of the type shown in Figs. G-3 and G-5. The pressure exerted collapses the lifter, permitting the clearance between the end of the rocker arm and the end of the valve stem to be measured with a feeler gauge. While measuring the clearance, be sure to maintain pressure on the valve lifter.

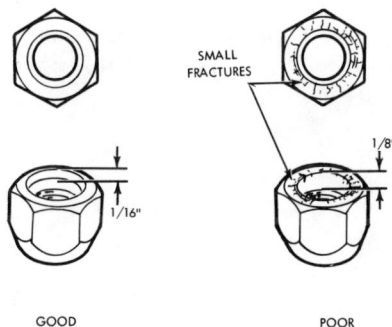

Fig. G-4a. Comparison of good and poor rocker arm stud nuts. Note fractures in poor or defective nut.

On some engines, instead of providing an adjustment, a positive stop rocker arm stud eliminates the necessity for adjusting valve lash. However, to obtain specified valve lash, all valve components must be in serviceable condition, properly installed and correctly torqued. Each stud nut should be carefully inspected. Rotate the engine to get the piston of the cylinder to be checked on the compression stroke and at top dead center. Remove the stud nut and inspect it for conditions shown in Fig. G-4a. If defective, install a new nut on the stud. Turn the nut clockwise until it contacts the stop. Torque the nut to 17-25 ft. lb.

## Fix Your Ford

The following instructions apply to Ford V-8 engines with the forged type rocker arms, Fig. G-3, and a firing order of 1-5-4-2-6-3-7-8. The valve arrangement is E-I-E-I-I-E-I-E. Push rods which are .060 in. shorter and .060 in. longer are available for service to provide means of compensating for dimensional changes in the valve mechanism. The specified clearance for these Ford V-8 engines is as follows:

| Displacement | Year | Clearance |
| --- | --- | --- |
| 352 cu. in. V-8 | 1960-1962 | .087-.218 in. |
| 352 cu. in. V-8 | 1963 | .083-.183 in. |
| 352 cu. in. V-8 | 1964-1966 | .050-.150 in. |
| 390 cu. in. V-8 | 1963 | .083-.183 in. |
| 390 cu. in. V-8 | 1964-1966 | .050-.150 in. |
| 390 cu. in. V-8 | 1967-1969 | .100-.200 in. |
| 390 cu. in. V-8 | 1970-1971 | .100-.150 in. |
| 410 cu. in. V-8 | 1965-1966 | .050-.150 in. |
| 428 cu. in. V-8 | 1967-1969 | .100-.200 in. |

The following clearance specifications for checking lash of hydraulic lifters apply to Ford V-8 engines with spherically mounted rocker arms, Fig. G-5. Firing order for these engines is 1-5-4-2-6-3-7-8. Valve arrangement is: Left - E-I-E-I-E-I-E-I. Right - I-E-I-E-I-E-I-E.

If clearance is incorrect: On 1970 302 cu. in. engines, install shorter or longer push rods. On 429 cu. in. engines, replace working parts as needed. On all other engines, adjust rocker arm stud nuts.

| Displacement | Year | Clearance |
| --- | --- | --- |
| 289 cu. in. V-8 | 1965-1966 | .082-.152 in. |
| 289 cu. in. V-8 | 1967-1968 | .067-.167 in. |
| 302 cu. in. V-8 | 1968-1969 | .067-.117 in. |
| 302 cu. in. V-8 | 1971 | .096-.190 in. |
| 302 cu. in. V-8 | 1970 | .068-.117 in. |
| 302 cu. in. V-8 | 1972-1976 | .090-.140 in. |
| 302 cu. in. V-8 | 1977-1978 | .096-.168 in. |
| 429 cu. in. V-8 | 1969-1970 | .075-.175 in. |
| 429 cu. in. V-8 | 1971-1973 | .105-.150 in. |
| 460 cu. in. V-8 | 1973-1976 | .075-.125 in. |
| 460 cu. in. V-8 | 1977 | .100-.150 in. |

(1t) = One turn down after contact.

On 351 cu. in. engines, a .060 in. shorter or longer push rod is used to bring clearance within specifications. The following engines have a firing order of 1-3-7-2-6-5-4-8. Valve arrangement is I-E-I-E-I-E-I-E on the right bank and E-I-E-I-E-I-E-I on the left bank. Clearances are:

## Tappet Adjustment

| Displacement | Year | Clearance |
|---|---|---|
| 351 cu. in. | 1969 | .083-.183 in. |
| 351C cu. in. | 1970 | .100-.200 in. |
| 351W cu. in. | 1970 | .083-.113 in. |
| 351C, 400 cu. in. | 1971-1976 | .100-.150 in. |
| 351W cu. in. | 1971 | .100-.200 in. |
| 351W cu. in. | 1972-1976 | .106-.156 in. |
| 351W cu. in. | 1977-1978 | .096-.168 in. |
| 351M cu. in. | 1975-1976 | .100-.200 in. |
| 351M cu. in. | 1977-1978 | .125-.175 in. |
| 400 cu. in. | 1977-1978 | .096-.168 in. |

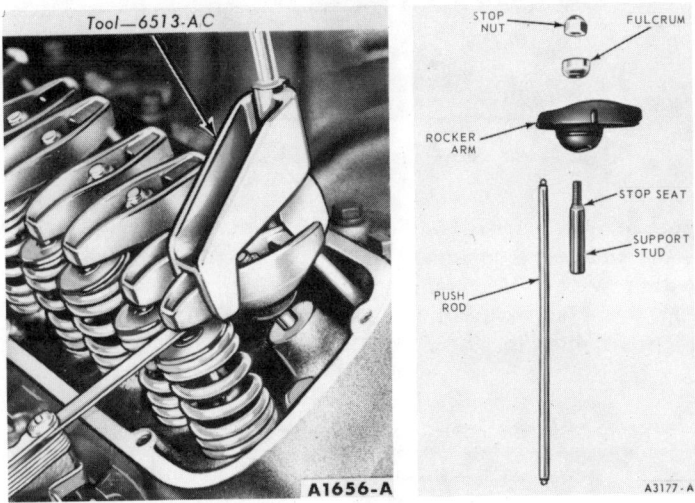

*Fig. G-5. Left. Collapse lifters as shown when checking valve lash on spherical rocker arms.*
*Fig. G-6. Right. Positive rocker arm stud installed on 1969-1971 351 cu. in. V-8 engine.*

## POSITIVE STOP ROCKER ARM STUD

All 1969-1970 351, 429 and 460 cu. in. V-8 engines are equipped with a different type of positive stop rocker arm stud, Figs. G-6 and G-7. This design eliminates the need for adjusting valve lash. All components must be installed correctly, with specified torque. On 351 cu. in. V-8 engines, Fig. G-6, first position piston of cylinder being worked on at TDC of compression stroke. Then, locate support stud properly with the special tool shown in Fig. G-7. Otherwise, valve lash will be incorrect.

In the case of the positive stop rocker arm stud used on the 429 and 460 cu. in. V-8 engines, it is very important that the correct push rod is installed and all components are installed and torqued as follows: Position the piston of the cylinder being worked on at top center on the

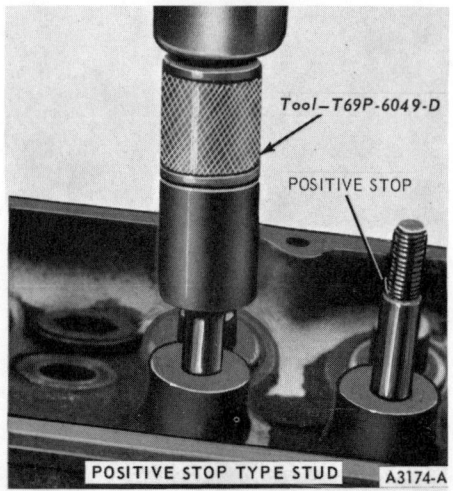

Fig. G-7. Tool used to install positive stop rocker arm stud.

compression stroke. Thread the positive stop stud, Fig. G-8, into cylinder head until the shoulder contacts the head. Torque the stud to 65 - 75 ft. lb. Lubricate the rocker arm components. Position the rocker arm and the fulcrum on the stud. Thread the nut onto the stud until it contacts the shoulder. Then tighten to 18 - 22 ft. lb.

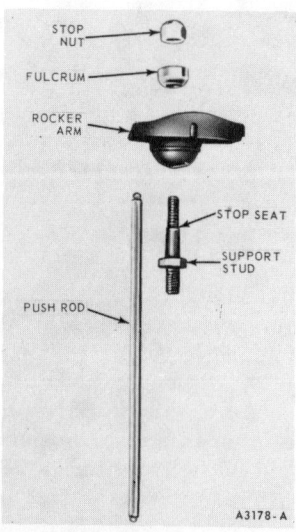

Fig. G-8. Type of positive stop rocker arm stud, as installed on 1969 429 and 460 cu. in. V-8 engine.

## Tappet Adjustment

*Fig. G-9. Valve springs may be replaced without removing cylinder head by introducing air pressure in cylinder and using a special spring compressor.*

## TIPS ON VALVE SPRING AND SEAL REPLACEMENT

Valve springs and seals can be replaced without removing the cylinder head from the engine and the time saving method is as follows: First remove the valve rocker cover. Then crank the engine until both valves of the particular cylinder are in the closed position. If the rocker arm is mounted on a ball stud, remove the rocker arm. If the rocker arm is on a rocker shaft, pull the rocker arm to one side and hold it in that position with a wire. If all new springs and seals are to be installed, use the special tool set available for this purpose, Fig. G-9.

To work on a particular cylinder, remove the spark plug for that cylinder. Next, install a threaded adapter that fits the spark plug opening, Fig. G-9. Connect an air line to the adapter and apply approximately 100 psi to the cylinder. This will prevent the valve from dropping into the cylinder when the valve spring, locks, seal and retainer are removed. The new spring and seal can then be installed.

The 1970 351 cu. in. engine, while having the same displacement as the previous model, has many new features. Cylinder heads and manifolds are completely new. Valves are of a flat head design with 2.19 in. intake and 1.71 in. exhaust. Water crossover passage is now in upper front of the cylinder block. In the 4-V version it develops 300 hp @ 5400 rpm.

# COOLING SYSTEM KINKS

Many of the troubles that occur in cooling systems can be eliminated by draining and flushing the cooling system every year or biannually. This is true even when modern coolants which protect the system against freezing and rust are used.

When water without antifreeze is used as the coolant, a rust inhibitor should always be added to the system to prevent the formation of rust and also prevent the precipitation of any minerals that the water may contain.

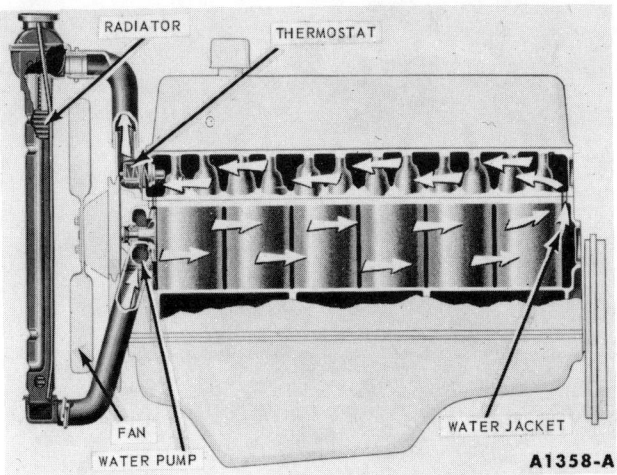

Fig. H-1. Direction of water flow in cooling system of Ford Six. (Typical)

## DRAINING, FLUSHING, TESTING THE COOLING SYSTEM

In order to drain the cooling system, it is required that the drain cock, located at the bottom of the radiator, be opened and also the drain cock in the cylinder block. In the case of the V-8 engines, there is a drain plug on each side of the block, Fig. H-2. On the 223 cu. in. engine, the drain plug is located at the left rear of the cylinder block and on the 144, 170, 200 and 240 cu. in. Six engines, it is located on the right side.

After the system has been drained, it should be thoroughly flushed in order to remove all traces of rust and old coolant. After flushing, clear water and rust inhibitor, or antifreeze solution, should be used to fill

# Fix Your Ford

the system. All antifreeze produced by reputable manufacturers contains rust inhibitor, so it is not necessary to add an inhibitor to the solution.

It is desirable to remove the cooling system thermostat, Figs. H-1 and H-3, from the system before flushing to insure a free flow of water.

If the cooling system is extremely dirty, flush it in reverse to normal flow. First, disconnect the radiator from the engine by removing the hose connections. Then, flush the radiator from bottom to top. NOTE: It is advisable to remove the radiator from the chassis and place it in an inverted position to flush out accumulated dirt.

Remove the thermostat, then flush the engine from top to bottom.

After reassembly, test the system by applying pressure by means of a special hand air pump. An attached gauge will indicate the applied pressure. Check the radiator cap separately. If pressure is not maintained in either case, a leak is indicated.

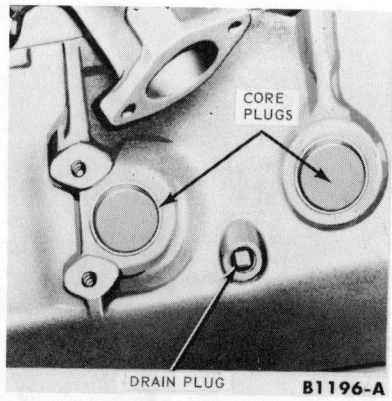

*Fig. H-2. Drain plugs are located on each side of the engine block on Ford V-8 engines.*

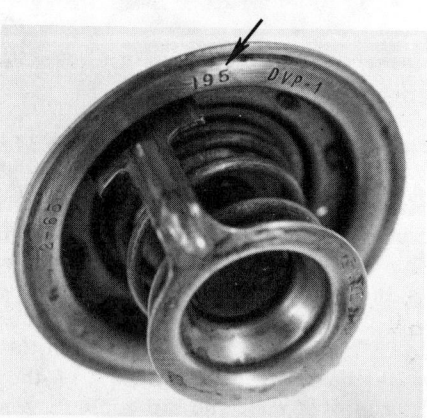

*Fig. H-3. Typical cooling system thermostat. Note opening temperature.*

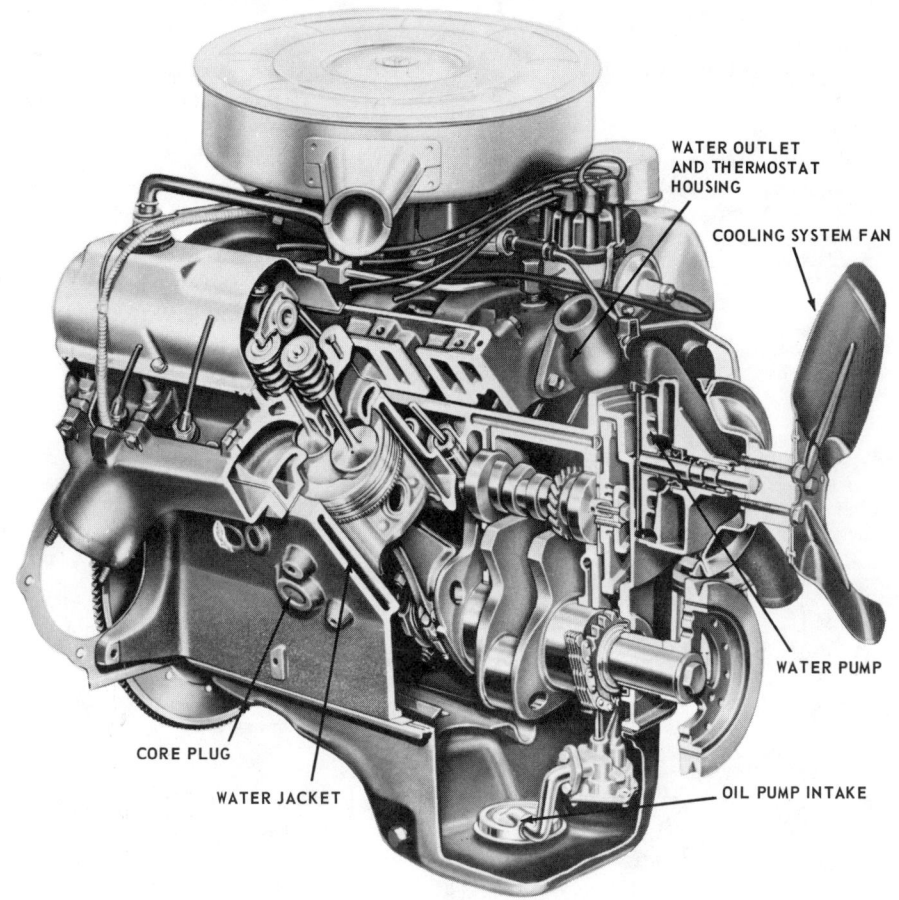

*Fig. H-4. Note location of water pump and other parts of cooling system.*

## HOW TO LOCATE LEAKS

In many cases, leaks in the cooling system are easily located. Leaks in the radiator core will discolor the surface of the core and the water leaking from the hose connections and water pump will be driven back over the engine where it is easily noticed. Leaking core plugs in the cylinder block, Figs. H-2 and H-4, are more difficult to spot (particularly on V-8 engines) because they are frequently hidden from view by accessories and manifolds.

Internal leakage from defective head gaskets can be detected by operating the engine at a fast idle, and looking for the formation of bubbles in the radiator upper tank. Oil in the upper tank may indicate leakage in the engine block, or a leak in the automatic transmission oil cooler. Water

# Fix Your Ford

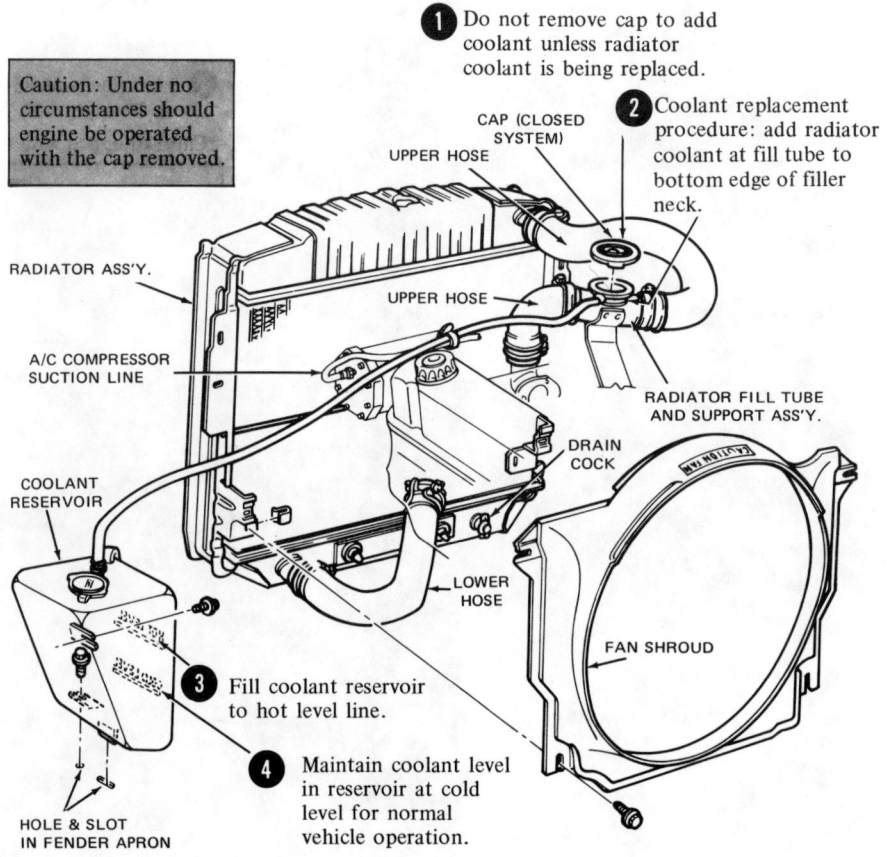

Fig. H-4a. Details of cooling system with coolant reservoir as installed on 1975–1978 Mustang II. Typical of other models.

formation on the oil level dipstick could also be an indication of internal leakage. If there is any suspicion of coolant leaking into the engine oil pan, drain the oil immediately into a receptacle and examine it carefully for evidence of coolant. Remember that water is heavier than oil and will be at the bottom of the container. If a permanent type antifreeze was being used, it will be necessary to disassemble the engine and thoroughly clean all parts, including the oil lines, to remove all traces of the permanent type antifreeze.

Small leaks in the cooling system can be fixed by means of special preparations designed to stop such leaks. In the case of leaking radiator hose connections, these are repaired by installing new hose, or tightening

## Cooling System Kinks

the clamps if the leak is not severe. If a core plug is leaking, new ones should be installed.

In the case of a leaking core plug, Fig. H-4, these are first removed by driving a screwdriver into the center of the plug, which then can be pried out. Clean the area to remove all traces of rust. Coat the new plug with litharge, or special cement designed for the purpose. Then drive it into position, using a round piece of metal the same diameter as the new core plug, Fig. H-5.

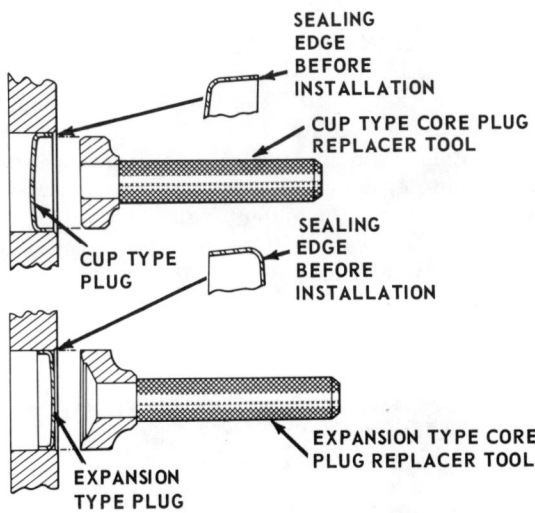

*Fig. H-5. Types of core plugs and installation tools.*

## CLEANING THE COOLING SYSTEM

When the coolant in the cooling system appears rusty, it should be cleaned with one of the chemicals which are available for that purpose. Directions for using that particular cleaner should be carefully followed.

In the event that no special cleaning preparation is available, oxalic acid in crystal form can be used, but special care must be taken to flush all traces of it out of the system, and then use a good rust inhibitor.

In cases of persistent overheating, it may be necessary to remove the radiator and have it cleaned by a specialist in such work. In such cases, it is usually advisable to remove the cylinder head also and have it reconditioned, which includes cleaning the water jacket. While the cylinder head is removed, the water jacket, Fig. H-4, in the cylinder block should be scraped as clean as possible and flushed repeatedly to remove as much rust as possible.

# Fix Your Ford

To fill cooling system after it has been drained, first close all drain openings and disconnect heater outlet hose at water pump to release trapped air. If car is not equipped with a heater, remove plug from water pump. Fill with coolant until coolant runs from hose or pump opening. Then reconnect hose or reinstall plug and complete filling operation. On cross flow radiators, fill only to COLD FILL mark. On vertical flow radiators, fill to 1 in. below lower flange of filler neck. Run engine to normal operating temperature. Recheck coolant level after engine has cooled.

If car has a radiator supply tank, Fig. H-4a, fill coolant reservoir to cold level mark. Run engine. Recheck reservoir with regard to hot level.

## AUTOMATIC TRANSMISSION OIL COOLER

Replacement of the automatic transmission oil cooler, Fig. H-11, usually is performed by a radiator specialty shop. This unit is located within the radiator tank. Should service be required, first remove the radiator from the vehicle, then the tank from the radiator core. The oil cooler can then be removed by unsoldering the connections.

Normally this unit requires no attention. Should oil leakage occur, it will be indicated by transmission oil being found in the radiator coolant.

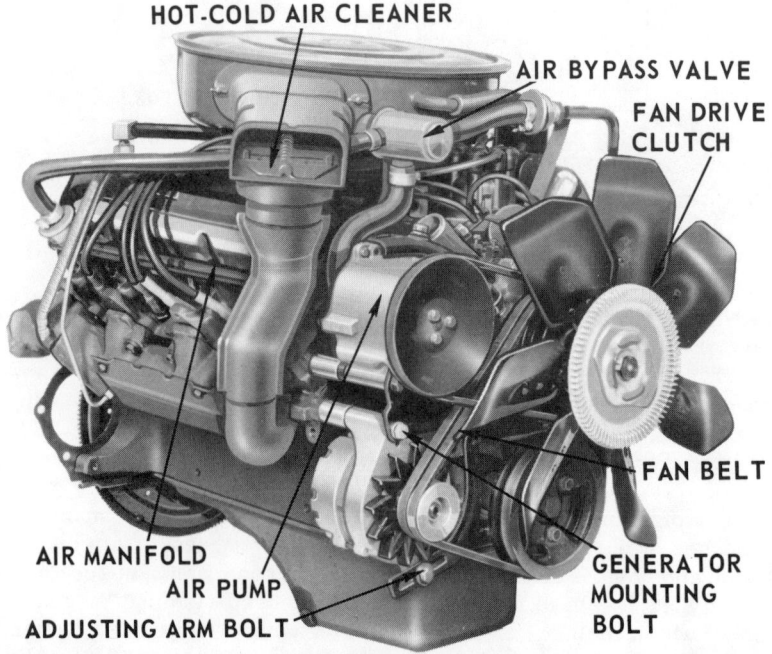

Fig. H-6. 289 cu. in. V-8 with fan drive clutch. Note fan belt and generator mounting bolt and adjusting arm bolt.

## Cooling System Kinks

### WHAT TO DO ABOUT THERMOSTATS

Ford cars are equipped with poppet type thermostats, Fig. H-3. High temperature thermostats, for use with permanent type antifreeze are designed to open at 188 to 195 deg. F. and be fully open at 210 to 212 deg. F. The low temperature thermostat designed for use with alcohol type antifreeze is designed to be fully open at 184 to 186 deg. F.

Thermostats are located in the water outlet from the engine. Fig. H-1 shows the thermostat in a six cylinder engine, and Fig. H-4 shows the location in a V-type engine. Some V-8 engines are provided with a single thermostat, while others have two.

To remove a thermostat, Fig. H-3, first drain the system until the water level is below the thermostat. Then remove the water outlet elbow, or the elbow to which radiator upper hose is connected. Thermostat can then be removed.

At room temperature, the valve of the thermostat should be in the closed position. If there is any doubt regarding the condition of the thermostat, place in a pan of water. When water reaches boiling point, the thermostat should open a minimum of 1/4 in. If not, it should be replaced. When fully closed, there should be no light leakage around valve.

Thermostats are stamped with a number indicating the temperature at which they are designed to open, Fig. H-3.

### CHECKING THE FAN BELT

Fan belts, when properly adjusted, should operate for at least 25,000 miles without giving any trouble. But it is well to anticipate their failure as the belt not only drives the water pump, but also the generator. As a result, should the fan belt break, not only will the engine overheat, but the battery will soon become discharged.

To adjust the tension of the fan belt, first loosen the generator mounting bolts, Fig. H-6. Then loosen the generator adjusting arm bolt. Swing the generator about its mounting bolts to obtain the desired belt tension. In most cases it is desirable to use a pry bar between the generator and the engine to obtain the desired tension. When the tension is correct, Figs. H-7 and H-8, tighten the mounting bolts and the adjusting bolt. In general a socket wrench and a ratchet handle are used to loosen and tighten the mounting bolts.

### WHICH TYPE ANTIFREEZE

Because of the claims made by the various manufacturers of antifreeze, it is difficult to select the best type. It is current practice of the Ford factory to fill the cooling system with a long-life coolant mixture which prevents freezing, keeps the cooling system clean, provides antifreeze protection to -20 deg. F. in winter and provides for summer operation at system temperatures up to 250 deg. F. without boiling.

# Fix Your Ford

It must be remembered that modern cooling systems operate under pressure and therefore at a temperature of 250 deg. F. Satisfactory operation could therefore not be maintained with only water as a coolant. For most effective operation the mixture strength of the coolant should be maintained throughout all seasons of the year. Correct mixture strength for most climates is 50 percent water and 50 percent ethylene glycol type antifreeze. However, in warm weather do not use mixtures with more than 50 percent antifreeze. In addition a rust inhibitor can also be used.

The radiator cap used on Ford engines is designed to maintain a pressure of 12 to 15 lbs. It is advisable to have the cap checked at least once a year to be sure it is capable of maintaining the desired pressure.

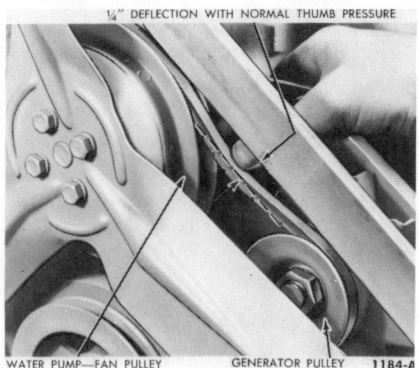

*Fig. H-7. Measuring fan belt tension on Ford Six and Falcon.*

*Fig. H-8. Measuring fan belt tension on 292, 312 and 352 cu. in. V-8 engines.*

## KINKS ON WATER PUMP SERVICE

Water pumps, Figs. H-4 and H-9, give good service for many thousands of miles of operation and need replacement only after they start to leak as a result of failure of the seal coupled with scoring of the shaft.

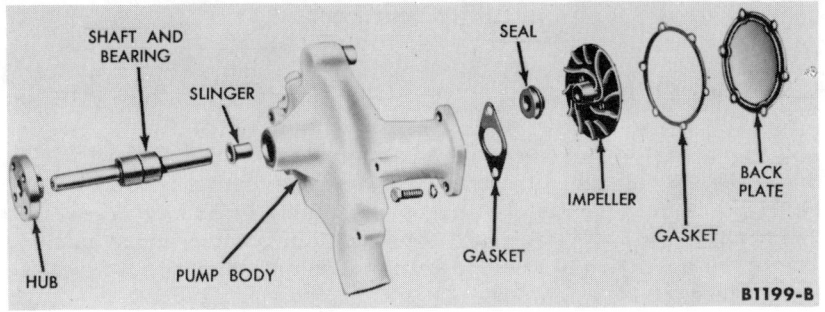

*Fig. H-9. Disassembled view of water pump used on 332, 352 and 390 cu. in. V-8 engines. Typical of other installations.*

Replacement parts are available for rebuilding water pumps, and in most cases all that is necessary is to replace the seal, shaft and bearing. However, most mechanics prefer to install a new or rebuilt pump rather than take the time to rebuild the worn unit.

To disassemble a water pump requires a puller to remove the hub and drive pulley from the shaft, and a press to push the shaft from the impeller.

The procedure for removing the water pump from the Falcon is as follows: Drain the cooling system. Disconnect the radiator lower hose at the water pump. Remove the drive belt, fan and water pump pulley. Disconnect the heater hose at the water pump. The water pump can then be removed. This is typical of the procedure on other engines.

## CHECK RADIATOR CAP

It is important that the radiator cap be checked at least once each year to be sure that it is operating correctly. The radiator caps used on Ford cars are of the pressure type. The caps used in 1953 and 1954 were designed to open at 7 lb. pressure. Since that time, 12 to 15 lb. pressure caps have been used. Most service stations have the necessary equipment for checking these caps.

Unless these caps open at the specified value, the pressure may become so great that the radiator may burst. This usually occurs at the seams of the radiator tank. If the caps open at a pressure lower than the specified value, coolant will be lost and overheating will then result.

## HOW TO REMOVE THE RADIATOR

Before removing the radiator, the cooling system should first be drained. Then disconnect the radiator hose connections. On cars with automatic transmissions, disconnect the automatic transmission fluid cooler lines at the radiator. Remove the radiator retaining bolts at the upper supports and loosen the bolts at the lower supports. Remove the fan guard upper retaining bolts, permitting the removal of the radiator assembly.

## Fix Your Ford

## FAN DRIVE CLUTCH

Some recent model Ford cars are equipped with special fans, Fig. H-6, which operate only when the engine is at full operating temperature. While the engine is cold the fan does not operate, and in that way saves fuel and also permits the engine to reach operating temperature more quickly. To control the operation of the fan, a bimetallic strip or a helical coil spring is used, Fig. H-10.

To make sure the fan is operating, run the engine at about 1,000 rpm until normal operating temperature is reached. This process can be speeded up by covering front of radiator with cardboard. Regardless of temperature, the unit must be operated for at least five minutes before being checked. Then, stop the engine. Using a cloth to protect your hand, immediately check the effort required to turn the fan. If considerable effort is required, it can be assumed the coupling of the fan is operating satisfactorily. If very little effort is required to turn the fan, it is an indication the coupling is not operating satisfactorily and should be replaced.

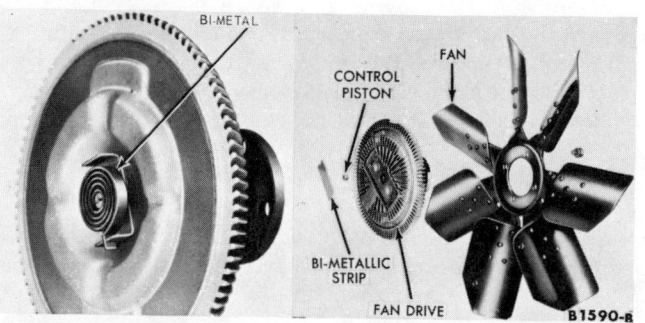

*Fig. H-10. Some of the fan drive clutches are fitted with a bimetallic strip to control the action of the fan, right, while others employ a helical spring, left.*

Another type of fan which provides a varying amount of air, depending on the speed of the engine, is known as the Flex-Blade fan. This fan has riveted flexible blades. As the engine speed increases, the blades flex so that less power is required to drive the fan which at the same time provides less air for cooling. No test or adjustment is therefore required, beyond keeping the fan belt adjusted to the correct tension.

## RADIATORS AND SUPPLY TANKS

Radiators of the six cylinder and smaller V-8 engines have tubes arranged vertically so that the flow is from the top to the bottom. On the larger V-8 engines the tubes are horizontal with the flow of the coolant from the left to the right. In addition, many cooling systems are provided

## Cooling System Kinks

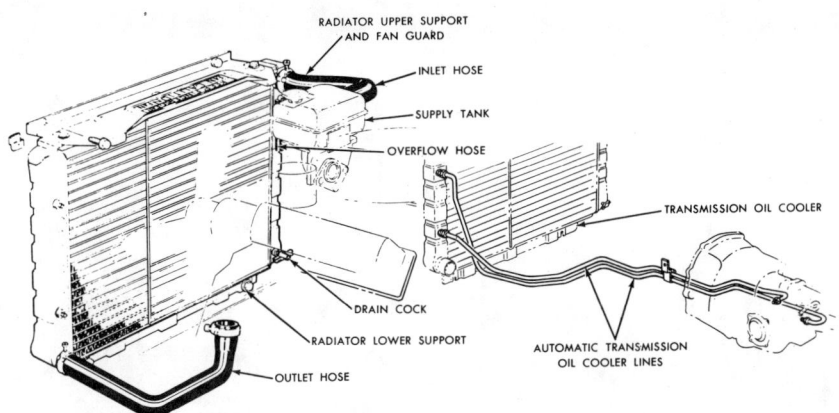

*Fig. H-11. Typical cross flow radiator as installed on larger V-8 engines. Note supply tank and transmission oil cooler.*

with a separate radiator supply tank which serves as an expansion chamber and supply reservoir, Figs. H-4a and H-11. The transmission oil cooler and oil cooler lines which form part of an automatic transmission installation are also shown in Fig. H-11.

## COOLING SYSTEM TROUBLE SHOOTING

### ENGINE OVERHEATS

Insufficient coolant. Loss of coolant. Belt tension incorrect. Radiator fins obstructed. Thermostat defective. Cooling system passages blocked by rust or scale. Water pump inoperative.

### ENGINE FAILS TO REACH OPERATING TEMPERATURE

Thermostat inoperative or of incorrect heat range. Temperature sending unit defective, causing gauge to indicate low temperature. Temperature gauge defective, not indicating true engine temperature.

### LOSS OF COOLANT

Leaking radiator. Loose or damaged hose connections. Water pump leaking. Cylinder head gasket defective. Improper tightening of cylinder head bolts. Cylinder, block core plugs leaking. Cracked cylinder head or cylinder block. Warped cylinder head or block surface. Radiator cap defective.

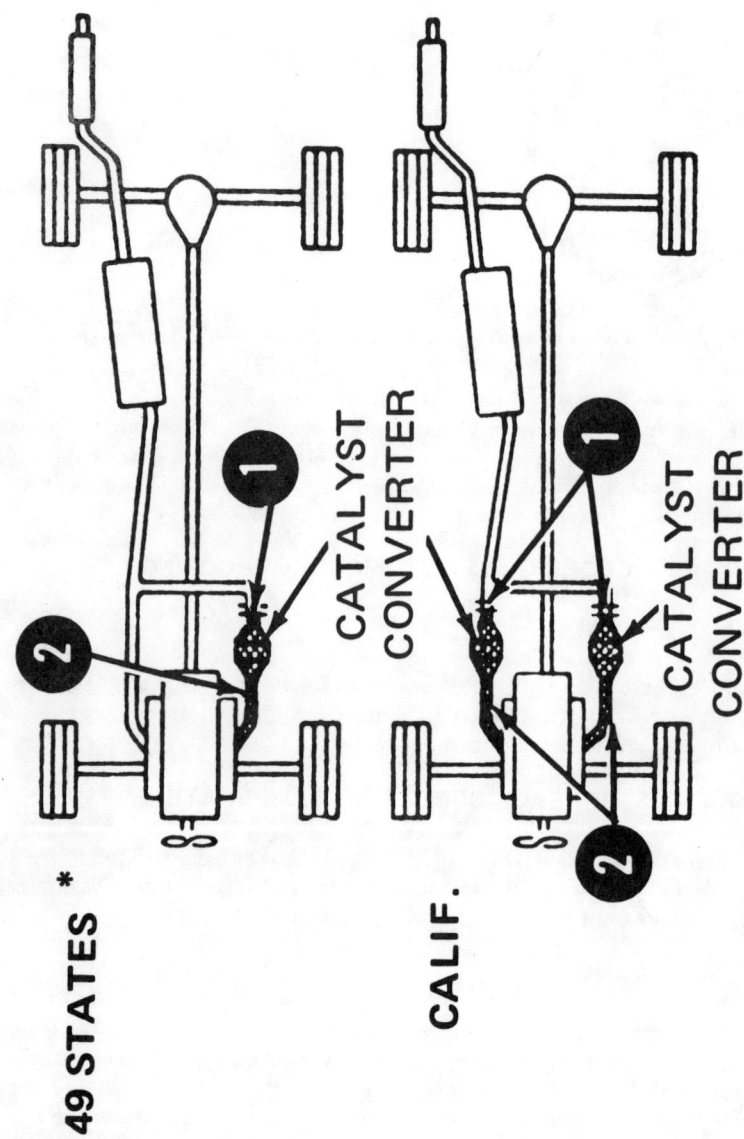

Fig. J-1. Typical layout of Ford chassis with catalytic converter. 1—Flat flange. 2—Inlet pipe welded to converter.

# EXHAUST SYSTEM SERVICE

The exhaust system varies with different models, but all include exhaust manifold, muffler(s), connecting pipes and tailpipe(s). Late models are equipped with catalytic converters, Figs. D-7 and J-1.

The life of mufflers and pipes is dependent largely on the type of service in which the vehicle is used. If it is used mostly in city type stop-and-go driving, with few trips exceeding 5 miles, the muffler will soon be rusted out. In most cases, on dual muffler installations on V-8 engines, the maximum mileage under such conditions is seldom in excess of 10,000 miles. On single muffler jobs, 20,000 to 25,000 miles may be expected. The reason for such short muffler life is that on short trips, condensed moisture from the engine exhaust gases, collects in the mufflers and pipes. As a result, the pipes and mufflers are soon corroded and have to be replaced.

If the car is driven mostly on longer trips, the muffler and pipes will get hot enough to evaporate this moisture. Consequently, corrosive action is retarded and exhaust system parts will last longer. The mufflers and pipes used on a single exhaust system will last much longer than a dual muffler installation, because all the exhaust gases pass through the single system, and as a result the temperature reaches a higher value more quickly. Consequently the corrosive moisture will be evaporated sooner.

On dual muffler systems, during the warm-up period, the exhaust gases from one exhaust system are deflected around the carburetor. As a result, the temperature of that one muffler system will take longer to reach operating temperature.

Mufflers and pipes should be replaced before they are rusted completely through for if there are any leaks in the system, the exhaust gases, which are poisonous, will escape into the interior of the car where they may cause the death of the occupants or a serious accident when the driver becomes affected by the gas.

Before mufflers and pipes are completely rusted through they will feel soft to the touch and will tend to bend when pressed. In addition, leaks in the system will often give a whistling sound, while a clogged system will give a hissing sound.

When the exhaust system becomes clogged with rust, it prevents the free escape of exhaust gases and consequently economy and performance are greatly reduced. In fact, when a system becomes sufficiently clogged, the engine will stop completely.

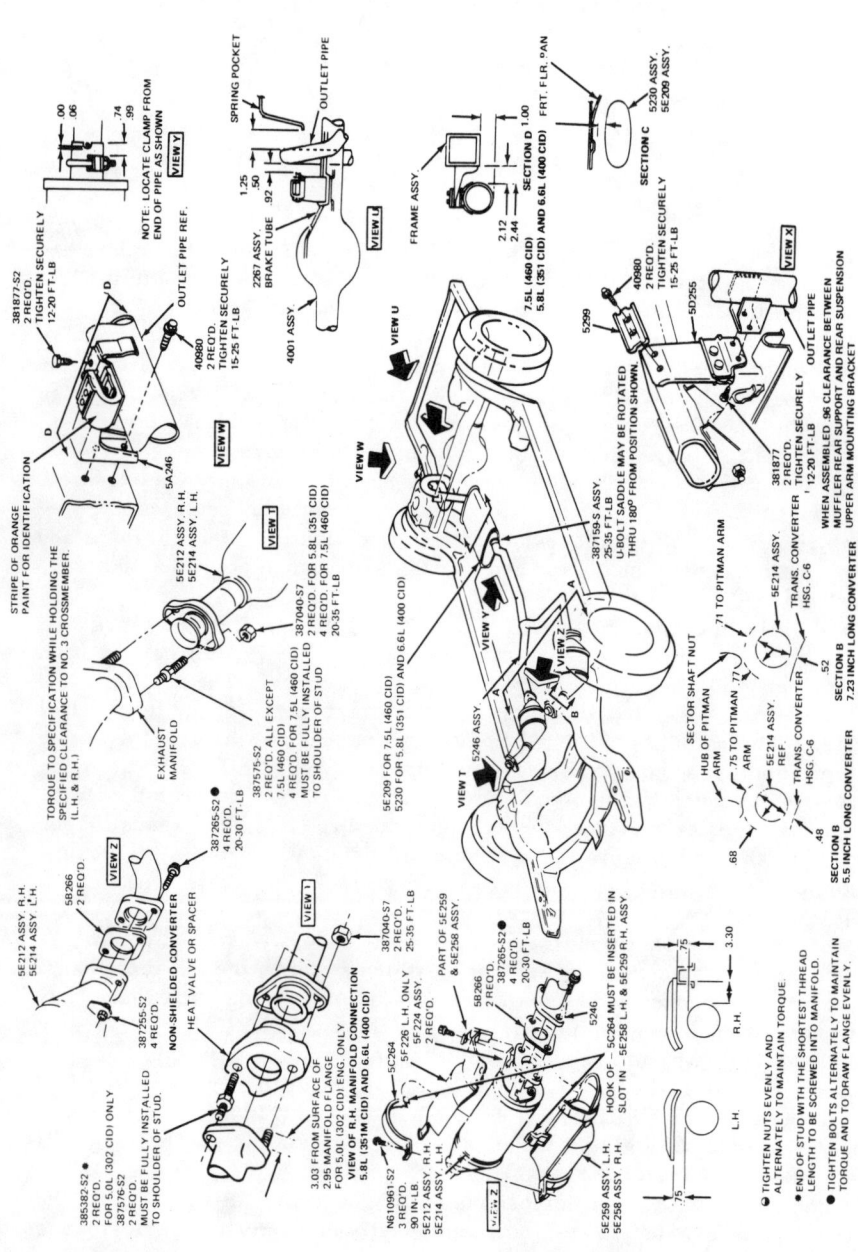

Fig. J-2. Exhaust system on 1978 Ford sedan with two catalytic converters.

## Exhaust Systems

Exhaust system vibration is usually caused by a broken or improperly aligned clamp.

The different sections of the pipes and mufflers are telescoped together and supported by brackets as shown in Fig. J-2. While the different sections are telescoped together (with the exception of the connection between the exhaust manifold and the inlet pipe, which are bolted together), they cannot be pulled apart because of accumulated rust.

To disassemble the system so that replacements can be made, it is usually necessary to cut them apart with a hacksaw, or by means of special cutters which are available, Fig. J-3. The procedure for replacing mufflers and pipes is as follows:

First apply penetrating oil to all the bolts and nuts of the support brackets and clamps.

Remove the inlet extension pipe clamp at the muffler. Then remove the bolts which attach the rear end of the muffler assembly to the frame mounted bracket. Separate the muffler from the inlet extension pipe and remove the muffler and tailpipe assembly. In order to separate the muffler from the inlet extension pipe, it may be necessary to cut this with a hacksaw, or, in many cases, it can be separated by driving a screwdriver between the two pipes until the rust is broken and the muffler can be separated from the pipe.

*Fig. J-3. Cutting tail pipe from muffler with a power chisel.*

The new muffler and tail pipe assembly can then be slid on the inlet extension pipe. Position the inlet extension pipe clamp. Position the muffler and outlet pipe assembly to the frame mounted bracket and install the retaining bolts. Tighten the inlet extension pipe clamp. Check the exhaust system for leaks by operating the engine.

The other pipes in the system can be replaced in the same manner, but in each case it will be necessary to first remove the muffler and tailpipe.

# Fix Your Ford

This work is greatly facilitated if the rear end of the car is raised by a bumper jack to provide maximum clearance between the car body and the axle.

It is generally advisable to use new clamps when replacing the muffler and tailpipe. When replacing the muffler, slide it forward until the slots in the muffler extension are blocked. Do not slide the muffler on the extension more than 1-3/4 in. Always check for possible interference between the kick-up of the outlet pipe and the floor pan and fuel tank. Reposition the outlet pipe of necessary and retighten all clamps.

Always make sure that the exhaust manifold heat control valve, Fig. J-4, is free and operating correctly.

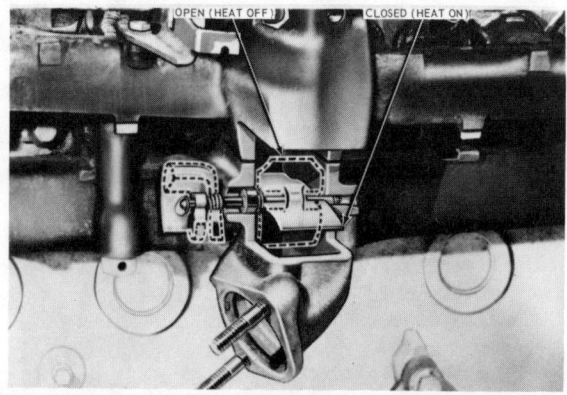

*Fig. J-4. The manifold heat control valve must be kept free and in good operating condition.*

A vacuum-operated exhaust heat control valve is used on late model Ford engines. See Fig. D-12. This type of heat control valve is designed to provide better evaporation and distribution of the air-fuel mixture. It is operated by the movement of a vacuum diaphragm rather than by means of a bimetal spring, as in earlier engines, Fig. J-4. Under high vacuum (low speed driving), the valve will close. Under low vacuum (high speed driving), the valve will open.

The proper procedure for testing the vacuum-operated exhaust heat control valve is illustrated in Fig. D-12. First, run engine to normal operating temperature. Then, disconnect hose at diaphragm housing and install vacuum-applying equipment to this port. Apply 15 in. Hg. to diaphragm. Valve should close. If not, lubricate shaft ends with graphite lube and recheck operation of valve. If valve is closed when vacuum is removed, install a new valve. On 302 and 351W CID engines, valve should start to close at 1-3 in. Hg. On other applications, it should start to close at 3-6 in. Hg.

## Exhaust Systems

## CATALYTIC CONVERTERS

The catalytic converter is an emission control unit installed in the exhaust system. It is designed to alter hydrocarbons and carbon monoxide in the exhaust gases into water and carbon dioxide. While this is a chemical action, the materials in the converter remain unchanged (provided nonleaded fuel is used). As the chemical action produces considerable heat, it is necessary in most installations to provide heat shields to protect the chassis and body.

A single converter is installed in single exhaust systems, while two are installed in dual exhaust systems. In general, the converters should last indefinitely and their effectiveness can be checked with an exhaust gas analyzer.

## CONVERTER REPLACEMENT

The procedure for removing and replacing a catalytic converter varies with different installations. The procedure for replacing a converter on the Ford, Torino and Elite may be considered typical.

Raise the car on a hoist and remove the exhaust shields from the converter. Support the exhaust inlet pipe in position by securing the pipe to a cross member. Remove the attaching nuts that hold the converter flange to the exhaust manifold and inlet pipe. Remove the attaching nuts holding the inlet pipe to the exhaust manifold (right side). Then, remove the converter.

**CATALYTIC CONVERTER OPERATION**

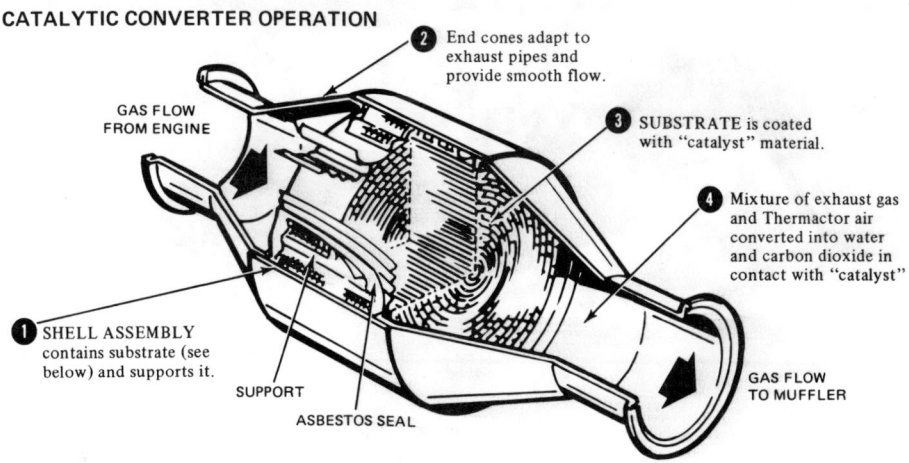

Catalytic converter used in exhaust system of late models converts exhaust gases into harmless carbon dioxide and water. Thermactor (air injection system) aids emission control by oxidizing gases leaving exhaust ports. Catalyst in converter completes conversion process.

Above. 1978 Ford **LTD** four-door hardtop has more than 70 options, including heavy duty towing equipment. Center. 1978 Mustang II Cobra with tricolor tape stripes. Below. 1978 Granada four-door sedan. Options include four-wheel disc brakes.

# Quick Tests on
# BATTERIES

When head lamps do not light to normal brilliance (when engine is not running), or when the engine is not cranked at normal speed, the first point to check is the starting battery.

First of all, the battery connections must be clean and tight. Corroded terminals, or loose connections provide a high resistance in the circuit so that full voltage is not available for lighting, starting and ignition, Fig. K-1.

To do a good job of cleaning the connections at the battery, the cable should be removed from the terminals and the terminals and battery connections are then cleaned by scraping with a knife, or with a wire brush designed especially for this purpose.

*Fig. K-1. Comparison of new cable terminal and a badly corroded and frayed terminal.*

The top surface of the battery must also be kept clean and dry, as any moisture and/or dirt will permit current leakage. This is a major cause of discharged batteries. After wiping the top of the battery with a cloth, then wipe with ammonia or other acid neutralizing material.

Also make sure that the battery ground connection is tight, not only at the battery but also where it is connected to the engine.

The level of the electrolyte should be checked every thousand miles and should never be permitted to get below the top of the battery plates. Use clean water, distilled if possible, to bring the electrolyte level up to the bottom of filler necks in the battery.

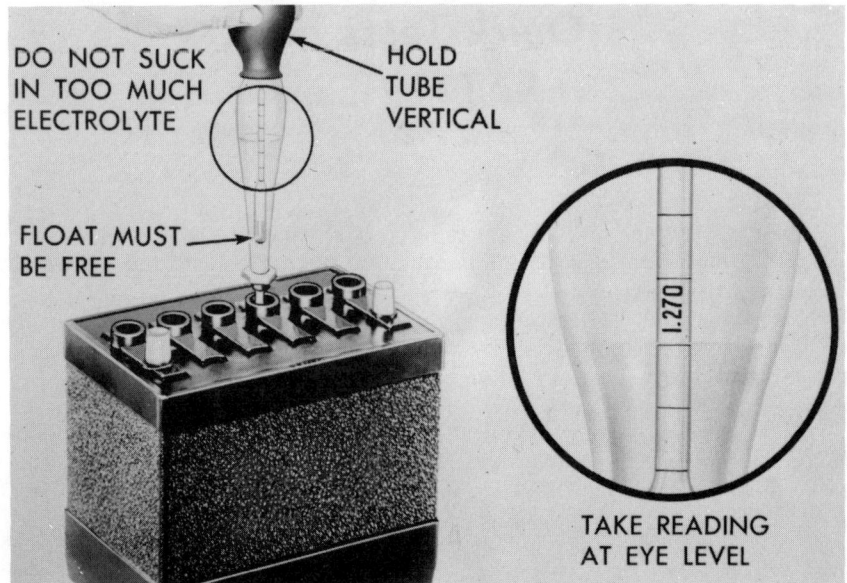

*Fig. K-2. Checking the condition of a starting battery with a hydrometer.*

It must be remembered that a discharged battery is not always due to defects in the charging system or in the battery. Excessive use of lights and accessories while the engine is either off or running at a slow idle; corroded battery cable and connectors; low water level in the battery, or prolonged disuse of the battery; a slipping generator drive belt or maladjusted regulator will all result in a battery which is not up to charge.

## HOW TO TEST THE BATTERY

There are many different types of equipment available for testing the condition of a starting battery. One of the most reliable tests is made with a hydrometer. The hydrometer can be used only when there is sufficient electrolite above the battery plate to fill the hydrometer tube. Do not take hydrometer readings immediately after filling a battery with distilled water. Instead, place the battery in operation for several hours and normal battery activity will disburse the water in the electrolite.

To check the condition of a battery with a hydrometer, the tube of the instrument is placed in the opening of the filler plug and electrolite is drawn into the instrument by means of the suction bulb, as shown in Fig. K-2. Draw the electrolite into the tube and force it out several times to bring the temperature of the hydrometer float to that of the electrolite. Then draw in just enough electrolite to lift the float. Read the specific gravity of the electrolite on the float, Fig. K-2. A specific gravity of 1.275 to 1.285 indicates a fully charged battery. A reading of 1.230 to 1.240 in-

## Batteries

dicates approximately 60 percent charge. If the specific gravity varies more than .025 between cells of the battery, the battery should be replaced.

Some batteries supplied to warm climates, have a specific gravity reading of 1.260 when fully charged. In such cases the battery is plainly marked.

As the specific gravity of the electrolite will vary with the temperature of the solution, many hydrometers are provided with a built-in thermometer so that the necessary correction is easily made. For temperatures above 80 deg. F, add .004 to the specific gravity reading for each 10 deg. that the battery temperature exceeds 80 deg. F. For temperatures below 80 deg. F., subtract .004 from the specific gravity readings for each 10 deg. that the battery temperature is below 80 deg. F.

Batteries that are not fully charged will freeze at low temperatures, while a fully charged battery will not freeze until the temperature exceeds -90 deg. F.

| Specific Gravity | Freezing Temperature |
|---|---|
| 1.280 | -90 deg. F. |
| 1.250 | -62 deg. F. |
| 1.200 | -16 deg. F. |
| 1.150 | + 5 deg. F. |
| 1.100 | +19 deg. F. |

## BATTERY VOLTAGE

Since starting batteries now have a hard cover, it is impossible to check the voltage of the individual cells with a conventional voltmeter. To check the voltage with a conventional voltmeter requires piercing the top of the battery terminal posts with the sharp prongs of the test connection. Service stations check all the cells at once by making a high rate discharge test of the entire battery. There is also a hand-held high rate discharge tester available for testing the voltage of the entire battery, which owners in isolated areas find convenient. Otherwise the hydrometer is used.

Another quick test is to turn on the headlights. They should burn steadily with normal brilliance. With the headlights burning, operate the starting motor. The lights should dim only slightly when the engine is cranked at normal speed. If the lights go out or dim considerably, the battery is probably in need of charging or replacing. However, the difficulty might be caused by poor connections at the battery and ground, or a partly defective starting motor.

## ELECTROLYTE LEVEL

The batteries in 1968-1971 Ford cars are equipped with a special device to indicate when the individual cells need water, Fig. K-3. The center of each cell cap contains a rod of refractive plastic that remains dark as long as the electrolyte level is high enough to cover the lower end of the cap. However, when the level of the electrolyte drops below a predetermined level, the cap will glow, indicating that additional water is needed.

On batteries not equipped with such an indicator, it is necessary to remove the cap and note the level of the electrolyte, which should cover the tops of the battery plates by approximately 1/2 in. When the level is below that point, water should be added.

Use of any water but distilled water will seriously shorten the life of the battery.

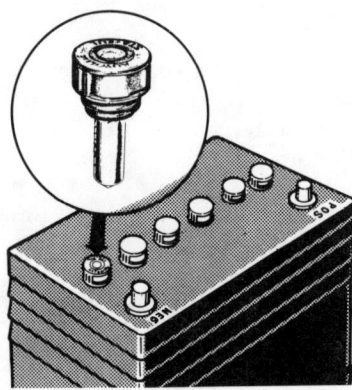

Fig. K-3. The filler caps on recent batteries will glow when water should be added to individual cells.

## CHARGING BATTERIES

If the car owner lives in an isolated area, where service stations are at some distance, it pays to have a battery charger of some type available for charging batteries in an emergency.

Battery chargers suitable for charging a single battery are available for approximately $15.00 up. Instructions for charging the battery accompany the charger, and these should be carefully followed.

### EVIDENCE OF OVERCHARGING

If it is necessary to add water to the battery at frequent intervals, it is usually an indication that the battery is being overcharged. In such cases a careful check of the voltage regulator should be made to make sure it is correctly adjusted.

### BATTERY TROUBLE SHOOTING

If head lamps dim considerably when engine is cranked, battery needs recharging or replacing, or there may be a high resistance in battery circuit. Check all connections carefully.

## Batteries

Undercharge of battery may be caused by incorrect adjustment of voltage regulator, or excessive use of electrical accessories. When it is necessary to add water to battery frequently, trouble is probably caused by charging rate being too high, or battery cells may be cracked.

Early battery failure may be caused by charging rate being too low. Too high a rate will also cause early battery failure.

Overcharging for a considerable time will cause the end covers of the cells to push up, indicating positive plates have swelled.

## BATTERY AND LIGHT TROUBLE SHOOTING

| | | |
|---|---|---|
| **DISCHARGED BATTERY** | **Verify the Malfunction**<br>1. Loose alternator drive belt.<br>2. Continuous drain on battery.<br>3. Defective wiring harness.<br>4. Defective battery. | 5. Defective alternator.<br>6. Defective regulator or voltage limiter out of adjustment. |
| **CHARGE INDICATOR LIGHT STAYS ON OR CHARGE INDICATOR GAUGE INDICATES CONSTANT DISCHARGE** | **Verify the malfunction**<br>1. Loose or broken drive belt.<br>2. Loose connections, or broken wires.<br>3. Grounded wiring from alternator to regulator. | 4. Open 15-ohm resistor across charge indicator light.<br>5. Defective alternator.<br>6. Defective regulator.<br>7. Defective gauge. |
| **LIGHTS FAIL PREMATURELY, BATTERY USES EXCESSIVE WATER** | **Verify the malfunction**<br>1. Loose or corroded connections in charging system wiring. | 2. Defective regulator, or high voltage limiter setting. |
| **CHARGE INDICATOR LIGHT FLICKERS OR CHARGE INDICATOR GAUGE FLUCTUATES** | **Verify the malfunction**<br>1. Loose or damaged connections at battery, starter relay or alternator. | 2. Loose bulb or defective socket.<br>3. Defective regulator. |
| **CHARGE INDICATOR LIGHT DOES NOT LIGHT WHEN IGNITION SWITCH IS TURNED ON** | **Verify the malfunction**<br>1. Burned out charge indicator bulb.<br>2. Defective wiring. | 3. Regulator connections loose or disconnected or defective regulator. |

Above. 1978 Ford Fairmont with 2.3 L engine is designed for fuel economy. Center. Ford Bronco four-wheel drive sports and utility vehicle. Below. Pinto station wagon with 57 cu. ft. cargo space.

# SIMPLIFIED ALTERNATOR SERVICE

Trouble shooting the charging system can be performed with or without elaborate testing equipment. The following instructions are limited primarily to determining whether trouble exists in the battery, alternator (ac generator) or regulator. Knowing the location of the trouble, a new unit can be obtained and installed. If more detailed tests are required, follow the instructions accompanying the test equipment.

Before making any tests on the alternator, when trouble is suspected, check the battery thoroughly as outlined in the chapter on Quick Tests On Batteries. If the battery and its wiring prove to be in good condition, make tests on the alternator and regulator. Be sure to observe correct polarity: positive to positive and negative to negative.

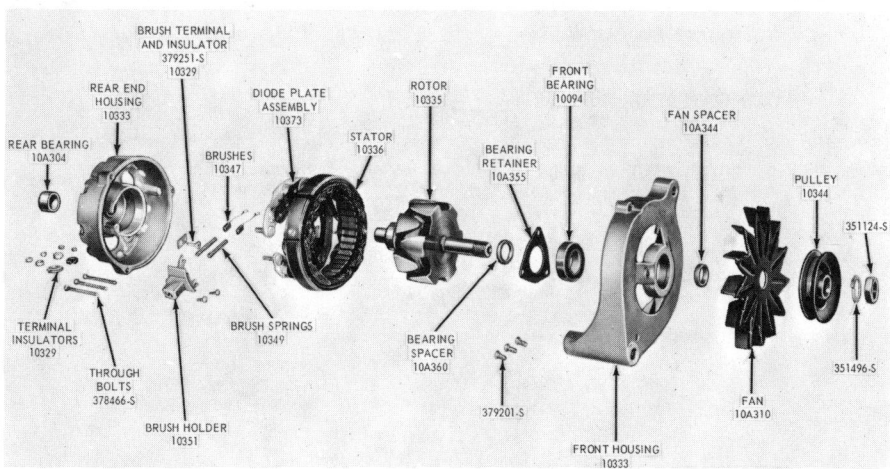

*Fig. L-1. Disassembled 42-45 amp. Ford alternator, also known as "rear terminal" alternator. Also available is a 70 amp. "side terminal" alternator.*

## FORD ALTERNATOR TESTS

The alternator charging system consists of an alternator, regulator, battery, charge indicator (light or ammeter), and the necessary wiring. Typical alternators are shown in Figs. L-1, L-2, L-3 and L-4, and a wiring diagram of the 1974 system is shown in Fig. L-5. The new Autolite alternator with integral regulator which is installed on the 1969 Thunderbird models is shown in Fig. L-4.

# Fix Your Ford

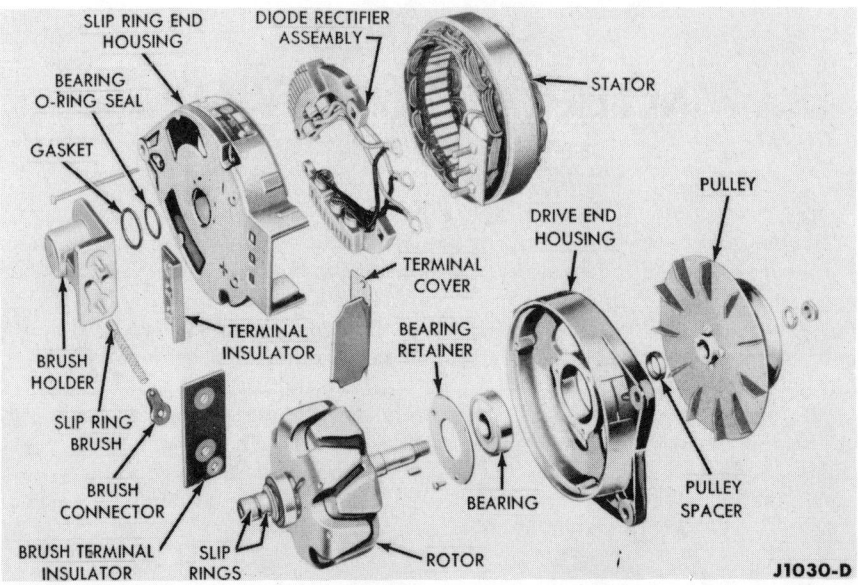

*Fig. L-2. Disassembled view of Leece Neville alternator used on some 1963–1969 Ford cars.*

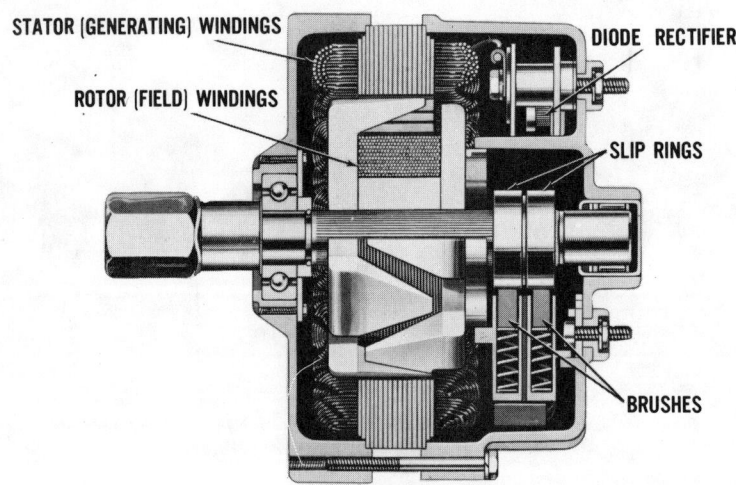

*Fig. L-3. Sectional view of 1967–1972 Autolite alternator. Most 1973 models are equipped with a 90 ampere output alternator.*

Alternators were first used as optional equipment on the 1962 cars and the 1963 cars with standard equipment on all models except the Falcon, and in 1965 was made standard on that model. The alternator produces alternating current which is then rectified for use in charging the starting battery, and supplying power to the ignition, lighting and accessory systems.

## Alternator Service

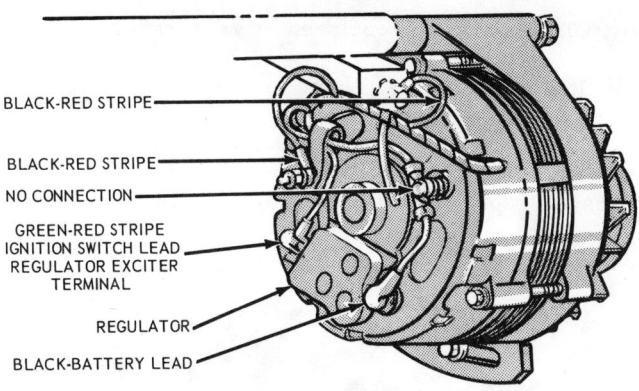

Fig. L-4. Alternator mounting and wiring connections of unit installed on 1969 Thunderbird. Note integral regulator which is of the transistor type.

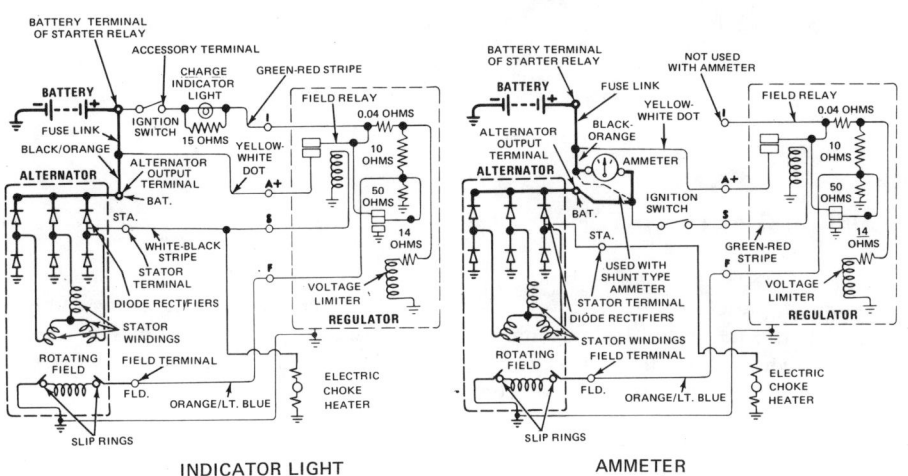

Fig. L-5. Alternator-based charging system. Left. With indicator lamp. Right. With ammeter. Models prior to 1973 did not have a choke heater.

One type of alternator regulator is composed of two control units: A sealed relay and a voltage limiter which are mounted as an assembly, Fig. L-6. The field relay serves to connect charging system voltage to the field circuit when the engine is running. The temperature compensating voltage limiter, Fig. L-6, is a double contact unit. Voltage limiting is accomplished by controlling the amount of current supplied to the rotating field.

Regulator used on Leece Neville alternators is shown in Fig. L-7.

## Fix Your Ford

Some models of Fords are equipped with a transistor voltage regulator instead of the electro-mechanical type. The transistor unit controls the alternator voltage output in the same manner as the electro-mechanical unit.

On the 1969 Thunderbird models, a transistor type regulator, Fig. L-4, was intergal with the alternator. It is sealed in plastic and cannot be adjusted. It must be replaced if it is not calibrated within specifications.

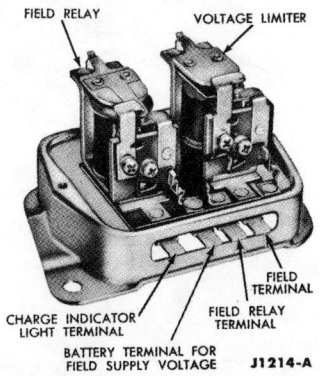

*Fig. L-6. Type of regulator used on Ford alternator.*

## CHECKING ALTERNATOR

Ford cars have an indicator light or an ammeter located on the instrument panel which will tell whether the alternator is delivering current. If the indicator light remains lighted, or the ammeter shows a discharge when the engine is operating at a faster than idle speed, it indicates that the alternator is not operating.

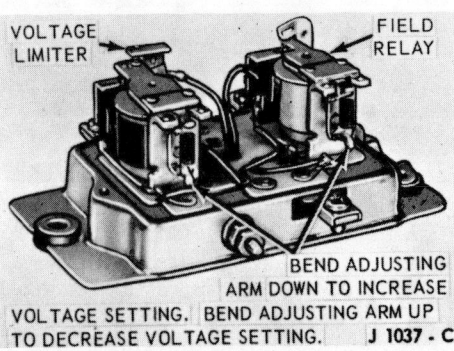

*Fig. L-7. Leece Neville regulator with adjustment points indicated.*

## Alternator Service

The recommended method of checking an alternator is to use a voltmeter. When making this test, connect the voltmeter positive lead to the battery positive terminal, and connect the negative lead to the battery negative terminal, Fig. L-9. Turn off all electrical loads, including interior lights in the car. Check and record the voltmeter reading.

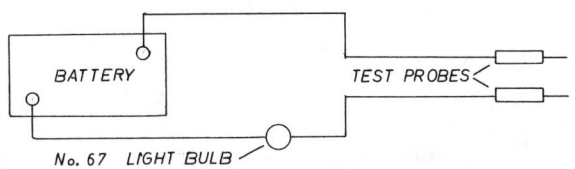

Fig. L-8. Equipment used for checking continuity of circuits.

Then, connect the red lead of a tachometer to the distributor terminal of the ignition coil and the black lead of the tachometer to a good ground. Place the transmission shift lever in neutral or park position and run the engine at 1800 to 2200 rpm for two to three minutes. Check and record the voltmeter reading. It should be one to two volts higher than the first reading. This is the regulated voltage reading.

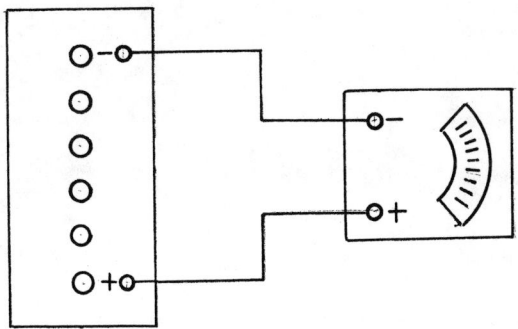

Fig. L-9. Test connections when making a check of the alternator, using the voltmeter method.

If the voltmeter reading is less than one volt or greater than 2 1/2 volts, replace the voltage regulator. If the reading is between one and two volts greater than the battery voltage, turn on the headlights and the heater blower. The voltage should not decrease more than 1/2 volt of the regulated voltage reading. Replace the regulator if voltage drop is greater than 1/2 volt below the regulated voltage.

Different parts of Ford electrical systems are connected together by

# Fix Your Ford

means of plug type connectors. These tend to make testing connections to the alternator and regulator difficult.

However, a simple continuity test of the field circuit is easily made and will in many cases disclose when an alternator is defective.

The only equipment needed to make such a test is a 12V No. 67 light bulb and socket, together with a starting battery and wiring as shown in Fig. L-8.

The procedure is to first disconnect the wiring harness at the alternator, taking care to note which wire is connected to the various terminals. Then connect one wire of the continuity tester to the frame of the alternator and the other to the terminal marked "F" or "FLD." The light bulb of the tester should light to full brilliance. If not, the field circuit is "open" and the alternator should be replaced.

## FORD AND AUTOLITE REGULATORS

As previously pointed out, the regulator, Fig. L-10, installed on the 1969 Thunderbird is of the transistor type and is integral with the alternator. It is not adjustable and if not calibrated correctly the entire unit is replaced.

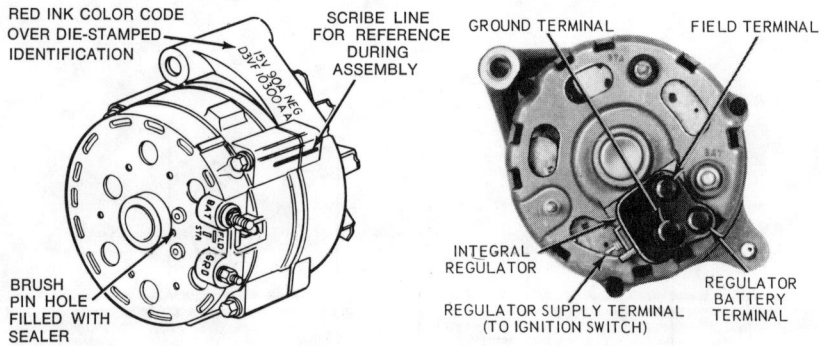

Fig. L-10. Left. 1973 alternator which has a capacity of 90 amp. Right. Note location of regulator as installed on some Autolite alternators.

The regulators installed on the 1968-1972 Ford cars, other than the Thunderbird unit are of the conventional type with a voltage limiter and field relay. However, these are not adjustable and a new unit is installed, should the charging rate be incorrect. On previous models, Fig. L-11, the Ford regulator is removed from the vehicle when making any adjustments. Unless accurate voltmeters are available, no attempt should be made to adjust the regulator.

To adjust the air gap of the field relay, remove the regulator from the vehicle and place a .010 to .018 in. feeler gauge on top of the coil core

## Alternator Service

closest to the contact points. Hold the armature down on the gauge. Do not push down on the contact spring arm. Bend the contact post arm, Fig. L-11, until the bottom contact just touches the upper contact.

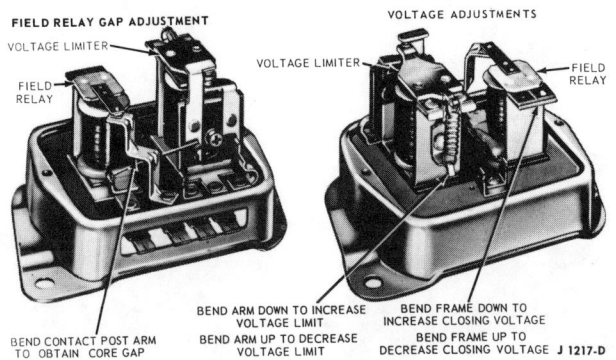

Fig. L-11. Adjustment points on regulator used on Ford alternator system 1964 to 1967. Starting with 1968 models, regulator was not adjustable.

The closing voltage adjustment is made by bending the relay frame, Fig. L-11. To increase the closing voltage bend the armature frame down, and to decrease the closing voltage bend the frame up.

The voltage limiter adjustment should be made on the regulator test stand and final adjustment must be made with the regulator at normal operating temperature. The voltage limiter is adjusted by bending the voltage limiter spring, Fig. L-11. To increase the voltage setting, bend the adjusting arm downward. To decrease the voltage setting bend the adjusting arm upward.

The erratic operation of the regulator, indicated by erratic movement of the voltmeter pointer during a voltage limiter test, may be caused by dirty or pitted regulator contacts. Vehicle ammeter pointer waver at certain critical engine speeds and electrical load is normal and is not a cause for regulator replacement.

## TRANSISTOR TYPE REGULATOR

A transistor type regulator, Fig. L-11a, was used on some 1968-1974 models. However, most models have been equipped with the electro-mechanical type regulator. The transistor type regulator controls the alternator voltage in a similar manner to the electro-mechanical type by regulating the alternator field current which is accomplished by the use of transistors and diodes. The only adjustment on the transistorized regulator is the voltage limiter adjustment. The adjustment is made with the regulator at normal operating temperature. Remove the top of the regulator mounting screws and remove the cover of the regulator. (Older

## Fix Your Ford

models remove the bottom of the regulator.) Use a fiber rod as a screwdriver to make this adjustment. Turn clockwise to increase voltage, Fig. L-11a.

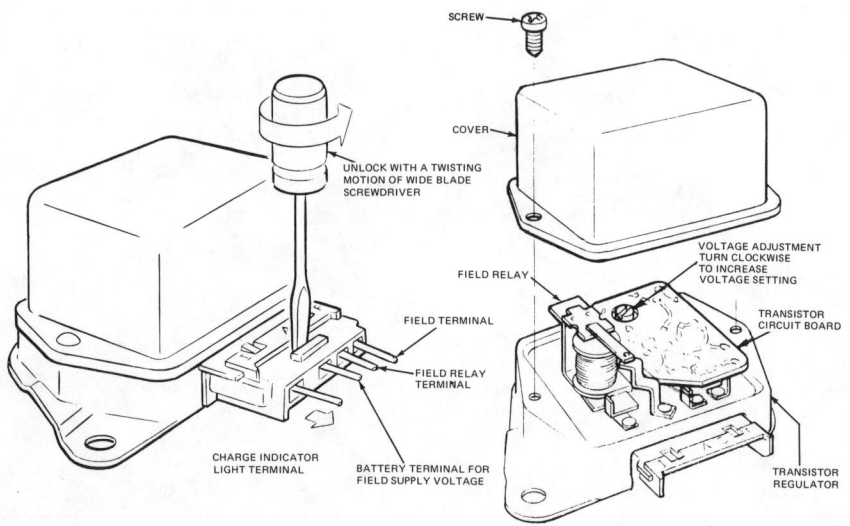

*Fig. L-11a. Transistorized alternator regulator.
(Courtesy Ford Customer Service. Div.)*

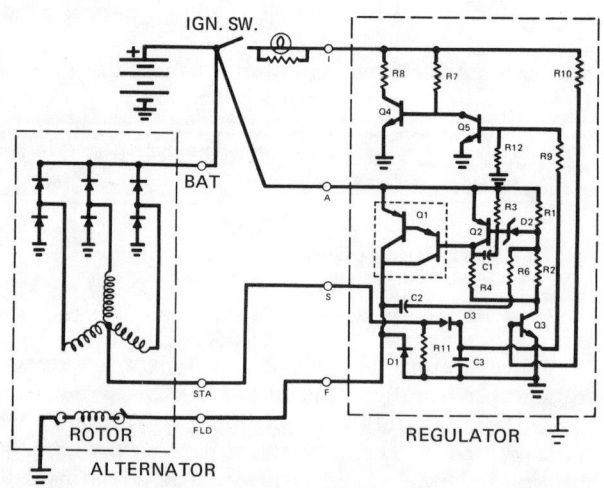

*Fig. L-11b. Charging system with electronic regulator and indicator lamp.*

## Alternator Service

### ALTERNATOR AND ELECTRONIC REGULATOR

A higher field current alternator and a completely solid state electronic voltage regulator were introduced in 1978. The regulator is used on systems that have an ammeter. It is color-coded for proper installation. No adjustment is required or possible.

Always use the correct alternator in the system being serviced. If the 1978 alternator is used on 1977 and prior systems, it will destroy the electromechanical regulator. Also, if an older model alternator is used with the new regulator, the system will have reduced output. NOTE: Never attempt to polarize or test alternator by grounding field circuit. This will destroy regulator.

### CHECKING THE DIODES

The diodes are devices which will carry current in one direction only and they are placed in the circuit of the alternator so that only direct current (current flowing in one direction) is supplied to the starting battery, ignition and other electrical equipment.

If special equipment is not available, the diodes can be tested simply for current flow. A diode in good condition will carry current in one direction only. To make such a test, connect the positive terminal of a 12V battery to one terminal of the diode. The other terminal of the diode is

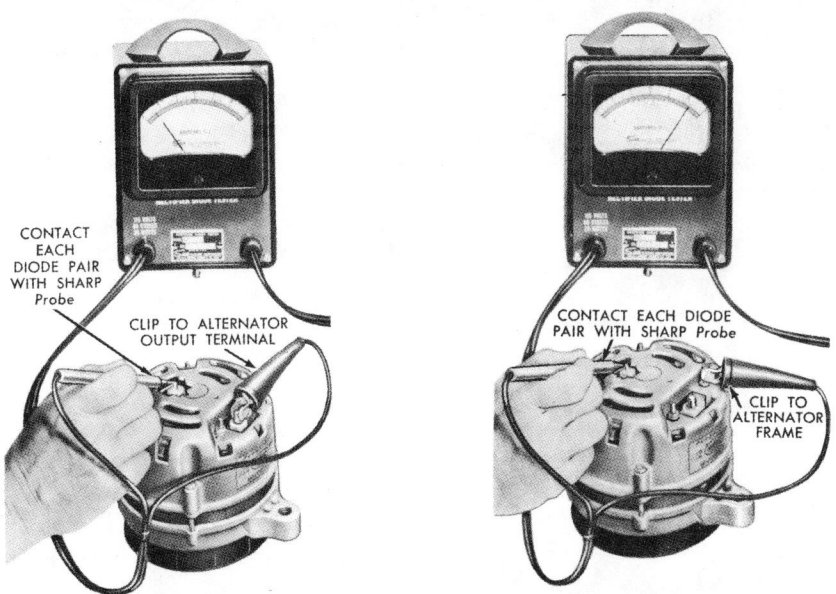

*Fig. L-12. Using an ohmmeter to check the condition of a diode.*

connected to a small No. 67 lamp bulb. The other terminal of the lamp bulb is then connected to the negative terminal of the battery. Then reverse the connections to the diode. Connected in one way the lamp bulb should light, but when the diode is connected in the opposite manner the lamp bulb should not light.

If an ohmmeter is available, such as shown in Fig. L-12, make the connections as shown. Each diode should show a reading of 60 ohms in one direction and infinity in the other.

## TROUBLE SHOOTING THE CHARGING SYSTEM

In case of discharged battery, check the following: Loose alternator or generator drive belt. Continued strain on battery. Defective wiring harness. Defective battery. Defective alternator or generator. Defective regulator or voltage limiter out-of-adjustment.

In case the charge indicator light stays on, or charge indicator gauge indicates constant discharge, check for the following conditions: Loose or broken drive belt. Loose connections or broken wires. Grounded wiring from alternator to regulator. Open 15 ohm resistor across charge indicator light. Defective alternator. Defective regulator. Defective gauge.

If lights fail prematurely, or battery uses excessive amount of water, check for the following conditions: Loose or corroded connections in charging system wiring. Defective regulator or high voltage limiter setting.

If charge indicator light flickers or charge indicator gauge fluctuates, check for the following conditions: Loose or damaged connections at battery, starter relay or alternator. Loose bulb or defective socket. Defective regulator.

If charge indicator light does not light when ignition switch is turned on, check for the following conditions: Burned out charge indicator bulb. Defective wiring. Regulator connections loose or disconnected. Defective regulator.

Check the drive belt to make sure that it has the proper tension. NEVER RUN THE ENGINE WITH THE BATTERY DISCONNECTED.

# Kinks on
# STARTER TESTING

Heavy cables, connectors and switches are used in the starting system because of the heavy current required while cranking the engine. The amount of resistance in the starting system must be kept at an absolute minimum to provide the maximum current for starter operation. Loose connections, corroded battery and relay contacts, and partly broken or undersize cables will result in slower than normal cranking speed and, in many cases, will prevent the starter from cranking the engine.

When the starter will not crank the engine, there are a number of tests which should be made before removing the starter for detailed examination. Starting motor trouble usually is evidenced by the failure of the starting motor to crank the engine or when the starter spins but does not crank the engine.

If the starting motor does not crank the engine when the ignition switch is turned on, the starting motor and starting circuit may be in good condition but the battery may be discharged. Therefore, the first point to be checked is the condition of the starting battery as outlined in the chapter entitled QUICK TESTS ON BATTERIES.

If the engine cranks but will not start, the trouble is in the engine, fuel system or ignition system and not in the starting system. If the engine will not crank, even with a booster battery connected, engine parts may be seized or the starter may be faulty. If the car has a manual shift transmission and will not start with a booster battery connected, attempt to start it by pushing or towing the car. If the engine starts, drive the car to a place where a complete check of the starting system can be made.

Do not tow or push a car equipped with an automatic transmission for more than 12 miles without raising the drive wheels from the ground. If a greater distance is necessary, disconnect the drive shaft.

If the engine will not crank and the starter relay does not click when the ignition switch is turned to "start" position, the battery may be discharged or the ignition switch, starter neutral switch or starter relay may be inoperative. In addition, the circuit may be open or contain a high resistance.

## STARTER TYPES

Two types of starters are used on recent model Ford cars. One is a positive engagement starter, Fig. M-1; the other is a solenoid actuated starter, Fig. M-2. The basic starter wiring diagram is shown in Fig. M-3.

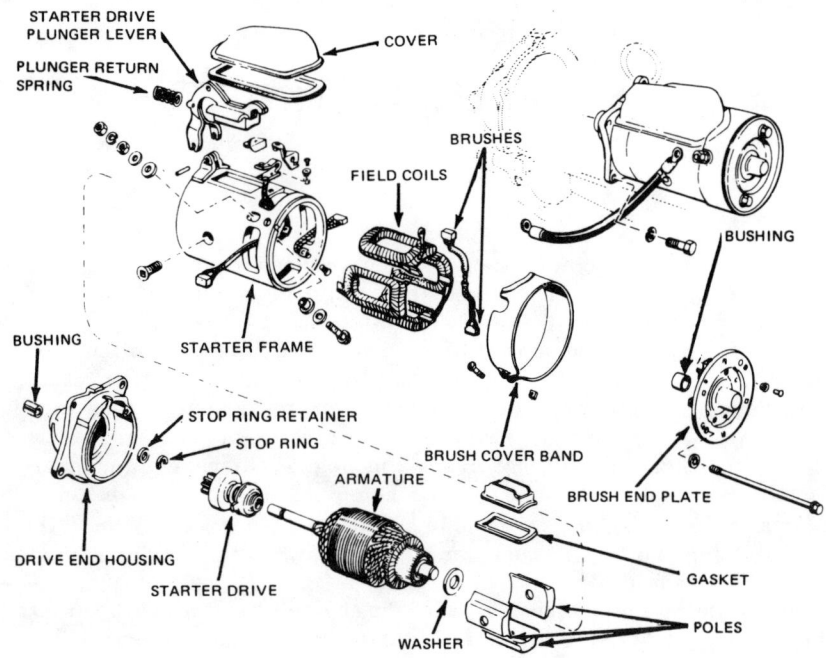

*Fig. M-1. Exploded view of positive engagement starter (except V-6 engine).*

## STARTER CIRCUIT CRANKING TEST

Excessive resistance in the starter circuit can be determined by making a starter circuit cranking test. Make the test connections as shown in Fig. M-4. Crank the engine with the ignition off. This is accomplished by disconnecting the push-on connector ("S") at the starter relay, and by connecting a remote control starter switch from the battery terminal of the starter relay to the "S" terminal of the relay.

The voltage drop in the circuit is indicated by the voltmeter (0 to 2 volt range). Maximum allowable drop is 0.5 volts with the voltmeter negative lead connected to the starter terminal and the positive lead connected to the battery positive post. See hookup No. 1 in Fig. M-4.

To make the next test, connect the voltmeter negative lead to the battery side of the starter relay. Leave the positive lead connected to the positive terminal of the battery. See hookup No. 2. Voltage drop should not exceed 0.1 volt. If greater, remove and clean battery cables. Clean post and relay terminal. Reinstall and retest.

Then, connect the voltmeter negative lead to the negative terminal of the battery. Again, leave the positive lead connected to the positive terminal of the battery. See hookup No. 3. Maximum allowable voltage

## Starter Testing

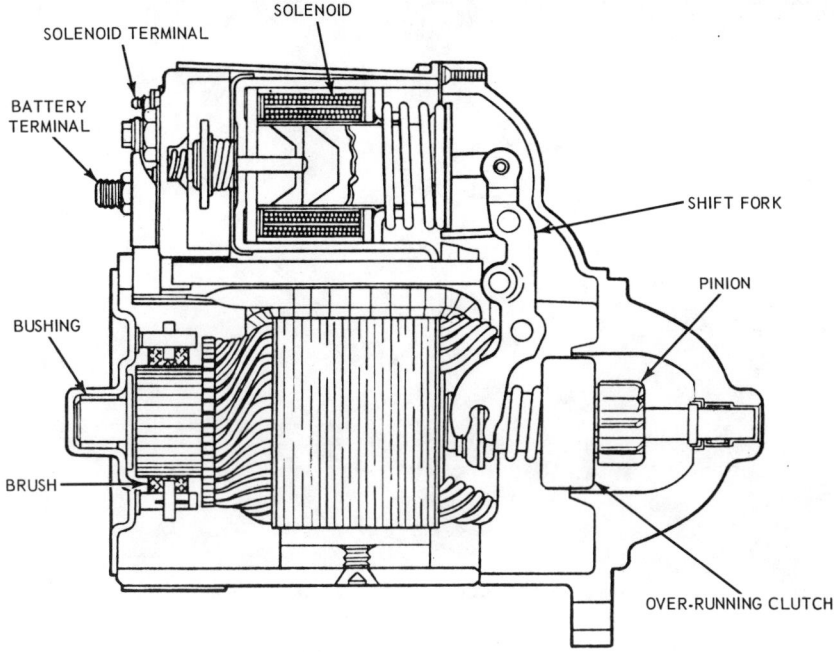

*Fig. M-2. Details of Autolite solenoid actuated starting motor as used on 400, 429 and 460 cu. in. engines, 1971–1975.*

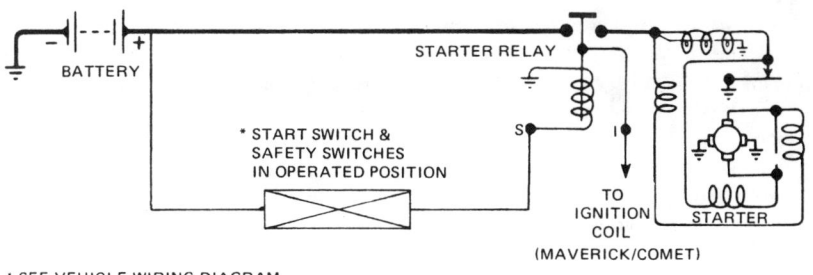

*Fig. M-3. Starting circuit of positive engagement starter.*

drop is 0.3 volt. If greater, replace relay and retest.

Finally, connect the voltmeter negative lead to the negative terminal of the battery. Move the positive lead to a good engine ground. See hookup No. 4 in Fig. M-4. Voltage drop should not exceed 0.3 volt. If greater, remove battery negative cable at engine ground connection. Clean cable and ground connection. Reinstall cable and retest.

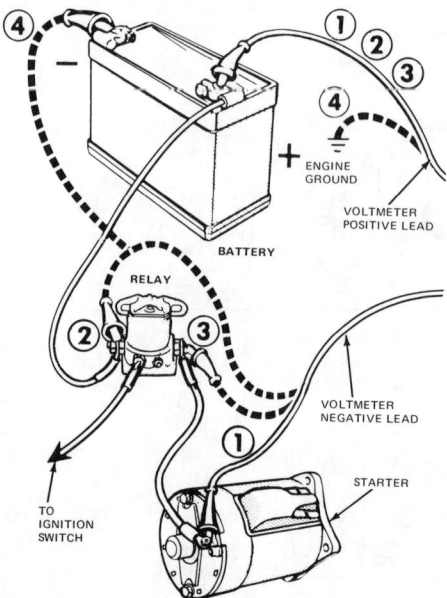

*Fig. M-4. Voltmeter test lead hookups to be used when making starter cranking circuit tests.*

## STARTER LOAD TEST

To make a starter load test, connect a carbon pile rheostat, a voltmeter and an ammeter as shown in Fig. M-5. Crank the engine with the ignition off and determine the exact reading on the voltmeter. This test is accomplished by disconnecting the push-on connector "S" at the starter relay, and by connecting a remote control starter switch from the positive battery terminal to the "S" terminal of the starter relay. The rheostat should be in maximum position. Stop cranking the engine and reduce the resistance of the carbon pile until the voltmeter indicates the same reading as obtained while the starter cranked the engine. The ammeter will show current draw under load.

## REMOVING THE STARTER

The procedure for removing the starter from the engine varies with different chassis and also with the type of engine. In most cases, it is a simple procedure. For example, consider the procedure on the 1978 Fairmont with the 2.3 litre engine and the Granada with the 250 cu. in. six cylinder engine. First, disconnect the negative battery cable. Then remove the positive battery cable from the engine compartment. Raise the vehicle on a hoist. Remove starter attaching bolts, permitting removal of the starter.

## Starter Testing

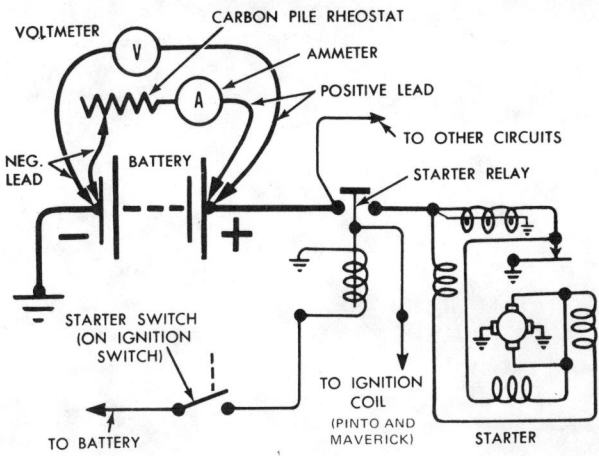

*Fig. M-5. Method of using a voltmeter, ammeter and carbon pile rheostat when making a starter load test.*

Starter removal on the 1978 Fairmont with the 200 cu. in. six cylinder engine requires a little different procedure. First, disconnect the negative battery cable from the battery terminal. Then, remove the top starter bolt. Also remove two nuts attaching the exhaust heat shield and remove the shield. Disconnect the starter cable from the starter. Raise the vehicle on a hoist. Remove wishbone brace. Remove the last two starter bolts. Remove the starter.

The procedure for removing the starter from the 1978 Granada with a 302 cu. in. V-8 is as follows: Disconnect negative battery cable. Raise vehicle on a hoist. Disconnect starter cable at starter. Remove through bolt and nut that attaches the engine mount insulator to the mounting bracket. Remove the two attaching bolts that hold the insulator to the engine block. Remove the insulator. Position a jack under the engine and raise it. Remove starter attaching bolts and remove starter.

# Fix Your Ford

For 1977: Above. Ford LTD Landau. Center. Maverick Sedan. Below. Mustang II 2 + 2.

# LIGHTING SYSTEM SERVICE

Cars with two headlamps use No. 2 sealed beam units. Each No. 2 unit has two filaments, one for low beam and one for high beam. Cars with four headlamps use No. 1 lamps inboard, No. 2 lamps outboard. Each No. 1 unit has only one filament. Locating tabs in both types of lamps permit installation in respective positions only.

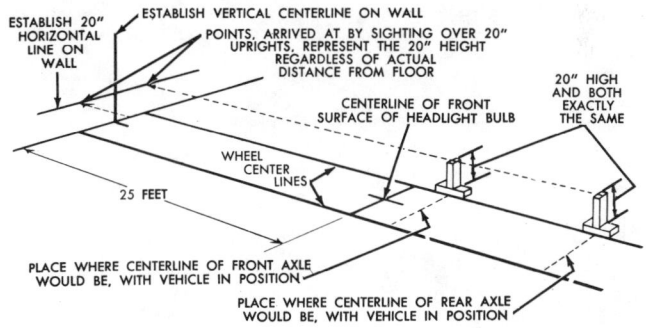

Fig. N-1. Floor plan used when aiming headlights.

## AIMING THE HEADLIGHTS

All headlight adjustments should be made with a half-full fuel tank plus or minus one gallon, with a person seated in the driver's seat, and a person seated in the right front passenger seat, the car unloaded and the trunk empty except for the spare tire and jacking equipment. Tires should be inflated to the recommended pressure. Before each adjustment bounce the car by pushing on the center of both the front and rear bumpers to level the car.

To align the No. 1 headlights by means to a wall screen, select a level portion of a shop floor and lay out the floor and wall as shown in Fig. N-1.

Establish the headlight horizontal center line by subtracting 20 in. from the actual measured height of the headlight lens center from the floor and adding this difference to the 20 in. reference line obtained by sighting over the uprights to obtain dimension B, Fig. N-2, and parallel to the headlight horizontal center line. Then draw the headlight vertical center lines on the screen as measured on the car, dimension A, Fig. N-2.

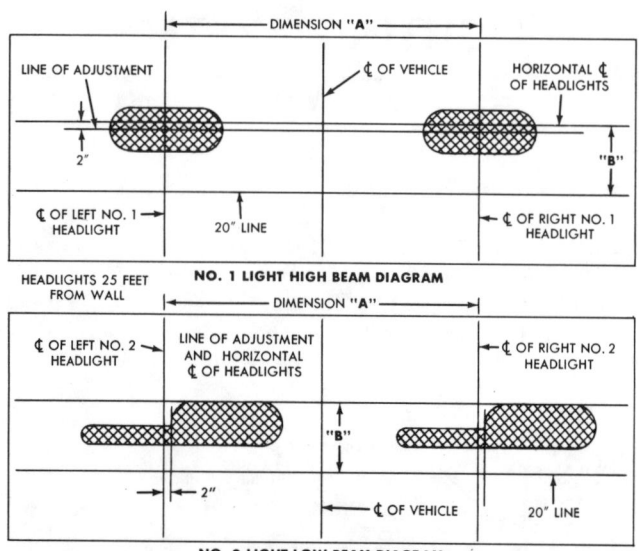

Fig. N-2. Light patterns for headlight aiming.

Adjust each No. 1 headlight beam as shown in Fig. N-2. Cover the No. 2 lights when making this adjustment. Some states may not approve of the two inch dimension for the No. 1 headlight. Check the law in the applicable state as a three inch dimension may be required.

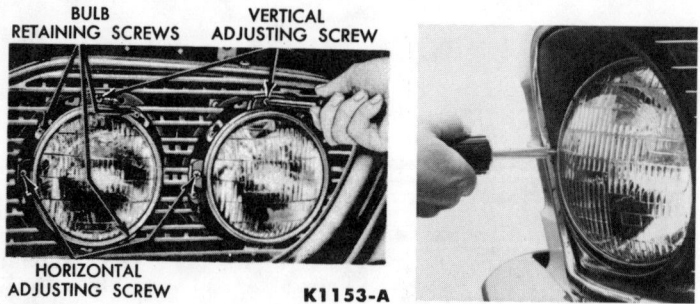

Fig. N-3. Left. Location of headlight adjustments. Fig. N-3a. Right. Externally adjustable headlights on some 1970 cars.

To adjust the No. 2, or outboard lights, a different wall chart, as shown in the lower portion of Fig. N-2 is required. Dimension B for the No. 2 lights in the same as B for the No. 1 lights. Dimension A is as measured on the car. Note that the line of adjustment of the No. 2 lights is the horizontal center line of the No. 2 lights. Turn the headlights to low beam and adjust each No. 2 light as shown in Fig. N-2.

Each headlight can be adjusted by means of two screws located under

## Lighting System Service

the headlight trim ring, as shown in Figs. N-3, and N-4. Always bring each beam into final position by turning the adjusting screws clockwise.

Some 1970 models can be adjusted without removing bezels or frames. Access holes are provided through which a screwdriver can be inserted to make the adjustment, Fig. N-3a.

### HEADLIGHT BULB REPLACEMENT

To replace the headlight bulbs which are of the sealed beam type, remove the retaining screws and headlight trim ring, Fig. N-4. Loosen the retaining ring screws, Fig. N-3, rotate the retaining ring counterclockwise and remove it. The headlight bulb can now be pulled forward far enough to disconnect the wiring assembly plugs. Plug in the new sealed beam light, making sure it is the correct type. Also be sure the locating tabs are placed in the positioning slots. Aim the headlights as described previously and then install the headlight bulb retaining ring and trim ring.

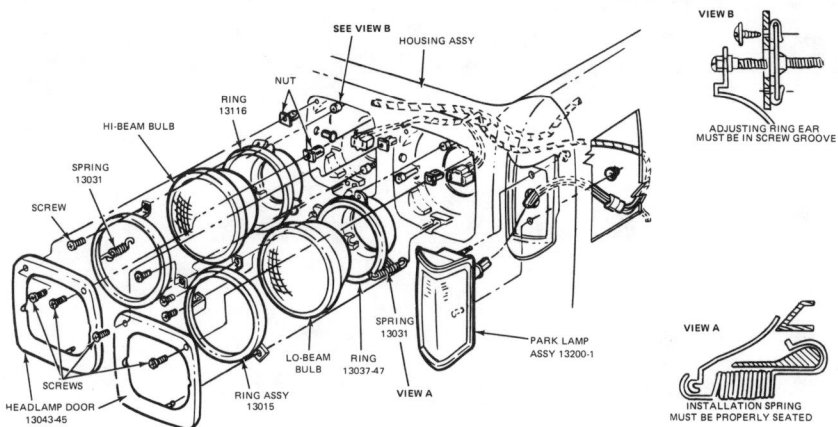

*Fig. N-4. Typical dual headlight bulb removal for recent models.*

### HEADLIGHT TROUBLE SHOOTING

When none of the headlights will light, check the following:
1. Loose battery cable.
2. Loose "disconnect" or broken wire from battery to headlight switch.
3. Defective headlight switch.
4. Disconnected or broken wire from headlight switch to high or low beam selector switch.
5. Loose or broken wire to headlamp.
6. Defective beam selector switch.
7. Defective or improperly adjusted alternator voltage regulator (if all headlamps are burned out).

# Fix Your Ford

When individual headlights do not light, check the following:
1. Burned out headlamp.
2. Loose or broken wire to headlamp.
3. Poor ground connection.

When headlamps burn out repeatedly, check the following:
1. Loose or corroded electrical connections.
2. Excessive vibration.
3. Defective or improperly adjusted alternator voltage regulator.

When both low beam headlamps do not light, check the following:
1. Defective beam selector switch.
2. Loose or broken wire to headlamps.
3. Both low beam filaments burned out.

When headlights are dim, check voltage at the lights. With the engine running and after the lights have been burning for approximately five minutes, the voltage at the headlights should be at least 11.25V for the

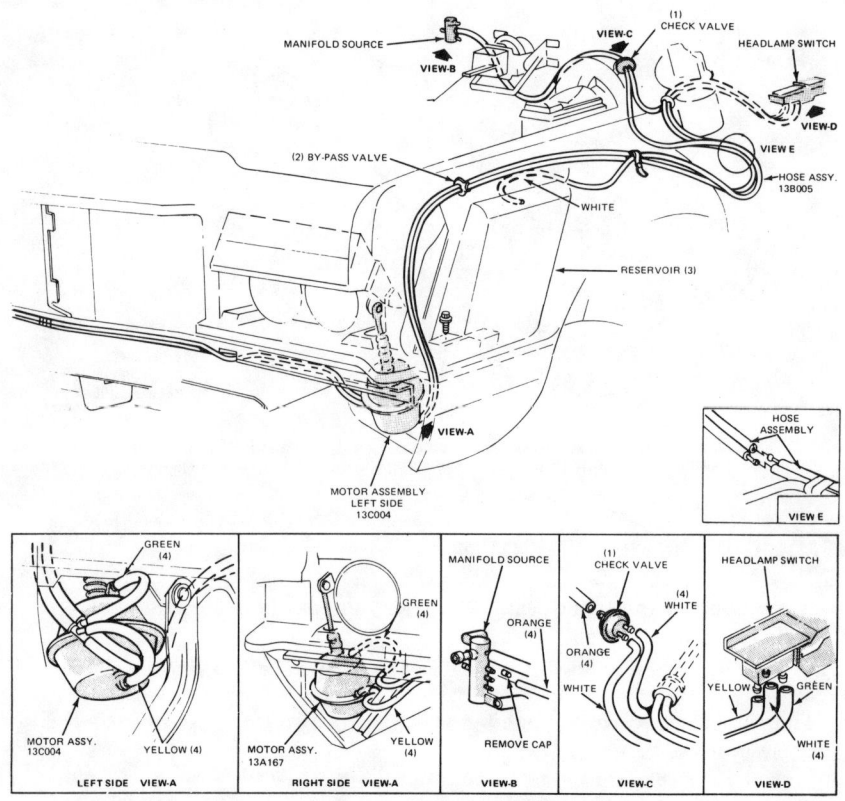

*Fig. N-5. Details of headlight covers and vacuum control system, typical of those used in 1978 and previous years.*

## Lighting System Service

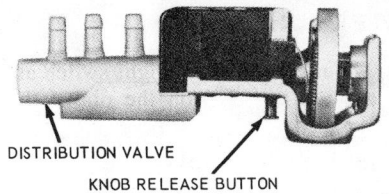

Fig. N-6. Headlight switch with distribution valve.

12V systems and 5.25V for the 6V systems. If the voltage is less than specified, there is a loose or dirty connection somewhere in the circuit which must be corrected. Also check the battery, paying particular attention to battery and ground connections.

## VACUUM CONTROLLED HEADLIGHT COVERS

The headlight covers on some late model Fords are opened and closed by the use of a vacuum motor, Fig. N-5. The headlight switch, when pulled full out, actuates a distribution valve located on the back of the headlight switch, Fig. N-6. The distribution valve applies vacuum to the vacuum motor operating the headlight covers. The distribution valve also provides a vacuum relief or exhaust port to that side of the vacuum motor diaphragm to which the vacuum is not applied.

A cover hinge spring, attached to each cover, functions as an over-center type spring which helps hold the covers in the open or closed position. Vacuum applied to either side of the vacuum motor diaphragm during opening or closing overcomes this spring tension.

In case of a vacuum loss, the covers can be opened or closed manually. To open the covers, pull the headlight switch full out and lift the covers by hand. To close the covers, push the switch all the way in and close the covers by hand.

Headlight covers should be opened when washing the car to clean the headlights for safer nightime driving.

If the headlight covers do not operate with the engine on or off, remove the white striped hose from the check valve that leads to the headlight switch and check for vacuum at the check valve. Check the reservoir and hose for leaks. Also check for vacuum through the green hose at the top of the cover control motor. If headlight covers do not operate with the engine off but do operate with the engine on, remove the vacuum hose from the center port of the junction block on the dash panel. With the headlight switch off, apply vacuum with a vacuum probe to the port on the junction block and check for a steady reading.

## DOME LIGHT

To replace the light bulb in the dome light, remove the two screws retaining the dome light lens and bezel. Remove the light and the bezel and then replace the bulb.

# Fix Your Ford

## INSTRUMENT CLUSTER BULBS

The instrument panel light bulbs, except for the right turn indicator and the seat belt bulbs, can be replaced by reaching under the instrument panel and pulling the light bulbs from the cluster. To replace the right turn indicator and/or seat belt bulb, it will be necessary to remove the ash tray and ash tray slide bracket and reach through the opening to replace the bulbs.

## MECHANICAL STOPLIGHT SWITCH

Prior to 1965, the stoplight switch was mounted on the end of the master cylinder and was hydraulically operated. In 1965 a mechanical stoplight switch, Fig. N-7, was adopted. The mechanical stoplight switch assembly is installed on the pin of the brake pedal arm so that it straddles the master cylinder push rod. The switch assembly is a slip fit on the pedal arm pin and thus the switch assembly moves with the pedal arm whenever the brake pedal is depressed.

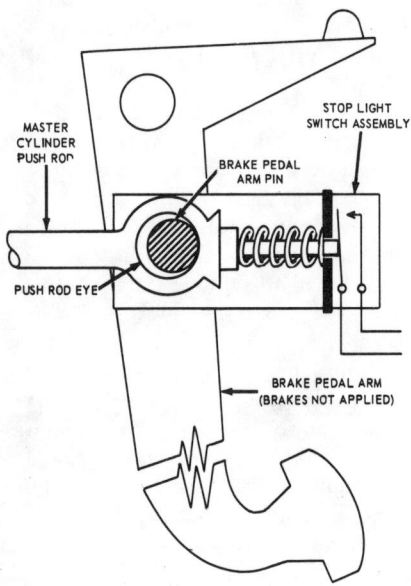

*Fig. N-7. Details of mechanical stoplight switch.*

The pedal arm pin has a designed-in clearance with the eye of the master cylinder push rod, Fig. N-7. Because of this clearance, whenever the brake pedal is pushed forward, the stoplight switch contacts, moving with the pedal arm, are actually pushed against the end of a master cylin-

## Lighting System Service

der push rod, through the switch actuating pin. It is this movement of the switch, with respect to the actuating pin and master cylinder push rod, that closes the switch contacts completing the circuit to the stoplight.

### BACK-UP LIGHT SWITCH

On vehicles equipped with a steering column gear selector lever, the switch is located on the lower end of the column in the passenger compartment. The switch can be replaced by removing the screws retaining the switch and disconnecting the lead wires.

On vehicles equipped with a shift lever directly over either the standard or automatic transmissions, the back-up light switch is located on the transmission.

### HEADLIGHT DIMMER SWITCH

To replace a headlight dimmer switch, Fig. N-8, lay the floor mat back from the area of the switch and remove the mounting screws, Fig. N-8. Disconnect the wire terminal block from the switch. The switch can then be lifted from its position.

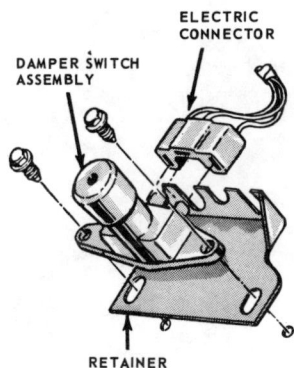

Fig. N-8. Headlight dimmer switch installation. Note electrical plug connector.

### HEADLIGHT SWITCH

To remove the headlight switch, first disconnect the battery ground cable. Remove the control knob and shaft by pressing the knob release button on the switch housing, Fig. N-9, with the knob in the full "On" position. Pull the knob out of the switch. Remove the bezel nut and lower switch assembly. Disconnect the multiple plug to the switch, also disconnect the three vacuum hoses, Fig. N-6, (if the vehicle is equipped with headlight doors). Remove the switch from the vehicle.

# Fix Your Ford

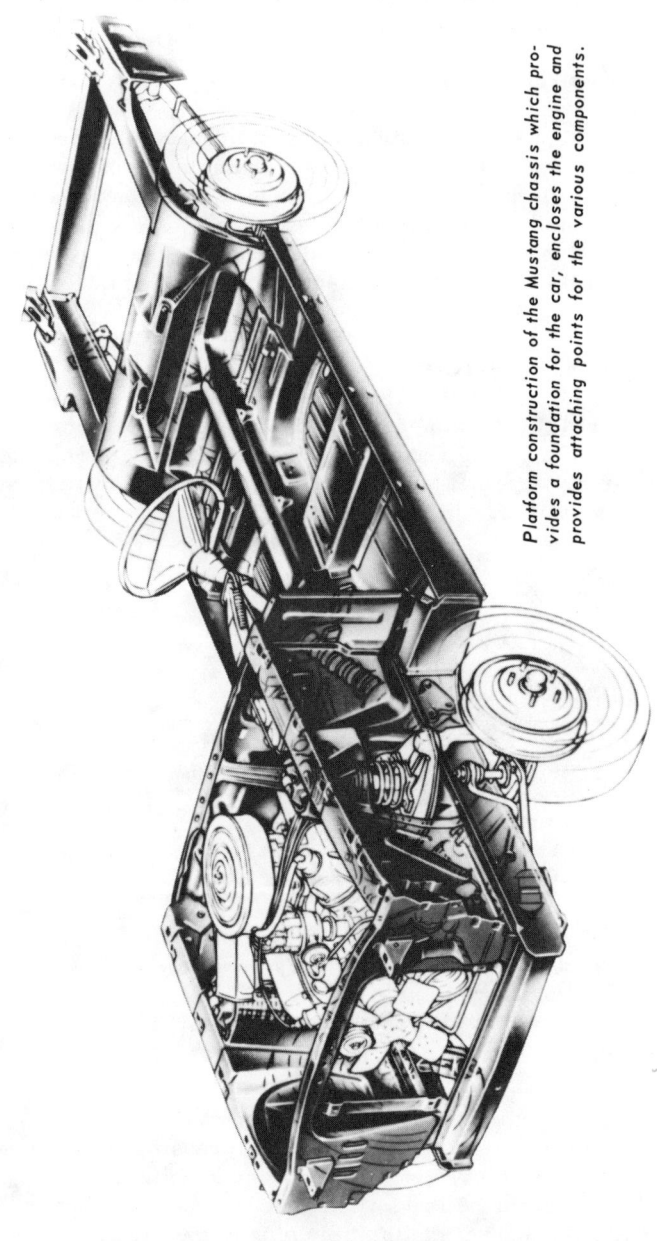

Platform construction of the Mustang chassis which provides a foundation for the car, encloses the engine and provides attaching points for the various components.

## Lighting System Service

To install the headlight switch, connect the multiple plug to the switch, also the vacuum hoses, if so equipped. Position the switch to the instrument panel and install the bezel nut. Install the knob and shaft assembly by inserting it all the way into the switch until a disconnect click is heard. In some instances it may be necessary to rotate the shaft slightly until it engages the switch contact carrier.

The job is completed after connecting the battery ground cable and checking the operation of the switch.

## CIRCUIT BREAKER AND FUSES

The electrical circuits of Ford vehicles are protected by circuit breakers, fuses and fuse links. Generally, two circuit breakers are employed. On older models, both units are incorporated in the headlight switch. On later models, one circuit breaker is mounted in the headlight switch to protect the taillights, parking lights, license plate lights and side marker lights. A separate circuit breaker protects the headlights, Fig. N-9. Other electrical circuits are protected by fuse links, Fig. N-10, or fuses, Fig. N-11. The fuse panel usually is mounted in the glove box or behind the instrument panel.

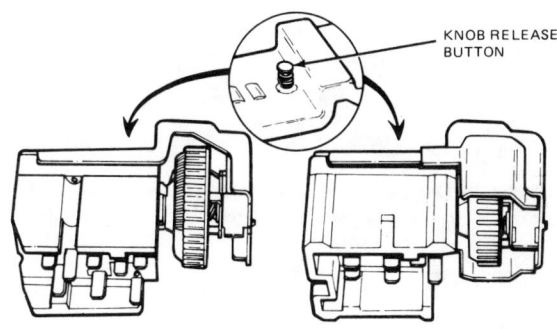

*Fig. N-9. Headlight switch on 1978 cars. Previous models are similar.*

## FUSE LINK

In addition to the conventional fuses, Fig. N-11, the electrical system is also protected by fuse links. The fuse link is a short piece of insulated wire, integral with the engine compartment wiring harness. It is several wire gages smaller than circuit which it protects. Production links are black. Replacement links are green or black depending on usage. All fuse links have the word FUSE LINK printed on the insulation.

The fuse link burns out, thus protecting the alternator or wiring, when heavy current flows such as when a booster battery is connected incorrectly, or a short or ground occurs in the circuit.

A burned out fuse link may have bare wire ends protruding from the insulation, or it may only have expanded, or bubbled the insulation. If a burned out fuse link cannot be located by visually inspecting the wiring harness, make a circuit continuity test.

On Ford, Fairlane, Falcon, LTD II, Maverick, Fairmont, Granada and Pinto, there are two fuse links, Fig. N-10. To test the link that protects the alternator, first check the battery and make sure it is up to voltage. Then use the voltmeter to test for voltage at the BAT terminal of the alternator. No voltage on the voltmeter indicates that the fuse link is probably burned out.

To check the fuse link that protects the vehicle equipment: First, check the battery's state of charge. If satisfactory, turn on the headlights. If the headlights do not light, the fuse link is probably "open." This test can also be used to check the single fuse link installed on Mustang cars. See Fig. N-10.

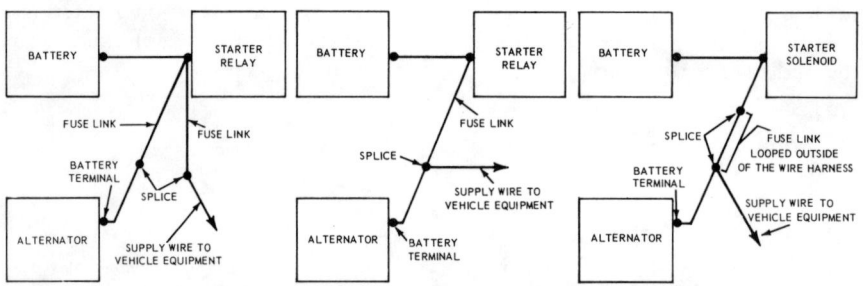

*Fig. N-10. Fuse link installations typical of setups used on various recent model Ford cars. Left. Ford, LTD II, Fairmont, Granada and Pinto. Center. Mustang II. Right. Thunderbird.*

## TURN SIGNAL SERVICE

The usual trouble with turn signals is burned out bulbs. A burnout generally is indicated by a change in the rate of clicking of the flasher, as well as failure of the bulb to light.

If turn indicator lights are inoperative, check for: Burned out bulbs. Loose sockets or poor ground at lamp housing. Burned out fuse. Loose or broken wire from ignition switch to flasher. Defective flasher. Loose or broken wire from flasher to indicator switch. Defective indicator switch. Broken, shorted or loose wires from switch to lights.

If turn lights operate incorrectly, look for: Broken, shorted or loose wires from switch to lights. Defective turn indicator switch. Faulty flasher. Burned out bulb.

If turn indicator cancels improperly, the trouble may result from the cam being improperly positioned on the steering wheel hub, or the coil spring on the switch plate assembly may be loose or weak.

# Lighting System Service

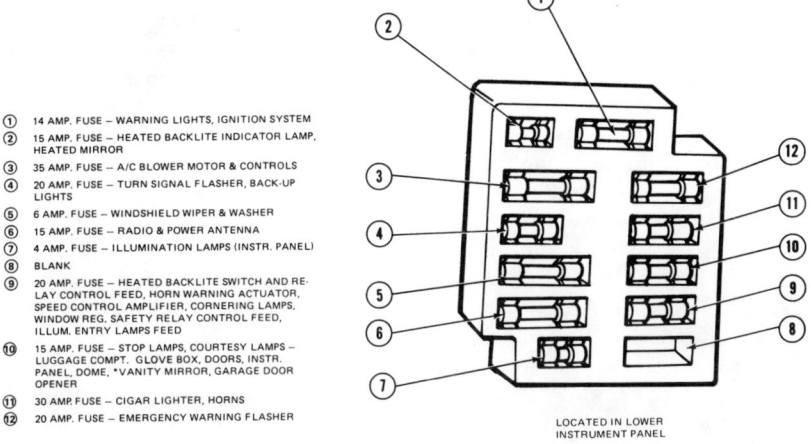

Fig. N-11. Fuse and circuit breaker panel as installed on 1978 Granada. Panels installed on other models vary in detail.

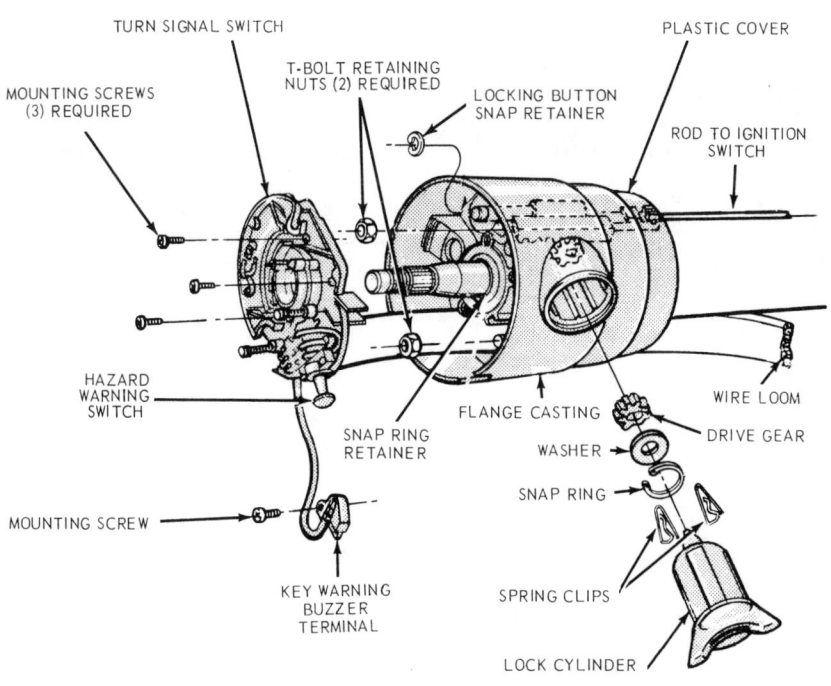

Fig. N-12. Details of turn signal switch as installed on some 1970–1976 models.

## Fix Your Ford

To replace the turn signal switch on 1966-68 models, disconnect the battery ground cable. Remove the horn button. Remove the steering wheel and turn signal handle. Next remove the screws and turn switch from the steering column tube. Remove connector blocks at steering column and release tabs one at a time and remove wires from block connectors. From lower portion of column, remove cover from wiring assembly and tie a cord to wire ends. Remove switch from top of column, feeding wire and cord up the column. Attach wire ends of new switch to cord and feed wires down through column. Remove cord and install wiring cover and complete the installation in reverse order.

In 1968-1970 on some models, the emergency warning flasher switch was incorporated with the turn signal, Fig. N-12. To remove the assembly, first disconnect the battery ground cable and then remove the steering wheel hub and steering wheel.

Remove the two screws retaining the steering column finish covers and remove covers. Pry the wire cover from the steering column. Disconnect the flasher switch, and multiple plug connector at the base of the steering column. Remove the wires and terminals from the connector plug. Record the color code and location of each wire before removing it from the connector plug. Remove the wire cover sleeve, if so equipped.

Unscrew the turn signal lever. If the vehicle is equipped with a speed control unit, it will be necessary to separate the speed control wires from the flasher switch wires to allow for removal of the turn signal lever. Remove the screws retaining flasher switch and wire assembly to the steering column and pull the assembly from the column.

To remove the turn signal switch on 1970 to 1972 models, Fig. N-12, disconnect negative battery cable, then remove the steering wheel trim pad and the steering wheel. To remove the steering wheel, work from underside of wheel spoke and remove the crash pad attaching screws. Lift pad from wheel. Remove the steering wheel nut and remove the wheel. Do not use a knock off type puller. Then remove the three screws attaching the turn signal switch. Disconnect the quick coupler at the lower end of the steering column. Remove the turn signal lever. Lift the turn signal switch over the steering shaft and lay to one side.

To remove the turn signal/hazard flasher switch and wire assembly on 1974-1977 cars: First, remove retaining screw from underside of each steering wheel spoke. Next, lift off horn switch trim cover and medallion as an assembly. Disconnect horn switch wires from terminals.

Remove steering wheel retaining nut. Pull steering wheel from shaft, using a puller designed for this purpose. Remove turn signal switch lever by unscrewing it from steering column. Remove shroud from underside of steering column. Disconnect steering column wire connecting plugs from bracket, Fig. N-14. Remove screws that secure switch assembly to steering column.

Most flasher units are slot-mounted. To remove, reach under dash panel and disconnect wiring plug. Rotate flasher unit 90 deg. counterclockwise to disengage it from slot. To install, reverse this procedure.

## Lighting System Service

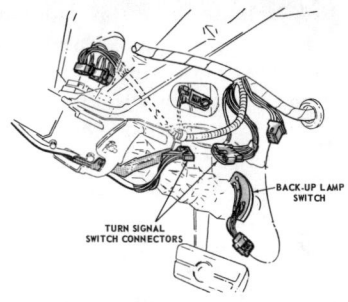

*Fig. N-14. Typical steering column wire connectors.*

## CHARGE INDICATOR LIGHT

Either an ammeter or a red light is used to indicate whether or not the alternator is charging. When the light glows, the alternator is not supplying current. The red indicator light is connected between the ignition switch and the "I" terminal of the regulator, Fig. L-5.

## DUAL BRAKE WARNING LIGHT

The dual brake system has a dual brake warning light and switch incorporated in the system. The function of the warning system is to indicate a failure of either the front or rear brake system.

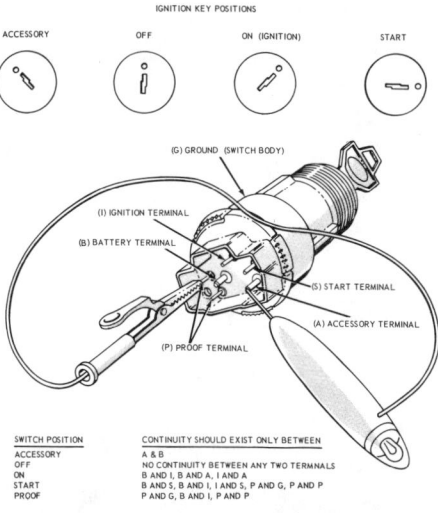

| SWITCH POSITION | CONTINUITY SHOULD EXIST ONLY BETWEEN |
|---|---|
| ACCESSORY | A & B |
| OFF | NO CONTINUITY BETWEEN ANY TWO TERMINALS |
| ON | B AND I, B AND A, I AND A |
| START | B AND S, B AND I, I AND S, P AND G, P AND P |
| PROOF | P AND G, B AND I, P AND P |

*Fig. N-15. Method of testing ignition switch.*

## Fix Your Ford

The switch assembly is located on the pressure differential valve on the master cylinder and activates a dual warning light located on the instrument panel. When the ignition switch is turned on to the "start" position, a dual brake warning light provides a visual indication that the warning light lamp is functional. If the dual brake warning light comes on when the ignition switch is turned to the "ON" or the "ACC" position, one portion of the dual brake system has become inoperative. If the light does not glow when the ignition switch is on, disconnect the bulb ground circuit at the sender switch and ground the switch side of the bulb. The light should glow. If the light checks satisfactorily, check for an open circuit in the wiring harness from the sender switch to the proof terminal of the ignition switch. If the light does not glow, install a new bulb. If that does not correct the trouble, check to be sure that current is reaching the bulb.

If brake warning light will not go out with the ignition switch on and the brakes in good condition, disconnect the ground circuit of the bulb at the sender switch. The light should go out. If the light continues to burn, check for an open circuit in the wiring harness and repair as required. If the light goes out, test the sender switch with a self-powered test light and if necessary replace the switch.

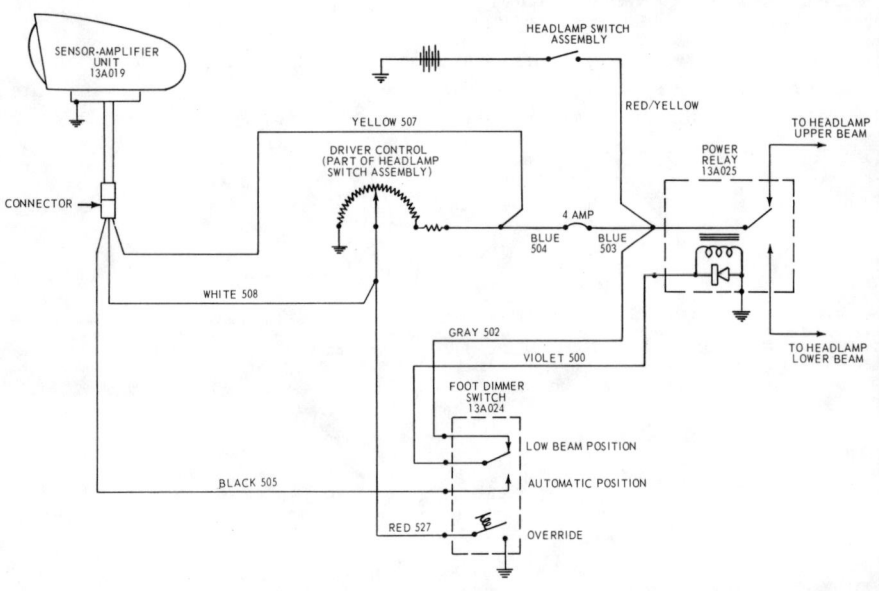

*Wiring diagram of 1971–1977 automatic headlight dimmer electrical system.*

# ACCESSORY AND INSTRUMENT SERVICE

## HEAT INDICATOR SERVICE

The temperature indicating system consists of a sending unit and a temperature gauge mounted on the instrument panel. The sending unit is located in the intake manifold on recent V-8s, in the engine block on 2800 cc engines, in the cylinder head on Sixes and on older engines in general. A circuit schematic is shown in Fig. O-1. The principle of operation is the same as for a fuel gauge. Test procedures are given on

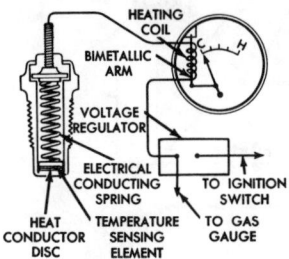

*Fig. O-1. Electrical circuit of temperature gauge.*

the following pages.

To test sending unit: Start engine and run to operating temperature. If no reading is indicated on gauge, check sending unit-to-gauge wire by removing it from sending unit and grounding it. If gauge still does not indicate temperature, wire is defective.

On recent models, the temperature indicating system provides the driver with a warning indication of engine coolant operating temperature by means of indicator lights. This system, Fig. O-2, consists of a temperature switch, or sending unit, mounted in the intake manifold on eight cylinder cars, or cylinder head for six cylinder cars, lead wires and two temperature indicator lights mounted on the instrument panel. The lights in the instrument panel are identified by words HOT or red color and COLD on blue color.

When the engine is cold and the ignition switch is on, the (cold) blue light glows and remains on until the engine begins to approach operating temperature. When the temperature of the engine coolant reaches approximately 125 deg. F., the cold light will go out indicating the engine has reached 125 deg. F. or more.

Should the temperature of the engine coolant reach approximately 245 deg. F., the (hot) red warning light will glow indicating that the engine is overheated. The (hot) red light does not indicate low coolant level.

These indicating lights are controlled by the temperature switch. The temperature switch has a temperature-sensitive bimetallic arm which completes the circuit through the switch body to the engine ground. With the ignition switch in start position, the (hot) red light should glow even though the engine is cold, thus proving that the light bulb is operable. A set of contacts in the ignition switch (normally opened) completes the proving circuit to ground in the start position.

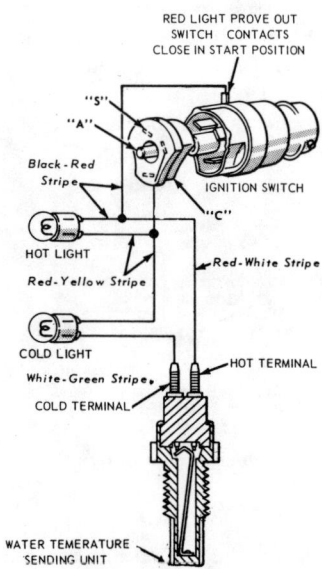

*Fig. O-2. Late type temperature indicating system.*

If the cold temperature light does not light when the ignition switch is on, Figs. O-2 and O-3, disconnect the bulb ground circuit lead at the cold terminal, Fig. O-3, of the temperature switch and ground the lead. The cold light should come on. If the cold light operates, then check the sender switch for proper ground and ground the switch as necessary. If the switch ground is satisfactory, it will be necessary to replace the temperature switch.

If the hot temperature light does not go out with the engine running, check as follows: With the engine temperature below 245 deg. F., turn the ignition switch on and the light should not come on. If the light does not come on, connect a 12V test light from the positive terminal of the battery to the hot terminal of the temperature switch, Fig. O-3. If the test light comes on, replace the temperature switch.

## Accessory, Instrument Service

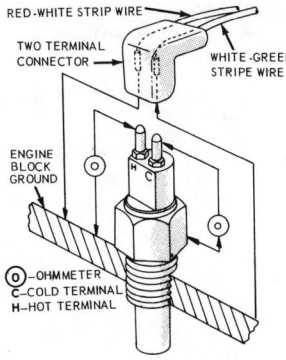

*Fig. O-3. Method of testing temperature switch and HOT and COLD lights.*

## HINTS ON SERVICING FUEL GAUGES

The fuel indicating system consists of a sender unit located in the fuel tank and a fuel gauge mounted on the instrument panel, Fig. O-4. Also,

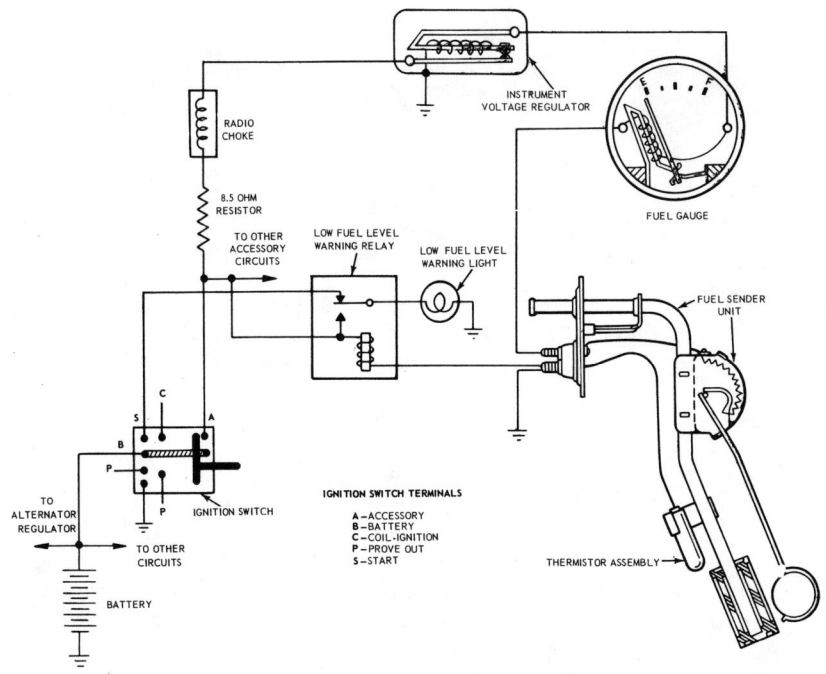

*Fig. O-4. Fuel level indicating and low fuel warning systems.*

## Fix Your Ford

most recent models are also equipped with a low level indicating system which consists of the thermistor assembly attached to the fuel sender outlet tube located in the fuel tank, Fig. O-4, the low fuel relay, a 45 ohm ballast resistor in parallel with the relay coil and the low level light(s) located on the instrument panel.

To test the fuel gauge, first check the instrument voltage regulator, Fig. O-4, by disconnecting the fuel gauge lead from the terminal of the sending unit. Connect the lead of a 12 volt test light or the positive lead of a voltmeter (20 volt scale) to the gauge lead that was disconnected from the sender unit, Fig. O-4. Connect the other test lead to the ground

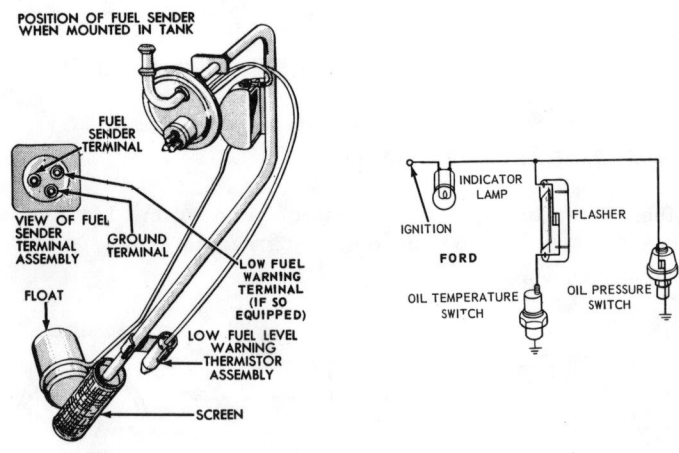

Fig. O-5. Left. Fuel level warning sender assembly.
Fig. O-6. Right. Oil pressure warning system.

and turn on the ignition switch. A flashing light or pulsating voltage will indicate that the voltage regulator is in good condition. If the regulator is satisfactory but the gauge is inaccurate, the gauge should be calibrated. If the voltage reading is steady or the test light stays on, the regulator should be replaced. If no voltage is indicated, check for proper ground or open circuit.

To test the sending unit, remove the unit from the tank, Fig. O-5. The resistance should be 8 to 12 ohms with the float in the upward position and 60-86 ohms in the empty or down position. If these specifications are not met, replace the unit.

Low fuel level system tests are made as follows: Turn the ignition switch to the ON position and the warning light should light. If not, test the bulb and the supply of current. To check the low level warning relay, shown in Fig. O-4, disconnect the electrical plug at fuel sender. With ignition switch on, ground the wire lead to the relay at the female plug.

## Accessory, Instrument Service

The relay should close and light the light. If the light is not lighted, replace the relay. To test the low fuel thermistor, remove the sending unit from the tank and with the sender still attached to the wire harness, turn ignition switch ON and indicator light should light. If light and relay had proved satisfactory in previous tests, but light does not now light, replace the fuel sender.

## OIL PRESSURE, CHARGE INDICATORS

All models are equipped with a red indicator light which flashes on when the oil pressure is below a safe value. The light should come on when the ignition switch is first turned on, and it should go out when the engine comes up to speed. The light is connected between the oil pressure switch unit and the coil or ignition terminal of the ignition switch, Fig. O-6.

To test the charge indicator light, turn the ignition switch on with the engine stopped. The light should come on. If it does not, the bulb is burned out or the wire to the light is defective.

An open resistor wire in the Ford alternator charging system wiring harness will usually cause the charge indicator light to stay on until the engine speed is increased to several thousand rpm. This effect will be noticed each time the engine is started. In some cases the light will not go out at all. The charge indicator light may be tested with the use of a test light containing a No. 67 bulb. Disconnect the regulator plug from the regulator. Turn the ignition switch to the "ACC" position. Touch one test probe from the test light to the ignition terminal and the other to the regulator base. The test light will come on if the circuit is in proper working order. If the 15 ohm resistor or circuit is open, the indicator light will operate at full brightness and the test light will be out. The voltage regulator should then be replaced.

## ELECTRIC CLOCK

On late model Ford cars, the adjustment of the clock is automatic. If the clock runs slow or fast, merely reset the clock to the proper time. This action adjusts the clock automatically. Turning the knob clockwise, the clock will go faster. By turning the knob counterclockwise, the clock will go slower. The clock fuse is in the fuse panel which is mounted on the dashboard above and to the right of the brake pedal.

## SPEEDOMETER SERVICE

Trouble with the speedometer will be caused by a defective speedometer instrument itself, or by breakage of the flexible shaft, or drive cable, which connects the instrument to the transmission.

In most cases, it will be found that the drive cable has broken. After disconnecting the cable at the transmission and at the instrument end, the two broken parts of the cable are withdrawn from housing.

# Fix Your Ford

It is usually necessary to cut replacement cables to the desired length and the necessary instructions for cutting the cable and attaching the end fittings to the cable are included in the kit parts.

Always lubricate the cable before installing it in the housing. Lubricants designed for the purpose are available.

After installing the cable in the housing, attach the housing end cable to the instrument head, taking care to turn the cable until it engages the tongue in the instrument. Then connect the lower end to the transmission.

## REMOVING SPEEDOMETER HEAD

On earlier models it was not difficult to remove the speedometer head from the instrument panel as it was held in position with small clips. On more recent models, because of the routing of the cable, it is usually necessary to remove the molding from the instrument panel. Then remove the panel. On some installations it is also necessary to remove other instruments in order to obtain access to the speedometer.

Repair of the speedometer is usually performed by specialists.

## WINDSHIELD WIPER ARM AND BLADE REMOVAL

To remove the windshield wiper arm and blade assembly on most models, swing the arm and blade away from the windshield and insert a 3/32 in. rod (a drill can be used) through the pin hole. The arm can now be pulled from the pivot shaft. Leave the pin in the shaft until after the installation of the new blade assembly. On other models the procedure is the same, except that it is not necessary to insert the 3/32 in. pin.

On 1974-1975 Ford, Thunderbird and Torino models, remove the windshield wiper blade as follows:

Raise the blade end of the arm off the windshield and move the slide latch away from the pivot shaft. This will unlock the wiper arm from the pivot shaft and hold the blade end of the arm off the glass at the same time.

The wiper arm can now be pulled off the pivot shaft without the aid of any tools.

To install the blade:

Position the auxiliary arm (if so equipped) over the pivot pin.

Hold it down and push the main arm head over the pivot shaft. Be sure the pivot shaft is in the park position.

Hold the main arm head on the pivot shaft while raising the blade end of the wiper arm and push the slide latch into the lock under the pivot shaft.

Then lower the blade to the windshield. If the blade does not touch the windshield the slide latch is not completely in place.

To remove the windshield wiper blade on recent Pinto, Maverick and Mustang models: swing arm and blade assembly away from windshield, hold and pull arm off pivot shaft.

## Accessory, Instrument Service

### WINDSHIELD WIPER BLADE ADJUSTMENT

Turn the ignition switch to the accessory position momentarily with the wiper control off. After bringing the pivot shafts to their rest positions, install the wiper blades so they lie flat against the lower edge of the windshield. Adjustment of the blade part position on the single-speed electric wiper may be made by moving the switch contact plate slightly.

### REMOVING WIPER MOTOR - FORD

To remove the electric wiper motor from the 1968-1978 Ford (which is typical), first disconnect the battery ground cable. Remove cowl intake screen. Disconnect the wiper links at the motor output arm pin. Disconnect the motor harness by removing the retention clip. Disconnect the motor harness connector and remove the motor. Remove the bolts retaining the wiper motor and bracket assembly and lower the motor. Assemble the new motor to the bracket assembly. Correct the position of the vapor seal gasket or replace if required. Connect the motor harness to the new motor. Position the motor and install the retaining bolts. Temporarily connect the motor and operate so that it is in a "park" position before connecting the linkage to the motor. Connect the wiper links at the motor output arm pin and connect the wiring connectors to the motor.

### REMOVING MOTOR - FAIRLANE, FALCON, MAVERICK, TORINO

On Fairlane and Falcon models, remove wiper arm and blade assemblies. Also remove cowl top grille panel. Disconnect battery ground cable and wiper motor wiring connections. Remove wiper arm retaining clips from wiper motor arm. Then, unscrew motor attaching bolts and remove motor.

On Maverick models with depressed park blades, first remove instrument cluster. If equipped with an air conditioning system, remove center connection and duct assembly. Then, working through cluster opening, disconnect both pivot shafts from motor drive arm. Disconnect wiring plug from motor. Unscrew attaching bolts and remove motor.

On Maverick and Torino models with nondepressed park, it is not necessary to remove instrument cluster. An exploded view of a typical wiper motor is shown in Fig. O-7.

### VACUUM WINDSHIELD WIPER

If service is required on the motor assembly, control assembly or pivot shaft assemblies, they can be removed separately.

To remove motor and mounting plate assembly, first remove cowl top ventilator grille, and weatherstrip assembly. Disconnect pivot shaft assembly links from motor shaft arm. Remove two motor mounting plate bolts. Drop motor down, disconnect vacuum line and control cable.

Since the wiper motor is serviced as an assembly, it is recommended that no further disassembly of the motor be attempted. Before removing the motor, make sure that all vacuum lines to the motor are clear and unobstructed as most of the trouble experienced with this type wiper results from broken vacuum lines.

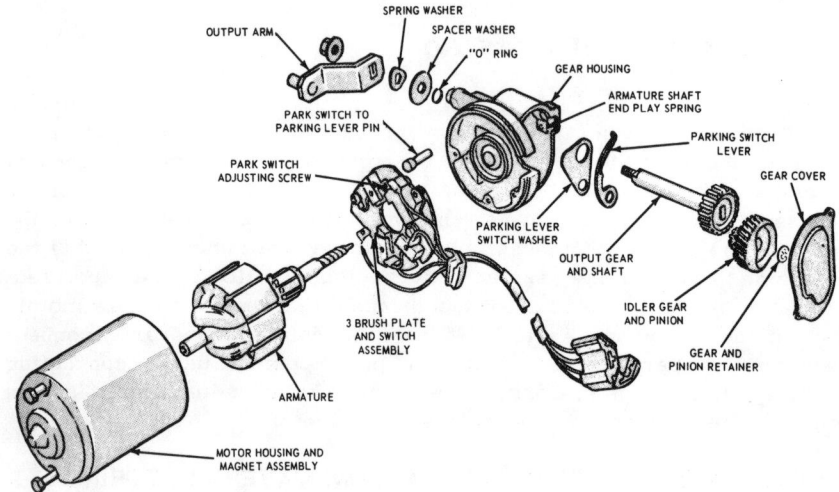

Fig. O-7. Disassembled windshield wiper motor.

## VACUUM DOOR LOCKS

The vacuum door lock system is composed of vacuum hoses which connect the functioning elements of the system. These include a reservoir assembly, a check valve, a control valve assembly, a control switch and the locking mechanism actuators, Fig. O-8.

All vacuum hoses are black rubber or nylon, with identifying colored stripes. The vacuum actuator is located within the door.

In the event of trouble with the vacuum door locks, the first place to check is the various vacuum hose connections to make sure they are tight and not leaking. A vacuum gauge, if available, can be used to make sure that full engine vacuum is reaching the check valve, control valve and reservoir.

## TIPS ON AIR CONDITIONING

The refrigerant used in Ford air conditioner systems, Fig. O-9, is nonpoisonous, noninflammable, noncorrosive and has practically no odor. It is also heavier than air. While it is classified as a safe refrigerant, certain precautions are necessary when servicing the system.

## Accessory, Instrument Service

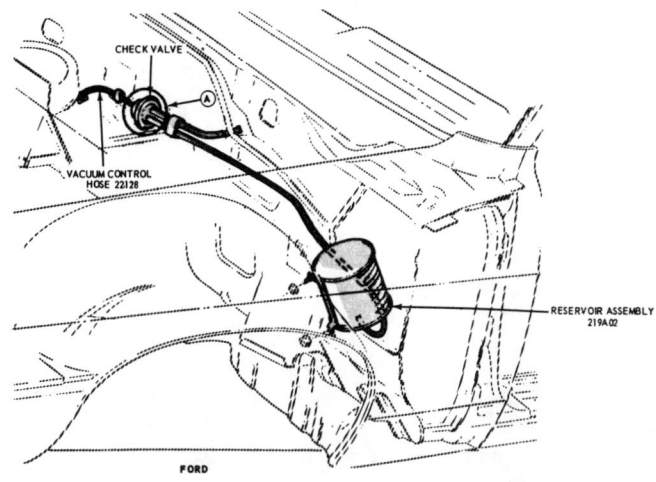

*Fig. O-8. Vacuum door lock supply installation.*

The Ford factory states that only Refrigerant 12 should be used. This evaporates so quickly that it tends to freeze anything that it contacts. Therefore, extreme care must be taken to prevent any refrigerant from coming in contact with the skin or eyes in the event that some emergency makes it necessary to service the system.

The refrigerant is readily absorbed by mineral oil and it is recommended that a bottle of sterile mineral oil be kept available.

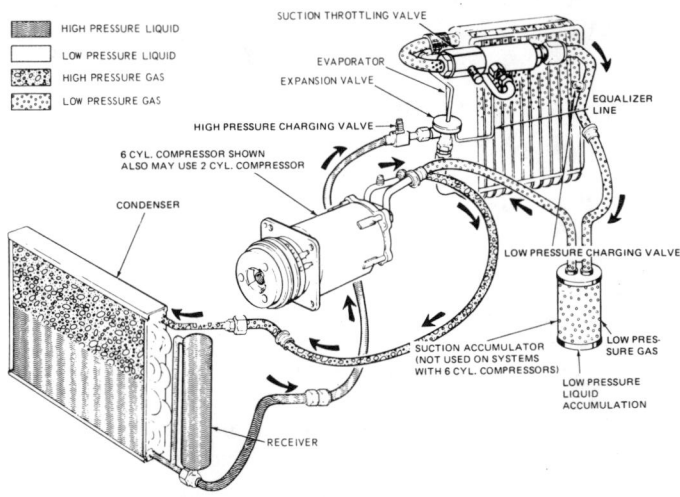

*Fig. O-9. Typical components of basic air conditioning system.*

## Fix Your Ford

While the refrigerant is nonpoisonous, the discharge of the refrigerant near an open flame can produce very poisonous gas.

Because of the need for a manifold pressure gauge set, vacuum pump and safety-type refrigerant can valve, car owners generally do not service their own vehicle's air conditioning system. However, a sight glass is provided to show whether there is sufficient refrigerant in the system. Run the engine at 1500 rpm with the controls set for maximum cooling and the blower operating at high speed. Observe the sight glass. A flow of bubbles indicates an undercharge of refrigerant.

The compressor must be isolated from the system for all compressor service operations except belt replacement.

To isolate the compressor from the system, turn both the high and the low pressure service valve to the extreme clockwise position. Loosen the cap on the high pressure service valve gauge port, and allow the gas to escape until the compressor is relieved of refrigerant pressure. Loosen the cap a small amount only, and do not remove it until the pressure is completely relieved.

To connect the compressor back into the system, evacuate the compressor at high pressure service valve gauge port, close the vacuum pump valve, turn both service valves to the maximum counterclockwise position and cap the high pressure service valve gauge port and service valve stems.

The oil level in the compressor should be checked after the system has been charged, and has been operating at an engine speed of 1500 rpm for 15 minutes at 60 deg. F. Turn off the engine and isolate the compressor, as described above. Remove the oil filter plug from the compressor and insert a flattened 1/8 in. diameter rod in the oil filler hole until it bottoms. The rod should show 3/4 in. of oil. This is equivalent to 9 oz. of oil. If additional oil is needed in the compressor, add Sunico 5G or Capella D refrigerator compressor oil, or equivalent.

## VENTILATING SYSTEM AND HEATER

Insufficient or no heat can result from any of the following causes: Blown fuse or loose or disconnected wires. Poor motor ground or a defective motor. Defective blower motor switch. Blower wheel loose on motor shaft or binding. Improperly connected heater water hoses, or low coolant level. Kinked, plugged or collapsed heater water hose. Plugged heater core or air trapped in the heater core. Improperly adjusted heater control cables. Defective heat sensor (Comfort Stream heater only). Vacuum leak in temperature control system (Comfort Stream heater only) or hoses kinked or incorrectly installed. Defective water valve (Comfort Stream heater only). Improperly installed or defective engine thermostat. Air leaks in the body or ventilating system. Incorrect installation of the heater.

Insufficient or no defrosting may result from any of the following causes: Improperly adjusted heat-defrost door control cable. Binding

## Accessory, Instrument Service

heat-defrost door. Disconnected or leaking defroster nozzle. Loose defroster nozzle or defroster openings or nozzle obstructed.

Erratic heater operation may result from any of the following causes: Temperature air door cable broken or disconnected (fresh air heater only). Temperature air door strap disconnected allowing the door to move from the heat position (Comfort Stream heater only). Defective heat sensor. Defective water valve.

In case considerable effort is required to operate the high heater control, check for the following conditions: Kinks in the control cables. Improper control cable wrapping. Binding door or valve in the heater.

## SPEED CONTROL SYSTEM

When making an inspection of the Bendix speed control system as installed on Ford built vehicles 1969-1971, it is necessary to check all items for abnormal conditions such as frayed wires, loose connections, and damaged vacuum hoses. Also for proper operation it is necessary that the speedometer cables be properly routed and securely attached to components. All vacuum hoses must be securely attached and routed with

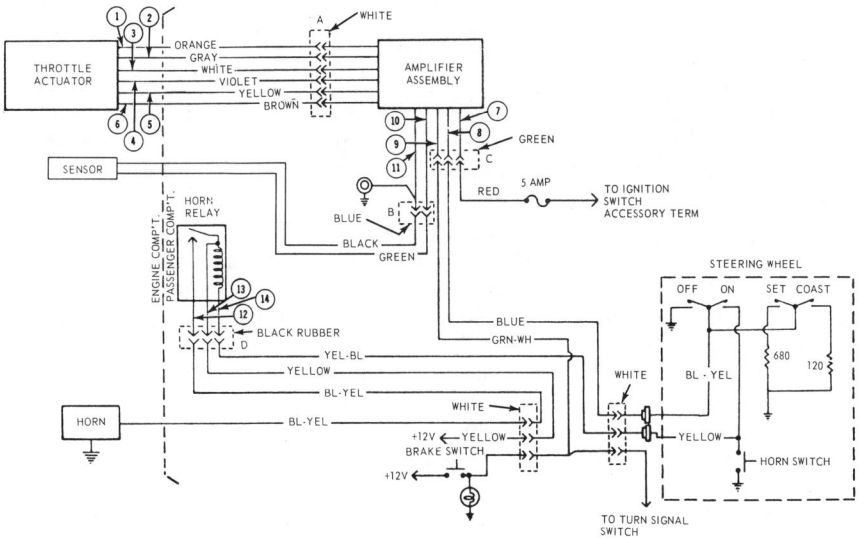

*Fig. O-10. Bendix speed control system wiring diagram.*

no sharp bends or kinks. The throttle actuator and throttle linkage must operate freely and smoothly. The bead chain should have no more than 1/4 in. free play.

To test the control switches, disconnect the blue lead from the control switches. Then, check the blue lead from the control switches as follows:

# Fix Your Ford

Check for battery voltage at the blue lead when the ON switch is depressed. Battery voltage should be available at the blue lead coming from the control switches, Fig. O-10. Connect an ohmmeter between the blue wire and the ground. Check the blue wire for continuity to ground when the OFF switch is depressed. If resistance is found, the wiring slip rings or the switch are at fault. Rotate the steering wheel back and forth and tilt the column up and down. If change in resistance is noted, clean the horn brush contacts and the ground brush. A good resistance reading should be obtained before proceeding with further tests.

With an ohmmeter connected between the blue wire and ground, depress the set-speed switch. A reading of approximately 680 ohms should be obtained. With the ohmmeter connected between the blue wire and the ground, depress the coast switch. A reading of approximately 120 ohms should be obtained.

The speed sensor test should be made as follows: Disconnect the speed sensor wires from the amplifier assembly and connect an ohmmeter between the wire connector terminals (green and black) at the speed sensor end. A reading of approximately 400 ohms should be obtained. A reading of zero ohms indicates a shorted coil and a maximum reading indicates an open coil. In either case replace the sensor. If the ohmmeter records 400 ohms and the speedometer operates properly within needle waver, the speed sensor is probably good.

To test the servo assembly: Disconnect the ball chain from the throttle linkage. Separate the servo to amplifier connector. Connect an ohmmeter between the orange and grey wire leads at the servo connector. A resistance of approximately 85 ohms should be obtained. Connect the ohmmeter between the orange and white leads. A reading of approximately 85 ohms should be obtained.

Start the engine. With the servo disconnected from the amplifier, connect the orange lead of the servo to the battery positive connection. Connect the white lead of the servo to the ground and momentarily touch the grey lead of the servo to the ground. The servo throttle actuator should tighten the bead chain and open the throttle. The throttle should hold that position or slowly release the tension on the chain. When white wire is removed from the ground, the servo should release the bead chain tension immediately. Replace the servo if any of these tests fail. If the orange lead is shorted to either the white or grey leads, it may be necessary to replace the amplifier.

If the ON circuit, OFF circuit, accelerator circuit, coast circuit are to be tested use only a 5000 ohm/voltmeter rating or higher. Do not use a test lamp to perform such tests as excessive current will damage electronic components inside the amplifier.

# Overhauling the FORD CLUTCH

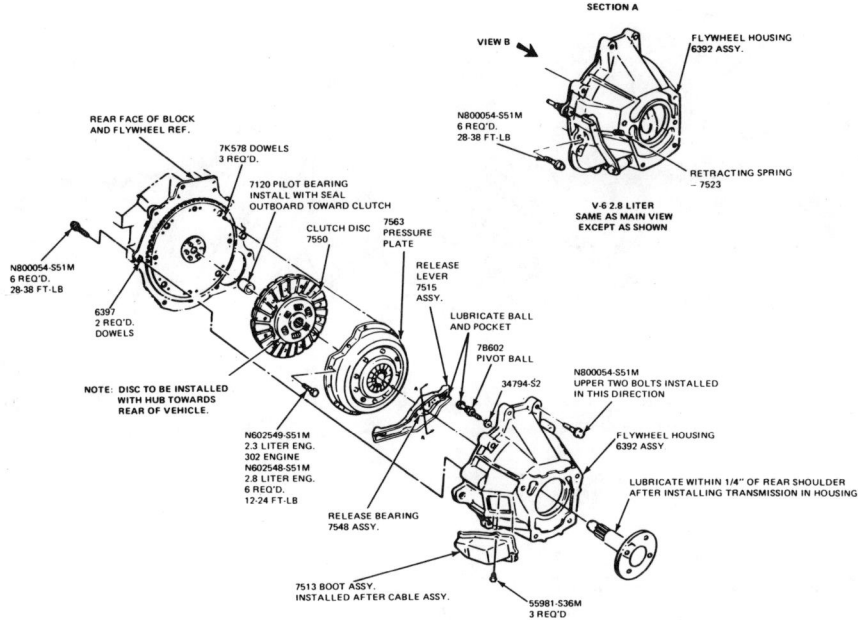

*Fig. P-1. Details are typical of clutch assembly installed on Mustang II with 2.3 litre, 2.8 litre or 302 cu. in. engine.*

The single plate clutch used on Ford cars with manual transmission is noted for giving exceptionally long life. Fig. P-1 shows a typical assembly used on the 1978 Mustang II with either 2.3 litre, 2.8 litre or 5 litre (302 cu. in.) engine. The Granada clutch assembly and flywheel housing are illustrated in Fig. P-2.

## PEDAL PLAY

Freedom from slipping and maximum clutch life can be obtained only if the clutch pedal is given sufficient free play. Pedal play on older cars should be maintained between 7/8 and 1 1/8 in. To check the amount

# Fix Your Ford

of free play, depress the clutch pedal by hand and measure the distance the pedal moves before the beginning of clutch disengagement is felt. The method of adjustment varies but, basically, it is made by adjusting the length of the clutch pedal-to-equalizer rod, Figs. P-3 and P-4. Shorten rod to increase free play; lengthen rod to decrease play.

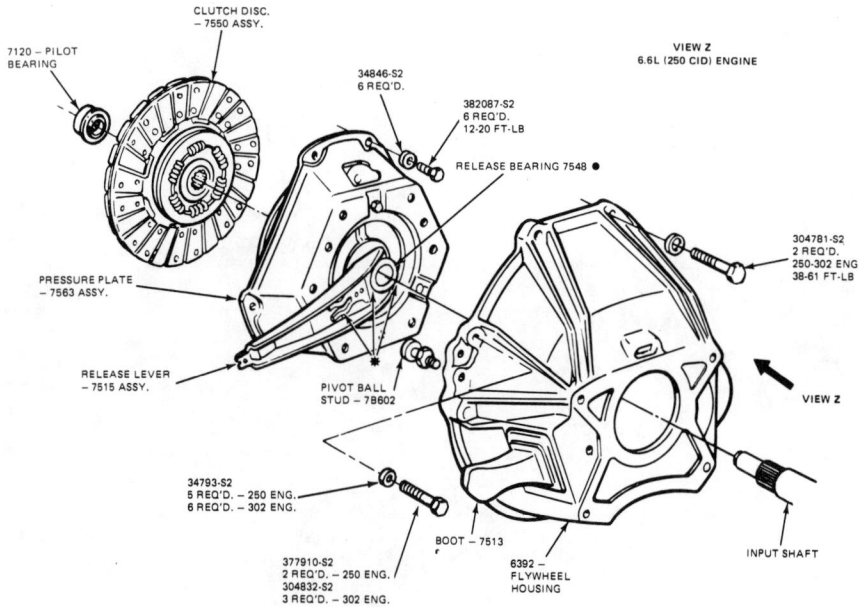

*Fig. P-2. Detail of flywheel housing, clutch release lever, release bearing, pressure plate, clutch disc and pilot bearing on Granada models.*

## 1968-1978 FORD CLUTCH ADJUSTMENT

The pedal assist spring on 1968-1978 Ford models extends from the equalizer bar to the clutch pedal bracket. To adjust free play: Disconnect clutch release lever spring from release lever. Loosen release lever rod lock nut and adjusting nut, Fig. P-4. Move clutch release lever rearward until release lever lightly contacts clutch pressure plate release fingers. Adjust adapter length until adapter seats in release lever pocket. Insert a feeler gauge against back face of rod adapter. On 1968-78 Ford models, the feeler gauge should be 0.194 in.
On 1968-1971 Fairlane, Falcon and Mustang models (except 0.178 in. on 390 and 428 cu. in. engines), the feeler gauge should be 0.136 in. On 1972-1976 Torino engines, clearance should be 0.194 in.; on 1972-1973 Mustang engines, 0.194 in.; on 1972-1977 Maverick engines, 0.136 in.

## Overhauling Clutch

On 1974-1975 Mustang II engines, clutch clearance should be 0.250 in.; on 1975-1978 Granada engines, 0.136 in.; on 1978 Fairmont engines, 0.136 in.; on Pinto and Mustang II engines since 1976, there is a built-in adjusting nut in the clutch linkage.

With feeler gauge in place, tighten adjusting nut finger-tight against against gauge. Tighten lock nut. Remove feeler gauge and install release spring. Finally, check with transmission in neutral and engine operating.

On models prior to 1974, free travel of clutch pedal should be a minimum of 1/2 in. On 1974 and later models (except Mustang), free travel should be 7/8 in. to 1 1/8 in.

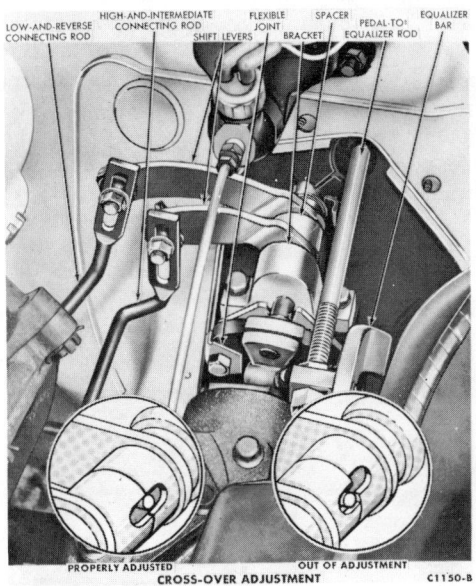

*Fig. P-3. Typical clutch and transmission linkage. Note pedal-to-equalizer rod which controls free play of clutch pedal.*

## CLUTCH REMOVAL

On 1969-1977 models, remove the drive shaft and transmission as described in the appropriate chapter. Then disconnect the clutch release lever retaining spring from the release lever. Loosen the clutch adjusting rod nuts and remove the adjusting rod. Remove the starter motor cable, then remove the starter from the flywheel housing. Remove the bolts that secure the engine rear plate to the front lower part of the flywheel housing. Remove the flywheel housing lower cover if so equipped. Remove the bolts that attach the housing to the cylinder block. Move the housing back just

# Fix Your Ford

far enough to clear the pressure plate, then move it to the right to free the pivot from the clutch equalizer bar. Be careful not to disturb the linkage and assist spring.

Loosen the six pressure plate cover attaching bolts evenly to release the spring pressure and avoid distortion of the cover. If the same pressure plate and cover are to be installed after the clutch is overhauled, mark the cover and flywheel so pressure plate can be installed in its original position. Then remove the pressure plate and clutch disc from the flywheel.

On the 1964-1968 Ford models, place the vehicle on jacks and remove the propeller shaft and transmission as described in the pertinent chapter. If removing a clutch from a car with an aluminum flywheel housing, remove the starter. Remove the bolts that attach the housing to the cylinder block. Move the housing back just far enough to clear the pressure plate, then move it to the right to free the pivot from the clutch equalizer bar. Be careful not to disturb the linkage and the assist spring. Remove the flywheel housing cover (cast iron housing only). Remove the release lever return spring. Then slide the release bearing and hub off the release lever. This applies only to cast iron flywheel housings. Loosen the six pressure plate attaching bolts evenly to release spring tension. Mark flywheel and cover so they can be replaced in original position. Remove pressure plate and clutch disc from flywheel.

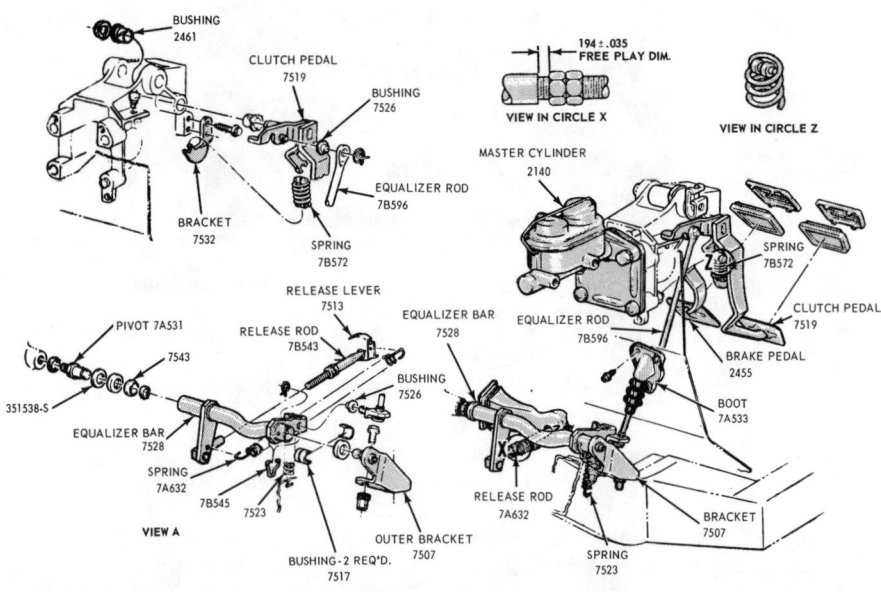

*Fig. P-4. Details of clutch pedal and linkage adjustments. Typical of 1969–1972 Ford cars.*

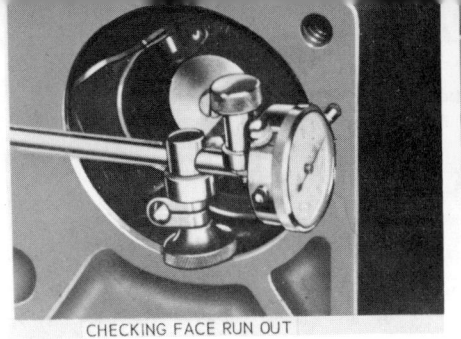
CHECKING FACE RUN OUT

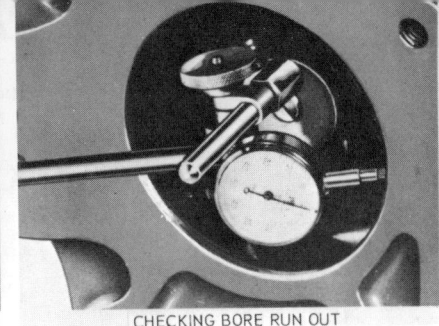
CHECKING BORE RUN OUT

Fig. P-5. Left. With the dial indicator installed as shown, the face of the flywheel can be checked for runout. Fig. P-6. Right. Showing installation of dial indicator when checking bore runout.

## FAIRLANE, FALCON AND MUSTANG

After removing the transmission as described in the Chapter on Transmissions, disconnect the clutch release lever return spring from the release lever. Remove the starter cable. Remove the starter motor from the flywheel housing. Remove the bolts that secure the engine rear plate to the front lower part of the flywheel housing. Remove the bolts that attach the flywheel housing to the cylinder block, and remove the housing and the release lever as a unit. Loosen the six pressure plate cover attaching bolts evenly to release the spring pressure. Mark the pressure plate and cover so that they can be reinstalled in their original position. Remove the six attaching bolts while holding the pressure plate cover, then remove the pressure plate and clutch disc.

If these models are equipped with a 390 cu. in. engine, the procedure is as follows: After removing the transmission, remove the flywheel housing cover. Remove the release lever retracting spring. Then slide the release bearing and hub off the release lever. Loosen the six cover attaching bolts evenly to release the spring pressure. Mark the clutch pressure plate and cover, then remove the cover and pressure plate and clutch disc through the opening at the bottom of the flywheel housing.

To remove the clutch on a 1960 to 1963 Falcon and Fairlane, first remove the transmission as described in the Chapter on Transmissions and disconnect the retracting spring and release rod. After removing the flywheel housing dust cover, remove the hub and release bearing assembly. Then remove the flywheel housing. Then remove the pressure plate and assembly from the flywheel. Note that the release bearing on this clutch is prelubricated and should not be cleaned in solvent.

## FLYWHEEL HOUSING ALIGNMENT

Alignment of the flywheel bore and the rear face of the engine should be checked as a possible cause of clutch pedal vibration, scrubby pedal feel, excessive pilot bushing wear, excessive clutch spin, transmission gear wear, and transmission jumping out of gear. Whenever any of these conditions exist the clutch housing should be given a complete inspection.

With the clutch release bearing removed clean the face of the flywheel

## Fix Your Ford

housing and remove all burrs, roughness and paint from the mating surfaces. Install a dial gauge, as shown in Fig. P-5, and adjust so that the button contacts just inside the transmission mounting holes. Remove the spark plugs to alleviate compression. Crank the engine through one complete revolution and while rotating be sure the crankshaft is pressed forward to remove all effects of end play. The indicator must return to zero to insure that no end play has affected the readings. Note the indicator reading and mark the maximum point of runout on the face of the housing.

Place the dial indicator to check the bore alignment, Fig. P-6. The bore must be clean and free from paint. Again crank the engine through one revolution. Note the indicator reading and mark the maximum point or runout on the face of the housing.

Remove the dial indicator. If the bore runout exceeds 0.015 in. and the face runout exceeds 0.010 in. and the positive readings occur at more than 90 deg. to each other, the housing should be replaced. The bore runout should not exceed 0.010 in. and the face runout should not exceed 0.006 in.

Since any change in face alignment will change bore alignment, it may be possible to correct bore alignment by changing face alignment. This can be done by installing U-shaped shims between the flywheel housing and the engine. The shim required is one-half the maximum minus indicator reading and should be located at the point of maximum minus indicator reading. If both bore and face alignment are out of limits, place shims between the flywheel housing and engine.

## CLUTCH TROUBLE SHOOTING

Loss of or excessive clutch pedal free play and inadequate reserve may be caused by any of the following conditions: Clutch linkage out of adjustment. Worn clutch disc. Bent or broken equalizer bar.

Clutch pedal hang up or excessive clutch pedal effort may be caused by any of the following conditions: Incorrect assist spring over center adjustment. Assist spring not positioned properly. Binding at pedal support bracket or equalizer rod at fire wall.

Clutch noisy when pedal is depressed to end of free travel and the engine running may be caused by any of the following conditions: Release bearing failure due to improper travel, bearing cocked on hub, release lever to fulcrum bracket loose or broken, flywheel housing misalignment, excessive crankshaft end play.

Clutch pedal actuation noisy with engine off may be caused by any of the following conditions: Insufficient lubricant on assist spring seats. Contamination or lack of lubricant on transmission input shaft bearing retainer. Binding at pedal support bracket or equalizer rod at fire wall.

Clutch slips or chatters may be caused by any of the following conditions: Incorrect pedal free travel, worn or contaminated clutch lining, grease or oil on clutch facings from release bearing, engine, pilot bearing, or transmission.

A heavy thud may be caused by excessive engine crankshaft end play.

# MANUAL SHIFT TRANSMISSIONS

## GENERAL TRANSMISSION SERVICE

Many of the troubles encountered with manual shift transmissions are relatively simple and can be performed without removing the transmission from the vehicle. The service procedure for all manual shift transmissions is basically the same.

One of the more frequent services results from leakage of lubricant from the rear of the transmission. To correct this condition:

First, remove drive shaft. Then, insert a puller in rear of transmission extension housing and pull out seal. Next, lubricate the new seal with transmission fluid. Then, using a cup type driver, install seal in transmission housing.

To replace rear bushing and rear seal: Remove drive shaft. Insert a special puller in rear of extension housing until it grips front end of bushing. Pull bushing from housing.

## ADJUSTING SHIFT LINKAGE

Adjusting the shift linkage should present no problem if it has not been bent and care was taken when it was removed from the transmission. When reinstalling the linkage: Move shift control lever into desired position. Then, move control lever on side of transmission case to desired position. Install shift rods.

## REMOVING THE TRANSMISSION

Raise car on jacks or hoist. Mark drive shaft so that it can be reinstalled in its original position. Disconnect drive shaft from rear universal joint. Slide drive shaft to rear and off transmission output shaft. Drain transmission to prevent fluid from leaking from transmission.

Disconnect speedometer cable. Disconnect all shift rods from transmission. Disconnect parking brake, if necessary. On some models, it will be necessary to disconnect clutch and brake operating mechanism. Remove bolts that attach extension housing to engine rear support. Jack up rear of engine and remove the engine rear support. Place jack under transmission. Remove bolts attaching transmission to flywheel housing. Replace two lower bolts with guide pins. Pull transmission to rear until input shaft is free.

NOTE: On some models, it is necessary to remove exhaust pipe and catalytic converter.

# Fix Your Ford

## TRANSMISSION ALIGNMENT

Alignment of the transmission or flywheel housing bore should always be checked. Misalignment could be the cause of transmission jumping out of gear, excessive transmission gear wear, vibration of the drive line, excessive pilot bushing wear, noisy release bearings or excessive clutch spin time. A dial gauge and a dummy pilot shaft and adapter plate are needed. Fig. Q-1 shows the way the measurements are made.

Face alignment can be changed by placing U-shaped shims between the flywheel housing and the engine. No more than 0.10 in. (2.54 mm) shim thickness should be used. Shims may also be placed between the transmission and the flywheel housing. This limit also is 0.10 in. (2.54 mm).

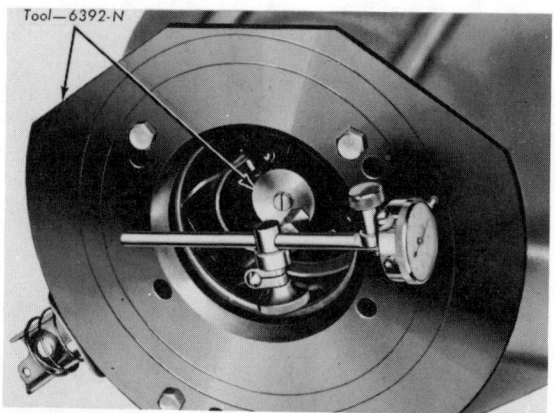

*Fig. Q-1. Checking runout of face of flywheel with a dial gauge.*

## 1968-1975 MODEL 3.03 TRANSMISSION DISASSEMBLY

To disassemble the 3.03 transmission, Fig. Q-2, used on some models of Ford, Falcon, Fairlane, Maverick and Mustang cars:

Mount transmission on a holding fixture and drain lubricant. Remove transmission cover and gasket. Remove extension housing from transmission case. Remove front bearing retainer and gasket from case. Remove either a long spring (later design) or setscrew and short spring (older design) that retains detent plug in case. Remove detent plug with a small magnet.

Remove lubricant filler plug from right side of case and, working through the plug opening, drive roll pin out of case and countershaft with a 1/4 in. punch.

On six cylinder vehicles with model RAN transmissions, tap countershaft from rear of case with a dummy shaft to remove expansion plug from countershaft bore at front of case. Hold countershaft gear with a

## Manual Shift Transmissions

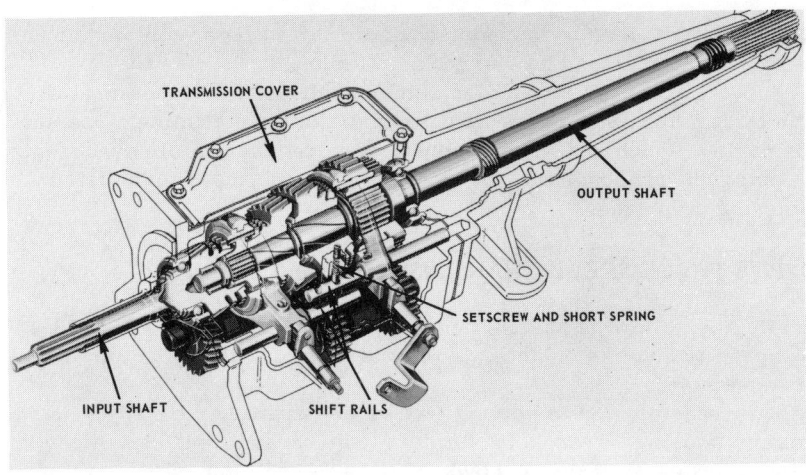

*Fig. Q-2. Phantom view of 3.03 three speed transmission.*

hook and use dummy shaft to push countershaft out of rear of case. Lower countershaft cluster gear and thrust washers to bottom of case.

Remove snap ring that secures speedometer drive gear on shaft. Slide speedometer gear off output shaft. Also, remove speedometer drive gear lock ball from shaft. Remove snap ring that retains output shaft bearing on shaft and remove bearing from case.

Place both shift levers in Neutral and remove setscrew that secures first and reverse shift fork to shift rail. Slide shift rail out rear of case.

Slide first and reverse synchronizer forward as far as possible, then rotate first and reverse shift fork upward and lift it from case.

Move second and third shift fork to second speed position, to gain access to setscrew. Remove setscrew from fork and rotate shift rail 90 deg. Lift interlock plug from case with a magnet. Tap on inner end of second and third shift rail to remove expansion plug from front of case and remove shift rail.

Remove second and third detent plug and spring from detent bore. Pull input gear and shaft forward until gear contacts case, then remove large snap ring. It is necessary to move gear forward to provide clearance when removing output shaft assembly in RAT models. On RAN models, input shaft and gear is removed from front of case at this time.

Rotate second and third shift fork upward and lift it from case. Carefully lift output shaft assembly out through top of case.

On RAT models, work input shaft bearing and gear back through bore in case and out at top.

Driving from front of case, remove reverse idler gear shaft from case, then lift gear and two thrust washers from case.

Remove stud ring from front of output shaft, then slide synchronizers and second speed gear off shaft.

# Fix Your Ford

Remove next snap ring and tabbed thrust washer from output shaft, then slide first gear and blocking ring off shaft.

Remove next snap ring from output shaft. NOTE: First and reverse synchronizer hub is a press fit on output shaft. To eliminate possibility of damaging synchronizer assembly, remove and install synchronizer hub, using an arbor press. Do not attempt to remove or install hub by hammering or prying.

## 1973-1978 THREE SPEED TRANSMISSION DISASSEMBLY

While the following instructions apply specifically to the 1973-1978 three speed transmission, they also can be applied to most earlier models. To disassemble:

Mount transmission in holding fixture and drain lubricant by removing extension housing lower bolt. Remove cap screws that attach cover to transmission case. Remove cover and gasket. Remove long coil spring that retains detent pin in case. With a magnet, pull detent pin from recess.

Remove cap screws and washers that attach extension housing to case. Remove housing. Remove attaching bolts from front bearing retainer and remove retainer from case. Remove lubricant filler plug from right side of case. Then, working through plug opening, use a 1/4 in. punch to drive roll pin out of countershaft.

Use a dummy shaft to tap countershaft from rear of case to remove expansion plug from countershaft bore at front of case. Support countershaft gear with a hook, then push countershaft out through front of case. Remove countershaft cluster gear from case.

Remove snap ring that secures speedometer drive gear to transmission output shaft, Fig. Q-3. Slide drive gear off shaft. Remove speedometer drive gear lock ball from shaft.

Remove snap ring that holds output shaft bearing on shaft. Then, remove bearing and shaft from case. Place both shift levers in central

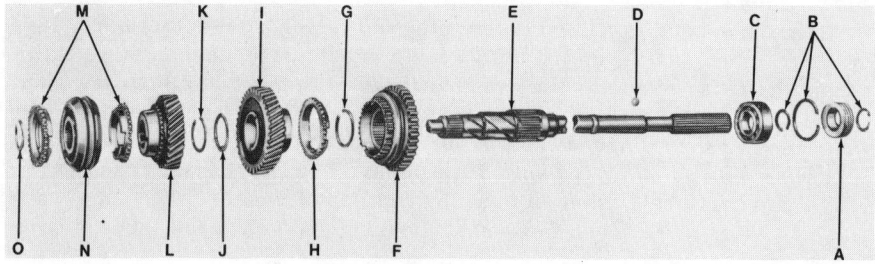

*Fig. Q-3. Output shaft of typical three speed manual shift transmission. A—Speedometer drive. B—Snap rings. C—Rear bearing. D—Lock ball. E—Output shaft. F—Reverse gear and sleeve. G—Snap ring. H—Blocking ring. I—First gear. J—Thrust washer. K—Snap ring. L—Second gear. M—Blocking rings. N—Synchronizer. O—Snap ring.*

## Manual Shift Transmissions

(Neutral) position. Remove setscrew that secures first and reverse shift fork to shift rail. Slide shift rail out through rear of case.

Slide first and reverse synchronizer forward as far as possible, rotate first and reverse shift fork upward, then lift fork from case.

Move second and third speed shift fork to second speed position for access to setscrew and remove it from fork. Rotate shift rail 90 deg. Pull input gear and shaft forward to separate input shaft and gear from front of case. Rotate second and third speed shift fork upward and lift it from case. Then, carefully lift output shaft assembly from case.

Remove idler gear shaft, driving from front of case. Lift reverse idler gear and two thrust washers from case. Lift countershaft gear, thrust washer and dummy shaft from case. Remove detent plug and spring from bottom of detent hole. Remove snap ring from front of output shaft and slide synchronizer and second speed gear off shaft.

Remove next snap ring from output shaft, Fig. Q-3. Then, slide first gear and blocking ring off shaft. Remove next snap ring from output shaft. The second and reverse synchronizer hub is a press fit on output shaft. To eliminate the possibility of damaging synchronizer assembly, use an arbor press to remove synchronizer hub. Do not hammer or pry.

## RAD FOUR SPEED TRANSMISSION DISASSEMBLY

To disassemble RAD transmission:

Mount transmission in a holding fixture and drain lubricant by removing extension housing lower bolt. Drive access plug from rear of extension housing. Unscrew nut that secures offset lever assembly and remove assembly. Unscrew remaining metric extension housing bolts, then remove housing from transmission case.

Remove cap screws that attach cover to transmission case, Fig. Q-4. Remove cover, shifter forks, shift rod assembly and cover-to-case gasket. Unscrew bolts that attach front bearing retainer to case. Remove retainer.

Pull spring clip that retains reverse lever assembly to pivot bolt. Remove pivot bolt and reverse lever assembly. Remove snap ring that secures input bearing to input shaft. Remove outer snap ring from input bearing. Locate a bearing removal tool in outer snap ring groove and remove bearing.

Remove snap ring that secures speedometer gear to output shaft. Slide gear off shaft. Remove lock ball from shaft. Remove snap ring that secures output shaft bearing on shaft. Remove outer snap ring from output shaft bearing.

Locate a bearing removal tool in outer snap ring groove and pull output shaft bearing from case. Remove input shaft through front bearing hole in case. Carefully lift output shaft and gear train through top of case.

Slide reverse idler gear shaft out through rear of case. Remove reverse gear. Use a dummy countershaft inserted from front of case

# Fix Your Ford

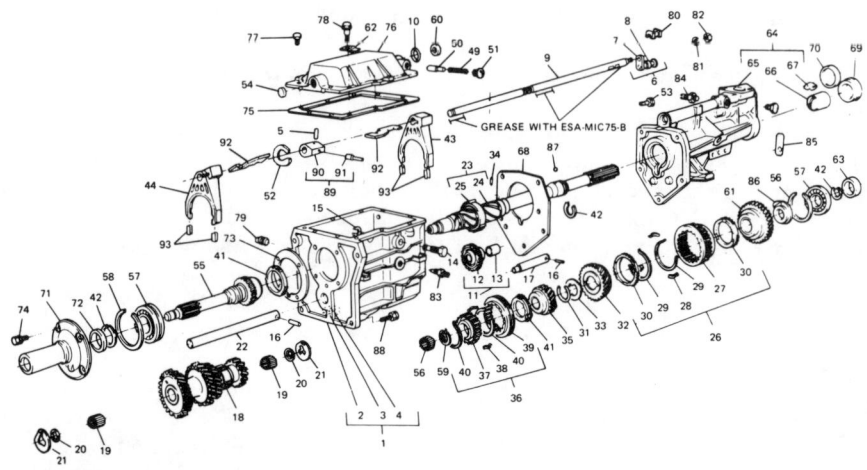

| ITEM | PART NAME | REQD. |
|---|---|---|
| 1. | CASE ASSY. – TRANS. | 1 |
| 2. | CASE – TRANS. | 1 |
| 3. | MAGNET – TRANS. CASE CHIP | 1 |
| 4. | NUT. SPRING 9/64 | 1 |
| 5. | PIN-3/16 DIA. X 13/16 ROLLED SPRING | 1 |
| 6. | LEVER ASSY.-TRANS. GEARSHIFT SHAFT OFFSET | 1 |
| 7. | LEVER-TRANS. GEARSHIFT SHAFT OFFSET | 1 |
| 8. | PIN-TRANS. GEAR SHIFT SHAFT OFFSET LEVER | 1 |
| 9. | SHAFT-TRANS. SHIFTER | 1 |
| 10. | SEAL-O-RING | 1 |
| 11. | GEAR & BUSH. ASSY.-TRANS. REV. IDLER SLIDING | 1 |
| 12. | GEAR-TRANS. REV. IDLER SLIDING | 1 |
| 13. | BUSHING-TRANS. REV. IDLER GEAR | 1 |
| 14. | PIN-TRANS. REV. GEAR SELECTOR FORK PIVOT | 1 |
| 15. | RING-7/16 RETAINING | 1 |
| 16. | PIN-1/4 X 1 SPRING | 2 |
| 17. | SHAFT-TRANS. REVERSE IDLER GEAR | 1 |
| 18. | GEAR-TRANS. COUNTERSHAFT | 1 |
| 19. | ROLLER-TRANS. C'SHAFT GEAR BEARING | 50 |
| 20. | WASHER-208 / .918 FLAT | 2 |
| 21. | WASHER-TRANS. C'SHAFT GEAR THRUST | 1 |
| 22. | COUNTERSHAFT-TRANSMISSION | 1 |
| 23. | SHAFT ASSY.-TRANS. OUTPUT | 1 |
| 24. | SHAFT-TRANS. OUTPUT | 1 |
| 25. | HUB-TRANS. SYN. 1ST & 2ND GEAR CL. | 1 |
| 26. | SHAFT & GEAR ASSY. - TRANS. OUTPUT | 1 |
| 27. | GEAR-TRANS. REVERSE SLIDING | 1 |
| 28. | INSERT-TRANS. SYNCHIRO. HUB | 3 |
| 29. | SPRING-TRANS. SYNCHIRO RETAINING | 2 |
| 30. | RING-TRANS. SYNCHIRO BLOCKING | 2 |
| 31. | RING-TRANS-2ND SPEED GEAR RET. SNAP | 1 |
| 32. | GEAR-TRANS. 2ND SPEED | 1 |
| 33. | WASHER-TRANS. 2ND SPEED GEAR THRUST | 1 |
| 34. | PIN - 1/8 x 3/8 ROLLED SPRING | 1 |
| 35. | GEAR-TRANS. 3RD SPEED | 1 |
| 36. | SYNCHRONIZER ASSY. - 3RD & 4TH SPEED | 1 |
| 37. | HUB-TRANS. SYNC. 3RD & 4TH GEAR CLUTCH | 1 |
| 38. | INSERT-TRANS. SYNC. HUB | 3 |
| 39. | SLEEVE-TRANS. 3RD & 4TH GEAR CLUTCH HUB | 1 |
| 40. | SPRING-TRANS. SYNCHRO. RETAINING | 2 |
| 41. | RING-TRANS. BLOCKING | 2 |
| 42. | RING-TRANS. M/D GEAR BRG. SHAFT-SNAP | 3 |
| 43. | FORK-TRANS. 1ST & 2ND GEAR SHIFT | 1 |
| 44. | FORK-TRANS. 3RD & 4TH GEAR SHIFT | 1 |
| 45. | LEVER ASSY.-TRANS. REV. GEAR SHIFT RELAY | 1 |
| 46. | RING.-TRANS. REV. GEAR SHIFT RELAY LEVER | 2 |
| 47. | LEVER-TRANS. REV. GEAR SHIFT RELAY | 1 |
| 48. | FORK-TRANS. REVERSE GEAR SHIFT | 1 |
| 49. | SPRING-TRANS. SHIFTER INTERLOCK | 1 |
| 50. | PLUNGER-TRANS. MESHLOCK | 1 |
| 51. | SCREW-M12 X 10 ROUND HEAD FLAT | 1 |
| 52. | PLATE-TRANS. GEAR SELECTOR INTERLOCK | 1 |
| 53. | SCREW & WASHER ASSY. M10 X 30 HEX. HEAD | 5 |
| 54. | PLUG - 3/4 DIA. WELSH TYPE | 1 |
| 55. | SHAFT-TRANS. INPUT | 1 |
| 56. | ROLLER-TRANS. M'SHAFT BEARING | 15 |
| 57. | BEARING ASSY.-TRANS. M/D GEAR BALL | 2 |
| 58. | RING-M/D GEAR BRG. RETAINING SNAP | 2 |
| 59. | RING - 1.00 RETAINING | 1 |
| 60. | SEAL-TRANS. SHIFT SHAFT | 1 |
| 61. | GEAR-TRANS. 1ST SPEED | 1 |
| 62. | CLIP-SPARK CONTROL SWITCH WIRE RET. | 1 |
| 63. | GEAR-SPEEDOMETER DRIVE | 1 |
| 64. | EXTENSION ASSY.-TRANS. | 1 |
| 65. | EXTENSION-TRANS. | 1 |
| 66. | BUSHING-TRANS. EXTENSION | 1 |
| 67. | STOP-TRANS. GEAR SHIFT LEVER REVERSE | 1 |
| 68. | GASKET-TRANS. EXTENSION | 1 |
| 69. | SEAL ASSY.-TRANS. EXTENSION OIL | 1 |
| 70. | PLUG-TRANS. EXTENSION | 1 |
| 71. | RETAINER-TRANS. INPUT SHAFT GEAR BRG. | 1 |
| 72. | SEAL ASSY.-TRANS. INPUT SHAFT OIL | 1 |
| 73. | GASKET-TRANS. INPUT SHAFT BRG. RETAINER | 1 |
| 74. | BOLT M8 X 20 HEX HEAD - LOCK | 4 |
| 75. | GASKET-TRANS. CASE COVER | 1 |
| 76. | COVER-TRANS. CASE | 1 |
| 77. | SCREW-M6 X 20 HEX. HEAD | 8 |
| 78. | BOLT-M6 X 32 HEX. WASHER HD. SHOULDER | 2 |
| 79. | PLUG-1 2-14 PIPE (FILLER) | 1 |
| 80. | BUSHING-TRANS. GEAR SHIFT DAMPER | 1 |
| 81. | NUT-HEXAGON | 1 |
| 82. | SWITCH ASSY. BACK-UP LAMP | 1 |
| 83. | SWITCH ASSY. TRANS. SEAT BELT WARNING SENSOR | 1 |
| 84. | TAG TRANS. SERVICE IDENTIFICATION | 1 |
| 85. | WASHER-TRANS. 1ST GEAR THRUST | 1 |
| 86. | BALL-.25 DIA. | 1 |
| 87. | SCREW & LOCKWASHER ASSY. M12 X 40 | 4 |
| 88. | ARM ASSY. TRANS. CONTROL SELECTOR | 1 |
| 89. | ARM-TRANS. CONTROL SELECTOR | 1 |
| 90. | PIN-TRANS. GEARSHIFT | 1 |
| 91. | PLATE-TRANS. GEARSHIFT SELECTOR ARM | 2 |
| 92. | INSERT-TRANS. GEARSHIFT FORK | 4 |

*Fig. Q-4. Details of model RAD four speed transmission as installed on Mustang II.*

to drive countershaft out through rear of case. Then, lift out countershaft gear, thrust washers and dummy countershaft through top of case.

To disassemble output shaft: Scratch alignment marks on synchronizer and blocker rings. Remove snap ring from front of output shaft.

## Manual Shift Transmissions

Slide third and fourth speed synchronizer assembly, blocker rings and third speed gear off shaft.
Remove next snap ring and second speed gear thrust washer from shaft, Fig. Q-4. Slide second speed gear and blocker ring off shaft. Take care not to lose sliding gear from first and second speed synchronizer assembly. First and second speed synchronizer hub cannot be removed from output shaft.
Working from rear of output shaft, remove first gear thrust washer (oil slinger). Remove spring pin which retains first speed gear on shaft. (Spring pin also locates and drives thrust washer type oil slinger.) Slide first speed gear from the output shaft along with first speed and second speed synchronizer assembly.

## 78ET FOUR SPEED TRANSMISSION

The 78ET transmission used on the 1978 Pinto and Fairmont is similar to the 75WT transmission used in previous years. To remove the 78ET from the 1978 Pinto:
Place gearshift lever in Neutral. Raise vehicle and remove back-up lamp switch from extension housing. Lower vehicle. Loosen gearshift lever knob lock nut and remove knob and lock nut. Remove two front attaching screws from each step plate. Also remove attaching screws from each kick pad and remove pads. Fold carpet or floor mat up against shift lever and remove shift lever boot through opening in floor mat. Compress corrugated rubber spring. Then, remove snap ring and slide spring upward on lever.
Bend shift lever lock tabs up, then carefully thread plastic dome nut from extension housing. Lift shift lever from extension housing.
To remove shift lever from Fairmont:
Place gear shift lever in Neutral position. Remove attaching screws at rear of coin tray and lift to release from front hold-down notch on boot retainer. Lift over gear shift lever boot.
Remove four cap screws attaching boot to floor pan and remove boot upward and out of way. Remove three lever attaching bolts. Then, remove lever and boot assembly from extension housing. Remove gear shift knob and lock nut, then slide boot off lever.
To remove the 78ET from the 1978 Fairmont:
Remove gear shift lever as previously described. Working under hood, remove upper bolts that attach flywheel housing to engine. Raise vehicle on a hoist. Mark drive shaft relative to rear axle companion flange. Remove drive shaft and install plug in extension housing to prevent leakage of lubricant from transmission. Remove clutch release dust cover. Disconnect clutch release cable from release lever. Remove starting motor.
Disconnect speedometer cable from transmission and lift cable from extension housing. Support rear of engine with a jack and remove bolts that attach cross member to body. Remove bolts that attach

## Fix Your Ford

cross member to extension housing, then remove cross member. Lower engine as required to permit removal of bolts that attach flywheel housing to engine. Slide transmission away from engine and from under vehicle.

NOTE: On some Fairmont installations, it may be necessary to slide mounting bracket forward from catalytic converter heat shield. This will provide additional clearance to permit transmission to move rearward for removal. Details of output shaft are shown in Fig. Q-4.

## DISASSEMBLING 78ET TRANSMISSION

Clean the exterior of the transmission, then mount it in a holding fixture. To disassemble the 78ET transmission:

Remove clutch release bearing, lever and clutch housing. Remove transmission cover and drain lubricant. Remove threaded plug, spring and shift rail detent plunger from front of transmission case. Drive access plug from rear of case. Then, drive interlock plate retaining pin from case. Remove roll pin from selector lever arm.

Tap front end of shift rail to displace plug at rear of extension housing. Withdraw shift rail from extension housing. Lift selector arm and shift forks from case.

Remove four extension housing attaching bolts. Tap housing with a plastic hammer to loosen it from case, then rotate housing to align countershaft with cutaway in extension housing flange. Using a brass drift, drive countershaft rearward until it just clears front of case. Install a dummy shaft in case and gear until countershaft gear can be

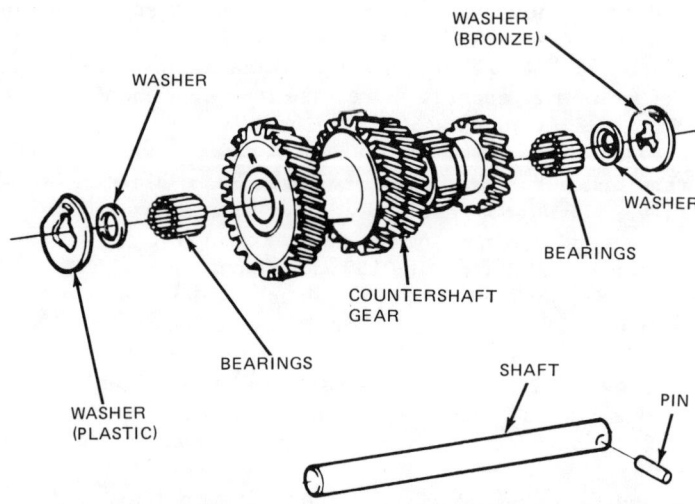

*Fig. Q-5. Countershaft gear cluster in model 78ET transmission.*

## Manual Shift Transmissions

lowered to bottom of case. Remove countershaft.

Lift extension housing and mainshaft from case as an assembly.

Remove input shaft retainer attaching bolts. Then, remove bearing and bearing retainer from case. Remove reverse idler gear shaft from rear of case. Also, remove reverse idler gear and spacer. Remove countershaft gear, Fig. Q-5. Remove bearing retaining washers, bearings and dummy shaft from countershaft gear.

Remove bearing retainer and pilot bearing from input shaft gear.

Do not remove ball bearing from input shaft unless replacement is necessary. Lift fourth gear blocker ring from front of output shaft. Remove snap ring from forward end of output shaft.

Slide third and fourth speed synchronizer assembly and third gear off output shaft, Fig. Q-6. Remove snap ring and washer. Then, slide second gear and blocker ring off output shaft. Etch alignment marks on hub and sleeve of synchronizer before disassembly.

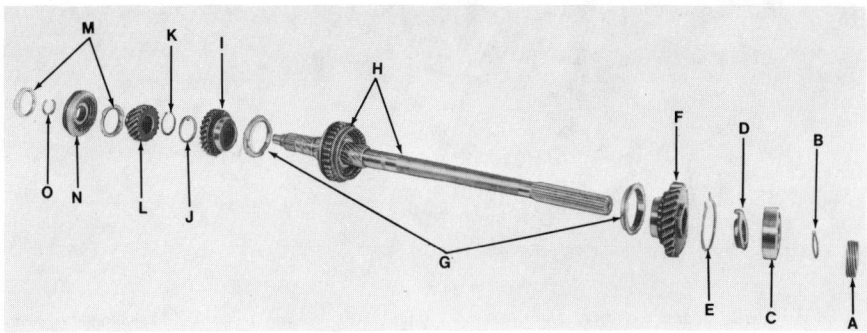

*Fig. Q-6. Output shaft of model 78ET four speed transmission. A—Speedometer gear. B—Snap ring. C—Shaft bearing. D—Spacer. E—Snap ring. F—First gear. G—Blocker ring. H—Output shaft and first and second speed synchronizer. I—Second gear. J—Thrust washer. K—Snap ring. L—Third gear. M—Blocker ring. N—Third and fourth speed synchronizer. O—Snap ring.*

## FOUR SPEED OVERDRIVE TRANSMISSION

Disassemble the four speed overdrive transmission, Fig. Q-7 as follows:

Remove transmission from case and mount it on a fixture. Drain fluid. Remove cover and long spring that retains detent plug in place. Remove plug with a small magnet. Remove extension housing. Remove intake shaft bearing retainer attaching screws, then slide retainer off input shaft. Support countershaft gear with a wire hook. Working from front of case, push countershaft out through rear of case, using a dummy shaft. Then, lower countershaft gear to bottom of case.

Remove setscrew from first and second speed shift fork and slide shift rail out rear of case. Using a magnet, remove interlock detent

# Fix Your Ford

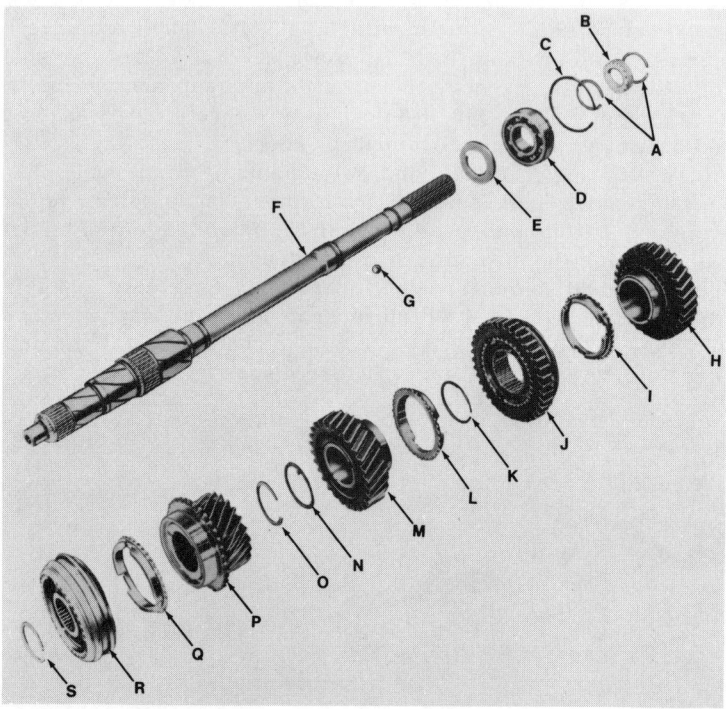

*Fig. Q-7. Four speed overdrive transmission output shaft. A—Snap rings. B—Speedometer gear. C—Snap ring. D—Bearing. E—Thrust washer. F—Output shaft. G—Speedometer gear drive ball. H—First speed gear. I—Blocker ring. J—First and second speed synchronizer. K—Snap ring. L—Blocker ring. M—Second speed gear. N—Thrust washer. O—Snap ring. P—Overdrive gear. Q—Blocking ring. R—Third and fourth speed synchronizer. S—Snap ring.*

spring from between first and second and from third and overdrive shift rails. Shift transmission into overdrive position. Remove setscrew from third and overdrive shift fork. Remove side detent bolt and detent plug and spring. Rotate third and overdrive speed shift rail 90 deg. clockwise and tap it out through front of case, using a punch and a hammer.

Remove interlock plug from top of case with a magnet. Remove snap ring that secures speedometer drive gear to output shaft. Slide gear off shaft. Then, remove speedometer drive ball, Fig. Q-7.

Remove snap ring that secures output shaft bearing to shaft. Remove snap ring from outside diameter of output shaft bearing. Remove output shaft bearing from output shaft using a special tool.

Remove snap ring that secures input shaft bearing to input shaft. Remove snap ring from outside diameter of input shaft bearing. Then

## Manual Shift Transmissions

remove input shaft bearing from input shaft and transmission case.

Move output shaft, Fig. Q-7, to right side of case, to provide clearance for forks. Rotate forks as they are removed from case. Support thrust washer and first speed gear to prevent them from sliding off the shaft, then lift output shaft assembly from case.

Remove reverse gear shift fork setscrew. Rotate reverse shift rail 90 deg. Slide shift rail out through rear of case, then lift fork from case. Use a magnet to remove reverse detent plug and spring from case. Then, remove reverse idler gear shaft from case. Lift countershaft gear and thrust washers from case, taking care not to drop bearings or dummy shaft from countershaft gear.

Lift reverse idler gear and thrust washers from case. Remove snap ring from front of output shaft. Slide third and overdrive synchronizer locking ring and gear from shaft. Remove next snap ring and second speed gear thrust washer from shaft. Slide second speed gear and blocking ring from shaft. Remove next snap ring. Remove thrust washer, first speed gear and blocking ring from rear of shaft. First and second synchronizer hub is a slip fit on output shaft.

## 1977-1978 FOUR SPEED OVERDRIVE TRANSMISSION

Model RUG-BP overdrive transmission, Fig. Q-8, is designed for Granada models having: 200-1V engine and 3.40 rear axle (1977 only); 250-1V engine with 3.00 rear axle; 302-2V engine with 3.00 rear axle.

RUG-BP is a four speed manual overdrive transmission, fully synchronized in all forward gears. The reverse sliding gear is not in constant mesh. The overdrive gear ratio is .81 to 1.00. This transmission is similar in design to Ford's earlier RUG four speed unit.

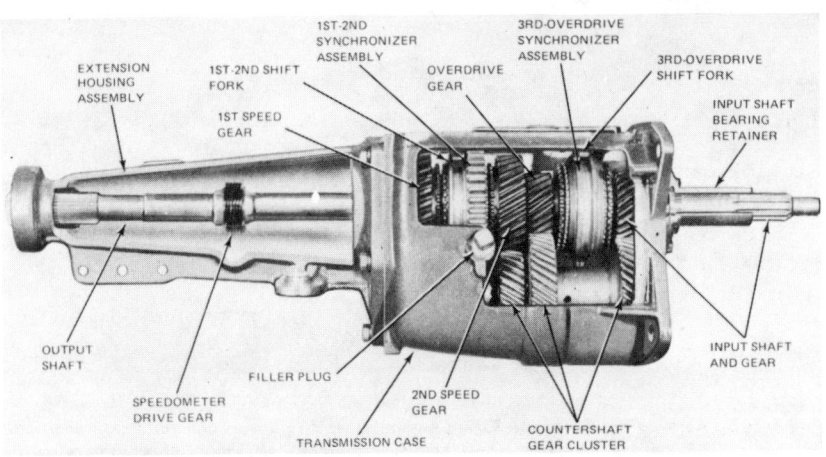

*Fig. Q-8. Details of RUG-BP four speed overdrive transmission.*

# Fix Your Ford

For 1976: Above. Ford Elite with 351-2V engine, front disc brakes and solid state ignition. Center. LTD Landau with four wheel power disc brakes optional. Below. Granada with improved ride and increased fuel mileage.

# AUTOMATIC TRANSMISSION SERVICE

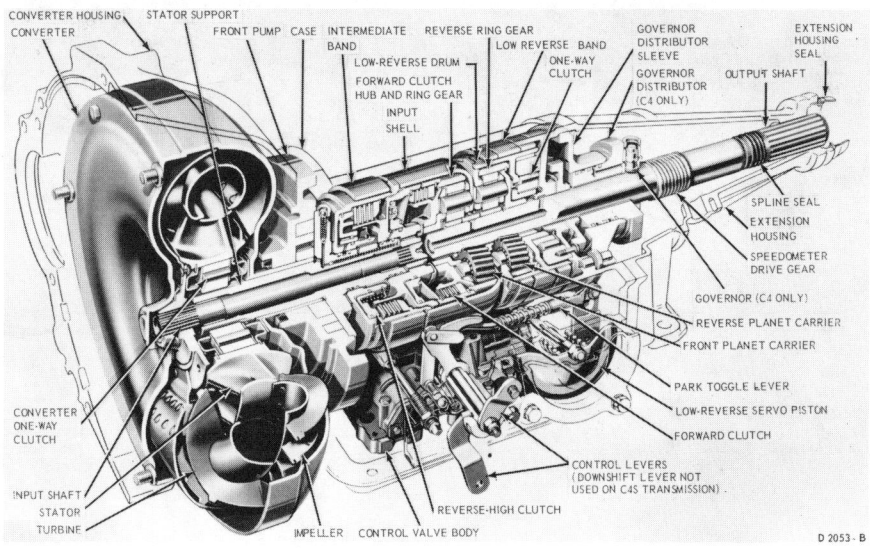

*Fig. R-1. Typical 1964-1978 Model C4 and C4S automatic transmission.*

Several different types of automatic transmissions have been used in Ford cars. These include the C4 and C4S as shown in Fig. R-1; model C6 as shown in Fig. R-2; the Cruise-O-Matic shown in Fig. R-3; and the Ford C3, three speed automatic transmission shown in Fig. R-4.

These transmissions require very little attention and external adjustments are usually all that are required. In the event major work is required, it is advisable to have the work performed by a shop having the necessary special tools and equipment; or, if preferred, a complete rebuilt unit can be installed.

Work that can be done by the average owner includes adjustment of engine idle speed, maintaining fluid at correct level, linkage adjustment and band adjustment.

# Fix Your Ford

## TRANSMISSION FLUID LEVEL CHECK

The latest official information covering the checking of the transmission fluid level is as follows: Make sure that the vehicle is standing level. Then firmly apply the parking brake.

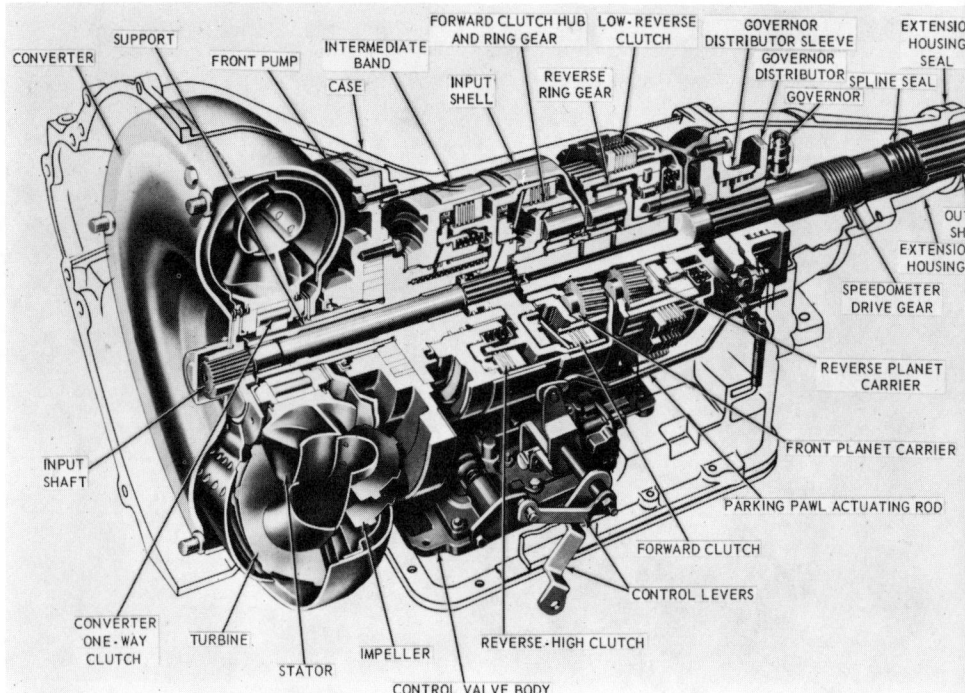

*Fig. R-2. 1966–1977 Model C6 dual range transmission, also available on Thunderbird with three manual up-and-down shifts. For 1977, C6 has a new forward clutch cylinder, forward ring gear and hub and some interior dimensional changes.*

Run the engine at normal idle speed. If the transmission fluid is cold, run the engine at fast idle until the fluid reaches its normal operating temperature. When the fluid is warm, slow the engine down to normal idle speed.

On a vehicle equipped with a vacuum brake release, disconnect the release line and plug the end of the line; otherwise the parking brake will not hold the transmission in any drive position.

Shift the selector lever through all positions, and place the lever at "Park" position. Do not turn off the engine during the fluid level check.

Clean all dirt from the transmission fluid dipstick cap before removing the dipstick from the filler tube.

# Automatic Transmission Service

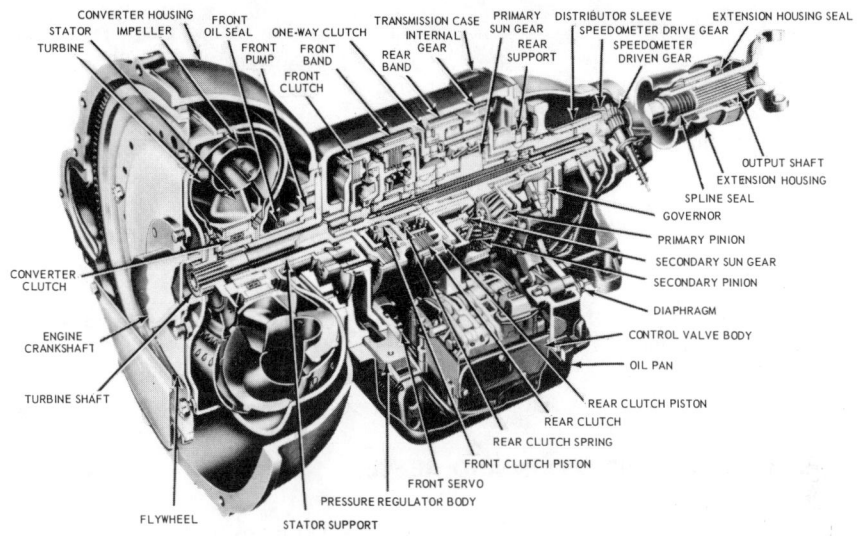

Fig. R-3. 1969–1978 FMX automatic transmission. Also typical of earlier models of the Cruise-O-Matic.

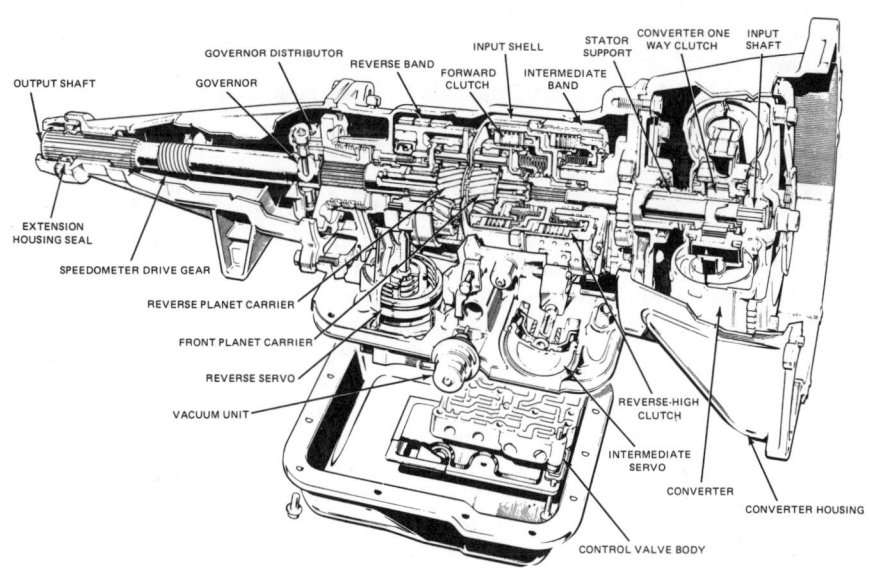

Fig. R-4. C3 automatic transmission 1974–1977, used primarily with 2300 cc and 2800 cc engines.

## Fix Your Ford

Pull the dipstick out of the tube and wipe it clean. Push it all the way back into the tube. Be sure that it is completely seated. Pull out the dipstick and check it for fluid level. If necessary, add enough approved automatic transmission fluid through the filler tube to raise the level to the full mark on the dipstick. Do not overfill. Then, reinstall the dipstick, making sure that it is fully seated.

A high fluid level will cause the fluid to become aerated, which will result in low control pressure. It also may force fluid out the vent. A low fluid level can affect transmission operation, and it may indicate fluid leakage that could lead to transmission damage.

Use only automatic transmission fluid approved for use in Ford automatic transmissions. Also note that a special fluid has been developed for use in 1977 C6 automatic transmissions. Use of a fluid other than the one specified could result in a transmission malfunction.

## TRANSMISSION FLUID DRAIN AND REFILL

Normal maintenance and lubrication requirements do not necessitate periodic automatic transmission fluid changes.

If a major failure, such as a clutch band, bearing, etc., has occurred in the transmission, it will have to be removed for service. At this time the converter, transmission cooler and cooler lines must be thoroughly flushed to remove any foreign matter.

When filling a dry transmission and converter, install five quarts of fluid. Start the engine, shift the selector lever through all positions and place it in the "Park" position. Then add fluid as required to bring it up to the full mark on the dipstick.

For partial drain and refill due to in-vehicle repair operations, such as band adjustment, proceed as follows:

C4 and C4S transmissions, PEA and PEF models, disconnect fluid filler tube from transmission oil pan to drain the fluid. On all other models, loosen the pan attaching bolts to drain the fluid. When the fluid has stopped draining, remove and thoroughly clean the pan and screen. Discard gasket. Install pan with new gasket.

Connect the filler tube to the pan and tighten the fittings securely.

Add three quarts of fluid to the transmission through the filler tube. Run the engine at idle speed for about two minutes and then run at a fast idle of about 1200 rpm until it reaches its normal operating temperature. Do not race the engine. Shift the selector lever through all positions and leave it in "Park" position. Then check the fluid level, and if necessary add enough fluid to transmission to raise the level to the "F" mark on the dipstick. Do not overfill the transmission.

Following are the procedures for partial drain and refill due to in-vehicle repair operation on the Cruise-O-Matic (which is also known as the FMX-MX) and C6 transmissions.

Raise the vehicle on a hoist or jack stand. Place a drain pan under the

## Automatic Transmission Service

transmission and loosen the pan attaching bolts to drain the fluid from the transmission.

After the fluid has drained to the level of the pan flange, remove the rest of the pan bolts working from the rear and both sides of the pan to allow it to drop and drain slowly.

When the fluid has stopped draining from the transmission, remove and thoroughly clean the pan and the screen. Discard the pan gasket. Replace a new gasket on the pan and install the pan on the transmission.

Add three quarts of fluid to the transmission through the filler tube. Run the engine at an idle speed for about two minutes, and at a fast idle of about 1200 rpm until it reaches normal operating temperature. Do not race the engine.

Shift the selector lever through all positions, place it in "Park" position and check the fluid level. If necessary, add enough fluid to the transmission to raise the level to the full mark on the dipstick. Do not overfill the transmission.

## OIL COOLER FLUSHING PROCEDURE

When a clutch or band failure has occurred in the transmission, remove any metal particles or clutch plate or band material which may have been carried into the cooler. This must be removed from the system by flushing the cooler and lines before the transmission is put back into service. In no case should an automatic transmission having a clutch or band failure, resulting in fluid contamination, be put back into service without first flushing the transmission oil cooler.

After installing a new or rebuilt automatic transmission and converter assembly into the vehicle, do not connect the cooler return line to the transmission. Place the transmission selector lever in "Park" position and connect the cooler inlet line to the transmission. Place a pan under the end of the cooler return line that will hold the transmission fluid. Do not start the engine. Install five quarts of automatic transmission fluid meeting Ford specifications. Start the engine and allow it to run at normal idle speed for three minutes, with the selector lever in "Park" position. Stop the engine and add additional transmission fluid required to complete the total fill. Start the engine and allow it to run at normal idle speed.

Allow approximately two quarts of transmission fluid to drain into the pan under the end of the cooler return line. If the fluid does not run clear after draining two quarts, shut off the engine and add two additional quarts to the transmission. Repeat that procedure until the fluid return line is clean.

If there is no fluid flow or the fluid does not flow freely, shut off the engine and disconnect both cooler lines from transmission and cooler. Use an air hose with not more than 100 psi air pressure to reverse flush the cooler lines and the cooler. After reverse flushing, connect both lines at the cooler and the cooler inlet line to the transmission.

# Fix Your Ford

Start engine and check flow of fluid as before. If it flows freely, allow fluid to drain until clear while maintaining correct level in transmission. If no fluid flows, check for pinched lines.

## QUICK SERVICE ON LEAKS

New high temperature resistant seals are used in all 1975 automatic transmissions. Do not install previous model seals in a 1975 transmission. If the transmission is used in severe service, drain and refill it every 30,000 miles.

Often, automatic transmission fluid leaks can be stopped by tightening bolts or by replacing a gasket or a seal. For example: Stop leakage at pan gasket by correctly torquing attaching bolts. Stop leakage at speedometer cable attachment by replacing the rubber seal. Stop leakage at the transmission fluid filler tube by replacing the O-ring.

In most applications, the transmission fluid is water-cooled by piping it to the radiator. Check the lines and fittings for leakage or looseness. Replace parts or tighten fittings, as required. Always use fitting wrenches to insure against distorting or crushing fittings.

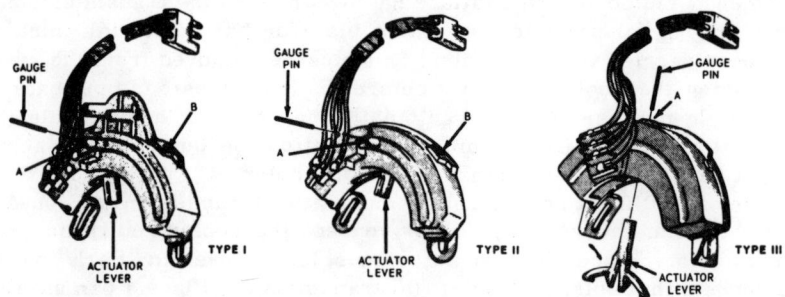

Fig. R-5. *Starter neutral switch for column shift installation.*

If there is transmission fluid within the radiator, the cooler in the tank is in need of service. To check the cooler, disconnect it and apply air pressure to the fittings. If necessary, replace the cooler.

Defective seals at the throttle lever shaft, and at the manual lever shaft, will result in leakage. If tightening the pipe plug in the case does not stop leakage at that point, a new plug should be installed. In some instances it may be necessary to install new threads in the case.

Leaks may also occur at the TV pressure port plug on the right rear of the C6 transmission.

When leakage occurs at the converter drain plugs, coat the threads with a sealing compound and then install the plugs, torquing them as specified. Fluid leakage from the converter housing may actually be oil leaking from the engine rear main bearing, or from oil gallery plugs.

## Automatic Transmission Service

As transmission fluid is usually red in color, it helps to distinguish fluid leaks from engine oil leaks. The sources of most other transmission fluid leaks will have their source within the transmission and it would be necessary to remove and disassemble the unit in order to make the necessary repairs.

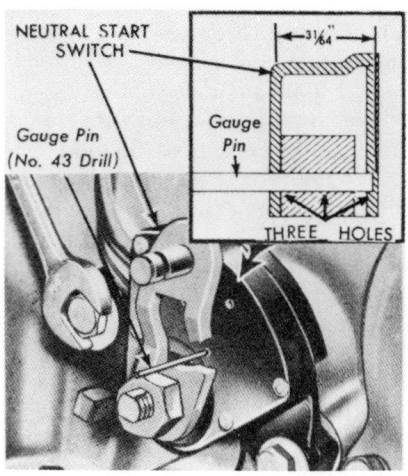

Fig. R-5a. Details of neutral start switch as installed on Maverick, Mustang and Pinto cars, equipped with C-4 or C-5 automatic transmissions.

## STARTER NEUTRAL SWITCH ADJUSTMENT

With the manual linkage properly adjusted on column shift cars, check the starter engagement circuit in all transmission selector lever positions. The circuit must be open in all positions except "Park" and "Neutral."

Set the parking brake and place the transmission selector lever tight against the neutral stop. Disconnect the starter neutral switch wires at the plug connector. Disconnect the vacuum hoses, if so equipped. Remove the two screws securing the starter neutral switch, Fig. R-5, to the steering column and remove the switch. If equipped with a type III switch, remove the actuator lever from the steering column and reinstall it in the switch, Fig. R-5. With the switch wires facing upward, move the actuator lever all the way to the left. Do not apply excessive pressure as internal damage to the switch may result.

Install a gauge pin (a No. 43 drill will do) and engage pin hole at point A, Fig. R-5. On type III switch, be sure the gauge pin is inserted to a depth of one-half inch. With the gauge pin in place, move the actuator lever to the right until a positive stop is engaged.

# Fix Your Ford

On type I and II, remove the gauge pin and install it at point B. On a type III switch, remove the gauge pin, align the two holes in the switch at point A and reinstall the gauge pin.

Position the starter neutral switch on the steering column and install the two attaching screws. Be sure the selector lever is tight against the neutral stop.

Connect the switch wires to the plug connector and the vacuum hoses to the switch, if so equipped. Remove the gauge pin and check the operation of the switch in each selector lever position. The starter should engage in only the neutral and park detent positions.

Whenever the manual linkage is adjusted, the starter neutral switch should be checked and, if necessary, adjusted.

To adjust the neutral start switch on Mustang, Maverick or Pinto cars equipped with C4 or C6 automatic transmission proceed as follows:

Remove the downshift linkage from the transmission downshift lever. Apply penetrating oil to the downshift lever shaft and nut. Remove the transmission downshift outer lever retaining nut and lever, Fig. R-5a. Remove the two neutral start switch attaching bolts. Disconnect the multiple wire connector. Remove the neutral switch from the transmission.

Install the neutral start switch on the transmission. Install the two attaching bolts. With the transmission manual lever in neutral, rotate the switch and install a No. 43 drill into the gauge pin hole, Fig. R-5a. Torque the switch attaching bolts 55-75 in. lb. Remove gauge pin. Install the outer downshift lever and attaching nut, torquing to 10-20 ft. lb. Install the downshift linkage rod to the downshift lever. Install the switch wires. Connect the multiple wire connector. Check operation of switch in each detent position. The engine should start only with the transmission in Neutral or Park positions. The starter neutral switch circuit MUST be open in all other detent positions.

## THROTTLE LINKAGE ADJUSTMENT

The object of throttle linkage adjustment is to adjust the linkage so there is correct relationship between the carburetor, throttle openings and the movement of the transmission throttle lever. If the linkage is correctly adjusted, the carburetor and transmission will combine to provide smooth shifting at proper speeds. If not, slippage, bunched shifts and rough shifting will result.

If care is taken whenever the throttle connections are detached from the carburetor or from the transmission to be sure their length is not altered, there will be no necessity for making any adjustments.

Making the complete adjustment is an involved procedure. Basically the adjustment is correct when the throttle lever is in the wide-open position and the downshift rod is through the detent stop. Adjustment should be made with the parking brake applied and the selector lever in neutral. In addition, engine idling speed must be correctly set in accordance with specifications.

# Automatic Transmission Service

## HOW TO ADJUST C4 AND C4S BANDS

To adjust the intermediate band, first clean all the dirt from the band adjusting screw area. Remove and discard the lock nut.

Install a new lock nut on the adjusting screw. With the tool shown in Fig. R-6, tighten the adjusting screw until the tool handle clicks. The tool is a pre-set torque wrench which clicks and overruns when the torque on

*Fig. R-6. Adjusting intermediate band on C4 and C4S transmission.*

the adjusting screw reaches 10 ft. lb. If the special tool is not available, use a conventional torque wrench and tighten as specified. Then back off the adjusting screw exactly one and three-quarter turns. Hold the adjusting screw from turning and torque the lock nut to 35-45 ft. lb.

To adjust the low-reverse band, Fig. R-7, on the C4 transmission, clean all the dirt from the band adjusting screw area. Remove and discard the lock nut. Install a new lock nut on the adjusting screw and tighten the adjusting screw to 10 ft. lb. Back off the adjusting screw exactly three full turns. Hold the adjusting screw from turning and torque the lock nut to 35-45 ft. lb.

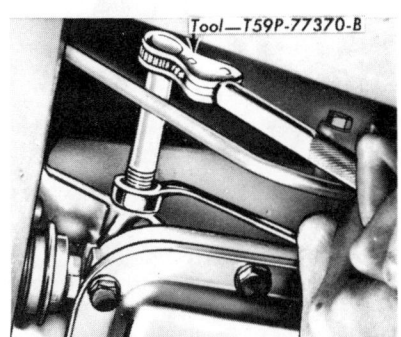

*Fig. R-7. Adjusting low-reverse band on C4 and C4S transmission.*

# Fix Your Ford

*Fig. R-8. Band adjustment on C6 transmission.*

## BAND ADJUSTMENT ON C6 TRANSMISSION

Clean all dirt from band adjusting screw area. Remove and discard lock nut. Install a new lock nut and tighten adjusting screw to 10 ft. lbs. torque. Back off adjusting screw 1 1/2 turns for 1971-1972 models; others, one turn, Fig. R-8. Hold adjustment and tighten lock nut to 35 ft. lbs.

## BAND ADJUSTMENT ON CRUISE-O-MATIC (FMX) TRANSMISSION

To adjust the front band, first drain the fluid from the transmission by loosening the pan attaching bolts starting at the rear of the pan and working toward the front. When most of the fluid has drained from the pan, remove the remainder of the attaching bolts. Use a clean drain can equipped with 100 mesh screen, if the fluid is to be reused.

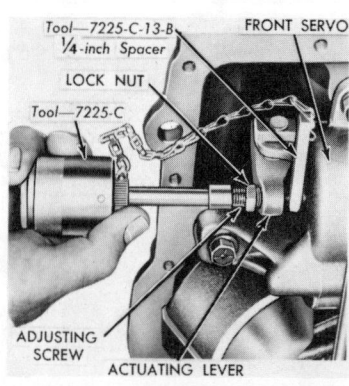

*Fig. R-9. Adjusting front band on FMX transmission. Cruise-O-Matic is similar.*

## Automatic Transmission Service

Remove the pan, then remove the fluid screen and clip from the transmission. Clean the inside of the pan. Remove all gasket material from the pan and pan mounting face of the case. Loosen the front servo-adjusting screw lock nut. Pull back on the actuating rod and insert a one-quarter inch spacer between the adjusting screw and the servo piston stem, Fig. R-9. Tighten the adjusting screw to 10 in. lb. torque. Remove the spacer and tighten the adjusting screw an additional three-quarter turn. Hold the adjusting screw stationary and tighten the lock nut securely. Replace the fluid screen and clip and install the pan using a new gasket. Refill the transmission to the full mark on the dipstick.

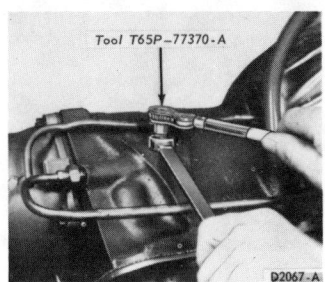

*Fig. R-10. Adjusting rear band on FMX transmission as installed on Ford models.*

To adjust the rear band on the Cruise-O-Matic (FMX) transmission, fold back the floor mat to expose the right side of the floor pan. Remove the access hole cover from the floor pan. Remove all dirt from the adjusting screw threads, then oil the threads.

To adjust rear band on FMX transmission on 1970-1976 Ford, Fairlane, Torino: Loosen reverse band adjusting screw lock nut. Torque tighten adjusting screw to 10 ft. lb., Fig. R-10. If screw is tighter than 10 ft. lb., loosen screw and retighten to 10 ft. lb. torque. Back off adjusting screw 1 1/2 turns and tighten lock nut to 35-45 ft. lb.

The rear band adjusting procedure on the 1969 Fairlane and Mustang is basically the same as above, except that the rear servo apply lever is pierced by an adjusting bolt. This permits the rear band to be adjusted either internally or externally. To make the internal adjustment of the rear band, drain the fluid from the transmission. Remove and thoroughly clean the pan and filter. Discard the pan gasket.

Loosen the rear servo adjusting screw and lock nut. Pull the adjusting screw end of the actuating lever away from the servo body and insert the spacer tool, Fig. R-9, between the servo piston and the adjusting screw. Using a torque wrench with an Allen head socket, Fig. R-11, tighten the adjusting screw to 24 in. lb. Back off the adjusting screw 1 1/2 turns. Hold the adjusting screw stationary and tighten the lock nut securely. Install the transmission fluid filter and clip. Replace the pan and gasket. Refill the transmission with fluid.

# Fix Your Ford

## HOW TO ADJUST FORDOMATIC BANDS

To adjust the front band on the Fordomatic transmission, Fig. R-4, the low band adjusting screw is threaded through the front left side of the case. Loosen the lock nut several turns. Tighten the adjusting screw to exactly 10 ft. lb. and then back off exactly two turns. Hold the adjusting

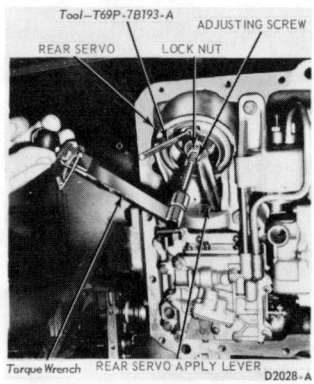

*Fig. R-11. Adjusting rear band on FMX transmission as installed on Fairlane and Mustang.*

screw in this position and tighten the lock nut to 35-40 ft. lb. If a torque wrench is not available, turn the adjusting screw until resistance is felt, indicating the band is snug against the drum. Then back off two full turns.

To adjust the reverse band, a special tool is required in order to make the required accurate adjustment.

## HOW TO ADJUST C3 BANDS

To adjust the front band on the C3 automatic transmission: Remove the downshift rod from the transmission downshift lever. Clean all dirt from the band adjusting screw area. Remove and discard the lock nut. With a torque wrench, tighten the adjusting screw to 10 ft. lb., Fig. R-12. Then back off the adjusting screw exactly 1 1/2 turns. Holding the adjusting screw, tighten the lock nut. Install the downshift rod on the transmission downshift lever.

## JATCO AUTOMATIC TRANSMISSION

The JATCO automatic transmission, Fig. R-13, is installed on the 1978 Granada. JATCO is a three speed unit providing automatic upshifts and downshifts through the three forward gear ratios. It also provides manual selection of first and second gears.

JATCO basically consists of a torque converter, planetary gear train, three multiple disc clutches, a one way clutch, one band and a hydraulic

## Automatic Transmission Service

control system. An adjustment for the intermediate band is provided. Make the adjustment after placing the vehicle on a hoist. Loosen the servo cover attaching bolts and remove the cover. Loosen the intermediate band adjusting screw lock nut and tighten the adjusting screw to 10 ft. lb. torque. Then, back off two turns. Hold the adjusting screw and torque tighten the lock nut to 22-29 ft. lb.

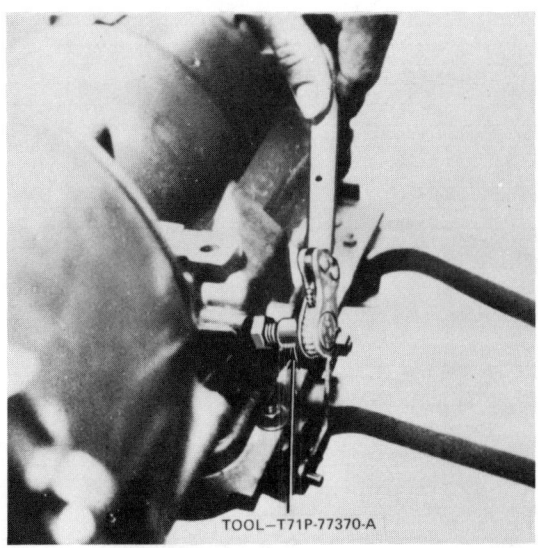

*Fig. R-12. Adjusting front band on C3 automatic transmission.*

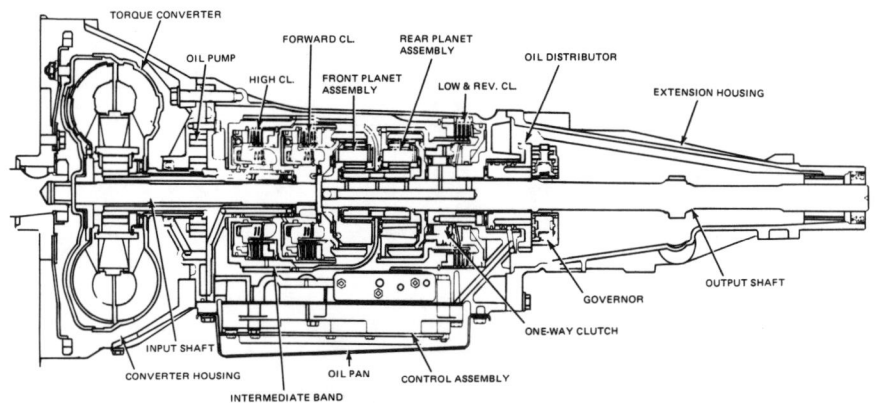

*Fig. R-13. Details of JATCO automatic transmission as installed on 1978 Granada.*

# Fix Your Ford

| Trouble Symptom | Items to Check | |
|---|---|---|
| | Transmission in Vehicle | Transmission Out of Vehicle |
| Rough Initial Engagement in D or 2 | K B W F E | |
| Rough Initial Engagement 2 Only | G J | |
| 1-2 or 2-3 Shift Points Incorrect | A L B C D W E | |
| Rough 2-3 Shift | B F E | |
| Engine Overspeeds on 2-3 Shift | B G W E F | r |
| No Shift Points | B C D E J | |
| No 2-3 Shift | C R D E | b r |
| No 3-1 Shift in D | B E | |
| No Forced Downshifts | L W E | |
| Runaway Engine on Forced Downshift | G F E J B | c |
| Rough 3-2 or 3-1 Shift at Closed Throttle | K B E | |
| Shifts 1-3 in D | G J | |
| No Engine Braking In First Gear—Manual Low Range | H I | |
| Creeps Excessively in D | K | |
| Slips or Chatters in First Gear, D | A B W F E | a c i |
| Slips or Chatters in Second Gear | A B G W F E J | a c |
| Slips or Chatters in R | A H W F E I | b c |
| No Drive in D Only | C E | i |
| No Drive in 2 Only | C | |
| No Drive in R Only | C H I E R | b c |
| No Drive in D, 2, or 1 | D W R | a |
| No Drive in Any Selector Lever Position | A C W F E R | c h |
| Lockup in 2 Only | H I | i |
| Lockup in R Only | | a g |
| Parking Lock Binds or Does Not Hold | C | g |
| Transmission Overheats | A O F | n |
| Maximum Speed Too Low, Poor Acceleration | | n |
| Transmission Noisy in N | F | d |
| Transmission Noisy in First, Second, and Reverse Gear | F | h d |
| Transmission Noisy in P | F | d |
| Fluid Leak | M N O P Q S U X | j m p |

**KEY TO DIAGNOSIS GUIDE**

| TRANSMISSION IN VEHICLE | |
|---|---|
| A | Fluid Level |
| B | Vacuum Diaphragm Unit or Tubes |
| C | Manual Linkage |
| D | Governor |
| E | Valve Body |
| F | Control Pressure Regulator Valve |
| G | Intermediate Band |
| H | Low-Reverse Band |
| I | Low-Reverse Servo |
| J | Intermediate Servo |
| K | Engine Idle Speed |
| L | Downshift Linkage |
| M | Convertor Drain Plugs |
| N | Oil Pan Gasket, or Filler Tube |
| O | Oil Cooler and Connections |
| P | Manual or Downshift Lever Shaft Seal |
| Q | 1/8-inch Pipe Plug in Side of Case |
| R | Perform Air-Pressure Check |
| S | Extension Housing to Case Gaskets and Lockwashers |
| U | Extension Housing Rear Oil Seal |
| W | Perform Control Pressure Check |
| X | Speedometer Driven Gear Adapter Seal |

| TRANSMISSION OUT OF VEHICLE | |
|---|---|
| a | Forward Clutch |
| b | Reverse-High Clutch |
| c | Leakage in Hydraulic System |
| d | Front Pump |
| g | Parking Linkage |
| h | Planetary Assembly |
| i | Planetary One-Way Clutch |
| j | Engine Rear Oil Seal |
| m | Front Pump Oil Seal |
| n | Converter One-Way Clutch |
| p | Front Pump to Case Gasket or Seal |
| r | Reverse-High Clutch Piston Air Bleed Valve |

*R-14. C4 automatic transmission diagnosis.*

# Automatic Transmission Service

| Trouble Symptoms | ITEMS TO CHECK (In the order indicated) See detailed possible causes below. | |
|---|---|---|
| | Transmission In Car | Transmission Out of Car |
| No Drive in D, 2 and 1 | C W E R | a c |
| Rough Initial Engagement in D or 2 | K B W F E | a |
| 1-2 or 2-3 Shift Points Incorrect or Erratic | A B L C D W E R | |
| Rough 1-2 Upshifts | B J G W E F | |
| Rough 2-3 Shifts | B J W F G E R | b r |
| Dragged Out 1-2 Shift | A B J W G E F R | c |
| Engine Overspeeds on 2-3 Shift | C A B J W E F G | b r |
| No 1-2 or 2-3 Shift | C L B D W E G J | b c |
| No 3-1 Shift in D | D E | |
| No Forced Downshifts | L E B | |
| Runaway Engine on Forced 3-2 Downshift | W J G F E B | c |
| Rough 3-2 or 3-1 Shift at Closed Throttle | K B J E F | |
| Shifts 1-3 in D | G J B E D R | |
| No Engine Braking in First Gear—1 Range | C H E D R | |
| Creeps Excessively | K | |
| Slips or Chatters in First Gear, D | A B W F E | a c i |
| Slips or Chatters in Second Gear | A B J G W F E R | a c |
| Slips or Chatters in R | A B H W F E R | b c r |
| No Drive in D Only | C W E | i |
| No Drive in 2 Only | A C W J E R | c |
| No Drive in 1 Only | A C W E R | c |
| No Drive in R Only | A C H W E R | b c r |
| No Drive in Any Selector Lever Position | A C W F E R | c d |
| Lockup in D only | | g c |
| Lockup in 2 Only | H | b g c i |
| Lockup in 1 Only | | g c |
| Lockup in R Only | | a g c |
| Parking Lock Binds or Does Not Hold | C | g |
| Transmission Overheats | O F B W | n s |
| Maximum Speed Too Low, Poor Acceleration | Y Z | n |
| Transmission Noisy in N and P | A F | d |
| Transmission Noisy in First, Second, Third or Reverse Gear | A F | h a d i |
| Fluid Leak | A M N O P Q S U X B J | j m p |
| Car Moves Forward in N | C | a |

Probable Trouble Sources

| | | | |
|---|---|---|---|
| A. | Fluid Level | U. | Extension Housing Rear Oil Seal |
| B. | Vacuum Diaphragm Unit or Tubes Restricted—Leaking—Adjustment | W. | Perform Control Pressure Check |
| C. | Manual Linkage | X. | Speedometer Driven Gear Adapter Seal |
| D. | Governor | Y. | Engine Performance |
| E. | Valve Body | Z. | Vehicle Brakes |
| F. | Pressure Regulator | a. | Forward Clutch |
| G. | Intermediate Band | b. | Reverse-High Clutch |
| H. | Low-Reverse Clutch | c. | Leakage in Hydraulic System |
| J. | Intermediate Servo | d. | Front Pump |
| K. | Engine Idle Speed | g. | Parking Linkage |
| L. | Downshift Linkage—Including inner Level Position | h. | Planetary Assembly |
| M. | Converter Drain Plugs | i. | Planetary One-Way Clutch |
| N. | Oil Pan Gasket, Filler Tube or Seal | j. | Engine Rear Oil Seal |
| O. | Oil Cooler and Connections | m. | Front Pump Oil Seal |
| P. | Manual or Downshift Lever Shaft Seal | n. | Converter One-Way Clutch |
| Q. | 1/8 Inch Pipe Plugs in Case | p. | Front Pump to Case Gasket or Seal |
| R. | Perform Air Pressure Check | r. | Reverse-High Clutch Piston Air Bleed Valve |
| S. | Extension Housing-to-Case Gasket | s. | Converter Pressure Check Valves |

*R-15. C6 automatic transmission diagnosis.*

|  | Items to Check | |
|---|---|---|
| Trouble Symptoms | Transmission in Car | Transmission Out of Car |
| Rough Initial Engagement in D or 2 | K B W F E G | |
| 1-2 or 2-3 Shift Points Incorrect | A B C D W E L | |
| Rough 2-3 Shift | B G F E J | |
| Engine Overspeeds on 2-3 Shift | B G E F | r |
| No 1-2 or 2-3 Shift | D E C G J | b c |
| No 3-1 Shift | K B E | |
| No Forced Downshifts | L W E | |
| Runaway Engine Forced Downshift | G F E J B | c |
| Rough 3-2 or 3-1 Shift at Closed Throttle | K B E | |
| Creeps Excessively | K | |
| Slips or Chatters in First Gear, D | A B W F E | a c i |
| Slips or Chatters in Second Gear | A B G W F E J | a c |
| Slips or Chatters in R | A H W F E I B | b c |
| No Drive in D | C E | i |
| No Drive in 2 | E R C | a c |
| No Drive in 1 | C E R | a c |
| No Drive in R | H I E R C | b c |
| No Drive in Any Selector Lever Position | A C W F E R | c |
| Lockup in D | C I J | b g c |
| Lockup in 2 | C H I | b g c i |
| Lockup in 1 | G J E | b g c |
| Lockup in R | G J | a g c |
| Parking Lock Binds or Does Not Hold | C | g |
| Transmission Overheats | O G | n |
| Maximum Speed Too Low, Poor Acceleration | | n |
| Transmission Noisy in N | F | a d |
| Transmission Noisy in First, Second, Third, or Reverse Gear | F | h a b d |
| Transmission Noisy in P | F | d |
| Fluid Leak | M N O P Q S T U X | j m p |

Probably Trouble Sources

| A. | Fluid Level | S. | Extension Housing to Case Gaskets and Lockwashers |
|---|---|---|---|
| B. | Vacuum Diaphragm Unit or Tubes | T. | Center Support Bolt Lockwashers |
| C. | Manual Linkage | U. | Extension Housing Rear Oil Seal |
| D. | Governor | W. | Perform Control Pressure Check |
| E. | Valve Body | X. | Speedometer Driven Gear Adapter Seal |
| F. | Pressure Regulator | a. | Front Clutch |
| G. | Front Band | b. | Rear Clutch |
| H. | Rear Band | c. | Leakage in Hydraulic System |
| I. | Rear Servo | d. | Front Pump |
| J. | Front Servo | g. | Parking Linkage |
| K. | Engine Idle Speed | h. | Planetary Assembly |
| L. | Downshift Linkage | i. | Planetary One-Way Clutch |
| M. | Converter Drain Plugs | j. | Engine Rear Oil Seal |
| N. | Oil Pan Gasket, Drain Plug or Tube | m. | Front Pump Oil Seal |
| O. | Oil Cooler and Connections | n. | Converter One-Way Clutch |
| P. | Manual or Throttle Lever Shaft Seal | p. | Front Pump to Case Gasket |
| Q. | 1/8-inch Pipe Plug in Side of Case | r. | Rear Clutch Piston Air Bleed Valve |
| R. | Perform Air Pressure Check | | |

*Fig. R-16. FMX Cruise-O-Matic automatic transmission diagnosis.*

# PROPELLER SHAFT AND UNIVERSAL JOINTS

Power is transmitted to the rear axle by means of an open propeller shaft and two universal joints. A slip yoke, Fig. S-1, is included in the design. These splines, Fig. S-2, in the yoke and on the transmission output shaft permit the drive shaft to move forward and backward as an axle moves up and down. All drive shafts are balanced. If the vehicle is to be undercoated, cover the drive shaft and universal joints to prevent application of the undercoating material as that would cause a state of unbalance which in turn causes vibration.

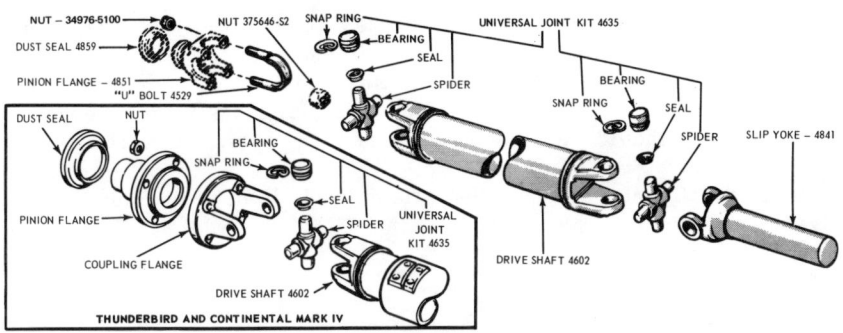

*Fig. S-1. Typical drive shaft and universal joints.*

## HOW TO REMOVE THE PROPELLER SHAFT

Before removing the propeller or drive shaft, mark the relationship of the rear drive shaft yoke and the drive pinion flange of the axle with the shaft so that they can be installed in their original positions. At time of manufacture, these parts are marked with a yellow alignment mark which may still be visible.

Disconnect the rear universal joint from the axle drive pinion flange. Wrap tape around the loose bearing caps to prevent them from falling off the spider, Fig. S-1. Pull the drive shaft toward the rear of the vehicle until the slip yoke, Fig. S-2, clears the transmission extension housing and the seal. Place a suitable plug in the extension housing to prevent leakage of the lubricant.

If either the rubber seal on the output shaft or the seal in the end of the transmission extension housing is damaged in any manner, replace the seal or seals as required. Also, if the lugs on the axle pinion flange are shaved or distorted so that the bearings slide, replace the flange.

Lubricate the yoke spline with special universal joint lubricant. This spline is sealed so that the transmission fluid does not wash away the spline lubricant, Fig. S-2. Remove the plug from the extension housing. Install the yoke on the transmission output shaft.

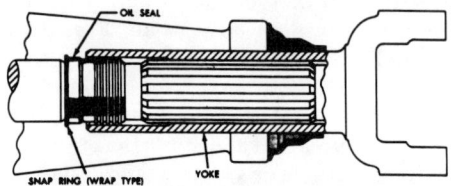

*Fig. S-2. Output shaft spline and seal.*

Install the drive shaft so that the marks placed on the yoke are in line with the yellow mark on the axle pinion flange. This prevents vibration which occurs when the balance of the shaft and the balance of the axle pinion flange become additive instead of neutralizing. If a vibration exists, the drive shaft should be disconnected from the axle, rotate at 180 deg. and reinstalled.

Install the U-bolts and nuts that attach the U-joint to the drive pinion flange.

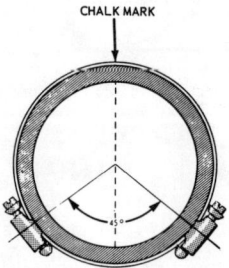

*Fig. S-3. Using Whittek type hose clamps to balance propeller shaft.*

## HOW TO BALANCE THE DRIVE SHAFT

If rotating the drive shaft 180 deg. does not eliminate vibration, the drive shaft may be balanced by using the following procedure:

Raise the vehicle so that the rear wheels are free to rotate. With the drive shaft rotating at a speedometer speed of approximately 40 mph,

## Propeller Shaft, Universal Joints

carefully bring a crayon or colored pencil up until it just barely contacts the rearward end of the drive shaft, Fig. S-3. This mark will indicate the heavy side of the shaft.

Install two Whittek type hose clamps on the drive shaft so that the heads are located 180 deg. from the crayon marks, Fig. S-3. Tighten the clamps.

Run the vehicle at about 65 mph speedometer speed. If no vibration is felt, lower the vehicle and road test. If unbalance still exists, rotate the clamp heads approximately 45 deg. away from each other and again test for vibration. Continue to rotate the clamp heads apart in small amounts until vibration is eliminated. Do not run the vehicle on the hoist for an extended period to avoid overheating.

## TROUBLE SHOOTING

U-joint noise may result from worn U-bolts, worn needle bearings, universal joint U-bolts loose, or lack of lubrication. Drive shaft vibration may result from any of the following conditions: Undercoating or other foreign material on shaft. Universal joint U-bolts loose. Universal joints worn or lack of lubricant. Drive shaft misalignment. Drive shaft and axle companion flange 180 deg. out of phase. Universal joint U-bolts over torqued or unevenly torqued. Broken rear spring. Rear springs not matched. Drive shaft damaged or out of balance. Sheared companion flange. Improper pinion angle.

Vibration or shudder which is noticeable either on fast acceleration or when coasting, using the engine as a brake, may be caused by the rear housing being loose on the rear springs or by improper pinion angle.

## REPLACING A U-JOINT

To replace a universal joint, first remove the snap ring, Fig. S-1, from under the yoke and around the needle bearing races. Then with a drift of approximately the same diameter as the needle bearing race, press one bearing race through the yoke. Using a pair of pliers, remove the opposite bearing, which is partly pushed out of the yoke. The spider can then be removed from the yoke. Repeat the same procedure on the other pair of bearings. To install the bearings, first pack the bearing and the holes in the end of the spider with universal joint grease. Place the spider in the yoke and press the bearings in place. Install a snap ring.

Reposition the drive shaft and install the new spider and two new bearings in the same manner as the rear yoke. Position the slip yoke on the spider and install two new bearings, nylon thrust bearings and snap rings. Check the joint for freedom of movement. If a bind has resulted from this alignment during the foregoing procedures, a sharp rap on the yokes with a brass hammer will seat the needle bearings and usually provide freedom of movement. Care must be taken to support the shaft end during this operation as well as preventing blows to the bearings and cells. Do not install the drive shaft unless the universal joints are free of bind.

# Fix Your Ford

For 1977: Above. Thunderbird Two-Door. Center. LTD II Two-Door. Below. Pinto Three-Door.

# REAR AXLE
## Service Kinks

Three different designs of rear axles are used on Ford cars. One of these, Fig. T-1, is of the removable carrier type, and the other two, Figs. T-2 and T-3, are of the integral carrier type. However, the integral carrier types differ in the method of removing the axle shafts.

### REMOVABLE CARRIER TYPE AXLE

This type axle, Fig. T-1, used primarily on cars with large displacement engines, is so designed that the rear axle shafts, wheel bearings, and oil seal can be replaced without removing the differential assembly from the axle housing.

HOW TO REMOVE THE SHAFTS: Removal and insertion of rear axle shafts must be performed with caution. The entire length of the shaft (including spline) up to the seal journal, must pass through the seal with-

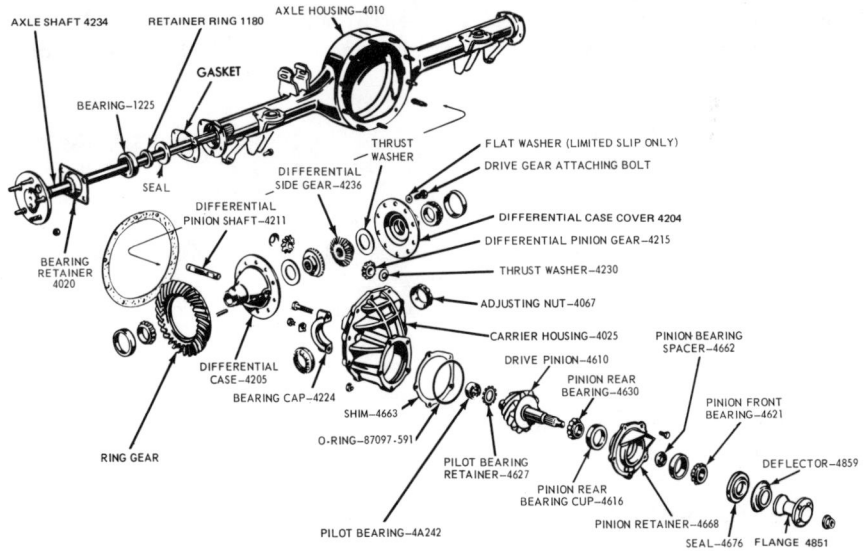

*Fig. T-1. Details of removable carrier type rear axle. Used on V-8 installations on Ford, Fairlane, Granada, Falcon and Mustang cars.*

out cutting off the seal element during axle removal or installation will result in early seal failure. Leather seals only are used as service replacement.

To remove the axle shaft, first remove the wheel cover, wheel and tire from the brake drum. Remove the nuts that secure the brake drum to the axle shaft flange, then remove the drum from the flange, after first removing the Tinnerman spring clips from the brake drum studs.

Working through the hold provided in each axle shaft flange, remove the nuts that secure the wheel bearing retainer plate. Then pull the axle shaft assembly out of the axle. An impact type hammer is used for pulling the axle shaft assembly from the housing. The brake backing plate must not be dislodged. Install one nut to hold the plate in place after the axle shaft is removed.

When replacing the axle shaft, use a new gasket between the housing flange and the backing plate, and then carefully slide the axle shaft into the housing so that the rough forging of the shaft will not damage the oil seal. Start the axle splines into the side gear, and push the shaft in until the bearing bottoms in the housing. Install the bearing retainer plate and the nuts that secure it. Then install the brake drum and the Tinnerman spring nuts. Install the wheel and tire on the drum and replace the wheel cover.

REMOVAL OF REAR WHEEL BEARING AND SEAL: Synthetic seals must not be cleaned, soaked or washed in cleaning solvents. Removal of the wheel bearings from the axle shaft makes them unfit for further use. If the rear wheel bearing is to be replaced, loosen the inner retainer ring by nicking it deeply with a cold chisel in several places. It will then slide off easily. The wheel bearing is then removed from the axle shaft by means of a press.

The seal may be removed by means of a slide hammer type tool which will engage the seal within the axle housing. The rear wheel bearing and seal are replaced by reversing the procedure, and new leather seals should be soaked in SAE 10 oil for one-half hour before installation.

To remove the carrier assembly, proceed as follows: Raise the vehicle on a hoist and remove the two rear wheels and tires. Remove both rear brake drum assemblies. Disconnect the propeller shaft at the rear end and the propeller shaft from the transmission, taking care to plug the transmission so that the lubricant will not come out. Clean the area around carrier-to-housing surface with a wire brush and wipe clean to prevent dirt entry into the housing. Place a drain pan under the carrier and housing, remove the carrier attaching nuts and drain the axle. The carrier assembly can then be lifted from the axle housing.

## LIGHT DUTY (WER) REAR AXLE

This rear axle is of the integral carrier type and used primarily on Ford passenger vehicles equipped with 240-1V and 289-2V engines and related transmissions.

## Rear Axle Service

REAR AXLE SHAFT REPLACEMENT: Raise the rear of the vehicle and remove the wheels, tires and brake drums. Place a drain pan and loosen the cover to the differential housing retaining bolts. Drain the housing. Remove the attaching Tinnerman spring nuts that secure the brake drums to the axle shaft flange and then remove the drums. Remove the differential housing cover bolts, cover and gasket. Discard the gasket.

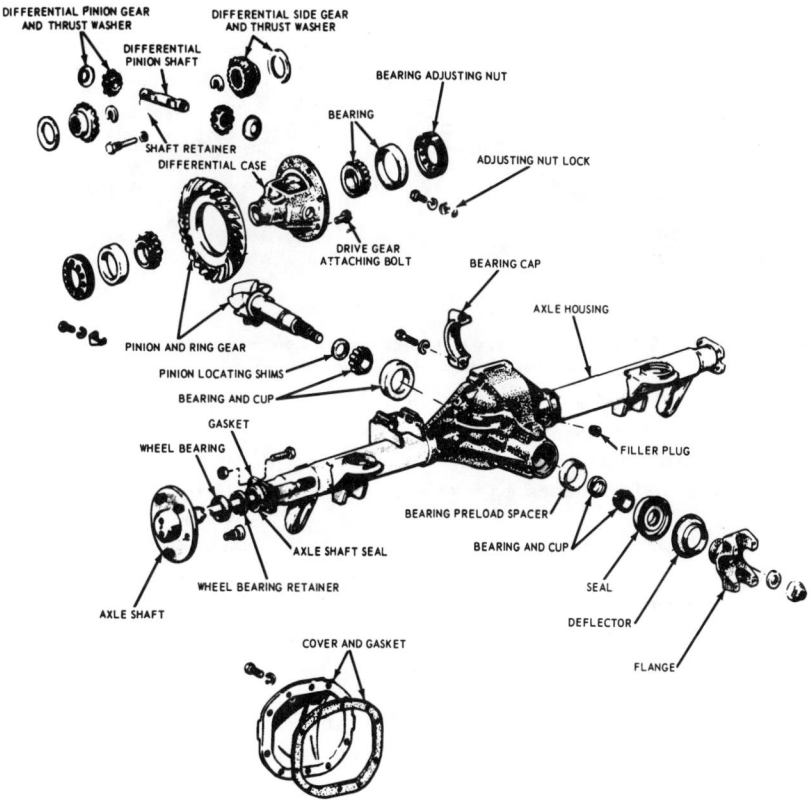

*Fig. T-2. Light-duty (WER) rear axle as installed on 240-1V and 289-2V engines and related transmissions. Axle shafts are retained at inner ends with "C" locks.*

Position safety stands under the rear frame member and lower the car and allow the axle to lower as far as possible. Working through the differential case opening, remove the pinion shaft lock bolt and the pinion shaft, Fig. T-2. Push the axle shafts toward the center of the axle housing and remove the axle shaft C-washers from the inner ends of the axle. The axle shafts can then be withdrawn from the housing. Extreme care must be used to avoid contact of the axle shaft seal lip with any portion of the axle shaft except the seal journal.

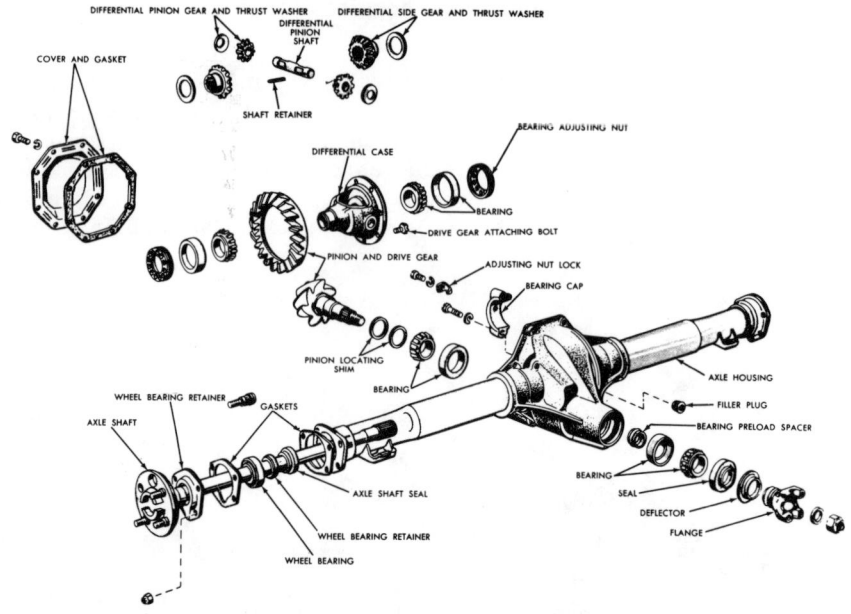

*Fig. T-3. Details of integral carrier type rear axle, used on Falcon, Granada, Maverick and Mustang cars using six cylinder engines.*

Replacement of the axle shaft is performed by reversing the procedure, taking care that splines or any portion of the axle shafts do not damage the oil seals and that they engage with the splines of the differential side gears.

BEARING AND OIL SEAL REPLACEMENT: The removal of the wheel bearing and oil seal from the axle shaft housing is accomplished by means of a slide type puller, Fig. T-4.

Inspect the machine surface of the axle shaft and the axle housing for rough spots or other irregularities, which would affect the sealing action of the oil seal. Check the axle shaft splines for burrs, wear or damage.

REMOVING DIFFERENTIAL CASE: First remove the axle shafts as previously described. Remove the pinion side gears and the side gear thrust washers. Remove both side bearing adjusting nut locks (bolts). Install a dial indicator and check and record the backlash and ring gear run-out. Mark one differential bearing cap and the case to help in positioning the parts properly during assembly. Remove the bearing cap retaining bolts. Remove the bearing cap cups, adjusting nuts and case assembly.

Then, to remove the drive pinion, hold the drive pinion flange and remove the pinion nut. Remove the pinion flange. Drive the pinion out of the front bearing cone and remove it from the carrier housing. Remove and discard the bearing spacer. With a hammer and drift remove the pinion shaft oil seal out to the front of the carrier housing. Remove the pinion rear bearing from the drive pinion shaft. Measure the shim, which is found under the bearing cone with a micrometer. Record the thickness of the shim.

# Rear Axle Service

## INTEGRAL CARRIER TYPE AXLE

This type rear axle is illustrated in Fig. T-3 and differs primarily from the other integral carrier type axle in the method of removing the axle shafts. This type axle is used primarily on Maverick, Falcon and Mustang cars with engines of lower horsepower.

REMOVING THE AXLE SHAFT: The rear axle shafts, wheel bearings and oil seal can be replaced without removing the differential assembly from the axle housing. Remove the wheel cover, wheel and tire from the brake drum. Remove the Tinnerman nuts that secure the brake drum to the axle housing flange, then remove the drum from the flange. Working through the hole provided in each axle shaft flange, Fig. T-3, remove the nuts that secure the wheel bearing retainer plate. Then remove the axle shaft assembly out of the axle housing using a slide type puller. Entire length of the axle shaft must pass through the seal without contact as any roughing of the seal will cause early seal failure.

The brake backing plate must not be dislodged. Install one nut to hold the plate in place after the axle shaft is removed. If the rear wheel bearing is to be replaced, loosen the inner retainer ring by nicking it deeply with a cold chisel in several places. It will then slide off easily. The bearing is then pressed from the shaft in a hydraulic press or a similar device.

REPLACING THE OIL SEAL: Whenever a rear axle shaft is replaced, the oil seal must also be replaced. The seal is removed from the axle housing by means of an impact type puller, Fig. T-4.

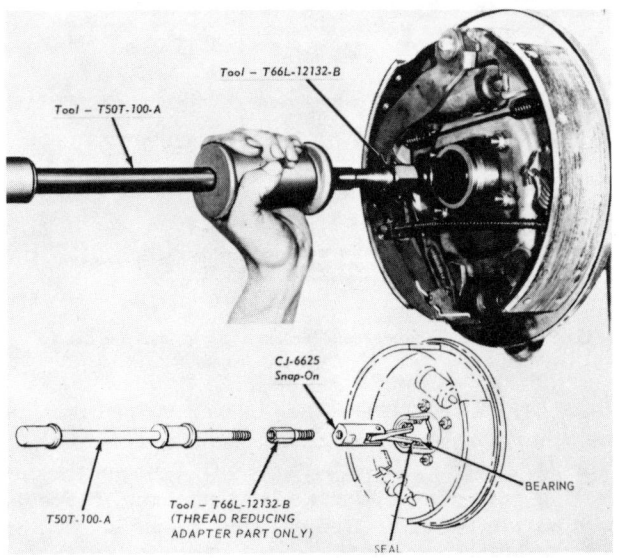

Fig. T-4. Using a slide type puller to withdraw oil seal from axle housing.

# Fix Your Ford

REMOVING DRIVE PINION OIL SEAL: Replacement of the pinion oil seal involves removal and installation of only the pinion shaft nut, and the universal joint flange. However this operation disturbs the pinion bearing preload and this preload must be carefully reset when assemblying. To remove the drive pinion oil seal, raise the vehicle and install safety stands, then remove the rear wheels and brake drums. Scribe marks on the drive shaft end yoke and the axle U-joint flange to insure proper position of the drive shaft and assembly. Remove the drive shaft using an inch-pound torque wrench on the pinion nut, record the torque required to maintain rotation of the pinion shaft through several revolutions. Then while holding the flange from rotation, remove the integral pinion nut and washer. Clean the pinion bearing retainer around the oil seal. Place a drain pan under the seal, then remove the pinion U-joint flange. The drive pinion oil seal can then be pulled from the housing by means of an impact type puller. Clean the oil seal seat. Pinion oil seals have preapplied oil resistant sealer. The new seal can then be installed.

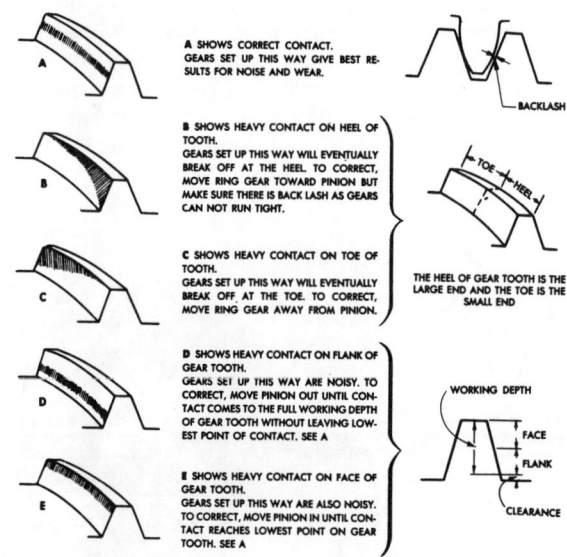

Fig. T-5. How to obtain correct tooth contact of pinion and ring gear.

REMOVAL OF DIFFERENTIAL CASE AND DRIVE PINION: Raise the vehicle and support it on the underbody so that the rear axle drops down as far as the springs and shock absorbers permit. Remove the cover from the carrier casting rear face and drain the lubricant. Remove the axle shafts. Remove both oil seals. Remove the drive shaft. Remove the differential bearing adjusting nut locks, Fig. T-3. Mark one differential bearing cap and the case to help position the parts properly during

## Rear Axle Service

reassembly. Remove the differential bearing cap bolts and the bearing caps. Hold the differential case assembly in the housing after the caps are removed. The differential case and bearing cups can then be removed from the housing. Remove the drive pinion nut and remove the drive pinion flange. With a soft faced hammer, drive the pinion out of the front bearing cone and remove it through the rear of the carrier casting. Drive against the pinion front bearing cone and drive the pinion flange seal and the bearing cone out of the front of the carrier casting. Use a press to remove the rear bearing cone. Measure the shim which is found under the bearing cone with a micrometer and record the thickness of the shim.

## INSPECTING DIFFERENTIAL PARTS

The differential case assembly and the drive pinion should be inspected before they are removed from the housing. These inspections can help to find the cause of the trouble and to determine the correction needed.

Wipe the lubricant from the internal working parts and visually inspect the parts for wear or damage. Rotate the gears to see if there is any roughness which would indicate defective bearings or chipped gears. Check the gear teeth for scoring or signs of abnormal wear.

Check the differential case and the drive pinion for end play. Using a dial indicator, check the backlash at several points around the ring gear. Backlash should be limited to .008-.012 in.

To check the gear tooth contact, paint the gear teeth with the special compound furnished with each service ring gear and pinion, or if that is not available make a paste of dry red lead and oil. A mixture that is too wet will run and smear, while mixtures that are too dry cannot be pressed out between the teeth. The procedure is to paint the gear teeth with the mixture and then rotate the gears until a clear tooth contact is obtained. It is advisable to make five complete revolutions in both directions, or until a clear tooth contact pattern is obtained. The different types of tooth patterns are shown in Fig. T-5. Both drive and coast patterns should be fairly well centered on the tooth. Some clearance between the pattern and the top of the tooth is desirable.

On integral carrier type axles, a thinner shim with the backlash set to specification moves the pinion farther from the ring gear. A thicker shim with the backlash set to specifications moves the pinion closer to the ring gear. If the patterns are not correct, make the changes as indicated. The differential case and drive pinion will have to be removed from the carrier casting to change a shim. When reinstalling the pinion and ring gear, be sure that the marked tooth on the pinion indexes between the marked teeth on the ring gear.

REMOVABLE CARRIER TYPE AXLE: Thicker shim with the backlash set to specifications moves the pinion farther from the ring gear. Thinner shim with the backlash set to specifications moves the pinion closer to the ring gear. If the patterns are not correct, make the changes as indicated. The pinion need not be disassembled to change a shim. All that is required

Fix Your Ford

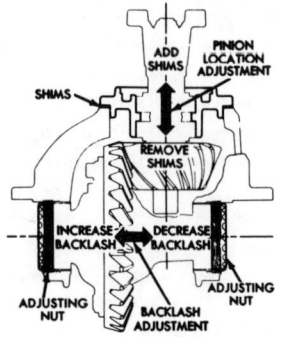

*Fig. T-6. Pinion and ring gear tooth contact adjustment on removable carrier type differential.*

is to remove the pinion, bearing and retainer assembly and install a different shim. When reinstalling the pinion and retainer assembly, be sure the marked tooth on the pinion indexes between the marked teeth in the ring gear.

## BACKLASH AND PRELOAD ADJUSTMENTS

In both types of axles, Figs. T-6 and T-7, the ring gear is moved away from or toward the piston as described in the following procedure. Remove the adjusting nut locks, loosen the differential bearing cap bolts, then torque the bolts to 15 ft. lb. on integral carrier type axles and 20 ft. lb. on removable carrier type axles before making adjustments. The left adjusting nut is on the ring gear side of the carrier. The right nut is on the pinion side.

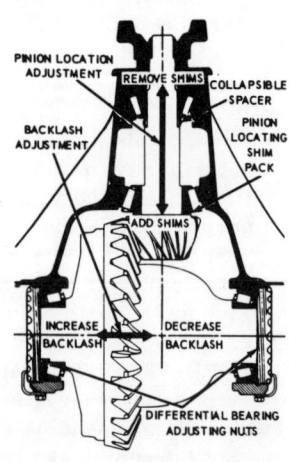

*Fig. T-7. Pinion and ring gear tooth contact adjustment on integral carrier type differential.*

## Rear Axle Service

Loosen the right nut until it is away from the cup. Tighten the left nut until the ring gear is just forced into the pinion with zero backlash, then rotate the pinion several revolutions to be sure no binding is evident. Recheck the right nut at this time to be sure that it is still loose. Tightening the left nut moves the ring gear into the pinion to decrease backlash and tightening the right nut moves the ring gear away.

Tighten the right nut until it first contacts the bearing cup. Then as measured with a dial gauge, preload the bearings from .008 to .012 in. case spread. Rotate the pinion gear several revolutions in each direction while the bearings are loaded, to seat the bearings in their cups to be sure no bind is evident. This step is important. Again loosen the right nut to release the preload. If there is any backlash between the gears, as shown by the dial indicator, tighten the left nut just enough to remove this backlash. At this time, make sure that one of the slots in the left nut is so located that the lock can be installed without turning the nut. Carefully tighten the right nut until it just contacts the cup. On integral carrier axles, tighten the differential bearing cap bolts to 40-55 ft. lb. and on removable carrier type to 55-70 ft. lb. on the 7-3/4 and 8 in. gears, and 70-85 ft. lb. on the 9 in. gears.

On integral carrier type axles, set a preload of .008 to .012 in. case spread for new bearings, and .003 to .005 for the original bearings. On removable carrier type axles, the preload is .008 to .012 in. case spread for new bearings, and .005 to .008 in. for the original bearings. As preload is applied from the right side, the ring gear is forced away from the pinion and usually results in correct backlash. Measure the backlash on several teeth around the ring gear. If the measurements vary more than .003 in. (both integral and removable carrier) there is excessive run-out in the gear or their mountings which should be corrected to obtain a satisfactory unit.

### NEW PINION AND RING GEAR INSTALLATION

If either the pinion or ring gear is damaged, both gears will have to be replaced as these gears are sold only in matched sets. At the same time, obtain the correct shims for the installation of the drive pinion for that particular set of gears, together with the necessary instructions for its installation. Pinion gears are marked with the size shim that is needed.

With the shim correctly installed, the proper mesh is then obtained by adjusting the position of the ring gear to the right or left as required. When adjusting the position of the ring gear, wipe a thin coating of lubricating oil over the bearing bores so the differential bearing cups will move easily.

Place the cups on the bearings and set the differential assembly in the carrier. Slide the assembly along the bores until a slight amount of backlash is felt between the gear teeth. Set the adjusting nuts in the bores so that they just contact the bearing cups. The nuts should be engaging about the same number of threads on each side.

Carefully position the bearing caps on the carrier. Match the marks made when the caps were removed. Install the bearing cap bolts and alternately torque them to 70-80 ft. lb. If the adjusting nuts do not turn freely as the cap bolts are tightened, remove the bearing caps and again inspect for damaged threads or incorrectly positioned caps. Tightening the bolt to the specified torque is done to be sure that the cup and adjusting nut are seated. Loosen the cap bolts and torque them to only 20 ft. lb. before making adjustments.

Loosen the right nut until it is away from the cup. Tighten the left nut until the drive gear is just forced into the pinion with no backlash. Recheck the right nut at this time to be sure that it is still loose. The left adjusting nut is on the drive gear side of the carrier. The right nut is on the pinion side. Tightening the left nut drives the pinion gear into the pinion to decrease backlash. Tightening the right nut moves the drive gear away. Tighten the right nut two notches beyond the position where it first contacts the bearing cup. Rotate the drive gear several revolutions in each direction while the bearings are loaded, to seat the bearings in their cup. This step is important.

Again loosen the right nut to release the preload. If there is any backlash between the gears, tighten the left nut just enough to remove this backlash. Carefully tighten the right nut until it just contacts the cup. Set preload of two or three notches tight by the right nut. As preload is applied from the right side, the drive gear is forced away from the pinion and usually results in a correct backlash, which should be .008 in. to .012 in. Torque the differential cap bolts.

Measure the backlash on several teeth around the drive gear. If the measurements vary more than .003 in., there is excessive run-out in the gears or their mountings which must be corrected to obtain a satisfactory unit. If backlash is out of specifications, loosen one adjusting nut and tighten the opposite nut an equal amount to remove the drive gear away from or toward the pinion. When moving the adjusting nuts, the final adjustment should always be made in a tightening direction. For example, if the left nut has to be loosened one notch, loosen the nut two notches, then tighten it one. After making these adjustments, recheck the mesh of the gears by painting them with red lead as previously described.

## LIMITED SLIP DIFFERENTIAL

A constant friction limited slip differential is used as optional equipment on some models. This unit, Fig. T-8, employs automatic transmission type clutch plates to control differential action. Under conditions with one or both wheels on icy surface, the friction between the clutch plates will transfer a portion of the usable torque to the wheel with the most traction. For that reason, care must be exercised when one wheel is jacked up as the car can be driven off the jack by power on the other wheel. To disassemble the limited slip differential, first mark one differential bearing cap and the mating bearing support to help position the part properly during assembly of the carrier.

## Rear Axle Service

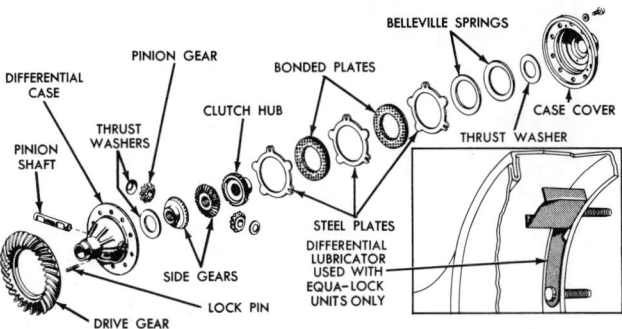

Fig. T-8. Limited slip type differential.

Remove the adjusting lock nut, bearing caps and adjusting nuts. Then lift the differential assembly out of the carrier. Remove the differential bearing, Fig. T-8. Loosen alternate drive gear attaching bolts evenly to release the spring pressure between the differential case and cover. A hydraulic press may be used to contain the spring pressure while the bolts are removed. Apply one ton pressure across the case bearing hubs while the drive gear bolts are removed.

Remove the differential case cover, then remove the drive gear. Remove the two Belleville springs. Remove the spring and bonded clutch plates. Remove the differential clutch hub, side gear and thrust washer. Remove the drive gear from the differential case. Drive out the differential pinion shaft lock pin. With a punch, drive out the differential pinion shaft. Then remove the pinion gear and thrust washers. The remainder of the unit is disassembled in the conventional manner.

## TRACTION-LOK DIFFERENTIAL

The Traction-Lok differential, Fig. T-9, is a torque sensitive locking type differential which permits one wheel to drive while the other is stationary. In effect, it is similar to the limited slip differential. The service procedure is as follows:

Remove the differential case from the carrier and remove the bearings from the differential case in the same manner as in the conventional differential case.

Remove ten bolts securing the ring gear to the differential case assembly. The ring gear must be removed in order to separate the case halves.

Remove the ring gear by tapping the gear with a soft hammer or press the gear from the case.

Place the differential case in a press to preload the bearing journals so that the preload of the springs is overcome. If a press is not available, two 7/16 in. bolts and nuts can be used in the ring gear mounting holes, one on each side to compress the halves together and overcome preload

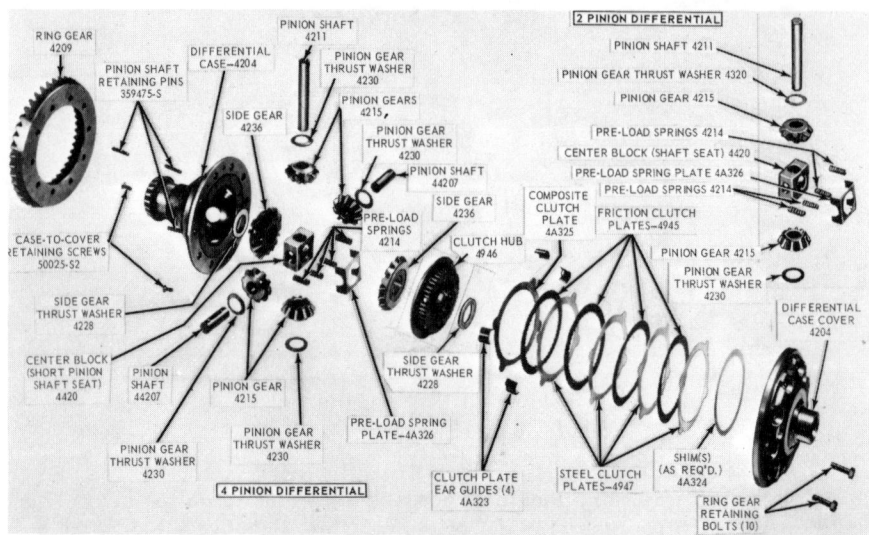

*Fig. T-9. Traction-Lok type differential.*

spring pressure. Then while the case is still under pressure, loosen the two Allen or Phillips head screws which hold the case halves together, until one or two threads of the screws remain engaged. Remove the case assembly from the press. Tap on the cover to spring it loose. Then remove both screws.

With the cover facing down, lift off the case. Remove the preload spring plate and four preload springs. From the cover, remove the side gear, four clutch plate ear guides, clutch hub, friction and steel plates and shims.

With a drift, drive out the pinion shaft lock pins from the case. With a brass drift, drive out the long pinion shaft from the case. Drive from the end opposite the lock pin hole.

Remove the two short pinion shafts, using a drift, driving each shaft from the center outward. Lift out the center block, then remove the pinion gears, thrust washers and side gear and thrust washer.

When reassembling and pressing the bearing on the cover, be sure to support the case under the bearing area to avoid damage to the cover.

## REAR AXLE TROUBLE SHOOTING

## EXCESSIVE REAR AXLE NOISE

Before road testing the car, make sure the tire pressures and the rear axle lubricant level are normal. Then drive the car far enough to warm the rear axle lubricant to its normal operating temperature.

With the car stopped, and the transmission in neutral, run the engine at various speeds. If the noise still exists during this test, the noise probably comes from the engine or from the exhaust system.

To determine if the noise is being caused by the rear axle or tires,

## Rear Axle Service

drive the car over several different types of road surfaces. Smooth asphalt or blacktop roads minimize tire noises. Tire noises may be changed and sometimes eliminated by cross-switching the tires. Snow tires often cause noises not heard from conventional tires.

Noise caused by a worn or damaged wheel bearing is often the loudest when the car is coasting at low speed, and it usually stops when the brakes are gently applied. To find the noisy bearing, provided the car is equipped with a conventional differential, jack up each wheel and check each bearing for roughness while the wheel is rotating.

If all possible external sources of noise have been checked and eliminated, and the noise still exists, road test the car under all four driving conditions of drive, cruise, float, and coast. Then remove, disassemble and inspect the axle.

### EXCESSIVE REAR AXLE BACKLASH

Excessive backlash in the axle driving parts may be caused by worn axle shaft splines, loose axle shaft flange nuts, loose universal joint flange mountings, excessive backlash between the drive pinion and drive gear, excessive backlash in the differential gears, or bearings, which are worn or out of adjustment.

### DRIVE LINE NOISE OR VIBRATION

Excessive noise or vibration may be caused by lack of lubrication, worn universal joint bearings, missing drive shaft balance weights, and sprung or damaged drive line.

### ONE WHEEL SPINS

This applies only to Equa-Lock or limited slip rear axle: If the torque required to rotate one rear wheel is less than 100 ft. lb., the differential is not functioning properly. To repair this unit it must be removed from the housing.

### HIGH PITCHED, CHATTERING NOISE

Drive the car in a fairly tight circle, making five circles in one direction and five in the opposite. If the noise continues, drain and refill with correct type of lubricant.

# Fix Your Ford

Above. 1976 Maverick Stallion. Center. 1976 F-150 4 x 4 Pickup. Below. 1976 Mustang II Stallion.

# Quick Service on
# SHOCK ABSORBERS AND SPRINGS

It is very important, both from a standpoint of safety and comfort, that the shock absorbers be maintained in good condition. Unless the shock absorbers, Figs. U-1 and Fig. U-2, control the rebound of the car, steering becomes hazardous, tire wear is increased, chassis spring life is shortened and riding comfort is sacrificed.

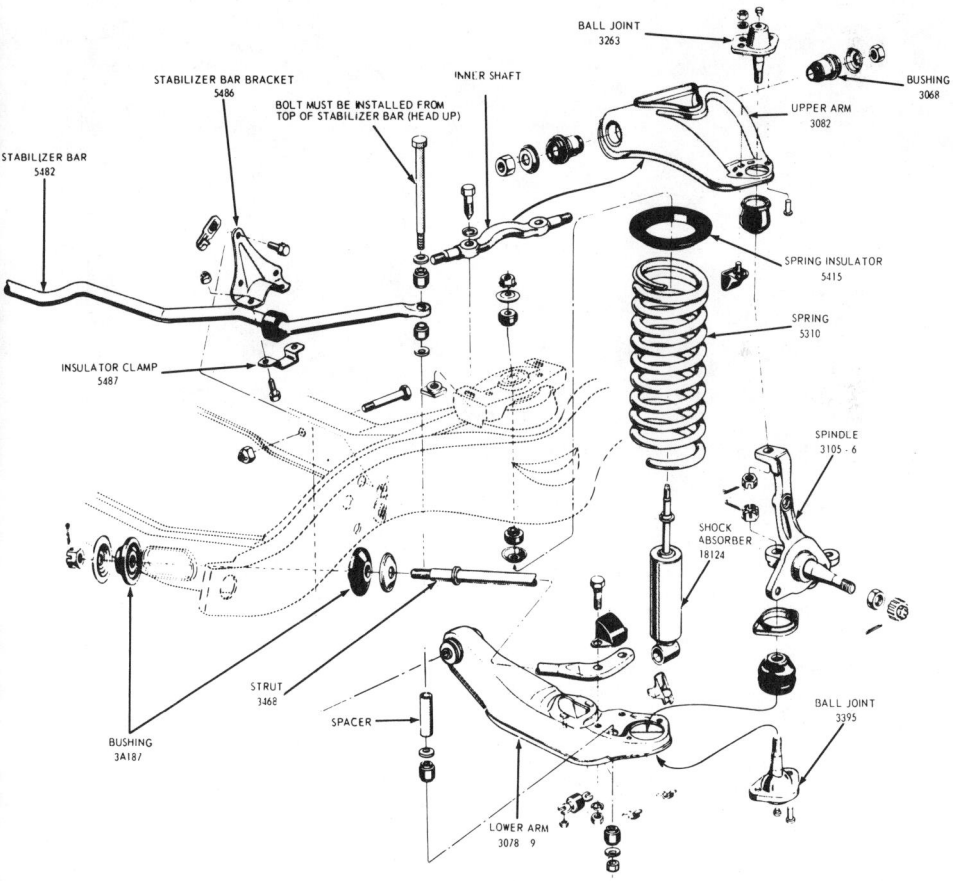

*Fig. U-1. Type of front suspension system with the spring between the control arms. See also Fig. U-3.*

# Fix Your Ford

The shock absorbers used on Ford built vehicles are of the direct acting type and are nonadjustable and nonrefillable and cannot be repaired. Before replacing a shock absorber, check the action of the shock absorber. Checking information follows.

## SHOCK ABSORBER CHECKS

Check the shock absorber to be sure it is securely and properly installed. Check the shock absorber insulators for damage and wear. Replace any defective insulators and tighten attachment to 20-28 ft. lb. for the upper attachment and 8-12 ft. lb. for the shock absorber lower arm. On a shock absorber which incorporates integral insulators, replace the shock absorber.

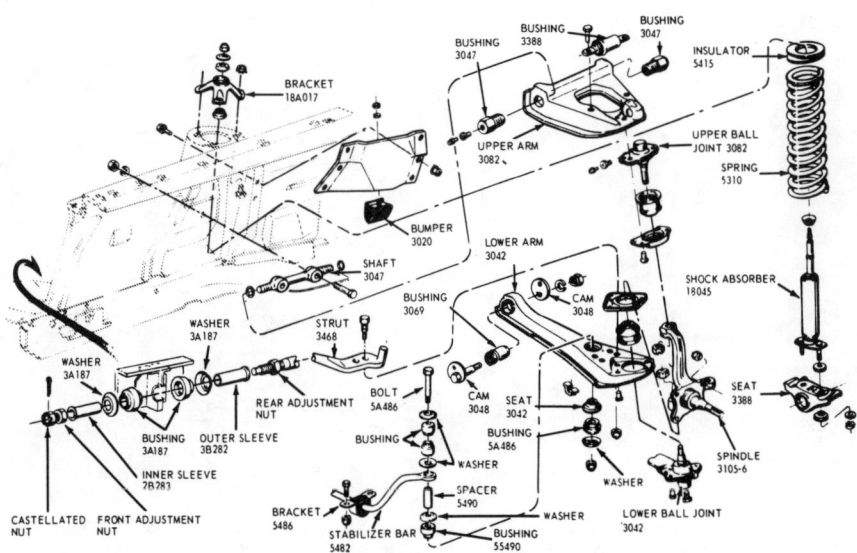

*Fig. U-2. Typical of Maverick and Granada front suspension is system with spring placed above upper control arm.*

Inspect the shock absorber for evidence of fluid leakage. A light film of fluid is permissible, but be sure any fluid observed is not from sources other than the shock absorber. Replace the shock absorber if leakage is severe.

A quick test of the condition of the shock absorbers can be made by grasping the bumper of the car and jouncing the car up and down. If the shock absorbers are in good condition, the car will immediately settle to normal position after the bumper is released. If the car continues to bounce or remains displaced, remove the shock absorber for further testing.

## Shock Absorber and Spring Service

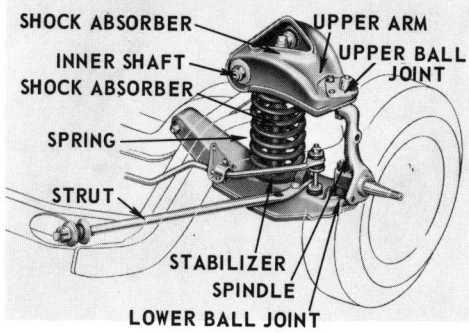

*Fig. U-3. Assembled front suspension system with the spring between the control arms. See also Fig. U-1.*

To further test the shock absorber, disconnect one end of the shock absorber. Extend and compress the shock absorber as fast as possible, using as much travel as possible. Action should be smoother and uniform throughout each stroke. Higher resistance on extension and on compression is normal condition. Any "swish" noises are also normal.

Remove the shock absorber for a bench test if the action is erratic. If the action is smooth, the shock absorbers are suspected of being weak. Compare the action of the tests with the shock absorber on the opposite side of the vehicle or with a new shock absorber.

It is advisable to replace shock absorbers in pairs, that is, both front shock absorbers, or both rear shock absorbers as the case may be.

### FRONT SHOCK ABSORBER REMOVAL

To remove the front shock absorbers from the suspension system used on full size Fords, which have the springs located between the upper and lower control arm, Fig. U-3, proceed as follows: Remove the nut washer and bushing from the shock absorber upper end. Raise the vehicle on a hoist and install safety stands. Remove two bolts attaching the shock absorber to the lower arm and remove the shock absorber. Installation is accomplished by reversing the procedure. Take care to place the washers and bushings in their correct position.

To remove the front shock absorbers from the suspension system used on the compact models (Falcon, Mustang, Fairlane and Maverick) which have the springs located above the upper control arm, as shown in Fig. U-2, proceed as follows: Raise the hood and remove the shock absorber upper mounting bracket to spring tower attaching nuts. Raise the front of the vehicle and place safety stands under the lower arms. Remove the shock absorber lower attaching nuts and washers. The shock absorber and upper bracket can then be lifted from the spring tower. When installing a new shock absorber, install the upper mounting bracket

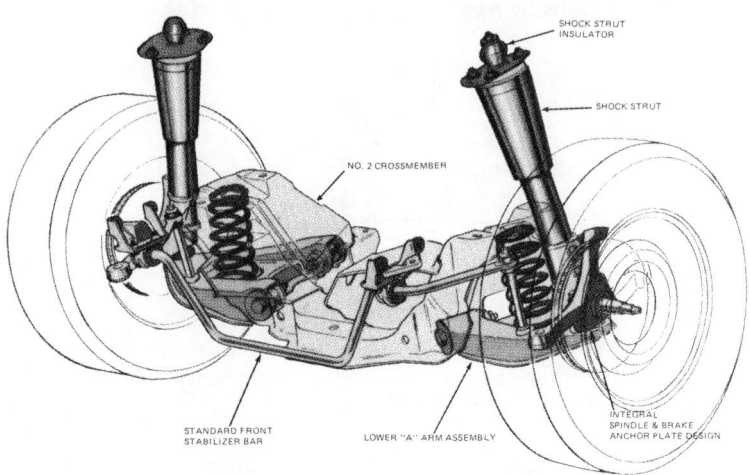

*Fig. U-4. Front suspension on 1978 Fairmont is known as single arm type. This setup is a modification of MacPherson strut design.*

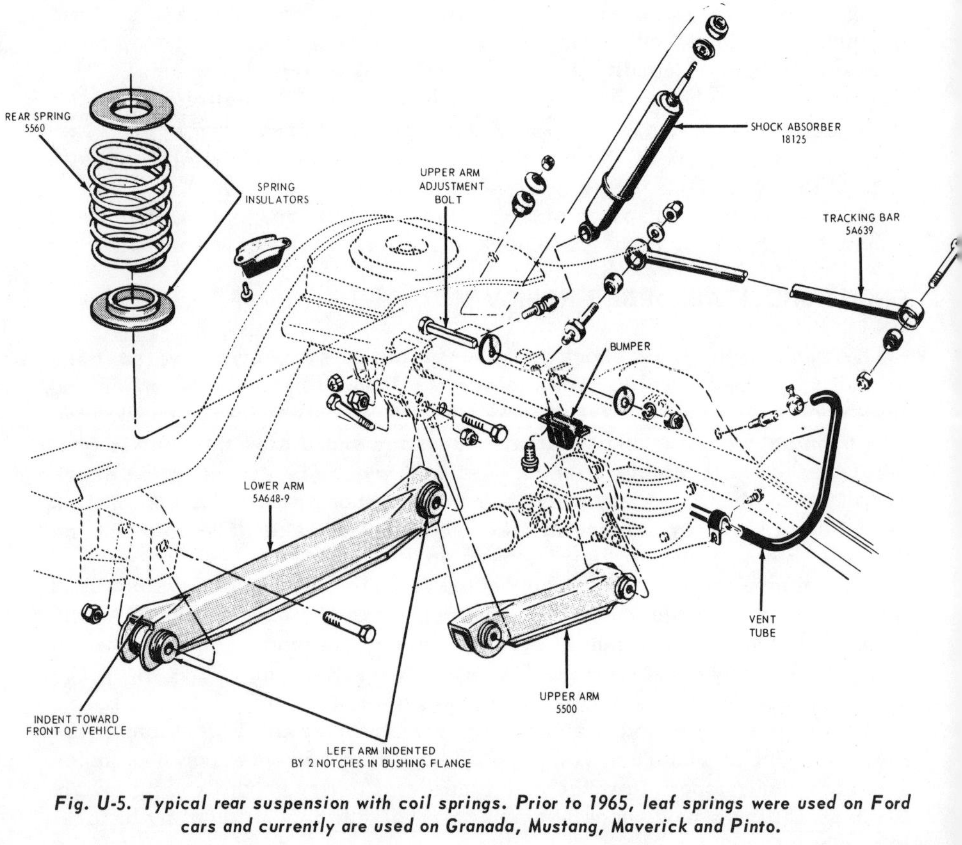

*Fig. U-5. Typical rear suspension with coil springs. Prior to 1965, leaf springs were used on Ford cars and currently are used on Granada, Mustang, Maverick and Pinto.*

## Shock Absorber and Spring Service

on the shock absorber and position the shock absorber and upper mounting bracket in the spring tower, making sure the shock absorber lower studs are in the pivot plate holes. Install the washers and attaching nuts on the shock absorber lower studs and then install the shock absorber upper mounting bracket to spring tower attaching nuts.

## SINGLE ARM FRONT SUSPENSION

The front suspension system utilized on the 1978 Fairmont is a modified MacPherson strut design. This particular design, Fig. U-4, features shock struts with coil springs mounted between the lower arm and a spring pocket on the No. 2 cross member.

The shock struts are not repairable. They must be replaced as a complete unit. Also make note that the ball joints and lower suspension arm bushings are not separately serviced. When faulty, they must be replaced as a suspension arm, bushing and ball joint assembly. The ball joint seal, however, can be replaced.

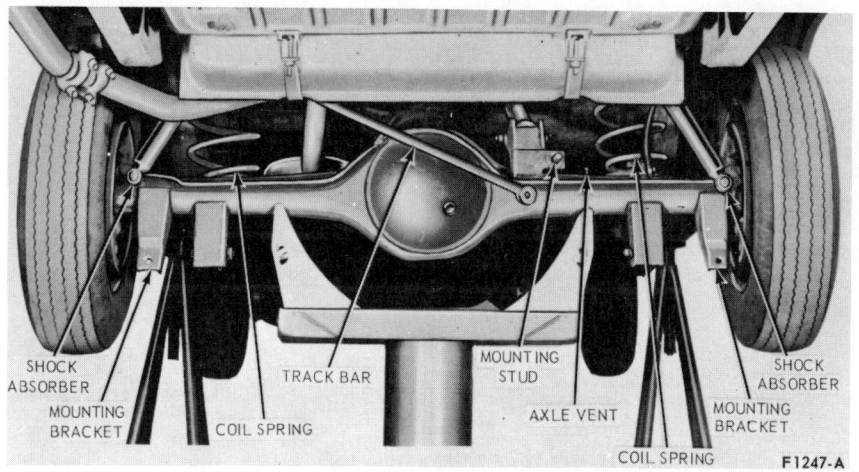

Fig. U-6. Coil spring rear suspension as installed on 1965-1970 Ford cars.

## REAR SHOCK ABSORBER REMOVAL

To remove rear shock absorbers from full size Ford cars, hoist vehicle. Remove nut, washer and insulator from upper stud. Compress shock to clear hole in spring seat and remove inner insulator and washer from upper stud. Remove self-locking nut and disconnect lower stud from mounting bracket on axle housing. See Figs. U-5 and U-6. Reverse procedure to install shock absorber.

# Fix Your Ford

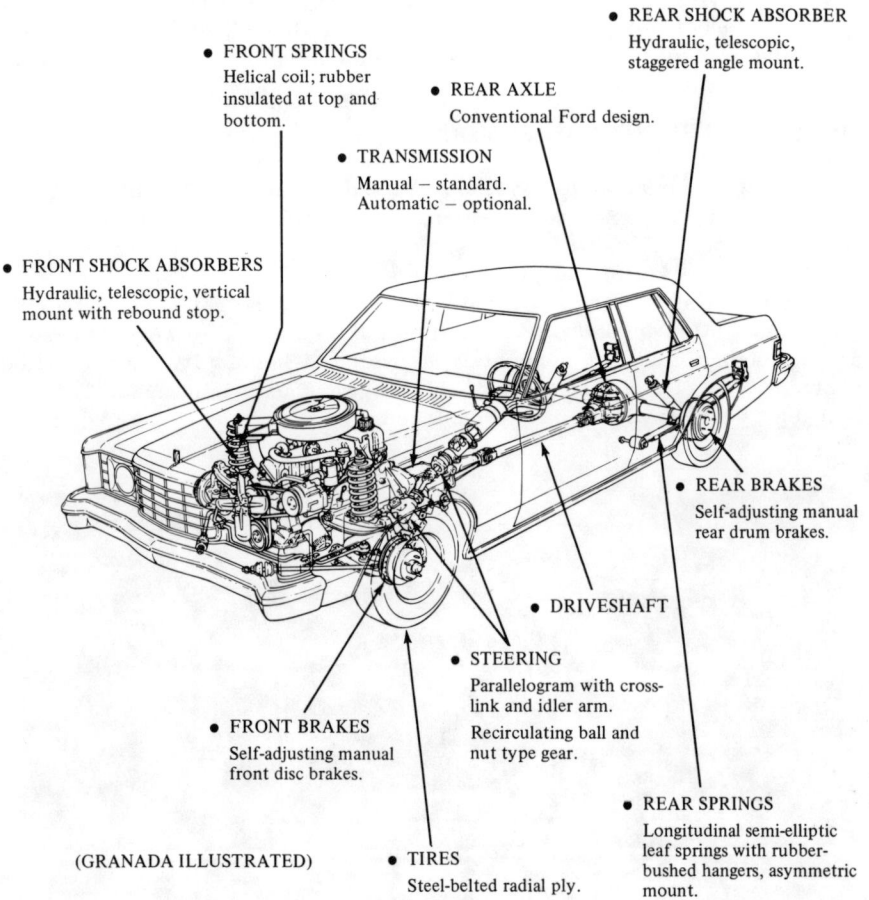

Details of running gear and steering, suspension and brake systems are shown in this phantom view of 1975 Granada.

To remove the rear shock absorbers from the compact models, such as the Falcon, Fairlane and Mustang, Fig. U-9, it is first necessary to remove the spare tire and access cover from the luggage compartment. On the Ranchero, remove the spare tire and wheel assembly. Next, remove the attaching screws and lift the forward half of the floor panel from the body. Then, remove the access cover from the opening in the floor pan over the shock absorber. Remove the attaching nuts. On station wagons, remove the access cover from the opening in the seat riser over

## Shock Absorber and Spring Service

the shock absorber. Then remove the nut outer washer and rubber bushing that attach the shock absorber to the upper mounting. Then remove the attaching nut outer washer and bushing from the shock absorber at the spring clip plate, Fig. U-7. Compress the shock absorber and remove it from the vehicle. Installation of the new shock absorber is accomplished by reversing the procedure.

### FRONT SPRING SERVICING

To remove a front spring, Fig. U-1, raise the front of the car so that the front wheels are about eight inches from the floor. Place supports under both frame side members just back of the lower arms. Remove the wheel and tire assembly. Place a jack under the lower arm to support it. Disconnect the lower end of the shock absorber from the lower arm. Re-

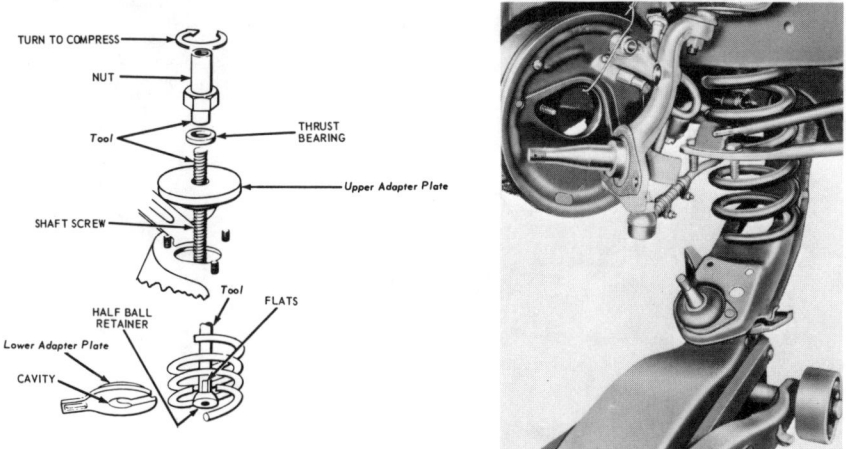

Fig. U-7. Left. Type of tool used to compress front chassis springs as installed on Falcon, Fairlane and Mustang. Fig. U-8. Right. Removing coil spring from between upper and lower control arms.

move the bolts that attach the strut and the rebound bumper to the lower arm. Disconnect the lower end of the sway bar stud from the lower arm. Remove the nut and bolt that secure the inner end of the lower arm to the cross member. Carefully lower the jack slowly to relieve the spring pressure on the lower arm and then remove the spring, Fig. U-8.

To install a front spring of the type illustrated in Fig. U-1, place the spring upper insulator on the spring and secure with tape. Position the spring on the lower arm so that the lower end properly engages the seat. The end of the spring must be no more than 1/2 in. from the end of the depression in the arm. Raise the lower arm carefully with a jack while guiding the inner end to align with the bolt hole in the cross member. In-

# Fix Your Ford

sert the attaching bolt in the cross member and through the lower arm. Install and torque the nut to 100-140 ft. lb. Secure the lower end of the shock absorber to the lower arm with two attaching bolts, torquing them to 8-15 ft. lb. Secure the strut and rebound bumper with two attaching bolts, torquing to 80-115 ft. lb. If so equipped, connect the sway bar to the lower arm with the attaching washer and insulators, as shown in Fig. U-1.

To replace the spring on the compact models of Ford cars, such as the Falcon, Figs. U-2 and U-4, proceed as follows:

1962-65 FALCON, AND 1965-66 MUSTANG: Raise the front of car by placing on stands under the frame. Remove wheel and shock absorber. Also on V-8's, remove carburetor air cleaner to gain access for spring compressor tool, Fig. U-7. Compress spring until it clears the upper control arm. Remove upper control arm shaft retaining nuts from arm, shaft and retaining bolts from under body. Carefully note number of shim thickness at each inner shaft retaining bolt. Swing upper arm and shaft 180 deg. to provide clearance for spring removal. Remove spring compressor tool and then take out spring.

1962-65 FAIRLANE: After raising arm, remove wheel, suspension bumper and bracket. Also remove shock absorber and bracket. Install one

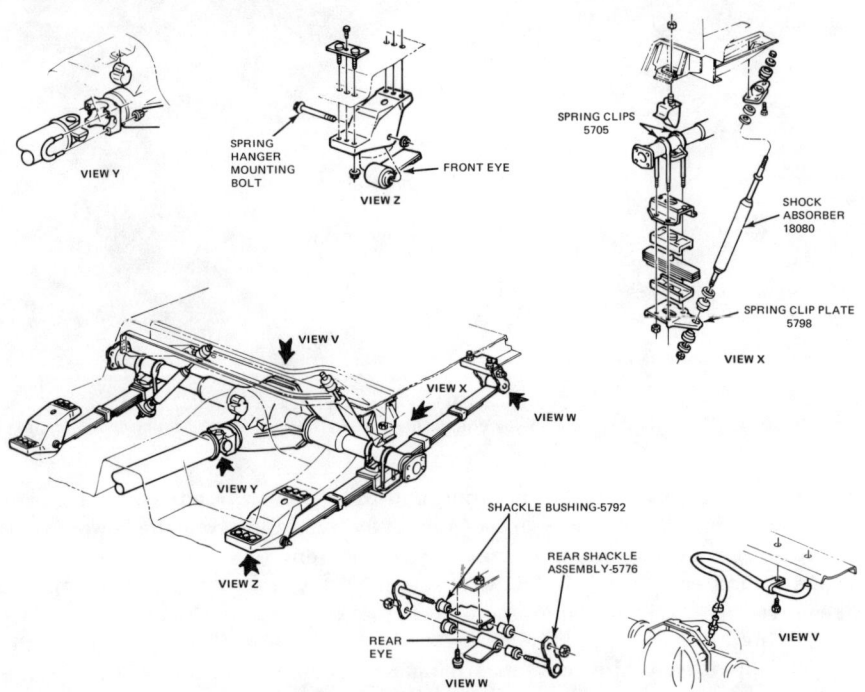

Fig. U-9. Leaf spring type of rear suspension is used on Granada, Mustang, Maverick and Pinto models. Suspension used on older Fords, Falcons and Fairlanes is similar. (Courtesy Ford Customer Service Div.)

## Shock Absorber and Spring Service

shock absorber mounting bracket bolt to hold spring upper seat to spring housing while spring is being compressed. Remove bolt that holds upper seat to housing, then remove spring and compressor tool.

1967-69 FALCON, FAIRLANE AND MUSTANG: Remove the shock absorber and upper mounting bracket as an assembly and place the car on safety stands. Remove wheel and brake drum assembly. Install the spring compressor, Fig. U-7, and compress spring. Remove upper arm to spring tower attaching nuts and swing the upper arm outboard from the spring tower. Release the spring compressor and remove the tool from the spring which will permit the removal of the spring from the vehicle.

### REPLACING BALL JOINTS

To remove the ball joints, first raise front of car with a bumper jack. Ball joints on Ford cars, Figs. U-1 and U-2, are riveted to the control arms. The ball joints can be replaced by drilling out the rivets. Bolts and nuts furnished with the replacement ball joint are then used to fasten the new ball joint in place. A pressing tool can be used to force the ball joint out of the spindle. Or strike the spindle in the ball joint area with a heavy hammer which will free it.

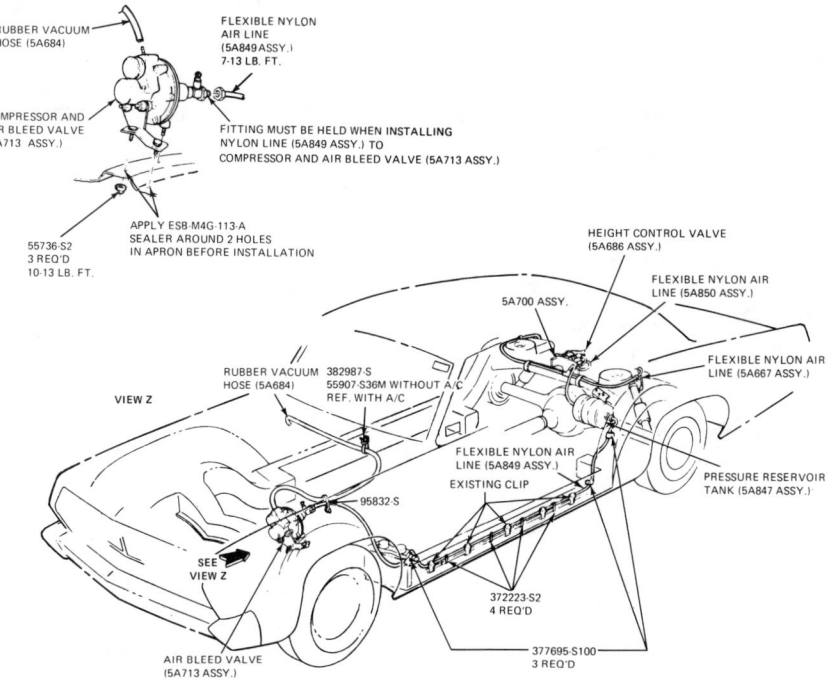

*Fig. U-10. Details of automatic loading system. Typical 1972-1978. (Courtesy Ford Customer Service Div.)*

## Fix Your Ford

The rear suspension automatic loading system, Fig. U-10, is designed to function only after a load of approximately three passengers is added to the vehicle. As load is added, the air sleeve rear shock absorbers inflate and extend, raising the vehicle to its designed height. The system consists of a compressor and air bleed valve, a pressure reservoir tank, a height control valve and link assembly, two air sleeve rear shock absorbers, three flexible nylon air lines and rubber vacuum hose. The air sleeve shock is essentially a conventional shock absorber enclosed in an air chamber.

The compressor operates because of the pressure difference between the engine manifold vacuum and the atmosphere. Due to the addition of a pressure reservoir tank on 1974 models, it takes 10 to 15 minutes longer to reach a balanced condition as opposed to the 1972 model which required two to three minutes.

To check the system, place the curb weight vehicle on a level surface. The vehicle should have a full fuel tank. Measure and record the rear fender opening height. Discharge the system completely by bleeding air through the air bleed valve at the compressor. Place a 400 lb. weight in the trunk. Again measure and record the rear fender opening. Start and idle the engine. Make sure compressor is operating. If it fails to work, replace it. Let engine idle until compressor stops. Measure and record rear fender opening height. The difference between the two measurements must be 3/4 in. minimum. If less, accelerate and decelerate engine and again compare fender opening heights. Remove load from vehicle. After two minutes measure and record fender opening height. The difference between the original measurement and the final must not be greater than 1/4 in.

If greater than that amount, check adjustment of control valve.

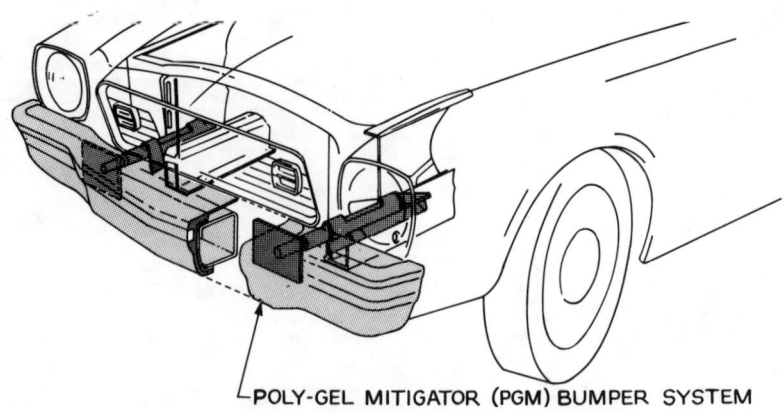

POLY-GEL MITIGATOR (PGM) BUMPER SYSTEM

*Details of 1974 Ford bumper system.*

# Shortcuts on
# WHEEL ALIGNMENT

To do an accurate job of aligning front wheels requires specialized equipment. Accuracy is a must if tire wear is to be kept to a minimum. In an emergency, however, approximate adjustments can be made.

Before altering the alignment of the front wheels, it is important to make sure what is causing the tire wear, or other steering difficulties. In many cases the difficulty results from some simple, easily remedied condition.

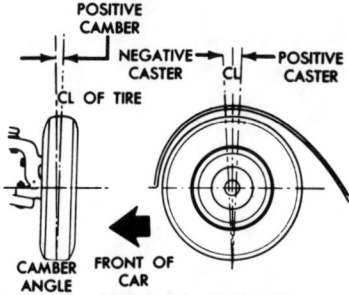

*Fig. V-1. Caster is the inclination or degree of tilt of steering axis forward or backward from the vertical center line of the wheel. Camber is the amount the front wheel is tilted at the top.*

First of all, make sure that all tires are correctly inflated, as this is a major cause of tire wear. Many authorities recommend that the tire pressures be maintained two pounds higher than the specified value. This not only increases tire life but also makes the car steer easier, but at a slight sacrifice of riding comfort. Further in regard to the tires, make sure that the tire valve cap is in place, as it is the cap that seals the valve and prevents leakage of air.

Next, jack up the front of the car using a bumper jack. Shake each front wheel grasping it at the top and bottom. Any looseness indicates the front wheel bearings need adjusting. Also it may indicate that the ball joints need replacing. Be sure to check the front suspension ball joints and mountings for looseness, wear and damage. Make sure there is no looseness or wear in the tie rod ends. Check the brake backing plate for looseness. Make sure the steering gear housing is bolted tight to the frame. The wheels should be balanced and the shock absorbers should be in good condition.

After all of these points have been checked and corrected, if necessary, the alignment of the wheels can be checked.

# Fix Your Ford

## CASTER, CAMBER AND TOE-IN

The conditions that are included in wheel alignment are caster, and camber, Fig. V-1, toe-in, Fig. V-2, and the inclination of the ball joints.

Caster, Fig. V-1, is the angle the ball joints are tilted to the front or rear. Tilting to the front is called negative caster, and tilting to the rear is positive caster.

Camber is the angle that the wheel is tilted to the side, Fig. V-1, or the angle between the center line of the wheel and the vertical.

Toe-in, Fig. V-2, is the difference between dimension A and dimension B. This is the most important factor in controlling tire wear. Ball joint inclination is the angle the center line of the ball joints make with the vertical.

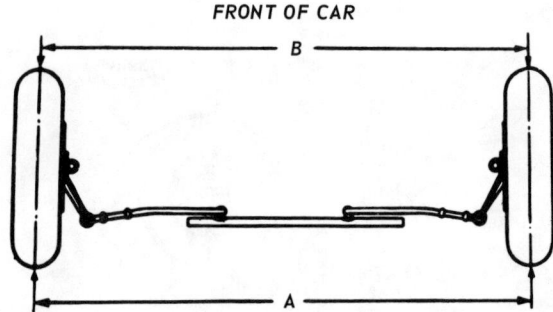

*Fig. V-2. Toe-in is the difference between dimensions A and B.*

Before attempting to align the front wheels, the car should always be rolled forward several feet to place the wheels in normal straight and running position.

Caster and ball joint inclination cannot be measured accurately without special equipment, but an approximation of camber angle can be made by placing the car on a level floor and then placing a large carpenter's square against the hub and tire rim. Then measure the distance from the square to the rim at the top and also at the bottom. The difference between these measurements is the camber in fractions of an inch. Unfortunately, there are no factory specifications available for camber measurements of this type. However, the difference in measurements should be approximately 1/16 in. and it must be emphasized that checking camber by this method is an emergency method only.

In an emergency, the following method of measuring toe-in can be used: With the car on a level floor, jack up the front wheels and with the wheels spinning hold a piece of chalk against the tire. Then with the wheels still spinning, hold a pointed tool, such as an ice pick against the chalk mark to scribe a fine line. Do this to both front wheels. Lower the car from the

## Wheel Alignment

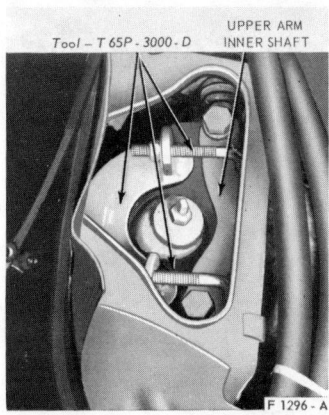

*Fig. V-3. Adjusting caster and camber on 1968–1976 Ford, T-Bird and Torino models.*

jacks and roll the car forward a few feet. Then suspend a plumb bob from the scribe line at the rear of the tire and make a mark on the floor where it is contacted by the point of the plumb bob. Repeat this operation at the front of the wheel and also on both wheels. Measure the distance between the two marks at the front of the tires and also at the back of the tires. The difference between these two measurements will be the toe-in, and obviously these measurements should be made with a high degree of accuracy. Toe-in for the various models is given in the specification changes in this book.

## CASTER AND CAMBER ADJUSTMENTS

1965-1978 Ford, 1972-1976 Torino, 1975-1976 Elite: Caster and camber are adjusted by loosening bolts attaching upper suspension inner shaft to frame, and moving inner shaft in or out in the bolt holes, Fig. V-3. The illustration shows a tool being used to make the adjustment which greatly simplifies the operation. However, the same effect can be obtained by means of a lever to pry the inner shaft in or out as required.

To adjust the camber angle, the inner shaft is moved in or out as required. To adjust the caster angle, hold one end of the inner shaft while the other end is moved in or out to obtain the desired caster.

1974-1978 Mustang II, Pinto: Adjust caster and camber with a special tool as shown in Fig. V-4. Proceed as follows:

Working from inside front wheel housing, install special tool at each end of control arm inner shaft. Turn special tool inward until bolt ends contact body metal. Loosen two upper arm inner shaft-to-body attaching nuts. Upper arm inner shaft will move inboard until it is stopped by bolt ends of special tool. Turn special tool bolt(s) inward or outward until caster and camber are within specifications. Then, torque upper arm inner shaft-to-body attaching nuts 95-110 ft. lb.

# Fix Your Ford

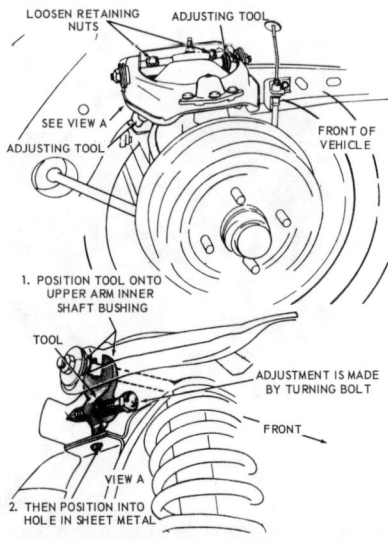

Fig. V-4. Adjusting caster and camber on Pinto and Mustang II.

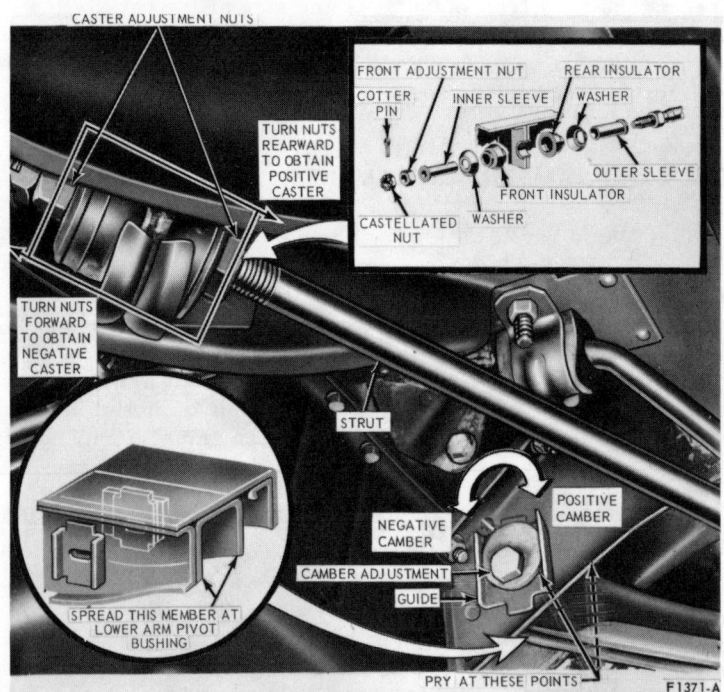

Fig. V-5. Caster and camber adjustments on Fairlane, Falcon, Mustang, Maverick and Granada models.

## Wheel Alignment

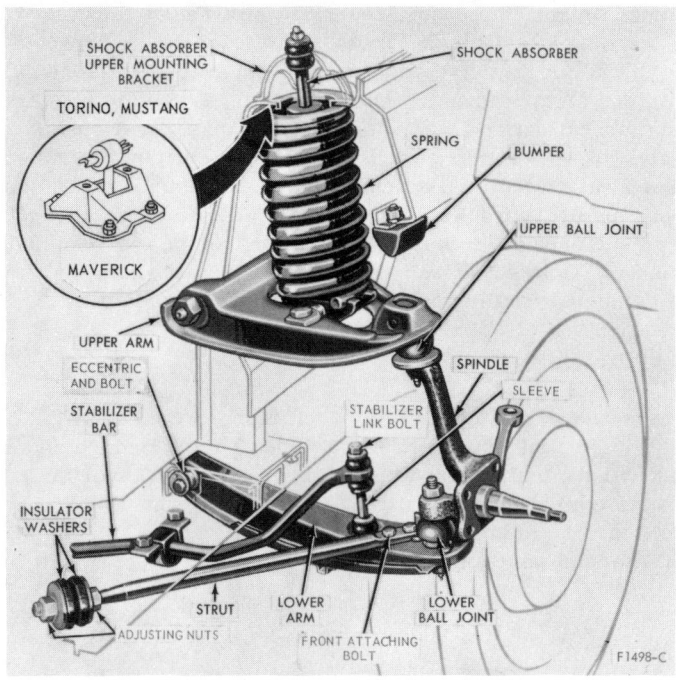

*Fig. V-6. Front suspension setup typical of system used on Fairlane, Torino, Falcon, Mustang II, Maverick and 1978 Granada.*

To adjust toe-in on 1972-1976 Mustangs: Check to see that steering shaft and steering wheel marks are in alignment and in top position. Loosen clamp screw on tie rod bellows, Fig. V-8, and free seal on rod to prevent twisting bellows. Use an open end wrench on flats of tie rod socket to prevent socket from turning while you are loosening tie rod jam nut. Then, select a suitable pliers and turn inner end of adjusting sleeve to get toe-in within specifications. Lock adjustment in place by tightening jam nut 35-50 ft. lb. of torque. Also tighten bellows clamp screw.

1975-1978 Granada: Caster and camber adjustments on Granada models are cam-operated type similar to those shown in Fig. V-5.

1965-1978 Thunderbird: Caster and camber are adjusted in the same manner as described for the 1965-1976 Ford cars, Fig. V-3.

1961-1964 Thunderbird: Adjusting shims are placed between pivot bracket of lower control arm and mounting bracket on underbody in engine compartment. Removal of shims will increase camber, and installing shims will decrease camber. Caster adjustment is made by repositioning strut on lower control arm. Adjust caster by loosening rear retaining bolts and lift strut serrations free from serrations on lower arm.

# Fix Your Ford

Fairlane, Falcon, Mustang, Maverick and Granada models: Caster and camber are controlled by the front suspension strut, Fig. V-5 and Fig. V-6. To adjust for positive caster, the first step is to loosen strut rear nut and tighten strut front nut against bushing. To obtain negative caster, loosen strut front nut and tighten strut rear nut against bushing. Camber is controlled by eccentric cam located at lower arm attachment to side rail, Figs. V-5 and V-6. To adjust camber, loosen camber adjusting bolt nut at rear of body bracket. Spread body bracket at camber adjustment bolt area just enough to permit lateral travel of arm when adjustment bolt is turned. Rotate bolt and eccentric clockwise from high position to increase camber; counterclockwise to decrease camber.

## TOE-IN ADJUSTMENT

Toe-in is one of the most important factors in the control of tire wear and adjustments must be accurately made. The procedure on all models is to first roll the car forward two or three feet on a level floor, with the wheel in the straight ahead position. The steering wheel spokes must also be in the position for straight ahead driving, Fig. V-7. If the spokes are not in the normal position, they can be properly adjusted while toe-in is adjusted, Fig. V-7.

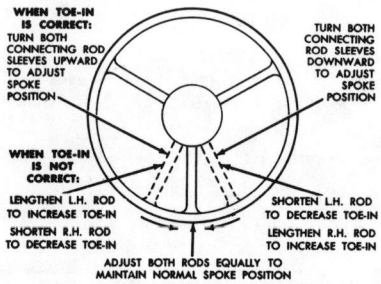

*Fig. V-7. Toe-in and steering wheel spoke adjustments.*

Loosen the two clamp bolts, Fig. V-9, on each spindle connecting rod sleeve. Adjust toe-in in accordance with the specifications in the back of this book. If the steering wheel spokes are in their normal position, lengthen or shorten both rods equally to obtain the correct toe-in, Fig. V-9. If the steering wheel spokes are not in their normal position, make the necessary rod adjustment to obtain correct toe-in and steering wheel position, Fig. V-7. Tighten clamp bolts after obtaining correct adjustment.

Toe-in adjustment on late model Mustang and Pinto models utilizes a socket and jam nut setup, Fig. V-8. Loosen jam nut while holding flats of tie rod socket. Then, use pliers to turn inner end of adjusting sleeve to obtain correct toe-in setting. Tighten jam nut.

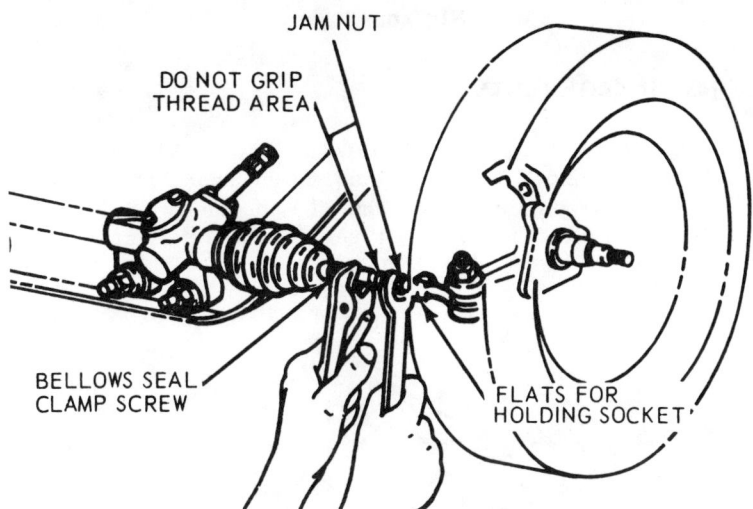

*Fig. V-8. Toe-in adjustment on 1973–1974 Mustang, 1974–1978 Mustang II, 1978 Pinto and Fairmont.*

Caster and camber angles on the 1978 Fairmont are set at the factory and cannot be adjusted in the field. Toe-in adjustments are made in the same manner as on the Pinto, Fig. V-8.

## HOW TO BALANCE WHEELS

If specialized wheel balancing equipment is not available, in an emergency, a fairly satisfactory job can be done by mounting the wheel to be balanced on the front wheel spindle. The procedure is to first back off on the brake adjustment until the wheel rotates freely. If the wheel bearing adjustment is tight, it might be necessary to loosen that adjustment also.

With the wheel in position on the spindle, allow it to rotate until it comes to a stop. The "heavy" area of the wheel will be at the bottom. Temporarily attach a wheel balance weight to the rim at the top. Again allow the wheel to rotate. If the weighted area of the wheel now stops at the bottom, the weight is too heavy. Change the weight until the wheel always stops in a different position. If it is found that a 2 oz. weight, for example, is required to balance the wheel, take two 1 oz. weights and place one on the outer side of the rim and the other on the inner side of the rim.

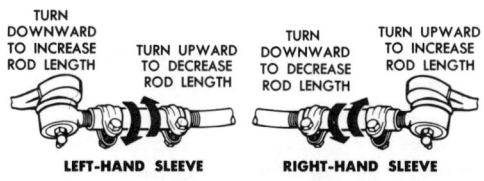

*Fig. V-9. Illustrating how sleeves should be adjusted when adjusting toe-in.*

# Fix Your Ford

## STEERING LINKAGE HINTS

The spindle connecting rod ends, threaded into adjusting sleeves have nonadjustable ball ends. On Ford, Torino and Thunderbird models, the procedure for removing these ends when they become worn is as follows:
1. Raise the front of the vehicle and remove the cotter pin and nut from the end of the ball stud, Fig. V-10.

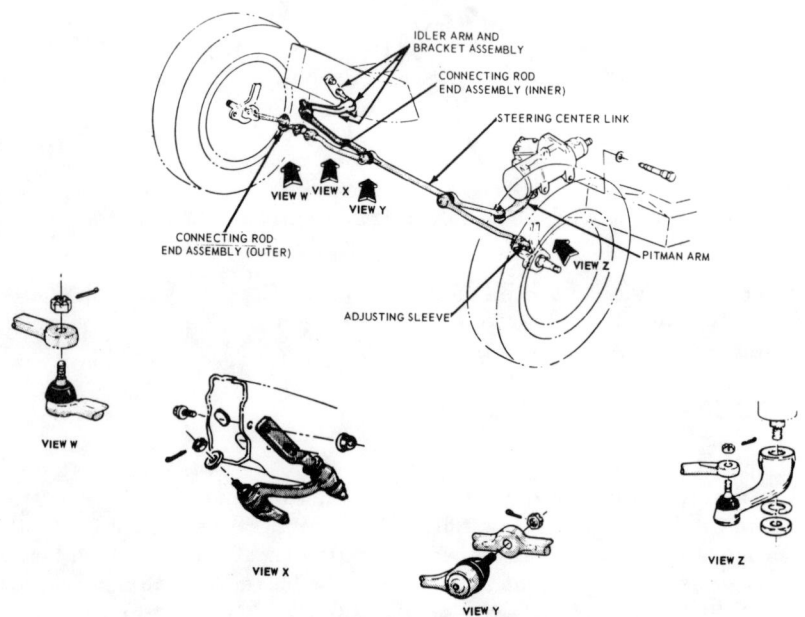

*Fig. V-10. Typical steering linkage. W—Connecting rod outer end assembly. X—Idler arm. Y—Connecting rod inner end assembly. Z—Pitman arm.*

2. Loosen connecting rod sleeve clamp bolts and remove assembly from sleeve, counting number of turns required.
3. Discard all parts removed from sleeve.
4. Thread new rod end into sleeve same number of turns required for removal. Do not tighten sleeve clamp bolts.
5. Install a new seal on a new rod end ball stud.
6. Install stud and stud nut. Torque to 30-40 ft. lb.
7. Install a new cotter pin.
8. Check toe-in and adjust, if necessary. Loosen clamps from sleeve and oil sleeve, clamps, bolts and nuts. Torque to specifications.

Always replace adjusting sleeve if worn or damaged. Install new seals when seals are used. Be sure to check toe-in after performing any replacement parts operation.

# Wheel Alignment

## RACK AND PINION STEERING GEAR

The rack and pinion steering gear installed on Mustang II, Pinto and Fairmont cars is illustrated in Fig. V-11. The gear input shaft is connected to the steering shaft by a U-joint shaft and flexible coupling. A pinion gear machined on the input shaft engages the rack. Rotation of the input shaft causes the rack to move laterally. The gear must be removed from the chassis to make an adjustment. Two adjustments are possible. Both are made by removing or adding shims.

To adjust the rack and pinion steering gear:

First, clean exterior of gear and mount it in a holding fixture. Remove yoke cover, gasket, shims and yoke spring. Clean cover and flange area thoroughly. Reinstall cover and yoke, but omit shims. Measure gap between cover and housing flange. With gasket, add selected shims to give a combined thickness .005 to .006 in. (.127 to .152 mm) greater than measured gap. Then reassemble, using correct shim thickness. Check to see if rack and pinion steering gear operates smoothly without binding.

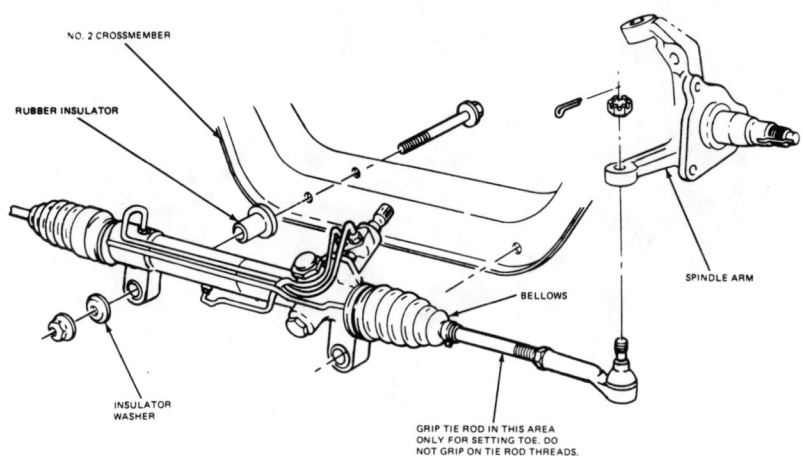

Fig. V-11. Details of rack and pinion steering gear.

To set bearing preload:

Loosen bolts of yoke cover to relieve spring pressure on rack. Remove pinion cover and gasket. Clean area. Remove spacer and shims. Install a new gasket and fit shims between upper bearing and spacer until top of spacer is flush with gasket. Check with a straight edge. Add or remove shims until spacer and gasket are flush. Then, add a .005 in. (.127 mm) shim to preload the bearing. Finally, reassemble unit and test operation.

# Fix Your Ford

## HOW TO ADJUST STEERING GEAR

The steering gear used on Ford, Falcon, Fairlane, Galaxie, Torino, Mustang and Maverick models is of the ball bearing type. Two adjustments can be made on this gear as follows:

On Ford cars, disconnect the pitman arm from the steering pitman-to-idler arm rod, and on other models disconnect the pitman arm from the sector shaft. On all models, loosen the nut which locks the sector adjusting screw, Fig. V-12, and turn the adjusting screw counterclockwise. Measure the worm bearing preload by attaching an inch-pound torque wrench to the steering wheel nut. With the steering wheel off center, read the pull required to rotate the input shaft approximately one and one-half turns either side of center. On manual steering cars this should be 4-5 in. lb.; on power steering gear it should be 2-7 in. lb.; on Saginaw power steering it should be 4-7 in. lb. If the torque or preload is not within specifications, loosen the steering shaft bearing adjust lock nut and tighten or back off the bearing adjuster and bring the preload within the specified

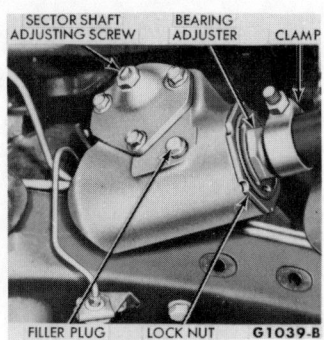 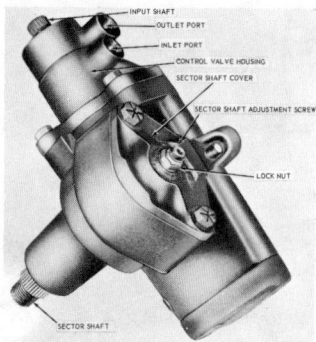

*Fig. V-12. Left. Manual steering gear.*
*Fig. V-13. Right. Power steering gear.*

limits. Then tighten the steering shaft bearing adjuster lock nut and recheck the preload. Turn the steering wheel slowly to either stop. Turn gently against the stop to avoid possible damage to the ball return guides. Then rotate the wheel 2 3/4 turns to center the ball nut on Ford cars, and 2 1/4 turns on other cars. Turn the sector adjusting screw clockwise until the specified torque is necessary to rotate the worm past center. While holding the sector adjusting screw, tighten the sector adjusting screw lock nut to specifications and recheck the backlash adjustment. Position the pitman arm on the sector shaft. Install the lockwasher and nut. Attach a foot-pound torque wrench to the nut and tighten it to 150-225 ft. lb. Check the tightness of the steering gear-to-side rail bolts. The torque specification is 50-65 ft. lb.

# Wheel Alignment

## ROTARY POWER STEERING GEAR

A rotary power steering gear was introduced as standard equipment on 1975 Thunderbird and Ford cars, and as optional equipment on Torino models. It is identical in external appearance to the previous model. The sector shaft adjustment is the same, and some parts are interchangeable with parts used in the previous design. However, do not attempt to intermix shafts and valves. These are designed specifically for the respective application and substitutions cannot be made.

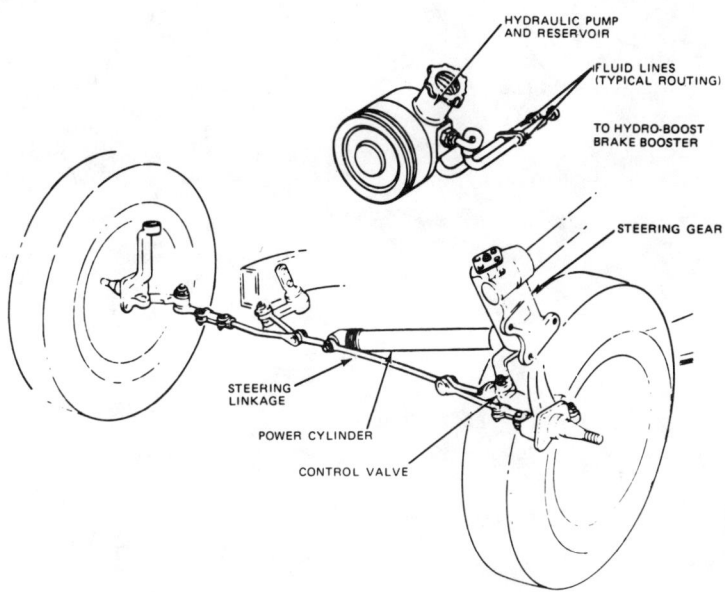

*Fig. V-14. Layout of non-integral power steering gear on Granada.*

## NON-INTEGRAL POWER STEERING

The non-integral power steering gear is used on Maverick and Granada models. This unit is a hydraulically controlled, linkage type steering system. It includes an integral pump and fluid reservoir, a control valve, a power cylinder and connecting fluid lines, Figs. V-14 and V-15.

Be sure the power steering drive belt is correctly adjusted. To adjust belt tension, loosen the mounting bolts and move the pump to obtain desired belt tension. Do not pry against the reservoir since this would damage the unit.

To center the control valve, first raise the vehicle. Remove two attaching screws. Remove spring cap and discard gasket. NOTE: Never start engine with cap removed. Torque centering spring adjusting nut

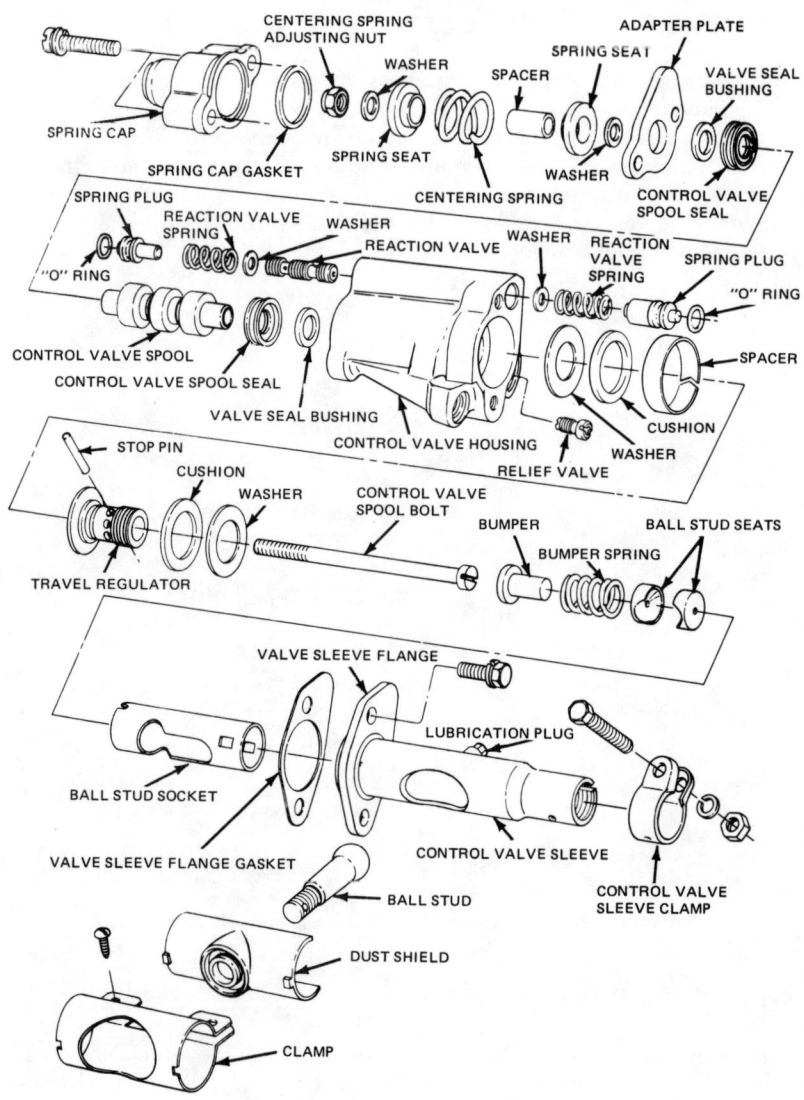

*Fig. V-15. Exploded view of control valve of non-integral power steering gear.*

90 to 100 ft. lb. Then, loosen adjusting nut 1/4 turn. NOTE: Control valve spool nut may turn slightly before centering spring adjusting nut turns. Position cap screw and a new spring cap gasket on valve housing. Lubricate and install two attaching screws and washer assembly. Torque screws 72 to 100 ft. lb.

# Wheel Alignment

## FORD INTEGRAL TYPE POWER STEERING

The integral type of power steering system is installed primarily on the full size Ford cars. The integral system is of the torsion bar, hydraulic assist type. Fig. V-16 shows the construction of the power steering pump used with this system.

The only adjustment which can be made in the vehicle is the total overall center position load to eliminate excessive lash between the sector and rack teeth. Disconnect the pitman arm from the sector shaft. Disconnect the fluid return line at the reservoir and cap the reservoir return line pipe.

Place the end of the return line in a clean container and cycle the steering wheel in both directions as required to discharge the fluid from the gear.

Remove the ornamental cover from the steering wheel hub and turn the steering wheel to 45 deg. from the left stop. Using an inch-pound torque wrench, determine the torque required to rotate the shaft slowly through an approximate 1/8 turn from the 45 deg. position.

Turn the steering gear back to the center, then determine the torque required to rotate the shaft back and forth across the center position. Loosen the adjuster nut and turn the adjuster screw until the reading is 8-9 in. lb. greater than the torque 45 deg. from the stop. Tighten the lock nut while holding the screw in place. Recheck the reading.

Reconnect the line and fill the reservoir.

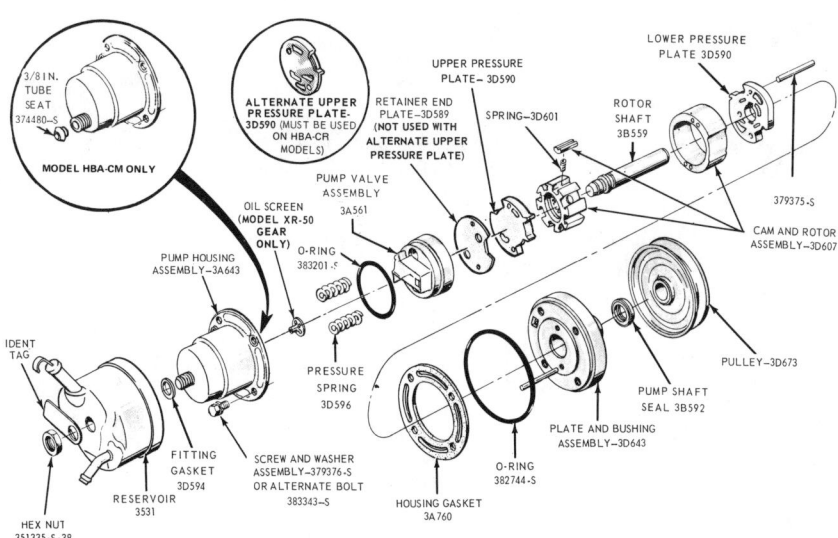

*Fig. V-16. Disassembled power steering pump. Ford-Thompson type. (Courtesy Ford Customer Service Div.)*

# Fix Your Ford

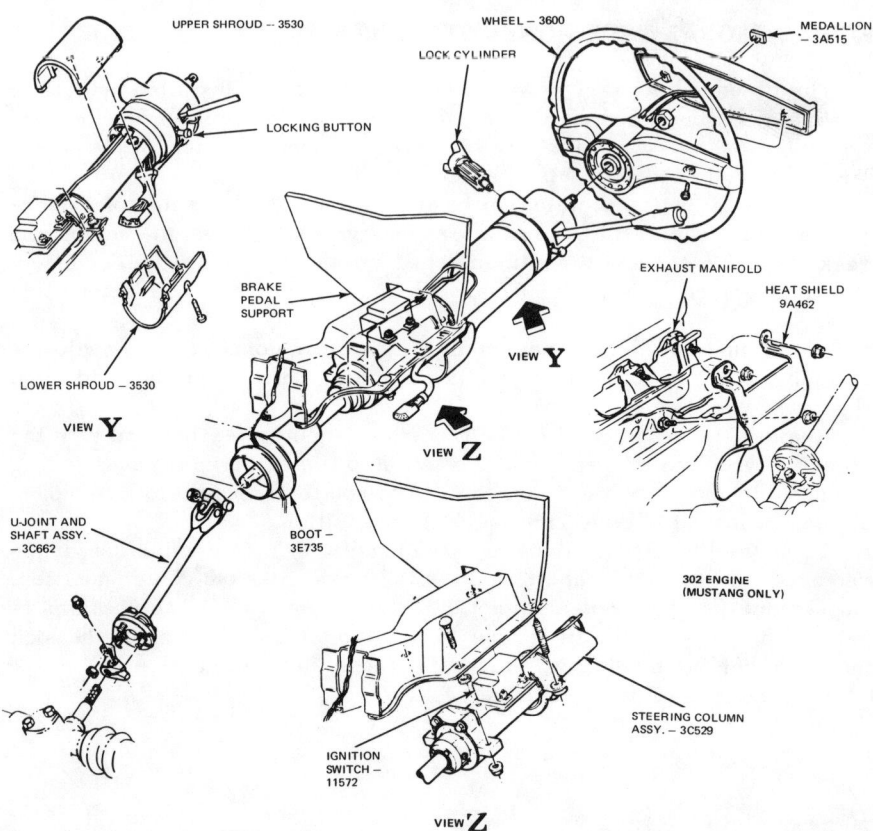

*Fig. V-17. Steering column installed on 1978 Mustang II and Pinto. Column on Granada, Thunderbird and Ford LTD are similar.*

Ford states that drive belt tension cannot be checked accurately without the use of a belt tension gauge. On belts that have been in use more than 15 minutes, the correct tension should be 90 to 120 lb.

To replace a pump drive belt, loosen the idler pulley attaching bolts and remove the compressor, if equipped with an air conditioner. Loosen three bolts and one nut attaching the power steering pump to the pump bracket and remove the drive belt. Position the new drive belt on the pulleys, and adjust the belt tension. Then tighten pump attaching bolts and nuts.

## POWER STEERING FLUID

When filling the power steering gear system, only automatic transmission fluid Type A, Suffix A, should be used.

# Wheel Alignment

## STEERING COLUMN

The Mini (extruded absorber type) steering gear used on Mustang II and Pinto cars is the fixed type. See Fig. V-17. A similar column used on Granada, Thunderbird and Ford LTD models is either tilt or fixed type.

To remove column from Mustang II and Pinto, first disconnect starting battery. Remove steering wheel and trim shrouds that cover steering column at instrument panel. Also remove section of instrument panel located beneath steering column. Disengage dust boot at base of steering column. Remove bolts attaching steering column lower shaft and U-joint assembly to flange on steering gear input shaft. Disengage safety strap. Remove bolts that attach steering column support bracket to brake pedal support. Remove column by withdrawing it from beneath dash panel.

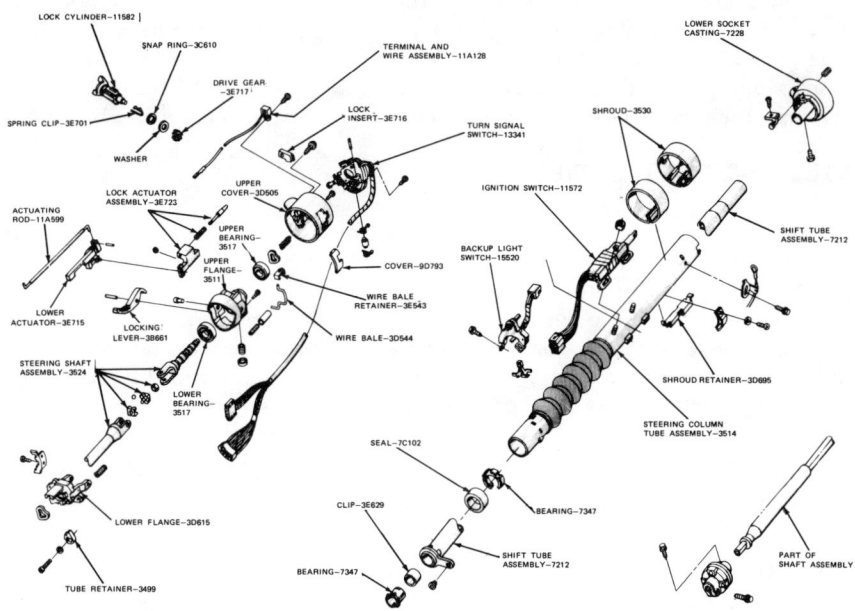

*Fig. V-18. Typical tilt steering column on 1973–1978 cars. (Courtesy Ford Customer Service Div.)*

The tilt steering column, Fig. V-18, is of the collapsible type. Upon hard impact, the lower end of the steering column at the bellows area will collapse approximately 6 in. The shaft tube and the steering shaft will also collapse in proportion. Once the steering column has collapsed, a complete new column must be installed, together with new brackets which will shear on impact. Fig. V-19 shows a 1970-1971 tilt steering column.

The 1973-1974 column features five driving positions (two up and two

## Fix Your Ford

down from a central position). The column has a turn signal switch with a lane changer indicating position and an emergency warning flasher control.

To remove a tilt column: Disconnect battery. Remove steering wheel. Remove lower instrument panel. Remove steering column trim. Disconnect all electric wiring from column. Remove toe plate from dash. Disconnect transmission control rod from steering column shaft. Remove nuts securing column to brake pedal support bracket. Remove steering column.

## TROUBLE SHOOTING

### CAUSE OF EXCESSIVE TIRE WEAR

Under-inflation. Worn kingpins and bushings or ball joints. Loose tie rod ends and steering rods. Overloaded car. High speed driving. Wheel balance. Tire balance. Incorrect toe-in or toe-out. Unequal brake adjustment. Spring sag. Bent or shifted rear axle housing. Bent frame. Dragging brakes. Incorrect camber. Incorrect caster. Defective shock absorbers.

### STEERING DIFFICULTIES

Steering difficulties including wander, wheel tramp, road sway, shimmy and hard steering may be caused by the following: Incorrect tire pressure. Tight spindle bearings or ball joints. Loose spindle bearings or ball joints. Loose connecting rod ends and connections. Broken chassis spring. Loose steering gear mountings. Wheels and tire assemblies out of balance. Incorrect caster, camber and toe-in. Incorrect kingpin angle. Dragging brakes. Steering gear off center. Spring sag. Loose or worn shock absorbers. Tires of unequal sizes. Bent rear axle housing. Tight wheel bearings. Loose or worn stabilizer. Bent frame.

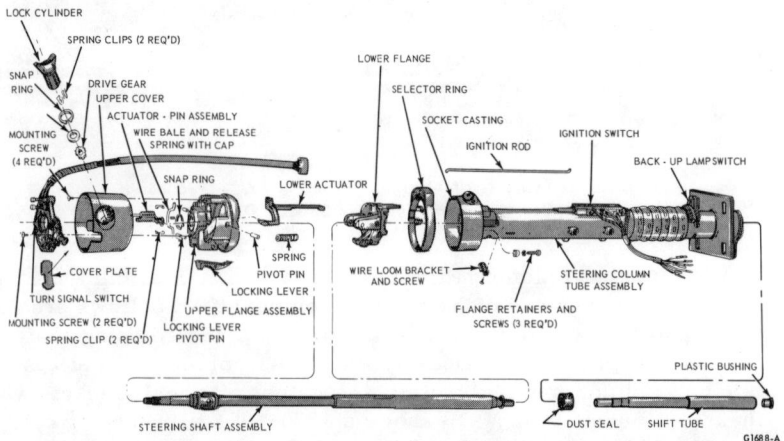

*Fig. V-19. Typical 1970–1971 tilt steering column. (Fixed column is similar.)*

# Quick Service on BRAKES

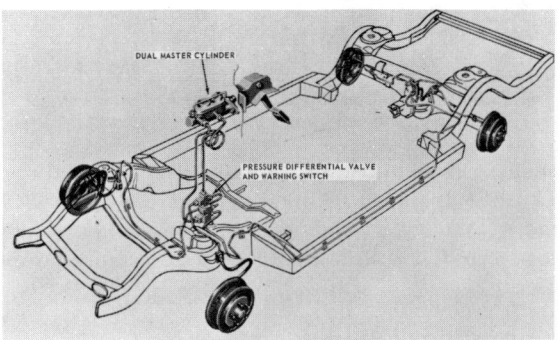

Fig. W-1. Typical drum brake system with dual master cylinder. Prior to 1967, a single type master cylinder was used.

A typical hydraulic brake system is shown in Fig. W-1. Dual master cylinder and drum brakes on all four wheels were standard for all cars until recently when disc brakes were installed on the front wheels. In 1975 and 1976, only the Maverick had drum brakes front and rear.

Brake adjustment and brake relining on Ford built cars are relatively simple. Relining requires about three hours and adjusting one-half hour.

In general, Ford brakes of the manually adjusted type require adjustment when the pedal goes to about 2 in. from the floor when the brakes are applied. New brake shoes should be installed when the lining is worn to 1/32 in. of the rivets in the case of riveted lining, and to 1/16 in. of brake shoe when cemented lining is used. Brake shoes with new lining attached to the shoes are available from Ford dealers and from auto parts jobbers.

When new shoes are installed, the hydraulic system should be flushed and refilled with new fluid. Details on servicing the hydraulic system will be given later in this chapter.

## REMOVING FRONT BRAKE DRUMS

In order to install new brake lining on brakes, it is first necessary to remove the brake drums. To remove the front brake drums on Ford cars, remove the hub cap or wheel cover, then remove the grease cap from the hub, Fig. W-2. Remove the cotter pin, nut retainer, adjusting nut and flat washer from the spindle, then remove the outer bearing cone and roller assembly, Fig. W-2.

## Fix Your Ford

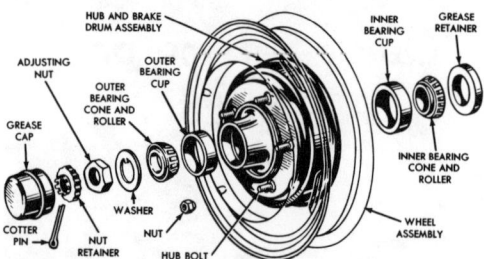

Fig. W-2. Front wheel hub and bearing. Note nut retainer and adjusting nut used on recent models. Earlier models used only a castellated nut for adjusting.

Pull the wheel, hub and drum assembly off the wheel spindle. In some cases when the brake drum has become severely worn, it will be necessary to readjust the clearance of the shoes before removing the drum so that the shoes are contracted within the drum. To do this, see the instructions on brake adjusting.

### ADJUSTING WHEEL BEARINGS

Drum Type Brakes: Whenever the front brake drums have been removed from the wheel spindle, it is necessary to adjust the wheel bearings. The procedure is as follows: Raise the vehicle until the tire clears the floor. Pry off the hub cap or wheel cover and remove the grease cap from the hub. Wipe the excess grease from the end of the spindle and remove the cotter pin and nut lock. While rotating the wheel assembly, torque the adjusting nut to 17-25 ft. lb. to seat the bearing, Fig. W-3.

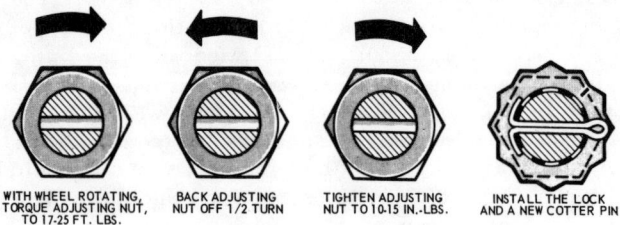

Fig. W-3. Adjusting nut used to adjust wheel bearings.

Back off the adjusting nut one-half turn. Retighten the adjusting nut to 10-15 in. lb. with a torque wrench or finger tight. Position the nut lock on the adjusting nut so the castellations on the lock are aligned with the cotter pin hole on the spindle. Bend the ends of the cotter pin around the castellated flange of the nut lock. Check wheel for smooth quiet rotation. If rough or noisy replace bearings.

# Brakes

Disc Type Brakes: To adjust the front wheel bearings when vehicle is equipped with disc type brakes proceed as follows: Raise the vehicle until the wheel clears the floor. Pry off the wheel cover and remove the grease cap. Wipe off excess grease from the end of tne spindle and remove the adjusting nut cotter pin and nut lock. Loosen the bearing adjusting nut

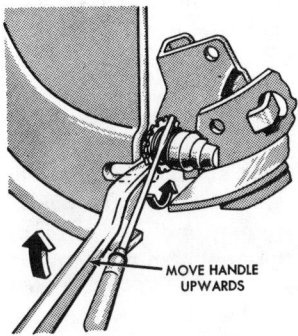

*Fig. W-4. Backing off brake adjustment on self-adjusting brakes.*

three turns. Then rock the wheel hub and rotor assembly in and out several times to push the shoe and linings away from the rotor. While rotating the wheel and hub assembly, torque the adjusting nut to 17-25 ft. lb. to seat the bearings. Back the adjusting nut off one-half turn. Retighten the adjusting nut to 10-15 in. lb. with a torque wrench or finger tight. Locate the nut lock on the adjusting nut so the castellations on the lock are aligned with the cotter pin hole in the spindle. Install a new cotter pin and bend the ends around the castellated flange of the nut lock. Check the front wheel for quiet rotation. If noisy or rough replace the bearing. Before driving the vehicle, pump the brake pedal several times to obtain normal lining to drum clearance.

## HOW TO REMOVE THE REAR BRAKE DRUMS

With the car raised from the floor, remove the hub cap and wheel and tire assembly. Remove the three Tinnerman spring nuts and the brake drum. Tinnerman nuts, which are flat spring type nuts, can be pulled off the stud. The brake drum can then be removed by pulling directly outward.

If the brake drum will not come off easily, turn the adjusting wheel (star wheel) to bring the brake shoes together. On brakes of the self-adjusting type, insert a narrow screwdriver through the brake adjusting hole in the carrier or backing plate and disengage the adjusting lever from the adjusting screw, Fig. W-4. While thus holding the adjusting lever away from the adjusting screw, back off the adjusting screw with the brake adjusting tool. Back off the adjustment only if the drum cannot be removed.

# Fix Your Ford

Be very careful not to burr, chip or damage the notches in the adjusting wheel, otherwise the self-adjusting mechanism will not operate correctly.

## SELF-ADJUSTING BRAKES 1961-1977

With the exception of the Falcon models, self-adjusting brakes are installed on all models since 1961, inclusive. On the Falcon, the self-adjusting brake was adopted in 1963. These brakes require adjustment only after new brake shoes have been installed, or when the length of the adjusting screw, Fig. W-6, has been changed while performing some other service operation.

The adjusting procedure is as follows: Remove the adjusting hole cover from the backing plate and turn the adjusting screws upward to expand the shoes, Fig. W-4. Expand the shoes until a slight drag is felt as the brake drum is rotated. Then remove the brake drum and while holding the adjusting lever out of engagement with the adjusting screw, back off the adjusting screw a three-quarter turn with the fingers. If finger movement will not turn the screw, free it up by lubrication, otherwise, the self-adjusting lever will not be able to turn the screw. The screw should be

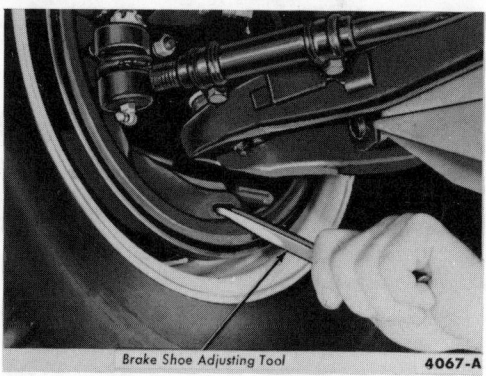

Fig. W-5. Using brake adjusting tool to adjust shoe-to-drum clearance. Self-adjusting brakes almost eliminate need for manual adjustment.

lubricated with special lubricant. These self-adjusting brakes have a self-adjusting shoe mechanism that assures correct lining to drum clearance at all times. The automatic adjusters operate only when the brakes are applied as the car is moving backward. As a result of excessive brake application with the car moving backward, it is possible that brake shoe to drum clearance will be reduced to such an extent that the brakes will drag. If such is the case, remove the covers from the adjusting holes in the backing plate and using a thin-bladed screwdriver to raise the adjusting lever from the adjusting screw, the brake adjustment can be backed off in the conventional manner, Fig. W-4.

# Brakes

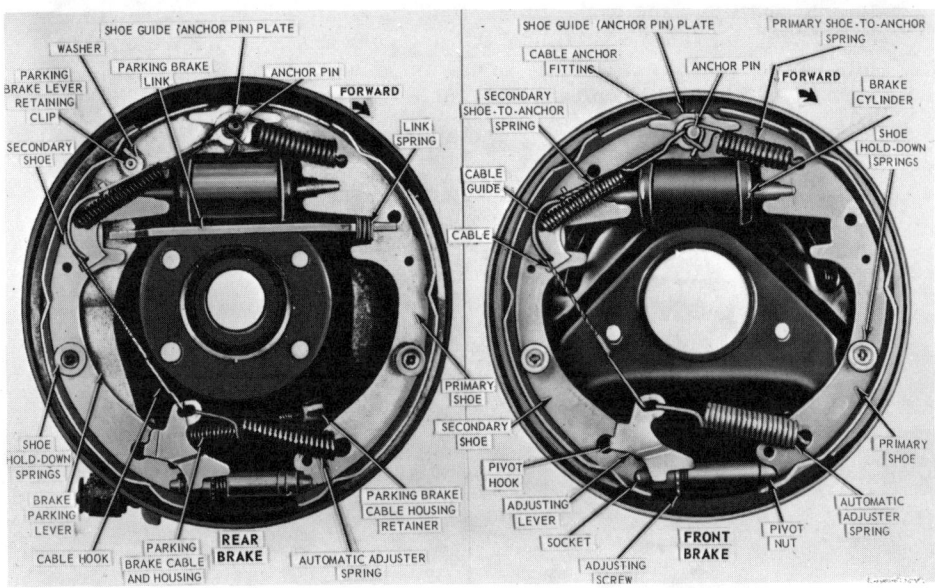

*Fig. W-6. Details of self-adjusting brake as used on recent models.*

On some recent models, the adjusting slot was omitted from the brake backing plate. The brake backing plates have a partly stamped knock-out slot for use only when the brake drums cannot be removed in the normal manner. The knock-out slot can then be knocked out and the brakes adjusted in the normal manner, after which a rubber plug should be used to close the opening.

## WHEN TO RELINE DRUM BRAKES

Just how often brakes should be relined depends largely on the driver of the vehicle, the rate at which the car is stopped, the frequency of stops,

*Fig. W-7. When brake lining is badly grooved, it should be replaced.*

# Fix Your Ford

and the quality of the brake lining. If the car is frequently driven through wet gravel, or sandy roads, brake lining wear will be more rapid.

It is necessary to reline drum brakes when the lining has become worn to 1/32 in. of the rivet heads or to 1/16 in. of the brake shoe in the case of cemented shoes. The brakes should also be relined when the lining becomes grooved, as shown in Fig. W-7, or when the brake drums have become scored as shown in Fig. W-8. Another reason for relining brakes is when the lining becomes soaked with oil, grease or brake fluid.

Fig. W-8. Example of a badly scored brake drum. Such drums should be reconditioned, but in no case should more than .060 in. of metal be removed.

When the drums are scored or become out-of-round, or bell-mouthed, they should be reconditioned, but in no case should more than .060 in. of metal be removed from the drum.

## HOW TO REMOVE BRAKE SHOES

With the wheel and drum removed, it is advisable to install a clamp over the ends of the wheel cylinder. Should the brakes be applied with the drums off, the hydraulic fluid would force the pistons from the cylinders and fluid would be lost. Then remove the shoe-to-anchor springs. Brake pliers, or other special tool, Fig. W-9, or a screwdriver can be used as a lever, to unhook the springs. Also unhook the cable eye from the anchor pin. Remove the shoe guide (anchor plate), Fig. W-6. Remove the shoe hold-down springs. Then the shoes can be pulled apart from the anchor pin and removed from the backing plate. The adjusting screw and automatic adjustment parts are also removed.

On rear brakes, remove the parking brake link, spring and retainer. Disconnect the parking brake cable from the parking brake lever. After removing the rear brake secondary shoe, Fig. W-6, disassemble the

## Brakes

*Fig. W-9. Removing a brake retracting spring with a special tool. A heavy screwdriver can also be used, if a special tool is not available. (Courtesy Ford Customer Service Div.)*

parking brake lever from the shoe by removing the retaining clip and spring washer.

### INSTALLING SHOES ON SELF-ADJUSTING BRAKES

In the case of self-adjusting brakes, Fig. W-6, before installing the rear brake shoes, assemble the parking brake lever to the secondary shoe and secure with the spring washer and retaining clip. Apply a light coating of high temperature grease at the points where the brake shoes contact the backing plate.

Position the brake shoes on the backing plate, and install the hold-down spring, pins, springs and cups. On the rear brake, install the parking brake link and spring. Connect the parking brake cable to the parking brake lever.

Install the shoe guide (anchor pin) plate on the anchor pin when so equipped. Place the cable eye over the anchor pin with the crimped side

*Fig. W-10. Installing a retractor spring with a special tool. Note that tool is being used as a lever. A heavy screwdriver can be used in same manner. Also note clamp on ends of wheel cylinder used as a precautionary measure to prevent pistons and cups being pushed from cylinder.*

toward the backing plate.

Install the primary shoe to the anchor spring as shown in Fig. W-10: Install the cable guide on the secondary shoe web with the flanged hole fitted into the hole in the secondary shoe web. Thread the cable around the cable guide groove, Fig. W-6. It is imperative that the cable be positioned in this groove, and not between the guide and the shoe web.

Install the secondary shoe to anchor spring, Fig. W-10. Be certain that the cable end is not cocked, or binding on the anchor pin when installed. All parts should be flat on the anchor pin.

Apply high temperature grease to the threads and the socket end of the adjusting screw. Turn the adjusting screw into the adjusting pivot nut to the limit of the threads and then back off one-half turn.

Interchanging the brake shoe adjusting screw assembly from one side of the car to the other would cause the brake shoe to retract rather than to expand each time the automatic adjusting mechanism operates. To prevent installation on the wrong side of the car, the socket end of the adjusting screw is stamped with an R or an L. The adjusting pivot nut can be distinguished by the number of lines machined around the body of the nut. Two lines indicate a right-hand nut, and one line indicates a left-hand nut.

Place the adjusting socket on the screw, and install this assembly between the two ends with the adjusting screw nearest the secondary shoe.

Hook the cable hook into the hole into the adjusting lever. The adjusting levers are stamped with an R and L to indicate their installation on right or left-hand brake assemblies.

Position the hook end of the adjuster spring into the large hole in the primary shoe web, and connect the looped end of the spring to the adjuster lever hole.

Pull the adjust lever, cable and automatic adjuster spring down, and toward the rear to engage the pivot hook in the large hole in the secondary shoe web.

After installation, check the action of the adjuster by pulling the section of the cable between the cable guides and the adjusting lever toward the secondary shoe web far enough to lift the lever past the tooth on the adjusting screw wheel. The lever should snap into position between the next teeth, and release of the cable should cause the adjuster spring to return the lever to its original position. This return action of the lever will turn the adjusting screw one tooth.

If pulling the cable does not produce the action described, or if the lever action is sluggish instead of positive and sharp, check the position of the lever on the adjusting screw toothed wheel. With the brake in a vertical position, the lever should contact the adjusting wheel 3/16 in. above the center line of the screw. If the contact point is below this center line, the lever will not lock on the teeth in the adjusting screw wheel, and the screw will not be turned as the lever is actuated by the cable.

To determine the cause of this condition, check the cable end fittings. The cable should completely fill, or extend slightly beyond the crimped section of the fittings. If it does not meet this specification, possible dam-

## Brakes

age is indicated and the cable assembly should be replaced.

Check the cable length. On Ford models the cable should measure 11 1/8 in. (plus or minus 1/64 in.) from the end of the cable anchor to the end of the cable hook. On Fairlane, Falcon and Mustang models, the cable should measure 8 13/32 in. on 9 in. brakes and 9 3/4 in. on 10 in. brakes. The cable groove should be parallel to the shoe web and the body of the guide should be flat against the web. Replace if damaged.

Self-adjusting brakes require a manual adjustment only after the brake shoes have been relined, replaced or when the length of the adjusting screw has been changed by performing some other service operation. After the shoes have been installed, or the adjusting screw has been turned, install the drum. Be sure all excess grease, oil and other foreign materials are wiped off the backing plate and drum. Remove the adjusting hole cover from the backing plate. From the backing plate side, turn the adjusting screw upward to expand the shoes. Expand the shoes until a slight drag is felt when the drum is rotated. Then remove the drum. While holding the adjusting lever out of engagement with the adjusting screw, Fig. W-4, back off the adjusting screw three-quarters turn with the fingers. If finger movement will not turn the screw, free it up, otherwise the self-adjusting lever will not turn the screw. Lubricate the screw with oil and coat the wheel with bearing grease.

## DISC BRAKES

In 1968, a single piston type disc brake, Figs. W-11 and W-15, was adopted for optional equipment on Ford built vehicles. This superceded the double piston type, Fig. W-12, which was available as optional equipment

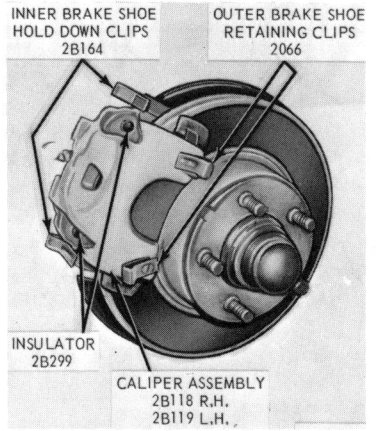
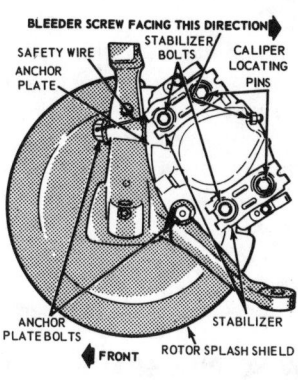

*Fig. W-11. Left. Assembled view of single piston disc brake which is also known as floating caliper disc brake. Right. Construction of single piston disc brake showing location of locating pins.*

# Fix Your Ford

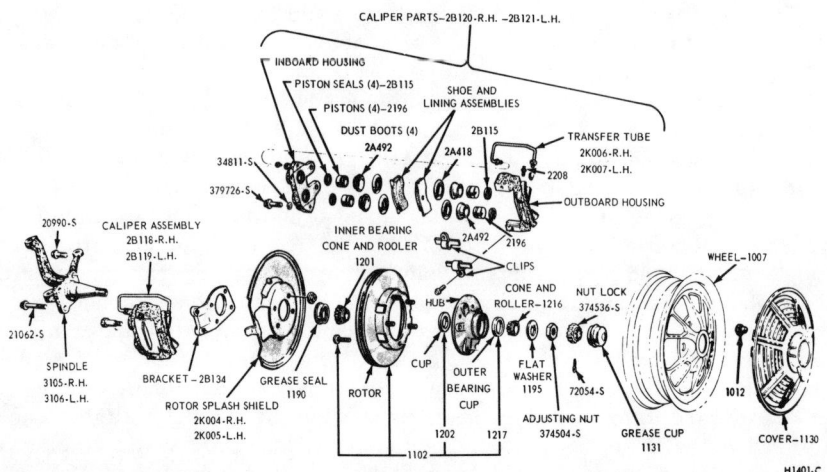

*Fig. W-12. Details of fixed caliper double piston type disc brake used on some 1967-1969 models.*

1965 through 1967. The 1968, single piston type disc brake has brake linings on both sides of the rotor which are actuated by a single piston. When hydraulic pressure is applied in braking, movement of the wheel cylinder piston causes equal and opposite motion of the caliper housing, thus forcing, with equal pressure, the linings against both sides of the revolving rotor. In the previous design, two pistons were required to accomplish the same effect.

## DISC BRAKE SHOE AND LINING REPLACEMENT 1968-1978

DISC BRAKE SERVICE PRECAUTIONS: Grease or any other foreign material must be kept off the caliper assembly, surfaces of the rotor and external surfaces of the hub during service operations. Handling of the rotor and caliper assembly should be done in a way to avoid deformation of the brake rotor and nicking or scratching of the brake linings. If the piston is removed for any reason, the piston seal must be replaced. During removal and installation of the wheel assembly, exercise care not to interfere with and damage the caliper splash shield or the bleeder screw fitting. Front wheel bearing end play is critical and must be within specifications. The proportioning valve should not be disassembled or adjustments attempted on it. Riding of the brake pedal which is common on left foot applications should be avoided during vehicle operation.

## REMOVING DISC BRAKE CALIPER ASSEMBLY

The following instructions apply particularly to 1972-1978 sliding disc brakes, Figs. W-13, W-14 and W-16a. They are not applicable to the pin

## Brakes

slider caliper brake, Fig. W-17, installed on the 1978 Fairmont.

Raise the vehicle and place on safety stands. Block both rear wheels if a jack is used. Remove wheel and tire assemblies from the hub. Disconnect the flexible brake hose from the caliper. To disconnect the hose, loosen the tubing fitting which connects it to the brake tube at its bracket on the frame. Remove the horseshoe-type retaining clip from the hose and bracket. Disengage the hose from the bracket. Then unscrew the entire hose assembly from the caliper.

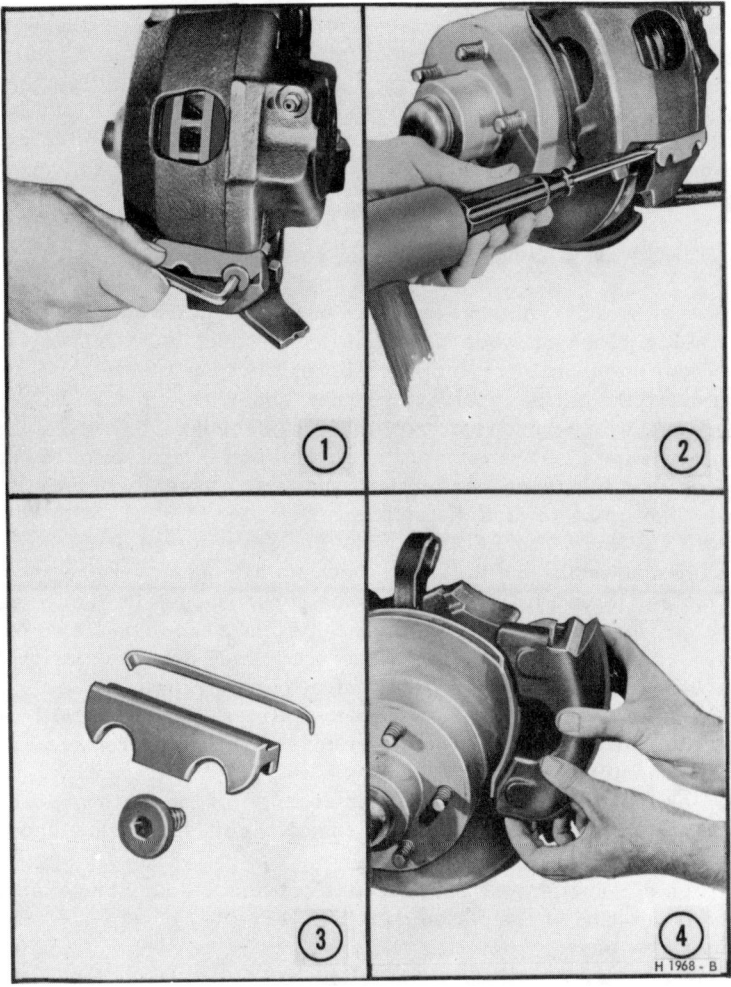

*Fig. W-13. 1—Removing retaining screw from caliper retaining key. 2—Removing caliper retaining key. 3—Retaining key and support spring. 4—Lifting caliper from anchor plate.*

## Fix Your Ford

Remove the retaining screw from the caliper retaining key, Fig. W-13. Slide the caliper retaining key and support spring either inward or outward from the anchor plate. Use a hammer and drift if necessary, taking care not to damage the key. Lift the caliper away from the anchor plate by pushing the caliper downward against the anchor plate and working the upper end upward and out of the anchor plate, Fig. W-13.

Remove the inner shoe and lining assembly from the anchor plate. The brake shoe anti-rattle clip (inner shoe only) may become displaced at this time. If so, reposition it on the inner shoe, Fig. W-13. Tap lightly on the outer shoe and lining assembly to free it from the caliper.

Clean the caliper, anchor plate and rotor assemblies. Inspect them for signs of brake fluid leakage, excessive wear or damage. Lightly sand or wire brush any rust or corrosion from the caliper and anchor plate sliding surfaces. Inspect brake shoes for wear. If either lining is worn within 1/32 in. of any rivet head, both shoe-and-lining assemblies must be replaced. Also if shoes and linings are replaced on one wheel, they must be replaced on both wheels to maintain equal braking.

## INSTALLING NEW LINING ASSEMBLIES

If new shoe and lining assemblies are to be installed, use a 4 in. C-clamp and a block of wood 1 3/4 in. x 1 in. and approximately 3/4 in. thick to seat the hydraulic piston in its bore. This must be done to provide clearance for the caliper to fit over the new shoes when installed. Be sure that the brake shoe anti-rattle clip is in place on the lower end of the inner brake shoe with the loop of the clip toward the inside of the anchor plate. Position the inner brake shoe and lining assembly on the anchor plate with the lining toward the rotor.

Install the outer brake shoe with the lower flange ends against the caliper leg abutments and the brake shoe upper flanges over the shoulders on the caliper legs, Fig. W-14. The shoe upper flanges fit tightly against the shoulder machined surfaces. If the same brake shoe and lining assemblies are reused, be certain the shoes are installed in their original locations as marked for identification prior to removal.

Remove the C-clamp (if used) from the caliper. The piston will remain seated in the bore. Position the caliper housing lower V-groove on anchor plate lower abutment surface, Fig. W-14, step 1. Pivot the caliper housing upward toward the rotor until the outer edge of the piston dust boot is approximately 1/4 in. from the upper edge of the inboard brake shoe, Fig. W-14, step 2.

Position clean, lightweight cardboard between inboard brake shoe and over the lower half of the piston dust boot, Fig. W-14, step 3. Cardboard is required to prevent pinching the dust boot between the piston and the inboard shoe during caliper installation to the rotor and anchor plate.

Rotate the caliper housing toward the rotor until a slight resistance is found. Pull the cardboard downward toward the rotor center line while rotating the caliper over the rotor, Fig. W-14, step 4. Remove the card-

## Brakes

board and rotate the caliper down over the rotor, Fig. W-14, step 5. Slide the caliper up against the anchor plate upper abutment and center it over the lower anchor plate abutment, Fig. W-14, step 6.

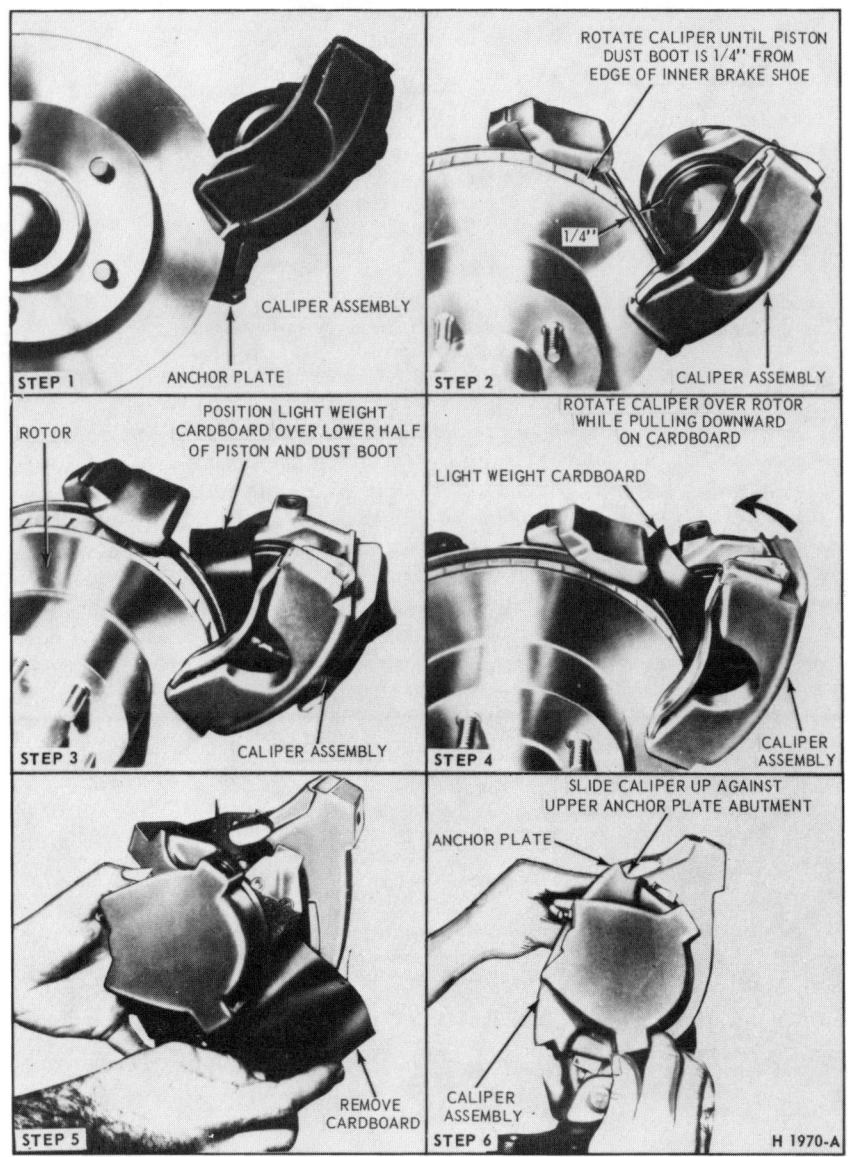

Fig. W-14. Steps in installing caliper assembly. (Courtesy Ford Customer Service Div.)

## Fix Your Ford

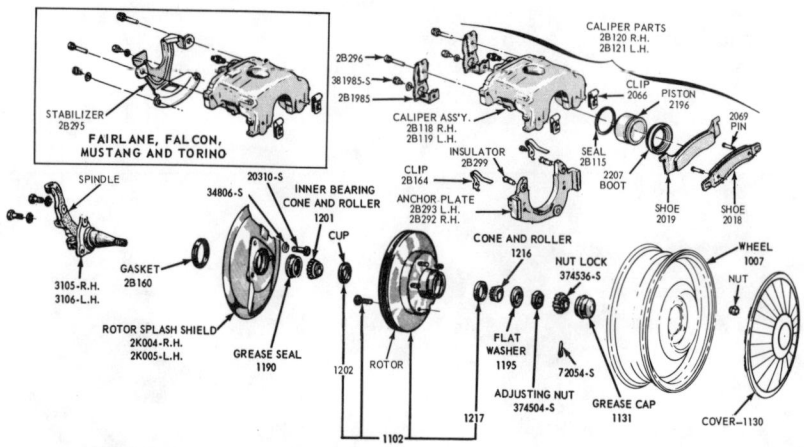

*Fig. W-15. Single piston caliper type disc brake as installed on 1968-1971 cars.*

Position the caliper support spring and key in the key slot and slide them into the opening between the lower end of the caliper and the lower anchor plate abutment. Align the semi-circular hole in the anchor plate. Install the key retaining screw and tighten to 12-16 ft. lb. Thread the flexible brake hose and gasket into the fitting on the caliper. Torque the hose fitting to 12 to 20 ft. lb. Position the upper end of the flexible brake hose in its bracket and install the retaining clip. Do not twist the hose. Remove the plug from the brake tube. Connect the brake tube to the hose with the tube fitting nut and tighten to 10 to 15 ft. lb.

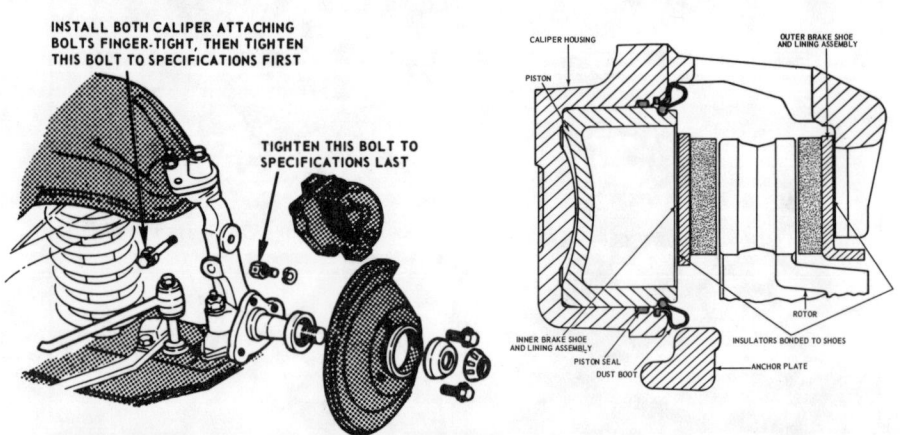

*Fig. W-16. Left. Removing fixed caliper. Note sequence for tightening bolts on reassembly.*
*Fig. W-16a. Right. Sectional view of sliding caliper assembly, 1975-1978.*

# Brakes

Bleed the brake system and install the wheel and tire assembly. Be sure there is a firm brake pedal, then road test car.

## FRONT WHEEL HUB AND ROTOR ASSEMBLY REMOVAL 1968 - 1978

Remove the wheel and tire from the hub and the caliper assembly from the spindle and the rotor. If the caliper does not require servicing, it is not necessary to disconnect the brake hose or remove the caliper from the vehicle. Position the caliper out of the way and support it with a wire to avoid damaging the caliper or stretching the hose. Remove the grease cap from the hub. Remove the cotter pin, nut lock, adjusting nut and flat washer from the spindle. Remove the outer bearing cone and rotor assembly. The hub and rotor assembly can then be removed from the spindle.

## 1978 PIN SLIDER CALIPER DISC BRAKE

The pin slider caliper disc brake is installed on the 1978 Fairmont. See Fig. W-17. The pin slider design consists of a caliper housing, inner and outer shoe and lining assemblies and a single piston. In operation, the caliper assembly slides on two locating pins, which also serve

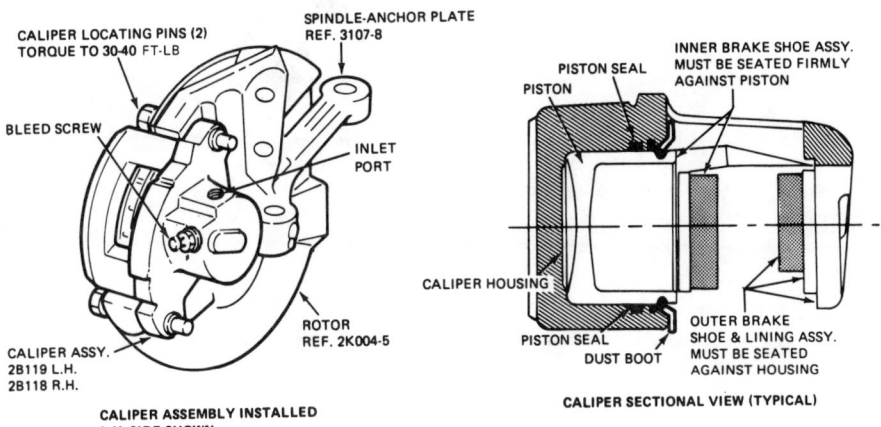

Fig. W-17. Details of component parts of a pin slider caliper used on 1978 Fairmont models. Left. Note caliper locating pins and important 30—40 ft. lb. torque tightening specification. Also note integral spindle-anchor plate. Right. Cross-sectional view of caliper shows piston, cylinder and shoe and lining assemblies.

as attaching bolts between the caliper and the combination anchor plate and wheel spindle, Fig. W-17.

Both inner and outer shoe and lining assemblies, Fig. W-18, are attached by spring clips riveted to the shoe surfaces. The inner shoe is

325

attached to the caliper by installing the spring clips to the inside of the caliper piston. The outer shoe, in turn, clips directly to the caliper housing.

A metal wear indicator is attached to the outer shoe and lining assembly. The indicator emits noise when the lining is worn to a point where replacement is needed.

The anchor plate is an integral part of the spindle.

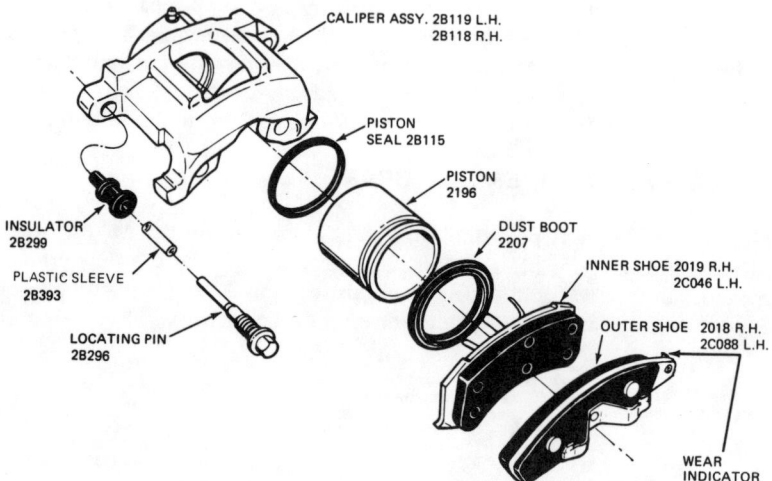

Fig. W-18. Exploded view of pin slider caliper assembly of 1978 Fairmont disc brake. Disassembled right-hand side is shown.

## REMOVING FAIRMONT BRAKE SHOES

To remove the front disc brake shoes and lining assemblies from the 1978 Fairmont:
1. Remove master cylinder filler cap and check fluid level in the primary (large) reservoir.
2. Remove and discard fluid until level is half full.
3. Remove tire and wheel assembly, taking care to avoid damage to splash shield and bleeder valve.
4. Remove caliper locating pins.
5. Lift caliper assembly from integral spindle.
6. Remove outer brake shoe from caliper assembly.
7. Remove inner shoe and lining assembly.
8. Inspect rotor.

Minor scoring or buildup of lining material does not indicate that the rotor must be reconditioned or replaced. Remove and discard plastic sleeves located inside caliper locating pin insulators. Also replace caliper locating insulators.

# Brakes

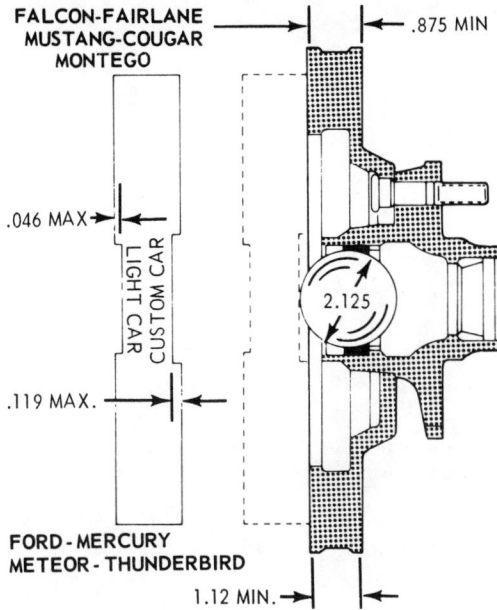

Fig. W-19. Reconditioning limits for disc brake rotor for various models shown. Maximum stock removal is: Custom—.119 in. (3.02 mm); compact—.046 in. (1.17 mm). Minimum thickness is: Custom—1.12 in. (28.45 mm); compact—.875 in. (22.23 mm).

## DISC BRAKE ROTOR SERVICE

To check rotor run-out, first eliminate the wheel bearing end play by tightening the adjusting nut. After tightening the nut, check to see that the rotor can still be rotated. Clamp a dial gauge to the caliper housing, so that the stylus of the gauge contacts the rotor at a point approximately one inch from the outer edge. Rotate the rotor and take an indicator reading. If the reading exceeds .003 in., total lateral run-out on the indicator, replace or resurface the disc brake rotor.

Only specialized equipment should be used to recondition rotors. The finished braking surface of the rotor must be flat and parallel within .0007 in. The lateral run-out must not exceed .003 in. total indicator reading, and the surface finish of the braking surfaces are to be 80-15 micro inches. The minimum limiting dimensions, Fig. W-19, must be observed when removing material from the rotor braking surfaces.

## WHEN TO REPLACE DISC BRAKE SHOES

On 1968-1972 disc brakes, make thickness measurements with a micrometer across the thinnest section of the shoe and lining. If the assembly has worn to a thickness of a .230 in. (shoe and lining together), or

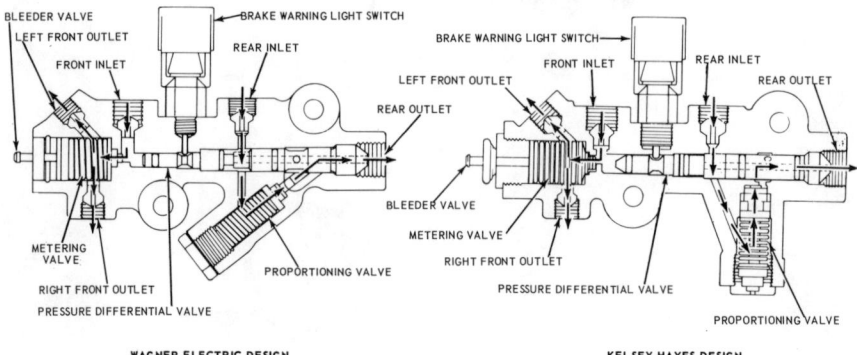

*Fig. W-20. Details of combined pressure differential valve and proportioning valve, known as the control valve. (Courtesy Ford Customer Service Div.)*

.030 in. (lining material only) at any one of three measuring locations, or if the lining shows evidence of brake fluid contamination, replace all four shoe and lining assemblies on both front wheels.

On 1965-1967 installations, make three thickness measurements with a micrometer across the metal section of the shoe and lining. Take one reading at each side and one in the center. If the assembly has worn to a thickness of .195 in. for the shoe and lining together, or .030 in. for the lining material only, at any one of the three measuring locations, or if the lining shows evidence of brake fluid contamination, replace all four shoe and lining assemblies on both front wheels.

## PRESSURE DIFFERENTIAL AND PROPORTIONING VALVE

The pressure differential valve, Fig. W-20, is combined with the proportioning valve. It senses unbalanced pressure between the front and the rear brakes. A pressure loss in either system will move the valve off center, causing a warning light to come on.

The proportioning valve is installed in a separate angular or vertical bore at the bottom of the valve casting between the rear brake system inlet and outlet ports. The proportioning valve functions to regulate rear brake system hydraulic pressure. With the piston in the centralized position, the switch contacts remain open. The complete unit is serviced as an assembly and is never overhauled or repaired.

## HYDRAULIC BRAKE SYSTEM

Two basic types of hydraulic brake systems have been used on Ford built cars. Prior to 1967, the single master cylinder system was standard and since that time the dual master cylinder has been used. The latter

## Brakes

system, Fig. W-1, consists of a dual master cylinder assembly, Fig. W-21, and switch. The switch on the differential valve, Fig. W-20, activates a dual brake warning light located on the instrument panel. The dual master cylinder brake system, Fig. W-21, is similar to the familiar single cylinder system, Fig. W-22. In the dual system, two master cylinders are combined in a single cast iron unit. One portion actuates the front brake system while the other actuates the rear brake system.

Hydraulic fluid leakage or failure of one of the systems, does not affect the operation of the other system. A dual brake warning light signals a failure of either the front or rear systems.

On disc brake equipped vehicles, a proportioning valve is included in the system and is connected to the differential valve by inlet and outlet tubes. The brake hose bracket serves as a junction point for the individual brake lines that lead to the wheel cylinders of right and left rear brake components.

## HOW TO BLEED BRAKES

Bleeding brakes is a process whereby any air in the hydraulic system is removed. It is very important that there be no air in the hydraulic system, as such air would be compressed instead of transmitting the motion of the fluid. When there is air in the system, the brake pedal will have a spongy feel, instead of the normal feel when the brakes are applied. This spongy feel results from the air being compressed.

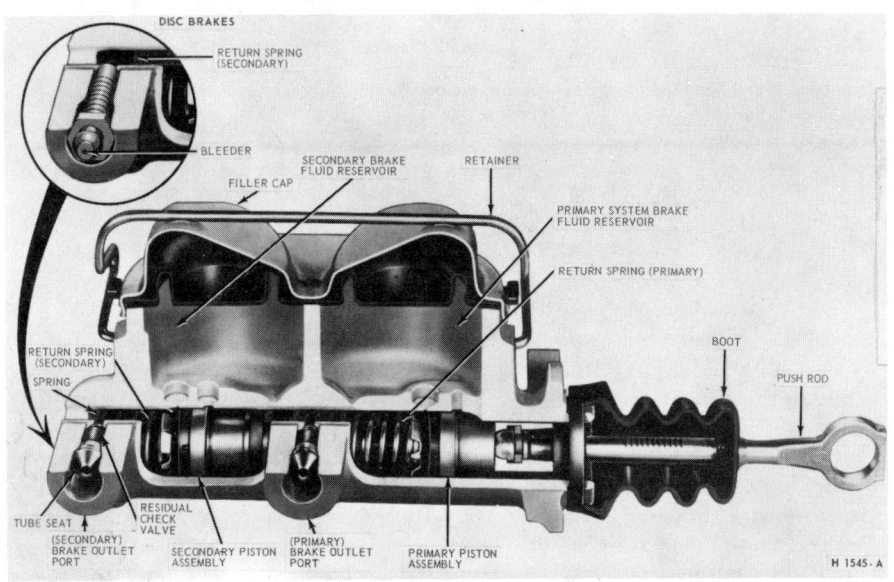

Fig. W-21. Sectional view of dual type master cylinder used on both drum and disc type brakes 1967–1971.

# Fix Your Ford

To bleed the hydraulic brake system, a small valve is provided in each of the wheel cylinders, Fig. W-23, and in the master cylinder, Fig. W-21.

On dual master cylinder systems used since 1967, the front and rear hydraulic brake systems are individual systems and are bled separately.

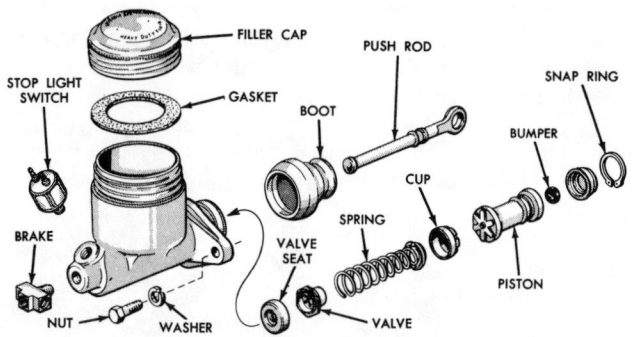

Fig. W-22. Disassembled single type master cylinder.

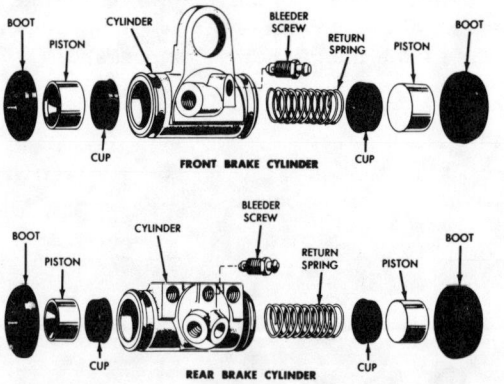

Fig. W-23. Typical front and rear wheel cylinders.

Bleed the longest line first, on the individual system being serviced. During the complete bleeding operation, do not allow the reservoir to run dry. Keep the master cylinder reservoirs filled with extra heavy-duty brake fluid, meeting SAE specifications. The disc brake heavy-duty brake fluid is colored blue for identification purposes. Do not mix low temperature brake fluids with the specified fluid during the bleeding operations. Never reuse brake fluid which has been drained from the hydraulic system.

If the master cylinder is equipped with a bleed screw, loosen the bleed screw. Push the brake pedal down slowly through its full travel. Close the bleeder fitting and return the pedal to the fully released position. Repeat

## Brakes

this operation until the fluid is free from bubbles. Then tighten bleeder screw. Do not use the secondary piston stop screw located on the bottom of the master cylinder to bleed the brake system as that would result in damage to the secondary piston or stop screw.

To bleed the rear brake system, position a suitable 3/8 in. box wrench on the bleeder fitting on the brake wheel cylinder, Fig. W-23. Attach a rubber drain tube to the bleeder fitting. The end of the tube should fit snugly around the bleeder fitting.

Submerge the free end of the tube in a container partly filled with clean brake fluid and loosen the bleeder fitting approximately 3/4 turn. Push the brake pedal down slowly through its full travel. Close the bleeder fitting. Then return the pedal to the fully released position. Repeat this operation until air bubbles cease to appear at the submerged end of the bleeder tube.

When the fluid is completely free of air bubbles, close the bleeder fitting and remove the bleeder tube.

Repeat this procedure at the brake wheel cylinder on the opposite side. Refill the master cylinder reservoir after each wheel cylinder is bled and install the master cylinder cover and gasket.

Be sure the diaphragm type gasket is properly positioned in the master cylinder cover.

Repeat these procedures on the right front brake caliper or cylinder, and then at the left front brake caliper or cylinder. Be sure that the front brake pistons are returned to their normal positions and that the shoe and lining assemblies are properly seated by depressing the brake pedal several times until normal pedal travel is established. When the bleeding operation is completed, the fluid level should be filled to within one-quarter to one-half in. from the top of the reservoirs.

## CENTRALIZING THE DIFFERENTIAL VALVE

After bleeding it is necessary to centralize the pressure differential valve which is done as follows:

Turn the ignition switch to the ACC position. Loosen the differential valve assembly brake tube nut at the outlet port on the opposite side of the brake system that was bled last. Depress the brake pedal slowly to build line pressure until the pressure differential valve is moved to a centralized position, and the brake warning light goes out. Then immediately tighten the outlet port tube nut. Recheck the fluid level in the master cylinder.

## BLEEDING THE 1954-1967 BRAKES

To bleed the single master cylinder type brake system, which was used prior to 1967, the procedure is the same as that described for the dual system which was just described, except that the master cylinder does not have a bleeder valve. Fig. W-24 shows a bleeding operation being performed on such a system.

Fix Your Ford

FLUSHING THE BRAKE SYSTEM

The hydraulic system should be flushed annually, or every 10,000 miles, and the procedure is the same as bleeding. However sufficient fluid should be bled from each line until the color of the fluid is clear, and the same as new fluid. When flushing a brake system, it is generally advisable to draw approximately one pint of fluid from the first cylinder bled. This will insure that all the fluid contained in the master cylinder has been drained. On subsequent cylinders, it is then necessary to drain the line until clear fluid is obtained.

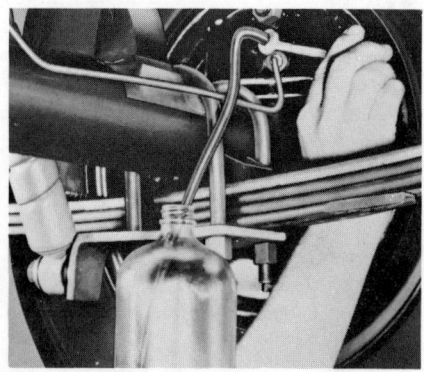

Fig. W-24. Method of bleeding brakes. Note bleeder hose carrying brake fluid to glass container. End of hose must remain below surface of fluid in the container.

QUICK SERVICE ON WHEEL CYLINDERS

The life of wheel cylinders can be prolonged by more frequent flushing of the hydraulic system and by the use of quality brake fluid meeting the SAE specifications. It is necessary to service the wheel cylinders when they start to leak fluid. This becomes apparent when the brake pedal gradually goes to the floor when the brakes are applied and "pumping" the pedal becomes necessary in order to stop the car.

The condition of the brake wheel cylinders may be properly checked by pulling back the boots from the ends of the cylinders as shown in Fig. W-25. If the inside of the boot is wet with fluid, there is leakage present and it will be necessary to recondition the cylinder.

Kits of the necessary parts are readily available and their installation is not difficult. The procedure is to remove the links and the rubber boots from the end of the brake cylinder. The pistons, cups and return spring can then be pushed from the cylinder bore, Fig. W-23. Remove the bleeder screw from the cylinder. Wash all parts with clean brake fluid and dry with compressed air if available. Replace scored pistons. Always replace the

Fig. W-25. If brake fluid has leaked into cups on wheel cylinders, the cylinders should be overhauled or replaced.

rubber cups and dust boots. Inspect the cylinder bore for score marks or rust. If either condition is present, the cylinder bore must be honed or replaced. However, the cylinder should not be honed more than .003 in. oversize.

It is not necessary to remove the brake cylinder from the backing plate to disassemble, inspect, or hone and overhaul the cylinder. Removal is only necessary when the cylinder is damaged or scored beyond repair.

When reassembling a wheel cylinder, apply a light coating of heavy-duty brake fluid to all internal parts. Thread the bleeder screw into the cylinder and tighten securely. Insert the return spring, cups, and pistons into their respective positions in the cylinder bore, Fig. W-23. Then place a boot over each end of the cylinder and bleed the brake cylinder.

Should it become necessary to replace the wheel cylinder, first disconnect the brake line from the brake cylinder. On a vehicle with a vacuum brake booster, be sure the engine is stopped and there is no vacuum in the booster system before disconnecting the hydraulic lines.

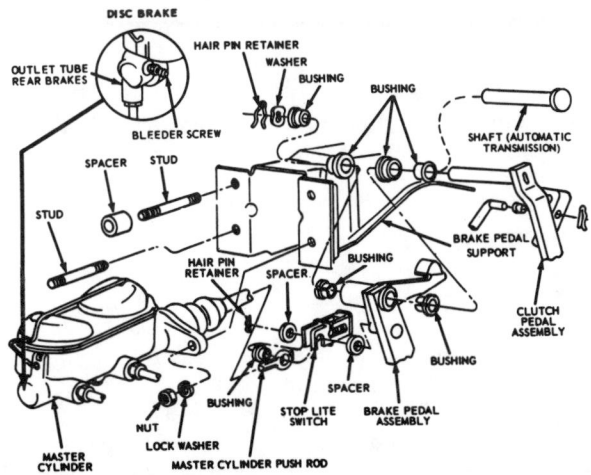

Fig. W-26. Installation of dual type master cylinder as used with drum type brakes.

# Fix Your Ford

To disconnect the hose at a front cylinder, loosen the tube fitting that connects the opposite end of the hose to a brake tube at a bracket on the frame. Remove the horseshoe type retaining clip from the hose and bracket. Disengage the hose from the bracket, then unscrew the entire hose assembly from the front wheel cylinder.

At a rear cylinder, unscrew the tube fitting that connects the tube to the cylinder. Do not pull the metal tube away from the cylinder. Pulling the tube out of the cylinder connection will bend the metal tube and make installation difficult. The tube will separate from the cylinder when the cylinder is removed from the backing plate.

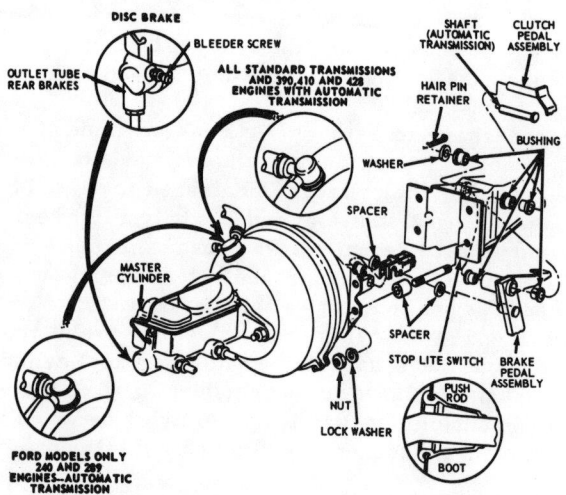

*Fig. W-27. Installation of dual type master cylinder as used with disc type brakes.*

On the rear wheel, remove the wheel cylinder attaching bolts and lock washers and remove the cylinder. On the front wheel, remove the nut and washer that attaches the cylinder to the anchor pin. Remove the cylinder from the anchor pin.

## MASTER CYLINDER TIPS

The master cylinder is mounted directly, Fig. W-26, or indirectly, Fig. W-27, on the dash panel. With a split hydraulic system, one part of the master cylinder supplies hydraulic pressure to the front brakes; the other part supplies the rear brakes. Installation of a dual master cylinder with a Hydro-Boost unit is shown in Fig. W-28.

In general, master cylinders require servicing when: all brakes drag; pedal gradually goes to the floor on brake application; brakes do not apply; fluid is found in boot on cylinder.

## Brakes

Kits for rebuilding master cylinders contain all necessary parts and instructions needed to make the repairs. However, some mechanics prefer to install rebuilt units to save time.

In order to overhaul a master cylinder, it is first necessary to remove it from the dash panel or from the power brake unit, as the case may be. To remove a conventional single type master cylinder: Disconnect rubber boot from rear end of master cylinder in passenger compartment. Disconnect brake line from master cylinder. Disconnect stoplight switch wires from switch. Remove bolts that secure master cylinder to dash panel. Lift cylinder from push rod. Remove rubber boot from push rod.

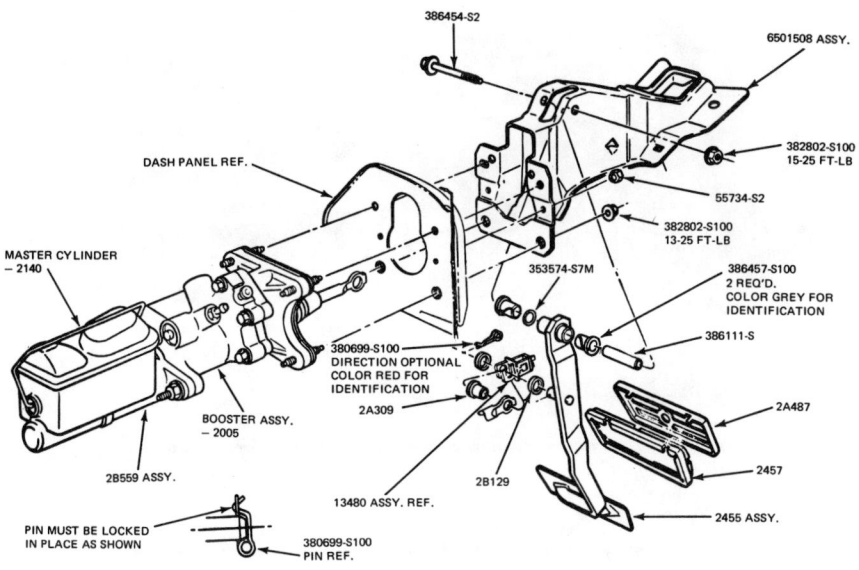

Fig. W-28. Dual master cylinder with Hydro-Boost power unit as installed on recent model Ford cars.

Clean the outside of the cylinder and remove the filler cap and gasket. Pour out any brake fluid that may remain in the cylinder or reservoir. Remove the stoplight switch and fitting from the forward end of the cylinder, Fig. W-22. Remove the snap ring from the bore at the rear of the cylinder. The piston cup, spring and seat can then be withdrawn from the cylinder bore. If necessary the bore should be honed before installation of the new parts.

To disassemble a dual type master cylinder, clean the outside of the master cylinder and remove the filler cover and diaphragm. Pour out any brake fluid that remains in the cylinder. Remove the secondary piston stop bolt from the bottom of the cylinder, Figs. W-29 and W-30. Remove the bleed screw if required. Remove the snap ring from the retainer groove

# Fix Your Ford

at the rear of the master cylinder bore. Remove the push rod and the primary piston assembly from the master cylinder bore. Do not remove the screw that retains the primary return spring retainer, return spring, primary cup and protector on the primary piston. This assembly is factory adjusted and should not be disassembled. Remove the secondary piston assembly. Do not remove the outlet tube seats, outlet check valves and outlet check valve springs from the master cylinder body.

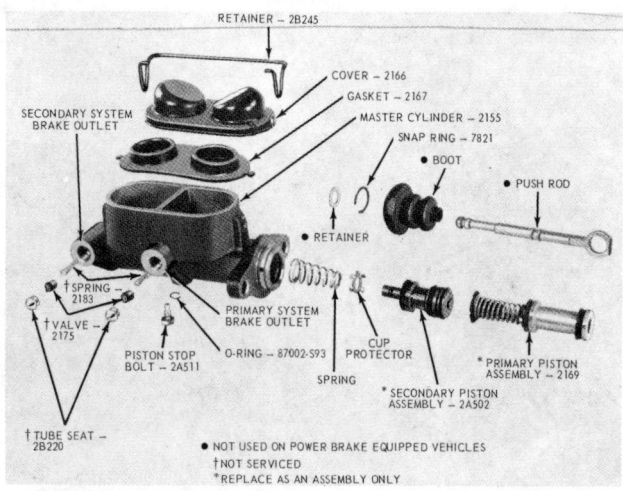

Fig. W-29. Dual master cylinder disassembled. Drum brake installation.

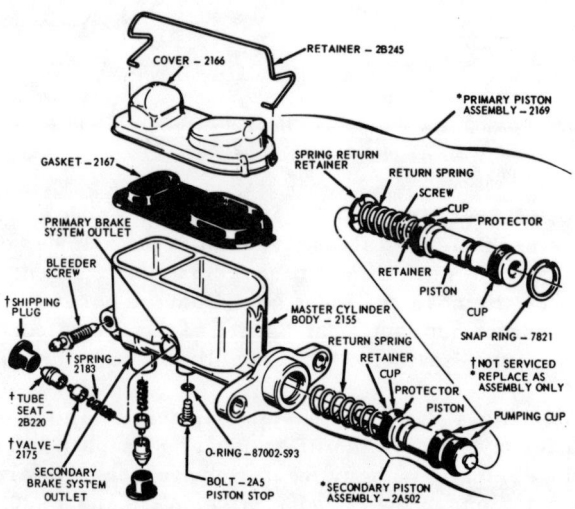

Fig. W-30. Type of master cylinder as used with disc brakes.

## Brakes

Clean all parts in clean, denatured alcohol and inspect the parts for chipping, excessive wear or damage. When using a master cylinder repair kit, install all the parts supplied. Make sure all recesses, openings and internal passages are free of all foreign matter. If necessary, hone the master cylinder bore to repair damage. When reassembling the master cylinder, dip all parts except the master cylinder body in clean, heavy-duty brake fluid. Carefully insert the complete secondary piston and return spring assembly in the master cylinder bore. Install the primary piston and return spring assembly in the master cylinder bore. Install the push rod retainer on the push rod, if so equipped. Install the push rod assembly in the master cylinder bore. Make sure the retainer is properly seated and holding the push rod securely. Depress the primary piston and install the snap ring in the cylinder bore groove. Position the inner end of the push rod boot, if so equipped, in the master cylinder body retaining groove. Install the secondary piston stop bolt and gasket in the bottom of the master cylinder. Install the bleed screw, if so equipped. Install the gasket in the master cylinder filler cover. Make sure the gasket is securely seated. Install the cover and gasket on the master cylinder and secure the cover in position with the retainer.

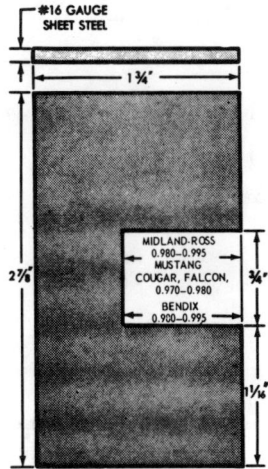

Fig. W-31. Details of gauge used when adjusting push rod of power brakes.

## BRAKE HOSE REPLACEMENT

A flexible brake hose should be replaced if it shows signs of softening, cracking or other damage.

When installing a new front brake hose, position the hose to avoid contact with other chassis parts. Place a new copper gasket over the hose fitting and thread the hose assembly into the front wheel cylinder. Engage

## Fix Your Ford

the opposite end of the hose to the bracket on the frame. Install a horseshoe type retaining clip, and connect the tube to the hose with a tube fitting nut.

A rear brake hose should be installed so that it does not touch the muffler outlet pipe or shock absorber. Place a new gasket over the rear hose fitting and thread the hose into the rear brake tube connector. Engage the front end of the hose to the bracket on the frame. Install the horseshoe-type retaining clip, and connect the tube to the hose with the tube fitting nut.

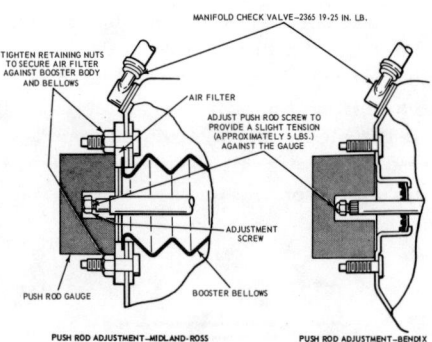

*Fig. W-32. Using gauge to adjust push rod on Midland-Ross type power brake on left and Bendix power brake on right.*

### TIPS ON POWER BRAKE SERVICE

There are two types of power (booster) brakes used on Ford cars. The first type, Figs. W-27 and W-33, utilizes intake manifold vacuum to amplify the power applied to the brake pedal. The other type makes use of the hydraulic power provided by the power steering pump. The latter type, known as Hydro-Boost, Figs. W-28 and W-34, has been used on some models with power steering since 1977.

Neither vacuum operated nor Hydro-Boost can be repaired. When either is found defective, a new unit must be installed.

The vacuum suspended type uses intake manifold vacuum and atmosphere pressure for its power. Push rod adjustment, Fig. W-32, is the only service permitted on the unit. When defective, the old unit can be exchanged for a new one.

The push rod is provided with an adjustment screw to maintain the correct relationship between the booster control valve plunger and the master cylinder. Failure to maintain this relationship will prevent the master cylinder piston from completely releasing hydraulic pressure and can cause the brakes to drag. Under normal service the adjustment screw does not require any further attention providing the original push rod assembly

## Brakes

remains in the original unit. To check the adjustment of the screw, fabricate a gauge, as shown in Fig. W-31. On the Midland-Ross booster unit, remove the master cylinder and air filter assembly and push the bellows back into the booster body. Reinstall the air filter directly against the booster body and then place the gauge against the master cylinder mounting surface on the air filter assembly, as shown in Fig. W-32. The push rod screw should be adjusted so that the end of the screw just touches the inner edge of the slot in the gauge.

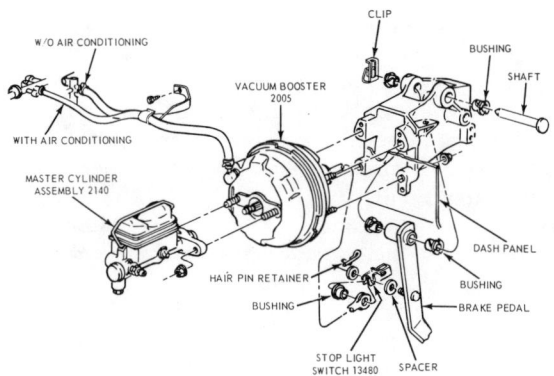

*Fig. W-33. Master cylinder and power brake installation. Typical.*

To check the Bendix type booster, remove the master cylinder and fit the gauge against the master cylinder mounting surface, as shown in Fig. W-32.

This is an approximate adjustment. To verify the adjustment, look through the make-up (rear) port of the master cylinder when installing the master cylinder to the booster. The master cylinder piston should not move more than .015 in. as it contacts the push rod. No movement is ideal.

## TROUBLE SHOOTING POWER BRAKES

To check to see if the vacuum power unit is operating: with the engine stopped, depress the brake pedal several times to eliminate all vacuum from the system. Apply the brakes and, while maintaining pressure on the pedal, start the engine. If the unit is operating, the brake pedal will move forward slightly when engine vacuum is added to the foot pressure on the pedal. If the unit is not operating, there will be no brake pedal reaction when the engine is started.

If this check shows that the unit is not working, check for the following conditions: Brake pedal linkage sticking. Collapsed or leaking vacuum hose. Leaking vacuum chamber. Vacuum leaking automatic transmission throttle valve vacuum line connection or fitting. If none of those conditions prove to be the trouble, the power unit should be replaced.

# Fix Your Ford

## HYDRO-BOOST SYSTEM

Hydro-Boost, Figs. W-28 and W-34, is a hydraulic assist power brake unit. It receives its hydraulic pressure from the power steering pump. Since the system operates hydraulically, it eliminates the familiar vacuum booster. To maintain satisfactory fluid temperature, cooler lines carry the fluid from the Hydro-Boost unit to the power steering gear, then to the front of the radiator for air cooling before returning it to the power steering pump reservoir.

In order for the Hydro-Boost system to operate correctly, the engine must idle smoothly and be tuned to specifications listed on the decal in the engine compartment. If excessive brake pedal effort is required, check for a loose power steering pump belt, low power steering fluid level (leakage), fluid contamination, low pump pressure or restriction of hoses. Also check for binding brake pedal or nicked or burred spool valve in the Hydro-Boost unit.

The Hydro-Boost cannot cause noisy brakes, fading brake pedal nor pulling brakes. If any of these conditions exist, the cause of the trouble will be found in the basic brake system.

To check the Hydro-Boost unit, first place the transmission in Neutral. Stop the engine and apply the brakes several times. Hold the pedal depressed with medium pressure and start the engine. If the booster unit is operating properly, the brake pedal will fall away slightly, then push back against the foot. If no reaction of this kind is felt, the Hydro-Boost unit probably is at fault.

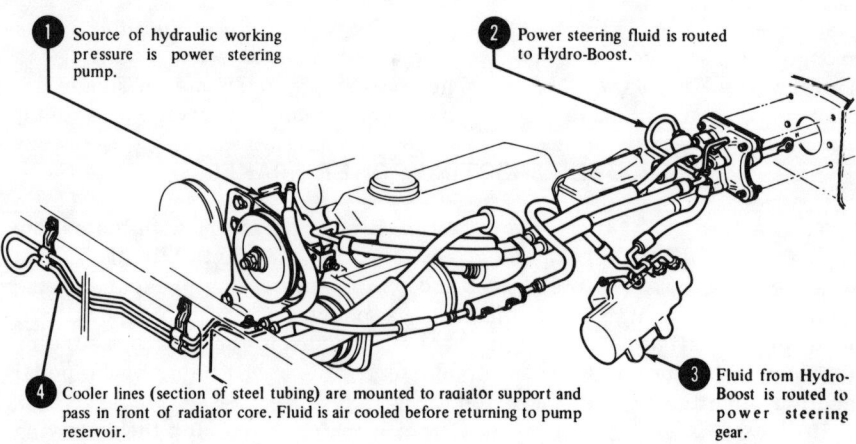

*Fig. W-34. Flow of power steering fluid is traced in Hydro-Boost power brake system that replaces conventional vacuum power brake unit on some models.*

# Brakes

## DRUM BRAKE (AND GENERAL SYSTEM) TROUBLE SYMPTONS AND POSSIBLE CAUSES

| POSSIBLE CAUSES OF TROUBLE | One Brake Drags | All Brakes Drag | Hard Pedal | Spongy Pedal | Car Pulls to One Side | One Wheel Locks | Brakes Chatter | Excessive Pedal Travel | Pedal Gradually Goes to Floor | Brakes Uneven | Shoe Click After Release | Noisy or Grabbing Brakes | Brakes Do Not Apply | Brakes for the Respective System Do Not Apply | Warning Lamp Stays Lit | Pedal Gradually Moves Toward Floor or Dash Panel | Warning Lamp Does Not Light |
|---|---|---|---|---|---|---|---|---|---|---|---|---|---|---|---|---|---|
| Mechanical Resistance at Pedal or Shoes | | X | X | | | | | | | | | | | | | | |
| Brake Line Restricted | X | X | X | | X | | | | | | | | | | | | |
| Leaks or Insufficient Fluid | | | | X | | | | X | X | | | X | | | | X | |
| Improper Tire Pressure | | | | | X | | | | | | X | | | | | | |
| Distorted or Improperly Adjusted Brake Shoe | X | X | X | | X | X | | X | | | | X | | | | | |
| Faulty Retracting Spring | X | | | | X | | | | | | | | | | | | |
| Drum Out of Round | X | | | | X | | X | | | | | | | | | | |
| Lining Glazed or Worn | | X | | | X | X | X | | | | | X | X | | | | |
| Oil or Grease on Lining | | | | | X | X | X | | | | X | X | X | | | | |
| Loose Carrier Plate | X | | | | | X | X | | | | | | | | | | |
| Loose Lining | | | | | | | X | | | | | | | | | | |
| Dirt on Drum-Lining Surface | | | | | | | | | | | | X | | | | | |
| Faulty Brake Cylinder | X | | | | X | X | | | | | | X | | | | | |
| Dirty Brake Fluid | X | X | | | | | | | | X | | X | | | | | |
| Faulty Master Cylinder | | X | | | | | | X | X | | | X | | | X | | |
| Air in Hydraulic System | X | | | X | | | | X | | | | X | | | | | |
| Self Adjusters Not Operating | | | | | X | | | X | | | | | | | | | |
| Insufficient Shoe-to-Carrier Plate Lubrication | X | | | | | | | | | | | | X | X | | | |
| Tire Tread Worn | | | | | X | | | | | | | | | | | | |
| Poor Lining to Drum Contact | | | | | | | X | | | | | | | | | | |
| Loose Front Suspension | | | | | | | X | | | | | | | | | | |
| Threads Left by Drum Turning Tool Pulls Shoes Sideways | | | | | | | | | | | X | | | | | | |
| Cracked Drum | | | | | | | | X | | | | | | | | | |
| One Section Dual Brake System Is Inoperative | | | | | | | | | | | | | | X | X | | |
| Differential Pressure Valve Not Centered | | | | | | | | | | | | | | | X | | |
| Wiring to Warning Lamp Switch Is Grounded | | | | | | | | | | | | | | | X | | |
| Warning Lamp Switch Is Grounded | | | | | | | | | | | | | | | X | | |
| Warning Lamp Is Burned Out | | | | | | | | | | | | | | | | | X |
| Warning Lamp Switch Has an Open Circuit | | | | | | | | | | | | | | | | | X |
| Wiring to Warning Lamp Has Open Circuit | | | | | | | | | | | | | | | | | X |

# Fix Your Ford

## DISC BRAKE TROUBLE SYMPTOMS AND POSSIBLE CAUSES

| POSSIBLE CAUSES OF TROUBLE | Excessive Pedal Travel | Brake Roughness or Chatter (Pedal Pumping) | Excessive Pedal Effort | Pull | Rattle | Brakes Heat Up During Driving and Fail to Release | Leaky Wheel Cylinder | Grabbing or Uneven Braking Action | No Braking Effect When Pedal Is Depressed | Brakes for the Respective System Do Not Apply | Pedal Gradually Moves Toward Floor or Dash Panel | Warning Lamp Stays Lit | Warning Lamp Does Not Light |
|---|---|---|---|---|---|---|---|---|---|---|---|---|---|
| Shoe and Lining Knock-back after Violent Cornering or Rough Road Travel | X | | | | | | | | | | | | |
| Shoe and Lining Assembly not Properly Seated or Positioned | X | | | | | X | | | | X | | | |
| Leak or Insufficient Fluid in System or Caliper | X | | X | | | | | | | X | X | | |
| Loose Wheel Bearing Adjustment | X | | | X | | | | | | | | | |
| Damaged or Worn Caliper Piston Seal | X | | | | | | X | | X | | | | |
| Improper Master Cylinder Push Rod Adjustment | X | | | | | | | | | | | | |
| Excessive Rotor Runout or Out of Parallel | | X | | | | | | | | | | | |
| Incorrect Tire Pressure | | | | X | | | | X | | | | | |
| Frozen or Seized Pistons | | | X | X | | X | | X | | | | | |
| Brake Fluid, Oil or Grease on Linings | | X | X | X | | | | X | | | | | |
| Shoe and Lining Worn Below Specifications | | X | | | | | | | | | | | |
| Proportioning Valve Malfunction | | X | | | | | | | X | | | | |
| Booster Inoperative | | X | | | | | | | | | | | |
| Caliper Out of Alignment with Rotor | | | | X | | | | X | | | | | |
| Loose Caliper Attachment | X | X | | X | X | | | X | | | | | |
| Metering Valve Seal Leaks | | | | | | | | X | | | | | |
| Excessive Clearance Between Shoe and Caliper or Between Shoe and Splash Shield | | | | | X | | | | | | | | |
| Shoe Hold Down Clips Missing or Improperly Positioned | | | | | X | | | | | | | | |
| Operator Riding Brake Pedal | | | | | | X | | | | | | | |
| Scores in the Cylinder Bore | | | | | | | X | | | | | | |
| Corrosion Build-Up in the Cylinder Bore or on the Piston Surface | | X | X | | | | X | | | | | | |
| Bleeder Screw Still Open | | | | | | | | | | X | X | | |
| Caliper Out of Parallel with Rotor | | X | | | | | | | | | | | |
| One Section Dual Brake System Is Inoperative | | | | | | | | | | X | | X | |
| Differential Pressure Valve Is not Centered | | | | | | | | | | | | X | |
| Wiring to Warning Lamp Switch Is Grounded | | | | | | | | | | | | X | |
| Warning Lamp Switch Is Grounded | | | | | | | | | | | | X | |
| Warning Lamp Is Burned Out | | | | | | | | | | | | | X |
| Warning Lamp Switch Has an Open Circuit | | | | | | | | | | | | | X |
| Warning Lamp Switch Is Inoperative | | | | | | | | | | | | | X |
| Wiring to Warning Lamp Has Open Circuit | | | | | | | | | | | | | X |

# LUBRICATION AND TIRES

## TIPS ON LUBRICATION

Latest Ford recommendations for engine oil changes are: L6 and V-8, every six months or 7500 miles; 4 and V-6, every six months or 10,000 miles. The oil filter should be replaced first at 6000 miles, then at every oil change. However, if all driving is of the short trip type (severe service), the oil should be changed every three months or 3000 miles to avoid valve and valve lifter sticking trouble.

The latest Ford recommendations for engine oil are: Use of SAE 10W-30 oil will provide proper viscosity for all normal ranges of outside temperatures. For operation at standard temperatures below -10 deg. F., a 5W-20 oil should be used. Use only oils which have been tested by the maker as satisfying auto manufacturer's specifications, for API SERVICE SE or SE-CC, Ford No. ESE-MZC144-A.

## OIL FILTER REPLACEMENT

A typical oil filter installation is shown in Fig. X-1. On most engines both Six and V-8, the oil filter is located on the left side of the engine.

Instructions for removing and replacing the oil filter element are as follows: Raise the car on a jack or hoist and drain the oil. Unscrew the filter element from the cylinder. On all the 352 and 390 cu. in. engines, check to see that the filter adapter plate is properly positioned, Fig. X-2. Clean the cylinder block filter recess. Coat the gasket on the new filter with oil, and position it on the cylinder block. Hand tighten the filter until the gasket contacts the adapter face, then advance it one-half turn. Fill the crankcase with the required amount of oil. Then operate the engine at a fast idle and check oil pressure. Also check for oil leaks around the filter.

On high performance engines the engine oil cooler should be cleaned every 24,000 miles.

## TRANSMISSION LUBRICATION

Current recommendations say to check level of fluid in automatic transmissions first at five months or 5000 miles, then every 15 months or 15,000 miles. On manual shift transmissions, check fluid level first at six months or 6000 miles, then every 12 months or 12,000 miles. Add Ford Rotunda automatic transmission fluid or manual transmission lubricant as required (see chapters on automatic and manual transmissions).

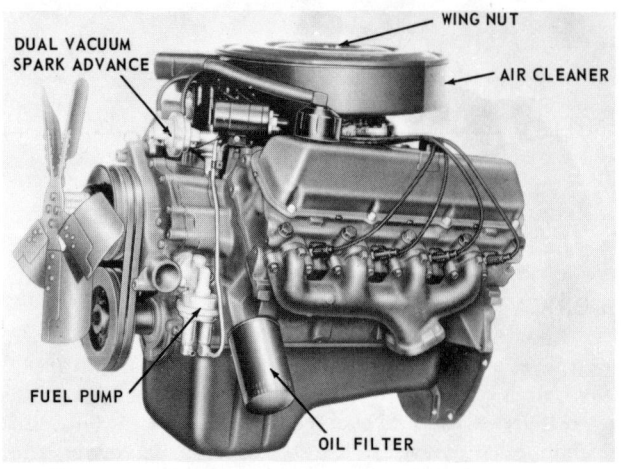

*Fig. X-1. Note location of the oil filter on this 429 cu. in. V-8 Ford engine.*

## REAR AXLE LUBRICATION

Check the level of the lubricant every 6000 miles and add lubricant as required to maintain the correct level. The Ford Motor Company recommends the use of FoMoCo Hypoid Gear Lubricant.

## LUBRICATING WHEEL BEARINGS

The front wheel bearings, Fig. W-2, should be lubricated each time the brakes are relined. When removing the bearings, care must be taken that no dirt or grit gets on the bearings. Only new bearing grease should

*Fig. X-2. When replacing the oil filter cartridge, make sure the filter adapter plate is correctly positioned.*

### Lubrication and Tires

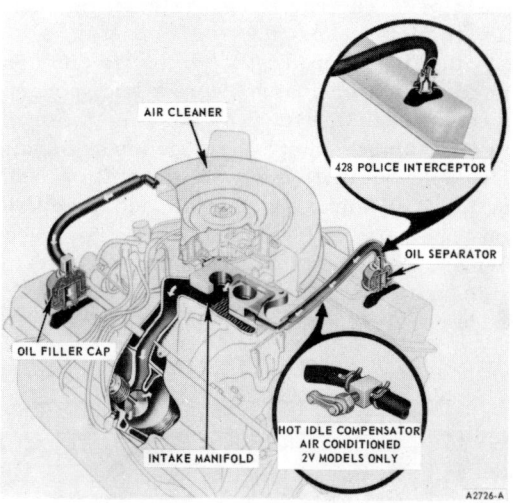

*Fig. X-3. Typical closed crankcase ventilating system as installed on V-8 engine.*

be used. This should be worked around the rollers with care. Do not apply any grease to the wheel spindle. Pack the inside of the hub with specified lubricant until flush with inside diameter of both bearing cups.

## CARBURETOR AIR CLEANER

Ford cars are equipped with a dry type filter that has a replaceable cellulose fibre filter element. This element should be cleaned at 6000 mile intervals or more often if a car is operated in a dusty atmosphere. To remove the element, remove the wing nut from the center of the pan covering the cleaner, Fig. X-1. The pan and element can then be lifted out. To clean, direct clean compressed air against the element in the opposite direction from normal air flow; that is, from the inside out. Before replacing the element, start the engine, then as the filter is placed in position, note if engine speed is materially reduced. If it is, install a new element.

## CRANKCASE BREATHER CAP AND FILTER

These should be cleaned every 6000 miles by washing in solvent.

## EMISSION CONTROL SYSTEMS

Since 1961, some form of crankcase emission control system has been used on Ford engines. Since 1968, devices have been included to control exhaust emissions and, since 1971, an evaporative emission control system has been installed. For 1975, a catalytic converter is used.

Since 1968, a closed recirculating system has been used to prevent the escape of fumes from the crankcase. It consists of a hose connecting the air cleaner to the filler cap, Fig. X-3, a hose and control valve, connecting the intake manifold to the rocker arm cover. In that way, the fumes from the crankcase are drawn into the intake manifold and then into the combustion chamber where they are burned again.

The control valve modulates the system air flow to maintain the correct air-fuel ratio. It is important that all tubing be kept clean and free from obstruction. The regulator valve should be replaced when defective.

There are two systems used to control the emission of exhaust gases: The improved combustion system (IMCO), Fig. X-7, and the Thermactor system which were described in a previous chapter.

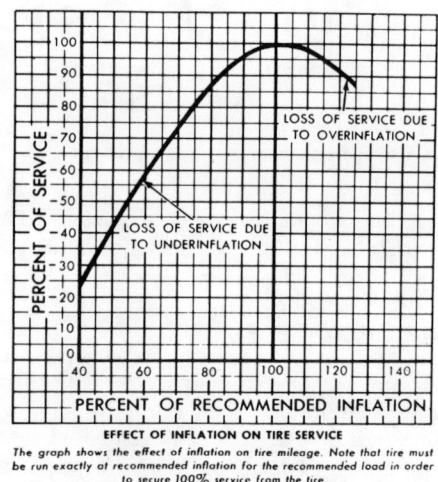

Fig. X-5. Effects of inflation on tire life.

Beginning with 1971 models, all passenger car fuel systems are equipped with a means of controlling evaporative emissions. System control and operation are accomplished through three separate basic functions. Fill Control Vent System; Vapor Vent and Storage System; Pressure and Vacuum Relief System in Fuel Cap. Care must be taken that the fill cap is not damaged in any way, as that would render it inoperative. All component parts of the fuel system are serviced by a simple nut, bolt, or screw part for removal or installation.

For complete coverage of exhaust emission systems, see the chapter on "Reducing Exhaust Emissions." A decal in the engine compartment of recent model cars contains instructions for adjusting units that pertain to emission systems. Follow these instructions.

## Lubrication and Tires

## WHAT TO DO ABOUT TIRES

In order to get maximum mileage from tires, they must be correctly inflated to the specified amount, driving speed must be conservative, brakes applied gently and acceleration must be conservative.

Rapid tire wear results when the tires are operated in an underinflated condition, Fig. X-5. Many authorities advise operating the tires at 2 pounds more than the specified amount in order to obtain better than average tire life. It is also important that the valve caps always be installed, as it is a cap which seals the air in the tire.

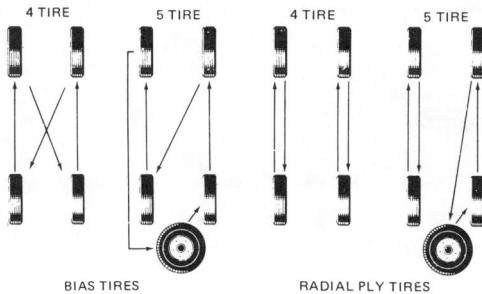

Fig. X-6. Rotation pattern for bias and radial ply tires.

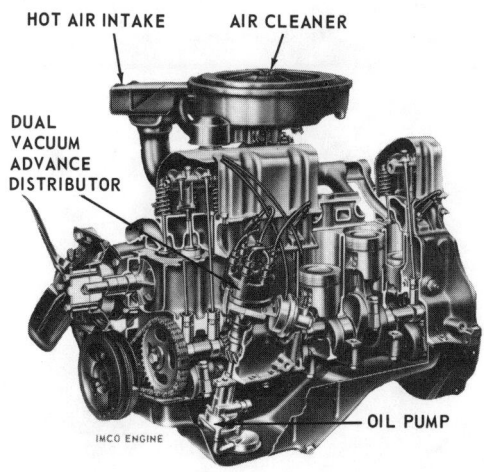

Fig. X-7. Typical six cylinder engine equipped with IMCO exhaust emission control system.

# Fix Your Ford

By rotating tires regularly, every 5000 miles, tire life will be materially increased. Rotation of tires should be made as shown in Fig. X-6. Also regularly inspect the tire treads for cuts and bruises and remove all stones, nails, glass and other objects from the tread. Leaks in a tire can be located by immersing the tire in a tub of water. The leaks will be indicated by a stream of air bubbles. Small leaks can be repaired without removing the tire from the rim, by inserting special plugs. Instructions accompanying the repair material should be followed.

If special equipment is not available to remove the tire from the rim, a bumper jack can be used. The procedure is as follows: Place the tire and wheel on the ground under the car bumper. Place the base of the bumper jack on the tire close to the rim and the head of the jack under the bumper of the car. Then as the jack is raised, the tire tread will be forced from the tire rim. Tire irons used to pry the tire from the rim must be smooth so that the rim will not be marred in any way.

## ENGINE OIL COOLER

Some of the high performance engines are equipped with oil coolers which are mounted behind the cooling system radiator and are designed to reduce the temperature of the engine oil thereby improving engine lubrication.

To remove the unit, first disconnect the inlet and outlet lines from the oil cooler and drain them into a container. Remove the hold down bracket from the top of the cooler, Fig. X-8. The cooler can then be lifted from the lower mount.

To install the oil cooler, first position the cooler on the lower mount. Install the upper hold down bracket. Connect the inlet and outlet lines. Fill the engine crankcase with specified oil. Start the engine and check for oil leaks.

*Fig. X-8. 1970 302 Boss, engine oil cooler.*

# Emergency
# TROUBLE SHOOTING AND REPAIRS

When the engine suddenly stops, or the brakes fail, or the horn continues to blow, or some similar trouble occurs, the situation may range from extreme danger to one of annoyance. What to do in such emergencies is described in the following pages. It is, of course, impossible to describe all possible emergencies that may occur, but the more usual ones are listed here, together with suggestions on ways and means of overcoming the trouble. For complete details on diagnosing troubles and making permanent repairs, the car owner is referred to other chapters in this volume. In presenting this material, it is assumed the car owner has become familiar with the automotive terms by studying the other chapters in this volume which will also discuss ways and means of effecting permanent repairs. In addition, more complete trouble shooting directions are given in the individual chapters. This chapter deals only with emergency conditions.

## ENGINE STOPS SUDDENLY

This condition, often described as the engine "conking out," usually is caused by running out of fuel, and the first check to be made is to note the fuel indicator gauge or light on the instrument panel. Another reason is failure of the fuel pump, and still another reason is known as vapor lock. This latter condition is caused by fuel vaporizing in the fuel lines, fuel pump or float chamber of the carburetor, and is most likely to occur during the spring or summer months. The remedy is to wait until the engine has cooled, and then it will usually start easily. A contributing factor to vapor lock is the air conditioning system, particulary when the engine has not been equipped with a larger radiator which is needed for the increased amount of heat that is generated under the hood by the air conditioning equipment.

To check for the failure of the fuel pump takes a little bit longer, and it is necessary to disconnect the fuel line from the carburetor. Then with the end of the fuel line directed into a container, crank the engine for several revolutions. If the fuel pump is working, fuel will spurt from the end of the fuel line in a strong stream.

A loose connection in the primary circuit of the ignition system will also cause the engine to "conk out" suddenly. A defective switch or a burned resistor are possible causes of this trouble. Wiring around the switch will permit the engine to start in case the switch is defective. If the resistor, or resistor wiring, is burned out, running a wire from the "C" connection to the "B" terminal on the coil will permit the engine to start. This should never be done except in the case of an extreme emergency, as this will place full battery voltage on the coil, and operation for more than a short time will ruin the coil and ignition breaker points.

## ENGINE WON'T CRANK

Cranking trouble may be due to defective starting battery, corroded battery connections, faulty starter relay, seat belts not buckled in proper sequence or automatic transmission not in PARK. To test relay, bypass it with a heavy wire from "B" terminal to starter terminal of relay. Relay is bad if engine starts when ignition switch is turned on.

## ENGINE CRANKS BUT WON'T START

Typical causes of this condition are as follows: No fuel in the fuel tank. Defective fuel pump. Check by disconnecting fuel line at carburetor and with the line directed into a container, crank the engine. A pump in good condition will deliver a strong stream of fuel provided there is fuel in the tank.

Excessive moisture on the ignition wiring and/or in the distributor will also cause this trouble. If the wiring is wet, mop up excess moisture at both areas with cloth and then spray with carbon tetrachloride to hasten drying.

Loose or defective connections in primary ignition system. The remedy is to tighten connections.

Burned out primary resistor, or resistor wire. Cut unit or wire out of circuit as an emergency measure only. Prolonged operation will ruin coil and breaker points.

Worn or badly adjusted breaker points. Points should be smoothed with a file and cleaned. Correct gap on V-8 engines is .015 in. and on Sixes is .025 in. If points are severely pitted, the condition can be improved by filing. A nail file can be used in an emergency.

Dirty or incorrectly adjusted spark plugs will prevent engine from starting. Correct gap is .035 in.

A flooded carburetor will prevent engine from starting. In most cases, a strong odor of fuel will be noted when the carburetor is flooded. The best procedure is to wait for 10 minutes and then try again. Or depress accelerator to floor and hold it there while engine is started in the usual manner. In some cases it may be necessary to remove air cleaner and note position of choke plate in the carburetor. If it is in a closed position, work carburetor linkage to make sure choke valve is open.

If engine is being cranked at less than normal speed, most likely the cause is a partly discharged battery or loose or corroded battery connections.

## Emergency Trouble Shooting

### SUDDEN BRAKE FAILURE

If brakes fail suddenly while car is in motion, shut off ignition, apply hand brake and leave transmission in gear or in drive position, as the case may be. Sudden and complete failure of brakes is caused by a break in the hydraulic line or leakage of fluid at some other point. The only remedy is replacement of the defective parts.

### SPONGY BRAKE PEDAL

If, when pressing on the brake pedal it has a spongy feel, there is air in the hydraulic line, and it is necessary to bleed the system to remove the air. Complete instructions for bleeding the brake system are given in the Chapter on Brakes.

### BRAKE PEDAL SINKS TO THE FLOOR

If the brake pedal sinks to the floor when the brakes are applied, the trouble is probably caused by a defective master cylinder or lack of fluid in the system. The remedy is replacement of parts.

### BRAKES WILL NOT HOLD

If this condition occurs suddenly and the brakes have been operating satisfactorily before that time, the condition may result from the car being driven through puddles of water with the result that there is considerable water in the brake drums. The condition can be minimized by driving with the brakes slightly applied for a short distance.

### BRAKES GRAB

When brakes tend to grab for several applications after the car has been parked for several hours, the trouble is probably caused by moisture absorbed by the brake lining and is a characteristic of many different makes of lining. There are many other causes of grabbing brakes which are discussed in the Chapter on Brakes.

### NOISY BRAKES

Brakes will make many different types of noises, but all are an indication that the brakes need servicing of some kind.

### GENERATOR OR ALTERNATOR FAILURE

When the generator fails as indicated by the ammeter, or indicator light on the instrument panel, the first point to check is the belt which drives the fan and generator or alternator. If the belt is loose or broken, no current will be produced and as a result the battery will quickly become discharged. If the same belt is driving the water pump, the engine will overheat with probable damage to the engine bearings, pistons and cylinder walls. The remedy is to install a new belt or tighten the existing belt, if it is not broken.

## RADIATOR BOILS OVER

This condition is usually caused by insufficient water in cooling system and is indicated by temperature gauge, or temperature warning light. Trouble can be caused by a leaking radiator, water pump, hose connections, car heater, defective core plugs in engine water jacket, or a loose or broken belt driving water pump and fan. Condition is also aggravated by excessive use of air conditioner and/or by pulling a trailer. The best procedure is to shut off engine and let it cool. While it is cooling, look for leaks in system. Tighten hose connections if necessary, then place cloth over radiator cap and remove cap. Cap must be removed slowly to avoid burst of steam in high pressure system. Start and idle engine and add water slowly until system is full. If leak has been noted in radiator core or core plugs, special radiator sealing compounds can be used to stop leak.

## HIGH PITCHED SQUEAL

A high pitched squeal when engine is started, and apparently coming from front of engine is often caused by a worn or glazed fan belt, or water pump seal that needs lubrication. The fan belt can be salvaged by applying belt dressing, or in an emergency soap can be used. For a complete cure, the belt should be replaced. In the case of the water pump seal, it can be lubricated by adding a water pump lubricant and rust inhibitor to the coolant in the radiator.

## HARSH RATTLE

A harsh rattling noise at the front of the engine can be caused by a dry or defective fan belt. To check, stop the engine and press on the belt with a hammer handle in the area between the two pulleys. A harsh rasp or creaky noise will be made if the belt is dry. Laundry soap can be used as a lubricant on the belt in an emergency.

## THROBBING ROAR

A throbbing roar coming from under the car is generally caused by muffler and pipes that have been rusted through, permitting the escape of poisonous gases. Defective parts should be replaced immediately, as the escaping exhaust gases are highly toxic and lethal. Noise is usually accompanied by odor of exhaust gases in the car.

## Emergency Trouble Shooting

### NO LIGHTS

When lights in one circuit, such as headlights, will not light, the trouble is usually caused by a burned-out fuse or a defective circuit breaker. On late models, the fuses are located on the left-hand air duct, and circuit breaker is built into the headlight switch. On older models, headlight switch assembly includes fuses and circuit breaker.

### NO OIL PRESSURE

If no oil pressure is indicated by the oil pressure gauge or indicator light on the instrument panel, the difficulty is most likely caused by insufficient oil in the engine crankcase. Stop the engine immediately and fill the crankcase with a specified amount of oil. If the gauge or light still fails to indicate pressure, the difficulty is caused either by a defective gauge or light, or the oil pump is defective. If the failure occurs at a distance from a shop where repairs can be made, add an extra quart of oil and drive slowly to the nearest shop where repairs can be made. If overheating is also indicated, stop the engine until it is cool before starting again. Without oil pressure there is every possibility of burning out the engine bearings and scoring the cylinder wall, so drive the car only if there is no other alternative.

### HORN KEEPS BLOWING

When horn keeps blowing, the cause is usually a defective horn button or ring, as the case may be. To overcome the trouble, stop the engine and disconnect the wires from the horn.

### WINDSHIELD WIPER WILL NOT STOP

This condition only occurs on electric type windshield wipers, and to overcome the trouble in an emergency, disconnect the wires from the windshield wiper motor.

### MAKE YOUR OWN SAFETY CHECK

There are many conditions contributing to the safety of the car that can be checked by the average driver and which should then be corrected either by the driver, or by the mechanic.

Before starting on a drive, adjust the rear view mirror or mirrors for comfortable viewing. For safety, the car should be equipped with two side view mirrors, in addition to the usual mirror located above the windshield.

If your inside mirror vibrates as the car is driven on a smooth road, it is an indication of an unbalanced condition of some rotating part. Therefore the wheels should be checked for roundness and a bent condi-

## Fix Your Ford

tion. Wheels should not be more than 1/16 in. out-of-round, or more than 1/16 in. laterally. Also check tires after they are mounted on the wheels for out-of-round. Also make sure they are accurately balanced. For slow speed driving, static balance is usually satisfactory. For higher speeds dynamic balance is recommended. Be sure that tires are inflated to the factory's specified value.

Also check the steering wheel, making sure there is not excessive play. Don't take a chance on the condition of the brakes. With self-adjusting brakes, the height of the brake pedal is not a gage to the condition of the brakes. The only sure way of determining the condition of the brakes is to remove a drum and look at the thickness of the brake lining and the condition of the drums. If when applying the brakes the pedal has a spongy feel, it indicates there is air in the system and servicing is indicated.

Make sure the engine is in good condition and has ample power for emergency passing. The passing capacity of an untuned engine is reduced considerably. In addition, economy of operation is seriously affected. It pays to have the engine tuned every 10,000 miles. If the car is pulling a trailer, remember that the added weight will reduce your available power for acceleration. Also the stopping ability will be decreased. The added weight of the trailer will tend to tilt the headlights upward and will blind approaching drivers. The lights should be readjusted to take care of that condition.

For safety's sake, the level of the driver's eyes should be several inches above the rim of the steering wheel. So adjust your seat accordingly, or use a cushion.

## SEAT BELT INTERLOCK SYSTEM

To start the engine and drive a vehicle with a seat belt interlock system, lap belts must be extended and/or buckled at all occupied seats. Transmission selector must be in Park (automatic) or Neutral (manual). Then, ignition key can be turned to start the engine.

If the engine stalls, it can be restarted as long as the ignition key is not turned to the OFF position. If the driver or passenger unfastens a belt after the engine starts, the engine will not stop but the buzzer and warning light will be activated. To start the engine for test purposes, reach through the window or door and turn the key. When you sit in the seat, the warning light and buzzer will operate but the car can be driven.

For emergency use when starter will not crank, an emergency starter interlock override switch is provided on the fender apron under the hood. The red push button is identified by a prominent decal. To use this override switch, depress the button, then release it. If the cause of the no-start was a starter interlock system malfunction, the starter can now be operated for one complete cycle of the ignition switch from OFF to START and back to OFF.

# Tips on
# BODY SERVICE

The outside finish of the body should be washed frequently. Never wipe the painted surfaces with a dry cloth, as that will scratch the surface and quickly remove its high luster. To keep the finish bright and attractive, and eliminate the necessity of using polish, wash the car whenever it has accumulated a moderate amount of dirt and road salt. In the past, Ford cars were painted with a baked enamel and currently, acrylic enamel is used. Both types of finish maintain a high luster without any polishing.

Fig. Y-1. Drain holes in the body panels must be kept open to prevent rusting. View of underside of quarter panel and door, showing location of drain holes.

If it is decided to use a polish, it must be remembered that the paint is only a few thousandths of an inch thick and can be quickly worn away if power polishing is used. Normally all that is required to keep the finish bright and attractive is to wash the car whenever it has accumulated a moderate amount of dirt and road salt.

The bright metal parts of the car ordinarily require no special care. Periodic cleaning will preserve the beauty and life of these finishes. Wash with clear water, or if the parts are very dirty, use a mild soap or special cleaning preparation designed for automotive bodies. Do not scour chrome finished parts with steel wool or polish them with polish containing abrasives.

## CLEANING THE INTERIOR

Use a broom or a vacuum cleaner to remove dust and dirt from the upholstery or floor covering. Vinyl and woven plastic trim that is dusty can usually be cleaned with a damp cloth.

## Fix Your Ford

Dirty or stained upholstery can be cleaned with special cleaner designed for the purpose. Some special cleaners are available which can be used on leather, plastic, vinyl, imitation leather, fabric upholsteries, rubber mats, and carpeting. However, if such special cleaner is not available to remove grease spots, a volatile type of cleaner such as carbon tetrachloride or benzine can be used.

### HOW TO REMOVE SPOTS

In case of battery acid getting on the upholstery, immediately apply ordinary household ammonia, saturating the area thoroughly, permitting the ammonia to remain on the spot so that it will have ample time to neutralize the acid, then rinse the spot by rubbing with a clean cloth saturated with cold water.

In the case of chewing gum, first harden the gum with an ice cube and then scrape off the particles with a dull knife. If the gum cannot be removed completely by this method, moisten it with benzine or carbon tetrachloride and work it from the fabric with a dull knife while the gum is still moist.

Fruit stains and stains from liquor can usually be removed with very hot water. Wet the stains well by applying hot water to the spot with a clean cloth. If the spot and stain is an old one, it may be necessary to pour very hot water directly on the spot, and then follow by scrapping and rubbing. However, care must be exercised as hot water in many cases will discolor the fabric.

To remove blood spots, wash the stain with a clean cloth saturated with cold water until no more of the stain can be removed. Then, if necessary, apply a small amount of household ammonia, using a brush or cloth, then rub the stain again with a clean cloth saturated with water. Do not use hot water or soap on blood stains, as they will tend to set the stain, thereby making it practically impossible to remove.

Candy stains, other than stains made from chocolate candy, can be removed by rubbing the area with a cloth soaked with very hot water. This, if necessary, can be followed with a volatile type of cleaner. In the case of stains made from chocolate candy, use a cloth soaked in lukewarm soap suds and scrape while wet, using a dull knife.

### WHAT TO DO ABOUT RATTLES

Most rattles are caused by a loose bolt or nut. Objects such as bolts, and small pieces of body deadener material in a door well, pillars and quarter panels, often cause rattles. Door wells can be checked by striking the underside of the door with a rubber mallet. The impact made by the mallet will cause loose parts to bounce in door well.

All bolts and screws should be tightened periodically. In the event that tightening the bolts and screws located on such assemblies as the doors, hood and deck lid, does not eliminate the rattle, the trouble is probably

## Body Service

caused by misalignment. The position of the doors, hoods and deck lids is adjustable and rubber bumpers are provided to help eliminate the possibility of rattles. Make sure that such bumpers are in position.

Rattles and squeaks are sometimes caused by the weatherstripping and antisqueak material that is out of position on the doors. Apply additional cement or other adhesives and install the material in the proper location to eliminate this difficulty.

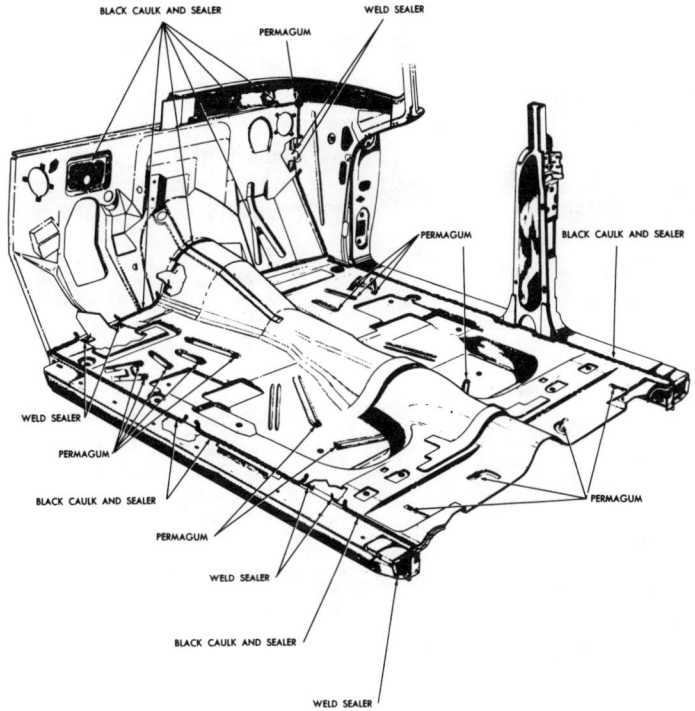

*Fig. Y-2. Showing location of sealers in typical front floor pan, cowl side and dash panel.*

## HOW TO KEEP BODIES FROM RUSTING

One of the major causes of body rusting is failure to keep open the drain holes located on the underside of each rocker panel, quarter panel and door, Fig. Y-1. These drain holes are provided so that water will not accumulate within the panels. When the drain holes are not open, the accumulation of water will soon rust the body panels from the inside.

Such drain holes soon become clogged with road dirt and they should be checked periodically to make sure that they are open to permit the drain-

# Fix Your Ford

age of water. Such drain and dust valves on recent models are so designed that the weight of the water will open the valve and allow the water to escape from the panel. After the water has drained the valve will close and prevent the entry of dust.

## FLOOR PAN PLUGS AND GROMMETS

Many plugs and grommets are used in the floor pan and dash panel. The floor pan plugs seal the various body access holes. If any plugs are missing or improperly installed, a dust or water leak may result. This also applies to the grommets used on the dash panel.

## FIXING DUST AND WATER LEAKS

The forward motion of the car creates a slight vacuum within the body, particularly if a window or ventilator is partly open. Any unsealed crevice or small opening in the lower section of the body will therefore permit air

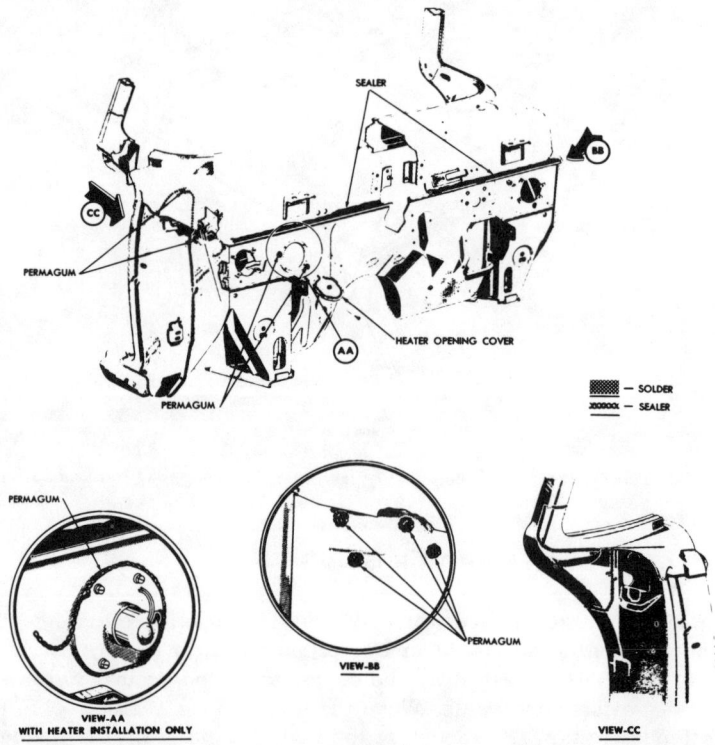

Fig. Y-3. Typical body pillar and dash. In case of water or dust leaks, check sealer at points indicated.

## Body Service

to be drawn into the body. If dust or moisture is present in the air, it will follow any path taken by the air from the point of entry into the passenger or luggage compartments. Opening the ventilator air ducts, will equalize these pressures. Dust may work its way into the hollow, box type rocker panel, which extends along the edge of the floor, below the doors. Dust

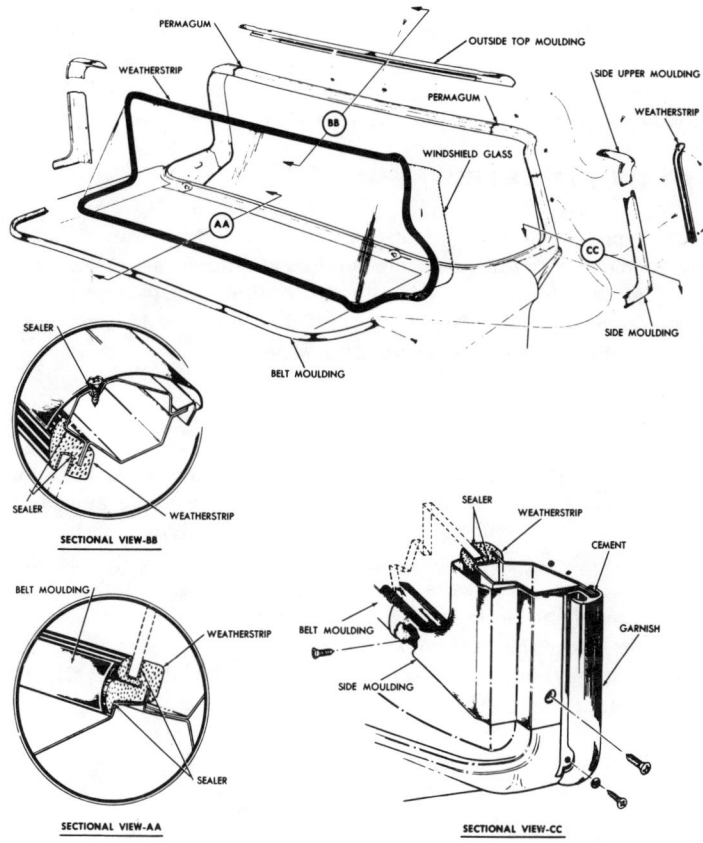

Fig. Y-4. Note location of weatherstrip and sealers used to prevent dust and water leakage.

accumulates in the rocker panel and may eventually work its way into the kick-up, or the rear body pillar, and follow the contour of the wheel house into the luggage compartment. The point of dust entrance can usually be determined by careful observation, noting the trail which will be heaviest at the point of entrance.

Under certain conditions, water can enter an automobile body at any point where dirt or dust can enter. Any consideration of water leakage must take into account all points covered under dust leaks.

# Fix Your Ford

The location of dust and water leaks can be greatly facilitated by removing interior trim, including the quarter trim panel, rear seat back and seat cushion, luggage compartment floor mats, spare wheel and side trim panel. After removing the trim, the location of most leaks will be readily evident. These leaks should then be sealed with cement or a sealer.

Similarly, water leaks can also be spotted in the same manner, but in such cases it is often easier to apply a stream of water to the exterior of the vehicle and have an observer on the inside to note where the water is entering. In most cases, such water leaks can be remedied by installing new weatherstripping or sealer. Some of the points where leaks usually occur are shown in Figs. Y-2, Y-3 and Y-4.

## WOOD GRAIN TRANSFERS

Never wipe the panels or trim rails with a dry cloth. This method of cleaning tends to rub dust into the finished surface and leave fine scratches. Flush off all loose dirt and other elements and wipe the body panels with a sponge and plenty of cold water. If desired a mild soap can be used. Rinse thoroughly with clear water and wipe dry.

## DOOR ALIGNMENT

The door hinges provide sufficient adjustment latitude to correct most misalignment conditions. The holes of the hinge and/or the hinge attaching points are enlarged or elongated to provide for hinge and door alignment, Fig. Y-5. To adjust: Remove the cowl trim panel and/or door trim panel and access covers. Loosen the hinge bolts just enough to permit movement of the door with a padded pry bar.

Move the door the distance estimated to be necessary. Tighten the hinge bolts and recheck the door fit. Repeat until desired fit is obtained. Then check striker plate alignment for proper door closing.

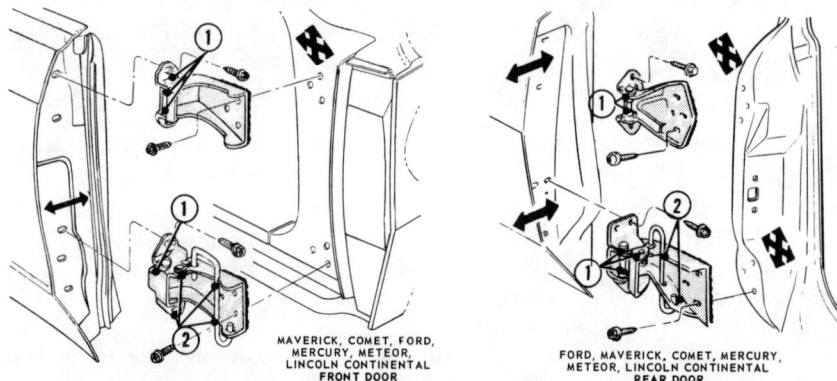

Fig. Y-5. Illustrating points of hinge adjustment on side doors and points of lubrication. At 1, use Polyethylene lubricant and at points 2, use lock lubricant. (Recent models.)

# SERVICING THE PINTO

This special section is included in FIX YOUR FORD because of the strong interest that is being exhibited in this sub-compact Ford-built vehicle. Every effort has been made to supply as complete information as possible on such phases of maintenance which are most frequently encountered. Therefore, service data on tune-up, ignition, carburetor adjusting, valve lash, cooling system, periodic lubrication, brakes, and shock absorber maintenance are particularly stressed.

As much of the basic service procedure is similar to that used on the larger Ford cars, it is recommended that the reader study those sections of this book for such information which may not be contained in these special pages. This applies particularly to such areas as trouble shooting and the reconditioning of parts after they have been removed from the vehicle.

## PINTO ENGINES

The 1600 cc (97.6 cu. in.), the 2000 cc (122 cu. in.) and the 2300 cc (140 cu. in.) engines are all four cylinder types, while the 2800 cc (171 cu. in.) is a V-Six (see page 4). The 1600 cc and 2800 cc engines have

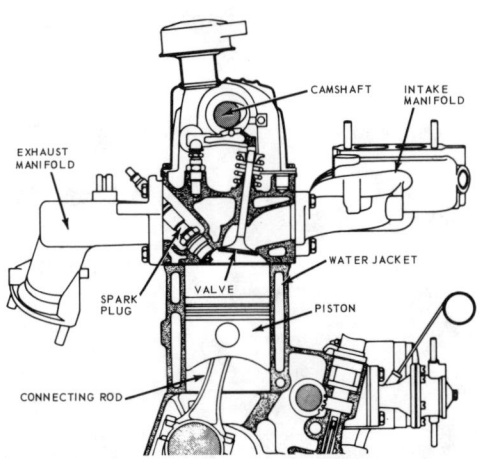

*Fig. 1. Sectional view of Pinto engine. Note overhead camshaft.*

valves operated by push rods; the other engines are overhead camshaft type, Fig. 1.

Compression ratio of the 1600 cc engine is 8.0 to 1. It develops 75 hp @ 5000 rpm, or 0.77 hp per cu. in. displacement. Compression ratio of the 2000 cc engine is 8.6 to 1. It develops 100 hp @ 5600 rpm, or 0.82 hp per cu. in. displacement. Compression ratio of the 2300 cc engine is 9.0 to 1. It develops 92 hp @ 5000 rpm, or 0.66 hp per cu. in. displacement. Compression ratio of the 2800 cc engine is 8.7 to 1. It develops 103 hp @ 4400 rpm, or 0.60 hp per cu. in. displacement. On California cars with a 2800 cc engine, the hp rating is 99 @ 4400.

## IGNITION TUNE-UP

All 1975-1978 Pinto engines are equipped with the breakerless ignition system described in detail on page 31.

The 1600 cc engine is equipped with an Autolite dual diaphragm dual advance distributor and the 2000 cc engine uses a similar distributor of Bosch manufacture. The Autolite unit revolves counterclockwise and the Bosch clockwise.

Mechanical operation of the advance mechanism of both distributors can be checked by turning the rotor in the direction of shaft rotation and then releasing it. The rotor should return quickly to its original position if the mechanism is free and the springs are in good condition.

The 1974 2000 cc engine is equipped with a single vacuum advance distributor; the distributor in the 2300 cc engine has a dual diaphragm vacuum advance. Both distributors are equipped with centrifugal advance units. Diaphragm advance units are preset at the factory and cannot be adjusted. To adjust centrifugal advance, bend the spring adjustment bracket by reaching through the opening in the breaker plate. Bend the adjustment bracket away from the distributor shaft to retard the spark and toward the shaft to advance the spark.

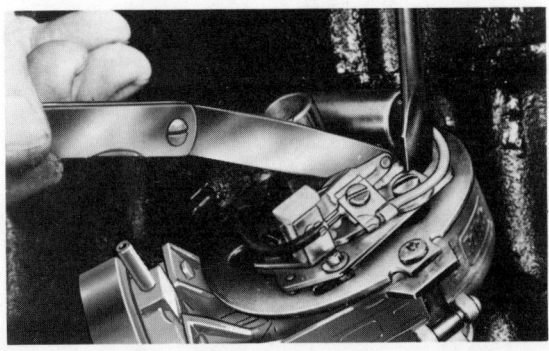

*Fig. 2. Adjusting the ignition breaker point gap.*

## Servicing the Pinto

### ADJUSTING BREAKER POINT GAP

To adjust point gap, remove distributor cap and crank engine until rubbing block is on high point of cam. Loosen point retaining screws and insert correct size feeler gauge between points, Fig. 2. Insert screwdriver in notch in points and advance plate, then twist to alter point gap. Correct gap for 1600 cc and 2000 cc engines is .025 in.; 2300 cc engine, .027 in. Starting in 1975, breakerless ignition is used.

### REPLACING BREAKER POINTS

Points and condenser are usually replaced at the same time. Remove breaker point and condenser mounting screws and remove the point assembly and condenser. On the Bosch distributor, when removing the condenser, it is also necessary to work the wire grommet out of the distributor body and disconnect the ignition wire at the coil.

*Fig. 3. Timing mark location on the 1600 cc engine.*

### ADJUSTING IGNITION TIMING

Be sure breaker point gap is correct. Rotate crankshaft until No. 1 piston is on compression stroke and crankshaft pulley is in line with the specified initial advance setting, Figs. 3 and 4. Initial setting for the 1600 cc engine is 12 deg. BTDC and for the 2000 cc engine is 6 deg. BTDC. Lift distributor cap, loosen distributor clamp bolt and rotate distributor body until contact points are just starting to open. When timing 1974-1976 engines, follow instructions on decal in engine compartment.

### SPARK PLUGS

Correct spark plug type and gap are: 1600 cc engine, AGR 22 plug, .030 in.; 2000 cc engine, BRF 42 plug, .034 in.; 2300 cc engine, AGRF 52 plug, .034 in.; 2800 cc engine, AGR 42 plug, .034 in.

*Fig. 4. Timing mark location on the 2000 cc engine.*

## FUEL SYSTEM

### DECEL VALVE

To adjust, bring engine to operating temperature. Remove fuel-air mixture hose from the decel valve, Fig. 5, and connect a vacuum gauge, using a tee fitting. With the transmission in Park or Neutral, raise engine speed to 3000 rpm. Hold for two seconds. Then release throttle

*Fig. 5. Decel valve showing the nylon adjuster.*

## Servicing the Pinto

suddenly. A vacuum reading should be noted immediately on vacuum gauge. Record elapsed time when throttle was released until reading reaches zero. If time is more than five seconds, turn nylon adjuster on top of decel valve clockwise approximately 1/2 turn. If the time is less than three seconds on 1600 cc engine or 1-1/2 seconds on the 2000 cc engine, turn the adjuster counterclockwise 1/2 turn and recheck the operation.

## AUTOLITE 1-V CARBURETOR

To adjust the idle fuel mixture and idle speed on the Autolite 1-V carburetor as installed on the 1600 cc engine, first bring the engine up to operating temperature. Set the idle speed at 820 rpm. Then turn the idle mixture adjustment screw until maximum rpm is obtained, Fig. 6. The idle mixture adjustment screw, due to internal restriction, can only be turned out a certain distance. Do not attempt to withdraw the screw any further. Next, screw the idle mixture adjustment screw in until the idle speed is reduced by 20 to 40 rpm. Leave the screw in that position. Reset engine idle speed, if necessary, by means of the curb idle adjustment to 870 rpm.

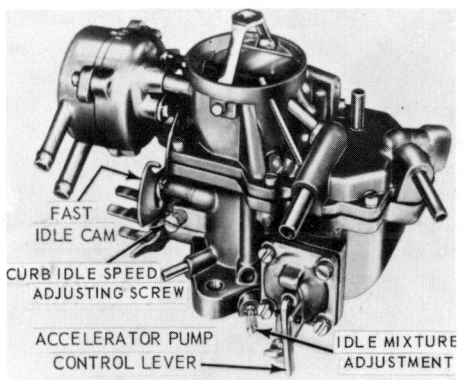

Fig. 6. Location of adjustments on the Autolite carburetor used on the 1600 cc Pinto.

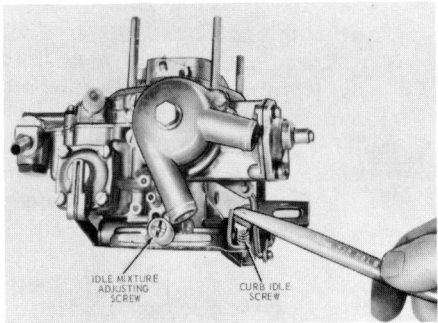

Fig. 7. Location of adjusting screws on Autolite 5200 2-V carburetor.

The float level adjustment of this carburetor is made as follows: Remove carburetor upper body assembly and hold it in a vertical position with the float hanging down. Measure the distance from the bottom of the float to the upper gasket and adjust to 1.09 to 1.11 in. by bending the tab resting against the needle valve. Turn the upper body to a horizontal position and measure the distance from the bottom of the float to the gasket. Adjust to 1.35 to 1.37 in. by bending tab resting against needle valve housing.

## AUTOLITE 5200 CARBURETOR

To adjust the idle speed and fuel mixture on the Autolite model 5200 carburetor as installed on 2000 cc and 2300 cc engines, run engine for 20 minutes to stabilize engine and underhood temperatures. Check the ignition timing. Adjust curb idle speed to 700 rpm with solenoid energized or to 500 rpm with the solenoid deenergized, Fig. 7. Turn the idle mixture adjustment screws inward to obtain the smoothest idle possible within the range of the idle limiter. Under no circumstances are the limiters to be mutilated in any way to render the limiters inoperative.

To adjust the position of the float, hold carburetor cover in normal position and measure the distance between the bowl cover and the lowest point of the float. Distance should be 1.9 in. To adjust, bend the drop tang up or down as required. Adjust dry float setting to 27/64 in.

Instructions for overhauling carburetor are contained in repair kit of parts.

## TUNE-UP TIPS

Adjust all idle speeds on Pinto engines with headlights off, automatic transmission in DRIVE or manual transmission in NEUTRAL. If car is air conditioned, place A/C controls in OFF position.

With the engine at normal operating temperature, adjust low idle speed as follows: Disconnect throttle solenoid wire. Turn idle adjusting screw to specification shown on tune-up decal in engine compartment.

To adjust high idle speed, reconnect solenoid wire and slowly increase engine idle speed until solenoid plunger is fully extended. Allow lever to recontact solenoid plunger and check tachometer reading. Turn solenoid plunger to obtain correct high idle speed.

When checking ignition timing, be sure to disconnect and plug one or both (depending on engine application) vacuum advance hoses. Set timing according to specification on tune-up decal. Unplug and reconnect vacuum hoses.

## FUEL PUMPS

Fuel pumps used on Pinto engines are of the permanently sealed type. In case of failure, a new pump should be installed. The fuel pump used on the 1600 cc engine should deliver a minimum of one pint of fuel in 38 seconds; 2000 cc pump, one pint in 43 seconds. Pumps used on 2300 cc and 2800 cc engines should deliver one pint of fuel in 25 seconds.

## AIR CLEANER DUCT SYSTEM

Both engines are equipped with temperature operated duct and valve assemblies for the air cleaners. To check the operation of this system proceed as follows: With the system installed on the engine and ambient

## Servicing the Pinto

temperature in the engine compartment less than 100 deg. F and the engine cold, the valve plates should be in the HEAT ON position, see Fig. 8. If the plate is not in the HEAT ON position, check for possible interference of plate and duct. Correct by realigning plate. Remove duct

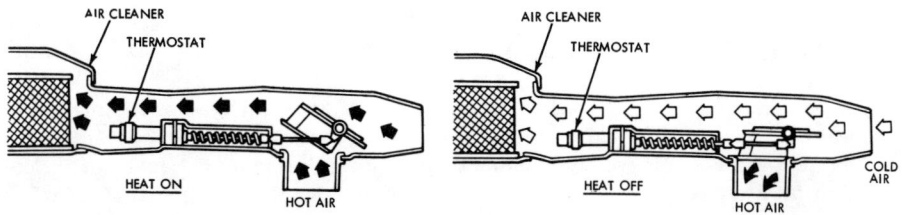

Fig. 8. Details of temperature operated duct and valve assembly.

and valve assembly and immerse in water so that thermostat capsule is covered. Raise water temperature to 100 deg. F. After five minutes check valve plate position which should be in the HEAT ON position. Increase water temperature to 135 deg. F and valve plate should be in the HEAT OFF position. If not, replace duct and valve assembly.

## FUEL VAPOR CONTROL SYSTEM

The fuel vapor emission control system consists of a two-way vented fill cap, fuel vapor separator, fuel vapor lines and a carbon filled canister for storing fuel and vapor. Diagnosis of troubles is limited to locating leaks, pinched lines or inoperative fill cap. Indication of system trouble would be restricted fuel flow or a deformed main fuel supply tank.

## FUEL FILTERS

Both types of engines use an in-line, disposable fuel filter inserted between the fuel pump and the carburetor. The 1600 cc uses a plastic filter and the 2000 cc uses a steel cylindrical filter. Filters should be replaced every 12,000 miles. To remove filter, loosen the two retaining clamp nuts securing the filter to the fuel line. Disconnect filter and discard.

## COOLING SYSTEM

The cooling system should be kept filled with coolant to 3/4 to 1-1/2 in. below the lower flange of radiator filler neck. The freeze protection level should be maintained at least to zero degrees F to provide adequate corrosion and boiling protection. Factory recommendation is to drain and refill the cooling system with new coolant every 24 months. As de-

# Fix Your Ford

livered in the United States, Pinto cars are filled with antifreeze and water solution to provide protection to -20 deg. F and in Canada the protection is to -35 deg. F. Cooling system capacity of 1600 cc engine is 6 3/4 qt. and the 2000 cc engine is 7 qt.

## 1600 cc ENGINE

### REMOVING CYLINDER HEAD

Disconnect the hot air and crankcase ventilation hoses at the air cleaner and remove air cleaner. Remove fuel line. Drain coolant. Disconnect spark plugs. Disconnect heater and vacuum hoses at intake manifold. Disconnect hose at choke housing. Disconnect temperature gauge sending unit. Disconnect exhaust pipe. Disconnect throttle linkage and distributor advance pipe from carburetor. Remove thermostat housing, pull aside and remove thermostat. Remove rocker arm cover and gasket. Remove rocker arm shaft bolts evenly and lift off rocker

*Fig. 9. Cylinder head bolt tightening sequence on the 1600 cc engine.*

shaft assembly. Lift out push rods, keeping them in correct order. Remove cylinder head bolts and lift off cylinder head and gasket. Take care not to mar gasket surface. When replacing head, tighten cylinder head bolts evenly to 65 to 70 ft. lbs. and in sequence indicated in Fig. 9.

### VALVE LASH ADJUSTMENT

Valve lash can be adjusted on 1600 cc engines hot or cold. When cold, set intake valve lash 0.008 to 0.010 in., exhaust lash 0.018 to 0.020 in. When hot, set intake lash 0.010 in., exhaust lash 0.017 in. Be sure valves are closed when making the cold adjustment. Fig. 10 shows the self-locking screw adjustment with correct feeler gauge blade in position. Valve

*Fig. 10. Adjusting the valve lash on the 1600 cc engine.*

lash on 2300 cc engines is 0.008 in. for intake and 0.010 in. for exhaust, with engine cold. Valve lash on V-Six engines is 0.014 in. for intake, 0.016 in. for exhaust, with engine hot.

## FRONT COVER OIL SEAL

To install a cylinder front cover oil seal in the event of leakage, drain engine coolant. Disconnect radiator hoses at engine. Remove radiator and fan belt. Then remove fan and water pump pulley and water pump. Use suitable puller and remove crankshaft pulley. Remove front cover. Oil seal is removed by supporting cover around the seal and driving the seal out the rear. New seal is driven in position from the rear, using a driver of a diameter the same as the seal.

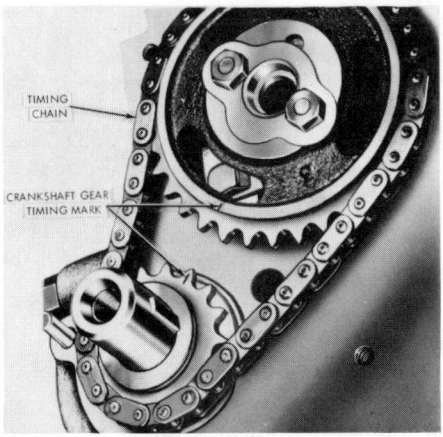

*Fig. 11. When timing the valves on the 1600 cc engine, timing marks should be as indicated.*

Fix Your Ford

## TIMING CHAIN REPLACEMENT

To replace the timing chain it is first necessary to remove the cylinder front cover. A single row timing chain with an automatic mechanical tensioner is used. The timing chain runs across a synthetic rubber pad on the tensioner arm. In use, the links wear two grooves in the pad so that the chain runs directly on the rollers. Do not dress the surface of the pad to remove the grooves. The sprockets incorporate timing marks, Fig. 11. After removing the front cover, remove the crankshaft oil slinger and then the camshaft sprocket. Then disconnect the timing chain. When installing a timing chain, position it over the camshaft and crankshaft sprockets so that the timing marks are correctly aligned, Fig. 11. Tighten bolts to 12 to 15 ft. lbs. torque. Bend up locking tabs.

## CONNECTING RODS AND PISTONS

To remove the connecting rod and piston assemblies, first remove the cylinder head and oil pan. Then remove the ridge at the top of the cylinder bore with a ridge remover. Push the piston and rod assemblies up through the cylinders after disconnecting the lower ends of the rods. Examine wear marks on piston to determine whether the rods are bent. A heavy mark on the piston skirt above the pin on one side, together with a corresponding mark below the pin on the opposite side indicates a bent rod. Bent rods should be straightened or replaced.

When fitting pistons it should require 7 to 11 lbs. pull on a 1/2 in. wide feeler blade to pull it from between the piston and the cylinder wall.

## OIL PAN REMOVAL

To remove the oil pan, first drain the crankcase. Remove oil level dipstick. Disconnect battery. Disconnect throttle linkage from the carburetor. Disconnect steering cable from the rack and pinion. Disconnect the rack and pinion from the cross member and move it forward to provide clearance for oil pan. Remove the starting motor. Remove left bottom bolt from the lower rear cover. Remove the cover. Remove oil pan attaching bolts and remove pan and gasket. When replacing the oil pan, tighten the bolts to 7 to 9 ft. lbs. torque and first follow the alphabetical and then the numerical sequence shown in Fig. 12.

## OIL PUMP AND FILTER

The oil pump and filter assembly is bolted to the right side of the cylinder block and can be removed after draining the oil and removing the three attaching bolts. Either of two types of pumps is fitted. One a bi-rotor type and the other a sliding vane type.

## Servicing the Pinto

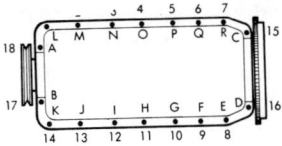

Fig. 12. First follow the alphabetical sequence and then the numerical when tightening the oil pan bolts on the 1600 cc engine.

## 2000 cc ENGINE

### CYLINDER HEAD REMOVAL

Drain cooling system. Remove air cleaner and valve rocker arm cover. Remove exhaust manifold. Remove intake manifold, carburetor and decel valve as an assembly. Remove camshaft drive belt cover. Loosen belt tensioner and remove drive belt. Remove water outlet elbow from cylinder head. Remove cylinder head attaching bolts. Lift cylinder head and camshaft from engine. When replacing cylinder head use two guide pins in place of bolts to insure easy alignment of head with block. Install attaching bolts. First finger tighten and then torque bolts to 65 to 80 ft. lbs. in sequence shown in Fig. 12.

When replacing parts, make sure crankshaft is at top center and the camshaft drive gear and distributor are at the positions shown in Fig. 4. Install camshaft drive belt and release the tensioner. Rotate crankshaft two full turns to remove slack from belt. The timing marks should again be in the same position as when the belt was installed. Complete the job by installing the rest of the parts.

### VALVE LASH ADJUSTMENT

Remove air cleaner and rocker arm cover. Rotate crankshaft until the high point of number one cam lobe is in the uppermost position, Fig. 13. Remove rocker arm retaining springs, Fig. 13, before setting valve lash to relieve spring tension from rocker arm. Then loosen lock nut and turn adjustment screw in or out to obtain clearance of 0.008 in. for the intake valves and 0.010 in. for the exhaust valves. (Adjustments made while the engine is cold.) Repeat this procedure on all valves. When replacing the valve rocker cover be sure the two screws provided with rubber coated washers are installed at the front and at the vertical attaching surface.

### CAMSHAFT DRIVE BELT

To remove the camshaft drive belt, Fig. 4, place the camshaft at top dead center. Remove the camshaft belt cover. Loosen the belt tensioner adjustment bolt and relax belt tension. Then tighten bolt. Lift the belt off the sprockets. Do not rotate crankshaft or camshaft, as that would alter

## Fix Your Ford

timing. Before replacing drive belt, make sure timing marks are properly aligned as shown in Fig. 4. Also, after the belt is installed, rotate crankshaft two full turns and recheck location of timing marks.

### OIL PAN REMOVAL

Drain the crankcase. Remove the oil level dipstick and the flywheel housing inspection cover. Disconnect the steering cable from the rack and pinion. Disconnect the rack and pinion from the cross member and move it forward for clearance. Remove the oil pan attaching bolts and remove the oil pan and gasket.

*Fig. 13. Checking the valve lash on the 2000 cc engine.*

### CRANKSHAFT REAR SEAL REPLACEMENT

Remove the transmission, clutch, and flywheel or the automatic transmission, converter and flywheel. Remove the crankshaft rear seal by punching a hole in the seal and inserting a sheet metal screw. Prying against the screw will force out the seal. The new seal is driven in position with the aid of a circular drift.

### PISTONS AND CONNECTING RODS

To remove the pistons and connecting rods, first remove the cylinder head and oil pan. Then after removing the ridge and deposits at the top of the cylinder bore, the piston and connecting rod can be pushed up through the top of the cylinder after removing the connecting rod bearing bolts.

### ALTERNATOR

The alternator and regulator used on the Pinto are the same as installed on current model Ford cars and servicing is discussed in detail

## Servicing the Pinto

in the main section of this book. These units are illustrated in Figs. L-1 and L-6, pages 187 and 190.

## STARTER

The starter used as standard equipment on the Pinto is the same as used on Ford cars and the servicing is discussed in the main section of this book. The starter is illustrated in Fig. M-3, page 205.

## FUSES AND FUSE LINKS

Most of the electrical equipment on the Pinto is protected by fuses and the fuse panel is located on a bracket attached to the brake pedal support to the right of the steering column.

In addition to fuses, the system is protected by fuse links. A fuse link is a short piece of insulated wire several gauges smaller than the regular wiring. The fuse link is integral with the engine compartment wiring. All fuse links have the word FUSE LINK stamped on the insulation. A diagram of the system is shown in Fig. N-10, page 216.

## BRAKES

The original Pinto was equipped with drum type brakes on all four wheels. See Fig. 14. Current models have disc brakes at the front and drum brakes at the rear. Details covering the service procedures for these brake systems are given in the chapter Quick Service on Brakes. Highlights of the procedures are explained in the following paragraphs.

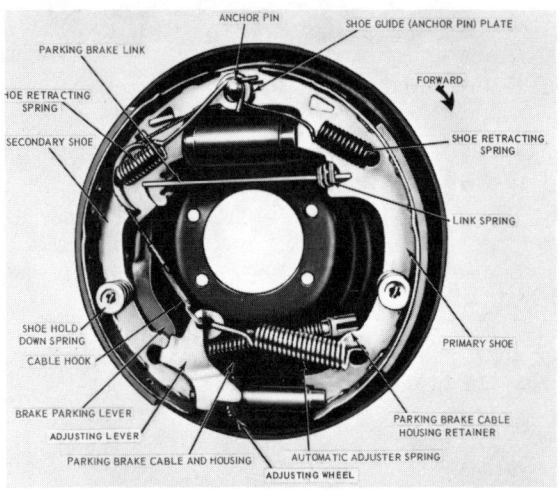

*Fig. 14. Details of service brakes.*

## DRUM BRAKE ADJUSTMENT

The drum brakes are self-adjusting and require a manual adjustment only after the brake shoes have been relined or when the length of the adjusting screw has been changed. The same instructions given in the main section of this book can be used should it be desired to adjust the brakes.

Disc Brake: To remove the disc brake shoes and lining, raise the car and install safety stands. Remove the wheel and tire assembly. Remove the two stainless steel cotter pins from the caliper retaining key, Fig. 15. Slide the caliper retaining key inward or outward from the anchor plate. Use a hammer and drift if necessary, taking care not to damage the key. Press the caliper assembly inward and upward against the caliper support springs and lift the assembly from the anchor plate. Suspend the assembly from the upper suspension arm. The shoe and lining assembly can now be removed from the anchor plate.

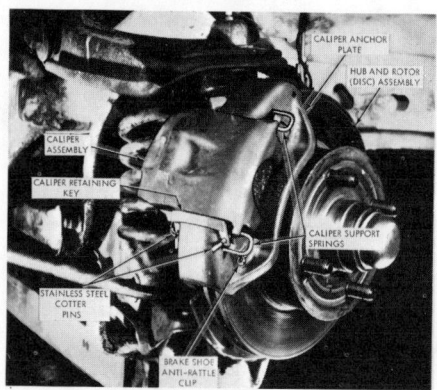

*Fig. 15. Details of the single piston sliding caliper disc brake available as optional equipment on the Pinto.*

## REMOVING THE BRAKE DRUMS

Follow the procedure given in the main section of this book.

## REPLACING THE BRAKE SHOES

Follow the procedure under the heading SELF-ADJUSTING BRAKES, 1961-1974, page 314 in the main section of this book.

## CLUTCH

To adjust the free play of the clutch pedal: From under the car, pull the flexible cable, Fig. 16, toward the front of the car until the C clip can be

## Servicing the Pinto

removed from the cable. Remove the C clip. Continue to pull the flexible cable forward until all free movement of the clutch release bearing is eliminated. While holding the cable in that position, place a 0.135 in. spacer against the flywheel boss on the engine side and install the C clip into the closest possible groove next to the spacer. Remove the spacer and release the cable. The pedal should have approximately 1 in. free play.

## TRANSMISSIONS

The automatic transmission used as special equipment on the Pinto is the model C4 described and illustrated in Fig. R-1, page 251, and the adjustments of the intermediate and the low-reverse bands are illustrated in Figs. R-6 and R-7, page 259, in the main section of this book.

## FOUR SPEED TRANSMISSIONS

To remove the four speed transmission, first remove the shift lever. Working from under the hood, remove the flywheel housing-to-engine upper attaching bolts. Raise the engine on a hoist. Remove the drive shaft and plug extension housing to prevent lubricant leakage. Disconnect back-up light wires and remove switch. Disconnect clutch release cable

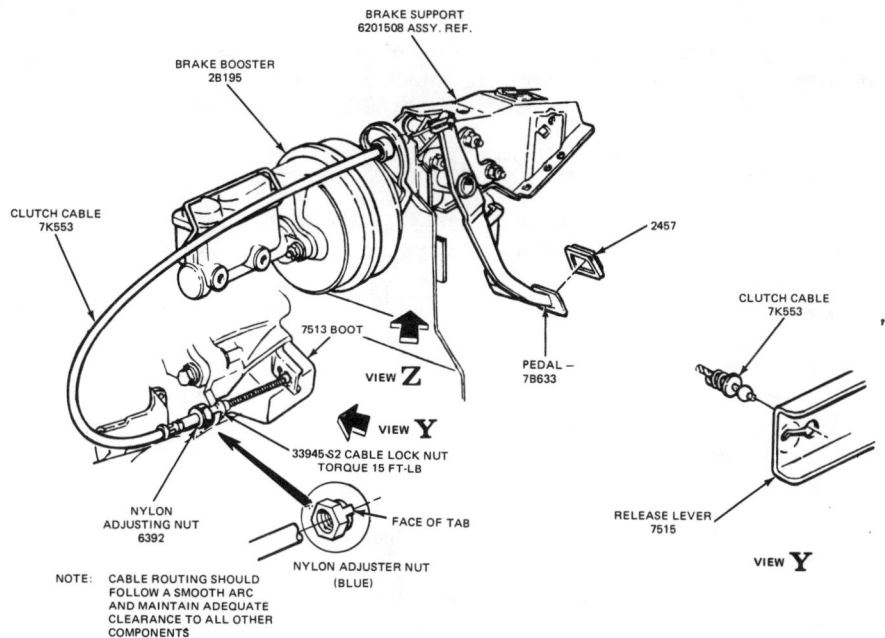

Fig. 16. Details of clutch linkage as used on the 1978 Pinto.

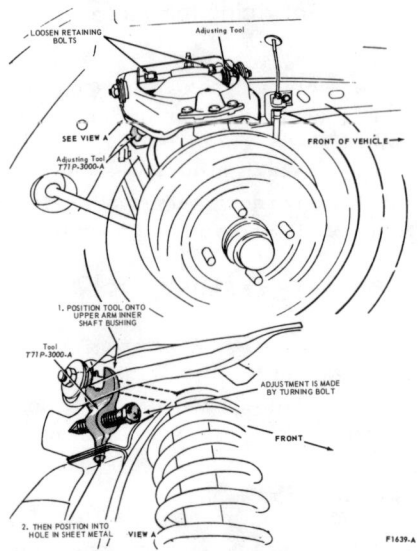

*Fig. 17. Showing method of adjusting caster and camber.*

from the release lever. Remove starting motor. Disconnect speedometer cable from extension housing. Plug opening. Support the rear of the engine with a jack and remove the bolts that attach the cross member to the body. Remove the cross member to extension housing attaching bolt and remove the cross member. Lower the engine as required to gain access to the flywheel-to-housing attaching bolts. Remove the bolts and slide the transmission from the engine and from under the vehicle.

## SHOCK ABSORBERS

To remove front shock absorbers, first remove the nut, washer and bushing from the upper end of the shock absorber. Raise the front of the car and place on safety stands. Remove the bolt and nut attaching the lower end of the shock absorber to the lower arm. It may be necessary to use a pry bar to free the T-shaped end of the shock absorber from the lower end permitting the removal of the shock absorber.

To remove the rear shock absorbers, first disconnect the lower end of the shock absorber from the spring plate. Remove the three bolts retaining the mounting bracket at the upper end of the shock absorber. Compress the shock absorber and remove it from the vehicle.

## WHEEL ALIGNMENT

Before adjusting wheel alignment, read the description of caster, camber and toe-in which starts on page 295. A special tool is used to adjust caster and camber on the Pinto. The purpose of the tool is to move the upper control arm in or out as needed to obtain the desired caster

## Servicing the Pinto

or camber adjustment. The preferred caster is +1 1/2 deg. and the preferred camber is +3/4 deg.

The preferred toe-in of 1/8 in. is obtained by turning the tie-rod inner end to obtain the desired toe-in. The procedure is to first loosen the clamp screw on the tie-rod bellows and free the seal on the rod. See Fig. 17. Then loosen the tie-rod jam nut. Turn the tie-rod inner end with suitable pliers to obtain the 1/8 in. toe-in. With the tie-rod correctly set and the steering wheel in the straight ahead position, hold the socket and tighten the jam nut to 35-50 ft. lbs. torque. Tighten bellows clamp screw. This procedure applies to both left and right tie-rod ends.

## LUBRICATION AND GENERAL MAINTENANCE

Inspect cooling system hoses for deterioration, leaks and loose hose clamps every 12,000 miles. Drain, flush cooling system and replace coolant every 6000 miles. Clean crankcase oil filler breather cap every 6000 miles. Replace fuel system filter and inspect for leaks every 12,000 miles. Replace carburetor air cleaner filter every 12,000 miles. Clean crankcase emission system, hoses, tubes, fittings and replace valve every 12,000 miles. Replace crankcase filter in air cleaner every 6000 miles. Clean and repack front wheel bearings every 30,000 miles. Change engine oil and filter every 6000 miles. Check transmission oil level every 6000 miles. Check rear axle fluid level every 6000 miles. Lubricate front suspension ball joints every 36,000 miles. Check rear axle fluid level every 6000 miles. Check brake master cylinder fluid level every 12,000 miles.

*1978 Pinto features 2.3 L overhead cam engine and four speed manual transmission. Optional equipment includes white forged aluminum wheels and accent tape stripe.*

# QUICK SERVICE ON FIESTA

The Fiesta differs greatly from other Ford models. The overhead valve, four cylinder engine, Fig. 1, has a displacement of 97.6 cu. in. (1.6 L). It is mounted transversely at the front and drives the front wheels through a four speed transmission. The "four speed" is combined with the drive axle to form a "transaxle."

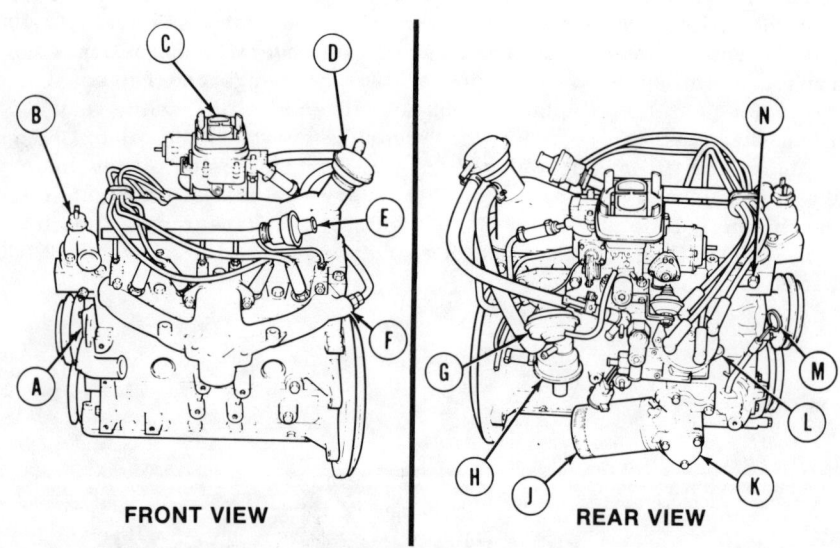

Fig. 1. Fiesta 1.6 L engine. A—Water pump. B—Cooling fan temperature switch. C—Carburetor. D—Oil filler cap/PCV system. E—Thermactor check valve. F—Exhaust manifold. G—EGR valve. H—Fuel pump. J—Oil filter. K—Oil pump. L—Distributor. M—Oil level dipstick. N—Intake manifold.

The engine is equipped with Dura-Spark II ignition, which features a solid state control module, Fig. 2. Details of Dura-Spark are given on page 35.

The engine is integral with the front drive assembly, Fig. 3, and transmits power to the front wheels through intermediate shafts and constant velocity universal joints.

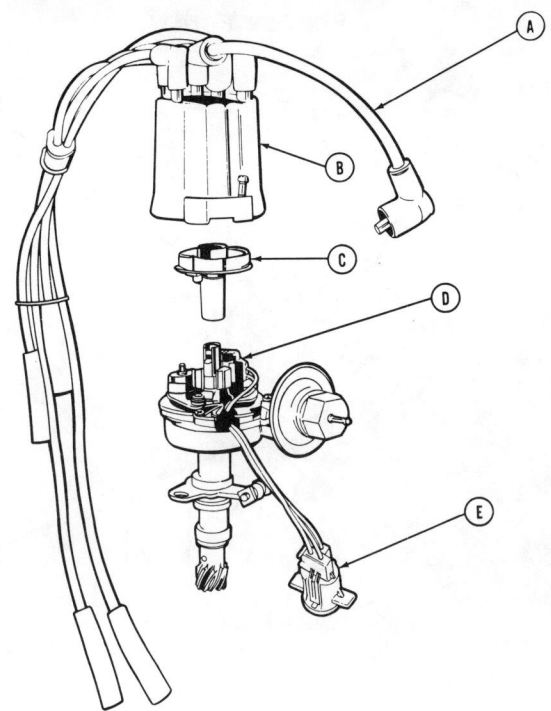

*Fig. 2. Dura-Spark ignition installed on 1978 Fiesta engine. A— Ignition secondary wires. B—Distributor cap. C—Rotor. D—Electronic pick-up assembly. E—Harness multiplug.*

## FRONT SUSPENSION

Front suspension, Fig. 4, is of the MacPherson strut design with bolt-on forged knuckles or spindle carriers. The main strut incorporates a rubber top mount, a coil spring mounted between the two seats and an integral shock absorber. This is all combined in a single assembly.

Caster, camber and toe-in are factory set and cannot be altered. The Fiesta front suspension system also has what is known as "negative scrub radius." This is the difference between the actual contact point of the tire on the road and the contact point that would be projected by drawing a line through the spindle. When the projected point falls outside the actual tire contact point, the suspension is said to have negative scrub geometry, Fig. 5.

Correct caster is 0 deg. 20 min. Camber is 2 deg. 15 min. Toe-in should be 0.10 in. (2.5 mm).

## IGNITION SERVICE

It is important to note that the Fiesta ignition system amplifier module and coil are ON when the ignition switch is in the ON position.

# Fix Your Ford

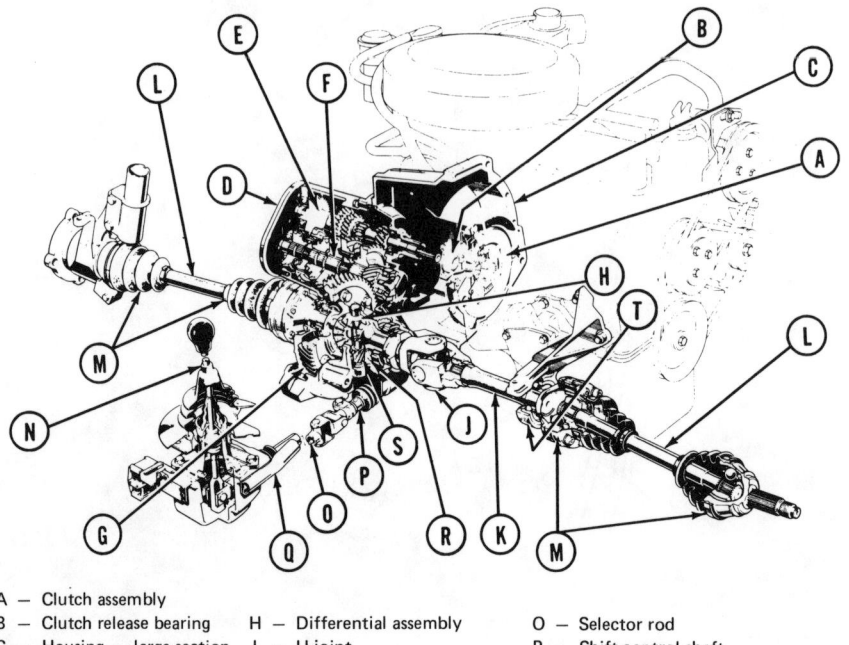

| | | |
|---|---|---|
| A — Clutch assembly | H — Differential assembly | O — Selector rod |
| B — Clutch release bearing | J — U-joint | P — Shift control shaft |
| C — Housing — large section | K — Inner drive shaft | Q — Stabilizer |
| D — Housing — small section | L — Outer driver shaft (2) | R — Speedometer drive gear |
| E — Input shaft assembly | M — Constant velocity joints (4) | S — Speedometer driven gear |
| F — Output shaft assembly | N — Gearshift assembly | T — Inner drive shaft bracket and bearing |
| G — Differential gear | | |

*Fig. 3. Fiesta engine is integral with front drive assembly.*

As a result, the ignition system may generate a spark when the key is turned OFF because of the collapse of the magnetic field of the coil. This action verifies continuity of the primary coil system.

Some other service operations, such as removing the distributor cap with the switch ON, may also cause the system to fire. Therefore, the ignition switch should be in the OFF position (or disconnect the battery during underhood operations) unless the specific operation requires the switch to be in the ON position.

## IGNITION TIMING

The distributor is located on the carburetor side of the engine. The firing order is 1-2-4-3, and the distributor rotates counterclockwise. Ignition timing is provided for the 1.6 litre engine as follows: With No. 1 piston approaching top dead center on the compression stroke, rotate the crankshaft clockwise until the notch on the crankshaft pulley aligns with the 12 deg. timing mark on the engine front cover, Fig. 6.

## Quick Service on Fiesta

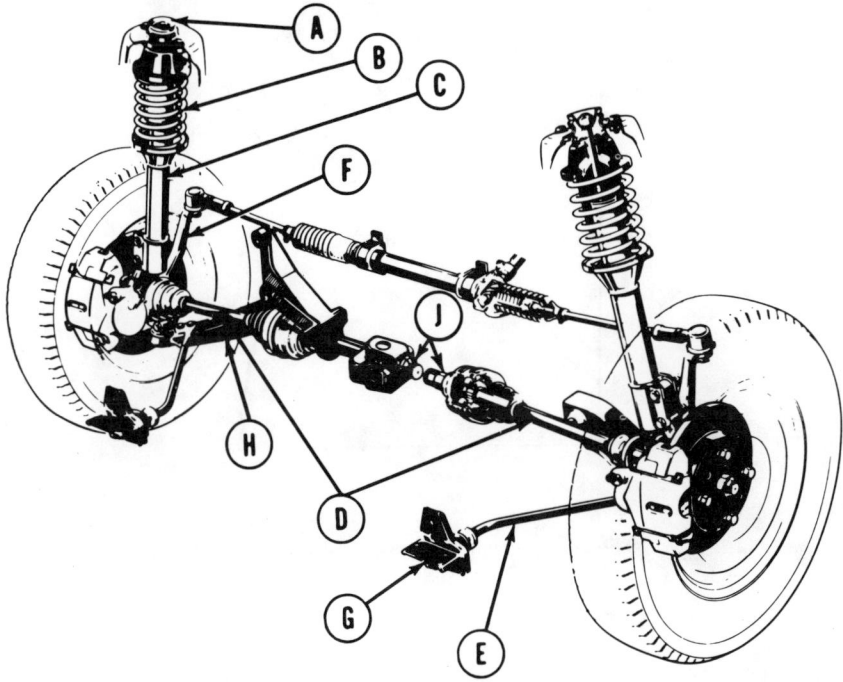

*Fig. 4. Front suspension on Fiesta is MacPherson strut design with bolt-on forged knuckles. A—Top mount. B—Coil spring. C—Strut. D—Intermediate drive shafts. E—Tie bar. F—Forged knuckle. G—Tie bar mounting bracket. H—Lower (track control) arm. J—Inner drive shafts.*

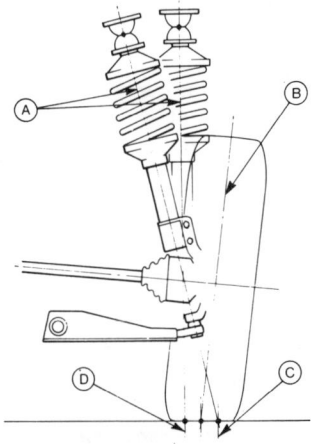

*Fig. 5. Front wheel geometry has negative scrub radius. A—Suspension pivot center line. B—Center of tire. C—Pivot center outside contact point (negative scrub radius geometry). D—Pivot center inside contact point (positive scrub radius geometry).*

Fix Your Ford

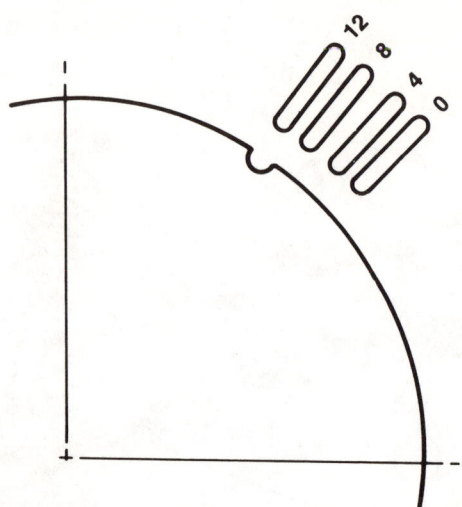

*Fig. 6. Ignition timing marks on the Fiesta.*

## HIGH TENSION IGNITION WIRING

Spark plug wires are "resistance type." Do not puncture them when making electrical tests. Resistance of these wires should be 4100 ohms per foot (30.48 cm). When disconnecting these wires, follow the usual precaution of pulling on the molded cap on the end of the wire; not on the wire itself. See page 42. Each spark plug wire on the Fiesta engine is numbered for its respective cylinder.

## CARBURETOR AND FUEL SYSTEM

The carburetor used on the Fiesta engine is Weber model 740 double venturi, two stage design with primary and secondary bores of equal size. The fuel pump is the sealed mechanical type. It is driven by an eccentric on the camshaft.

If the fuel pump does not provide 4.3-5.8 psi (30-40 kPa) pressure at 850 rpm, it should be replaced.

## ADJUSTING IDLE MIXTURE

The idle mixture adjustment screws, Fig. 7, are provided with screws so that the idle mixture must be adjusted within specified limits. If the idle limiter caps are removed, install new limiter caps at the maximum rich stop. Special equipment is needed so that Federal requirements can be met.

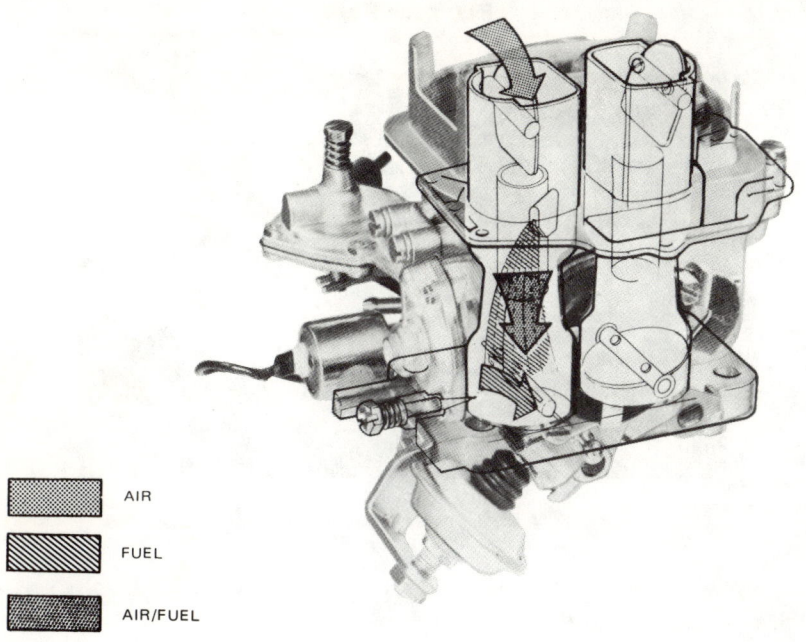

Fig. 7. Phantom view shows air, fuel and air-fuel flow, along with location of idle mixture adjustment screw on Weber carburetor.

## EMISSION CONTROL SYSTEMS

The Fiesta is equipped with the following exhaust emission controls: crankcase ventilating system; exhaust gas recirculating system; thermactor air injector system; spark control system. None of these systems is adjustable. However, all connections must be tight and vacuum lines must be clear and unobstructed.

## ADJUSTING VALVE CLEARANCE

Valve lifters in the Fiesta engine are the mechanical type. The valves require clearance adjustment at regular service intervals, Fig. 8: First, bring engine to operating temperature. Next, remove air cleaner and rocker arm cover. Torque tighten rocker arm shaft attaching screws to 25-30 ft. lb. (33.8-40.8 Nm). Then, check valve clearance. It should be 0.010 in. (0.254 mm) for intake valves and 0.022 in. (0.508 mm) for exhaust valves. When checking clearance, be sure the valves are in the fully closed position.

## CYLINDER HEAD

When torquing cylinder head bolts, start at the center and work progressively to each end. First, tigthen head bolts to 5 ft. lb. (7.75 Nm);

## Fix Your Ford

*Fig. 8. Adjusting valve lash on Fiesta engine.*

then, 20-30 ft. lb. (31-46 Nm); next, 50-55 ft. lb. (77-85 Nm); finally, 65-70 ft. lb. (101-109 Nm).

If it is necessary to remove the cylinder head, be sure to note the location of each push rod so it can be replaced in its original location. Before replacing the cylinder head, make sure all gasket surfaces are clean and not damaged in any way. Also check the surfaces for flatness, which should be 0.0015 in. (0.038 mm) in any 12 in. (30 cm) span.

## COOLING SYSTEM

The fan used in the Fiesta cooling system is electrically driven, Fig. 9. A plastic coolant expansion tank is installed on the left fender apron. A coolant temperature switch is mounted in the coolant outlet elbow just above the thermostat. This switch causes the fan to operate when the coolant temperature exceeds a predetermined temperature of 223 deg. F (106 C).

Cooling system capacity is 14 pt. (6.6 L). Specified pressure of the radiator cap is 13 psi (90 kPa). Opening temperature of the cooling system thermostat is 185-193 deg. F (85-90 C).

Check the level of the coolant in the cross flow radiator at regular service intervals. Make this inspection when engine is cold. The coolant level should be maintained 1 3/16 in. (30 mm) from the internal flange of the filler neck.

When a Fiesta is equipped with an air conditioner system, the thermostat housing is replaced with a longer unit to provide space for clearance of the ignition wires. Therefore, a special procedure must be followed when filling the system with coolant: Fill radiator through filler neck. Place radiator cap on neck. Remove bolt in top of thermostat housing.

## Quick Service on Fiesta

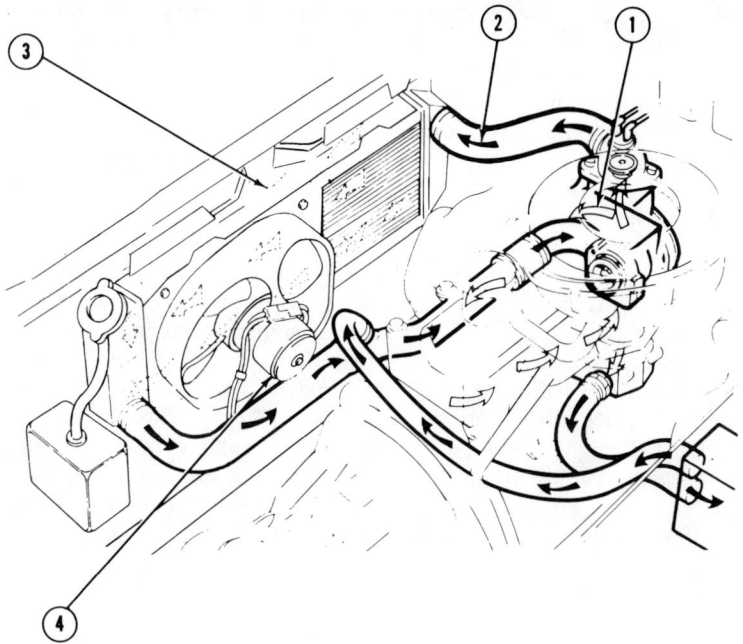

*Fig. 9. Fiesta engine cooling system. 1—Thermostat. 2—Water circulating to radiator. 3—Radiator. 4—Cooling system fan driven by electric motor which is controlled by thermostat.*

Add coolant through this opening until system is completely full. Replace the bolt and tighten it.

### ELECTRICAL SYSTEM

The Fiesta electrical system has a one piece wiring harness that eliminates many of the multiple connections found in most systems. Alternators of 40, 55 or 60 amp. capacity are used, depending on the accessories installed on the vehicle. The battery is see-through type, permitting inspection of the level of the electrolyte without removing filler caps. The negative battery terminal is grounded.

The fuse box is located on the lower edge of the left side of the instrument panel. Circuit breakers are mounted on a central bracket under the instrument panel. A fuse link is included in the Fiesta wiring harness. Some models are provided with a tachometer.

### ENGINE AND TRANSMISSION REMOVAL

The engine and transmission are removed as a single unit: Prior to removal, engage fourth gear (to insure subsequent gearshift assembly adjustment). Next, remove starting battery. Drain coolant. Disconnect radiator and heater hoses. Remove carburetor controls. Disconnect fuel lines, vent hoses, emission hoses and servo hoses from carburetor. Disconnect temperature sending unit, oil pressure switch, distributor, ignition coil, choke and fan switch.

Disconnect speedometer cable and clutch cable. Remove exhaust manifold heat stove. Disconnect and remove complete exhaust system. Disconnect ground wire at air pump. Remove gear selector rod. Unhook spring between selector rod and longintudinal member. Back off nuts on stabilizer rubber insulators and engine mounts.

Loosen stud lock nut and remove stud from transmission. Remove shift lever from floor pan. Rotate gear selector rod with stabilizer halfway around and suspend on wire. Disconnect alternator and starting motor leads. Disconnect left axle drive shaft at coupling with stub shaft. Separate coupling. Disconnect right hand drive shaft at inner U-joint.

Support engine and transmission on a floor jack. Remove engine mountings and right upper engine mounting rubber insulator. Remove engine-to-body bracket in engine compartment. Remove left engine mounting and bottom engine mounting strap. Raise hoist and lift vehicle away from engine and transmission. Withdraw assembly from under vehicle.

## OIL PAN REMOVAL

The oil pan can be removed without removing the engine assembly from the chassis. Proceed as follows: Drain crankcase. Remove oil dipstick. Remove battery cables. Disconnect throttle linkage at carburetor. Disengage steering cable from rack and pinion, then disconnect rack and pinion from cross member and move it forward to provide clearance for the pan. Remove starting motor. Unscrew left bottom bolt from lower rear cover and remove cover. Disassemble engine rear plate from engine rear plate assembly. Unscrew oil pan attaching bolts and remove pan and gasket.

When replacing oil pan, tighten pan bolts in order shown in Fig. 10. Tighten first in alphabetical order, then in numerical order.

## CONNECTING RODS AND PISTONS

Connecting rods and pistons can be removed from the Fiesta engine after removing the engine assembly from the chassis. The pistons are unusual in that the combustion chamber of a semi-spherical shape is formed in the head of the piston.

## CLUTCH

The clutch is a single plate with a diaphragm spring pressure plate, Fig. 11. The clutch disc has four torsion springs. It is operated by an automatic self-adjusting device and a release shaft with a thrust bearing in the clutch housing. Clutch cable adjustment is not required.

*Fig. 10. When installing oil pan, first tighten bolts shown in alphabetical order, then those in numerical order.*

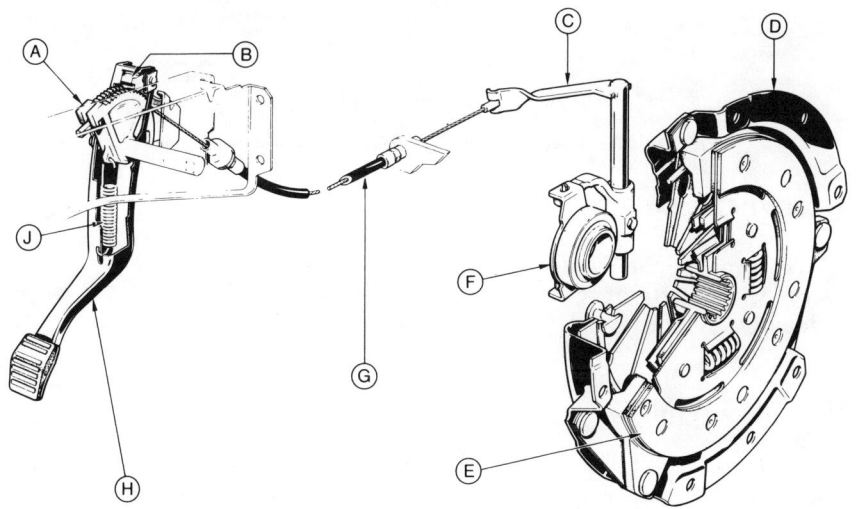

*Fig. 11. Details of Fiesta single plate clutch. A—Automatic adjusting device toothed segment. B—Automatic adjusting device pawl. C—Release shaft. D—Pressure plate. E—Clutch disc. F—Release bearing with fork. G—Clutch cable. H—Clutch pedal. J—Toothed segment tension spring.*

## BRAKING SYSTEM

Disc brakes are installed on the front wheels of the Fiesta; drum brakes at the rear. These brakes are hydraulically operated and separate circuits are provided for each pair of diagonally positioned wheels (left front and right rear; right front and left rear).

Front calipers, Fig. 12, are single piston units operated by a sliding piston. Diameter of the cast iron disc is 8.7 in. (221 mm). Calipers are self adjusting during operation of the brake pedal. Rear drums are 7.00 in. (178 mm) in diameter. The brakes are self adjusting.

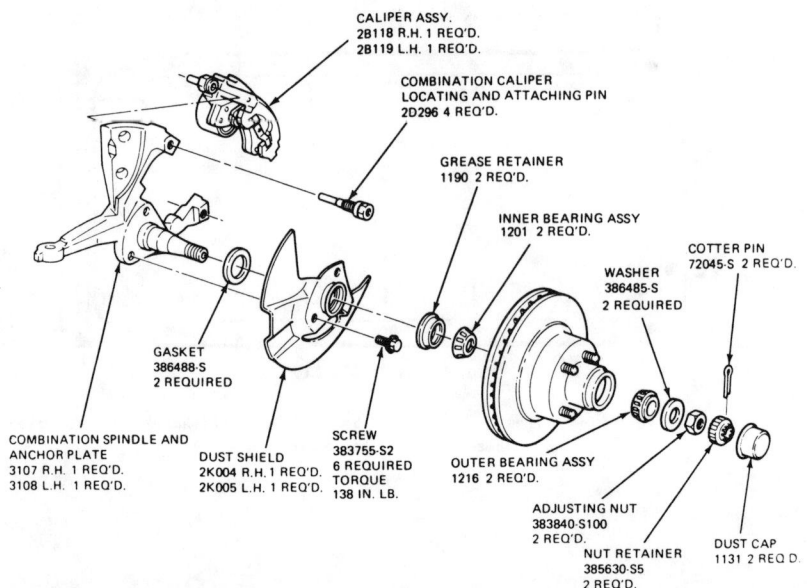

*Fig. 12. Disc brake assembly installed on front wheels of Fiesta.*

## REMOVING BRAKE DISC

To remove the brake disc (rotor): Jack up front of vehicle and remove wheel. Remove two caliper mounting nuts and detach caliper assembly. Suspend caliper assembly from vehicle body. Remove disc retaining screw, then remove disc.

## BLEEDING BRAKES

To bleed the Fiesta hydraulic brake system: First, bleed left front brake, then right rear. Next, bleed right front brake, then left rear.

## REPLACING DISC BRAKE PADS

To replace disc brake pads: Place front of vehicle on stands and remove wheel. Remove retaining pins and discard. Apply light pressure to piston housing against caliper tension springs, then slide out keys and discard. Remove piston housing and suspend from vehicle with a wire of suitable length. Withdraw brake pads and anti rattle clips from pad housing.

To install new pads, reverse this procedure.

## REAR BRAKE SHOE SERVICE

To remove rear brake shoes: First, place rear of car on jack stands. Fully release parking brake. Disconnect parking brake cable from brake

## Quick Service on Fiesta

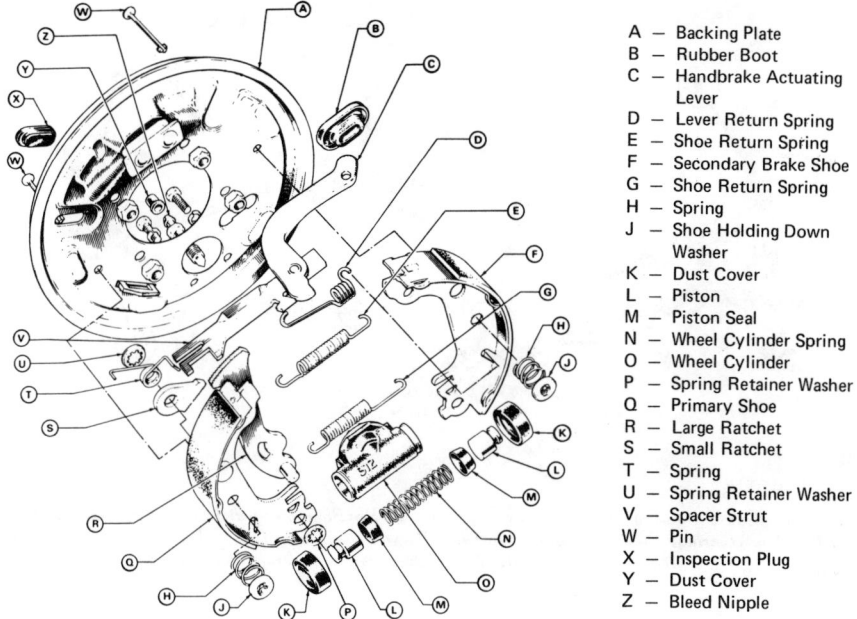

A — Backing Plate
B — Rubber Boot
C — Handbrake Actuating Lever
D — Lever Return Spring
E — Shoe Return Spring
F — Secondary Brake Shoe
G — Shoe Return Spring
H — Spring
J — Shoe Holding Down Washer
K — Dust Cover
L — Piston
M — Piston Seal
N — Wheel Cylinder Spring
O — Wheel Cylinder
P — Spring Retainer Washer
Q — Primary Shoe
R — Large Ratchet
S — Small Ratchet
T — Spring
U — Spring Retainer Washer
V — Spacer Strut
W — Pin
X — Inspection Plug
Y — Dust Cover
Z — Bleed Nipple

*Fig. 13. Exploded view of drum brake assembly used on rear wheels of Fiesta.*

assembly. Remove spindle and bearing dust cap, cotter pin, adjusting nut, washer and outer bearing. Slide brake drum clear of spindle.

Next, remove shoe hold-down spring from primary shoe, Fig. 13, by depressing and turning washer through 90 deg. Remove spring and washer, then withdraw pin from brake carrier plate. Twist primary shoe outward, away from carrier plate, taking care not to damage cylinder dust cover. Detach shoe and remove springs. Remove shoe hold-down spring from secondary shoe. Slide lower end of spacer strut out from slot in carrier plate. Move secondary shoe assembly upward and away from carrier plate. Remove brake operating lever and shoe assembly from carrier plate.

Disassemble primary shoe as follows: Remove spring washer P, Fig. 13 and discard separate longer ratchet R from brake shoe. Remove spring washer from shorter ratchet S and discard. Remove spring T and ratchet from brake shoe. Separate the secondary brake shoe from spacer strut by twisting. Remove spring.

## STEERING AND SUSPENSION SYSTEMS

Details of the steering and suspension system are shown in Fig. 14. The steering system consists of the rack and pinion steering gear and the steering shaft and column assembly. The rack and pinion steering

# Fix Your Ford

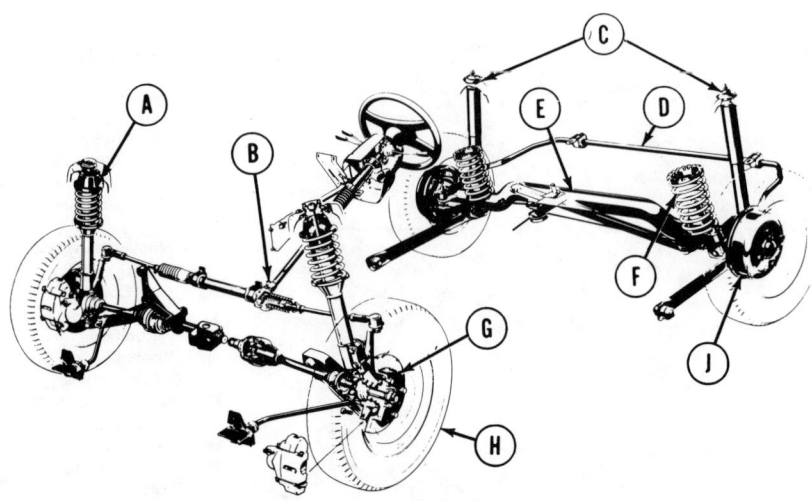

*Fig. 14. Fiesta steering and suspension systems. A—MacPherson strut front suspension. B—Rack and pinion steering. C—Rear shock absorbers. D—Stabilizer bar. E—Solid axle. F—Coil springs. G—Disc front brakes. H—Front wheel drive. J—Drum rear brakes.*

gear is similar to that installed on the Pinto and Mustang, except that the pinion load is pre-fixed and the lubricant is a special type to reduce the possibility of leakage.

The front suspension system is attached at the top by two bolts which retain the top mount to the side apron panel. The lower end of the assembly is held in a lateral direction by a fabricated track control or lower arm.

The rear axle has a transverse tubular steel member with its center positioned upwards to provide clearance for the exhaust. A stub is welded to each end on which run the tapered roller wheel bearings.

## TRANSAXLE DETAILS

The transaxle assembly is a combination unit consisting of a transmission and a driving axle attached to the engine. The four speed transmission and the driving axle gears are contained in a single housing. See Fig. 3. Power from the engine is transmitted to the transmission input shaft (designed as a countershaft cluster) and from there (with gear engaged) to the output shaft (mainshaft). The output shaft drives the differential drive gear.

## EMISSION CONTROL EQUIPMENT

Thirteen different emission control devices (PCV, EGR, Thermactor, etc.) are utilized on Fiesta models.

## ENGINE TUNE-UP SPECIFICATIONS

| YEAR AND MODEL | Displacement Cu. In. | Number of Cylinders Bore and Stroke | Brake Horsepower | Compression Ratio | Compression Pressure | Spark Plug Make and Model | Spark Plug Gap | Timing Mark Location | Ignition Timing Degrees BTDC* | Breaker Point Gap | VALVE LASH Intake | VALVE LASH Exhaust |
|---|---|---|---|---|---|---|---|---|---|---|---|---|
| 1967 240 No Ex. Emission, Auto. Trans. | 240 | 6-4.00x3.180 | 155@4200 | 9.2 | 175 | AL BF42 | .035 | V | 10 | .025 | .117W | .117W |
| 1967 240 Ex. Emission Man. Trans. | 240 | 6-4.00x3.180 | 155@4200 | 9.2 | 175 | AL BF42 | .035 | V | 0 | .025 | .117W | .117W |
| 1967 240 Ex. Emission Auto. Trans. | 240 | 6-4.00x3.180 | 155@4200 | 9.2 | 175 | AL BF42 | .035 | V | 4 | .025 | .117W | .117W |
| 1967 240 Police, Taxi | 240 | 6-4.00x3.180 | 155@4200 | 9.2 | 175 | AL BTF6 | .035 | V | - - | .025 | .117W | .117W |
| 1967 289 No Ex. Emission Man. Trans. | 289 | V8-4.00x2.870 | 200@4400 | 9.3 | 150 | AL BF42 | .035 | V | 6 | .015 | .018H | .018H |
| 1967 289 No Ex. Emission Auto.Trans. | 289 | V8-4.00x2.870 | 200@4400 | 9.3 | 150 | AL BF42 | .035 | V | 6 | .015 | .018H | .018H |
| 1967 289 Ex. Emission Man. Trans. | 289 | V8-4.00x2.870 | 200@4400 | 9.3 | 150 | AL BF42 | .035 | V | 0 | .015 | .018H | .018H |
| 1967 289 Ex. Emission Auto. Trans. | 289 | V8-4.00x2.870 | 200@4400 | 9.3 | 150 | AL BF42 | .035 | V | 0 | .015 | .018H | .018H |
| 1967 390 (2V) No Ex. Emission | 390 | V8-4.05x3.780 | 270@4400 | 9.5 | 180 | AL BF42 | .035 | V | 10 | .015 | .150W | .150W |
| 1967 390(4V) Ex. Emission | 390 | V8-4.05x3.780 | 315@4600 | 10.5 | 190 | AL BF42 | .035 | V | 6 | .015 | .150W | .150W |
| 1967 390(2V) Ex. Emission | 390 | V8-4.05x3.780 | 270@4400 | 9.5 | 180 | AL BF42 | .035 | V | 6 | .015 | .150W | .150W |
| 1967 390(4V) No Ex. Emission | 390 | V8-4.05x3.780 | 315@4600 | 10.5 | 190 | AL BF42 | .035 | V | 10 | .015 | .150W | .150W |
| 1967 410(4V) No Ex. Emission | 410 | V8-4.05x3.980 | 330@4600 | 10.5 | 190 | AL BF42 | .035 | V | 10 | .015 | .150W | .150W |
| 1967 410(4V) Ex. Emission | 410 | V8-4.05x3.980 | 330@4600 | 10.5 | 190 | AL BF42 | .035 | V | 6 | .015 | .150W | .150W |
| 1967 427 (4V) | 427 | V8-4.23x3.780 | 410@5600 | 11.1 | 180 | AL BF32 | .035 | V | 8 | .015 | .025H | .025H |
| 1967 427 (8V) | 427 | V8-4.23x3.780 | 425@6000 | 11.1 | 180 | AL BF32 | .035 | V | 8 | .015 | .025H | .025H |
| 1967 428 (4V) | 428 | V8-4.13x3.980 | 345@4600 | 10.5 | 190 | AL BF42 | .035 | V | 12 | .015 | .150W | .150W |
| 1967 428 (4V) Police | 428 | V8-4.13x3.980 | 360@5400 | 10.5 | 190 | AL BF32 | .035 | V | 12 | .015 | .150W | .150W |
| 1968 | 170 | 6-3.50x2.94 | 105@4400 | 9.1 | 175 | AL BF82 | .035 | V | 6 | .027 | .117WN | .117WN |
| 1968 | 200 | 6-3.68x3.13 | 120@4400 | 9.2 | 175 | AL BF32 | .035 | V | 6 | .027 | .145W | .145W |
| 1968 | 240 | 6-4.00x3.00 | 150@4000 | 9.2 | 175 | AL BF82 | .035 | V | 6 | .027 | .117W | .117W |
| 1968 Police | 240 | 6-4.00x3.00 | 155@4200 | 9.2 | 175 | AL BTF6 | .035 | V | 6 | .027 | .117W | .117W |
| 1968 Taxi | 240 | 6-4.00x3.00 | 155@4200 | 9.2 | 175 | AL BTF6 | .035 | V | 6 | .027 | .117W | .117W |
| 1968 289 (2V) | 289 | V8-4.00x2.870 | 200@4400 | 9.3 | 150 | AL BF42 | .035 | V | 6 | .021 | .117W | .117W |
| 1968 302 (2V) | 302 | V8-4.00x3.000 | 210@4400 | 9.5 | 150 | AL BF32 | .035 | V | 6 | .021 | .117W | .117W |
| 1968 302 (4V) | 302 | V8-4.00x3.000 | 235@4800 | 10.5 | 150 | AL BF32 | .035 | V | 6 | .021P | .117W | .117W |
| 1968 390 (2V) | 390 | V8-4.05x3.780 | 270@4400 | 9.5 | 180 | AL BF32 | .035 | V | 6 | .021P | .150W | .150W |
| 1968 390 (4V) GT | 390 | V8-4.05x3.780 | 320@4800 | 10.5 | 190 | AL BF32 | .035 | V | 6 | .016 | .150W | .150W |
| 1968 390 (2V) Pre Fuel | 390 | V8-4.05x3.780 | 280@4400 | 10.5 | 190 | AL BF32 | .035 | V | 6 | .021 | .150W | .150W |
| 1968 427 (4V) | 427 | V8-4.23x3.780 | 390@5600 | 10.9 | 180 | AL BF32 | .035 | V | 6 | .021 | .150W | .150W |
| 1968 428 (4V) | 428 | V8-4.13x3.980 | 345@4600 | 10.5 | 190 | AL BF32 | .035 | V | 6 | .021P | .150W | .150W |
| 1968 428 Police | 428 | V8-4.13x3.980 | 360@5400 | 10.5 | 190 | AL BF32 | .035 | V | 6 | .017 | .150W | .150W |
| 1969 | 170 | 6-3.50x2.94 | 105@4400 | 9.10 | CP | AL BF82 | .035 | V | 6 | .027 | C | C |
| 1969 | 200 | 6-3.50x3.12 | 120@4400 | 8.10 | CP | AL BF82 | .035 | V | 6 | .027 | C | C |
| 1969 | 240 | 6-4.00x3.18 | 150@4000 | 9.20 | CP | AL BF42 | .035 | V | 6 | .027 | .117 | .117 |
| 1969 Police | 240 | 6-4.00x3.18 | 155@4200 | 9.20 | CP | AL BTF6 | .035 | V | 6 | .027 | .117 | .117 |
| 1969 | 250 | 6-3.68x3.91 | 155@4000 | 9.00 | CP | AL BF82 | .035 | V | 6 | .025 | .145 | .145 |
| 1969 Std. Trans. | 302 | V8-4.00x3.00 | 210@4400 | 9.50 | CP | AL BF42 | .035 | V | 6 | .021 | C | C |
| 1969 | 302 | V8-4.00x3.00 | 210@4400 | 9.50 | CP | AL BF42 | .035 | V | 6 | .017 | C | C |
| 1969 (2V) | 351 | V8-4.00x3.50 | 250@4600 | 9.50 | CP | AL BF42 | .035 | V | 6 | .017 | .113 | .113 |
| 1969 (4V) | 351 | V8-4.00x3.50 | 290@4800 | 10.70 | CP | AL BF32 | .035 | V | 6 | .017 | .113 | .113 |
| 1969 (2V) | 390 | V8-4.05x3.78 | 270@4400 | 9.50 | CP | AL BF42 | .035 | V | 6 | .017 | .150 | .150 |
| 1969 Police | 390 | V8-4.05x3.78 | 280@4400 | 10.50 | CP | AL BF42 | .035 | V | 6 | .017 | .150 | .150 |
| 1969 (4V) | 390 | V8-4.05x3.78 | 320@4600 | 10.50 | CP | AL BF32 | .035 | V | 6 | .017 | .150 | .150 |
| 1969 Police | 428 | V8-4.13x3.98 | 360@5400 | 10.50 | CP | AL BF32 | .035 | V | 6 | .017Y | .150 | .150 |
| 1969 Cobra Jet | 428 | V8-4.13x3.98 | 335@5200 | 10.60 | CP | AL BF32 | .035 | V | 6 | .017Y | .150 | .150 |
| 1969 (2V) | 429 | V8-4.36x3.59 | 320@4400 | 10.50 | CP | AL BF42 | .035 | V | 6 | .017Y | .125 | .125 |
| 1969 (4V) | 429 | V8-4.36x3.59 | 360@4600 | 11.00 | CP | AL BF42 | .035 | V | 6 | .017Y | .125 | .125 |
| 1970 | 170 | 6-3.50x2.94 | 105@4400 | 9.1 | CP | AL BF82 | .035 | V | 6 | .027 | .091W | .091W |
| 1970 | 200 | 6-3.68x3.13 | 120@4400 | 8.1 | CP | AL BF82 | .035 | V | 6 | .027 | .091W | .091W |
| 1970 | 240 | 6-4.00x3.18 | 155@4200 | 9.2 | CP | AL BF42 | .035 | V | 6 | .027 | .091W | .091W |
| 1970 | 250 | 6-3.68x3.91 | 155@4000 | 9.1 | CP | AL BF82 | .035 | V | 6 | .027 | .091W | .091W |
| 1970 | 302-2V | V8-4.00x3.00 | 210@4400 | 9.5 | CP | AL BF42b | .035 | V | 6 | .021 | .092W | .092W |
| 1970 Boss | 302-4V | V8-4.00x3.00 | 290@5800 | 10.5 | CP | AL AF32 | .035 | V | 16 | .020 | .025H | .025H |
| 1970 351W | 351-2V | V8-4.00x3.50 | 250@4600 | 9.5 | CP | AL BF42 | .035 | V | 10 | .021 | .133W | .133W |
| 1970 351C-2CV | 351-2V | V8-4.00x3.50 | 250@4600 | 9.5 | CP | AL AF42 | .035 | V | 10 | .021 | .125W | .125W |
| 1970 351C-4CV | 351-4V | V8-4.00x3.50 | 300@5400 | 11.0 | CP | AL AF32 | .035 | V | 10 | .021 | .125W | .125W |
| 1970 390-2V | 390-2V | V8-4.05x3.78 | 270@4400 | 9.5 | CP | AL BF42 | .035 | V | 10 | .021 | .125W | .125W |
| 1970 428-4V (P) | 428-4V | V8-4.13x3.98 | 360@5400 | 10.5 | CP | AL BF32 | .035 | V | 10 | .021 | .125W | .125W |
| 1970 428-4V (CJ) | 428-4V | V8-4.13x3.98 | 335@5200 | 10.6 | CP | AL BF32 | .035 | V | 10 | .021 | .125W | .125W |
| 1970 429-2V | 429-2V | V8-4.36x3.59 | 320@4400 | 10.5 | CP | AL BF42 | .035 | V | 6 | .021 | .019H | .019H |
| 1970 429-4V (CJ) | 429-4V | V8-4.36x3.59 | 360@4600 | 11.0 | CP | AL AF32 | .035 | V | 10 | .021 | .019H | .019H |
| 1970 429-4V Boss | 429-4V | V8-4.36x3.59 | 370@5200 | 10.5 | CP | AL AF32 | .035 | V | 10 | .020 | .013C | .013C |
| 1971 | 170 | 6-3.50x2.94 | 100@4200 | 8.70 | CP | AL BRF82 | .035 | V | 6 | .027 | .091W | .091W |
| 1971 | 200 | 6-3.68x3.13 | 115@4000 | 8.70 | CP | AL BRF82 | .035 | V | 6 | .027 | .097W | .097W |
| 1971 | 240 | 6-4.00x3.18 | 140@4000 | 8.90 | CP | AL BRF42 | .035 | V | 6 | .027 | .117W | .117W |
| 1971 | 250 | 6-3.68x3.91 | 145@4000 | 9.00 | CP | AL BRF82 | .035 | V | 6 | .027 | .145W | .145W |
| 1971 | 302 | V8-4.00x3.00 | 210@4400 | 9.00 | CP | AL BRF42 | .035 | V | 6 | .017 | .140W | .140W |
| 1971 302 HO | 302HO | V8-4.00x3.00 | 275@6000 | 9.40 | CP | AL ARF32 | .035 | V | 16 | .020 | .025H | .025H |
| 1971 351 W | 351W | V8-4.00x3.50 | 240@4600 | 9.00 | CP | AL BRF42 | .035 | V | 6 | .021G | .150W | .150W |
| 1971 351 C | 351C | V8-4.00x3.50 | 240@4600 | 9.00 | CP | AL BRF42 | .035 | V | 6 | .021G | .150W | .150W |
| 1971 | 400 | V8-4.00x4.00 | 260@4000 | 9.00 | CP | AL ARF42 | .035 | V | 10j | .021 | .150W | .150W |
| 1971 | 390 | V8-4.05x3.78 | 255@4600 | 8.60 | CP | AL BRF42 | .035 | V | 4 | .021G | .150W | .150W |
| 1971 429-2V | 429-2V | V8-4.36x3.59 | 320@4400 | 10.50 | CP | AL BRF42 | .035 | V | 4 | .021G | .150W | .150W |
| 1971 429-4V | 429-4V | V8-4.36x3.59 | 360@4600 | 11.00 | CP | AL BRF42 | .035 | V | 4 | .021G | .150W | .150W |
| 1972 170 | 170 | 6-3.50x2.94 | 82@4000 | 8.30 | CP | AL BRF82 | .034 | V | 6 | .027 | .125W | .125W |
| 1972 200 | 200 | 6-3.68x3.13 | 91@4000 | 8.30 | CP | AL BRF82 | .034 | V | 6 | .027 | .125W | .125W |
| 1972 240 | 240 | 6-4.00x3.18 | 103@3800 | 8.50 | CP | AL BRF82 | .034 | V | 6 | .027 | .125W | .125W |

# ENGINE TUNE-UP SPECIFICATIONS (Continued)

| YEAR AND MODEL | Displacement Cu. In. or cm³ | Number of Cylinders Bore and Stroke | Brake Horsepower | Compression Ratio | Compression Pressure | Spark Plug Make and Model | | Spark Plug Gap | Timing Mark Location | Ignition Timing Degrees BTDC* | Breaker Point Gap | VALVE LASH ## | |
|---|---|---|---|---|---|---|---|---|---|---|---|---|---|
| | | | | | | | | | | | | Intake | Exhaust |
| 1972 250 | 250 | 6-3.68x3.91 | 98@3600 | 8.0 | CP | AL | BRF82 | .034 | V | 6 | .027 | .125W | .125W |
| 1972 302-2V | 302 | V8-4.00x3.00 | 140@4000 | 8.5 | CP | AL | BRF42 | .034 | V | 6 | .017 | .115W | .115W |
| 1972 351 W | 351 | V8-4.00x3.50 | 153@3800 | 8.6 | CP | AL | ARF42 | .034 | V | 6 | .017 | .130W | .130W |
| 1972 351 C-4V | 351 | V8-4.00x3.50 | 248@5400 | 8.6 | CP | AL | ARF42 | .034 | V | 10# | .017 | .125W | .125W |
| 1972 351 C HO | 351 | V8-4.00x3.50 | 266@5400 | 8.8 | CP | AL | ARF42 | .034 | V | 10# | .017 | .125W | .125W |
| 1972 400-2V | 400 | V8-4.00x4.00 | 172@4000 | 8.4 | CP | AL | ARF42 | .034 | V | 6 | .017 | .150W | .150W |
| 1972 429 | 429 | V8-4.36x3.59 | 212@4400 | 8.5 | CP | AL | BRF42 | .034 | V | 10 | .017 | .150W | .150W |
| 1973 200-1V | 200 | 6-3.68x3.13 | 84@3600 | 8.3 | CP | AL | BRF82 | .035 | V | 6 | .027 | .144W | .144W |
| 1973 250-1V | 250 | 6-3.68x3.91 | 92@3200 | 8.0 | CP | AL | BRF82 | .035 | V | 6 | .027 | .144W | .144W |
| 1973 302-2V | 302 | V8-4.00x3.00 | 138@4200 | 8.0 | CP | AL | BRF42 | .035 | V | 6 | .017 | .130W | .130W |
| 1973 351-2V | 351 | V8-4.00x3.50 | 158@3800 | 8.0 | CP | AL | ARF42 | .035 | V | 10 | .017 | .150W | .150W |
| 1973 351-4V | 351 | V8-4.00x3.50 | 246@5400 | 8.0 | CP | AL | ARF42 | .035 | V | 16F | .017 | .150W | .150W |
| 1973 400-2V | 400 | V8-4.00x4.00 | 171@3600 | 8.0 | CP | AL | ARF42 | .035 | V | 6 | .017 | .150W | .150W |
| 1973 429-4V | 429 | V8-4.36x3.59 | 201@4400 | 8.0 | CP | AL | ARF42 | .035 | V | 10 | .017 | .125W | .125W |
| 1973 460 | 460 | V8-4.36x3.85 | 208@4400 | 8.8 | CP | AL | ARF42 | .035 | V | 14 | .017 | .125W | .125W |
| 1974 200 | 200 | 6-3.68x3.13 | 84@3800 | 8.0 | CP | AL | BRF82 | .034 | V | CD | .025 | .104W | .104W |
| 1974 250 | 250 | 6-3.68x3.91 | 91@3200 | 8.0 | CP | AL | BRF82 | .034 | V | CD | .025 | .145W | .145W |
| 1974-1976 2.3 L | 2300 | 4-3.78x3.126 | 88@5000 | 9.0 | CP | AL | AGRF52 | .034 | V | CD | .027 | .008C | .010C |
| 1974-1976 2.8 L | 2800 | V6-3.66x2.70 | 105@4600 | 8.7 | CP | AL | AGR42 | .034 | V | CD | .024 | .014H | .016H |
| 1974 302-2V | 302 | V8-4.00x3.00 | 140@3800 | 8.0 | CP | AL | BRF42 | .034 | V | CD | .017 | .015W | .015W |
| 1974 351W | 351 | V8-4.00x3.50 | 163@4200 | 8.0 | CP | AL | BRF42 | .034 | V | CD | .017 | .131W | .131W |
| 1974 351C-2V | 351 | V8-4.00x3.50 | 173@4200 | 8.0 | CP | AL | ARF42 | .044 | V | CD | .017 | .125W | .125W |
| 1974 351C-4V | 351 | V8-4.00x3.50 | 246@5400 | 8.0 | CP | AL | ARF42 | .034 | V | CD | .017 | .125W | .125W |
| 1974 400 | 400 | V8-4.00x4.00 | 170@3400 | 8.0 | CP | AL | ARF42 | .044 | V | CD | PL | .125W | .125W |
| 1974 460 | 460 | V8-4.36x3.85 | 195@3800 | 8.0 | CP | AL | ARF52 | .052 | V | CD | PL | .100W | .100W |
| 1975 200 | 200 | 6-3.68x3.13 | 84@3800 | 8.3 | CP | AL | BRF82 | .034** | V | CD | PL | .104W | .104W |
| 1976 200 | 200 | 6-3.68x3.13 | 81@3400 | 8.3 | CP | AL | BRF82 | .044** | V | CD | PL | .104W | .104W |
| 1975-1976 250 | 250 | 6-3.68x3.91 | 81@3000 | 8.0 | CP | AL | BRF82 | .044** | V | CD | PL | .104W | .104W |
| 1975-1976 302 | 302 | V8-4.00x3.00 | 137@3600 | 8.0 | CP | AL | ARF42** | .044** | V | CD | PL | .137W | .137W |
| 1975-1976 Granada | 351 | V8-4.00x3.50 | 143@3600 | 8.0 | CP | AL | ARF42 | .044** | V | CD | PL | .137W | .137W |
| 1975-1977 351M | 351 | V8-4.00x3.50 | 152@3800 | 8.0 | CP | AL | ARF42 | .044** | V | CD | PL | .150W | .150W |
| 1975-1978 400 | 400 | V8-4.00x4.00 | 166@3800 | 8.0 | CP | AL | ARF42 | .044** | V | CD | PL | .150W | .150W |
| 1975-1976 460 | 460 | V8-4.36x3.85 | 202@3800 | 8.0 | CP | AL | ARF42 | .044** | V | CD | PL | .150W | .150W |
| 1977 2.3 L | 2300 | 4-3.78x3.126 | 89@4800 | 9.0 | CP | | AWRF42 | .034 | V | CD | PL | .010C | .010C |
| 1977 2.8 L | 2800 | V6-3.66x2.70 | 93@4200 | 8.7 | CP | | AWSF42 | .034 | V | CD | PL | .014H | .016H |
| 1977-1978 200-1V | 200 | 6-3.68x3.13 | 85@3600 | 8.5 | CP | | CD | CD | V | CD | PL | .135W | .135W |
| 1977-1978 250-1V | 250 | 6-3.68x3.91 | 97@3200 | 8.1 | CP | | CD | CD | V | CD | PL | .140W | .140W |
| 1977-1978 302-2V | 302 | V8-4.00x3.00 | 139@3600 | 8.4 | CP | | CD | CD | V | CD | PL | .132W | .132W |
| 1977-1978 351W-2V | 351 | V8-4.00x3.50 | 144@3200 | 8.3 | CP | | CD | CD | V | CD | PL | .132W | .132W |
| 1977-1978 460-4V | 460 | V8-4.36x3.85 | 210@4200 | 8.3 | CP | | CD | CD | V | CD | PL | .125W | .125W |
| 1978 2.3 L | 2300 | 4-3.78x3.126 | 88@4800 | 9.0 | CP | | CD | CD | V | CD | PL | .045W | .045W |
| 1978 2.8 L | 2800 | V6-3.66x2.70 | 90@4200 | 8.7 | CP | | CD | CD . | V | CD | PL | .014C | .016C |
| 1978 351M | 351 | V8-4.00x3.50 | 152@3600 | 8.0 | CP | | CD | CD | V | CD | PL | .150W | .150W |

**ABBREVIATIONS:**

- \* - Ignition diaphragm hose or hoses must be disconnected and plugged when timing ignition with the engine running.
- \*\* - See decal in engine compartment.
- \# - Applies to manual transmission, Automatic 16 deg.
- \#\# - Average values are given for valve lash for hydraulic lifters. A tolerance of + or - .030 in. is permissible.
- a - Applies to manual transmission, Automatic 6 deg.
- b - With air conditioning.
- C - Hydraulic lifter adjustment - one turn down after contact.
- CD - See decal on engine.
- CP - Lowest reading should be within 75 percent of highest reading.
- d - If equipped with mechanical lifters, adjust lash to .025 in. with engine at operating temperature.
- F - Applies to manual transmission, Automatic 18 deg.
- G - Applied to dual diaphragm distributor.
- H - Hot.
- hy - Hydraulic lifters.
- j - 6 deg. for California registration.
- k - For California: D4PF-SA, .054 in. gap.
- l - For California: D4PF-NA, .054 in. gap.

- L - If equipped with hydraulic lifters, valve clearance should be .067-.167 in. obtained at valve stem tip with tappet collapsed.
- N - For mechanical tappet adjust lash to .018 in. with engine at operating temperature.
- N.A. - Not available.
- P - Applies to engine with Thermactor. For IMCO equipped engines point gap should be .017 in.
- PL - Breakerless.
- S - If equipped with hydraulic lifters, valve clearance should be .082-.152 in. obtained at valve stem tip with tappet collapsed.
- TC - Top Center.
- V - Crankshaft pulley.
- W - Hydraulic lifters. Clearance specified is clearance with a tolerance of approximately .030 in. and is obtained at valve spring tip with tappet collapsed. On some engines, oversize or undersize push rods are available, in others the rocker arms are adjustable.
- Y - Standard transmission .021 in.

## ENGINE TIGHTENING SPECIFICATIONS

Specifications are for clean, undamaged and lightly lubricated threads only. Dirty, damaged and dry threads produce undue friction which prevents accurate measurement of torque required to tighten bolt or nut.

| YEAR | Engine | Cylinder Head Bolts ft. lb. | Main Bearing Bolts ft. lb. | Connecting Rod Bolts ft. lb. |
|---|---|---|---|---|
| 1960-63 | 144, 170 | 65-75 | 60-70 | 19-24 |
| 1961-66 | 352, 390 | 95-105 | 95-105 | 40-45 |
| 1963 | 221 | 65-70 | 60-70 | 19-24 |
| 1963-65 | 260 | 65-70 | 60-70 | 19-24 |
| 1963-64 | 223 | 105-115 | 95-105 | 40-45 |
| 1963 | 406 | 100-110 | 95-105 | 53-58 |
| 1964-72 | 170 | 70-75 | 60-70 | 19-24 |
| 1964-77 | 200 | 70-75 | 60-70 | 19-24 |
| 1964-67 | 289 Hi | 65-70 | 60-70 | 19-24 |
| 1964-67 | 289 | 65-72 | 60-70 | 19-24 |
| 1964-67 | 427 | 100-110 | 95-105 | 53-58 |
| 1965-67 | 240 | 70-75 | 60-70 | 40-45 |
| 1966 | 410 | 80-90 | 95-105 | 40-45 |
| 1966-67 | 428 | 80-90 | 95-105 | 40-45 |
| 1968-72 | 240 | 70-75 | 60-70 | 19-24 |
| 1968 | 289 | 65-72 | 60-70 | 19-24 |
| 1968-72 | 302 | 65-72 | 60-70 | 19-24 |
| 1968-71 | 390 | 80-90 | 95-105 | 40-45 |
| 1968-70 | 427 | 100-110 | 95-105 | 40-45 |
| 1969-78 | 250 | 70-75 | 60-70 | 21-26 |
| 1969 | 351 | 75-100 | 95-105 | 40-45 |
| 1969-72 | 429 | 130-140 | 95-105 | 40-45 |
| 1970-78 | 302 2V | 65-72 | 60-70a | 19-24 |
| 1970-71 | 302 Boss | 65-72 | 95-105 | 40-45 |
| 1970-74 | 351 C | 95-100 | 95-105a | 40-45 |
| 1970-71 | 351 W | 95-100 | 95-105 | 40-45 |
| 1971-78 | 400 | 95-105 | 95-105 | 40-45 |
| 1973-78 | 351W | 105-112 | 95-105 | 40-45 |
| 1973-78 | 460 | 130-140 | 95-105a | 40-45 |
| 1975-78 | 351M | 95-100 | 95-105a | 40-45 |

a - Applies to inner bolts. Outer bolts 34-40 ft. lb.
Hi - High performance engine.

## WHEEL ALIGNMENT SPECIFICATIONS

| YEAR | Caster Degree | Camber Degree | Toe-in Inches |
|---|---|---|---|
| **Ford** | | | |
| 1966-68 | +1 | +1/2 | 3/16 |
| 1969 | +1 | +1/2 | 3/16 |
| 1970-73 | +1 | +1/2 | 3/16 |
| 1974 | +2 | L+1/2, R+1/8 | 1/8 |
| 1975-78 | +2 | L+1/4, R+1/4 | 3/16 |
| **Falcon** | | | |
| 1968 | +1/4 | +1/4 | 1/4 |
| 1969 | -3/4 | +1/4 | 3/16 |
| 1970 | -3/4 | +1/4 | 1/4 |
| **Fairlane** | | | |
| 1968 | +1/4 | +1/4 | 1/4 |
| 1969 | -3/4 | +1/4 | 1/4 |
| 1970 | -3/4 | +1/4 | 1/4 |
| **Thunderbird** | | | |
| 1966-68 | -1-1/2 | +1/2 | 3/8 |
| 1969 | +1 | +1/2 | 3/16 |
| 1970-72; | +1 | +1/2 | 3/16 |
| 1973 | +1-1/4 | +3/4 | 1/4 |
| 1974 | +2 | +3/4 | 1/4 |
| 1975 | +4 | L+1, R+1/4 | 1/4 |
| 1976-77 | +2 | L+1/2, R+1/4 | 3/16 |
| 1978 | +4 | L+1/2, R+1/4 | 1/8 |
| **Mustang** | | | |
| 1968 | +1/4 | +1/4 | 3/16 |
| 1969 | +1/4 | +3/4 | 1/4 |
| 1970 | 0 | +1 | 3/16 |
| 1971 | 0 | +3/4 | 1/4 |
| 1972 | 0 | +3/4 | 3/16 |
| 1973 | +1-1/4 | +3/4 | 3/16 |
| 1974 | +3/4 | +1/4 | 1/8 |
| **Maverick** | | | |
| 1970-73 | -1/2 | +1/4 | 3/16 |
| 1974-75 | -1/2 | +1/4 | 3/16 |
| 1976-77 | -1/2 | +1/4 | 3/16 |
| **Torino** | | | |
| 1971 | -3/4 | +3/4 | 3/16 |
| 1972 | +1-1/4 | +3/4 | 3/16 |
| 1973 | +1-1/4 | +3/4 | 1/4 |
| 1974-75 | +2 | L+5/8, R+5/8 | 1/8 |
| 1976-77 | +4 | L+1/2, R+1/4 | 1/8 |
| **Mustang II** | | | |
| 1975-78 | +7/8 | +1/2 | 1/8 |
| **Granada** | | | |
| 1975-78 | -1/2 | +1/4 | 1/4 |
| **Fairmont #** | | | |
| 1978 | +7/8 | +3/8 | 5/16 |

# - Caster and camber not adjustable.

## COOLING AND LUBRICATION SPECIFICATIONS

| YEAR | Engine | Cooling System Capacity with Heater Quarts | Radiator Cap Relief Pressure | Refill Capacity, Quarts | Crankcase Capacity, Quarts |
|---|---|---|---|---|---|
| 1968-69 | 170 Six | 9.3 | 12-15 | 4-1/2 | 5 f |
| 1968-69 | 200 Six | 9.1 | 12-15 | 4-1/2 | 5 f |
| 1968 | 240 Six | 12.8 | 12-15 | 5 | 5 f |
| 1968 | 302 V-8 | 13.6 | 12-15 | 5 | 5 f |
| 1968 | 390 V-8 | 20.2 | 12-15 | 5 | 5 f |
| 1968 | 427 Mustang | 20.6 | 12-15 | 6 | 5 f |
| 1968 | 427 Fairlane | 20.6 | 12-15 | 5 | 5 f |
| 1968 | 428 V-8 | 19.4 | 12-15 | 4-1/2 | 5 f |
| 1969 | 240 | 9.9 | 12-15 | 4-1/2 | 5 f |
| 1969 | 302 Mustang, Fairlane | 13.5 | 12-15 | 5 | 5 f |
| 1969 | 302 Ford | 15.4 | 12-15 | 5 | 5 f |
| 1969 | 351 | 14.6 | 12-15 | 5 | 5 f |
| 1969 | 390 Fairlane | 20.9 | 12-15 | 5 | 5 f |
| 1969 | 390 Mustang, Ford | 19.7 | 12-15 | 5 | 5 f |
| 1969 | 390 Thunderbird | 20.5 | 12-15 | 5 | 5 f |
| 1969 | 390 Police | 19.1 | 12-15 | 5 | 5 f |
| 1969 | 428 Fairlane | 19.3 | 12-15 | 5 | 5 f |
| 1969 | 428 Mustang | 19.7 | 12-15 | 5 | 5 f |
| 1969 | 428 Ford | 18.6 | 12-16 | 5 | 7 f |
| 1969 | 429 | 9.2 | 12-16 | 4-1/2 f | 7 f |
| 1970 | 170 | 9.0 | 12-16 | 4-1/2 f | 5-1/2 f |
| 1970 | 200 | 11.4 | 12-16 | 4-1/2 f | 5-1/2 f |
| 1970 | 240 | 9.8 | 12-16 | 4-1/2 f | 5 f |
| 1970 | 250 Mustang | 11.4 | 12-16 | 5 f | 5 f |
| 1970 | 250 Fairlane | 13.5 | 12-16 | 5 f | 5 f |
| 1970 | 302 Falcon | 15.4 | 12-16 | 5 f | 5 f |
| 1970 | 302 Ford, Fairlane | 15.6 | 12-16 | 5 f | 5 f |
| 1970 | 302 Boss Mustang | 15.6 | 12-16 | 5 f | 5 f |
| 1970 | 351 Fairlane | 14.6 | 12-16 | 5 f | 5 f |
| 1970 | 351 Ford | 16.5 | 12-16 | 5 f | 5 f |
| 1970 | 390 Ford | 20.0 | 12-16 | 5 f | 5 f |
| 1970 | 428 Ford | 19.3 | 12-16 | 5 f | 5 f |
| 1970 | 428 Mustang CJ | 19.5 | 12-16 | 5 f | 5 f |
| 1970 | 429 Fairlane CJ | 18.5 | 12-16 | 5 f | 5 f |
| 1970 | 429 SCJ | 18.5 | 12-16 | 8 | 5 f |
| 1970 | 429 Mustang Boss | 18.5 | 12-16 | 6 f | 5 f |
| 1970 | Torino | 19.4 | 12-16 | 5 f | 5 f |
| 1971 | 170 | 9.0 | 12-16 | 4-1/2 f | 5 f |
| 1971-72 | 200 Thunderbird | 14.0 | 12-16 | 5 f | 5 f |
| 1971-72 | 240 | 10.0 | 12-16 | 4-1/2 f | 5 f |
| 1971-72 | 250 Maverick | 11.2 | 12-16 | 4-1/2 f | 5 f |
| 1971-72 | 250 Mustang | 15.5 | 12-16 | 5 f | 5 f |
| 1971-72 | 302 | 15.5 | 12-16 | 5 f | 5 f |
| 1971-72 | 302 Torino | 16.5 | 12-16 | 5 f | 5 f |
| 1971-72 | 351 | 16.5 | 12-16 | 5 f | 5 f |
| 1971-72 | 351 Torino | 21.0 | 12-16 | 7 f | 5 f |
| 1971 | 390 | 17.5 | 12-16 | 5 f | 5 f |
| 1971 | 400 | 19.0 | 12-16 | 5 f | 5 f |
| 1971 | 429 Ford | 19.5 | 12-16 | 5 | 5 f |
| 1972 | 429 | 17.5 | 12-16 | 5 | 5 f |
| 1972 | 400 | 19.0 | 12-16 | 5 | 5 f |
| 1972 | 429 Ford | 9.7 | 12-16 | 5 | 5 f |
| 1973-74 | 200 Maverick | 11.5 | 12-16 | 5 | 5 f |
| 1973 | 250 Maverick | 13.4 | 12-16 | 5 | 5 f |
| 1973 | 250 Torino | 16.3 | 12-16 | 5 | 5 f |
| 1973 | 302 Ford | 15.6 | 12-16 | 5 | 5 f |
| 1973-74 | 302 Torino | 15.6 | 12-16 | 5 | 5 f |
| 1973 | 351 2V Mustang | 15.8 | 12-16 | 5 | 5 f |
| 1973 | 351 2V Ford | 15.7 | 12-16 | 5 | 5 f |
| 1973-74 | 351 4V Mustang | 17.7 | 12-16 | 5 | 5 f |
| 1973-74 | 351 4V Torino | 18.0 | 12-16 | 5 | 5 f |
| 1973 | 400 Ford | 18.8 | 12-16 | 5 | 7 f |
| 1973 | 429 T-bird | 18.9 | 12-16 | 5 | 7 f |
| 1973-74 | 429 Torino | 19.5 | 12-16 | 5 | 7 f |
| 1973-74 | 460 T-bird | 19.5 | 12-16 | 5 | 7 f |
| 1973-74 | 460 Torino | 9.0 | 12-16 | 4 | 5 f |
| 1974 | 2300 cc Mustang | 13.0 | 12-16 | 4-1/2 f | 5 f |
| 1974 | 2800 cc Mustang | 19.5 | 12-16 | 5 | 5-1/2 f |
| 1974 | 460 Ford | 8.5 | 12-16 | 4-1/2 f | 5 f |
| 1975-77 | 2300 cc Mustang II | 12.3 | 12-16 | 4-1/2 f | 5 f |
| 1975-77 | 2800 cc Mustang II | 9.0 | 12-16 | 5 f | 5 f |
| 1975-77 | 300 Maverick | 10.7 | 12-16 | 5 f | 5 f |
| 1975-77 | 250 Granada | 13.4 | 12-16 | 5 f | 5 f |
| 1975-77 | 302 Granada | 14.5 | 12-16 | 5 f | 5 f |
| 1975-77 | 302 Ford | 17.1 | 12-16 | 5 f | 5 f |
| 1975-77 | 351M Torino | 18.1 | 12-16 | 5 f | 5 f |
| 1975-77 | 400 Torino | 18.5 | 12-16 | 5 f | 5 f |
| 1975-77 | 460 T-bird | 19.2 | 12-16 | 5 f | 5 f |
| 1975-77 | 460 Torino | 8.8 | 12-16 | 5 f | 5 f |
| 1978 | 2.3 L Mustang II | 8.4 | 12-16 | 5 f | 5 f |
| 1978 | 2.8 L Mustang II | 14.6 | 12-16 | 6 f | 5 f |
| 1978 | 302 Mustang II | 8.6 | 12-16 | 5 f | 5 f |
| 1978 | 2.3 L Fairmont | 9.0 | 12-16 | 4-1/2 f | 5 f |
| 1978 | 200 Fairmont | 13.9 | 12-16 | 4-1/2 f | 5 f |
| 1978 | 302 Fairmont | 10.5 | 12-16 | 4-1/2 f | 5 f |
| 1978 | 250 Granada | 14.2 | 12-16 | 5 f | 5 f |
| 1978 | 302 Granada | 14.3 | 12-16 | 5 f | 5 f |
| 1978 | 302 Ford LTD | 15.4 | 12-16 | 7 f | 5 f |
| 1978 | 351W Ford LTD | 16.5 | 12-16 | 7 f | 5 f |
| 1978 | 351M Ford LTD | 15.2 | 12-16 | 5 f | 5 f |
| 1978 | 302 Ford | 16.3 | 12-16 | 5 f | 5 f |
| 1978 | 351W Ford | 17.0 | 12-16 | 5 f | 5 f |
| 1978 | 351M Ford | 17.0 | 12-16 | 5 f | 5 f |
| 1978 | 400 Ford | 18.6 | 12-16 | 5 f | 5 f |
| 1978 | 460 Ford | 19.0 | 12-16 | 5 f | 5 f |

f - Includes one quart with filter replacement.

## PINTO SPECIFICATIONS

| | 1600 cc | 2000 cc | 2300 cc | 2800 cc |
|---|---|---|---|---|
| Bore and stroke | 3.188 x 3.056 in. | 3.575 x 3.029 in. | 3.78 x 3.126 in. | 3.66 x 2.70 in. |
| Displacement cc | 1600 | 2000 | 2300 | 2800 |
| Displacement cu. in. | 97.6 | 122 | 140 | 170.8 |
| Brake horsepower | 75 @ 5000 rpm | 100 @ 5600 rpm | 88@4800 | 90@4200 |
| Compression ratio | 8.0 to 1 | 8.6 to 1 | 9.0 to 1 | 8.7 to 1 |
| Initial ignition timing | 12 deg. BTDC | 6 deg. BTDC | 6 deg. BTDC | 12 deg. BTDC |
| Spark plug | AGR-22 | BRF-32 | AGRF-52 | AGR-42 |
| Spark plug gap | 0.030 in. | 0.034 in. | 0.034 in. | 0.034 in. |
| Valve seat/face angle | 45 deg./44 deg. | 45 deg./44 deg. | 44.5 deg./45.5 deg. | 44.5 deg./45.5 deg. |
| Valve spring assem. ht. | 1.263 in. | 1.417 in. | 1.5625 in. | 1.5781 in. |
| Valve spring pressure | 44-49 @ 1.263 in. | 60-64 @ 1.417 in. | 78-86 @ 1.56 in. | 143 @ 1.22 in. |
| Valve spring free length | 1.48 in. | 1.77 in. | 1.816 in. | 1.91 in. |
| Valve lash, intake | 0.010 in. hot | 0.008 in. cold | 0.008 in. cold | 0.014 in. hot |
| Valve lash, exhaust | 0.017 in. hot | 0.010 in. cold | 0.010 in. cold | 0.016 in. hot |
| Valve lobe lift, intake | 0.2108 in. | 0.2519 in. | 0.2493 in. | 0.373 in. |
| Valve lobe lift, exhaust | 0.2176 in. | 0.2519 in. | 0.2493 in. | 0.373 in. |
| Main bearing bore diam. | 2.2710-2.2715 in. | 2.2432-2.2440 in. | 2.5902-2.5910 in. | 2.2437 in. |
| Rod journal diam. | 1.9368-1.9376 in. | 2.0464-2.0472 in. | 2.0464-2.0472 in. | 2.1252-2.1260 in. |
| Piston clearance | 0.0016-0.0022 in. | 0.001-0.002 in. | 0.0013-0.0021 in. | 0.001-0.002 in. |
| Oil pan capacity | 3.5 qt. | 5 qt. | 5 qt. | 5 qt. |
| Cooling capacity 1971-72 | 6 3/4 qt. | 7 1/2 qt. | . . . . | . . . . |
| Cooling capacity 1973 | 7.8 qt. | 8.5 qt. | . . . . | . . . . |
| Cooling capacity 1974-75 | . . . . | 8.5 qt.-1974 | 8.5 qt. | 12.5 qt.-1975 |
| Cooling capacity 1976-77 | . . . . | . . . . | 8.7 qt. | 12.5 qt./8.5-1977 |
| Cooling capacity 1978 | . . . . | . . . . | 8.6 qt. | 8.5 qt. |
| Torque cyl. head bolt | 65-70 ft. lb. | 65-80 ft. lb. | 80-90 ft. lb. | 65-80 ft. lb. |
| Torque con. rod bolt | 30-35 ft. lb. | 29-34 ft. lb. | 30-36 ft. lb. | 21-25 ft. lb. |
| Caster | +1 1/2 deg. | +1 1/2 deg. | +1 1/4 deg. | +1 1/4 deg. |
| Camber | +3/4 deg. | +3/4 deg. | +3/4 deg. | +3/4 deg. |
| Toe-in | 1/8 in. | 1/8 in. | 1/8 | 1/4 in. |

## Specifications

### FIESTA SPECIFICATIONS

| | |
|---|---|
| Bore and stroke | 3.18 in. (80.8 mm) x 3.056 (77.6 mm) |
| Displacement | 97.6 cu. in. (1.6 L) |
| Compression ratio | 8.6 to 1 |
| Firing order | 1-2-4-3 |
| Spark plug gap | 0.050 in. (1.27 mm) |
| Valve seat angle | 45 deg. |
| Valve spring assembled height | 1.25 in. (31.8 mm) |
| Valve spring free length | 1.48 in. (37.6 mm) |
| Valve lash, intake (cold) | .010 in. (.254 mm) |
| Valve lash, exhaust (cold) | .022 in. (.559 mm) |
| Valve lift, intake | .3536 in. (8.98 mm) |
| Valve lift, exhaust | .3553 in. (9.03 mm) |
| Piston clearance | .0009-.0017 in. (.023-.432 mm) |
| Oil pan capacity | 3.5 qt. (3.3 L) |
| Cooling system capacity | 7 qt. (6.6 L) |
| Cylinder head bolt torque | 65-70 ft. lb. (87.7-94.5 Nm) |
| Connecting rod bolt torque | 30-35 ft. lb. (40.5-47 Nm) |

A — TIV Valve
B — EGR Valve
C — Bi-metal Sensor
D — TVS Valve (Normally Operated)
E — Vacuum Reservoir
F — Air Bypass Valve
G — Air Cleaner
H — Oil Filler Cap
J — Vacuum Vent Valve
K — Check Valve
L — Delay Valve
M — Distributor
N — Hot Idle Compensator (HIC)

*Fiesta engine emission control system.*

# INDEX

## A

Accessory service, 221
Air bypass valve, 82, 83
Air cleaner,
 cleaning, 72
 hot and cold intake, 70, 366
 testing, 345, 366
Air conditioner schematic drawing, 229
Air conditioning tips, 228, 229, 230
Alternator,
 disassembled view, 191, 192
 Leece Neville, 198
 regulators, 196
 service, 191, 372
 test, 191
 voltmeter check, 194
Antifreeze, 173
Anti-stall dashpot adjustment, 56, 60
Autolite
 alternator diagram, 193
 alternator, sectional view, 192
 regulators, 196, 198
 solenoid actuated starter, 202, 206
 1-V carburetor, 365
 1101 1-V carburetor, 51, 54
 2100 2-V carburetor, 57
 4100 carburetor, 58
 5200 carburetor, 366
Automatic choke, 62, 63
Automatic load leveler, 294
Automatic transmission
 band adjustment, 259, 260, 261
 diagnosis, 263, 264, 265
 service, 251, 254, 375
Axle shaft,
 removal, 275
 seal replacement, 275

## B

Back-up light switch, 213
Balancing wheels, 301
Ball joint replacement, 293
Band adjustment, automatic
 transmission, 253, 259, 260, 261
Battery, 185
 charging, overcharging, 188
 testing, 186
 trouble shooting, 188, 189
 voltage, 187
Bleeding, brakes, 329, 330, 331, 388
Body rust prevention, 357
Body service, 355
Bolt tightening sequence, cylinder
 head, 100, 101, 383
Bolt torque, cylinder, 137, 393
Brake
 adjustment, 314, 374
 bleeding, 329, 330, 388

differential valve, 328
 disc type, 319, 325, 341, 388
 drum removal, 311, 313
 hose replacement, 337
 Hydro-Boost, 340
 master cylinder, 334, 335
 power, 338
 reconditioning rotors, 327
 relining drum brakes, 315, 388
 replacing pads, 327
 self-adjusting, 314, 317
 service, 311, 387
 servicing disc, 320, 322, 325, 388
 shoe installation, 316, 317, 388
 system, flushing, 332
 system, hydraulic, 311, 328, 387
Brakes, trouble shooting, 341, 342
Breaker points,
 adjusting, 25
 alignment, 20, 21
 checking, 20
 service, 20, 24, 25, 363
 spring tension, 22, 23
Breakerless ignition, 13, 30, 31
Bumper system, 294

## C

Caliper brake assembly, 320, 325, 387
Camber, 296, 376, 393
Cam lift measurement, 108
Cam performance, 368
Camshaft drive belt, 371
Camshaft removal, 108, 109
Carburetor
 adjustment, 48, 49, 50, 51, 52, 53, 382
 air cleaner, 72, 345
 Autolite 1-V, 365
 Autolite 1101 1-V, 51, 54
 Autolite 2100 2-V, 57, 62
 Autolite 4100, 58, 62
 Autolite 5200, 366
 Carter YFA 1-V, 54, 55
 high altitude, 70
 Holley dual carburetor, 64, 65, 66
 Holley four barrel, 67, 68
 Holley 1946 1-V, 59, 60
 Motorcraft 2700 VV, 52
 Rochester 4 MW, 68
 service, 47, 74, 362, 364, 382
 variable venturi, 52, 69
Carter carburetor, 48, 49, 54, 55
Caster, 295, 296, 376, 393
Catalytic converter, 9, 86, 88, 178, 183
Centrigual advance distributor, 26, 27
C3 automatic transmission, 253
C4 automatic transmission, 263
C6 automatic transmission, 252, 264
Charge indicator light, 219

# Index

Charge indicators, 219, 225
Charging
  batteries, 188
  system, trouble shooting, 191, 196, 200
Choke, automatic, 62, 63
Circuit
  alternator, 193
  breaker, 215, 217
  fuel gauge, 223
  fuel level warning, 223
  ignition, 13
  starter, 203
  temperature gauge, 221, 222
Circuits, test equipment, 195
Circulating ball type steering gear, 303
Cleaning,
  air cleaner, 72
  cooling system, 171
  cylinder head, 123
  fuel filter, 73
  interiors, 355
  spark plugs, 16
Clearance, piston skirt, 128
Clock, electric, 225
Clutch, 233
  adjustment, 233, 234, 374
  and transmission linkage, 235
  overhauling, 233
  pedal linkage, 236
  removal, 235, 237
  trouble shooting, 238
Coil spring rear suspension, 288, 289
Cold start spark advance, 91
Compression
  test procedure, 9
  test specifications, 10
Connecting rod
  alignment, 131
  and piston assembly, 104, 370
  assembly installation, 136, 145
  caps, replacement, 146
  fit, 133, 135
  removal, 103, 104, 105
Cooling specifications, 393
Cooling system, 167, 367, 384
  cleaning, 171
  draining flushing, testing, 167, 168
  leak location, 169
  thermostat, 168
  trouble shooting, 177
Crankcase breather cap and filter, 345
Crankcase ventilating valves, 79, 80, 81
Crankshaft, checking, 133
Cruise-O-Matic transmission, 253, 265
CTAV system, 87
Cylinder balance test, 11, 12
  catalytic converter warning, 11
Cylinder head
  bolt tightening sequence, 100, 101, 383
  bolt torque, 383, 393
  cleaning, 123
  removal, 94, 368, 371
Cylinder reconditioning, 144

**D**

Deceleration valve, 40, 364

Differential,
  limited slip, 280
  part inspection, 277
  Traction-Lok, 281
  transaxle, 390
Dimmer switch, 213, 220
Diode checking, 199
Disassembly, engine, 93
Disc brake
  caliper assembly, 320, 326, 387
  differential valve, 328
  double piston type, 320
  rotor service, 325, 327, 388
  shoe replacement, 322, 325, 327, 388
  single piston type, 319, 320, 325
Disc brakes, 319, 387
  pad replacement, 327
  pin slider, 325, 326
  rotor reconditioning, 327
Distributor
  cap removal, cleaning, 18, 36
  dual advance, 18, 25
  dual diaphragm, 29, 30
  Loadomatic, 22, 23, 24
  modulator, 42, 84
  point service, 20, 24, 25
  removal, 36
  shaft rotation, 41
  V-Six, 31, 32
  vacuum control valve, 39
Dome light, 211
Door locks, vacuum, 228
Drain holes, 355
Drain plugs, 96, 168
Draining cooling system, 167
Drive shaft, 267
  balancing, 268
Drum brake relining, 315, 388
Dual
  advance distributor, 18, 25, 26
  advance distributor, service, 25, 26
  brake warning light, 219
  carburetor, 50
  diaphragm distributor, service, 28, 29, 30
  exhaust system, 180
Dust leaks, 358

**E**

Electric choke, 64
Electric clock, 225
Electrical system, overdrive
  transmission, 249
Electrolyte level, 187
Emergency trouble shooting, 349
Emergency warning flasher switch, 217, 218
Emission controls, 38, 79, 85, 345, 383, 395
Engine
  bearing fit, 133, 135
  bearing replacement, 131, 137
  bearing wear, 132, 140
  disassembly, trouble shooting, 93, 153
  idle speed, 51, 52, 53
  keeps running, 155
  removal, 109, 110, 385
  repairs, trouble shooting, 113, 150
  tightening specifications, 137, 393

# Fix Your Ford

torque tables, 137, 393
tune-up specifications, 391, 392, 394, 395
Exhaust
  catalytic converter, 86, 88, 178, 183
  emission control, Thermactor, 82, 83, 89
  gas recirculating system, 85, 91
  system service, 179, 180, 181

## F

Fan belt check, 173
Fan drive clutch, 176
Fiesta, servicing, 378
Fiesta specifications, 395
Firing order, 11, 12, 44, 380
Flushing,
  brake system, 332
  cooling system, 167, 168, 171
  oil cooler, 255
Flywheel runout, checking, 246
FMX automatic transmission, 253, 265,
Ford cars,
  1978 Fairmont wagon, 112
  1978 LTD, 184
  1978 Mustang II Cobra, 184
  1978 Granada, 184
  1978 Fairmont, 190
  1978 Bronco, 190
  1978 Pinto wagon, 190
  1978 Pinto, 377
  1977 LTD, Maverick, Mustang II, 206
  1977 Thunderbird, LTD II, Pinto 270
  1976 Elite, LTD, Granada, 250
  1976 Maverick, Pickup, Mustang II, 284
Ford single barrel carburetor, 51, 52
Four-speed transmission, 243
Front spring removal, 291
Front suspension, 285, 378, 381, 389
Fuel, 187
  carburetor adjustments, 48, 53
  economy graph, 8
  filter cleaning, 73
  gauge service, 223
  level warning, 223, 224
  pump service, 76, 366
  system service, 47, 364, 382
  tips, 367
  vapor control, 367
Fuse, 215
  link, 215, 216
  panel, 217

## G

Gauge, fuel, 223
Gauge, temperature, 221
Gear tooth contact, 276
Generator, ac
  charge indicator light circuit, 219
  service, 191

## H

Headlight
  adjusting, 208
  aiming, 207
  light pattern, 208
  bulb replacement, 207, 209
  covers, 209, 211
  dimmer switch, 213
  retainers, 209

  switch, 211, 213
  trouble shooting, 189, 209
  vacuum control system, 210, 211
Heat indicator service, 221
Heater, 230
High altitude option, 70
Holley
  dual carburetor adjustment, 64, 65
  four barrel carburetor, 67, 68
  single barrel carburetor, 64, 65
  1946 1-V carburetor, 59, 60
Hydraulic brake system, 311, 328, 387
Hydraulic valve
  clearance, 160, 161, 162
  lifter service, 148, 149, 150
  specifications, 160
Hydro-Boost system, 340

## I

Idle speed, 53
Ignition
  breaker points, 20, 21, 22, 363
  breakerless, 13, 30, 31
  cable care, checks, 42, 43, 382
  circuit, 13
  Dura-Spark, 35
  primary checks, 44
  resistors, 44
  solid state, 13, 30, 31, 379
  switch testing, 219
  timing, 34, 35, 380
  transistor, 44, 45
  trouble shooting, 46
  tune-up, 9, 13, 47, 362, 379
IMCO exhaust emission control, 84
Impact absorbing bumper, 294
Inflation, tires, 346
Instrument cluster bulbs, 212
Instrument service, 221
Integral carrier rear axle, 275
Interior cleaning, 355

## L

Leaf type rear suspension system, 292
Leece Neville alternator, 198
Light pattern, headlight aiming, 208
Lighting system service, 207
Limited slip differential, 280
Linkage,
  clutch pedal, 236
  steering, 302
Load leveler, automatic, 294
Loadomatic distributor, service, 24, 25
Locks, vacuum door, 228
Lubrication, 343, 377
  rear axle, 344
  specifications, 393
  transmission, 343
  wheel bearings, 344

## M

Main bearing, checking, 137
Main bearings, replacement, 137, 138, 139
Manifold heat control valve, 75, 92, 182
Manual transmission removal, 239
Master cylinder tips, 334, 335
Model C4 automatic transmission, 251, 263
Model C6 dual transmission, 252, 264

# Index

Model FMX transmission, 253, 265
Model 78ET transmission, 246
Model 3.03 transmission, 240
Model RUG-BP overdrive, 249
Motor,
  starting, 203
  windshield wiper, 226

## O

Oil
  cooler flushing procedure, 255
  filter replacement, 343, 370
  leak test, 140
  pan removal, 101, 370, 372, 386
  pressure indicator, 225
  pump service, 147, 370
  seal replacement, 369, 372
Overcharging batteries, 188
Overdrive transmission, 248, 249

## P

Pin slider caliper, 325
Pinion and ring gear tooth contact
  adjustment, 278
Pinto, servicing, 361
Piston clearance, 128, 129, 370
Piston pins, checking, 131
Piston ring
  fitting, 126
  gap specifications, 127
  groove cleaning, 125
  installation, 124
Piston skirt clearance, 128, 129
Pistons, expanding, 130
Positive
  crankcase ventilating system, 79
  stop rocker arm stud, 163, 164
Power brake service, 338
Power brakes, 338
  Hydro-Boost, 340
  trouble shooting, 339, 340, 341
Power steering, 305
  drive belt, 308
  fluid, 308
  integral, 307
  non-integral, 305
  pump disassembled, 307
Pressure check, valve spring, 120
Primary ignition circuit checks, 43, 44
Propeller shaft removal, 267
Propeller shafts, 267
Proportioning valve, 328

## R

Rack and pinion, 303
Radiator
  cap check, 174, 175
  filling, 172, 176
  removal, 175
  supply tanks, 170, 172, 176
Rattles, 356
Rear axle
  backlash adjustments, 278
  exploded view, 271, 273
  light duty (WER), 272
  lubrication, 344
  pinion and ring gear installation, 279
  preload adjustments, 278
  service, 271
  trouble shooting, 282
Rear main oil seal replacement, 141, 372
Rear suspension system, 288
Reconditioning,
  engine cylinders, 144
  engine valves, 117, 118
Refacing valves, 117, 118
Regulator adjustment points, 198
Regulator, electronic, 198, 199
Regulators, Autolite, 196
Regulators, transistor type, 198
Removable carrier type axle, 271
Resistors, ignition, 44
Rochester carburetor, 69
Rocker arm and shaft, 115, 157
Rotary power steering gear, 305
Rotating tires, 347
Rust prevention, 357

## S

Seat belt interlock system, 354
Self-adjusting brakes, 314
  shoe installation, 317, 388
Shock absorber
  checks, service, 285, 289, 393
Single exhaust system, 178
Single piston type disc brake, 319, 320, 325
Smog control systems, 79, 85, 345, 383
Solid state ignition, 13, 30, 31, 35
Spark control system, 40, 92
Spark control valve, 53
Spark delay valve, 42
Spark plugs, 14
  checking, 16
  gap adjustment, 17, 363
  installation, 17, 18
  service, 17, 18, 380
Spark quick test, 13
Specifications, 391, 392, 393, 394, 395
Specifications, compression pressure, 10
Specifications, idling speeds, 53
Specifications, piston ring gap, 127
Specifications, spark plugs, 14
Specifications, valve lash, 160, 368, 371, 383
Specifications, valve springs, 122
Speed control system, 231, 232
Speedometer
  service, 226, 227
Spot removal, 356
Spring service, 285
Spring tension, breaker point, 22, 23
Starter
  circuits, 202
  neutral switch adjustment, 257
  testing, 201, 202, 203, 204
Starting control circuit test, 202
Starting motor, 201, 202, 203
  removing, 204, 205
Steering
  columns, 308, 309, 389
  gear adjustment, 304
  linkage hints, 302
  power, 305, 308
  rack and pinion, 303
  tilt wheel, 309

trouble shooting, 310
wheel spoke adjustments, 300
Stoplight switch, 212
Suspension system, 285, 288, 379, 381
Switch, emergency warning flasher, 217, 218
Switch, headlight, 213

**T**
Table, engine torque, 137, 393
Table, piston clearance, 128, 129
Tappet adjustment, 157, 368, 371, 383
Temperature gauge electrical circuit, 221
Thermactor exhaust emission
 control system, 82, 83, 88
Thermal sensing valve, 42
Thermostat, cooling system, 168, 173
Three-speed transmission
 disassembly, 240, 241, 242, 244
Throttle linkage adjustment, 258
Timing
 case cover removal, 106, 369
 chain replacement, 107, 147, 370
 ignition, 34, 35, 363
 marks, 37
Tires, 347
 trouble shooting, 310
Toe-in, 296
 adjustment, 299, 300, 376, 393
Traction-Lok differential, 281
Transistor ignition, 44, 45
 system schematic, 44
Transistor regulator, 198
Transmission, 239
 alignment, 240
 and clutch linkage, 235, 239
 automatic, 251, 375
 Cruise-O-Matic, 253, 266
 fluid drain and refill, 254
 fluid leaks, 256
 fluid level check, 252
 FMX, 253, 265
 four speed, 243, 247, 375
 JATCO, 262, 263
 manual shift, 239
 model C3, 253, 262
 model C4, 251, 263
 model C6, 252, 264
 model RUG-BP, 249
 model 3.03, 240
 model 78ET, 246
 overdrive, 248, 249
 removal, 239, 385
 three speed, 242
TRS System, 40
Trouble shooting,
 battery, 188, 189
 brakes, 341, 342
 charging system, 196
 clutch, 238
 cooling system, 177
 emergency, 349
 engine disassembly, 111, 148

engine repairs, 150
headlights, 209
ignition, 45, 46
rear axle, 282
power brakes, 341, 342
propeller shaft, 269
steering, 310
tires, 310
universal joints, 269
wheel alignment, 310
Tune-up steps, 9
Tune-up tips, 7, 47, 362
Turbochargers, 372
Turn signal indicator, 216, 217

**U**
Universal joints, 267
Universal joint replacement, 269

**V**
V-Six distributor, 31, 32
Vacuum
 advance control valve, 39
 door locks, 228
 heat control valve, 92, 182
 windshield wiper, 227
Valve
 assembly, 113
 critical dimensions, 118
 guides, 122
 heat control, 92, 182
 reconditioning, 113, 117, 118
 removal, 114, 165
 seal replacement, 165
Valve spring
 assembled height, 122
 checks, 120, 121
 compressor, 116
 replacement, 154, 165
Valve tappet adjustment, 157, 368, 371, 383
Variable venturi carburetor, 51, 52, 69
Vent type crankcase ventilating
 system, 79
Ventilating system, 230

**W**
Water leaks, 169, 358
Water pump service, 174
Wheel alignment, 295, 297, 376, 393
 specifications, 377, 393
 trouble shooting, 310
Wheel balancing, 301
Wheel bearing
 adjustment, 312
 lubrication, 344
Wheel cylinder service, 332
Wheel hub and bearing, 312
Wheel hub and rotor assembly
 removal, 325, 327
Windshield wiper blade,
 adjustment, 226
 replacement, 226
Wiper motor removal, 227
Wood grain transfers, 360